Progress in Zoology

Volume 38

Fortschritte der Zoologie
Progress in Zoology

Herausgegeben im Auftrag
der Deutschen Zoologischen Gesellschaft
von Martin Lindauer

Volume 38

Biology and Physiology of Amphibians

Proceedings of the First International Symposium on Biology and Physiology of Amphibians held at Karlsruhe, Federal Republic of Germany, August 31–September 3, 1988

Edited by
WILFRIED HANKE

215 figures and 35 tables

SEMPER BONIS ARTIBUS
Gustav Fischer Verlag · Stuttgart · New York · 1990

The Symposium was supported by the University of Karlsruhe, FRG, the Deutsche Gesellschaft für Endokrinologie, and by the Akademie der Wissenschaften und der Literatur, Mainz. It was a Satellite meeting of the 14th Conference of European Comparative Endocrinologists.

Sponsored by
Bundesministerium für Forschung und Technologie, Bonn,
and Bayerisches Staatsministerium für Wissenschaft und Kunst, München.

Edited by Wilfried Hanke, with help of Sabine Albrecht.
With the assistance of the organizing committee C. Barker Jorgensen, Uri Katz, Lis Olesen Larsen, Per Rosenkilde.

CIP-Kurztitelaufnahme der Deutschen Bibliothek

Biology and physiology of amphibians : proceedings of the First International Symposium on Biology and Physiology of Amphibians, held at Karlsruhe, Federal Republic of Germany, August 31 – September 3, 1988 ; [a satellite meeting of the 14th Conference of European Comparative Endocrinologists] / ed. by Wilfried Hanke. – Stuttgart ; New York : Fischer, 1990
(Progress in zoology ; Vol. 38)
ISBN 3-437-30622-7 (Stuttgart)
ISBN 0-89574-314-0 (New York)
NE: Hanke, Wilfried [Hrsg.]; Symposium Biology and Physiology of Amphibians ⟨01, 1988, Karlsruhe⟩; Conference of European Comparative Endocrinologists ⟨14, 1988, Karlsruhe⟩; Fortschritte der Zoologie

Library of Congress Card-No. 89-37373

All business correspondence should be made with:
Gustav Fischer Verlag GmbH & Co KG, Wollgrasweg 49, D-7000 Stuttgart 70
For USA and Canada:
Verlag Chemie International Inc., 303 N.W. 12th Avenue, Deerfield Beach, Florida 33441

Printed by: Laupp & Göbel, Nehren/Tübingen
Printed in Germany

Preface

This book contains papers which are read at the symposium "Biology and Physiology of Amphibians" held at the Department of Zoology, University of Karlsruhe in August/Sept. 1988. The conference was a satellite symposium of the 14th Conference of European Comparative Endocrinologists and thus supposed to primarily attract endocrinologists. However, we had the aim to establish a forum for discussion of amphibian biology within a wider framework and therefore, also invited workers from the fields of ethology and ecology. In this way the symposium became multidisciplinary in its approach to an understanding of amphibian functions. It covers all levels of analysis from the cell to the Amphibia in its natural environment.

Amphibia have often been used for analyses where function in man was the ultimate point of interrest, and sometimes even because some species are cheap and easy to keep in the laboratory. However, this group of invited research workers had a genuine interest in amphibians as such.

The physiology of Amphibia is especially interesting because of several facts related to the phylogenetic status of this class of vertebrates. The transition from aquatic to terrestrial life marks definitively the physiology of Amphibia. The two most important groups, the Anura and the Urodela, have different adaptational types despite of having also clear correlations. Both groups are characterized by aquatic larvae and terrestrial adults, in the typical form, from which exceptions exist.

The metamorphosis does not only include the development of criteria of the adult animal, like development of the gonads or reproductive behavior or calcification of the skeleton as in most other vertebrate groups. It includes also typical adaptational phenomenons accompanied by special hormonal activities like the counteraction of growth, promoted by prolactin or growth hormone, and differentiation depending on the thyroid system. The development of metabolic directions is a speciality influenced by the shift from herbivorism to carnivorism which mostly occurs.

The adaptational capacity of the adult – not too much is known about that of the larvae – is characterized by the highly permeable skin, an effective sodium uptake mechanism and the tool of water retention (Brunn-effect) by the skin or bladder. The Amphibia do not live in sea water, except *Bufo cancrivora* which finds the food in salty water, or sometimes *Bufo viridis*, which is distributed near salt lakes. But, the adaptational capacity varies strongly between the species. There are species like *Xenopus laevis*, which live aquatil for the whole life and can only survive for half a day outside the water. Examples for water-bound life despite of spending time outside the water are frogs belonging to the group of *Rana ridibunda – lessonae – esculenta*, called the water frogs. A few species like *Bufo calamita* and *viridis* can survive in arid regions. These different adaptations have physiological and hormonal backgrounds. Osmo- and electrolyte regulation are important features of the Amphibian life.

Many adaptations exist for the reproduction. There are seasonal rhythmicity, reproductive behavior and special characteristics like clustering the eggs with jelly coats, ripening of the oocytes etc. All these features make up the "Biology of Amphibians" to a very interesting and glittering story.

The wide spectrum of knowledge gave rise to many fruitful discussions during the symposium. We hope that the reader will also gain new understanding and inspiration from the many facets of amphibian biology illustrated in this book which at the same time covers a broad field and goes into great depth at several points.

The Organizers: W. Hanke, Karlsruhe
U. Katz, Haifa
L. Olesen Larsen, Copenhagen
P. Rosenkilde, Copenhagen

Participants

ABRAHAM, M.: Zoology Department, The Hebrew University, Jerusalem, 91904, Israel

ACCORDI, F.: Dept. of Animal and Human Biology, Viale dell'Universita 32, I-00185 Rom, Italy

ALONSO-BEDATE, M.: Facultad Biologia, Dept. Fisiologia, Univers. Complutense, 28040, Madrid, Spain

BARKER JØRGENSEN, C.: Zoophysiological Lab. A, August Krogh Institute, University of Copenhagen, 13, Universitetsparken, DK-2100 Copenhagen, Denmark

BICIOTTI, M.: Dipart. Biologia Animale, Via Acc. Albertina 17, I-10123 Torino, Italy

BÖHMER, J.: Institut für Zoologie, Universität Hohenheim, D-7000 Stuttgart 70, FRG

BOUJARD, D.: Lab. Biologie de Reproduction, Université de Rennes, Av. Général Leclerc, F-35042 Rennes, France

CAYROL, C.: 4, Rue Jean Breffel, F-31400 Toulouse, France

CHANOINE, C.: Lab. de Biologie du Developpement, 45, Rue des St. Pères, F-75270 Paris Cedex 06, France

COLUCCI, D.: Dipart. di Biologia Animale, Via A. Albertina 17, I-10123 Torino, Italy

DEGANI, G.: Migal, Galilee Technological Center, Kiryat Shmona 10-200, Israel

DELARUE, C.: Mol. Endocrinol. Lab. UA CNRS 650, Unité Affiliée INSERM, Université de Rouen, F-76134 Mont-Saint-Aignan Cedex, France

DELGADO, M.J.: Dept. Fisiologia Animal II, Fac. Biologia, Univ. Complutense, Madrid 28040, Spain

DEPARIS, P.: 3, Impasse des Genévrier, F-31400 Toulouse, France

DORE, B.: Dipart. di Biologia Animale, Via A. Albertina 17, I-10123 Torino, Italy

GALLIEN, C.L.: Lab. de Biologie du Développement, 45, rue des Saints Pères. F-75720 Paris Cedex 06, France

GIANNETTI, M.: Institut für Angewandte Zoologie, An der Immenburg 1, D-5300 Bonn 1, FRG

GORBMAN, A.: Zoology Dept. NJ-15, University of Washington, Seattle WA 98195, USA

GRACIA-NAVARRO, F.: Dept. Biologia Celular, Universidad de Cordoba Av. San Alberto Magno, E-14004 Cordoba, Spain

GUASTALLA, A.: Dipart. Biologia Animale, Via A. Albertina 17, I-10123 Torino, Italy

HAIDER, S.G.: Anatomie II der Universität Düsseldorf, Universitätsstr. 1, D-4000 Düsseldorf, FRG

HANKE, W.: Zoologisches Institut II der Universität Karlsruhe, Kaiserstr. 12, D-7500 Karlsruhe, FRG

HARTWIG, H.G.: Anatomie II der Universität Düsseldorf, Universitätsstr. 1, D-4000 Düsseldorf 1, FRG

HERTWIG, I.: Zoologisches Institut, Poppelsdorfer Schloß, D-5300 Bonn, FRG

HÖDL, W.: I. Zoologisches Institut der Universität Wien, Dr. Karl-Lueger-Ring 1, A-1010 Wien, Austria

HOFFMAN, J.: Biology Dept., Technion Haifa, Haifa, Israel

JACOBS, G.: Zoologisch Institut, Naamsestraat 61, B-3000 Leuven, Belgium

JENKS, B.: Dept. Animal Physiology, University of Nijmegen, Toernooiveld, N-6525 ED Nijmegen, The Netherlands

JOLY, J.: Lab. Biologie de Reproduction, Université de Rennes, Av. Général Leclerc, F-35-42 Rennes, France

KATZ, U.: Dept. Biology, Technion Haifa, Haifa, Israel

KLOAS, W.: Zoologisches Institut II der Universität Karlsruhe, Kaiserstr. 12, D-7500 Karlsruhe, FRG

Kühn, E.: Lab. Comparative Endocrinology, Zoological Institut, Naamsestraat 61, B-3000 Leuven, Belgium
Lange, C.: Auguststr. 23, D-6500 Mainz, FRG
Leloup, J.: Laboratoire de Physiologie, Museum Nat. d'Histoire Naturelle, 7, Rue Cuvier, F-75231 Paris Cedex 05, France
Leloup-Hatey, J.: Laboratoire de Physiologie, Museum Nat. d'Histoire Naturelle, 7, Rue Cuvier, F-75231 Paris Cedex 05, France
Leucht, T.: Zoologisches Institut II, Universität Würzburg, Röntgenring 10, D-8700 Würzburg, FRG
Martin, U.: Zoologisches Institut II, Universität Würzburg, Röntgenring 10, D-8700 Würzburg, FRG
Merkle, S.: Gesellschaft für Strahlen- und Umweltforschung, Institut für Säugetiergenetik, D-8042 Neuherberg, FRG
Milano Grassi, E.: Animal and Human Biology, Viale dell'Universita 32, I-00185 Roma, Italy
Müller, R.: Zoologisches Institut II der Universität Karlsruhe, Kaiserstr. 12, D-7500 Karlsruhe, FRG
Olesen Larsen, L.: Zoophysiological Lab. A, August Krogh Inst., University of Copenhagen, 13, Universitetsxparken, DK-2100 Copenhagen, Denmark
Olivereau, M.: Laboratoire de Physiology, Institut Oceanographique, 195, rue St. Jaques, F-75005 Paris, France
Passia, D.: Anatomie II der Universität Düsseldorf, Universitätsstraße 1, D-4000 Düsseldorf, FRG
Peyrot, A.: Dipart. di Biologia Animale, Via A. Albertina 17, I-10123 Torino, Italy
Plisetskaya, E.: Dept. of Zoology NJ 15, University of Washington, Seattle, WA 98195, USA
Podufal, C.: III. Zoologisches Institut, Entwicklungsbiologie, Universität Göttingen, Berliner Straße 28, D-3400 Göttingen, FRG
Rahmann, H.: Institut für Zoologie, Universität Hohenheim, D-7000 Stuttgart 70
Rainteau, D.: Cell Biologie, Faculté de Médicine, Lab. R 285, 45, rue des St. Pères, F-75720 Paris Cedex 06, France
Rascher, C.: Anatomie II der Universität Düsseldorf, Universitätsstr. 1, D-4000 Düsseldorf, FRG
Rosenkilde, P.: Zoophysiological Lab. A, August Krogh Institute, University of Copenhagen, 13, Universitetsparken, DK-2100 Copenhagen, Denmark
Sawar, S. A.: Institut für Anatomie und Zytobiologie, Aulweg 123, D-6300 Gießen, FRG
Schneider, H.: Zoologisches Institut, Poppelsdorfer Schloß, D-5300 Bonn 1, FRG
Shpun, S.: Department of Biology, Technion Haifa, Haifa, Israel
Sinsch, U.: Zoologisches Institut, Poppelsdorfer Schloß, D-5300 Bonn 1, FRG
Thünker, H.: Institut für Angewandte Zoologie, Universität Bonn, An der Immenburg 1, D-5300 Bonn 1, FRG
Thurmond, W.: Biological Science Dept., Cal. Polytech. State Univ., San Luis Obispo, Ca. 93401, USA
Tonon, M. C.: Mol. Endocrinol. Lab., UA CNRS 650, Un. Aff. INSERM, Université de Rouen, F-76134 Mont-St. Aignan Cedex, France
Trux, A.: Institut für angewandte Zoologie, Universität Bonn, An der Immenburg 1, D-5300 Bonn 1, FRG
Ussing, A.: Zoophysiological Lab. A, August Krogh Institute, University of Copenhagen, 13, Universitetsparken, DK-2100 Copenhagen, Denmark
Vandorpe, G.: Zoologisch Institut, Naamsestraat 61, B-3000 Leuven, Belgium

VAUDRY, H.: Mol. Endocrinol. Lab., UA CNRS 650, Un. Aff. INSERM, Université de Rouen, F-76134 Mont-St.-Aignan Cedex, France
VELLANO, C.: Dipart. Biologia Animale, Via A. Albertina 17, I-10123 Torino, Italy
WARBURG, M.: Biology Department, Technion Haifa, Haifa, Haifa 32000, Israel
ZIMMERMANN, E.: Institut für Zoologie, Universität Hohenheim, D-7000 Stuttgart 70

Contents

I. Reproduction

II. Metamorphosis

III. Neural and Endocrine Regulation

IV. Osmoregulation and Adaptation

I. Reproduction

Fortschritte der Zoologie, Band/Vol. 38 · Hanke, W. (Hrsg.), Biology and Physiology of Amphibians
Gustav Fischer Verlag · Stuttgart · New York · 1990

Thyroid function and a possible thyroidal-gonadal interaction in reproduction and circannual rhythmicity

EDUARD KÜHN, GRETA JACOBS, GREET VANDORPE

Laboratory of Comparative Endocrinology, Zoological Institute, Naamsestraat 61, B-3000 Leuven, Belgium

1. Introduction

Reproductive cycles of frogs living in the temperate regions have been known for long to correspond closely to seasonal changes in climate and an extensive literature deals with seasonal variations in physiological and metabolic activity of amphibians. Annual variations in the secretory activity of the pituitary gland have been observed and are usually ascribed to seasonal alterations in temperature but other environmental factors such as humidity and photoperiod may be of importance as well.

Seasonal variations in the reproductive capacity however become particularly intriguing when we deal with animals submitted to relatively constant environmental conditions such as exist in some tropical areas.

In the following account annual variations in reproduction and thyroid activity of frogs of the temperate region have been compared to the annual reproductive capacity of the giant swamp frog *Dicroglossus occipitalis* living on the equator in Zaïre under virtually constant climatic conditions.

The thyroid gland was studied because it has been implicated in many seasonal processes including body metabolism, reproduction, molt, migration and hibernation (see Kar and Chandola, 1985). This study was conducted at the peripheral organs (thyroid, gonad) and the hypothalamo-hypophyseal level.

2. Studies on the interaction of the thyroidal and gonadal axis

2.1. Interaction at the thyroidal-gonadal level

In teleostean fishes, a thyroid-gonadal interrelationship is well evidenced by the presence of a maturational effect of thyroxine upon the gonads and the existence of cyles of thyroid activity correlated with reproduction (Sage, 1973; Hurlburt, 1977). Effects of estrogens on the thyroidal axis are also described (Chakraborti and Bhattacharya, 1984; Mackenzie, 1986; Maclatchy et al., 1986). In the following experiments this interrelationship between the thyroidal and gonadal hormones has been studied in *Rana ridibunda*.

Castration of male frogs resulted in lower testosterone plasma concentrations after 21, 42 and 51 days in three separate experiments. Some parameters of the thyroidal axis were studied: Plasma T4 was measured by RIA; the thyroid glands of each frog were incubated in a medium containing TSH in order to examine the release of T4 by the thyroid glands into the medium and the 5′-monodeiodination (5′-D) activity, an enzymatic process in which T4 is converted to T3 was studied *in vitro* in kidney homogenates. No significant effects of castration on the studied parameters of the thyroidal axis were observed in the different experiments. The only difference noticed between the castrated and the sham operated frogs was an elevated plasma T4 value in the castrated animals of the 2nd experiment, but this observation was not confirmed by the 1st and the 3rd experiment.

Analogous to the castration experiments, female *Rana ridibunda* were ovariectomized and sacrificed after 11 days. Compared to the sham operated controls plasma oestradiol (E_2) levels of the ovariectomized frogs were decreased significantly. No differences between the two groups were noticed as to the 5′-D-activity in the kidney homogenates or plasma concentrations of T_3. However, a decrease in plasma T_4 was present at the 10% level in the ovariectomized frogs and T_4 plasma concentrations were significantly positively correlated with E_2 plasma concentrations. A subcutaneous implantation of silastic tubings containing oestradiol-17β, resulted in a gradual release of E_2 into the circulation. E_2-tubings were implanted for 30 days in the experimental group and empty tubings were implanted in the control group. The E_2-tubing frogs compared to the control frogs, not only showed a sharp significant increase of plasma and ovarian E_2 concentrations after 30 days, but some clear effects were seen on the thyroidal axis as well: plasma T4 and T3 concentrations and the 5′-D-activity in the kidneys were significantly lower (Fig. 1).

In order to decrease the thyroid hormone concentrations some antithyroid compounds have been used. In methimazole (MMI) treated male *Rana ridibunda* plasma concentrations of T4 and the 5′-D activity in kidney homogenates were depressed. No influence however was seen on plasma testosterone concentrations. In female *Rana temporaria* iopanoic acid (IOP), a drug which blocks 5′-D-activity, was injected subcutaneously during 4 consecutive days. IOP treatment resulted in a significant decrease of the 5′-D-activity in the kidneys and a significant increase of plasma T4. Plasma E_2 levels dropped significantly in the IOP treated frogs. Silastic tubings were filled with IOP and implanted subcutaneously for 7 days in male and female *Rana ridibunda*. Both males and females with IOP tubings showed a significant increase of the plasma T_4 values, compared to control frogs with empty tubings. In IOP males the 5′-D-activity was declined but no alternations in plasma and testicular testosterone levels took place. In IOP females similar effects were noticed: a decreased T_3/T_4 ratio, indicating a decline of the T_4-T_3 conversion, but the ovarian and plasma E_2 levels were unaltered.

These results do indicate that no simple interaction exists between the thyroid hormones and the gonadal steroids of frogs. Mild changes in thyroid hormone levels do not influence the gonadal axis, nor do mild alterations in sex hormone levels influence the thyroidal axis. Only a high and long-term administration of sex hormones in female frogs seems to have an impact on the thyroidal axis (Vandorpe and Kühn, 1989).

In birds and reptiles «progonadal» and «antigonadal» effects of thyroid hormones have been observed. Progonadal effects have been found in seasonally breeding birds and reptiles since thyroidectomy causes gonadal regression which can be overcome with thyroid hormones (Thapliyal and Garg, 1969; Chaturvedi and Thapliyal, 1979; Haldar-Misra and Thapliyal, 1981). In some birds however, e.g. the spotted munia, antigonadal effects of the thyroid glands have been described and thyroidectomy will abolish normal seasonal regression (Thapliyal and Pandha, 1965; Thapliyal, 1969; Thapliyal and Chandola, 1972); whereas thyroxine (T_4) administration suppresses gonadal development and precipitates regression. Consequently, low T_4 plasma concentrations are found during reproduction, and they only rise when the gonads begin to regress. Circulating levels of

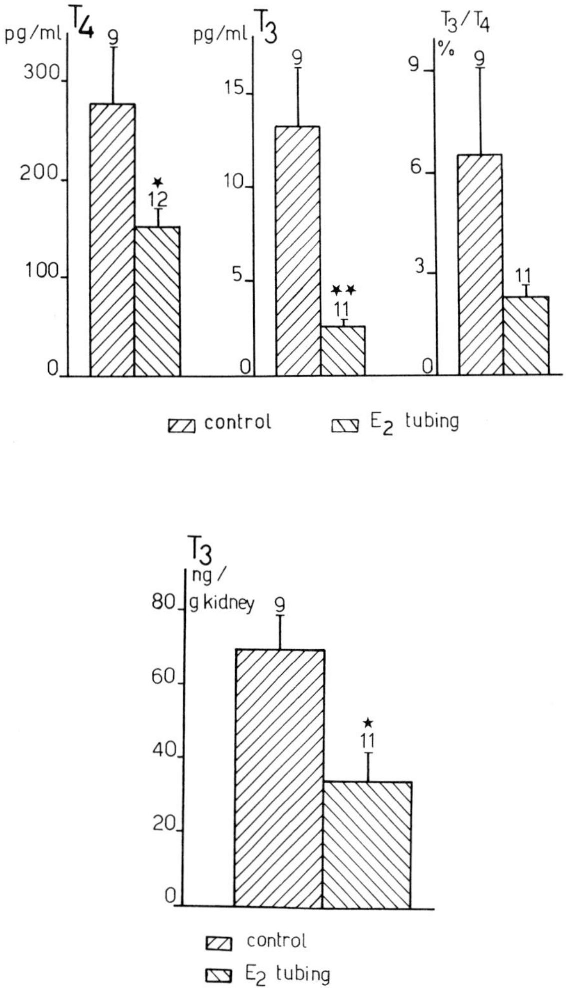

Fig. 1: Plasma T_3, T_4, the T_3/T_4 ratio and the kidney 5′-D activity in female *Rana ridibunda* with an implant of empty (control) or E_2-filled (E_2 tubing) silastic tubings. Mean ± S.E.M.
★ $P < 0.05$, ★★ $P < 0.01$ (ANOVA)

triiodothyronine (T_3) on the other hand parallel gonadal development. Moreover, T_4 but not T_3 may decrease gonadal volume when injected into thyroidectomised spotted munia. In lizards, where the thyroid is progonadal, only T_4 can maintain gonadal function in thyroidectomised animals (Kar and Chandola, 1985).

These findings may be of great importance since they attribute to T_4 a physiological role distinct from T_3.

Triiodothyronine may act as a cohormone for estradiol-17β induction of vitellogenin in *Xenopus laevis*, which is the precursor protein of the major egg yolk proteins (Wangh and Schneider, 1982). Moreover, glucocorticoids may act together with estrogens and thyroid hormones in regulating the synthesis of *Xenopus* vitellogenins, serum albumin and fibrinogen (Wangh, 1982). It may be of interest that when the conversion of T_4 into T_3 is blocked by propylthiouracil in *Xenopus laevis* tadpoles, undergoing metamorphosis, the estradiol-17β induction of vitellogenin is also inhibited (May and Knowland, 1980).

2.2. The hypothalamic control of thyroid and gonadal function

2.2.1. The thyrotropin releasing hormone (TRH)

In the hypothalamus of the frog immunoreactive thyrotropin releasing hormone (TRH) has been found (Jackson and Reichlin, 1974) and this may be able to stimulate the release of several pituitary hormones.

a) **Thyroid-stimulating hormone**: For long, strong evidence existed› in amphibians against a thyrotropin-releasing function of the mammalian and avian TRH or pGlu-His-ProNH$_2$ (Rosenkilde, 1979). So attempts to accelerate metamorphosis with TRH injections in tadpoles of *Rana catesbeiana* and *Notophtalmus viridescens* (Gona and Gona, 1974) or in the neotenic axolotl (Taurog et al., 1974) have been negative and injections of TRH into the dorsal lymph sac of adult *Rana temporaria* or directly on the pars distalis failed to increase the ^{125}I uptake by the thyroid gland (Vandesande and Aspeslagh, 1974). Even stimulation of TRH on the TSH release from frog pituitaries *in vitro* could not be demonstrated (Taurog et al., 1974). However, a few years ago, TRH has been proposed as a possible thyrotropin releasing factor in the frog *Rana ridibunda* (Darras and Kühn, 1982). The vena abdominalis of pentobarbital anesthetized female frogs (*Rana ridibunda*) was cannulated for injection of 10 μg TRH in these experiments performed during the months of April and May. Control levels of T_4 were low (0.35 ± 0.08 ng T_4) and increased after 1, 2, 4 and 8 hours following injection of 10 μg TRH with a maximal concentration of 2.65 ± 0.48 ng/ml after 4 hr. Control levels of T_3 were even ten times lower than of T_4 (0.029 ± 0.005 ng/ml) and were increased only after 4 hr (0.051 ± 0.007 ng/ml). Two days after removal of the pars distalis circulating levels of T_4 (but not T_3) in frog serum were significantly depressed, whereas T_3 and T_4 content of thyroids remained unchanged. An intravenous injection of 10 μg TRH in these hypophysectomized animals did not alter circulating levels of T_3 and T_4. These results indicate that the activity of the thyroid gland of *Rana ridibunda* is stimulated by intravenous injections of TRH and that this effect is mediated through the hypophysis (Darras and Kühn, 1982) (Fig. 2). Recently, these results have been confirmed by an *in vitro* study (Denver, 1988), whereas a morphometric study showed activation of the TSH cells after TRH administration (Gracia-Navarro et al., 1988, and this volume).

b) **Prolactin**: Hypothalamic extracts of frogs are able to stimulate the release of prolactin in rats (Kühn and Engelen, 1976) or increase its bioassayable activity in the serum of the frog itself (Singh and Singh, 1980). Hypothalamic extracts of frogs are also effective in stimulating the release of prolactin from the pituitary gland of frogs *in vitro* as measured by homologous radioimmunoassay (Seki and Kikuyama, 1984) and by densitometry of the prolactin band separated electrophoretically (Hall and Chadwick, 1984). Moreover in frogs, TRH is able to promote the secretion of prolactin *in vitro* (Clemons et al., 1979; Kikuyama and Seki, 1983; Hall and Chadwick, 1984) and to cause degranulation of the PRL cells (Gracia-Navarro et al., 1988). This prolactin release is inhibited by dopamine (Hall and Chadwick, 1984). In *Rana ridibunda* an *in vivo* release of prolactin was also observed, together with the release of thyroid hormones, following injection of TRH (Kühn et al., 1985 c) (Fig. 3). However, in *Bufo bufo* TRH releases prolactin without a concomitant increase in plasma concentration of thyroid hormones (Kikuyama et al., unpublished observations).

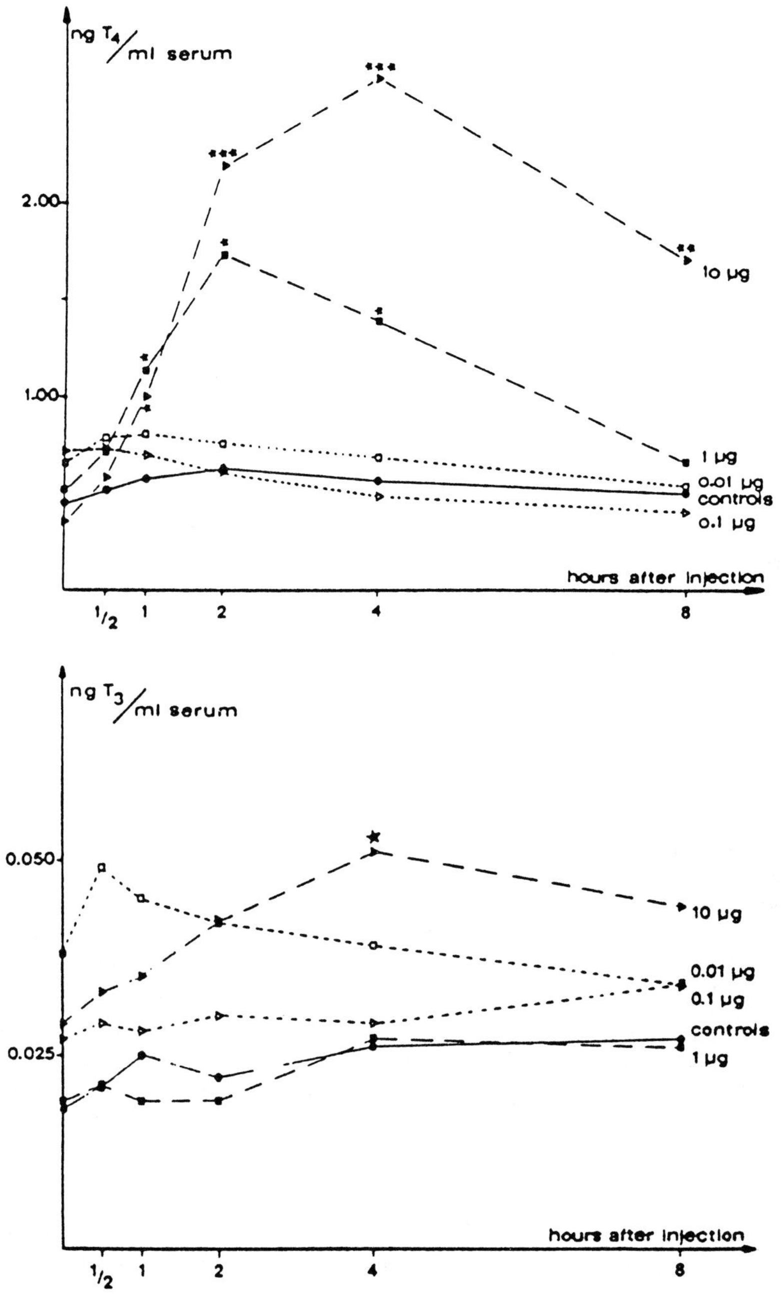

Fig. 2: Serum levels of T_4 and T_3 following injection of frog Ringer solution 0.01, 0.1, 1 and 10 μg TRH (mean values, n=8).
★ $P < 0.05$, ★★ $P < 0.01$, ★★★ $P < 0.001$.

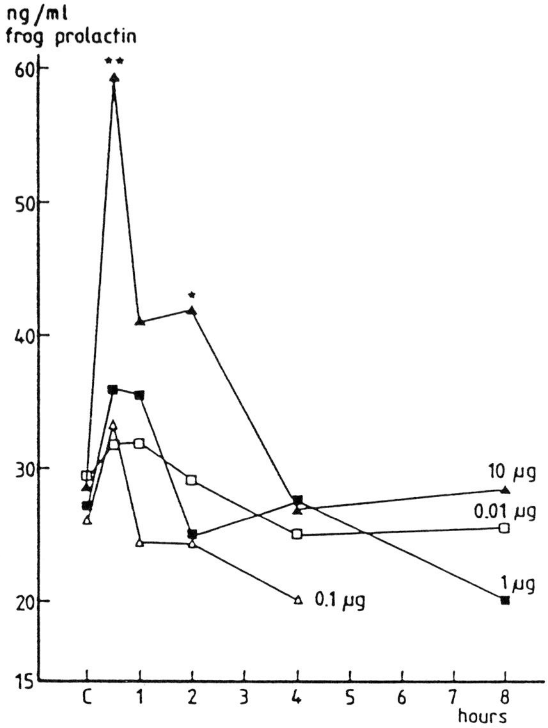

Fig. 3: Influence of an injection of several doses of TRH on serum concentrations of prolactin (n=5–7).
★ $P < 0.05$, ★★ $P < 0.02$ (paired t-test).

c) **Growth hormone:** In several frog species TRH or hypothalamic extracts stimulate the secretion of GH *in vitro*, as assayed by densitometry. Somatostatin by itself has no apparent effect on the release, but it inhibits the TRH- or hypothalamic extract-stimulated release of GH (Hall and Chadwick, 1984). Gracia-Navarro et al. (this volume) find the same with pituitaries of *Rana perezi in vitro*.

d) **α-Melanophorotropin:** TRH also stimulates the release of α-MSH from frog neurointermediate lobes *in vitro*. The concentrations of TRH required to promote a significant release of α-MSH are consistent with the high concentrations of TRH in blood and in the neurointermediate lobe complex of these animals (Leroux et al., 1983).

2.2.2. *The gonadotropin releasing hormone (GnRH)*

Recently, a possible second thyrotropic candidate has been proposed (Jacobs et al., 1988a; Denver, 1988): the gonadotropin-releasing hormone the dominant form of which in frogs and salamanders is chromatographically and immunologically indistinguishable from mammalian GnRH (Sherwood et al., 1986).

Plasma concentrations of T_4 were raised significantly 2 and 4 hrs after intravenous injection of synthetic luteinizing hormone-releasing hormone (GnRH) in *Rana ridibunda* (1 and 10 µg on two consecutive days) and in *Rana esculenta* (10 µg). A dose of 1 µg GnRH was not so effective as 50 µg synthetic TRH when injected in *Rana ridibunda* in

November. However 10 μg GnRH was equipotent to 50 μg TRH. Injection of GnRH into *R. temporaria* in February did not cause the same pronounced T_4 increase as in the other frogs: about half of the group was responsive to the decapeptide. GnRH or TRH did not influence plasma T_3 concentrations. Pre-injection levels of T_3 and T_4 were higher during the breeding season (April) in *R. esculenta* (resp. 35.4 ± 1.4 pg/ml; 744 ± 134 pg/ml; n=22) compared to the basal concentrations in the very closely related *R. ridibunda* (November) (resp. 15.2 ± 1.1; 162 ± 24 pg/ml; n=28). Four days after removal of the pars distalis plasma T_4 concentrations were significantly decreased in *R. esculenta*, whereas T_3 could stay longer in circulation, probably by peripheral T_4 conversion. T_3 and T_4 content of the thyroids was not altered by the short-term hypophysectomy. Injection of 10 μg GnRH had no influence on plasma T_4 nor testosterone concentrations in these frogs, contrary to the shamectomized animals. The results suggest that the stimulatory effect of intravenously injected GnRH on thyroidal (and gonadal) activity in the frog, is primarily mediated through the pars distalis of the hypophysis. They also point to a possible correlation between the gonadal and thyroidal axis (Jacobs et al., 1988 a).

Uptill now it seemed to be impossible to stimulate the release of T_4 with TRH in the neotenic axolotl (Darras and Kühn, 1983; Jacobs et al., 1988 b). However, when 10 μg GnRH was administered intravenously in male neotenic axolotls (*Ambystoma mexicanum*) plasma concentrations of T_4 and testosterone were increased 2 and 4 hr after injection. A dose of 50 μg only influenced plasma T_4 levels which allows to conclude that the elevation of T_4 was not caused indirectly by testosterone. This observation suggests for the first time that a hypothalamic hormone is capable of stimulating the thyroidal axis in the neotenic axolotl (Jacobs and Kühn, 1988). Therefore, three attempts were made to induce metamorphosis by repeated injections of GnRH. First, female axolotls were injected intraperitoneally on 5 consecutive days with 100 μg GnRH (July). However nothing else but egg deposition could be observed. In a second (December) and third experiment (April), male and some female axolotls received 5 intravenous injections of 10 μg GnRH every other day. Although significant elevations of the plasma concentrations of T_4 could be observed 2 hrs after injection, these were not sufficient to trigger off metamorphosis (Fig. 4). In some cases, the responsiveness of gonads and thyroids to the GnRH injections was not necessarily coupled. T_4 could be enhanced without concomitant increase of testosterone, and vice versa. Therefore, this observation is not in contradiction with the hypothesis that testosterone and T_4 may be increased by a different factor, resp. LH (Licht, 1979) and TSH.

These results may support the hypothesis of Sage (1973) that a gonadotropin-releasing hormone was the original controlling hormone of the gonadal and thyroidal axis. In the female sea lamprey plasma T_4 was raised after injection of a GnRH analog (Sower et al. 1985). However the question remains which hypothalamic hormone is capable of controlling the thyroid gland in teleost fish since it was demonstrated that a rise in blood gonadotropin after injection of GnRH was not accompanied by a change in thyroid activity (Brown et al., 1985; MacKenzie et al., 1987). TRH itself apparently is not effective in fish since four injections of different doses performed in our laboratory in carp, Tilapia or Clarias did not result in increased thyroid hormone concentrations.

3. Peripheral monodeiodination in amphibians

3.1. Existence of a 5′-monodeiodination activity

In mammals and in birds it is widely accepted that T_4 is a prohormone which is only physiologically active after deiodination to 3,3′,5-triiodothyronine (T_3), whereas conver-

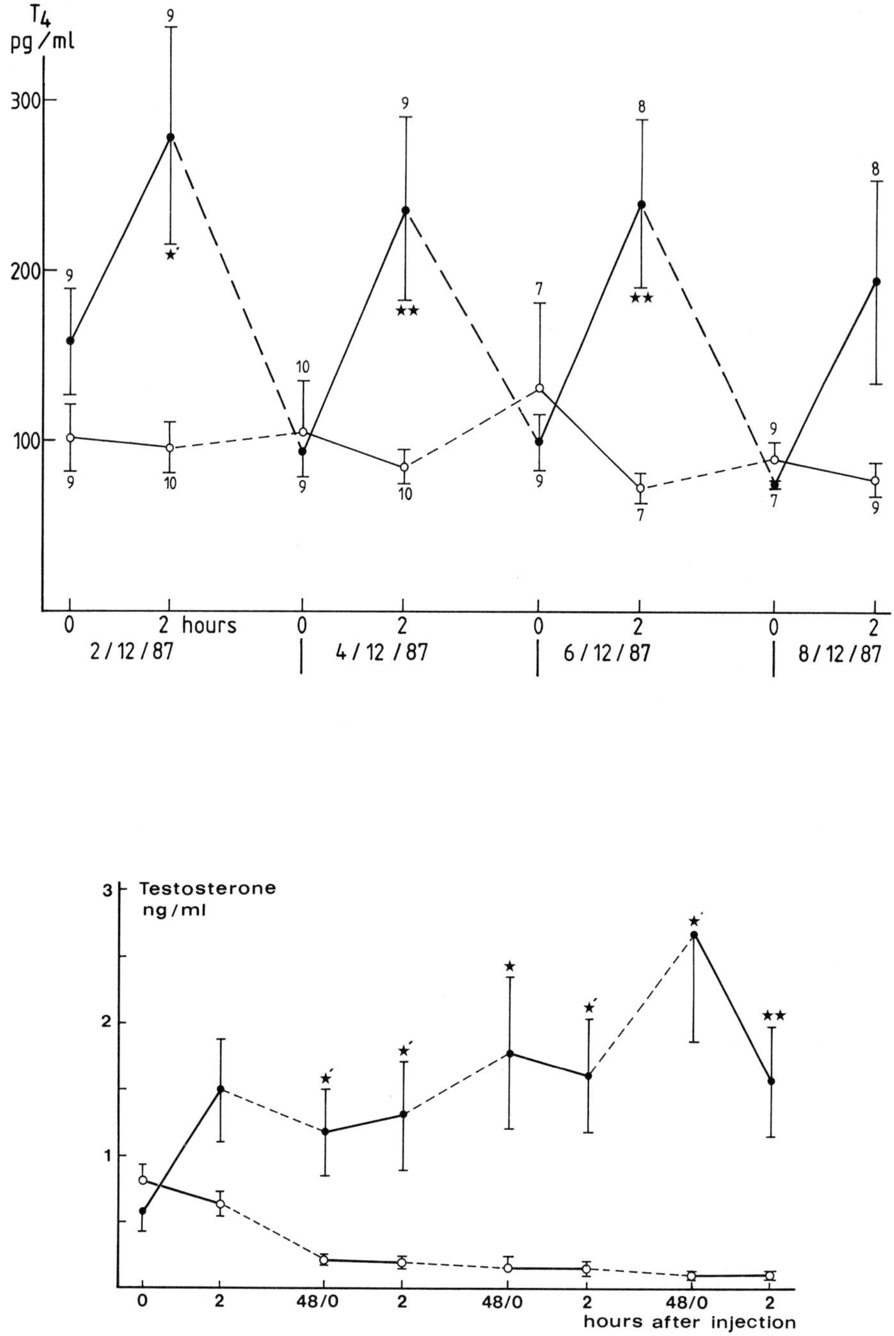

Fig. 4: The influence of 4 injections of 10 μg LHRH every other day on plasma T_4 and testosterone concentrations in the mexican axolotl. Mean ± S.E.M.
★ $P < 0.05$, ★' $P < 0.025$, ★★ $P < 0.01$.

sion to 3,3′5′-triiodothyronine (reverse T_3, rT_3) leads to its metabolic inactivation (Cavalieri, 1980; Kühn et al., 1984a). This conversion occurs peripherally, mainly in the liver. Thus, it is demonstrated qualitatively that exogenous treatment with T_4 of thyroidectomized ducks results in the appearance of T_3 in the serum of these animals (Astier and Newcomer, 1978). In the chicken it is shown that the conversion rate of T_4 into T_3 even exceeds that found in mammals, with up to 70% of the T_4 secreted by the thyroid gland being converted into T_3 (Rudas and Pethes, 1984, a, b), compared to 40% found in the rat (Schwartz et al., 1971).

In amphibians, this conversion plays an important role during metamorphosis (Buscaglia et al., 1985). The surge of plasma T_3 observed at climax cannot be explained by direct thyroid secretion of T_3, since the thyroidal T_3/T_4 ratio is very low and does not change significantly throughout metamorphosis in *Xenopus* (Leloup et al., 1977; Schultheiss, 1980), *Rana catesbeiana* (Suzuki and Suzuki, 1980) and *Rana esculenta* (Schultheiss, 1980). An injection of $^{125}I-T_4$ into tadpoles of *Xenopus* from late premetamorphosis to the end of climax demonstrates clearly the peripheral production of $^{125}I-T_3$ which increases towards climax (Leloup and Buscaglia, 1980; Galton and Munck, 1981). Moreover, when this peripheral conversion is inhibited by the use of a competitive inhibitor (iopanoic acid) of the T_4 5′-monodeiodinase, the significant reduction of the peripheral production of T_3 leads to a delayed metamorphosis which indicates that T_3 is the major metamorphic hormone in amphibians (Buscaglia et al., 1985).

The existence of a T_4 5′-monodeiodination activity has also been demonstrated in adult *Rana catesbeiana*, *Necturus maculosus* (Galton, 1985) and *Xenopus laevis* (Buscaglia et al., 1985) following injection of labelled T_4 and in adult *Bufo marinus* (Sawin et al., 1981) following injection of unlabelled T_4 and consequent T_3 radioimmunoassay. The presence of a peripheral monodeiodination in *Rana ridibunda* activity is suggested by the occurrence of an extremely low T_3 content of the thyroid gland together with a much higher plasma T_3/T_4 ratio, which indicates that practically all circulating T_3 in adult frogs is derived from peripheral monodeiodination (Kühn et al., 1983a) (Fig. 5).

In amphibians *in vitro* deiodination of T_4 was first reported in liver and muscle homogenates (Tata, 1960) and later studies confirmed T_4 deiodination, but T_3 was not a detected product (Dowling and Rasevska, 1966). In these studies general deiodination rather than monodeiodination is considered to take place.

The exact location for the peripheral monodeiodination of T_4 into T_3 in adult male *Rana ridibunda* was investigated using a method described for rats and chicken in which unlabelled T_4 was added to a tissue homogenate. The production of T_3 was measured by radioimmunoassay, taking into account the presence of T_3 in the homogenate before the addition of T_4, and the cross reaction of the T_3-Ab with T_4 (Chiraseveenuprapund et al., 1976; Chopra, 1977; Decuypere et al., 1982). Studies on mammals have revealed that monodeiodination of T_4 occurs by an enzymatic reduction reaction (Chiraseveenuprapund et al., 1976). The presence of thiol groups in the cytoplasma, probably of glutathion, determines the activity of this monodeiodinase, which may contain itself SH-groups (Visser, 1978).

In the following study this method was used in order to look for the presence of T_4-5′-monodeiodination activity in liver and kidney homogenates of *Rana ridibunda* (March). Reducing conditions were obtained by adding 1,4-dithio-DL-treithol (DTT) to the incubation medium. EDTA was also added since it is known that some enzymes with essential SH-groups are inhibited by metal ions (Lehninger, 1979).

The results indicate that a very low T_3 production occurred in liver homogenates examined by this *in vitro* system. Addition of EDTA or DTT did not influence the liver monodeiodination, but DTT anhanced the basal kidney monodeiodination activity and

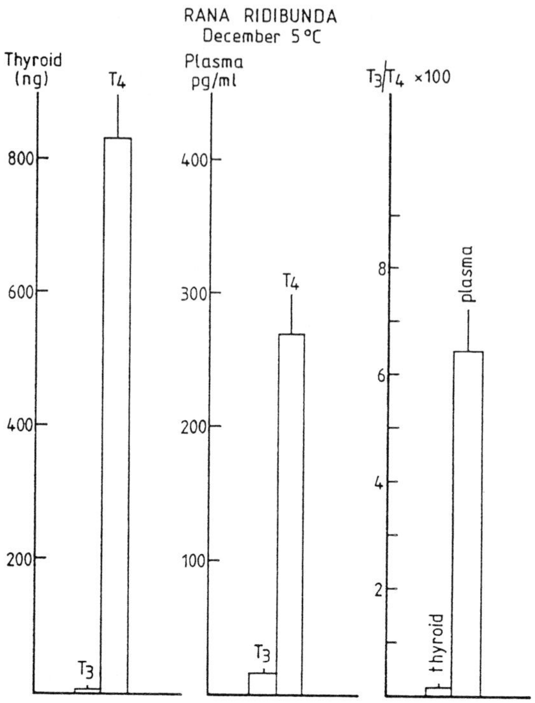

Fig. 5: Comparison between thyroid content (ng) and plasma concentrations (pg/ml) of T_3 and T_4 in December frogs.

even more in combination with EDTA. EDTA alone did not increase the T_4 conversion. It is suggested that although a 5′-D is present in the kidneys, the cofactor (endogenous SH-groups) either may occur in a low concentration or may be inhibited in its natural action due to the *in vitro* system (oxidation, dilution) (Table 1). In a second experiment (Vandorpe et al., 1987) T_4 5′-monodeiodinating activity was found in the skin of adult *Rana ridibunda* (Table 2). Interestingly this activity exhibits monthly variations. Our findings are not completely in agreement with those of Galton (1988), who used an alternate *in vitro* technique with addition of labeled T_4 to the tissue homogenates. She reported that the major organs responsible for the production of T3 from T4 in *R. catesbeiana* are gut and skin while 5′D-activity is absent in liver and kidney. On the other hand, significant amounts of ^{125}I–T3 were found in the serum and also in the liver of *Rana catesbeiana* following injection of $^{125}I–T_4$ (Galton, 1985). Thus, a discrepancy may exist between *in vivo* and *in vitro* experiments, even between different *in vitro* techniques or between different species.

3.2. Hormonal regulation of the T_4 5′-monodeiodination activity

The involvement of the hypophysis in the control of the peripheral monodeiodination of T_4 into T_3 has become more and more obvious in recent years. It was first observed that a peripheral conversion of T_4 into T_3 is stimulated by ovine prolactin and ovine GH in the adult eel (Leloup and de Luze, 1980; de Luze and Leloup, 1983; de Luze et al., 1984),

Table 1: Influence of DTT (4 mM) and EDTA (3 mM) on the production of T_3 (ΔT_3: pg/mg tissue) in liver and kidney homogenates of *Rana ridibunda* (March). Homogenates were incubated with 2500 pg T_4/mg liver or 8000 pg T_4/mg kidney (representing for both organs 595 ng T_4/ml incubate during 1 or 2 hr at 37 °C. Mean ± S.E.M. of 4 different experiments.

pH = 6.55	T_4 alone	T_4 + DTT	T_4 + EDTA	T_4 + EDTA + DTT
Liver 1 hr	0.09 ± 2.68	4.26 ± 2.00	0.80 ± 2.12	5.59 ± 2.13
Liver 2 hr	12.48 ± 4.53	10.67 ± 2.34	10.03 ± 1.51	12.66 ± 2.12
Kidney 1 hr	–3.20 ± 8.79	140.17 ± 50.88	5.06 ± 7.54	349.08 ± 57.22
Kidney 2 hr	17.54 ± 2.06	260.47 ± 61.16	29.13 ± 10.66	476.64 ± 78.34

Table 2: T_3 production (ng/g skin) in skin homogenates of male *Rana ridibunda* incubated for 1 hour at 37 °C with 1 µg T_4/g skin alone or with 1 µg T_4/g skin in the presence of DTT and EDTA (0.211M and 0.158M respectively). Mean ± S.E.M., number of animals as indicated, *$P < 0.05$, **$P < 0.01$, ***$P < 0.001$, compared to unstimulated values (ANOVA).

	T4 alone		T4+DTT+EDTA	
JUN	–1.13 ± 1.34	(10)	7.69 ± 1.61	(9)***
JUL	–2.72 ± 1.17	(9)	1.22 ± 1.43	(9)
AUG	0.61 ± 1.05	(10)	6.94 ± 2.37	(10)*
SEP	–0.89 ± 0.52	(10)	5.94 ± 1.73	(10)**
OCT	–1.25 ± 0.73	(10)	3.22 ± 0.81	(10)***
NOV	0.49 ± 0.77	(8)	6.17 ± 1.88	(8)*
DEC	–0.49 ± 0.63	(8)	8.02 ± 2.01	(9)**

whereas fish GH but not fish prolactin stimulates this conversion (de Luze and Leloup, 1984). In the chick embryo and adult chicken activation of thyroid function as evidenced by a peripheral conversion of T_4 into T_3 and an increased liver 5′-monodeiodination is induced by GH (Kühn et al., 1987c, 1986). Moreover, hypothalamic hormones which release GH also stimulate the conversion of T_4 into T_3 in embryos (Kühn et al., 1988) or adult chicken (Kühn et al., 1988).

In mammals evidence for a control by GH, but not prolactin, in the peripheral conversion has been presented for newborn lambs (Kühn et al., 1986b) and adult rats (Kühn et al., 1986a).

In amphibians the stimulation of the 5′-monodeiodination process during metamorphosis correlates with the increase of circulating T_4 and T_3 (Buscaglia et al., 1985) suggesting that T_4 5′-D- may be regulated by thyroid hormones as shown in mammals (Larsen et al., 1981). When the thyroid hormone synthesis is blocked in premetamorphic tadpoles of *Xenopus laevis* for at least 2 months by immersion in perchlorate, the plasma T_4 is undetectable and the monodeiodination activity remains low. Addition of T_4 or T_3 however increases this activity. When T_3 or T_4 is withdrawn from such tadpoles, the 5′-monodeiodinase falls again to the low premetamorphic level, despite the fact that their morphology corresponds to that of climax (Buscaglia and Leloup, 1982).

In order to investigate a possible involvement of the hypophysis in the control of peripheral monodeiodination, an injection was made of 1.5 µg bullfrog GH and prolactin on respectively two and three consecutive days in *Rana ridibunda* and plasma concentration of thyroid hormones were measured. The injections did not influence this parameter, nor could the 5′-D activity be altered in kidneys, skin, liver or adipose tissue. If however frogs were hypophysectomized, a decrease of this activity was observed in the kidney, together with decreased circulating levels of T_4. Since an exogenous cofactor was available, this decrease in the T_4 converting capacity may be due to a changed ability of the deiodination enzyme to exert its action. Whether or not a hypophyseal hormone or the thyroxine substrate is involved in the maintenance of this 5′-D activity needs further investigation.

4. Seasonal variation of steroid and thyroid hormones in frogs of the temperate region

4.1. Temperate region

4.1.1. Steroid hormones

In *Rana esculenta* the ovarian cycle usually starts in September with an active vitellogenesis up to December. During hibernation egg maturation slows down considerably whereas final maturation of the ova occurs before March. The breeding season occurs from April till June.

Plasma levels of several steroid hormones, e.g. progesterone, androstenedione, estrone and 17β-estradiol (E_2), were higher just before the first ovulatory wave in spring and lowest after the breeding season (Pierantoni et al., 1984a). Progesterone may play an important role in oocyte maturation (Wasserman and Smith, 1978) and usually high titers were found prior to ovulation (Thornton, 1972; Redshaw, 1972). It was also suggested that progesterone may be involved in retarding egg-laying until the formation of the jelly coat around the egg was completed during its passage through the oviduct (Wasserman and Smith, 1978). The role of estrogens in vitellogenesis has been discussed above.

The testes of *Rana esculenta* displayed a well-marked seasonal variation not only in their spermatogenic activity (Lofts, 1964) but also in their ability to secrete testosterone following administration of gonadotropin releasing hormone and a crude hypophyseal extract. The increase in testicular testosterone preceded the one found in plasma by 2 months (November versus January). The early increased steroid level in the testes may be necessary for its local action on spermatid formation (Pierantoni et al., 1984b). In nature, the quiescence of spermatogenesis apparently was due solely to low temperature. Under controlled experimental conditions a temperature of 4 °C whatever the photoperiod, impaired spermatogenesis or testosterone release at any time of the year (Rastogi et al., 1978; Iela et al., 1980). However, if winter animals were kept at a high temperature (24 °C) and exposed to a photoperiodic regimen of 24 L: 0 D or 12 L:12 D the hormone concentration increased, while no increase was detectable in animals kept in total darkness at the same temperature (Iela et al., 1980).

During the post-reproductive period a transitory refractoriness to several environmental cues appeared to be a common event in some vertebrates (see Polzonetti-Magni et al., 1984). So, in *Rana esculenta* populations testosterone and progesterone progressively decreased in the blood until July, while estradiol showed, in both sexes, an increase in the same month. Testosterone depletion accounted for thumb pad atrophy in the male and probably, in both sexes for the summer interruption of sexual behaviour. The estradiol increase could be responsible for the renewed vitellogenesis (Polzonetti-Magni et al., 1984).

4.1.2. *Thyroid and steroid hormones*

Several data indicated that the hypothalamo-hypophyseal-thyroidal axis of amphibians belonging to the temperate climatic zone also underwent seasonal variations in activity. Histological evidence for the seasonal secretory activity of the pituitary thyrotrophs and thyroid follicles existed for long (van Oordt et al., 1968; Rosenkilde, 1979) and it seemed that environmental factors may be responsible for the observed changes. In *Bufo bufo* cold decreased thyroidal iodine uptake to very low values (Egeberg and Rosenkilde, 1965), whereas in male *Rana temporaria* acclimation to higher temperatures resulted in an increased iodine uptake (Ceusters et al., 1978). Toads kept at 5 °C also had lower plasma T_4 concentrations, whereas in prebreeding animals circulating T_4 levels were more than double compared to their concentrations in early autumn (Rosenkilde and Jørgensen, 1977). On the other hand, a lower thyroidal T_3 and T_4 content was found in hibernating *Rana ridibunda* in January, whereas plasma levels of T_3 were maintained and plasma levels of T_4 were even higher compared to fed September or October frogs (Kühn et al., 1983). The increase in plasma T_4 during the month of January, with the coldest month still to come, together with a virtual depletion of hormone from the thyroids may be the result of a negative photostimulation: December frogs were kept at 4 °C and submitted to complete darkness or a different photoperiod and light intensity during 4 weeks (at 4 °C). The animals which had been in complete darkness showed higher plasma T_4 concentration than those submitted to the different light conditions. Moreover, frogs adapted to 8 hours

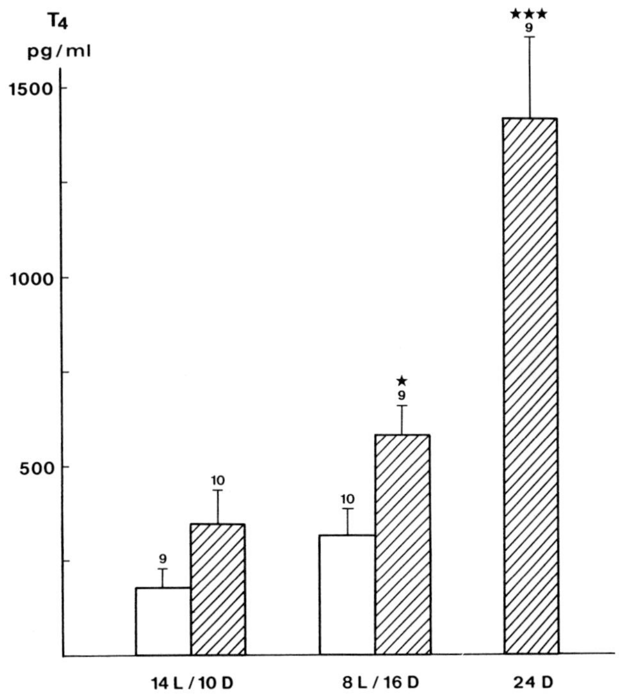

Fig. 6: The influence of different photoperiod and light intensities (□ 2500 lux, ▨ 500 lux) on plasma concentrations of T_4 in *Rana ridibunda*.
★ $P < 0.05$, ★★★ $P < 0.001$ (ANOVA).

light with low intensity (500 Lux) had higher T_4 values than frogs which had been living under the same photoperiod but with higher intensity (2500 Lux). If they had been subjected to a 14L: 10D photoperiod, T_4 levels were low and did not differ between the two light intensities (Fig. 6). Apparently the deprivation of light during hibernation and not the lack of food or the low temperatures, may increase plasma concentration of T_4. Plasma concentrations of T_3 however were not affected by the light intensities but were doubled in the animals conditioned to the dark. The hypothesis was put forward that T_4 released this way, may act as a trigger in the activation of the hypothalamo-hypophyseal-thyroidal axis (Kühn et al., 1984b). In these experiments, two days after a single injection of 10 μg T_4 a seven-fold increase in the ability of the thyroid gland to release T_4 following TSH-stimulation was observed. It is known that a similar dose will induce metamorphosis in *Ambystoma tigrinum*, when injected peripherally but also when a much lower dose is injected into the hypothalamus (Norris and Gern, 1976). It has also been shown that this T_4 exerts a positive feedback on the hypophyseal TSH-cells in *Ambystoma mexicanum* (Gunsbourg, 1971). We therefore conclude that the depletion of the thyroid gland of T_4 observed at the end of hibernation may be essential for the reactivation of the hypothalamo-hypophyseal-thyroidal axis.

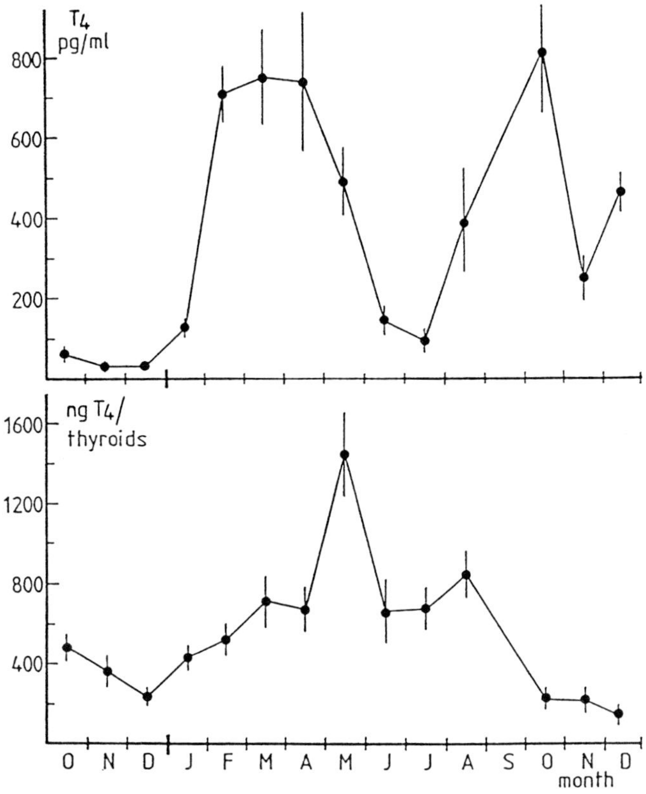

Fig. 7: Plasma concentrations of T_4 (ng/ml) and thyroid content (ng) of samples collected every month (n=10) between October 1982 and December 1983. Mean values ± S.E.M.

Whether or not this reactivation of the thyroid gland is also necessary for the activation of the gonadal axis however remains questionable. In a following experiment, circulating levels of T_4 and testosterone were studied in male frogs each month between October 1982 and December 1983 (Fig. 7 and Fig. 8). Maximal and minimal temperatures of the unheated room where the frogs were kept are also provided. Low plasma concentrations of T_4 were found in November and December 1982, but higher ones in these months the next year. During the month of January these levels increased and reached maximal levels (> 700 pg/ml) in February although the temperature was still decreasing. During the month of May, T_4 levels dropped to winter values which were reached in June–July. At this time, plasma testosterone values were high indicating the breeding period of this animal. The high thyroid T_4 content when plasma values are declining could be indicative for an increased peripheral monodeiodination to T_3. After the breeding period both plasma T_4 and testosterone concentration were increasing again, which may be related to an increased spermatogenesis as observed for *Rana esculenta* (Pierantoni et al., 1984b).

The plasma concentrations of T_4 however may depend also on the capacity of the thyroid gland itself to release T_4. When tested in an *in vitro* system it was found that the thyroids will release more T_4 in March or May, following administration of a given dose of TSH (Kühn et al., 1985b).

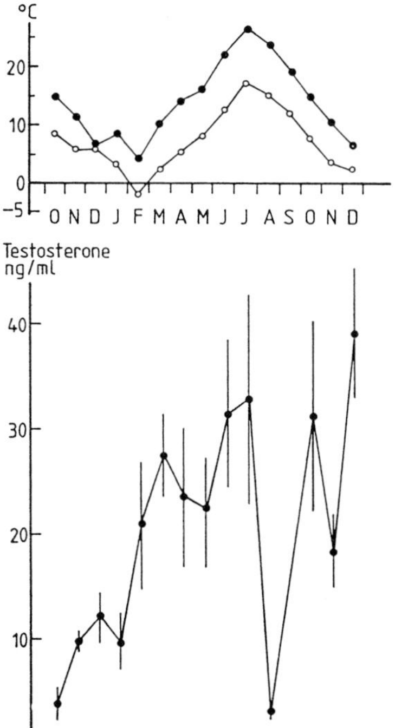

Fig. 8: Testosterone values (ng/ml) of same experiment together with minimal (○) and maximal (●) environmental temperatures.

4.1.3. *Peripheral monodeiodination activity*

As was demonstrated above, kidney and skin homogenate of *Rana ridibunda* contain a T_4-5′-monodeiodination activity. In the following experiment male *Rana ridibunda* were acclimated for one month to 4.5 °C and 20 °C respectively under a regimen of 8 L:16 D (December–January). Following this, the kidney T_4 5′-monodeiodination activity was measured in the presence of DTT and EDTA (Fig. 9). The results obtained with the warm adapted frogs suggest that extrathyroidal conversion of T_4 into T_3 may display a circadian rhythmicity, because an increase in enzyme activity could be observed towards the dark period.

Considering all T_3 production values together, it seems that at a given photoperiod an increase in temperature alone may be able to stimulate the peripheral conversion of T_4 into T_3. As was discussed earlier, the quiescence of spermatogenesis is due solely to low temperature (Rastogi et al., 1978; Iela et al., 1980) whereas a high temperature will increase testosterone production also in a constant light or a given photoperiod, but not in constant darkness (Iela et al., 1980).

In a following experiment the kidney 5′-monodeiodination activity was studied in male *Rana ridibunda* between January and December, each time using 10 animals (Fig. 10). With the addition of T_4 alone, no conversion is present in the homogenate. Together with DTT + EDTA a T_4 to T_3 conversion can be seen in each month studied. This activity is low in January–March and July–December, but high during reproduction in April–June (Vandorpe et al., 1987)

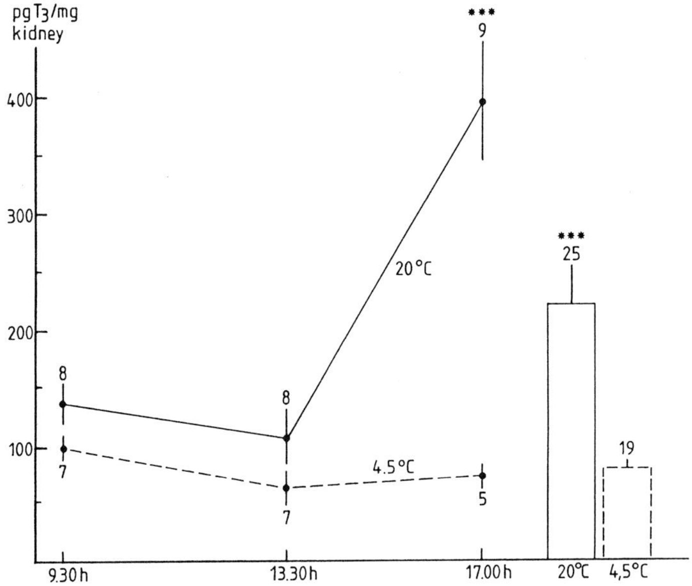

Fig. 9: Monodeiodinating activity (pg T_3/mg kidney) in the presence of EDTA (3 mM) and DTT (4 mM) in kidney homogenate of December frogs (male *Rana ridibunda*) acclimatized for one month to a temperature of 20 °C or 4.5 °C and to a light schedule of 8L:16D (Light 8.45h → 16.45h).

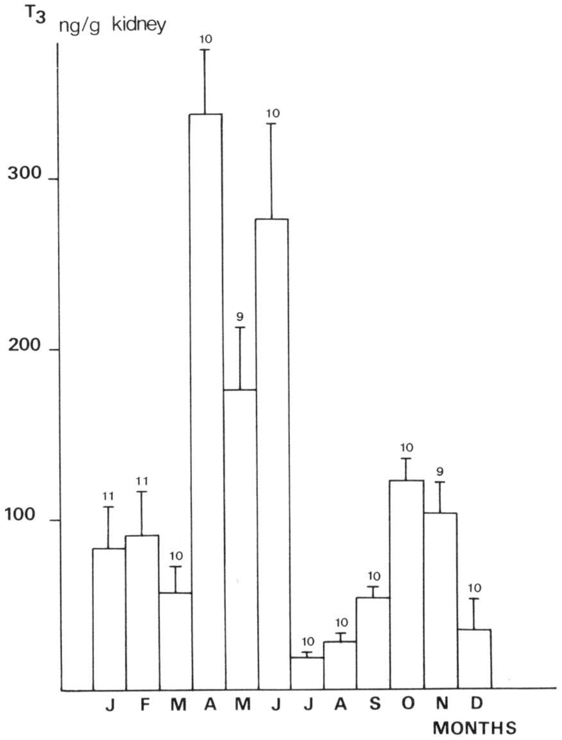

Fig. 10: Monthly T_3 production (ng/g kidney) in kidney homogenate incubated with 8 μg T_4/g kidney for 1 hour at 37 °C in the presence of DTT and EDTA in male *Rana ridibunda*.

4.2. The thyroid and the reproductive cycle of the giant swamp frog Dicroglossus occipitalis at the equator (Kühn et al., 1987b, c)

Females of the giant swamp frog (*Dicroglossus occipitalis*: Ranidae) were captured monthly during the night in the swamps and tributaries of the River Zaïre close to Kisangani, a town located on the equator (00° 31 N) with virtually constant conditions as to photoperiod, temperature, precipitations and relative humidity. Egg size groups according to Church (1960) and the gonadosomatic index (GSI) were closely related (Table 3). Though females with mature eggs could be found in every month, not all months were represented in the same way. A reproductive quiescence with a low GSI, undeveloped eggs and minimal plasma concentrations of E_2 and P_4 were found from October to January (Fig. 11). It is interesting to notice that in a separate study performed in the same area on the toad *Bufo regularis*, a quiet reproductive period was also found between September and November (Gevaerts and Kazungu, unpublished observations). Annual variations in thyroid content and plasma concentrations of T_4 were present in our study without concomitant changes in temperature or photoperiod, contrary to results described above on frogs of the temperate regions where temperature may control thyroid function (Ceusters et al., 1978) and where several data also pointed to the involvement of light intensity and photoperiod in the release of T_4 from the thyroid gland (Kühn et al., 1983a, 1985b).

Table 3: GSI and egg size grouping according to Church (1960).

	Grouping	GSI	n
Group I:	small unpigmented ova	0.61 ± 0.10 (0.21 – 1.17)	10
Group II:	variabel pigmentation	1.24 ± 0.14 (0.76 – 1.95)	7
Group III:	all eggs pigmented – no distinction between animal and vegetal hemispheres	1.92 ± 0.16 (1.33 – 2.64)	9
Group IV:	difference of distinction between animal and vegetal hemispheres	4.67 ± 0.22 (2.74 – 8.90)	42
Group V:	large eggs – clearly distinguishable animal and vegetal hemispheres	9.73 ± 0.55 (5.74 – 22.93)	42
Group VI:	post-ovulation – some unovulated group V ova are present	0.40 ± 0.06 (0.03 – 0.70)	11
			121

In the present study an inverse relationship existed between the thyroid content and plasma concentrations of T_4 throughout the year, which was even more pronounced when T_4 concentrations were compared to egg size groups or GSI (Fig. 12). So, thyroid content increased with proceeding of egg development, whereas plasma concentrations of T_4 were decreasing. This inverse relationship was already suggested in a previous study, where blood samples and thyroids of the giant swamp frog were assayed for T_4 in January, April, July and November (Kühn et al., 1985 c) and may be the consequence of an increased T_4 to T_3 conversion during reproduction as has been demonstrated for frogs of the temperate regions (Vandorpe et al., 1987).

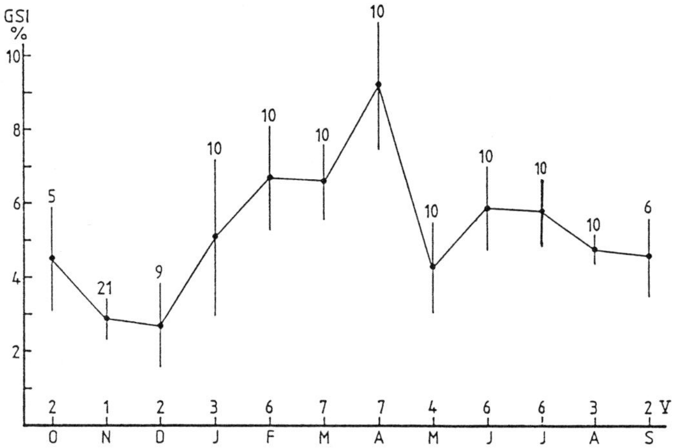

Fig. 11: Annual variations in GSI of female *Dicroglossus occipitalis*. Means ± S.E.M. Number of animals as indicated. Number of individuals belonging to egg size group V are also indicated.

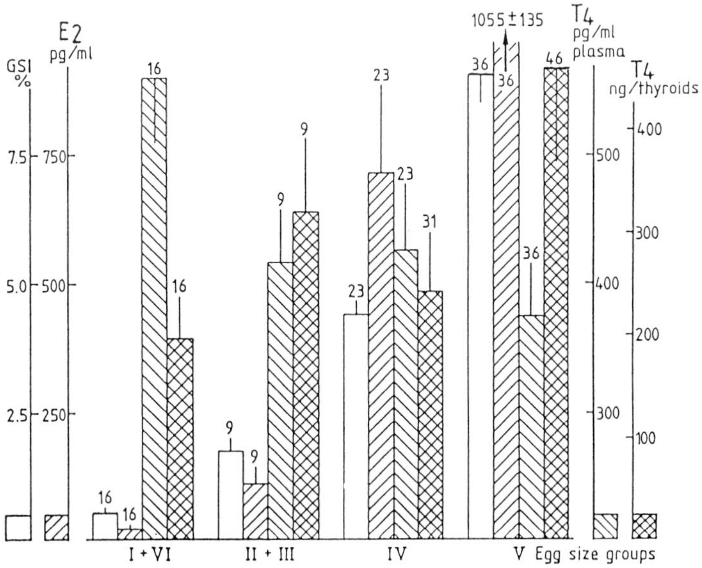

Fig. 12: GSI (▭) plasma concentrations of E_2 (pg/ml) (▨), and T_4 (pg/ml) (▧), and thyroid T_4 content(ng) (▩) in egg size groups of female *Dicroglossus occipitalis* as indicated. Means ± S.E.M.

In male *Dicroglossus occipitalis* a significant variation in plasma concentrations of testosterone was found during the year with a minimum in October and gradual increase to a maximum in March. Thereafter values dropped to a low in May, increased slightly again in July and August, and dropped again in September. This means that high values of testosterone in males coincided with the reproductive period of females (Kühn et al., 1987b). As has been discussed above, high testosterone plasma concentrations in males of the temperate region, also coincided or preceded the breeding season of females e.g. in *Rana esculenta* (Pierantoni et al., 1984a, b) and *R. ridibunda* (Vandorpe et al., 1987). Plasma concentrations of T_4 however were highly variable and no significant variations could be calculated. There is however a weak positive correlation present with testosterone, which may be related to the observation that in male *R. ridibunda* plasma concentration of T_4 are also high when high levels of testosterone were found (Vandorpe et al., 1987).

Conclusions

Temperate-zoned amphibians show seasonal variations in the activity of their thyroids and gonads. During hibernation circulating levels of steroids and thyroxine are minimal. After a period of low light intensity, T_4 is released from the thyroid gland, even though outside temperatures remain low. This T_4 may be responsible for a reactivation of the thyroidal axis. During the reproductive period an increase in the peripheral 5′-monodeiodination activity occurs in the kidney and high circulating levels of steroid hormones are found. After this period, the thyroid and gonadal axis may be reactivated again which is necessary for an active vitellogenesis and spermatogenesis.

In the frog *Dicroglossus occipitalis* living on the equator at virtually constant climatic conditions a reproductive quiescence is described. During active reproduction plasma oestradiol-17β and progesterone are increased together with the thyroidal T_4 content, whereas T_4 in plasma is decreased. It is concluded that the peripheral monodeiodination of T_4 into T_3 may play an important role in reproduction of frogs from the temperature or equatorial regions.

The parallel increases in plasma concentrations of steroid hormones and thyroxine which are observed in frogs of the temperate and tropical regions may be the result of a common hypothalamic control since LHRH is able to stimulate the gonadal and thyroidal axis at the same time. However, interaction between the hormones of the target organs itself is minimal and only high levels of oestradiol are able to decrease plasma concentrations of thyroid hormone and the converting activity for T_4 into T_3 in the kidney (Fig. 13).

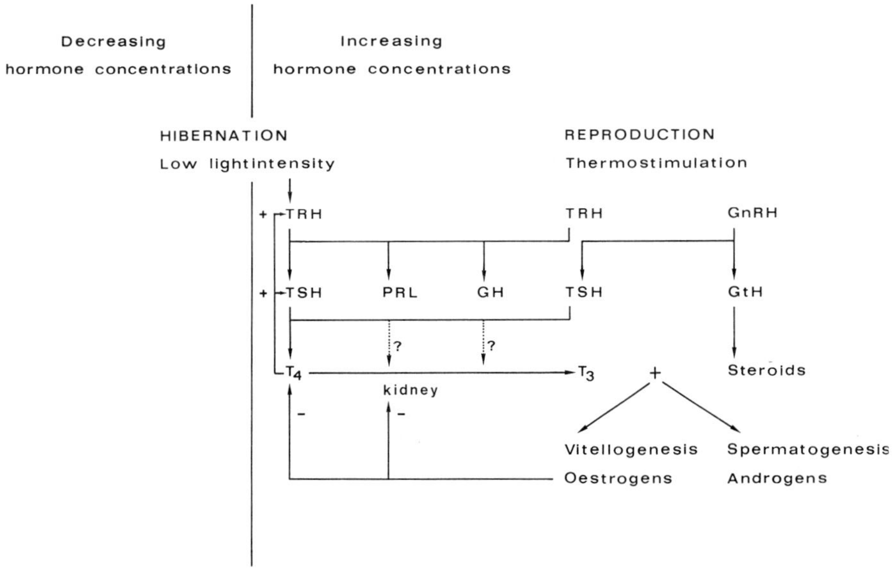

Fig. 13: Evolution and interrelation of thyroid and gonadal hormones during hibernation and reproduction in the frog *Rana ridibunda*.

Acknowledgment

We wish to thank Prof. S. Kikuyama of the Waseda university in Tokyo for his kind gift of bullfrog prolactin and growth hormone. G. Jacobs was supported by the Belgian National Fund of Scientific Research, whereas G. Vandorpe was supported by the IWONL institute.

References

Astier, H. Newcomer, W. S. (1978). Extrathyroidal conversion of thyroxine into triiodothyronine in a bird: the Peking duck. Gen. Comp. Endocrinol. *35*, 496–499.

Brown, C. L., Grau, E. G., Stetson, M. H. (1985): Functional specificity of gonadotropin and thyrotropin in *Fundulus heteroclitus*. Gen. Comp. Endocrinol., *58*, 252–258.

Buscaglia, M., Leloup, J. (1982): Inhibition of T_4-induced metamorphosis by telepaque administration to *Xenopus laevis* tadpoles. Experientia *38*, 712.

Buscaglia, M., Leloup, J., de Luze, A. (1985): The role and regulation of monodeiodination of thyroxine to 3,5,3′-triiodothyronine during amphibian metamorphosis. In: Metamorphosis. (M. Balls, M. Bownes, eds.), pp. 273–293. Clarendon Press, Oxford.

Cavalieri, R. R. (1980): Peripheral metabolism of thyroid hormones. Thyroid Today *3/7*, 1–5.

Ceusters, R., Darras, V. M., Kühn, E. R. (1978): Difference in thyroid function between male and female frogs (*Rana temporaria* L.) with increasing temperature. Gen. Comp. Endocrinol. *36*, 598–603.

Chakraborti, P., Bhattacharya, S. (1984): Plasma thyroxine levels in freshwater perch: Influence of season, gonadotropins, and gonadal hormones. Gen. Comp. Endocrinol. *53*, 179–186.

Chaturvedi, C. M., Thapliyal, J. P. (1979): Thyroidectomy and gonadal development in common Myna, *Acridotheres tristis*. Gen. Comp. Endocrinol. *39*, 327–329.

Chiraseveenuprapund, P., Buergi, U., Goswami, A. Rosenberg, I. N. (1976): Formation of triiodothyronine from L-thyroxine in rat kidney homogenate. In: Thyroid Research (J. Robbins, I. E. Braverman, eds.), pp. 244–247. American Elsevier, New York.

Chopra, I. J. (1977): A study of extrathyroidal conversion of thyroxine (T_4) to 3,3′,5-triiodothyronine (T_3) *in vitro*. Endocrinology *101(2)*, 453–463.

Church, G. (1960): Annual and lunar periodicity in the sexual cycle of the Javanese toad, *Bufo melanostictus* Schneider. Zoologica: New York Zoological Society *45*, 181–189.

Clemons, G. K., Russell, S. M., Nicoll, C. S. (1979): Effect of mammalian thyrotropin releasing hormone on prolactin secretion by bullfrog adenohypophysis *in vitro*. Gen. Comp. Endocrinol. *38*, 62–67.

Darras, V. M., Kühn, E. R. (1982): Increased plasma levels of thyroid hormones in a frog *Rana ridibunda* following intravenous administration of TRH. Gen. Comp. Endocrinol. *48*, 469–475.

Darras, V. M., Kühn, E. R. (1983): Effects of TRH, bovine TSH, and pituitary extracts on thyroidal T_4 release in *Ambystoma mexicanum*. Gen. Comp. Endocrinol. *51*, 286–291.

Decuypere, E., Kühn, E. R., Clijmans, B., Nouwen, E. J., Michels, H. (1982): Prenatal peripheral monodeiodination in the chick embryo. Gen. Comp. Endocrinol. *47*, 15–17.

de Luze, A., Leloup, J. (1983): Stimulation de la conversion périphérique de la thyroxine en triiodothyronine par l'hormone somatotrope ovine chez l'anguille (*Anguilla anguilla* L.). Comptes Rendus Hebdomadaires des Séances de l'Académie des Sciences, Séries D *296*, 409–412.

de Luze, A. and Leloup, J. (1984): Effects of ovine prolactin on iodide metabolism and thyroid activity in the eel. J. Comp. Endocrinol. *B 154*, 199–205.

de Luze, A., Leloup, J. and Olivereau, M. (1984): Fish growth hormone enhances peripheral conversion of thyroxine to triiodothyronine in the eel (*Anguilla anguilla* L.). Gen. Comp. Endocrinol. *56*, 308–312.

Dowling, J. T., Rasevska, D. (1966): Thyroxine metabolism by amphibian skin during metamorphosis and moulting. Gen. Comp. Endocrinol. *6*, 162–169.

Egeberg, J. C., Rosenkilde, P. (1965): Iodine uptake and ultrastructure of the thyroid gland in cold-exposed toads, *Bufo bufo*. Gen. Comp. Endocrinol. *5*, 673 (Abstract).

Galton, V. A. (1985): 3,5,3′-Triiodothyronine receptors and thyroxine 5′-monodeiodinating activity in thyroid hormone insensitive Amphibia. Gen. Comp. Endocrinol. *57*, 465–471.

Galton, V. A. (1988): Iodothyronine 5′-deiodinase activity in the amphibian *Rana castesbeiana* at different stages of the life cycle. Endocrinology *122*, 1746–1750.

Galton, V. A., Munck, K. (1981): Metabolism of thyroxine in *Rana catesbeiana* tadpoles during metamorphic climax. Endocrinology *109*, 1127–1131.

Gona, A. G., Gona, O. (1974): Failure of synthetic TRF to elicit metamorphosis in frog tadpoles or red-spotted newts. Gen. Comp. Endocrinol. *24*, 223–225.

Gracia-Navarro, F., Garcia-Navarro, S., Malagon, P. M., Ruiz-Navarro, A., Castano, J. (1988): Cellular and subcellular responses of pituitary cells to hypothalamic stimulation. Symposium on Biology and Physiology of Amphibians, Karlsruher Beiträge zur Zoophysiologie, Vol. 14, Abstract M 5.

Gunsbourg, N. (1971): Etude de la variation de charge de péricaryons neurosécréteurs au cours de la métamorphose provoquée chez *Ambystoma mexicanum* (Shaw). Ann. Endocrinol. *32*, 705–708.

Haldar-Misra, C., Thapliyal, J. P. (1981): Thyroid in reproduction of reptiles. Gen. Comp. Endocrinol. *43*, 537–542.

Hall, T. R., Chadwick, A. (1984): Effects of synthetic mammalian thyrotropin releasing hormone, somatostatin and dopaminie on the secretion of prolactin and growth hormone from amphibian and reptilian pituitary glands incubated *in vitro*. J. Endocrinol. *102*, 175–180.

Hurlburt, M. E. (1977): Role of the thyroid gland in ovarian maturation of the goldfish, *Carassius auratus* L. Canad. J. Zool. *55*, 1906–1913.

Iela, L., Pierantoni, R., Rastogi, R. K. (1980): Effect of temperature and light on androgen production in the male *Rana esculenta*. Experientia *36*, 256.

Jackson, I. M. D., Reichlin, S. (1974): Thyrotropin-releasing hormone (TRH): Distribution in hypothalamic and extrahypothalamic brain tissues of mammalian and submammalian chordates. Endocrinology *95*, 854–862.

Jacobs, G. F. M., Goyvaerts, M. P., Vandorpe, G., Quaghebeur, A. M. L., Kühn, E. R. (1988 a): Luteinizing hormone-releasing hormone as a potent stimulator of the thyroidal axis in ranid frogs. Gen. Comp. Endocrinol. *70*, 274–283.

Jacobs, G. F. M., Michielsen, R. P. A., Kühn, E. R. (1988 b): Thyroxine and triiodothyronine in plasma and thyroids of the neotenic and metamorphosed axolotl *Ambystoma mexicanum*: influence of TRH injections. Gen. Comp. Endocrinol. *70*, 145–151.

Jacobs, G. F. M., Kühn, E. R. (1988): Luteinizing hormone-releasing hormone induces thyroxine release together with testosterone in the neotenic axolotl *Ambystoma mexicanum*. Gen. Comp. Endocrinol. *71*, 502–505.

Kar, A., Chandola, A. (1985): Seasonality in birds and reptiles, the involvement of thyroxine and triiodothyronine. In: The Endocrine System and the Environment. (B. K. Follett, S. Ishii, A. Chandola, eds.) pp. 117–126.

Kikuyama, S., Seki, T (1983): Dopamine and serotonin control of prolactin release in bullfrogs. In: Integrative Neurohumoral Mechanisms. (L. Endroczi, D. Angelucci, D. Deurid, U. Scapagnirai, eds.), pp. 317–324. Hungarian Academic Press, Budapest.

Kühn, E. R., Darras, V. M., Gevaerts, H. (1985 a): Circadian and annual hormonal rhythms in amphibians. In: The Endocrine System and the Environment. B. K. Follett, S. Ishii, A. Chandola, eds.) pp. 55–69. Japan Sci. Soc. Press, Tokyo/Springer-Verlag, Berlin.

Kühn, E. R., Darras, V. M., Verlinden, T. M. (1985 b): Annual variations of thyroid reactivity following thyrotrophin stimulation and circulating levels of thyroid hormones in the frog *Rana ridibunda*. Gen. Comp. Endocrinol. *57*, 266–273.

Kühn, E. R., Decuypere, E., Iqbal, A., Luysterborgh, D., Michielsen, R. (1988 a): Thyrotropic and peripheral activities of thyrotrophin and thyrotrophin-releasing hormone in the chick embryo and adult chicken. Horm. Met. Res. *20*, 158–162.

Kühn, E. R., Decuypere, E., Rudas, P. (1984 a): Hormonal and environmental interactions on thyroid function in the chick embryo and posthatching chicken. J. Exp. Zool. *232*, 653–658.

Kühn, E. R., Delmotte, N. M. J., Darras, V. M. (1983): Persistence of a circadian rhythmicity for thyroid hormones in plasma and thyroid of hibernating male *Rana ridibunda*. Gen. Comp. Endocrinol. *50*, 383–394.

Kühn, E. R., Engelen, H. (1976): Seasonal variation in prolactin and TSH releasing activity in the hypothalamus of *Rana temporaria*. Gen. Comp. Endocrinol. *28*, 277–282.

Kühn, E. R., Gevaerts, H., Jacobs, G., Vandorpe, G. (1987 a): Reproductive cycle, thyroxine and corticosterone in females of the giant swamp frog *Dicroglossus occipitalis* at the equator. Gen. Comp. Endocrinol. *66*, 137–144.

Kühn, E. R., Gevaerts, H., Vandorpe, G., Jacobs, G. F. M. (1987 b): Plasma concentrations of testosterone and thyroxine in males of the giant swamp frog *Dicroglossus occipitalis* at the equator. Gen. Comp. Endocrinol. *68*, 492–493.

Kühn, E. R., Jacobs, G. F. M., Michielsen, R. P. A. (1984 b): Thyroxine as the trigger for thyroid activation in the hibernating frog *Rana ridibunda*. IRCS Med. Sci. *12*: 168.

Kühn, E. R., Kikuyama, S., Yamamoto, K., Darras, V. (1985 c): *In vivo* release of prolactin in *Rana ridibunda* following an intravenous injection of thyrotropin-releasing hormone. Gen. Comp. Endocrinol. *60*, 86–89.

Kühn, E. R., Peeters, R., Pauwels, J. (1986 a): Stimulation of the hepatic 5′-monodeiodination activity in the adult male rat following injection of ovine growth hormone. IRCS Med. Sci. *14*, 804.

Kühn, E. R., Van Osselaer, P., Siau, O., Decuypere, E., Moreels, A. (1986 b): Thyroid function in newborn lambs: influence of prolactin and growth hormone. J. Endocr. *109*, 215–219.

Kühn, E. R., Verheyen, G., Chiasson, R. B., Huts, C., Huybrechts, L., Van den Steen, P., Decuypere, E. (1987 c): Growth hormone stimulates the peripheral conversion of thyroxine into triiodothyronine by increasing the liver 5′-monodeiodinase activity in the fasted and normal fed chicken. Horm. metabol. Res. *19*, 304–308.

Kühn, E. R., Huybrechts, L. M., Decuypere, E., Mérat, P. (1986 d): Endocrinological effects of sex-linked dwarf gene. 3. Prolactin and growth hormone fail to increase the liver T_4-5′-monodeiodinase activity in the sex-linked dwarf chick embryo. In: 7th European Poultry Conference, Paris 24–28 August 1986, 965–969.

Kühn, E. R., Vanderpooten, A., Huybrechts, L. M., Decuypere, E., Darras, V., Sharp, P. J. (1988 b): Hypothalamic hormones that release growth hormone stimulate hepatic 5′-monodeiodination activity in the chick embryo. J. Endocr. *118*, 233–236.

Larsen, P. R., Silva, J. E., Kaplan, M. K. (1981): Circulating and intracellular thyroid hormones: physiological and clinical implications. Endocrine Reviews *2*, 87–102.

Lehninger, A. L. (1979): Biochemistry. Second edition, Worth publishers, Inc., New York.

Leloup, J., Buscaglia, M. (1980): Thyroxine metabolism in *Xenopus laevis* tadpoles. In «Thyroid Research» (J. R. Stockigt, S. Nagataki, eds.), pp. 233–236, Austral. Acad. Sci. Canberra.

Leloup, J., Buscaglia, M., Horn, C., Lambergeon, M. (1977): Evolution of thyroid iodine and hormones in thyroid and plasma during the metamorphosis of *Xenopus laevis* tadpoles. Ann. Endocrinol. *38*; 21 A.

Leloup, J., de Luze, A. (1980): Prolactine et hormones thyroidiennes chez l'anguille (*Anguilla anguilla* L.). Comptes Rendus Hebdomadaires des Séances de l'Académie des Sciences, Séries D *291*; 87–90.

Leroux, P., Tonon, M. C., Stoeckel, M. E., Jégou, S., Leboulenger, F., Delarue, C., Perroteau, I., Netchitaïlo, P., Kupryszewski, G. and Vaudry, H. (1983): Role of TRH in the control of melanotropin release in amphibia. In: Thyrotropin-releasing hormone. (E. C. Griffiths, G. W. Bennett, eds.) pp. 229–240. Raven Press, New York.

Licht, P. (1979): Reproductive endocrinology of reptiles and amphibians: Gonadotropins. Annu. Rev. Physiol. *41*, 337–351.

Lofts, B. (1964): Seasonal changes in the functional activity of the interstitial and spermatogenetic tissues of the green frog, *Rana esculenta*. Gen. Comp. Endocrinol. *4*: 550–562.

Mackenzie, D. S. (1986): Effects of estradiol on thyroid hormone plasma protein binding in the goldfish. Am. Zool. *26*, 107 A.

Mackenzie, D. S., Sokolowska, M., Peter, R. E. and Breton, B. (1987): Increased gonadotropin levels in goldfish do not result in alteration in circulating thyroid hormone levels. Gen. Comp. Endocrinol. *67*, 202–213.

Maclatchy, D. L., Cyr, D. G., Eales, J. G. (1986): Estradiol-17β depresses T_4 to T_3 conversion in rainbow trout. Am. Zool. *26*, 24 A.

May, F. E. B., Knowland, J. (1980): The role of thyroxine in the transition of vitellogenin synthesis from noninducibility to inducibility during metamorphosis in *Xenopus laevis*. Develop. Biol. *77*, 419–430.

Norris, D. O., Gern, W. A. (1976): Thyroxine-induced activation of hypothalamo-hypophysial axis in neotenic salamander larvae. Science *194*, 525–527.

Pierantoni, R., Iela, L., Delrio, G., Rastogi, R. K. (1984 a): Seasonal plasma sex steroid levels in the female *Rana esculenta*. Gen. Comp. Endocrinol. *53*, 126–134.

Pierantoni, R., Iela, L., d'Istria, M., Fasano, S., Rastogi, R. K., Delrio, G. (1984 b): Seasonal testosterone profile and testicular responsiveness to pituitary factors and gonadotrophin releasing hor-

mone during two different phases of the sexual cycle of the frog (*Rana esculenta*). J. Endocr. *102*, 387–392.
Polzonetti-Magni, A., Botte, V., Bellini-Cardellini, L., Gobbetti, A., Crasto, A. (1984): Plasma sex hormones and post-reproductive period in the green frog, *Rana esculenta* complex. Gen. Comp. Endocrinol. *54*, 372–377.
Rastogi, R. K., Iela, L., Delrio, G., Di Meglio, M., Russo, A., Chieffi, G. (1978): Environmental influence on testicular activity in the green frog *Rana esculenta*. Journal of Experimental Zoology *206*, 49–64.
Redshaw, M. (1972): The hormonal control of the amphibian ovary. Amer. Zool. *12*, 289–306.
Rosenkilde, P. (1979): The thyroid hormones in Amphibia. In: Hormones and Evolution. (E. J. W. Barrington, ed.). Vol. 1, pp. 437–491. Academic Press, London/New York.
Rosenkilde, P., Jørgensen, I. (1977): Determination of serum thyroxine in two species of toads: Variation with season. Gen. Comp. Endocrinol. *33*, 566–573.
Rudas, P., Pethes, G. (1984a): The importance of the peripheral thyroid hormone deiodination in adaption to ambient temperature in the chicken (*Gallus domesticus*). Comp. Biochem. Physiol. *77/A*, 567–571.
Rudas, P., Pethes, G. (1984b): Studies on the conversion of thyroxine to 3,5,3′-triiodothyronine in normal and thyroidectomized chickens. Gen. Comp. Endocrinol. *54*, 154–161.
Sage, M. (1973): The evolution of thyroidal function in fishes. Amer. Zool. *13*, 899–905.
Sawin, C. T., Bolaffi, J. L., Bacharach, P., Lance, V. (1981): Conversion of thyroxine to triiodothyronine in an adult amphibian, *Bufo marinus*. Gen. Comp. Endocrinol. *43*, 17–19.
Schultheiss, H. (1980): T_3 and T_4 concentrations during metamorphosis of *Xenopus laevis* and *Rana esculenta* and in the neotenic Mexican Axolotl. Gen. Comp. Endocrinol. *40*, 372.
Schwartz, H. L., Surks, M. I., Oppenheimer, J. H. (1971): Quantitation of extrathyroidal conversion of L-thyroxine to 3,5,3′-triiodo-L-thyronine. J. Clin. Invest. *50*, 1124–1130.
Seki, T., Kikuyama, S. (1984): *In vitro* stimulation of bullfrog prolactin release by hypothalamic extract. Zool. Sci. *1*, 969.
Sherwood, N. M. (1986): Evolution of a neuropeptide family: Gonadotropin-releasing hormone. Amer. Zool. *26*, 1041–1054.
Singh, J. P., Singh, T. P. (1980): Regulation of prolactin secretion by hypothalamus in some cold blooded vertebrates. Endocrinology *76(1)*, 51–62.
Sower, S. A., Plisetskaya, E., Gorbman, A. (1985). Steroid and thyroid hormone profiles following a single injection of partly purified salmon gonadotropin or GnRH analogues in male and female sea lamprey. J. Exp. Zool. *235*, 403–408.
Suzuki, S., Suzuki, . (1980): Changes in thyroidal and plasma iodine compounds during and after metamorphosis of bullfrog (*Rana catesbeiana*). In: Thyroid Research VIII. J. R. Stockigt, S. Nagataki, eds.) pp. 229–232 Australian Academy of Science, Canberra.
Tata, J. R. (1960): The partial purification and properties of thyroxine dehalogenase. Biochem. J. *77*, 214–226.
Taurog, A., Oliver, C., Eskay, R. L., Porter, J. C., McKenzie, J. M. (1974): The role of TRH in the neoteny of the Mexican axolotl (*Ambystoma mexianum*). Gen. Comp. Endocrinol. *24*, 267–279.
Thapliyal, J. P. (1969): Thyroid in avian reproduction. Gen. Comp. Endocrinol., Supple. *2*, 111–122.
Thapliyal, J. P., Chandola, A. (1972): Thyroid in wild finches. Proc. Natl. Acad. Sci. India *B 42*, 1–11.
Thapliyal, J. P., Garg, R. K. (1969): Relation of thyroid to gonadal and body weight cycles in male weaver birds, *Ploceus philippinus*. Arch. Anat. Histol. Embryol. *516*, 689–695.
Thapliyal, J. P., Pandha, S. K. (1965): Thyroid-gonad relationship in spotted Munia, *Uroloncha punctulata*. J. Exp. Zool. *158*, 253–261.
Thornton, V. F. (1972): A progesterone-like factor detected by bioassay in the blood of the toad (*Bufo bufo*) shortly before ovulation. Gen. Comp. Endocrinol. *18*, 133–139.
Vandesande, F., Aspeslagh, M. R. (1974): Failure of thyrotropin-releasing hormone to increase ^{125}I uptake by the thyroid in *Rana temporaria*. Gen. Comp. Endocrinol. *23*, 355–356.
Vandorpe, G., Jacobs, G. F. M., Kühn, E. R. (1987): Seasonal changes of the 5′-monodeiodination activity in kidney and skin homogenates of male *Rana ridibunda*: Relation to plasma thyroxine (T_4) and testosterone. Gen. Comp. Endocrinol. *68*, 163–169.

Vandorpe, G., Kühn, E. R. (1989): Estradiol-17β silastic implants in female *Rana ridibunda* depress thyroid hormone concentrations in plasma and the *in vitro* 5′-monodeiodination activity in kidney homogenates. Gen. Comp. Endocrinol. *76*, 341–345.
van Oordt, P. G. W. J., van Dongen, W. J., Lofts, B. (1968): Seasonal changes in endocrine organs of the male common frog, *Rana temporaria*. I. The pars distalis of the adenohypophysis. Z. Zellforsch. *88*, 549–559.
Visser, T. J. (1978): A tentative review of recent *in vitro* observations on the enzymatic deiodination of iodothyronines and its possible physiological implications. Mol. Cell. Endocrinol. *10*, 241–247.
Wangh, L. J. (1982): Glucocorticoids act together with estrogens and thyroid hormones in regulating the synthesis and secretion of *Xenopus* vitellogenin, serum albumin, and fibrinogen. Develop. Biol. *89*, 294–298.
Wangh, L. J., Schneider, W. (1982): Thyroid hormones are corequisites for estradiol-17β *in vitro* induction of *Xenopus* vitellogenin synthesis and secretion. Develop. Biol. *89*, 287–293.
Wasserman, W. J., Smith, L. D. (1978): Oocyte maturation in nonmammalian vertebrates. In: The Vertebrate Ovary: Comparative Biology and Evolution. (R. E. Jones, ed.) pp. 443–468. Plenum Press, New York/London.

Fortschritte der Zoologie, Band/Vol. 38 · Hanke, W. (Hrsg.), Biology and Physiology of Amphibians
Gustav Fischer Verlag · Stuttgart · New York · 1990

Reproductive behavior and biology of Central European water frogs

HANS SCHNEIDER

Zoologisches Institut, der Universität, Poppelsdorfer Schloss, D-5300 Bonn 1 (FRG)

1. Introduction

Ever since the publication of Wahl's (1969) comprehensive analysis of the reproductive and calling behavior of the Central European water frogs, the subject has continued to arouse great interest, for many reasons. The calling period lasts for an unusually long time; the calling behavior is complex and depends on both external and internal factors. Although there are several distinct calls, their biological significance is difficult to demonstrate, because phonotactic responses are not as readily elicited in water frogs as in other anuran species. Therefore other kinds of experiments had to be devised.

An additional incentive to study these frogs emerged when Berger (1966) found that *Rana esculenta* is not a species in the classical sense but rather a hybrid. This view at first encountered opposition, but it was confirmed by subsequent research. The results of bioacoustic studies also corroborate the hybrid nature of *R. esculenta*. Some of the information that has been gathered about the water frogs is summarized here.

2. Calling and reproductive behavior

The water frog species native to Central Europe are *Rana lessonae, R. ridibunda* and their hybrid, *R. esculenta*. The field studies have comprised extensive observations of populations in the Neckar valley consisting mainly of *R. esculenta* (Wahl, 1969), others in lakes near Bonn with a majority of *R. lessonae* (Obert, 1975; Brzoska, 1980; Radwan and Schneider, 1988) and a non-autochthonous population of *R. ridibunda* in the botanical garden of the University of Bonn (Schneider and Inst. Wiss. Film, 1982; Kuhn and Schneider, 1984).

The annual activity period of the water frogs in Central Europe begins early if the weather is good, in the first half of March. Its onset is marked by the appearance of large adult frogs, mostly females, in the breeding waters. The males do not begin to call until the second half of April, both in the Rhine region and at higher altitudes in southern Germany. The calling period then continues for a long time, ending about the middle of July or even later. Calling behavior changes twice during this time, dividing the calling period into three sections: a main spawning phase and pre- and postspawning phases (Wahl, 1969; Obert, 1975; Radwan and Schneider, 1988).

The lower threshold for calling is the same for all three phenotypes, 10–12 °C water temperature (WT). The upper threshold varies. Radwan and Schneider (1988) found 26 °C for *R. lessonae*. Wahl (1969) noted that *R. esculenta* still called vigorously at 29 °C, the highest WT that occurred during his field observations; in subsequent laboratory measurements he found an upper threshold of 36.5 ± 0.5 °C for this species. Kuhn and Schneider (1984) recorded calls of *R. ridibunda* at 33.5 °C WT.

Male water frogs form calling groups composed of at least 8–10 and as many as 40 individuals. *R. esculenta* males at the edges of neighboring groups are separated from one another by 15–20 m, according to Wahl (1969). In a pond measuring 50 × 30 m *R. lessonae* were gathered into four calling groups, each comprising 20–30 males and occupying an area of ca. 1.5 m^2.

Each group calls in its own rhythm, with alternating activity maxima and minima. Single males are often to be found between the groups, and these call together with one of the adjacent groups. Occasionally these males transmit the rhythm of one group to the next, so that the two groups call in synchrony. Central European populations comprise only one species of water frog, usually *R. lessonae*, plus the hybrid *R. esculenta*. At Lake Skadar (Yugoslavia), on the other hand, *R. lessonae* and *R. ridibunda* are sympatric; in the calling groups, the two species are segregated. The males within the *R. lessonae* groups are 0.5–1.5 m apart, and those in *R. ridibunda* groups are separated by 2–10 m. The intermediate hybrids, phenologically similar to *R. ridibunda*, join the calling groups of *R. ridibunda* (Schneider and Joermann, 1988). There is a comparable situation at recently analyzed sites in western Greece, where *R. ridibunda* and the new species *R. epeirotica* (Schneider et al., 1984) are sympatric and segregate when they form calling groups (Sofianidou and Schneider, 1989).

The level of calling activity fluctuates over several days, depending on the overall weather conditions and the temperature, especially the water temperature. On any given day the level of calling activity is correlated with the weather on the preceeding day. After the onset of bad weather calling subsides at a variable rate; the frogs may stop calling after only 2–3 days or not until 1–2 weeks have elapsed, depending on the microclimatic conditions. Calling persists longer when the decline in water temperature is slow.

Except during the main spawning phase, calling activity reaches a peak each day when the water temperature is between 17.5 ± 1 °C and 22 ± 1 °C. During the prespawning phase, therefore, calling is most intense during the afternoon. At 21 °C the duration of the activity maxima averages 4.5 min and that of the activity minima, 2 min (Fig. 1). In the early evening, beginning ca. 1800 h, few if any calls are produced; at this time the frogs are hunting insects. Toward 2100 h calling activity resumes, because the WT has fallen into the optimal range. During the prespawning phase there is a striking change in the coloration of the male *R. lessonae*; the head and shoulders turn from dark green to a light yellow-green.

One to two days before onset of the main spawning phase the calling groups are disbanded. The frogs gather in shallow water and call as a single group. Under favorable weather conditions the spawning phase is completed in only 3–5 days. Spawning may be interrupted by deteriorating weather, and then continues when the weather improves. During the main spawning phase the level of calling activity is no longer closely related to the water temperature. High water temperatures do not inhibit calling; the males call vigorously at night as well as during the day.

The females not yet ready to mate stay near the calling group, on the shore or in the water. When ready to mate a female swims up to the calling group and is immediately clasped by a male. In many cases the eggs are laid as soon as 30 min after clasping.

Observations of *R. lessonae* indicate that all medium-sized and large males manage to

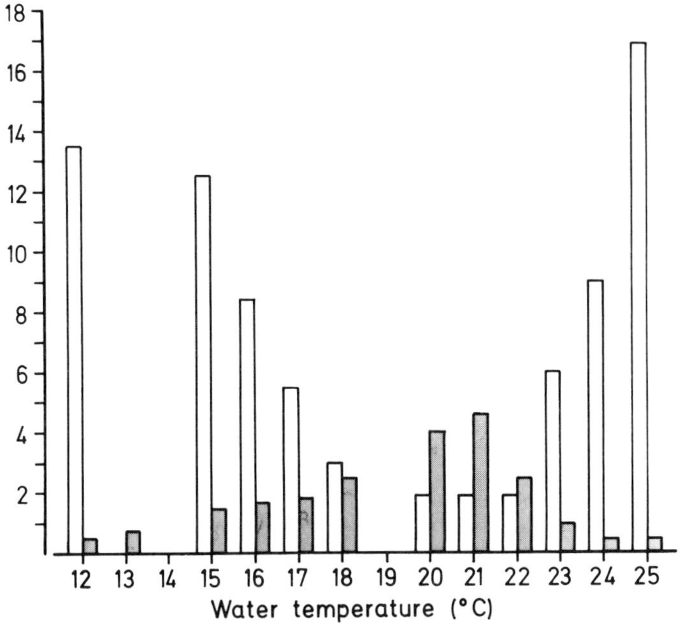

Fig. 1: Calling activity of *R. esculenta* during the prespawning phase, as a function of the water temperature. Shaded columns: activity maxima; white columns: activity minima. From M. Wahl, Oecologia (Berl.) 3 (1969) 14–55. By permission of the author and of Springer Verlag, Heidelberg, Berlin, New York.

mate, whereas some of the small males do not find females, and the remainder do so only toward the end of the main spawning phase. In the Kottenforst pond, where *R. lessonae* predominate, the male *R. esculenta* were found to call intensely but fail to mate; on the other hand, eight female *R. esculenta* were observed in amplexus with male *R. lessonae* (Radwan and Schneider, 1988).

The postspawning phase is variable, and appears most clearly when some males fail to achieve spawning and hence continue to call. As in the prespawning phase, calling activity is maximal in the range from 17.5 ± 1 °C to 22 ± 1 °C. Because the time course of water temperature during the day is different later in the season, calling is shifted to different times of day in the postspawning phase; now the longest activity maxima occur in the early morning. On days of bright sunshine the WT rises beyond the optimal range and the frogs do not call actively again until after 2000 h, when the water has cooled sufficiently. Calling activity can continue without interruption until 4–5 o'clock in the morning, when it is suspended for 1–2 hours; then the next day's calling begins.

3. The calls

3.1. Mating call

The most conspicuous call is the mating call of the male, which is composed of pulse groups (Fig. 2). The number of pulse groups is highest in *R. lessonae*; it is extremely variable, with 18–58 pulse groups per call. A group comprises 2-6 pulses, the higher pulse counts being found in the calls of the large males (Schneider et al., 1979; Schneider and Joermann, 1988; Radwan and Schneider, 1988). With so many pulse groups, the duration of the mating calls is considerable – an average of 1334.3 ms at 15 °C for the population in the Kottenforst, falling to an average of 1100 ms when the WT rises to 26 °C. The calls of the *R. lessonae* living in Lake Skadar are only slightly different, even though the two sites are separated by 1350 km. At Lake Skadar the mean call duration was found to be 1579.5 ms at 15 °C and 1334.3 ms at 26 °C. Under the influence of increasing WT the number of pulses per group, and hence the duration of the pulse groups, decreases, while the pulse-group repetition rate increases. The frequency spectrum of the mating calls exhibits two maxima, at 1132 ± 158.7 Hz and 2210 ± 227 Hz, measured at the end of the call with the water temperature between 18 and 23 °C. At a distance of 1 m the sound pressure averages 99 dB (re 20 μP). The males produce 3–11 calls in series. The pauses between the calls have an average duration of 1554.3 ms at 15 °C and only 1050 ms at 26 °C.

Because *R. ridibunda* is not so widespread in Central Europe as the two other phenotypes, animals from southern Yugoslavia were examined (Schneider, 1973; Kuhn and Schneider, 1984) and found to give mating calls nearly identical to those of water frogs in northern Greece near Thessaloniki (Schneider and Sofianidou, 1985). The comparative study has since been extended not only to populations in other parts of Greece (Schneider and Sofianidou, 1986) but also to some in Israel (Nevo and Schneider, 1983), in Turkey (Joerman et al., 1988), Egypt (Akef and Schneider, 1989) and in Armenia (Schneider and Egiasarjan, in prep.).

The mating calls of the frogs in the region of Thessaloniki consist of 4.05 ± 0.64 pulse groups; this call parameter is uninfluenced by WT. The males always produce their calls in series. Calls with a higher number of pulse groups – as many as eight, rarely more – appear toward the end of a series, when the territorial males leave their calling site and swim around. The number of pulse groups is also above average just before a female is clasped (Kuhn and Schneider, 1984). The pulse groups within a call are separated from one another by distinct intervals (Fig. 2). The sound pressure of the loudest calls is 110 dB at a distance of 1 m, though the intensity varies by as much as 20 dB. In the course of a call

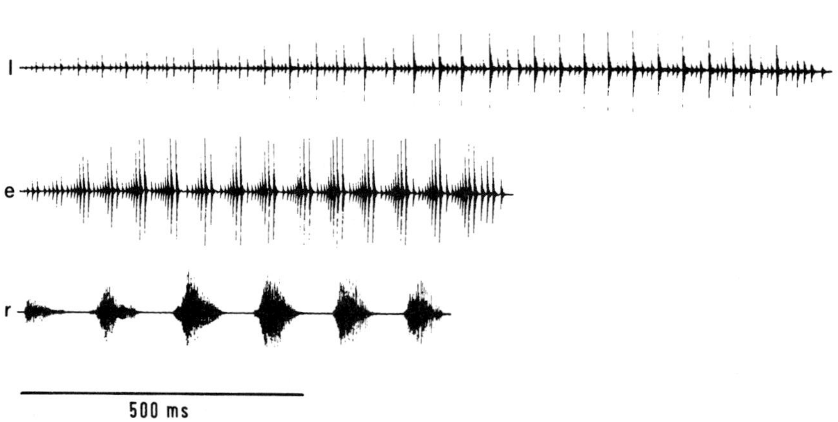

Fig. 2: Oscillograms of the mating calls of *R. lessonae* (l), *R. esculenta* (e) and *R. ridibunda* (r). From J. Brzoska, Behav. Processes 5 (1980) 113–141. By permission of the author and of Elsevier Publ. Co., Amsterdam.

series the intensity rises progressively, in correlation with the degree to which the vocal sac is filled (Brzoska, 1982).

The sound energy is concentrated in two frequency regions, the first around 400 Hz. The second is variable; it lies between 1500 and 2500 Hz, depending on the number of pulse groups per call and on the position of a call within the series. The greater the number of pulse groups in a call, the higher the frequency of the second energy maximum.

Several call parameters are correlated with temperature. As the WT rises, the pauses between the calls become shorter. The call duration also decreases, due to shortening of both the pulse groups and the intervals between them. The latter effect is very pronounced – an average reduction from 84.4 ms to 29.8 ms when the temperature rises from 16.5 to 33.5 °C.

The mating calls of *R. esculenta* are intermediate (Fig. 2). Those of the population in the Neckar valley have pulse groups consisting of 8–9 pulses, with very short intervals between the groups (Wahl, 1969). The sound pressure at 1 m averages 104 dB. The hybrids of *R. ridibunda* and *R. lessonae* at Lake Skadar also produce intermediate mating calls. Water temperature has a marked influence on the calls of *R. esculenta*.

3.2. Territorial calls

The call repertoire of *R. ridibunda* and *R. esculenta* includes three types of territorial calls and that of *R. lessonae* only two. The latter lacks the territorial call known as Type 2.

The males produce territorial calls spontaneously or in response to the calls of other water frogs engaging in aggressive behavior. These calls may be single or in series. In 10 min one *R. ridibunda*, uninfluenced by other males, produced 29 series of territorial calls, with a minimum of two and a maximum of 24 calls per series (Kuhn and Schneider, 1984).

The territorial call 1 of *R. ridibunda* consists of pulses arranged in more or less distinct groups. There is one frequency component at 400 Hz and a band rising from 600 to 1600 Hz (Fig. 3 a, b).

Territorial call 2 also has a component at 400 Hz and a frequency-modulated band; in this case the pitch of the latter rises from 1500 Hz to 2150 Hz in the middle of the call and then falls to 1800–1200 Hz (Fig. 3 a, b). An experienced listener can easily distinguish this call from Type 1 by the different frequency modulation. A tendency to form pulse groups is discernible but is not as clear as in calls of Type 1.

In *R. lessonae* the territorial calls 1 have a duration of 292 ± 58.79 ms in the intermediate temperature range, 18–23 °C (Radwan and Schneider, 1988). Although these calls are considerably shorter than the mating calls, their temporal structure is similar in that the pulses are grouped. The territorial calls are influenced by water temperature. Their spectrum includes components at 650 ± 60.23 Hz and at 1310.7 ± 123 Hz.

In *R. esculenta* the territorial calls 1 have a duration of 236–266 ms and consist of 45–58 pulses, the amplitude of which rises slightly toward the end of the call. The duration of territorial call 2 is 260–404 ms, averaging 322 ms; this call comprises 62–78 pulses (Wahl, 1969). As in *R. ridibunda*, Type 2 differs from Type 1 in its frequency modulation; the frequency of Type 2 decreases at the beginning of the second half of the call. Territorial calls 1 and 2 are almost as loud as the mating calls: *R. lessonae* 98 dB, *R. esculenta* 104 dB and *R. ridibunda* 108 dB SPL on average (Brzoska, 1982).

Territorial call 3 is the least common of these calls and is almost always produced singly following other territorial calls. In *R. ridibunda* it consists of a series of highly damped and hence brief pulses, separated by clear intervals (Fig. 3 a). Towards the end of this call the pulses are grouped. The amplitude is usually low at the beginning and then rises fairly

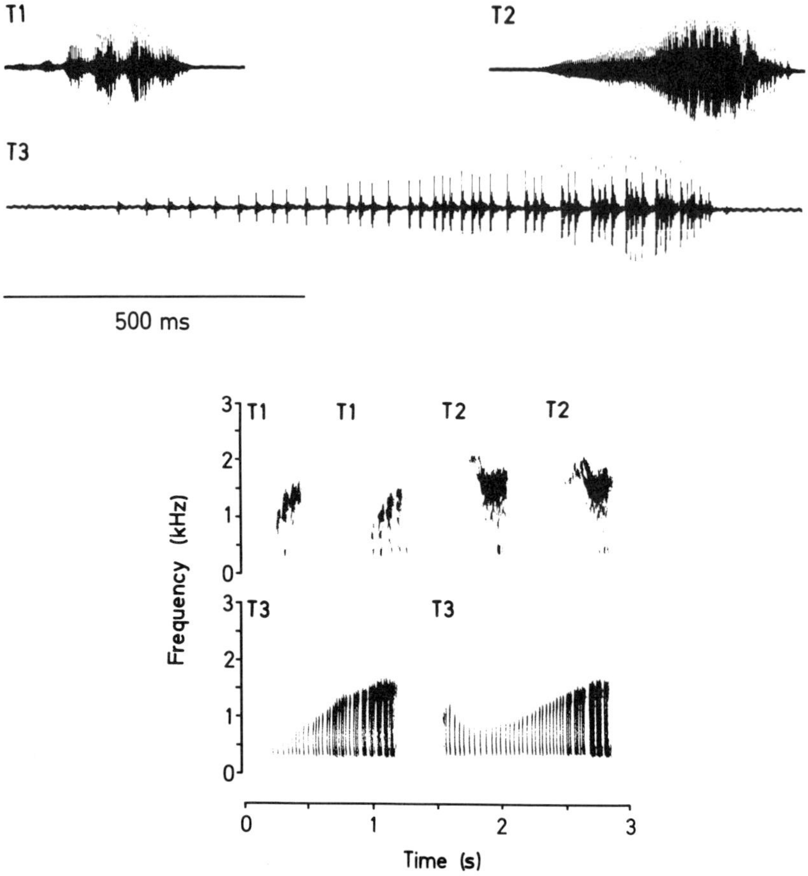

Fig. 3a–b: Oscillograms (above) and sonagrams (below) of the territorial calls 1, 2, 3 (T1, T2, T3) of *R. ridibunda*. From Kuhn and Schneider (1984). By permission of VEB Gustav Fischer Verlag, Jena.

steadily until near the end of the call, when it falls abruptly. The spectrum includes a component at 400 Hz and a higher-frequency, modulated component. The latter either rises uniformly from 500 Hz to 1650 Hz (Fig. 3b, left) or begins at 1350 Hz, falls to 850 Hz and then climbs to 1650 Hz (Fig. 3b, right). In comparison with territorial calls 1 and 2, Type 3 is noticeably less loud. In *R. lessonae* territorial call 3 is composed of 11–14 pulses, which are not grouped. In the intermediate temperature range the call duration is 671 ± 138 ms. the territorial call of *R. esculenta* closely resembles that of *R. lessonae*.

R. ridibunda also produces transitional calls in which features of territorial calls 1 and 2, or 1 and 3 or 2 and 3 are combined. The calls transitional between 1 and 2 are relatively common, while the rarest are those between 2 and 3 (Kuhn and Schneider, 1984). Calls transitional between 1 and 3 have also been noted in *R. lessonae* (Radwan and Schneider, 1988). *R. esculenta* has not yet been examined for the occurrence of transitional calls.

3.3. Release calls

These calls are typically produced by females as well as by males. The females employ this acoustic signal to prevent males from clasping them when they are not yet prepared to spawn or have already spawned.

In all three water frog phenotypes the release calls consist of very short pulses, the amplitude of which is low at first, rises rapidly and then varies only slightly (Fig. 4). At intermediate and high temperatures the release calls of the three phenotypes closely resemble one another. In *R. lessonae* the pulse train is slow and very uniform; in *R. ridibunda* it is more rapid and the pulses are arranged in distinct groups. The release calls of *R. esculenta* are intermediate, with a pulse repetition rate higher than that of *R. lessonae* but lower than that of *R. ridibunda*. However, *R. esculenta* also occasionally produces release calls like those of *R. ridibunda* or *R. lessonae*. In the crucial temperature range, 17–22 °C, the duration of most release calls is 340–450 ms. The spectrum is very broad, sometimes extending to 4000 Hz (Schneider and Brzoska, 1981).

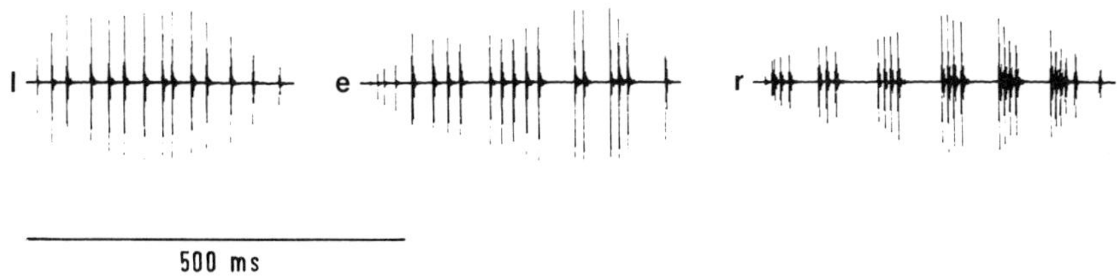

Fig. 4: Oscillograms of the release calls of *R. lessonae* (1), *R. esculenta* (e) and *R. ridibunda* (r). From Brzoska (1980) 113–141. By permission of the author and of Elsevier Publ. Co., Amsterdam.

4. The biological significance of the calls

According to the available field studies, when a female water frog is ready to mate she can choose a partner only in the sense that she swims into the group of calling males, where she is soon clasped (Wahl, 1969; Radwan and Schneider, 1988). It is not yet known whether females are attracted by the mating call of a single male, or whether these auditory signals are the only effective attractants, as is the case for *Hyla meridionalis* (Schneider, 1982).

On the other hand, due to the playback experiments of Brzoska (1982) the responses of male water frogs to con- and paraspecific mating and territorial calls are well known. These experiments were carried out over three years, during the main spawning phase of each breeding season. The test calls were broadcasted from the shore, with a loudspeaker 1–5 m away from a calling frog. To ensure that the response was actually to the test signal alone, such calls were presented only when no other frog was calling in the vicinity.

In each trial a series of mating or territorial calls of one of the three phenotypes was tested; each series lasted 4–6 s, and the series were separated by pauses of 20–60 s. A positive response was considered to have occurred when the male began to exhibit the following behavior within 5 s after the end of a series.

The first reaction was always to turn toward the loudspeaker while giving one or two calls. As playback continued, the male frog – still calling – swam to the speaker and then fixated it for 5–60 s or swam back and forth in front of it. Finally the male turned away. If another frog was in the vicinity during the approach to the speaker, it would be attacked by the responding male.

The calls produced during responses to the played-back signals included mating calls and the territorial calls 1, 2 and 3.

The responses to playback of mating calls depended on the intensity of the mating calls. At intensities above 80–90 dB, the frogs responded with territorial calls; at lower intensities 6 of the 27 animals tested gave mating calls and the others remained silent. The production of mating calls was not accompanied by turning toward the loudspeaker. Both *R. lessonae* and *R. esculenta* males responded to the mating calls of both phenotypes, but the threshold intensity for an aggressive response was lower for the conspecific than for the paraspecific call. By contrast, *R. ridibunda* was stimulated to produce mating calls only by presentation of the conspecific mating call.

The territorial calls elicited less clearly differentiated responses. That is, territorial calls of each of the three phenotypes caused all the frogs tested to produce calls in response, and almost without exception these were territorial calls. However, the threshold of *R. ridibunda* was higher than those of *R. lessonae* and *R. esculenta.*

These results have implications for the function of the water frog calls. Since mating calls above a certain intensity elicit responses of territorial males that fall into the category of aggressive behavior – it follows that in water frogs the mating calls have a territorial function. So do the territorial calls, which are produced in response to both territorial and mating calls. While the occupant of a territory is approaching a calling male or a loudspeaker, it gives territorial but not mating calls. Hence the territorial calls are associated with stronger aggression than the mating calls, and signal that a male is prepared to defend his calling site.

To investigate the significance of the calls in more detail, Brzoska (1980) developed a new approach, with great success. His method is based on the observation that acoustic stimuli affect the function of organs under the control of the autonomic nervous system. Kohlrausch and Schilf (1922) had found that the bioelectric phenomenon associated with the secretory activity of cutaneous glands, called the electrodermal response (EDR), can be induced by acoustic stimuli. In general, the EDR is a form (or a side effect) of flight or defense behavior. The secretions produced by the skin glands during the EDR could help the frog to escape the grasp of an aggressive conspecific or a predator. Experiments utilizing the EDR, however, can be carried out only in the laboratory.

Animals of all three phenotypes were tested, by presenting recorded mating, territorial and release calls of *R. lessonae*, *R. ridibunda* and *R. esculenta.* During the spawning period, at the beginnig of June, the threshold of male *R. lessonae* to the conspecific mating call was relatively high, 75 dB SPL. The thresholds to the other mating calls were lower, by an average of 3 dB for the call of *R. esculenta* and by as much as 12 dB for that of *R. ridibunda.*

As expected, the opposite picture emerged for the release calls, which are very effective in eliciting escape behavior. The conspecific release call produced an electrodermal reflex at a sound pressure of 66 dB, whereas the threshold to the call of *R. ridibunda* was 72 dB. The thresholds to the territorial calls of the three phenotypes were nearly the same, a relatively low 63–65 dB.

In October, after the end of the calling period, a fundamental change was observed. The EDR thresholds to the mating calls were now the lowest and those to the release calls the highest, with no appreciable change in the thresholds to the territorial calls.

The results found for *R. ridibunda* and *R. esculenta* were similar to those for *R. lessonae*.

It is understandable that the EDR thresholds to the mating call should be relatively high during the reproductive period, because the mating calls are thought to have a sexually stimulating action and to assist the establishment of territories, but do not elicit escape behavior. It is also significant that the EDR appeared in response to the release call. With this finding Brzoska (1980) provided the first documentation of a behavioral response of water frogs to the release call. It had previously been thought that the acoustic signal alone was insufficient to deter attempted clasping.

Brzoska (1980) also used a synthetic acoustic signal at various frequencies (100–4000 Hz) to obtain EDR threshold curves for the water frogs. Outside the calling period the shape of this threshold curve for *R. ridibunda* was like that of the neural auditory threshold curve measured by recording the electrical activity in the torus semicircularis of the midbrain at 20 °C (Hubl and Schneider, 1979). However, the EDR threshold curve lay 30–40 dB above the neural auditory threshold curve.

An additional function of the mating calls, previously demonstrated only for the grass frog, can also be relevant to the water frogs. When male grass frogs were exposed to electronically simulated mating calls, the androgenic tissue remained active longer than in the absence of such auditory stimulation (Brzoska and Obert, 1980). Hence the mating calls serve to extend the duration of male reproductive activity. As the water frogs have a very long calling period, this function could be even more important for them than for the grass frogs, which have a brief reproductive season.

5. Call recognition

To learn more about the central nervous mechanisms of call recognition, Diekamp and Schneider (1988) recorded from single units in the torus semicircularis in the midbrain of *R. ridibunda*. The stimuli tested included conspecific mating, territorial and release calls as well as the mating calls of *R. lessonae* and *R. esculenta*.

Of the 80 units they considered, 75% responded to at least one call, and most responded to two or three calls. Three cells were excited only by the mating call of *R. ridibunda*. The discharge in response to this call could be correlated with the call as a whole or with the pulse groups (Fig. 5), and in the latter case the synchronization was extremely precise. Most cells responded maximally to the conspecific mating call. The typical response to the mating calls of the other phenotypes was less well synchronized, consisting of a discharge maintained throughout the call with a high amplitude-modulation rate. Because the mating calls of the three water frog phenotypes have very similar frequency spectra, the temporal pattern of a call is an important identifying feature.

During stimulation with the territorial and release calls, the neuronal discharge was always synchronized with the call as a whole (Fig. 6). A phasic-tonic response pattern was typical. At high intensities the responses persisted into the interval between the calls.

Acknowledgments

I thank Dr. J. Brzoska for critically reading the manuscript.

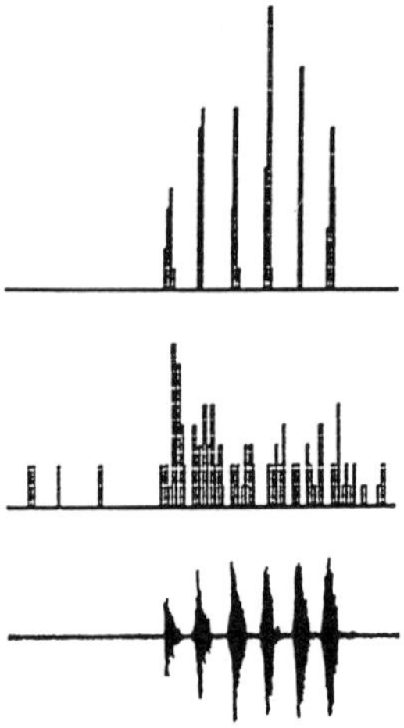

Fig. 5: Responses of neurons in the torus semicircularis to the conspecific mating call. PST histogram. Top: discharge synchronized with the pulse groups of the call. Middle: phasic-tonic response to the call as a whole. Bottom: Oscillogram of the call. Modified from Diekamp and Schneider (1988). By permission of Springer Verlag, Heidelberg, Berlin, New York.

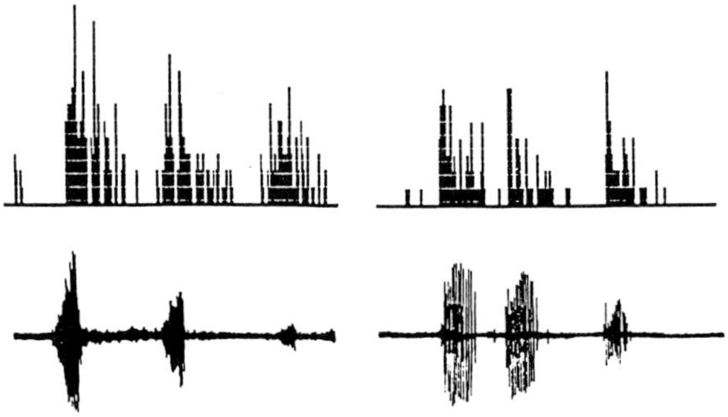

Fig. 6: Phasic-tonic responses of two single units to stimulation with three territorial calls (left) and three release calls (right). PST histogram. Modified from Diekamp and Schneider (1988). By permission of Springer Verlag, Heidelberg, Berlin, New York.

References

Akef, M. S. A., Schneider, H. (1989): The eastern form of *Rana ridibunda* (Anura: Ranidae) inhabits the Nile delta. Zool. Anz., Jena, *223*, 129–138.

Berger, L. (1966): Biometrical studies on the population of green frogs from the environs of Poznan. Annales Zool. *23*, 303–324.

Brzoska, J. (1980): Quantitative studies on the elicitation of the electrodermal response by calls and synthetic acoustical stimuli in *Rana lessonae* Camerano, *Rana r. ridibunda* Pallas and the hybrid *Rana «esculenta»* L. (Anura, Amphibia). Behav. Processes *5*, 113–141.

Brzoska, J. (1982): Vocal response of male european water frogs (*Rana esculenta* complex) to mating and territorial calls. Behav. Processes *7*, 37–47.
Brzoska, J., Obert, H.-J. (1980): Acoustic signals influencing the hormone production of the testes in the grass frog. J. Comp. Physiol. *140*, 25–29.
Diekamp, B., Schneider, H. (1988): Neuronal processing of conspecific and related calls in the torus semicircularis of *Rana r. ridibunda* Pall. (Anura): single-unit recordings. J. Comp. Physiol. *163*, 301–315.
Hubl, L., Schneider, H. (1979): Temperature and auditory thresholds: bioacoustic studies of the frogs *Rana r. ridibunda, Hyla a. arborea* and *Hyla a. savignyi* (Anura, Amphibia). J. Comp. Physiol. *130*, 17–27.
Joermann, G., Baran, I., Schneider, H. (1988): The mating call of *Rana ridibunda* (Amphibia: Anura) in western Turkey: Bioacoustic analysis and taxonomic consequences. Zool. Anz., Jena *220*, 225–232.
Kohlrausch, A., Schilf, E. (1922): Der galvanische Hautreflex beim Frosch auf Sinnesreizung. Pflügers Arch. *194*, 326–329.
Kuhn, B., Schneider, H. (1984): Mating and territorial calls of the frog *Rana ridibunda* and their temperature-dependent variability. Zool. Anz., Jena *212*, 273–305.
Nevo, E., Schneider, H. (1983): Structure and variation of *Rana ridibunda* mating call in Israel (Amphibia: Anura). Israel J. Zool. *32*, 45–60.
Obert, H.-J. (1975): The dependence of calling activity in *Rana esculenta* Linné 1758 and *Rana ridibunda* Pallas 1771 upon exogenous factors (Ranidae, Anura). Oecologica (Berl.) *18*, 317–328.
Radwan, N. M. M., Schneider, H. (1988): Social behaviour, call repertory and variation in the calls of the pool frog, *Rana lessona* (Anura, Ranidae). Amphibia/Reptilia *9*, 329–351.
Schneider, H. (1973): Die Paarungsrufe einheimischer Ranidae (Anura, Amphibia). Bonn. Zool. Beitr. *24*, 51–61.
Schneider, H. (1982): Phonotaxis bei Weibchen des Kanarischen Laubfrosches, *Hyla meridionalis*. Zool. Anz., Jena *208*, 161–174.
Schneider, H., Brzoska, J. (1981): Die Befreiungsrufe der mitteleuropäischen Wasserfrösche. Zool. Anz., Jena *206*, 189–202.
Schneider, H., Inst. Wiss. Film (1982): *Rana ridibunda* (Ranidae) – Rufe. Publ. Wiss. Film, Sekt. Biol., Ser. *15*, Nr. 5/E 2634.
Schneider, H., Joermann, G. (1988): Mating calls of water frogs (Ranidae) from Lake Skutari, Yugoslavia, and the relationship to water frogs of other regions. Z. zool. Syst. Evolut.-forsch. *26*, 261–275.
Schneider, H., Sofianidou, T. S. (1985): The mating call of *Rana ridibunda* (Amphibia, Anura) in northern Greece as compared with those of Yugoslavian and Israeli populations: proposal of a new subspecies. Zool. Anz., Jena *214*, 309–319.
Schneider, H., Sofianidou, T. S. (1986): Bioacoustic study of water frogs (Ranidae) in Greece. In: Studies in Herpetology. (Z. Roček, ed.), Proc. 3rd Meet, pp. 561–564, Soc. Europ. Herp., Prague.
Schneider, H., Egiasarjan, E. M. (1990): Bioacoustic investigations of lake frogs (Ranidae: *Rana ridibunda*) in Armenia contributing to the distribution of the eastern form. In prep.
Schneider, H., Tunner, H. G., Hödl, W. (1979): Beitrag zur Kenntnis des Paarungsrufs von *Rana lessonae* Camerano, 1882 (Anura, Amphibia). Zool. Anz., Jena *202*, 20–28.
Schneider, H., Sofianidou, T. S., Kyriakopoulou-Sklavounou, P. (1984): Bioacoustic and morphometric studies in water frogs (genus Rana) of Lake Ioannina in Greece, and description of a new species (Anura, Amphibia). Z. zool. Syst. Evolut.-forsch. *22*, 349–366.
Sofianidou, T. S., Schneider, H. (1989): Distribution range of the Epeirus frog *Rana epeirotica* (Amphibia: Anura) and the composition of the water frog populations in western Greece. Zool. Anz., Jena, *223*, 13–25.
Wahl, M. (1969): Untersuchungen zur Bio-Akustik des Wasserfrosches *Rana esculenta* (L.). Oecologia (Berl.) *3*, 14–55.

Fortschritte der Zoologie, Band/Vol. 38 · Hanke, W. (Hrsg.), Biology and Physiology of Amphibians
Gustav Fischer Verlag · Stuttgart · New York · 1990

Reproductive diversity in Amazonian lowland frogs

WALTER HÖDL

Institute of Zoology, University of Vienna, Althanstraße 14, A-1090 Wien, Austria

1. Introduction

High species diversity is a common trait of tropical rainforests, where ectothermic animals profit from constant high atmospheric humidity and temperatures. Long historical periods for evolution, recent speciation during short-term isolation in pleistocene forest refuges (Haffer, 1969) and stable, favourable climatic conditions have led to a biotic richness in the tropics. The frog fauna is no exception to this general pattern. 1545 (44%) out of 3533 currently recognized frog species occur in tropical America (Duellman, 1988). Selective pressures on eggs and early larval stages – such as predation and the habitat unpredictability of aquatic environments – have led to attainment of partial or total independence from water bodies in many neotropical anurans. From the generalized (and presumable primitive) pattern of aquatic eggs and aquatic larvae many specialized reproductive styles have evolved within various taxa under humid terrestrial conditions. With increasing terrestriality, however, problems of evaporative water loss were added to those of predation and larval transport; this eventually resulted in direct development (McDiarmid, 1978). Thus, the many (parallel evolved) alternative life-history styles in tropical anurans (summarized and discussed by Duellman, 1989) offer a prime example for the random character of variation and the strong canalization which works upon it through environmental conditions.

In his review on nesting and parental care in amphibians, Wunder (1932) already presented most of the bizzare reproductive patterns presently known in anurans. In a study on reproductive strategies in the neotropical anuran community at Santa Cecilia, Ecuador, Crump (1974) recognized ten different modes of anuran reproduction. Her classification system was modified and remodified by Duellman (1978, 1985) and adapted for all anuran reproductive patterns presently known (Duellman and Trueb, 1986). Based on the differences in the combination of «oviposition site, ovum and clutch characteristics, rate and duration of development, stage and size of hatchling and type of parental care, if any» Duellman (1985) recognized 29 reproductive modes worldwide. In a comparative study on species diversity patterns, Duellman (1988) identified 17 reproductive styles among anurans from 48 sites in the American tropics. The purpose of this review is to present the accumulated data on reproduction in 130 Amazonian lowland frog species. Detailed information is given on each of their 16 reproductive modes. Patterns of reproductive biology are compared for frog communities from four intensively studied areas in lowland Amazonia.

2. Methods for herpetological surveys

Herpetological surveys have been undertaken in several parts of lowland Amazonia (for summary, see Duellman, 1988), here considered as the area of the Amazon drainage system below an altitude of 400 meters.

Continuous long-term studies lasting at least twelve months at single sites are known only from Manaus, Brazil, (Hödl, 1977; Zimmerman, unpubl. data), Panguana, Rio Llullapichis, Peru, (Schlüter, 1983; Aichinger, 1985) and Santa Cecilia, Ecuador, (Crump, 1974; Duellman, 1978). The presently best studied frog fauna from Eastern Amazonia at Belém, Brazil, 01° 21'S, 48' 30'W, 12 m (Crump, 1971; Hödl, unpubl. data) and anurans occurring at Manaus, 03° 08'S, 60° 02'W, 50 m; Panguana, 09° 35'S, 74° 48'W, 260 m, and Santa Cecilia, 00° 03'N, 76° 59'W, 340 m, are included in the comparative analyses at the species level. Frog genera known from the Amazonian lowlands but not reported from these four areas are listed in a footnote to the appendix section. No changes in the reproductive mode classification system of Duellman (1985) are made. However, I include subdivisions (a, b, c) where separations are behaviourally and/or ecologically meaningful (Fig. 1). Together with the ecological assignment, reproductive data are listed for each species separately. For 42 species whose mode of reproduction remains unknown, evidence such as taxonomic status, laboratory or field observations, and ovarian egg numbers and pigmentation are utilized for a reasonable assumption (see also Duellman, 1978). Therefore the presumed category is placed before a questionmark in the appendix section and included in the comparative analyses.

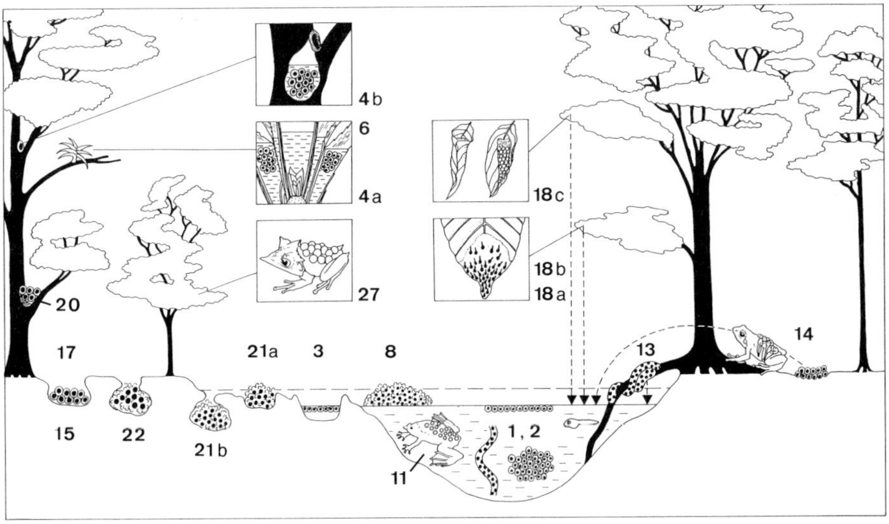

Fig. 1: Reproductive modes of frogs from lowland Amazonia (0–400 m above sea level). Numbers identify modes outlined in Duellman and Trueb, 1986. 1, 2, 3, 4a, 4b, 6: embryonic and larval development in water. 8, 13, 14, 18a, 18b, 18c, 21a, 21b: eggs out of water, larvae in water. 15, 17, 20, 22: eggs and larval/direct development on land. 11, 27: direct development on dorsum of female frog. – water level at time of oviposition, – – – water level necessary for survival of larvae. Adapted or modified from Duellman and Trueb, 1986; Hödl, 1986; Lamotte and Lescure, 1977; Lynch, 1979.

3. Reproductive modes of Amazonian lowland frogs (Fig. 1, Table 1)

3.1. Aquatic development (modes 1, 2, 3, 4 and 6)

Mode 1. Oviposition and larval development in unconstrained lentic waters.

Eggs and larvae of 47 out of 130 Amazonian lowland species are found in ponds, puddles or lakes (see Table 1). Most of the mode 1 species breed in temporary pools (Crump, 1971, 1974; Aichinger, 1985, 1987a).

Osteocephalus taurinus, an explosive breeder (sensu: Wells, 1977), breeds either in puddles, in pools left behind by receeding creeks and rivers, as well as in flooded forests. *Bufo marinus*, *B. granulosus* and *Hyla geographica* have been found breeding in large permanent water bodies. Clutches consist of strings (*Bufo spp.*), globular masses (e.g. *Hyla parviceps*, *H. minuta*, *Ceratophrys cornuta*) or – most commonly – of an egg film floating on the water surface (e.g. *Chiasmocleis ventrimaculata*, *Hamptophryne boliviana*, *Hyla lanciformis*, *H. marmorata*, *Ololygon rubra*, *Osteocephalus taurinus*, *Phrynohyas venulosa*).

Mode 2. Oviposition and larval development in lotic water.

Atelopus pulcher and *Osteocephalus buckleyi* are the only obligate stream breeding frogs from the Amazonian lowlands. In Central Amazonia, *Bufo granulosus*, *B. typhonius*, *Hyla geographica*, *H. granosa* and *H. calcarata* have been found breeding both in standing water and large forest creeks or rivers.

Mode 3. Oviposition in water basins constructed by males.

Eggs of *Hyla boans* are often deposited in male-made basins next to temporary ponds, streams or lakes (Fig. 2). Mud or sand nests are built at the end of the dry season. Flooding

Table 1: Reproductive modes among 130 Amazonian lowland frog species.

Reproductive mode	total	study areas: Belém	Manaus	Panguana	Santa Cecilia
1	47 (36.2%)	20 (51.3%)	31 (46.3%)	23 (34.8%)	31 (35.2%)
2	2 (1.5%)	–	2 (3.0%)	–	1 (1.1%)
3	1 (0.8%)	1 (2.6%)	1 (1.5%)	1 (1.5%)	1 (1.1%)
4	4 (3.1%)	1 (2.6%)	2 (3.0%)	2 (3.0%)	2 (2.3%)
6	1 (0.8%)	–	–	1 (1.5%)	1 (1.1%)
8	11 (8.5%)	5 (12.8%)	7 (10.4%)	5 (7.5%)	6 (6.8%)
11	2 (1.5%)	1 (2.6%)	2 (3.0%)	–	1 (1.1%)
13	1 (0.8%)	–	1 (1.5%)	1 (1.5%)	1 (1.1%)
14	10 (7.7%)	2 (5.1%)	3 (4.5%)	7 (10.6%)	6 (6.8%)
15	2 (1.5%)	–	2 (3.0%)	–	–
17/20	23 (17.7%)	1 (2.6%)	2 (3.0%)	12 (18.2%)	17 (19.3%)
18	18 (13.8%)	5 (12.8%)	7 (10.4%)	11 (16.7%)	15 (17.0%)
21	5 (3.8%)	2 (5.1%)	5 (7.5%)	1 (1.5%)	4 (4.5%)
22	2 (1.5%)	1 (2.6%)	2 (3.0%)	2 (3.0%)	1 (1.1%)
27	1 (0.8%)	–	–	–	1 (1.1%)
	130 (100.0%)	39 (100.1%)	67 (100.1%)	66 (99.8%)	88 (99.6%)

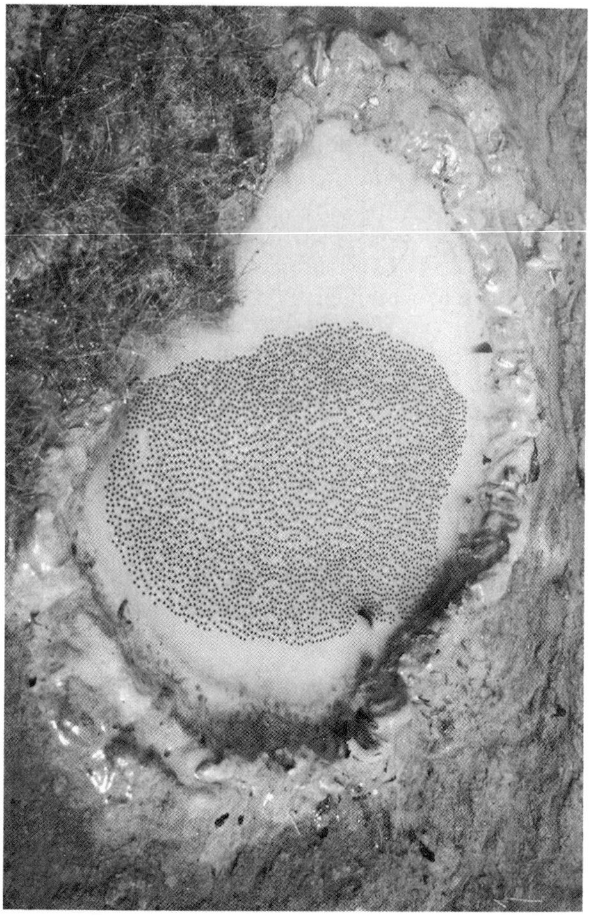

Fig. 2: Nest of *Hyla boans* showing surface film of eggs. Photo by the author, Lago Amaña, Brazil.

of the basins during heavy rains enables tadpoles to leave the nests. In rocky banks along the Tapajoz river, where basin formation is impossible, eggs are deposited in shallow water (Zimmerman, pers. comm.).

Mode 4. Oviposition in water-filled leaf axils (a) or tree holes (b). Feeding tadpoles.

Phrynohyas resinifictrix and *Nyctimantis rugiceps* represent mode 4. While floating on the water surface, widely spaced *P. resinifictrix* males call from water-filled tree cavities (Fig. 3a) (Zimmerman and Hödl, 1983), where mating occurs. *Osteocephalus sp.* (erroneously named *O. buckleyi* in Zimmerman and Bogart, 1988) breeds in bromeliads (Fig. 3b) and palms, where tadpoles develop in water basins formed by leaf axils (mode 4a).

Mode 6. Oviposition in water-filled bromeliads. Non-feeding tadpoles.

This mode of reproduction – as yet unknown for the neotropics – was recently observed in the microhylid *Syncope antenori* (Aichinger, pers. comm.; Henzl, pers. comm.). Large

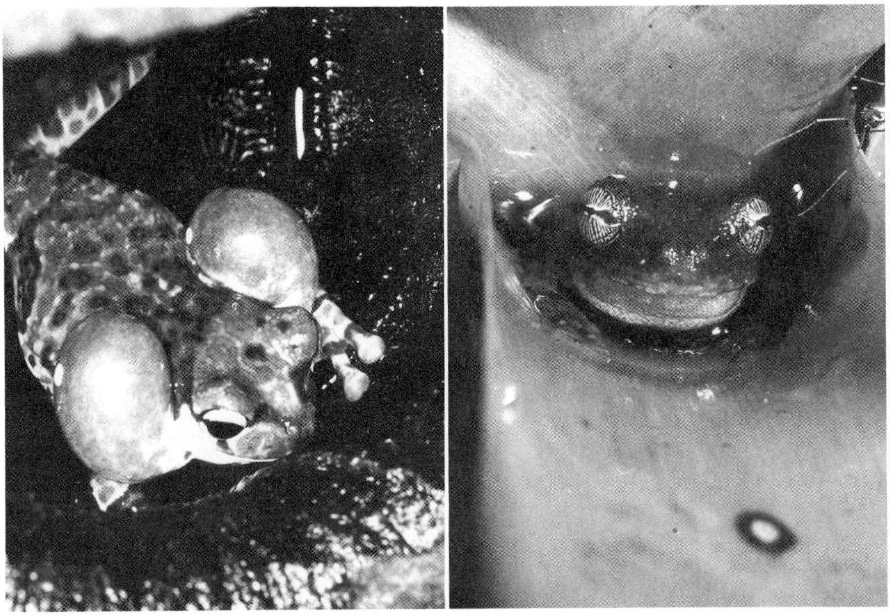

Fig. 3: Amazonian frogs at arboreal breeding sites.
a (left): *Phrynohyas resinifictrix* (Hylidae). Male calling in tree hole. Photo by M. Henzl, Panguana, Peru.
b (right): *Osteocephalus sp.* (Hylidae). Male at calling station in a bromeliad. Photo by the author, Reserva Ducke near Manaus, Brazil.

eggs were deposited in water-filled terrestrial, off-ground or arboreal bromeliads and artificial mimicks (Krügel, pers. comm.), where non-feeding tadpoles undergo metamorphosis.

3.2. Semiterrestrial development (modes 8, 13, 14, 15, 18 and 21)

Mode 8. Foam nest construction on water surface. Feeding tadpoles in lentic water.

In 11 out of 16 foam-nesting species, eggs may be deposited in foam chambers floating on the water surface (see also Heyer, 1969). A detailed behavioural analyses of aquatic foam nest construction in *Physalaemus ephippifer* is given by Hödl (1988, 1990). While floating close to the shoreline, the amplecting male beats oviductal secretions into a frothy mass. During the foam-beating motions, unpigmented eggs are fertilized and distributed within the foam. Among neotropical frogs, the foam-nesting *Lithodytes lineatus* is unique in its life history due to its close association with leaf-cutting ants (Schlüter and Regös, 1981).

Mode 13. Terrestrial oviposition next to or above water. Feeding tadpoles in lentic water.

The small diurnal bufonid *Dendrophryniscus minutus* is the only Amazonian lowland frog with egg deposition at ground/off ground level out of water (Fig. 4a) and feeding

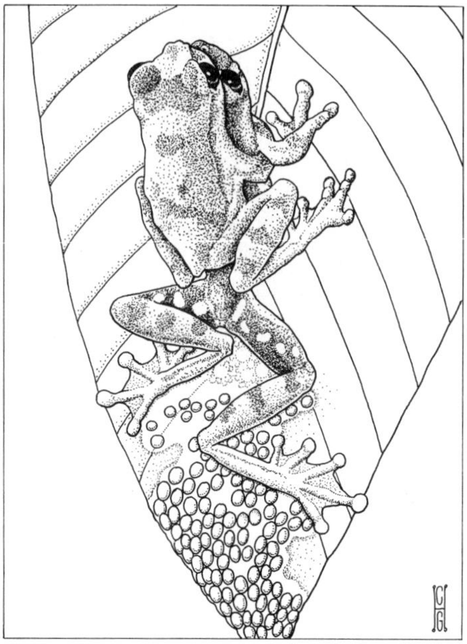

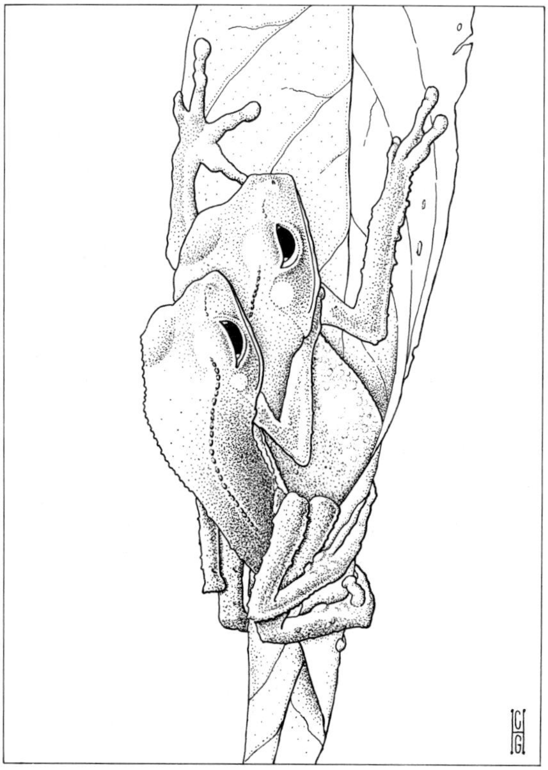

Fig. 4: Terrestrial oviposition in Amazonian frogs.
a (above left): *Dendrophryniscus minutus* (Bufonidae). b (above right): *Hyla brevifrons* (Hylidae). c (left): *Phyllomedusa vaillanti* (Hylidae). Drawn by H. C. Grillitsch after pictures taken by M. Henzl (a, c) and the author (b) at Panguana, Peru.

tadpoles (Schlüter, 1983; Aichinger, 1985). Eggs are deposited on roots, trunks and litter close to the shore-line of temporary ponds at the onset of the rainy season. Oviposition sites may be flooded later on during the rain period, thus enabling aquatic development of the hatching larvae.

Mode 14. Terrestrial oviposition. Tadpoles carried to lentic and/or lotic waters by adults.

All presently known dendrobatids lay their eggs on land and carry the larvae to water for development (Fig. 5). A thorough discussion on the evolution of parental care in the dart poison frogs is given by Weygoldt (1987). Dendrobatid species from the Amazonian lowlands are known to be highly territorial. Males may advertise territories through calling over several weeks (Hödl, 1983). In *Epipedobates* (= *Dendrobates*) *femoralis*, calling positions are found within territories of up to 26 m^2 in size, which may be occupied continuously by a single male for as long as 138 days (Roithmair, 1988). Following intensive courtship displays, *E. femoralis* and *E. trivittatus* oviposit during early morning hours in hidden places within the leaf litter. Eggs are deposited on leaves or palmspathices within the male territories (Roithmair, 1988; Zimmerman, pers. comm.). Larvae of most dendrobatid frogs are transported to ponds, puddles, water-filled ground-fallen palm-spathices or streamside puddles prior to flooding. *Dendrobates quinquevittatus* larvae also develop in arboreal waters, such as water-filled bromeliads or tree holes. Tadpoles of *Epipedobates petersi* are released into flowing streams (Henzl, pers. comm.). *Colostethus marchesianus* is known to release its tadpoles in ponds as well as in slow current forest creeks (pers. obs.).

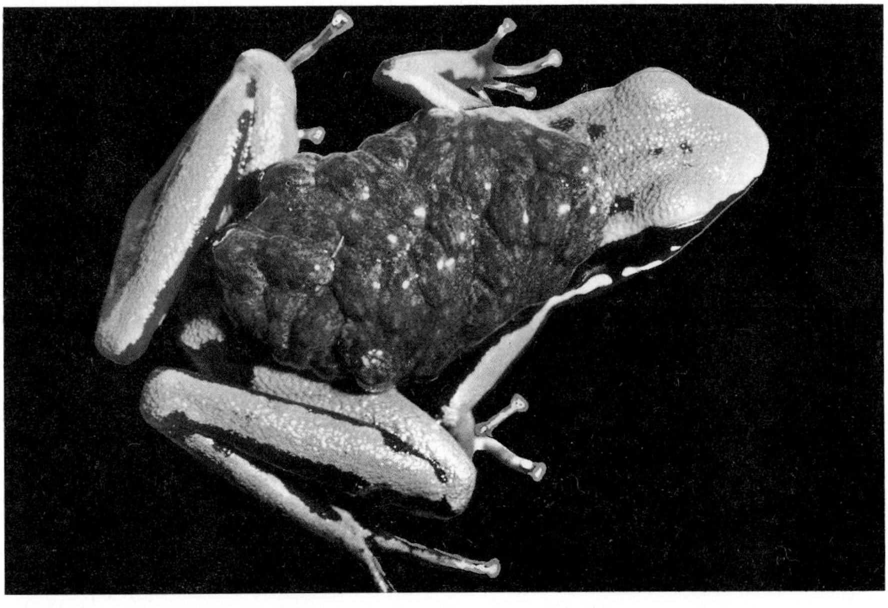

Fig. 5: Male *Epipedobates trivittatus* (Dendrobatidae) carrying tadpoles. Photo by the author, Panguana, Peru.

Mode 15. Terrestrial oviposition. Non-feeding tadpoles complete development in (flooded?) nest.

The two species of the fossorial genus *Synapturanus* are unique in laying large terrestrial eggs which develop into non-feeding tadpoles. Even though *Synapturanus mirandaribeiroi* and *S. salseri* are commonly heard during the rain season in Central Amazonian forests (Zimmerman and Bogart, 1988) little is known about their reproductive behaviour and life history (Pyburn, 1975). Presently it is uncertain whether flooding of the nest is obligate for successful development of the non-feeding larvae.

Mode 18. Oviposition on vegetation above water. Aquatic larval development.

All leaf-breeding members of the genus *Hyla* preferably deposit their pigmented eggs on the upper surface of leaves overhanging temporary ponds (mode 18 a). Aichinger (1987 b) presents detailed observations on reproductive behaviour of the leaf-breeding frog *Hyla brevifrons* (Fig. 4 b). *H. sarayacuensis* is known to lay its eggs on leaves (Duellman, 1978) or on moss-covered tree trunks or buttresses (Henzl, 1987) near ground level. All Amazonian lowland species of the hylid genus *Phyllomedusa* deposit non-pigmented eggs at the upper side of leaves (*P. palliata*) (mode 18 a) or in folded leaves which at least partly conceal the eggs (all other Amazonian *Phyllomedusa spp.*) (mode 18 c). Oviposition sites are above ponds, puddles and – as in *P. vaillanti* and *P. tomopterna* – occasionally streams (Henzl, pers. comm.). Fig. 4 c shows the onset of the oviposition process in *P. vaillanti* during which the female and the amplecting male start to roll up the distal part of the leaf into a cone with its hind legs. Eggs are laid on the upper surface of the leaf during this cone-shaping process; this side then forms the inner surface of the nest. Nests formed out of a single enrolled leaf are also found in *P. hypocondrialis* and *P. tomopterna* (Pyburn, 1980; Lamotte and Lescure, 1977). *P. tarsius* constructs a simple nest consisting of a large folded leaf or of several palm-leaf pinnae attached to the clutch. Centrolenids lay their eggs on foliage overhanging streams (mode 18 b). Egg clutches are usually deposited on the undersites of the leaves (Crump, 1974). *Centrolenella oyampiensis* males stay near the clutch until the tadpoles drop into the stream below (Zimmerman, pers. comm.). The tadpoles of the exclusively stream-dwelling family Centrolenidae are greatly modified and bury themselves in the detritus and gravel of the stream bottom (Scott and Limerick, 1983).

Mode 21. Terrestrial foam nests. Feeding tadpoles in lentic water.

Terrestrial foam nests with obligate subsequent flooding may be built in small depressions (mode 21 a), large holes or in small burrows constructed by the male (mode 21 b) (Heyer, 1969). When these structures are flooded, well-developed tadpoles leave the deteriorating nests. *Leptodactylus knudseni* produces its foam nest at the beginning of the rain season in depressions either in contact with small water bodies or on land (Fig. 6) next to water. *L. mystaceus* breeds both in litter-covered depressions or burrows (pers. obs.). *L. fuscus* places the foam nest in a burrow fashioned by the *male*. Detailed observations on the breeding behaviour of *L. fuscus* are given by Martins (1988).

3.3. Terrestrial development (modes 17, 20, 22)

Mode 17. Terrestrial oviposition. Direct development. Mode 20. Arboreal oviposition. Direct development.

All species of the genus *Eleutherodactylus* whose reproduction is known are characterized by direct development and large terrestrial eggs. Oviposition sites may be subterra-

Fig. 6: Foam nest construction in *Leptodactylus knudseni* (*L. pentadactylus*-group, Leptodactylidae). [From Hödl, 1986. By permission of the Charles Univ. Press, Prague]

nean, terrestrial, off-ground or arboreal (Stewart, 1988). Little is known about the life history of the Amazonian frogs of the two genera (*Eleutherodactylus*, *Ischnocnema*) associated with direct development. Oviposition in *E. altamazonicus*, *E. croceoinguinis*, *E. diadematus*, *E. lacrimosus*, *E. lanthanites*, *E. martiae*, *E. pseudoacuminatus*, and *E. variabilis* (Duellman, 1978) and *E. fenestratus* (Hödl, unpubl.) have been observed in the laboratory. No field observations on oviposition in Amazonian *Eleutherodactylus spp.* have been made. Based on small (ovarian) clutch size, large ovum diameter and lack of pigment in the eggs, Duellman (1978) assumes *Ischnocnema* to have terrestrial eggs which undergo direct development.

Mode 22. Terrestrial foam nesting. Non-feeding tadpoles complete development in nest.

Adenomera is the only known neotropical genus to produce terrestrial foam nests with few large-yolked eggs and non-feeding tadpoles. Foam nesting in *A. hylaedactyla* occurs in small, hidden depressions in grasslands and other open formations with low vegetation.

3.4. Egg deposition and direct development on dorsum of the female. (modes 11 and 27)

Mode 11. Direct development on dorsum of aquatic frogs.

Deposition of eggs on the back of the female and direct development of eggs is displayed in *Pipa pipa* (Rabb and Rabb, 1961; Schütte and Ehrl 1987) and in *P. arrabali* (Buchacher, pers. comm.). Young *P. pipa* and *P. arrabali* leave their mother's back from the place where the individual eggs were embedded.

Mode 27. Direct development on dorsum of terrestrial frogs.

In the hylid genus *Hemiphractus*, eggs develop on the dorsum of the female. Field observations on reproductive behaviour of Amazonian *Hemiphractus spp.* are lacking.

4. General considerations

4.1. Reproductive diversity and environment

It is accepted as a general rule that environmental factors constrain the diversity of reproductive modes in frogs (Duellman, 1989). The generalized mode of aquatic eggs and larvae is universal in all major environments. In temperate regions only a few modes (Palaearctis: 6, Nearctis: 4) are known (Duellman and Trueb, 1986). High humidity, rainfall and temperatures have influenced the evolution of alternative life histories in wet tropical forests. Less than 50% of Amazonian lowland frogs have an entirely aquatic development (Table 2). In 47 (36%) out of 130 species embryonic development occurs out of water and 26 (20%) species are reproductively independent from water bodies. Egg development out of water is dependent upon high humidity. In the two Upper Amazon basin sites (Santa Cecilia, Panguana) species with semiterrestrial and terrestrial reproduction account for more than 56% of the total local anuran community. Santa Cecilia lies in an area with high precipitation and aseasonal, erratic rainfalls with at least 200 mm per month. At Panguana, 80% of the rain falls within six months and the actual dry season (monthly rainfall less than 40 mm) is limited to three months (Aichinger 1985, 1987a). In Central (Manaus) and Lower Amazonia (Belém), where the dry seasons are more pronounced than in Upper Amazonia (Salati et al., 1978), less than 44% of anuran eggs are laid out of water bodies. An almost equal percentage of frog species exhibiting semiterrestrial development is found throughout the Amazon lowland (Table 2). Both highly humid-

Table 2: Developmental patterns among 130 Amazonian lowland frog species. [mean annual rainfall given for each study area in mm; data source: Belém (Crump, 1971), Manaus (Hödl, 1977), Panguana (Aichinger, 1985), Santa Cecilia (Duellman, 1978)]

Development	Amazonian lowlands	Belém (2858 mm)	Manaus (2568 mm)	Panguana (2634 mm)	Santa Cecilia (4279 mm)
Aquatic (modes 1,2,3,4,6)	55 (42.3%)	22 (56.4%)	36 (53.7%)	27 (40.9%)	36 (40.9%)
Semiterrestrial (8,13,14,15, 18,21)	47 (36.2%)	14 (35.9%)	25 (37.3%)	25 (37.9%)	32 (36.4%)
Terrestrial (17,20,22)	25 (19.2%)	2 (5.1%)	4 (6.0%)	14 (21.2%)	18 (20.5%)
Others (11,27)	3 (2.3%)	1 (2.6%)	2 (3.0%)	–	2 (2.3%)

ity-sensitive dendrobatids (mode 14) and leaf-breeding frogs (mode 18) account for two thirds of the semiterrestrial species in the Upper Amazon basin, whereas the more dry-resistant foam-nesting modes dominate in the Central (48%) and Lower (50%) Amazon basin (Table 1, Table 2).

The ecological distribution of anuran reproductive modes (Fig. 7) shows, that all open-area species undergo embryonic development in water (modes 1, 3, 11) or frothy foam (modes 8, 21, 22). Frogs typically associated with human activities («Kulturfolger») include *Bufo marinus*, *B. granulosus*, *Hyla marmorata*, *H. walfordi*, *Ololygon rubra*, *Phrynohyas venulosa* (mode 1), *Physalaemus ephippifer* (mode 8), *Leptodactylus fuscus* (mode 21) and *Adenomera hylaedactyla* (mode 22). Leaf-breeding frogs (mode 18) or species with direct development (modes 17, 20) are generally restricted to habitats with high humidity, such as floating meadows, flooded forests or terra firme woodland. With an occurrence of 4.6% (modes 2, 18 c), stream-dependant modes of reproduction are poorly represented in lowland Amazonia. As pool sites are scarce in mountainous areas, frogs with stream modes can make up to 53% of the anuran fauna in humid mountain forests (Duellman, 1989).

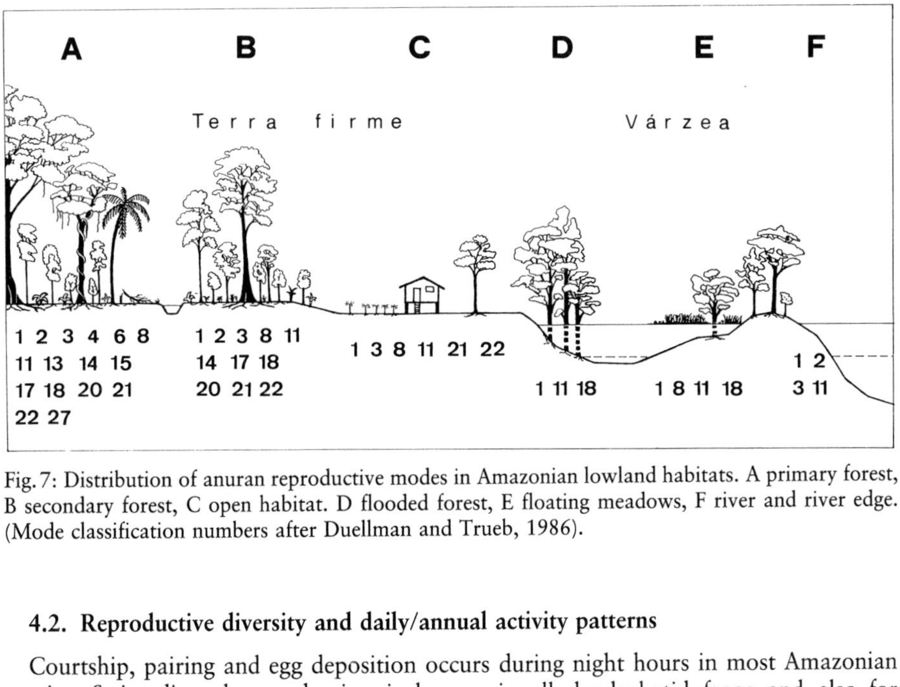

Fig. 7: Distribution of anuran reproductive modes in Amazonian lowland habitats. A primary forest, B secondary forest, C open habitat. D flooded forest, E floating meadows, F river and river edge. (Mode classification numbers after Duellman and Trueb, 1986).

4.2. Reproductive diversity and daily/annual activity patterns

Courtship, pairing and egg deposition occurs during night hours in most Amazonian species. Strict diurnal reproduction is known in all dendrobatid frogs and also for *Atelopus pulcher*. The otherwise exclusively diurnal *Dendrophryniscus minutus* oviposits preferably during the night (Aichinger, 1985). For other day-active frogs, e.g., *Edalorhina perezi*, *Eleutherodactylus nigrovittatus* and *E. sulcatus*, too little information on reproductive activities exist to confirm diel oviposition. The explosive breeders *Bufo typhonius*, *Chiasmocleis ventrimaculata* and *Hamptophryne boliviana* have been found breeding both during day and night hours (Schlüter, 1983). With the exception of mass breeding microhylids, *Bufo typhonius*, *Atelopus pulcher*, as well as the dendrobatid frogs, all species whose reproduction has been well studied are known to be nocturnal (Crump, 1971, 1974; Duellman, 1978; Schlüter, 1983; Aichinger, 1985, 1987a, 1987b).

Rainfall and the subsequent availability of waterbodies and terrestrial sites with high atmospheric humidity are probably the most important environmental factors influencing anuran reproduction. At Santa Cecilia 30% of the anurans – representing five reproductive modes – bred continuously and 49% sporadically throughout the year (Duellman, 1978). Only two species (*Epipedobates pictus* and *E. trivittatus*) were found to be reproductively active throughout the year at Panguana. 35.5% of the species studied were exclusively and a further 44.5% predominantely active throughout the six month «rain period» at the Peruvian site (Aichinger 1985). With the exception of *Hyla geographica* (Magnusson, pers. comm.), none of the frogs occurring at Manaus or Belém is known to be a continuous breeder (Crump, 1971; Hödl, 1977). *Epipedobates femoralis* taken from the Reserva Ducke near Manaus bred continuously over 24 months under laboratory conditions. Within a year, 24 clutches with a mean egg number of 14 were laid by a single pair at mean intervals of 15.2 (range 7–34) days (Hödl, unpubl. data). In Amazonia the breeding period of *E. femoralis* lasted five months at Manaus (Hödl, 1983), seven months at Panguana (Aichinger, 1985; Roithmair, 1988) and «with the possible exception of the period December–February evidently throughout the year» at Santa Cecilia (Duellman, 1978).

Some species exhibiting mode 1 tend to form dense breeding aggregations for a few days once the water bodies are established. This explosive opportunistic breeding pattern is known for hylids (e.g., *Hyla parviceps*, *H. riveroi*, *Ololygon rubra*, *Osteocephalus taurinus*, *Phrynohyas coriacea*), bufonids (*Bufo typhonius*), leptodactylids (*Ceratophrys cornuta*), and microhylid frogs (*Chiasmocleis ventrimaculata*, *C. shudicarensis*, *Hamptophryne boliviana* (Schlüter, 1983; Aichinger, 1985; Zimmerman and Bogart, 1988). Wet opportunistic breeders such as the hylid frogs *Hyla brevifrons*, *H. marmorata*, *H. rhodopepla*, *H. sarayacuensis*, *Ololygon cruentomma* and *O. funerea* breed repeatedly after rainfalls throughout the year. Frog species requiring a rising water level for survival of the larvae (comp. Fig. 1) breed at the end of the dry season or at the onset of the first heavy rains of the wet period (*Leptodactylus knudseni*, *L. fuscus*, *Dendrophryniscus minutus*) (Aichinger, 1985).

4.3. Reproductive diversity and fecundity

Thorough analyses of quantitative anuran reproductive variables are given by Crump (1974), Duellman (1978), and Salthe and Duellman (1973). Data on female snout-vent length, mature ovarian egg number and maximum ovarian egg diameter are presented in the appendix section. Table 3 summarizes relationships between clutch size, female snout-vent length and developmental pattern among Amazonian lowland frogs. Species with aquatic eggs have by far the largest ovarian complements. The number of ovarian eggs and the size of females is lowest for species reproducing in complete independence from water bodies. Maximum ovarian egg diameter increase with terrestriality and range from 1 to 4 mm (Appendix, Table 3).

Acknowledgements

Field work in Amazonia was supported by the Österreicher Fonds zur Förderung der Wissenschaftlichen Forschung (FWF, Proj. Nr. 5403, 6389B). I am grateful to B. Zimmermann and the many local helpers at Belém, Manaus (Brazil) and Panguana (Peru) for field assistance. Special thanks go to J. Koepcke and H.-W. Koepcke for permission to work at

Table 3: Mean female snout-vent length (SVL), mean egg number, and mean maximum ovarian egg diameter of Amazonian frog species with aquatic, semi-terrestrial and terrestrial development. (Number of species analyzed are given in brackets).

	Aquatic development		Eggs out of water, aquatic larvae		Terrestrial development	
Female SVL (mm)	50.3	(49)	45.5	(39)	31.0	(18)
Mature ovarian egg number	1279	(45)	264	(35)	22	(18)
Maximum ovarian egg diameter (mm)	1.3	(45)	2.1	(32)	2.9	(18)

their field station at Panguana. M. Aichinger, O. Buchacher, M. Henzl, M. Hero, W. Magnusson, A. Schlüter and B. Zimmerman offered insights into yet unpublished data on reproductive activities in Amazonian frogs. W. Duellman kindly provided me with a preprint of his publication (Duellman, 1989). I am especially thankful to H. C. Grillitsch for drawing Figs. 4 a to 4 c and improving Fig. 1. P. Weygoldt and M. Henzl kindly commented on drafts of the manuscript.

Appendix

Ecological and reproductive diversity of 130 anuran species from lowland Amazonia*.

Study areas: B Belém, Pará, Brazil (01° 21′S, 48° 30′W, 12 m); M Manaus, Amazonas, Brazil (03° 03′S, 60° 02′W, 50 m); P Panguana, Huánuco, Peru (09°35′S, 74° 48′W, 260 m); S Santa Cecilia, Napo, Ecuador (00° 03′N, 76° 59′W, 340 m). Ecological codes: AQ aquatic, AR arboreal (no differences are made between off-ground, low and high), FO fossorial, TE terrestrial. See text and Fig. 1 for number codes of reproductive modes. SVL mean snout-vent length of mature females, EN number of mature ovarian eggs (c egg number of entire clutch). ED maximal egg diameter.

Data sources: 1: Hödl, present study. 2: Aichinger, pers. communication. 3: Crump, 1974. 4: Aichinger, 1985. 5: Duellman, 1978. 6: Zimmerman, pers. communication. 7: Toft and Duellman, 1979. 8: Crump, 1971. 9: Zimmerman and Hödl, 1983. 10: Buchacher, pers. communication. 11: Martins, 1988. 12: Muedeking and Heyer, 1967. 13: Magnusson, pers. communication. 14: Pyburn, 1975. 15: Schütte and Ehrl, 1987.

Family, genus, species	*Study area*	*Ecology*	*Reprod. mode*	*SVL*	*EN*	*(n)*	*ED*	*Data source*
Bufonidae								
Atelopus pulcher	M	TE	2	25				1
Bufo								
glaberrimus	PS	TE	1?	110	11069	(1)	1.9	2
granulosus	M	TE	1/2	66	983c	(1)	1.0	1
marinus	BMPS	TE	1	133	8598	(5)	1.5	3
typhonius	BMPS	TE	1/2	74	1538	(14)	2.0	3
				67	1585	(10)	1.4	4
Dendrophryniscus								
minutus	MPS	TE	13	19	150	(19)	1.0	3
				20	284	(15)	0.5	4
Centrolenidae								
Centrolenella								
midas	PS	AR	18	27	28	(3)	1.5	3
munozorum	PS	AR	18	21				5
oyampiensis	M	AR	18					6
resplendens	S	AR	18					5
Dendrobatiade								
Colostethus								
marchesianus	MPS	TE	14	18	14	(14)	2.0	3
				17	13	(15)	1.5	4
peruvianus	P	TE	14?					7
sauli	S	TE	14	25	11	(40)	1.5	3
sp.	M	TE	14?	17				1
Dendrobates								
quinquevittatus	B PS	AR	14	17	7	(2)	1.5	4
Epipedobates								
femoralis	MPS	TE	14	26	23	(12)	2.0	3
				27	22	(15)	1.5	4
parvulus	S	TE	14	21	9	(109)	3.0	3
petersi	P	TE	14	29	10	(10)	3.0	4
pictus	PS	TE	14	23	18	(48)	2.0	3
				21	15	(15)	2.0	4
trivittatus	B P	TE	14	45	38	(15)	3.0	4
Hylidae								
Hemiphractus								
proboscideus	S	TE/AR	27?	50	26	(1)	2.5	5
Hyla								
alboguttata	S	AR	1?	41	440	(22)	1.5	3
baumgardneri	B	AR	1					8

Family, genus, species	*Study area*	*Ecology*	*Reprod. mode*	*SVL*	*EN*	*(n)*	*ED*	*Data source*
bifurca	S	AR	18	33	190	(20)	2.0	5
boans	BMPS	AR	3	99	3155	(23)	2.0	3
					3587c	(1)	2.0	1
bokermanni	B PS	AR	18	24	98	(24)	1.5	3
brevifrons	PS	AR	18	21	79	(15)	1.0	3
				22	80	(15)	1.5	4
calcarata	BMPS	AR	1	54	1144	(10)	1.5	3
fasciata	MPS	AR	1	47	569	(27)	1.5	3
favosa	S	AR	18	40	496	(1)		5
geographica	BMPS	AR	1/2	67	2797	(7)	2.0	3
goughi	B	AR	1					8
granosa	BMPS	AR	1/2	41	426	(11)	1.5	3
				36	400	(10)	2.0	4
haraldschultzi	M	AR	1	23	216	(7)	1.0	1
helenae	B	AR	1?					8
lanciformis	M S	AR	1	87	1618	(23)	2.0	3
leucophyllata	B PS	AR	18	42	588	(6)	1.5	3
				36	496	(3)	1.0	4
marmorata	B PS	AR	1	49	979	(7)	1.5	3
				44	687	(3)	1.0	4
melanargyrea	B	AR	1?	37				1
minuta	BMPS	AR	1	24	212	(5)	1.0	3
multifasciata	BM	AR	1	83	1343	(8)	1.0	1
parviceps	PS	AR	1	23	234	(101)	1.0	3
				25	290	(15)	1.0	4
punctata	M S	AR	1	37	325	(20)	1.5	3
raniceps	BM	AR	1	57	1272	(5)	1.0	1
rhodopepla	PS	AR	1	27	285	(52)	1.1	3
				26	383	(15)	1.0	4
riveroi	PS	AR	1	23	394	(10)	1.0	4
rossalleni	MPS	AR	18?	22	103	(7)	1.0	4
sarayacuensis	PS	AR	18	34	113	(14)	2.0	3
				34	113	(10)	1.5	4
triangulum	M S	AR	18	40	502	(23)	1.0	3
walfordi	BM	AR	1	20	181	(10)	1.0	1
Nyctimantis								
rugiceps	S	AR	4	61				5
Ololygon								
boesemani	BM	AR	1	39	480	(5)	1.0	1
cruentomma	MPS	AR	1	28	580	(18)	1.0	3
				29	511	(15)	1.0	4
funerea	PS	AR	1?	38	538	(38)	1.1	3
garbei	MPS	AR	1	42	550	(21)	1.5	3
				43	810	(4)	1.0	4
nebulosa	BM	AR	1	32	527	(5)	1.0	1
rubra	BMPS	AR	1	40	591	(66)	1.5	3
				39	1170	(10)	1.0	4

Family, genus, species	Study area	Ecology	Reprod. mode	SVL	EN	(n)	ED	Data source
Osteocephalus								
buckleyi	M S	AR	2	49	580	(1)	1.0	3
leprieurii	PS	AR	4?	60	848	(16)	1.0	3
				57	788	(2)	1.5	4
taurinus	BMPS	AR	1	76	550	(1)	1.0	3
				74	1479c	(1)	1.0	1
sp.	M	AR	4	56	437c	(1)	1.5	1
Phrynohyas								
coriacea	MPS	AR	*1*	66	1430	(1)	2.0	3
resinifictrix	BMP	AR	4					9
venulosa	BMPS	AR	1	71				5
Phyllomedusa								
bicolor	BM	AR	18	119	267c			10
hypocondrialis	B	AR	18	44				1
palliata	PS	AR	18	47	61	(15)	2.5	3
tarsius	MPS	AR	18	105	549	(15)	3.0	3
				84	435	(5)	3.0	4
					207c	(25)		10
tomopterna	MPS	AR	18	57	71	(5)	3.5	3
				62	49	(1)	3.0	4
					83c	(5)		10
vaillanti	BMPS	AR	18	79	1114	(5)	2.0	3
				59	703	(2)	2.5	4
Sphaenorhynchus								
carneus	M S	AQ/AR	1	23	143	(1)	1.0	3
				21	152	(7)	1.0	1
dorisae	M	AQ/AR	1	31	326	(7)	1.0	1
lacteus	BM S	AR/AQ	1	48	550	(1)	1.0	3
				46	478	(5)	1.0	1
Leptodactylidae								
Adenomera								
andreae	BMPS	TE	22	27	9	(12)	3.0	3
hylaedactyla	MP	TE	22	26	12	(6)	3.0	1
				26	14	(5)	3.0	4
					9c			1
Ceratophrys								
cornuta	MPS	TE	1	97	2270	(1)	2.0	4
Edalorhina								
perezi	PS	TE	8	38	93	(1)	2.0	3
Eleutherodactylus								
acuminatus	S	AR	20?	29	17	(6)	2.5	3
altamazonicus	PS	TE/AR	17/20?	28	18	(20)	2.5	3
carvalhoi	P	TE/AR?	17/20?					7

Family, genus, species	*Study area*	*Ecology*	*Reprod. mode*	*SVL*	*EN*	*(n)*	*ED*	*Data source*
croceoinguinis	S	AR	20?	20	5	(86)	3.0	3
diadematus	S	AR	20?	42	62	(3)	3.0	3
fenestratus	M	TE/AR	17/20?	45	48	(5)	2.5	1
imitatrix	P	TE/AR?	17/20?					7
lacrimosus	BMPS	TE	17?					5
lanthanites	PS	TE/AR	17/20?	39	30	(68)	3.0	3
martiae	S	TE	17?	22	8	(18)	2.0	3
mendax	P	TE/AR?	17/20?					5
nigrovittatus	S	TE	17?	22	9	(3)	2.5	3
ockendeni	PS	TE/AR	17/20?	27	13	(29)	3.0	3
				29	28	(13)	3.0	4
orphnolaimus	S	AR	20?					5
paululus	S	TE/AR	17/20?	19	5	(2)	2.0	3
peruvianus	PS	AR/TE	17/20?	42	43	(12)	3.5	3
(= conspicillatus)				36	38	(2)	2.0	4
pseudoacuminatus	S	AR	20?	21	7	(12)	3.0	3
quaquaversus	S	AR	20?	29	22	(1)	3.0	3
sulcatus	PS	TE	17?	49	32	(1)	2.5	1
toftae	P	AR	20?					7
variabilis	S	AR	20?	24	7	(148)	3.0	3
ventrimarmoratus	P	TE/AR	17/20?					7
Ischnocnema								
quixensis	PS	TE	17?	53	35	(34)	4.0	3
				45	35	(10)	4.0	4
Leptodactylus								
fuscus	M S	TE	21	40	232	(10)	2.0	11
knudseni	M	TE	21	136				1
longirostris	M	TE	8?					1
mystaceus	BM S	TE	21	55	281	(22)	2.5	3
ocellatus	BM	TE	8	78				1
pentadactylus	BMPS	TE	21?	125	952	(1)	2.9	12
podicipinus	M	TE	8?					13
riveroi	M	TE	8?					6
rhodomystax	BMPS	TE	8?	80	257	(1)	3.0	4
stenodema	M S	TE	21?					6
wagneri	BMPS	TE	8	68	1740	(6)	1.5	3
				46	1726	(8)	1.0	4
Lithodytes								
lineatus	MPS	TE/FO	8	51	195	(1)	2.0	3
				55	260	(1)	2.0	1
Physalaemus								
ephippifer	B	TE/FO	8	29	418	(8)	1.5	1
petersi	B PS	TE	8	33	563	(4)	1.0	4
Vanzolinius								
discodactylus	S	TE	8	33	235	(6)	1.2	5

Family, genus, species	*Study area*	*Ecology*	*Reprod. mode*	*SVL*	*EN*	*(n)*	*ED*	*Data source*
Microhylidae								
Chiasmocleis								
anatipes	S	FO?	1?					5
bassleri	S	FO	1	28	212	(3)	1.0	3
shudikarensis	M	FO	1	32	566	(2)	1.0	1
c.f. hudsoni	M	FO?	1?					6
ventrimaculata	PS	FO	1	24	421	(15)	1.5	4
Ctenophryne								
geayi	MPS	FO	1	54	1250	(1)	1.0	5
Elachistocleis								
bicolor	M	TE/FO	1	41	1380	(3)	1.0	1
Hamptophryne								
boliviana	PS	TE/FO	1	42	1788	(2)	1.0	3
				35	1487	(15)	1.0	4
Synapturanus								
mirandaribeiroi	M	FO	15?	42	8c	(1)	4.0	1
salseri	M	FO			5	(1)	4.0	14
Syncope								
antenori	PS	TE/AR	6	14	5	(5)	1.2	5
					6	(1)	2.0	2
Pipidae								
Pipa								
arrabali	M	AQ	11	45	7	(7)		10
pipa	BM S	AQ	11	138	139	(2)		15
Pseudidae								
Lysapsus								
limellus	M	AQ	1	24	147	(7)	1.0	1
Ranidae								
Rana								
palmipes	S	TE/AQ	1	117	2860	(25)	2.0	3

* Genera known from lowland Amazonia, but not known from at either of the four study areas: Allophrynidae: *Allophryne* at Balbina, Amazonas, Brazil (Martins, unpubl. data); Hylidae: *Gastrotheca* at Rio Cenepa, Perú (Duellman, 1988); Leptodactylidae: *Hydrolaetare* at the mouth of Rio Purus, Amazonas, Brazil (Hödl, unpubl. data); *Phyllonastes* (Heyer, 1977) and at Parque Nacional del Manu, Madre de Dios, Peru (Morales, pers. comm.); *Phyzelaphryne* (Heyer, 1977; Duellman, 1988); Pseudopaludicola (Lynch, 1989).

References

Aichinger, M. (1985): Niederschlagsbedingte Aktivitätsmuster von Anuren des tropischen Regenwaldes: Eine quantitative Studie durchgeführt im Forschungsgebiet von Panguana (Peru). Unpubl. Ph. D. thesis. Univ. Wien.

– (1987a): Annual activity patterns in a seasonal neotropical environment. Oecologia (Berl.) *71*, 583–592.

– (1987b): Freilandbeobachtungen zum Fortpflanzungsverhalten von *Hyla brevifrons* Duellman and Crump, 1974 (Anura: Hylidae). Salamandra *23*, 269–276.

Crump, M. L. (1971): Quantitative analysis of the ecological distribution of a tropical herpetofauna. Occ. Pap. Mus. Nat. Hist. Univ. Kansas *3*, 1–62.

– (1974): Reproductive strategies in a tropical anuran community. Misc. Publ. Mus. Nat. Hist. Univ. Kansas *61*, 1–68.

Duellman, E. D. (1978): The biology of an equatorial herpetofauna in Amazonian Ecuador. Misc. Publ. Mus. Nat. Hist. Univ. Kansas *65*, 1–352.

– (1985): Reproductive modes in anuran amphibians: phylogenetic significance of adaptive strategies. S. Afr. J. Sci. *81*, 174–178.

– (1988): Patterns of species diversity in anuran amphibians in the american tropics. Ann. Missouri Bot. Gard. *75*, 79–104.

– (1989): Alternative life-history styles in anuran amphibians: evolutionary and ecological implications. In: Alternative life-history styles of animals (M. N. Bruton ed.), pp. 101–126. Kluwer Acad. Publ., Dordrecht.

Duellman, W. E., Trueb, L. (1986): Biology of amphibia. McGraw-Hill Book Co., New York.

Haffer, J. (1969): Speciation in forest birds. Science *165*, 131–137.

Henzl, M. (1987): Zur Fortpflanzung von *Hyla sarayacuensis*. ÖGH Nachr. *12/13*, 45–51.

Heyer, W. R. (1969): The adaptive ecology of the species groups of the genus *Leptodactylus* (Amphibia, Leptodactylidae). Evolution *23*, 421–428.

– (1977): Taxonomic notes on frogs from the Madeira and Purus rivers, Brasil. Pap. avul. Zool., S. Paulo *31*, 141–162.

Hödl, W. (1977): Call differences and calling site segregation in anuran species from Central Amazonian floating meadows. Oecologia (Berl.) *28*, 351–363.

– (1983): *Phyllobates femoralis* (Dendrobatidae): Rufverhalten und akustische Orientierung der Männchen (Freilandaufnahmen). Wiss. Film *30*, 12–19.

– (1986): Foam nest construction in South American leptodactylid frogs. In: Studies in Herpetology (Z. Roček, ed.), pp. 565–570. Charles Univ. Press, Prague.

– (1988): *Physalaemus ephippifer* (Leptodactylidae): Schaumnestbildung. Wiss. Film *38/39*, 29–35.

– (1990): An analysis of foam nest construction in the neotropical frog *Physalaemus ephippifer* (Leptodactylidae). Copeia (in press).

Lamotte, M., Lescure, J. (1977): Tendances adaptives a l'affranchissement du milieu aquatique chez les amphibiens anoures. Terre et Vie *30*, 225–312.

Lynch, J. D. (1979): The amphibians of the lowland tropical forests. In: The South American Herpetofauna: Its origin, evolution, and dispersal (W. E. Duellmann ed.), pp. 189–215. Monogr. Mus. Nat. Hist. Univ. Kansas *7*, 1–485.

– (1989): A review of the leptodactylid frogs of the genus *Pseudopoludicola* in northern South America Copeia *1989*, 577–588.

Martins, M. (1988): Biologia reprodutiva de *Leptodactylus fuscus* em Boa Vista, Roraima (Amphibia: Anura). Rev. Brasil. Biol. *48*, 969–977.

McDiarmid, R. W. (1978): Evolution of parental care in frogs. In: The development of behavior: comperative and evolutionary aspects (G. M. Burkhardt, M. Bekoff eds.), pp. 127–147. STMP Press. New York.

Muedeking, M. H., Heyer, W. R. (1976): Description of eggs and reproductive patterns of *Leptodactylus pentadactylus* (Amphibia: Leptodactylidae). Herpetologica *32*, 137–139.

Pyburn, W. F. (1975): A new species of microhylid frog of the genus *Synapturanus* from Southeastern Colombia. Herpetologica *31*, 439–443.

– (1980): The function of eggless capsules and leaf in nests of the frog *Phyllomedusa hypochondrialis* (Anura: Hylidae). Proc. Biol. Soc. Wash. *93*, 153–167.

Rabb, G.B., Rabb, M.S. (1961): On the mating and egg-laying behavior of the Surinam toad, Pipa pipa. *Copeia* 1960, *271–276.*

Roithmair, M.E. (1988): Freilandstudie zur Territorialität und Fortpflanzungsbiologie von *Dendrobates femoralis* (Dendrobatidae, Anura). Unpubl. PhD thesis, Univ. Wien.

Salati, E., Marques, J., Molion, L.C.B. (1978): Origem e distribuiçâo das chuvas na Amazônia. Interciencia *3*, 200–205.

Salthe, S.N., Duellman, W.E. (1973): Quantitative constraints associated with reproductive mode in anurans. In: Evolutionary biology of the anurans: contemporary research on major problems (J.L. Vial ed.) pp. 229–249. Univ. Missouri Press, Columbia.

Schlüter, A. (1983): Ökologische Untersuchungen an einem Stillgewässer im tropischen Regenwald von Peru unter besonderer Berücksichtigung der Amphibien. Unpubl. PhD thesis, Univ. Hamburg.

Schlüter, A., Regös, J. (1981): *Lithodytes lineatus* (Schneider, 1799) (Amphibia: Leptodactylidae) as a dweller in nests of the leaf cutting ant *Atta cephalotes* (Linnaeus, 1758) (Hymenoptera: Attini). Amphibia-Reptilia 2, 117–121.

Schütte, F., Ehrl, A. (1987): Zur Haltung und Zucht der großen südamerikanischen Wabenkröte *Pipa pipa* (Linnaeus, 1758) (Anura: Pipidae). Salamandra *23*, 256–268.

Scott, N.J., Limerick, S. (1983): Reptiles and Amphibians. In: Costa Rican natural history. (D.H. Janzen ed.), pp. 351–382. Univ. Chicago Press. Chicago.

Stewart, M.M. (1988): Eleutherodactyline frogs: a medley of reproductive styles. SSAR meetings, Ann Arbor (abstract).

Toft, C.A., Duellman, W.E. (1979): Anurans of the lower Rio Llullapichis, Amazonian Peru: a preliminary analysis of community structure. Herpetologica *35*, 71–77.

Wells, K.D. (1977): The social behavior of anuran amphibians. Anim. Behav. *25*, 666–693.

Weygoldt, P. (1987): Evolution of parental care in poison dart frogs (Amphibia: Anura: Dendrobatidae). Z. Zool. Syst. Evolutionsforsch. *25*, 51–67.

Wunder, W. (1932): Nestbau und Brutpflege bei Amphibien. Ergebn. Biologie *8*, 180–220.

Zimmerman, B.L., Bogart, J.P. (1988): Ecology and calls of four species of Amazonian forest frogs. J. Herpetol. *22*, 97–108.

Zimmerman, B.L., Hödl, W. (1983): Distinction of *Phrynohyas resinifictrix* (Goeldi, 1907) from *Phrynohyas venulosa* (Laurenti, 1768) based on acoustical and behavioural parameters. Zool. Anz., Jena *211*, 341–353.

Note added in proof:

On the basis of an allozymic investigation Titus et. al. (1989) consider *Hyla favosa* to be a color pattern morph of *H. leucophyllata* and recommend that *H. favosa* be considered a junior synonym of *H. leucophyllata.*

Lit.: Titus, T.A., Hillis D.M., Duellman, W.E. (1989): Color polymorphism in neotropical treefrogs: an allozymic investigation of the taxonomic status of *Hyla favosa* Cope. Herpetologica *45*, 17–23.

Fortschritte der Zoologie, Band/Vol. 38 · Hanke, W. (Hrsg.), Biology and Physiology of Amphibians
Gustav Fischer Verlag · Stuttgart · New York · 1990

Behavioral signals and reproduction modes in the neotropical frog family Dendrobatidae

Elke Zimmermann

Institute of Zoology, University of Stuttgart-Hohenheim, D-7000 Stuttgart 70, FRG

1. Introduction

Usually temperate anurans like our brown frogs (Rana temporaria) or common toads (Bufo bufo) show a cyclic reproduction with explosive breeding induced by changing temperatures and day-night-cycles in spring. Frog species, however, living in wet tropical forests display in most cases a prolonged breeding mode. Reproduction in these species is often triggered by a sudden change in the abiotic environment, e.g. the beginning of the rainy season after a period of dryness (Zimmermann, 1983; Duellman and Trueb, 1986). Many members o the diurnal, terrestrial breeding dart-poison frogs (Dendrobatidae) occur in neotropical primary or secondary forests where climate conditions remain relatively constant throughout the whole year (Lüddecke, 1974; Duellman, 1978; Myers and Daly, 1978; Zimmermann, pers. obs.). Sexes don't migrate to special breeding water sites and thus can be found together in the same habitat where they may reproduce continousely in all months of the year (Lüddecke, 1974; Duellman, 1978; Wells, 1980; Schlüter, 1984).

Within this paper I will outline behavioral mechanisms assumed to be responsible for breeding activity and reproductive success in this frog family. First, I concentrate on acoustic signals, their variants and the behavioral alterations they evoke in conspecifics. Then, I demonstrate the complexity of behavioral signals which mates exchange during courtship to synchronize breeding activity. Finally, I focus on the elaborated brood care behavior and emphasize signals evolved for parent-offspring communication.

2. Calls, variants and effects on conspecifics

Vocalizations form an important part of behavioral signals during courtship and agonistic encounters. An oscillographic and spectrographic analysis of the acoustic pattern of these calls reveal two main differentiations (Zimmermann and Zimmermann, 1986; Zimmermann and Zimmermann, 1988). Peep- or trill like calls (Fig. 1) with tonal or harmonic structure are characteristic for all studied *Allobates*, *Colostethus*, *Epipedobates*, *Phobobates* and *Phyllobates* as well as for a few *Dendrobates*. They are used for advertisement or long-range courtship as well as for aggressive displays. Buzz like calls with a more broadband noisy structure are produced by *Allobates*, by some *Colostethus*, *Epipedobates* and *Phyllobates* (Tab. 1) whereby they are restricted to close range courtship interactions. In most *Dendrobates* buzz calls (Fig. 2) may be given in short- and long-range courtship as well as during agonistic interactions.

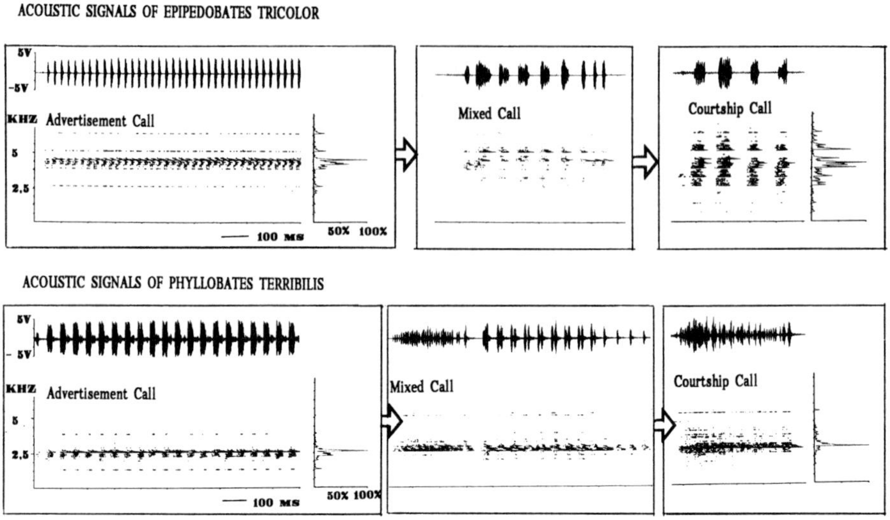

Fig. 1: Trill advertisement calls of *Epipedobates* and *Phyllobates* may grade over mixed calls into close-range courtship buzz calls.
Oscillogram (above), sonagram (below) and power spectrum (beneath sonagram) of representative call sequences (frequency resolution 20 Hz, temperature 24 °C).

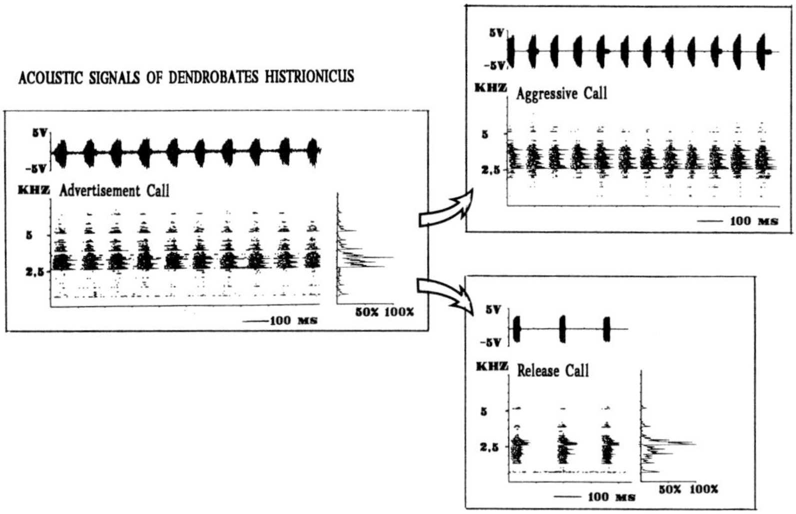

Fig. 2: Buzz advertisement calls of *Dendrobates* may grade to aggressive or defensive calls according to the motivation of the sender. Oscillogram (above), sonagram (below) and power spectrum (beneath) of representative call sequences (frequency resolution 20 Hz, temperature 22 °C).

Table 1: Synopsis of calls used by different dendrobatid taxa

Call/species	Advertisement Call	Courtship Call	Aggressive Call	Release Call
Colostethus inguinalis (1)	P	B	P	
C. palmatus (2)	P	B	P	
C. talamance	P	B	P	
C. trinitatis (3)	P	B	P	
Allobates femoralis	P	B	P	
Epipedobates anthonyi	T	B	T	
E. boulengeri-espinosai	T	B	T	
E. tricolor	T	B	T	
E. arvulus	P	P	P	
E. pictus	P	P	P	
E. pulchripectus	P	P	P	
Phyllobates lughubris	T	T	T	
Ph. terribillis	T	B	T	
Ph. vittatus	T	T	T	
Dendrobates auratus	T	T	T	
D. leucomelas	T	T	T	
D. azureus	B	B	B	
D. tinctorius	B	B	B	
D. imitator	B	B	B	
D. quinquevittatus	B	B	B	
D. reticulatus	B	B	B	
D. variabilis	B	B	B	
D. historinicus	B	B	B	B
D. lehmanni	B	B	B	B
D. speciosus (4)	B	B	B	B
D. pumilio	B	B	B	B

B = buzz call, P = peep call, T = trill call; according to own, partly unpublished data and (1) Wells 1980a, (2) Lüddecke 1974, (3) Wells 1980b, (4) Jungfer 1985

2.1. Long-range courtship or advertisement calls

These calls show little interinidividual variation in measured acoustic characters within a population (Tab. 2). Therefore, they are expected to be the most important candidates for species recognition. Among sympatrically occurring sister species they differ mostly in temporal patterns (pulse repetition rate, call duration and call repetition rate) and these differences are sufficient to prevent interbreeding. The same parameters, however, may fail to be distinguished apart by allopatric species, so, in captivity, interbreeding with fertile hybrids may result (Zimmermann and Zimmermann, 1988). Males of various dendrobatid species (e.g. all *Allobates, Colostethus, Epipedobates* and the *Dendrobates histrionicus* and *D. quinquevittatus*-group) defend small areas with suitable oviposition

Table 2: Acoustic characteristics of calls in *Dendrobates histrionicus*

Calls (analysed calls/males)	Advertisement call (220/11)	Aggressive call (40/4)	Release call (20/4)
Dominant frequency (kHz) mean, SD, range	3,37 ± 0,406 3,242 – 3,906	3,409 ± 0,451 2,66 – 4,03	2,777 ± 0,097 2,66 – 2,97
Frequency range (kHz)	2,538 – 4,686	2,5 – 4,14	1,25 – 4,53
Unit duration (ms) mean, SD, range	98 ± 10 68 – 133	61 ± 4 53 – 71	47 ± 10 28 – 66
Interunit interval (ms) mean, SD, range	124 ± 7 91 – 178	117 ± 12 105 – 168	285 ± 51 171 – 392

sites against conspecifics (e.g. Lüddecke, 1974; Wells, 1978; Hödl, 1983; Zimmermann and Zimmermann, 1981, 1988). The size of the territory may vary considerably and is most probably dependent on the calling intensity of the male, the abundance of suitable terrestrial oviposition sites and the abundance of food. In three different populations of *Epipedobates boulengeri-espinosai* at Ecuador we measured sizes between 0,3 and 5 m^2. Roithmair (1988) found territory sizes between 0,5 and 26 m^2 in *Allobates femoralis* at her study site at Peru where males with larger territories seem to have a higher reproductive success. Advertisement calls of all territorial dendrobatids are characterized by a high sound intensity as well as a high redundance by rhythmic repetition of calls. This structure together with the exposed position of the calling male permit reliable propagation over longer distances (e.g. several hundred meters in *Dendrobates histrionicus*, own obs.). Short-term behavioral responses of conspecifics toward species-specific advertisement calls are dependent on reproductive status, sex and sound pressure level. Froglets as well as sexually inactive frogs don't show any obvious reaction. Gravid females are attracted above a particular sound pressure level whereby their behavioral responses (head lifting, preservering, orienting by head and body movements, zig-zag-hopping toward sound source, tactile contact to sound source) are almost uniform (Zimmermann and Rahmann, 1987) and correspond well to those reported from different hyperolids and hylids (Rheinlaender et al., 1979; Schneider, 1982; Passmore et al., 1984; Rand, 1988; Gerhardt, 1988; Wells, 1988). Territorial males seem to discriminate between different call amplitudes in advertisement calls. A low sound pressure level releases antiphonal calling, above a distinct threshold level are phonotactic responses evoked often leading to agonistic encounters (Lüddecke, 1974; Gerhardt and Rheinlaender, 1980; Hödl, 1983; Zimmermann and Rahmann, 1987).

Playbacks of recorded calls have shown that male and female dendrobatid frogs can identify and localize their calling conspecifics solely on the basis of their advertisement calls (Gerhardt and Rheinlaender, 1980; Hödl, 1983; Zimmermann and Rahmann, 1985, 1987). Thus, play-back experiments with artificially altered advertisement calls were used to determine thresholds for inducing positive behavioral responses in conspecifics. Results of our study in *Epipedobates tricolor* are shown in Fig. 3. Stepwise alteration of dominant frequency, pulse duration, interpulse duration and call duration indicate that males of this species accepted a much broader variety of acoustic parameters as species-specific than it usually occurs within their own calls. As long as the dominant frequency lies in the species-

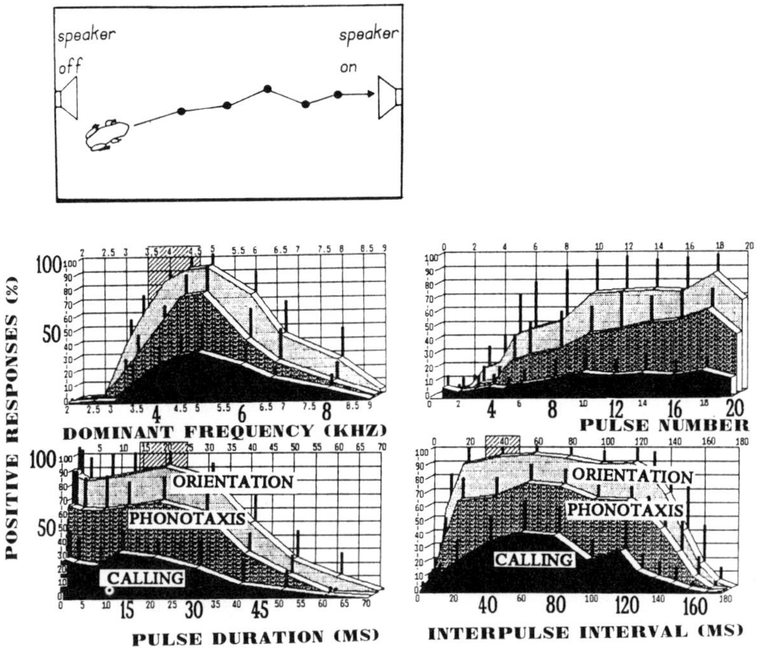

Fig. 3: Play-back experiments with stepwise altered natural advertisement calls demonstrate thresholds for the recipients behavioral response (orientation toward stimulus, phonotaxis, antiphonal calling) in *Epipedobates tricolor*. Experimental set-up (above) and measured percentage of positive responses toward each of the tested experimental paradigm in five tested males (below). Stripe patterning in the background shows natural variation of each parameter in the investigated population (according to Zimmermann, 1985 and Kost, 1988).

specific range (3,5–4,7 kHz), all tested males started to react positively when the call is given pulsed with at least 18 pulses (species minimum 40) of 0,5 ms duration (species minimum 14 ms) in 20 ms intervals (species minimum 30 ms).

Advertisement calling males always keep a particular distance from each other ranging from at least 10 cm in captive *Epipedobates tricolor* (Zimmermann and Rahmann, 1987) to at least 5 m at our studied *Dendrobates histrionicus* populations at Ecuador. When a territorial male recognizes an advertisement calling intruder at the border of its territory the advertisement call grade into the aggressive call (see Fig. 2, Tab. 2 and below). The same may be found in other territorial dendrobatid frogs (Zimmermann, 1985). These findings imply that advertisement calls in these species are not only used for mate attraction but also for rival spacing by regulation distances within a breeding chorus of sexually active males. Besides these two main functions widely distributed in territorial anurans (Wells 1988), a third was detected at least in *Epipedobates tricolor*, the maintenance of permanent breeding activity (Zimmermann and Rahmann, 1987). Adult territorial males living under optimal climate and food conditions in captivity produced advertisement calls from dawn to dust, but only if kept together in social groups. Adult females maintained with males under the above conditions are confronted with these calls throughout the whole active period. Consequently they oviposit at short intervals of one to three weeks (clutch size up to maximally 43 eggs) in all months of the year. However, exclusively on the day of oviposition they are obviously responsive to male advertisement calls and show positive phonotactic responses.

If sexually active male or female frogs were socioacoustically deprived for three months, males stopped calling, females stopped developing ripe eggs as histological sections verified. Taken together these findings indicate that advertisement calls may cause the permanent reproductive capability in socially living dendrobatids.

2.2. Short-range courtship calls

These calls with an acoustic pattern totally different from advertisement calls are given by males of some dendrobatid species (Tab. 1) either when a female nearby is detected to approach the caller or during tactile interactions (Lüddecke, 1976; Zimmermann and Zimmermann, 1982, 1986, 1988; Jungfer, 1985; Weygoldt, 1980; Roithmair, 1988; Wells, 1988). In all species they possess a noisy frequency structure and the lowest sound intensity of any call within the species repertoire. Behavioral responses are released only in gravide females already attracted by advertisement calls. They keep in following the caller leading them to a potential oviposition site or start egg-laying whereby the male clasps its mate in cephalic amplexus position (see Figs. 4, 5, 6). With regard to gravide females the function seems to be similar as in the advertisement call. The energy costs for the male, however, may be minimized. Thus, Taigen and Wells (1985) have pointed out, that advertisement calling is one of the most energy-demanding activities of males in hylids. Whenever an advertisement calling male recognizes an attracted mate willing to court it should therefore be favourable for him to shift from the advertisement to the less energy-consuming courtship call. Indeed, dendrobatids behaved in such a way. Interestingly, they can produce intermediate calls in conflict situations e. g. when the attracted female appears to turn away in the course of a courtship sequence (see Fig. 1).

2.3. Aggressive and release calls

These calls are used in territorial dendrobatids (Tab. 2) during short range agonistic encounters. The aggressive calls are graded signals slightly modified from advertisement calls (Fig. 2). Changes in temporal features are a function of the distance between interacting males as observed in hylids (Wells, 1988). In *Dendrobates histrionicus* call duration decreases and repetition rate increases (Tab. 2). In *Epipedobates tricolor* pulse duration and repetition rate remain constant whereas call duration decreases and call repetition rate increases (Zimmermann, 1985). A male shifts from advertisement calling to aggressive calling if an advertisement calling intruder is walking at the border of his territory. Aggressive calling he faces the intruder and walks toward him. In most cases the intruder is intimidated by this aggressive display and turns away without any fighting. If he resisted, a brief wrestling bout might follow with the opponents jumping against the other in a circle, hugging, pushing and overthrowing. At the end the winner, in all observed cases the resident, will jump onto the other's back clasping him dorsally or around the head giving aggressive calls. The looser remains either silently in a ducking position or gives, additionally, release calls (Fig. 2, Tab. 1, 2) differing from the other calls especially in their lower dominant frequency, the shorter call duration and the irregular repetition rate. This submissive signal induces the dominant male to loose its grip so that the submissive may retreat. Advertisement calling the dominant male returns to his calling site.

3. Behavioral signals exchanged during courtship

In contrast to most other anurans dendrobatids evolve a highly elaborated form of courtship. Thereby the exchange of various acoustic, tactile and visual signals is used to synchronize breeding activity in mates. During our comparative behavioral study of 32 species (Zimmermann and Zimmermann, 1988) three main courtship strategies could be identified, schematically displayed in Fig. 4, 5, 6. In all studied species males signalizes their motivation to court by giving species-specific advertisement calls. The behavioral decisions of conspecifics, then, determine further activites of the calling male. If there are no specific reactions as it is the case in silent males, unreceptive or unwilling females or froglets, he stops calling and turns away, if the calls are responded to by neighbouring males, antiphonal calling will result. If the recipient is a gravide female and signals interest by phonotactic behavior, he continous courting and tries to lead the mate to a potential spawning site while calling. A complex stimulus-reaction chain starts in which the behavior of one partner induces the behavior of the other and vice versa.

A relatively simple courtship ceremony seldomly lasting more than a few hours was found in the *Epipedobates*-group. After attraction by male's advertisement calls a gravide female shows her willingness to mate by crouching in a ducking position underneath the male. The male responds by cephalic amplexus and courtship calls. During the next 1–1

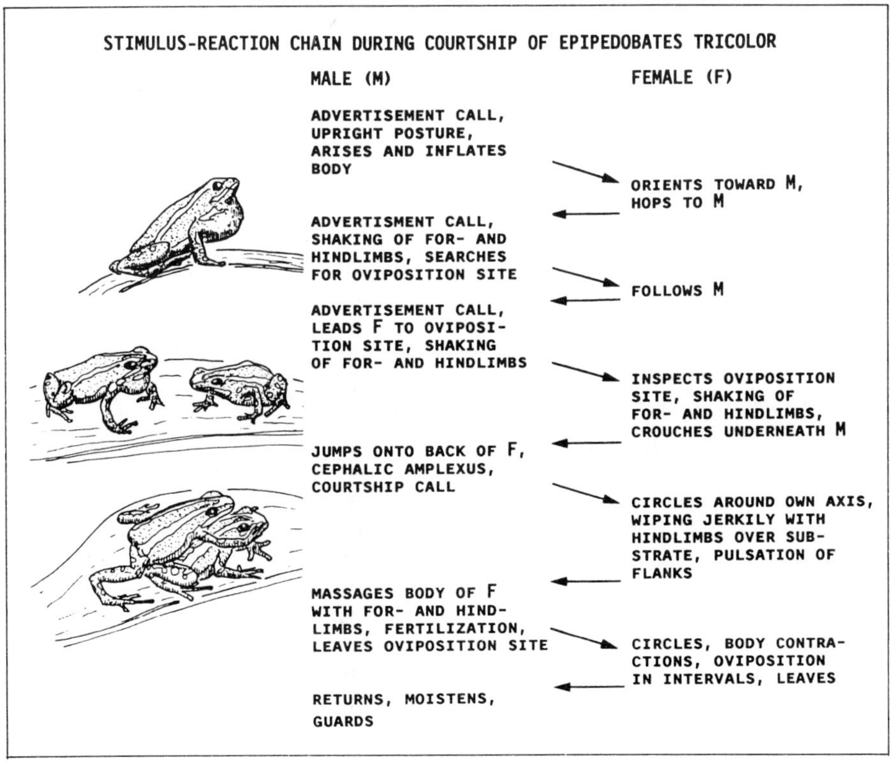

Fig. 4: Schematic representation of complex courtship stimulus-reaction chain in *Epipedobates*.

½ hours he massages her body with his limbs which apparently stimulates her to eject the eggs immediatly fertilized by the male. Whereas the female leaves the oviposition site shortly after spawning the male returns to moisten and guard the clutch for the next two weeks.

In *Phyllobates* and in the *Dendrobates leucomelas*-group courtship may last up to a whole day. An attracted, receptive female signalizes her interest to court by an other tactile signal, she strokes with her hand several times over the back of her mate. In the male, now, courtship calls and leading the female to a potential oviposition site are released. For maintaining courtship activity in the male, the female has to repeat this tactile signal during the whole courtship ceremony again and again. At a suitable oviposition site another sequence of tactile interactions begins. In contrast to the first group oviposition takes place without any amplexus. Eggs are laid either during a vent-to-vent position of the pair or after the male has left the spawning site. They are fertilized either immediately or after oviposition. Brood care is simple and involves solely the male who moistens the clutch irregularly and takes over tadpole transport.

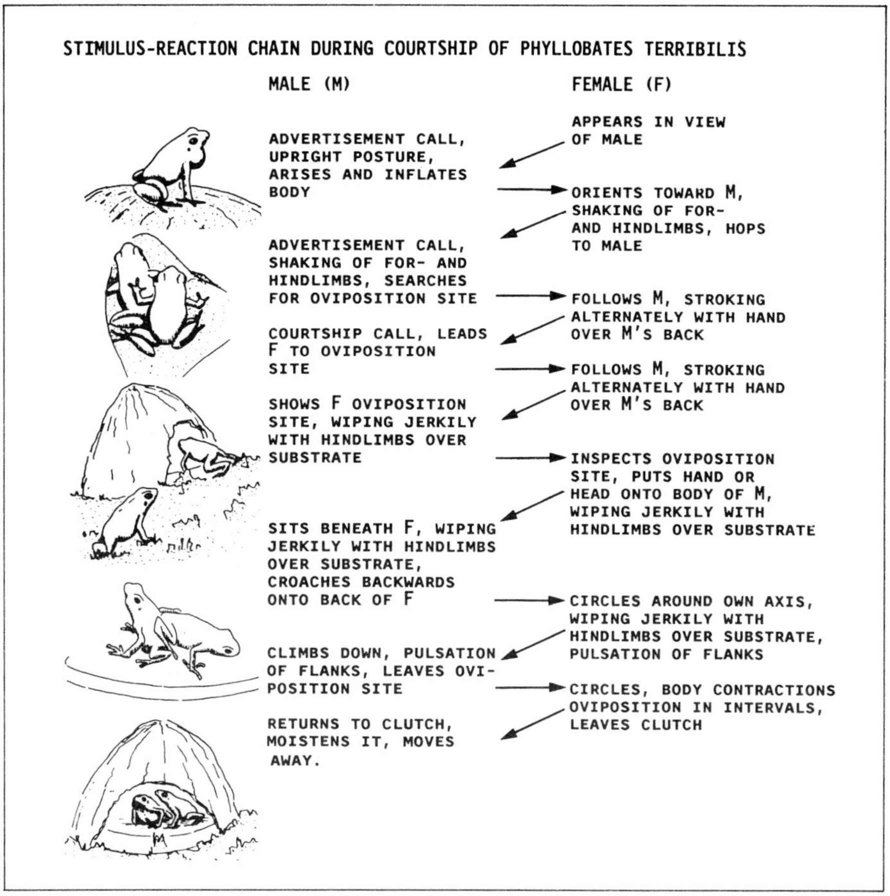

Fig. 5: Schematic representation of complex stimulus-reaction chain during courtship of *Phyllobates*.

In the *Dendrobates histrionicus*- and the *Dendrobates quinquevittatus*-group courtship is most highly elaborated and may extend to several days. Male and female have to stimulate each other by exchanging different acoustic (male), visual and tactile signals. Thereby the male shows several oviposition sites to the female. The female inspects these sites which are often under dead leaves or on bromeliads and then may turn away searching another male or spawning site until depositing her clutch. As in the second group there is no amplexus during the courtship ceremony of this group. Probably females of the *histrionicus*-group are so choosy since they have to take over a highly energy consuming brood care unique for frogs but characteristic for all species of this group. After oviposi-

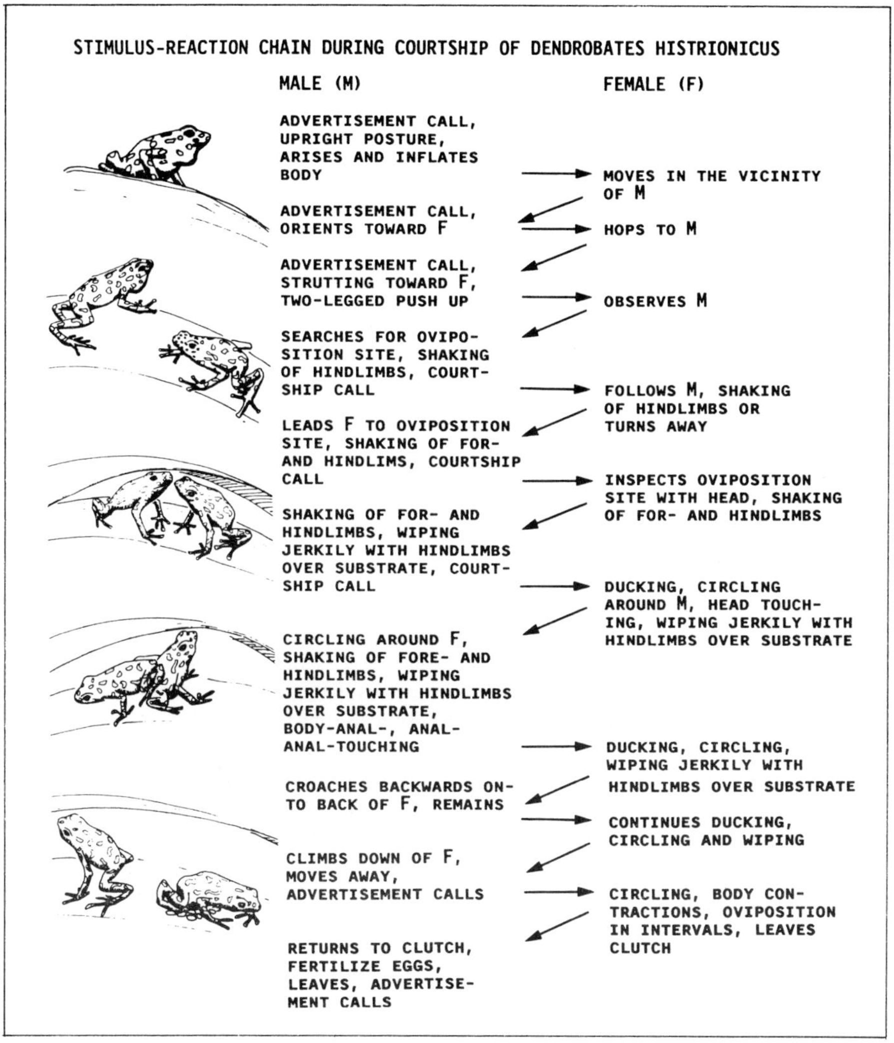

Fig. 6: Schematic representation of complex stimulus-reaction chain during courtship of the *Dendrobates histrionicus*-group.

tion the female and not the male returns to the clutch to moisten it in regular intervals (in *D. pumilio* the male may sometimes moisten the clutch (Weygoldt, 1980)) until the tadpoles emerge from their egg capsules after about two weeks. The female now transports each tadpole individually to a water filled bromeliad leaf axil where she feeds them once a week with specially produced nutritive eggs, 3–7 eggs/tadpole. For about 2 ½ months the female has to care in such a manner for her offsprings until they develop into froglets. Under terrarium conditions a female may have up to four reproductive clutches per year. In the average she cares for four tadpoles deposited into the same bromeliad. Tadpoles are so specialized for species-specific eggs that they can't digest any other item (except chicken egg yolk, given to them artificially). This extraordinary brood care strategy was firstly revealed by terrarium observations in five different species (Graef and Schulte, 1980; Weygoldt, 1980; Zimmermann and Zimmermann, 1981, 1982, 1988; Jungfer 1985) and could recently be confirmed for *D. histrionicus* during our field studies at Ecuador (Zimmermann and Zimmermann 1985, 1988).

4. Parent-offspring communication during brood care

All dendrobatid frogs exhibit a more or less differentiated brood care behavior involving clutch attendance (in most species), clutch moistening, tadpole transport to water on the back of the parent and in some species with the most advanced form of parental care tadpole feeding (Zimmermann and Zimmermann, 1985; Weygoldt, 1987; Zimmermann and Zimmermann, 1988). Do parents or offsprings evolve behavioral signals for these complex interactions?

Attendance of the clutch doesn't seem to require special signals besides the spatial information of the oviposition site. We have changed clutches in several dendrobatid species of each group maintained under terrarium conditions. As far as we place strange clutches of the same or even different species onto the original spawning site clutches at each developmental stage are accepted as their own and cared for by moistening, guarding or tadpole transport. Furthermore, if the clutch is removed, they still moisten the spawning sites for one or two further visits. Clutches introduced at other sites were eaten by male and female frogs of most species at any developmental stage.

Tadpole transport to water, however, appears to be dependent on visual, tactile and/or vibrational signals of the larvae. Tadpoles emerged from their egg capsule start to move very strongly by undulating tail movements as soon as they recognize a moist smooth object and try to climb on it by wriggling movements. In the caring parent these behaviors induce ducking, a bowl-back position and freezing so that the tadpoles can wriggle upon the back. Adhered there they are transported to a water site where they swim away shortly after recognizing water contact. Tadpoles can't discriminate between their own parent and other frogs or objects, they will try to climb on all moist and smooth objects even a human finger coming into their vicinity (Zimmermann, 1984). The egg-feeding dendrobatid frogs of the *Dendrobates histrionicus*-group have evolved a more complex form of communication which may be forced by the high maternal investment. The brood caring female, here, has to find the site at which she has deposited each tadpole and furthermore has to be sure that her offspring there is still alive. Again the female firstly orientates on the basis of visual cues to find the right way to her tadpoles (If the equipement of the terrarium is altered the female failed to find them (Zimmermann and Zimmermann, 1981, 1982)). The female, then, climbs backwards on into the leaf axil. A hungry tadpole thereby responds by a sort of begging behavior. It stiffened its tail and rapidly vibrated it, producing strong water surface waves. Then, it starts to move in such a way onto the mother's back again and again. This very conspicuous behavior of a hungry tadpole signalizes its presence and appears to induce ovulation in the mother. It was observed in all oophagous dendrobatid tadpoles (Weygoldt, 1980; Zimmermann 1983; Jungfer, 1985). Dead larvae or weak larvae were not able to show the begging behavior as well as leaf axils from which tadpoles were removed were not provided with nutritive eggs. The same was observed when tadpoles artificially placed in a bromeliad leaf axil beneath the site where the female usually feeds her own tadpole showed begging behavior (Weygoldt, 1980, own obs.). Thus both, the spatial information about the tadpole's depositing site together with the tadpole's begging behavior are necessary to trigger ovulation in the nursing female.

The egg-feeding omnivorous tadpoles of the *Dendrobates quinquevittatus*-group also try to swim onto the mother's back, however, the strong vibrational tail movements are lacking. In these species the male transports tadpoles to water-filled bromeliad leaf axils. During the development of the larvae (about 2 months) the male leads the female at regular intervals to the tadpole-occupied leaf axil while avertisement calling. There, he starts to display the normal range of courtship patterns. Thus, ovulation in the female seems to be released primarily by tactile and acoustic stimuli of the courting male (Zimmermann and Zimmermann, 1988).

5. Concluding remarks

Most species of the terrestrial breeding dart-poison frogs inhabit neotropical forests with relatively little annual climate fluctuations. Environmental timing factors for the induction of reproduction known to be important for temperate and subtropical anurans are therefore lacking. If sufficient food, oviposition sites and mates are available the best reproductive strategy for an terrestrial breeder should be to reproduce continously. Indeed, most dendrobatids display this strategy. Their highly elaborated courtship interactions where mates have to stimulate each other by a complex exchange of distinct acoustic, tactile and visual signals might have evolved as a consequence toward the pressure of synchronizing breeding activity without any external timing factor. Behavioral signals used during this display are required for releasing ovulation in the female and ejaculation in the male, at least in several *Epipedobates, Phyllobates* and *Dendrobates* species (Weygoldt, 1987; Zimmermann and Rahmann, 1987; Zimmermann and Zimmermann 1988). Furthermore, in *Epipedobates tricolor* species -specific stimulation with the advertisement call seems to maintain permanent breeding activity in a social group. It also effects certain brain areas involved in processing this acoustic key stimulus and most likely influence the hormonal status of the recipient (Zimmermann and Rahmann, 1987). However, more detailed research on this aspect is necessary to reveal the physiological mechanisms modifying reproduction in these social anurans.

The revealed stimulus-response chain between mother and offspring in dendrobatid species with the most advanced form of brood care is extraordinary for anurans. However, maternal investment by feeding tadpoles with own eggs is high since during the two to three month nursing time the female can't invest in new reproductive clutches. Strong selection should therefore favour a highly differentiated mother-larvae-communication signalizing to the mother the presence of a hungry oophageous tadpole and to the tadpole the presence of a potential feeder instead of a potential larvae predator. This is most likely the reason for the evolution of begging behavior in all oophageous tadpoles. The tactile part of this behavior is necessary to induce ovulation in the mother and seems to correspond in its tactile stimulations to that of a courting male. It may have evolved from «swimming against mother's back by chance» as it was discovered in the egg-feeding omnivorous tadpoles of the *D. quinquevittatus*-group.

Summary

In comparison to other anurans the neotropical terrestrial breeding poison-dart frogs show a highly complex social and reproductive behavior. During a prolonged courtship display mates have to synchronize their breeding activity by exchanging taxon-specific acoustic, visual and acoustic signals. At least in one species, *Epipedobates tricolor*, permanent reproduction could be maintained by stimulation with species-specific avertisment calls. Behavioral signals evolved in the oophageous tadpoles of the high advanced dendrobatid species are a prerequisite for the induction of egg-feeding behavior in the mother.

Acknowledgements

Research on dendrobatid behavior was done in collaboration with H. Zimmermann, who also maintained more than 24 species during the last 16 years. A. Zimmermann build up the computer sound analysis system. M. Kost conducted part of the play-back experiments. S. Kugel helped in call analysing. Prof. Dr. H. Rahmann gave valuable comments. Field studies at Ecuador were made possible by Prof. Dr. E. del Pino and Prof. Dr. T. de Vries, Universidad Catolica del Ecuador, Quito, and were financially supported by the Deutsche Forschungsgemeinschaft. I am deeply indepted to all of them.

References

Duellman, W. E. (1978): The biology of an Equatorial herpetofauna in Amazonian Ecuador. Univ. Kansas Publ. Mus. nat. Hist. *65*, 1–352.

Duellman, W. E., Trueb, L. (1986): Biology of amphibians. McGraw Hill Book Comp. New York.

Gerhardt, H. C. (1988): Acoustic properties used in call recognition by frogs and toads. In: The evolution of the amphibian auditory system. Eds.: B. Fritzsch, M. J. Ryan, W. Wilczynski, T. E. Hetherington, W. Walkowiak. New York: John Wiley & Sons. 455–484.

Gerhardt, H. C., Rheinlaender, J. (1980): Accurancy of sound localization in a miniature dendrobatid frog. Naturwiss. 67, 362.

Graeff, D., Schulte, R.: Neue Erkenntnisse zur Brutbiologie von *Dendrobates pumilio*. Herpetofauna *2*, 17–23.

Hödl, W. (1983): Rufverhalten und Phonotaxis bei Männchen von *Phyllobates femoralis*. Verh. dt. zool. Ges. 76, 172.

Jungfer, K.-H. (1985): Beitrag zur Kenntnis von *Dendrobates speciosus*. Salamandra *21*, 263–280.

Kost, M. (1988): Bioakustische Untersuchungen zur Charakterisierung akustischer Auslöser bei Pfeilgiftfröschen (Phyllobates tricolor) mittels sound-sampling. Diplomarbeit, Univ. Stuttgart-Hohenheim.

Lüddecke, H. (1974): Ethologische Untersuchungen zur Fortpflanzung von *Phyllobates palmatus*. Diss. Univ. Mainz.

Myers, C. W., Daly, J. W., Malkin, B. (1978): A dangerously new frog (*Phyllobates*) used by Embera indians of West Colombia, with discussion of blowgun fabrication and dart poisoning. Bull. amer. Mus. nat. Hist. *161*, 307–365.

Passmore, N. J., Capranica, R. R., Telford, S. R., Bishop, P. J. (1984): Phonotaxis in the painted reed frog (Hyperolius marmoratus). J. Comp. Physiol. A. *154*, 189–197.

Rand, A. S. (1988): An overview of anuran acoustic communication. In: The evolution of the amphibian auditory system (B. Fritzsch, M. J. Ryan, W. Wilczynski, T. E. Hetherington, W. Walkowiak, eds.) John Wiley & Sons, New York.

Rheinlaender, J., Gerhardt, H. C., Capranica, R. R., Yager, D. D. (1979): Accurancy of phonotaxis by the green treefrog (*Hyla cinerea*). J. Comp. Physiol. A, *133*, 247–255.

Roithmair, M. (1988): Freilandstudie zur Territorialität und Fortpflanzungsbiologie von *Dendrobates (Phyllobates) femoralis* Boulenger (*Dendrobatidae, Anura*). Diss. Univ. Wien.

Schlüter, A. (1984): Ökologische Untersuchungen an einem Stillgewässer im tropischen Regenwald von Peru unter besonderer Berücksichtigung der Amphibien. Diss., Univ. Hamburg.

Schneider, H. (1982): Phonotaxis bei Weibchen des Kanarischen Laubfrosches. Zool. Anz. *208*, 161–174.

Taigen, T. L., Wells, K. D. (1985): Energetics of vocalization by an anuran amphibian. J. Comp. Physiol. B *155*, 163.170.

Wells, K. D. (1977): The courtship of frogs. In: The reproductive behavior of amphibians (H. D. Taylor, S. I. Guttman, eds.) pp. 233–262. Plenum press, New York.

Wells, K. D. (1980a): Social behavior and communication of a dendrobatid frog (*Colostethus trinitatis*). Herpetologia *36*, 189–199.

Wells, K. D. (1980b): Behavioral ecology and social organisation of a Dendrobatid frog (*Colostethus inguinalis*). Behav. Ecol. Sociobiol. *6*, 199–209.

Wells, K. D. (1988): The effect of social interactions on anuran vocal behavior. In: The evolution of the amphibian auditory system (B. Fritzsch, M. J. Ryan, W. Wilczynski, T. E. Hetherington, W. Walkowiak, eds.) pp. 433–454: John Wiley & Sons, New York.

Weygoldt, P. (1980): Complex brood care and reproductive behavior in captive poison-arrow frogs *Dendrobates pumilio* O. Schmidt. Behav. Ecol. Sociobiol. *7*, 329–332.

Weygoldt, P. (1987): Evolution of parental care in dart poison frogs. Z. zool. System. Evol.-Forsch. *25*, 51–67.

Zimmermann, E. (1983): Das Züchten von Terrarientieren. Stuttgart: Franckh.

Zimmermann, E. (1985): Verhaltensphysiologische Studien zur akustischen Kommunikation sowie Einfluß akustischer Stimulationen auf den Glykokonjugatstoffwechsel im ZNS neotropischer Pfeilgiftfrösche (*Phyllobates tricolor*, Dendrobatidae, Anura). Diss., Univ. Stuttgart-Hohenheim.

Zimmermann, E., Rahmann, H. (1985): Acoustic key stimulus alters 3H-2-Deoxyglucose uptake in the brain of the frog *Phyllobates tricolor*. Naturwiss. *72*, 543.

Zimmermann, E., Rahmann, H. (1987): Acoustic communication in the poison-arrow frog *Phyllobates tricolor*: Advertisement calls and their effects on behavior and metabolic brain activity of recipients. J. Comp. Physiol. A *160*, 693–702.

Zimmermann, E., Zimmermann, H. (1982): Soziale Aktionen, Brutpflege und Zucht des Pfeilgiftfrosches *Dendrobates histrionicus*. Salamandra *18*, 150–167.

Zimmermann, E., Zimmermann, H. (1985): Brutpflegestrategien bei Pfeilgiftfröschen (Fam. *Dendrobatidae*). Verh. dt. zool. Ges. *78*, 220.

Zimmermann, E., Zimmermann, H. (1986): Zur Evolution akustischer Signale beim Fortpflanzungsverhalten von Pfeilgiftfröschen (*Dendrobatidae*). Verh. dt. zool. Ges. *79*, 194.

Zimmermann, H. (1984): Larventransport bei Pfeilgiftfröschen. Aqua. Mag. *18*, 116.

Zimmermann, H., Zimmermann, E. (1981): Sozialverhalten, Fortpflanzungsverhalten und Zucht der Färberfrösche *Dendrobates histrionicus* und *D. lehmanni* sowie einiger anderer Dendrobatiden. Z. Kölner Zoo *24*, 83–99.

Zimmermann, H., Zimmermann, E. (1985): Zur Fortpflanzungsstrategie des Pfeilgiftfrosches *Phyllobates terribilis* Myers, Daly & Malkin, 1978. Salamandra *21*, 281–297.

Zimmermann, H., Zimmermann, E. (1988): Etho-Taxonomie und zoogeografische Artengruppenbildung bei Pfeilgiftfröschen (Anura: Dendroabtidae). Salamandra *24*, 125–160.

Fortschritte der Zoologie, Band/Vol. 38 · Hanke, W. (Hrsg.), Biology and Physiology of Amphibians
Gustav Fischer Verlag · Stuttgart · New York · 1990

The orientation behaviour of three toad species (genus *Bufo*) displaced from the breeding site

Ulrich Sinsch

Zoologisches Institut der Universität, Poppelsdorfer Schloß, D-5300 Bonn 1, FRG

1. Introduction

Many animals possess the ability to find a path from a start point to a goal in some distance by processing sensory informations. This orientation behaviour bases either on a path integration or on a site localization mechanism. Path integration requires complete records of the movements between goal and present location (outward journey information) to calculate the position of the goal relative to present location. Many invertebrates have been shown to use this mechanism for homing (Mittelstaedt, 1985; Wehner and Wehner, 1986). Path integration is completely independent of location-specific stimuli. Other animals which have been displaced experimentally or by chance still accomplish homing by the interpretation of local informations at the start point. Site localization requires besides a local map a compass mechanism to maintain the direction to the goal. This mechanism has been found in many vertebrates (reviews: pigeons: Wallraff, 1984; amphibians: Able, 1981; Adler 1982; Ferguson 1971).

During the past 20 years the sensory base of orientation in Amphibia has been investigated thoroughly in many species, especially in those species which display conspicuous breeding migrations. A surprising variety of orientation cues demonstrates the multisensory mode of orientation in these vertebrates. In North American toads of the genus *Bufo* the main orientation cues are of olfactory (*B. boreas*, Tracy and Dole, 1969 a) or of visual nature (*B. americanus*, *B. valliceps*, *B. woodhousei*, Dole, 1972; Grubb, 1970; Ferguson and Landreth, 1966). In order to test the hypothesis that olfactory cues are more important for species with long distance breeding migrations (> 1.5 km), whereas visual ones serve better for short distance orientation (< 1 km), the orientation behaviour of another three species was studied: the common toad *B. bufo*, the natterjack toad *B. calamita* and the Andean toad *B. spinulosus*. *B. bufo* is an explosive breeder with summer habitats up to 3 km distance from the breeding site (Jungfer, 1943; Heusser, 1960 a, b; Sinsch, 1988 a), whereas the other two species are prolonged breeders with shorter breeding migrations (*B. calamita* males: < 1 km (Sinsch, 1988 b); *B. spinulosus* males: < 0.5 km, Sinsch, 1988 c). This paper reviews the studies on the sensory base of orientation in these species (Jungfer, 1943; Heusser, 1969; Sinsch, 1986, 1987 a, b, 1988 a, b, c, unpublished data) and in North American toads (Dole, 1972; Ferguson, 1963; Ferguson and Landreth 1966; Gorman and Ferguson, 1970; Grubb, 1970, 1973 a, b; Tracy and Dole, 1969 a, b).

2. Experimental design and statistical analysis

Any experimental approach to orientation behaviour in toads requires the solution of two main problems: (1) The position of the toads' goal relative to the release site has to be known to predict successfully the directional choice; (2) The migratory behaviour of toads, that is their route following experimental release, has to be quantified for statistical comparisons.

The first point can be solved easily by conducting the experiments during the reproductive period. The reproductive individuals of a population usually head towards the breeding site. All toads which are captured at their breeding site and are passively displaced to a release site in some distance, are expected to choose the direction of the breeding pond. However, this is only true, if the experimental toads meet three conditions: They are still willing to migrate, they show site-fidelity and they are capable of homing based on release-site specific informations. This has to be shown at first.

B. bufo was studied in 1985 and 1986 near Seewiesen (Bavaria, Germany), *B. spinulosus* in 1986 in the interandean Mantaro Valley (Department of Junin, Perú) and *B. calamita* since 1986 near Bonn (Rhineland, Germany). All species were tested using the same experimental design (Fig. 1). Four release sites were symmetrically distributed around the breeding site at distances between 90 and 150 m to avoid release site biases. The outward journey of the toads was passive in closed opaque plastic containers which neither permitted the perception of visual nor of olfactory information. At the release site groups of 14 to 20 toads were allowed to move actively again. All experimental displacements lasted from sunset to sunrise of the next day, because these species migrate nocturnally. In case of the prolonged breeders it was not possible to distinguish gravid females from non-reproductive ones by means of external features. Therefore, only males with dark pigmented nuptial pads participated in the experiments.

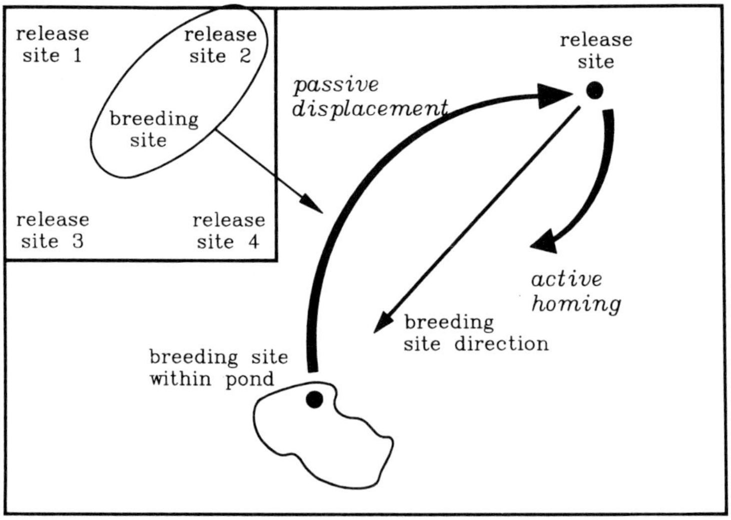

Fig. 1: Schedule of experimental displacements. Four release sites are distributed symmetrically around the breeding site at 90–150 m distance. For details see: Experimental design.

The movements of the toads were monitored using a mechanical tracking device which was fastened to the toads' back. The device consisted of a sewing machine bobbin within a holder which was tied around the toad's waist with an elastic tape. The bobbin contained about 60 m of thread. Further details are given in Dole (1965). Only toads of at least 30 g standard mass were trailed to minimize unspecific effects of the additional cargo (6.5 g) on the orientation behaviour. The path of each toad was marked by the thread becoming tangled with ground structures.

The quantitative analysis of data consisted in three steps (Fig. 2). The first step is the mathematical description of the path of a migrating toad by three parameters: chosen direction relative to the release site, line-of-sight distance between start and final position, and total migratory activity. Every release provided a bivariate data set on the directional choice of the toads which was analyzed by circular statistics in the second step of analysis. The mean direction of toads was calculated by bivariate methods (Batschelet, 1981), either relative to geographical north or to the breeding site. The standardized vector length r is a measure of dispersion: random directional choice results in values near zero, movements of all toads to the same direction give values of near one. The home component c measures the approach to the breeding site. A value of plus one means all toads chose the breeding site direction, minus one means they chose the opposite direction. Finally, the straightness of path (st) describes, if the toads approached their final position in a straight line (value near one) or in cycloid trails (values near zero). Third step of analysis summarizes the effect of a treatment by the calculation of the second order mean of all single releases and its corresponding 95% confidence ellipse (details in Sinsch, 1987b). The results of all field experiments are presented at this level.

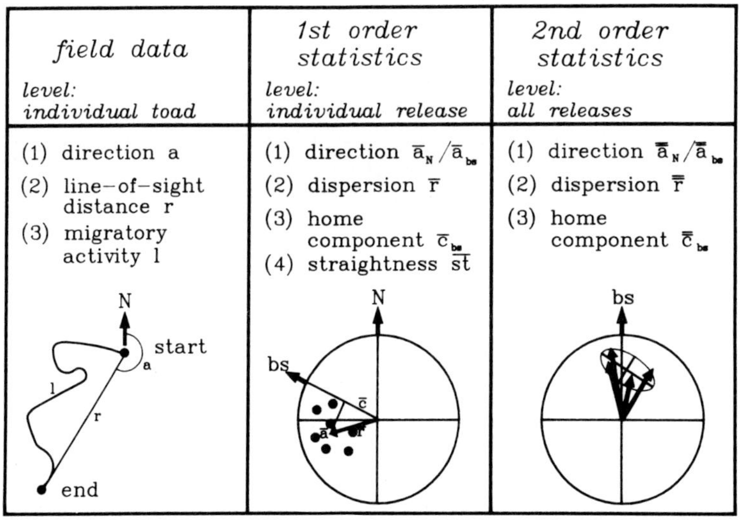

Fig. 2: Three steps of statistical analysis. In each step the measured or calculated parameters are listed and examples are given. For details see: Statistical analysis.

3. Orientation behaviour of untreated toads

Displaced toads without additional treatment headed straight towards their breeding site with almost the same precision in the three species (Fig. 3). This result agrees with similar data on *B. boreas* (Tracy and Dole, 1969 a), *B. valliceps* (Grubb, 1970, 1973 b) and *B. woodhousei* (Ferguson and Landreth, 1966) and demonstrates the impressive ability of toads to relocate the breeding site based on release site specific stimuli accompanied with fidelity to the breeding site. Whether free-ranging toads also use path integration or not, is unknown. The application of the mechanical tracking device obviously does not hinder the normal orientation behaviour, although the velocity of migration is markedly reduced (detailed discussion of this aspect in Sinsch, 1987 a).

The question remains whether the homing ability of toads is navigation from an unfamiliar site or not. Since orientation behaviour of all toads studied so far was usually tested at distances of 90 to 200 m, that means within the normal migratory range, it cannot be excluded that the individuals were familiar with the particular release sites. Ferguson (1963) displaced *B. fowleri* up to 3 km distance, but he did not recapture toads from releases of more than 1 km distance. However, a release of common toads *B. bufo* 3 km distant from their breeding site provided the strong indication that at least this species is capable of navigation (Sinsch, 1987 a). 7 out of 10 toads still headed towards their breeding site, although another pond was by far nearer and the migratory range of this population was lower than 2 km (Sinsch, 1987 b). Thus, the toads were most probably released at a site unfamiliar to them.

4. Sensory base of orientation

4.1. Auditory cues

Male natterjacks form large choruses which are audible over hundreds of meters and therefore, the possibility of a phonotactic approach to the breeding site has to be considered in *B. calamita*. In the other two species the intensity of calls is too low to be heard even at 50 m of distance. Orientation of natterjack males was slightly, but insignificantly better, if the breeding chorus was audible at the release site (Fig. 4). However, the directional choice of migrating *B. woodhousei fowleri* was biassed by a conspecific breeding chorus (Ferguson and Landreth, 1966). Nevertheless, in most *Bufo* species acoustical communication primarily serves for mate selection and not for long distance orientation. Thus, the role of auditory cues has to be evaluated carefully in each species. In male natterjack toads they are helpful for orientation, but not essential.

4.2. Magnetic cues

The effect of strong magnetic fields on initial orientation was tested by gluing bar magnets to the top of the toad's head with south of the artificial field pointing upwards (distal). The artificial field was about 100 times stronger (75 Gauss at 1 cm distance) than earth's natural field. This treatment excluded the perception of natural magnetic cues. Instead of bar magnets brass bars were attached to the head of control toads. The effect of magnets was significant in all species, whereas brass bars permitted normal orientation behaviour. In *B. bufo* and in *B. calamita* the main effect consisted in disorientation, with second order means which did not differ significantly from the start point (Fig. 5). The disorientation of the natterjack males is even more remarkable considering that the breed-

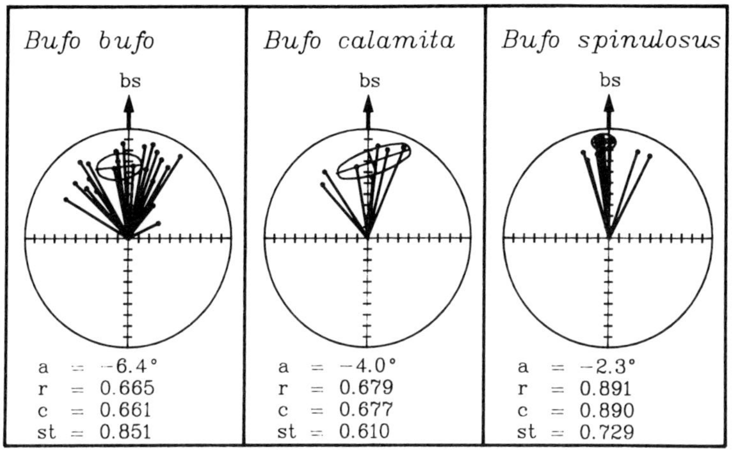

Fig. 3: Initial orientation of untreated toads towards the breeding site (bs). Every dot represents the bivariate mean of an individual release. The second order mean of these vectors corresponds to the centers of the 95% confidence ellipse. The numerical values of the second order mean (direction a and vector length r), home component (c) and straightness of path (st) are also given.

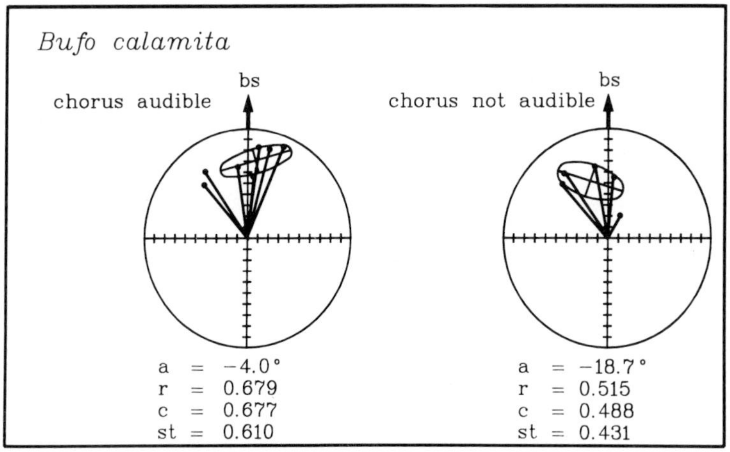

Fig. 4: Initial orientation of untreated *B. calamita* males towards the breeding site (bs) with respect to auditory cues. Chorus audible means that the breeding chorus of natterjack toads at the breeding pond could be heard by the experimenter at the release site. Chorus not audible means in two releases a chorus of less than 7 males (too faint to be heard) and in three release the absence of a breeding chorus. Presentation of data analogous to Fig. 3.

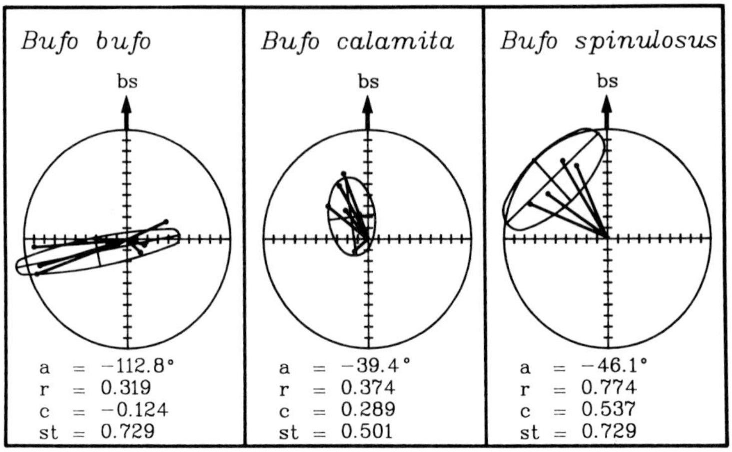

Fig. 5: Initial orientation of toads with bar magnets (magnetic south pointing upwards) with respect to the breeding site (bs). Presentation of data analogous to Fig. 3.

ing chorus gave correct directional information. This result emphasizes the low importance of auditory cues for orientation at least in this species. In *B. spinulosus*, however, magnets caused a directional bias to the left side from the correct direction. This effect was sometimes observed in common toads as well. Nevertheless, the individual paths were as straight as in the controls. These results demonstrate that the three toad species make use of the earth's magnetic field as a directional cue, most probably as a compass system as shown in several newt species (Phillips, 1977, 1986). Since comparable studies on other amphibians have not been performed, the general use of magnetic cues for orientation seems probable, but more experimental evidence is necessary.

Nevertheless, even toads with bar magnets still accomplish homing to the breeding site, as proved by the recapture of individuals of all species studied some days later. Following a period of initial disorientation other orientation cues apparently replace the magnetic ones providing evidence for the multisensory mode of orientation in toads.

4.3. Olfactory cues

The role of olfactory cues was studied by covering the olfactory epithelia of the nostrils completely with cyanoacrylate. Following such a treatment toads are anosmic as shown by behavioural tests (application of amylacetate, lack of wiping behaviour in anosmic toads, Sinsch, 1987 a). Breeding site orientation disappeared in anosmic *B. bufo*, whereas anosmic *B. spinulosus* still headed towards the breeding pond (Fig. 6). Moreover, wind blowing from the breeding site improved the initial orientation of common toads, whereas wind from the opposite direction reduced the home component (Sinsch, 1987 a). Specific pond odours seem to be responsible for this reaction (Jungfer, 1943). Incomplete data in *B. calamita* prevent a final evaluation, but two releases with anosmic males did not show any effect on initial orientation. These results support the hypothesis that only species with breeding migrations over large distances rely on olfactory cues for initial orientation. However, toad species such as *B. valliceps* and *B. woodhousei fowleri* also use the olfactory system for orientation (Grubb, 1973 a, b), but in these species other cues predominate

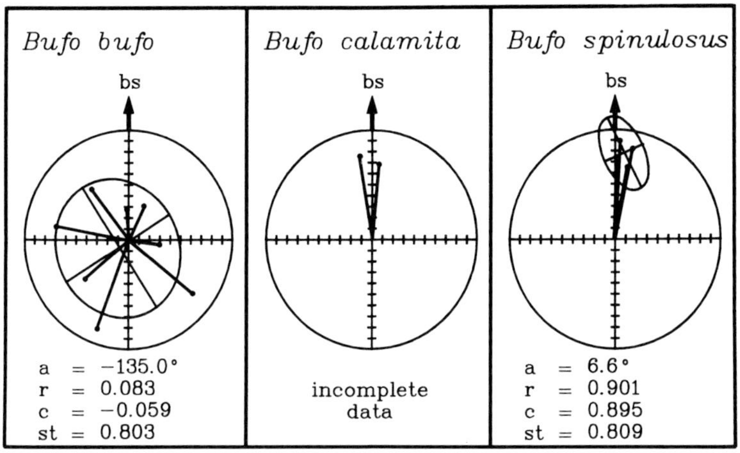

Fig. 6: Initial orientation of anosmic toads with respect to the breeding site (bs). Presentation of data analogous to Fig. 3.

the initial orientation. Olfactory information is apparently more useful for species breeding in permanent ponds than for those using ephemeral ones (*B. calamita*, *B. spinulosus*). Nevertheless, even the lack of olfactory information does not prevent *B. bufo* from homing (Heusser, 1969) – another evidence for multisensory orientation.

4.4. Visual cues

Toads were deprived of visual informations by blindfolding them with adhesive tape. These animals were still able to perceive olfactory information through the nostrils. Con-

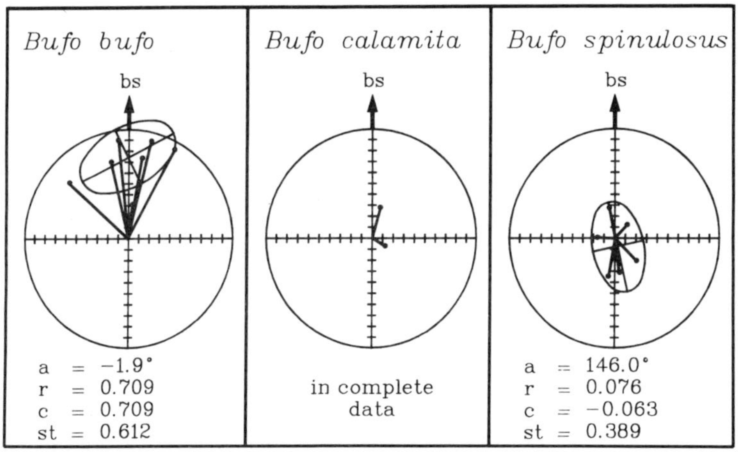

Fig. 7: Initial orientation of blindfolded toads with respect to the breeding site (bs). Presentation of data analogous to Fig. 3.

trols were treated similarly, but the adhesive tape did not cover the eyes. The orientation behaviour of controls and of blindfolded *B. bufo* remained unaffected, but blinded common toads migrated less straight than the controls (Fig. 7). In contrast, blinded *B. spinulosus* were completely disoriented and moved frequently in cycloid trails. Corresponding data of *B. calamita* are still incomplete, but two releases showed similar effects as in the Andean toad. Thus, visual recognition of landmarks is used for orientation in all species, in *B. bufo* as a control of straightness of path and in the other two species as primary cue for initial orientation. Species which permanently inhabit the adjacent areas of the breeding site, apparently rely on a visual map. However, in absence of visual informations olfactory ones can be used alternatively (Grubb, 1970).

Celestial cues does not appear to be of primary importance for any of the three species, as they orient with the same precision under any sky condition, even under completely overcast sky (Heusser, 1969, Sinsch 1987a, 1988c). Nevertheless, toads are capable of using such cues as shown in *B. boreas* (Gorman and Ferguson, 1970; Tracy and Dole, 1969b) and in *B. fowleri* (Ferguson and Landreth, 1966).

5. Concluding remarks

Toads of the genus *Bufo* employ a variety of orientation cues to relocate the breeding site following experimental displacement. Site localization and following initial orientation is based on multisensory information input. Visual and olfactory informations can replace each other in many species and are probably related to the map component of orientation. Visual cues are preferred for short distance orientation, olfactory cues for long distance orientation. Neither visual nor olfactory information can replace magnetic cues which are probably required for the compass component of orientation. Initial orientation bases on a hierarchial order of the different sensory inputs according to their relative availability within the habitat of every species. If the toads are experimentally deprived of an important sensory information, the specific hierarchy can be broken after a temporal delay and alternative cues are used. Thus, the differences in orientation behaviour of toads are probably due to a different hierarchy of sensory inputs and not to different sensory capacities.

References

Able, K. P. (1981): Mechanisms of orientation, navigation and homing. In: Animal migration, orientation and navigation (S. A. Gauthreaux, ed.), pp. 283–383. Acad. Press.

Adler, K. (1982): Sensory aspects of amphibian navigation and compass orientation. Vertebrata Hungarica *21*, 7–18.

Batschelet, E. (1981): Circular statistics in biology. Acad. Press NY.

Dole, J. W. (1965): Summer movements of adult leopard frogs, *Rana pipiens* Schreber, in northern Michigan. Ecology *46*, 236–255.

Dole, J. W. (1972): Homing and orientation of displaced toads, *Bufo americanus*, to their home sites. Copeia 1972, 151–158.

Ferguson, D. E. (1963): Orientation in three species of anuran amphibians. Ergebn. Biol. *26*, 128–134.

Ferguson, D. E. (1971): The sensory base of orientation in amphibians. ANN. NY Acad. Sci. *188*, 30–36.

Ferguson, D. E., Landreth, H. F. (1966): Celestial orientation of Fowler's toad, *Bufo fowleri*. Behaviour *26*, 105–123.
Gorman, R. R., Ferguson, J. H. (1970): Sun-compass orientation in the western toad, *Bufo boreas*. Herpetologica *26*, 34–45.
Grubb, J. C. (1970): Orientation in post-reproductive Mexican toads, *Bufo valliceps*. Copeia 1970, 674–680.
Grubb, J. C. (1973a): Olfactory orientation in *Bufo woodhousei fowleri, Pseudacris clarki* and *Pseudacris streckeri*. Anim. Behav. *21*, 726–732.
Grubb, J. C. (1973b): Olfactory orientation in breeding Mexican toads, *Bufo valliceps*. Copeia 1973, 490–496.
Heusser, H. (1960a): Über die Beziehungen der Erdkröte (*Bufo bufo* L.) zu ihrem Laichplatz I. Behaviour *12*, 208–232.
Heusser, H. (1960b): Über die Beziehungen der Erdkröte (*Bufo bufo* L.) zu ihrem Laichplatz II. Behaviour *14*, 90–109.
Heusser, H. (1969): Die Lebensweise der Erdkröte (*Bufo bufo* L.): Das Orientierungsproblem. Rev. Suis. Zool. *76*, 444–517.
Jungfer, W. (1943): Beiträge zur Biologie der Erdkröte (*Bufo bufo* L.) mit besonderer Berücksichtigung der Wanderung zu den Laichgewässern. Z. f. Morph. u. Ökol. d. Tiere *40*, 117–157.
Mittelstaedt, H. (1985): Analytical cybernetics of spider navigation. In: Neurobiology of arachnids (F. G. Barth, ed.) pp. 298–316. Springer Verlag, Berlin.
Phillips, J. B. (1977): Use of earth's magnetic field by orienting cave salamanders (*Eurycea lucifuga*). J. Comp. Physiol. A *121*, 273–288.
Phillips, J. B. (1986): Magnetic compass orientation in the eastern redspotted newt (*Notophthalmus viridescens*). J. Comp. Physiol. A *158*, 103–109.
Sinsch, U. (1986): Laichplatzwanderung der Erdkröte *Bufo bufo*: sensorische Basis der Orientierung. Verh. Deut. Zool. Ges. München 1986, 214 (Abstract).
Sinsch, U. (1987a): Orientation behaviour of toads (*Bufo bufo*) displaced from the breeding site. J. Comp. Physiol. A *161*, 715–727.
Sinsch, U. (1987b): Migratory behaviour of the toad *Bufo bufo* within its home range and after displacement. Proceed. 4th Ord. Gen. Meet. Societas Europaea Herpet. (Nijmegen) 361–364.
Sinsch, U. (1988a): Seasonal changes in the migratory behaviour of the toad *Bufo bufo*: direction and magnitude of movements. Oecologia (Berlin) *76*, 390–398.
Sinsch, U. (1988b): Temporal spacing of breeding activity in the natterjack toad, *Bufo calamita*. Oecologia (Berlin) *76*, 399–407.
Sinsch, U. (1988c): El sapo andino *Bufo spinulosus*: analisis preliminar de su orientacion hacia sus lugares de reproduccion. Boletin de Lima *57*, 83–91.
Tracy, C. R., Dole, J. W. (1969a): Orientation of displaced California toads, *Bufo boreas*, to their breeding sites. Copeia 1969, 693–700.
Tracy, C. R., Dole, J. W. (1969b): Evidence of celestial orientation by California toads (*Bufo boreas*) during breeding migration. Southern California Academy of Science Bulletin *68*, 10–18.
Wallraff, H. G. (1984): Migration and navigation in birds: a present-state survey with some digressions to related fish behaviour. In: Mechanisms of migration in fishes (J. D. McCleave, G. P. Arnold, J. J. Dodson, W. H. Neill, eds.) pp. 509–544, Plenum Publ. Corp.
Wehner, R., Wehner, S. (1986): Path integration in desert ants. Approaching a long-standing puzzle in insect navigation. Mon. zool. ital. (N. S.) *20*, 309–331.

Fortschritte der Zoologie, Band/Vol. 38 · Hanke, W. (Hrsg.), Biology and Physiology of Amphibians
Gustav Fischer Verlag · Stuttgart · New York · 1990

Hormonal control of oocyte maturation: role of pituitary and follicle cells

Daniel Boujard, Michel Charbonneau, Jean Joly

Laboratoire de Biologie de la Reproduction and Laboratoire de Biologie et Génétique du développement. URA 256 CNRS; Université de Rennes I, 35042 Rennes cedex, France

1. Introduction

Among vertebrates, amphibians, particularly *Xenopus* and *Rana*, represent a leading model system to study the regulation of the meiotic and mitotic cell cycles. Prophase – arrested amphibian oocytes resume meiosis in the ovary under hormonal control of the hypothalamo–pituitary–gonadal axis. Cytoplasmic maturation accompanies meiosis resumption, and both lead the oocyte to the metaphase II stage of meiosis, a second cell cycle blockade which is in turn released by the sperm, at the time of fertilization, thus producing a rapidly dividing embryo. The main advantage of experimenting on amphibian oocytes and eggs is that the regulation of the cell cycle can be controlled *in vitro*, and studied on a large number of cells. Thus, maturation and meiosis resumption can be triggered in oocytes or follicles isolated from the ovary by various hormonal stimuli, such as progesterone, insulin or gonadotropins. Extensive studies on the cytoplasmic transformations occurring at the time of maturation have appeared in the literature during the last few years (see a recent review by Maller, 1985) and very recently, the cytoplasmic factor responsible for the resumption of meiosis, the so-called maturation promoting factor or M-phase promoting factor (MPF), has been highly purified (Lohka et al., 1988).

However, the regulation of these events *in vivo* is less understood, due to a more difficult access to the oocyte and surrounding layers. For instance, the kinetics and extent of progesterone secretion, which is thought to be the natural inducer of oocyte maturation, are not known with precision, due to the fact that progesterone, secreted by the follicle cells, is difficult to measure in the narrow space surrounding the oocyte. The situation is even more complex, since additional layers of somatic cells are also in relation with the follicle cells, the whole system constituting, together with the oocyte, the so-called ovarian follicle, which is described in Fig. 1. *In vivo*, during the process of oocyte maturation, the oocyte is released from the ovary after rupture of the gap junctions previously established with the follicle cells. Oocyte maturation, as well as ovulation, are under the control of the steroids secreted by the follicle cells, which are themselves the target of other circulating hormones. The present review recapitulates the current knowledge about the hormonal control of pituitary gonadotropin and sex steroid secretion and their influence on oocyte maturation.

2. Hypothalamic control of pituitary-gonadal axis during oocyte maturation

As in other vertebrates, the major amphibian hormones regulating ovarian function and oocyte maturation are under the control of the hypothalamo-pituitary axis which includes a well-developed portal vascular system (Green, 1951). The strongest evidence for such a control is that various extracts from *Rana pipiens* brain were able, just as mammalian gonadotropin releasing hormone (GnRH), to stimulate gonadotropin release from *Rana pipiens* pituitaries (Thornton and Geschwind, 1974). Synthetic GnRH could also induce ovulation in *Xenopus laevis* (Thornton and Geschwind, 1974) and in the urodele *Triturus cristatus* (Vellano et al., 1974). Further studies demonstrated that molecules immunologically similar to mammalian GnRH were present in the hypothalamus of various amphibian species, including *Rana pipiens, Rana catesbeiana* (Alpert et al., 1976) *Rana esculenta* (Goos et al., 1976), *Xenopus laevis* (Doerr-Schott and Dubois, 1976) and *Bufo japonicus* (Jokura and Urano, 1985). Amphibian hypothalamic GnRH was found to be at its highest level during the breeding season (King and Millar, 1979). Moreover, GnRH was found in various parts of the brain, a localization that differed according to the reproductive activity (Crim, 1985; Jokura and Urano, 1985). There are also experiments about disrupture of the hypothalamo-pituitary connection which manifest such an influence.

In order to understand the regulation of the sexual cycles by the hypothalamus, several studies aimed at observing the effects of GnRH injection on the levels of pituitary gonadotropins. Artificial acute injections of GnRH to *Rana catesbeiana* females could induce small increases in gonadotropin levels independently from the ovarian cycle (Licht et al., 1983 a). On the other hand, males from the same species also displayed a good sensitivity to GnRH, as shown by the induction of spermiation following injection of GnRH (Daniels and Licht, 1987). However, when GnRH was applied continuously to canulated frogs, it induced a stimulation of the production of gonadotropins which was maximal during oocyte maturation (McCreery and Licht, 1983 a). It is to be noted that stimulation of *Rana* females with GnRH never produced a complete desensitization of GnRH receptors, contrary to what happens in mammals (McCreery and Licht, 1983 b; Porter and Licht, 1985). Thus, in amphibians, the production of gonadotropins during the periovulatory period might require a prolonged constant stimulation.

In addition to gonadotropin releasing function, it is possible that GnRH has other biological activities (stimulation of TSH-secretion from pituitaries of *Rana pipiens*, Denver, 1988). GnRH probably acts as a neuromediator, since it was also found to be located in discrete brain loci (reviewed by Barry, 1979). Moreover, in the amphibian brain, three or four forms of GnRH have been described, but their functions and localization are presently unknown (Eiden et al., 1982; King and Millar, 1986; Sherwood et al., 1986). Such multiple forms of GnRH might reflect the existence of multiple receptors to GnRH (reviewed by Sherwood, 1987). This localization of GnRH in the brain varies according to the reproductive activity (Crim, 1985; Jokura and Urano, 1985). GnRH might also act directly on the gonads. Indeed, Pierantoni et al. (1984 b) have shown a direct effect of GnRH on steroidogenesis in testicular explants from *Rana esculenta* incubated in *vitro*. A particular form of GnRH, similar to chicken II GnRH, was identified in the testis of the same species (Pierantoni et al., 1988). However, while GnRH has been found in mammalian ovary (Ying et al., 1981), studies on amphibian ovary failed to demonstrate a local action of GnRH. Indeed, Hubbard and Licht (1985) did not observe any effect of GnRH alone on LH-stimulated testosterone and progesterone secretions in *Rana pipiens* and *Rana catesbeiana*. In addition, progesterone-induced maturation of *Discoglossus* oocytes was not modified in the presence of GnRH, but GnRH stimulated oestradiol secretion by *Discoglossus* ovaries *in vitro* (Alonso-Bedate et al., 1989, and this volume).

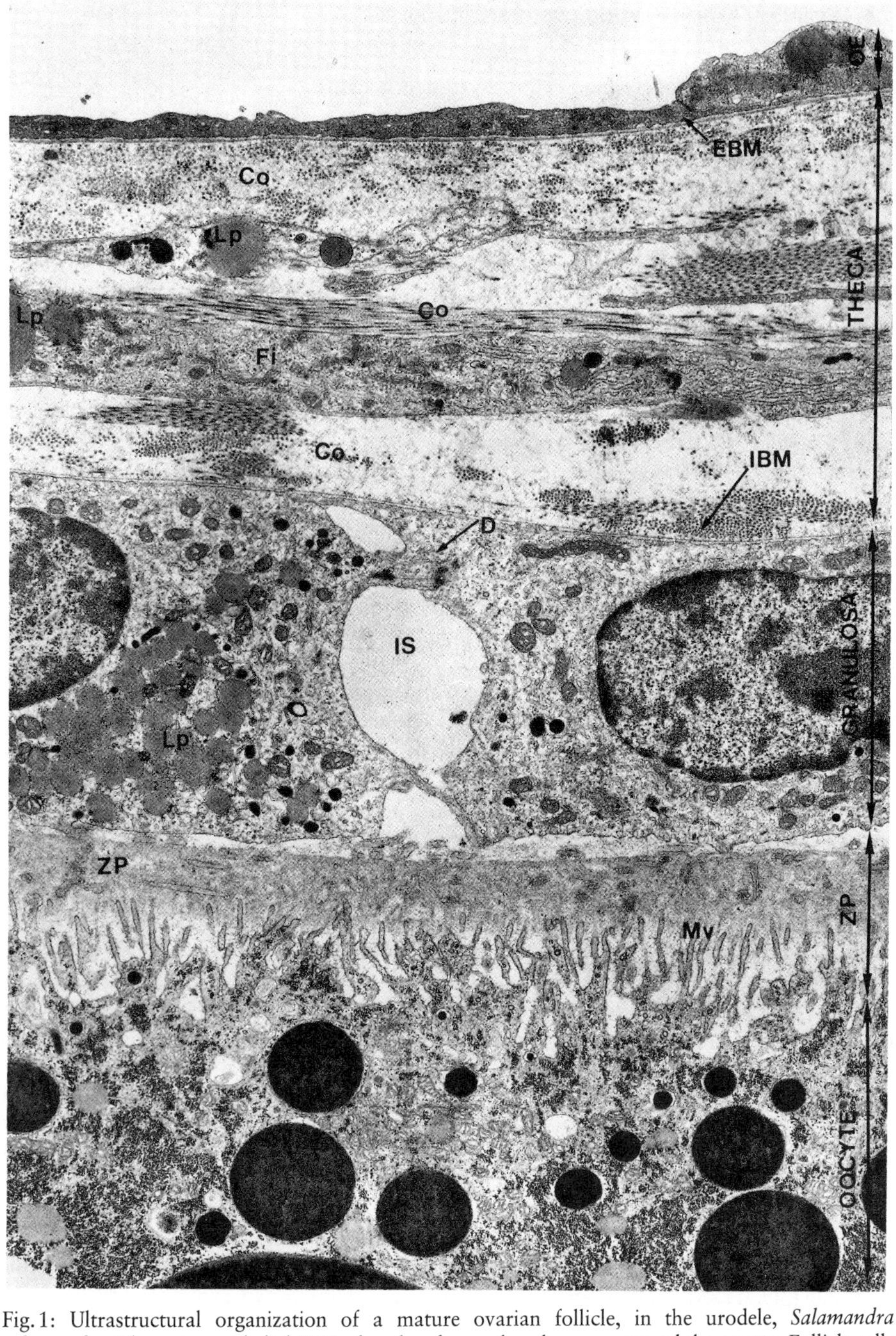

Fig. 1: Ultrastructural organization of a mature ovarian follicle, in the urodele, *Salamandra salamandra*. The outer epithelial (OE), thecal and granulosa layers surround the oocyte. Follicle cells establish gap junctions with the oocyte. Co, Collagen fibres; D, Desmosomes; EBM, External Basement Membrane; Fi, Fibroblast; IMB, Internal Basement membrane; Lp, Liposomes; Mv, Microvilli; zp, zona pellucida (adapted from Joly and Picheral).

3. Pituitary control of oocyte maturation

3.1. Induction of oocyte maturation by gonadotropins

Pituitary extracts have been known for a long time to induce, when injected in the homologous species, oocyte maturation and ovulation (Houssay, 1947). As in other vertebrates, a gonadotropin-like hormone is responsible for the induction of amphibian oocyte maturation. The hormonal target appears to be represented by the follicle cells, since their presence around the oocyte is necessary to the induction of oocyte maturation (Smith et al., 1968; Masui, 1967; Schuetz, 1967).

More recent work has demonstrated that two gonadotropins present in most tetrapods are homologous to the mammalian luteinizing hormone (LH) and follicle stimulating hormone (FSH) (Licht et al., 1977). This hypothesis is reinforced by the recent demonstration that also in fish (e.g. the chum salmon *Oncorhynchus keta*) two gonadotropins (GTH) chemically related to the family of the LH/FSH-like GTHs (Suzuki et al., 1988 a, b) exist. Prior to this work, fish represented the only class of vertebrates in which the presence of two glycoproteic gonadotropins had not been detected.

Two chemically distinct GTHs, showing characteristics similar to those of mammalian FSH and LH, have been identified in several amphibian species, including *Rana catesbeiana* (Licht and Papkoff, 1974), *Rana pipiens* (Farmer et al., 1977) and *Ambystoma tigrinum* (Licht et al., 1975). However, the difficulty to collect large amounts of material made it impossible to purify the large quantities of amphibian gonadotropins necessary to carry out extensive studies on their physiological roles. A diversity in the structure of amphibian gonadotropins and responsiveness of the gonads among the species may exist and complicates physiological investigations. For instance, some mammalian LHs were found to be as potent as amphibian gonadotropins in inducing oocyte maturation and ovulation in *Xenopus laevis*, whereas others were completely inefficient (Licht and Papkoff, 1976). Similarly, ovine LH was very efficient in inducing progesterone secretion in *Xenopus laevis* but relatively ineffective in *Rana catesbeiana* (Licht and Crews, 1976). So far, no phylogenetic pattern has been distinguished among the various related amphibian gonadotropins (Fontaine, 1980; Licht, 1983).

Alternative experiments to understand the physiological roles of pituitary hormones in the ovarian cycle consisted in measuring their levels after stimulation with GnRH. The most detailed studies in the matter have been carried out on *Rana catesbeiana*. They demonstrate that continuous infusion of GnRH into canulated frogs triggered an increase in FSH and LH which occurred concomitantly with oocyte maturation (McCreery and Licht, 1983 a). However, other studies demonstrated that oocyte maturation and ovulation depended on an LH-like hormone, rather than on an FSH-like hormone which was shown to have little or no effect, in *Rana catesbeiana* and *Ambystoma tigrinum* (Licht and Crews, 1976), as well as in *Xenopus laevis* (Fortune, 1983). Although LH is now currently believed to play the major role during the maturation process, it is not excluded that FSH may act by modifying the response to LH.

Another way to study the pituitary control of oocyte maturation is to analyze the functioning of the ovary in response to stimulation by pituitary gonadotropins. The technique of perifusion, adapted to study the dynamics of gonadal steroid secretion (Boujard and Joly, 1983), consists in continuously perifusing ovarian explants with a culture medium, supplemented with various substances, during a given period of time. Continuous perifusion of ovarian explants with gonadotropins resulted in the triggering of oocyte maturation in *Rana catesbeiana* and *Rana pipiens* (Hubbard and Licht, 1986 a), and in *Xenopus laevis* (Boujard et al., 1987; Elzein et al., 1988). On the other hand, pulsatile administration of gonadotropin also induced oocyte maturation, but only when high doses were applied (Elzein et al., 1988). This situation in amphibians is contrary to that in mammals in which pulsatile stimulation with gonadotropins, mimicking the natural endogenous pulsatile secretion of gonadotropins, is more efficient than continuous secretion of gonadotropins in stimulating ovarian function and triggering oocyte maturation (Brinkley, 1981; Kiehm et al., 1984). Such a fundamental difference between amphibians and mammals in the mode of stimulation of the gonads by gonadotropins has been recently confirmed by Licht (1986) who reported that preliminary attempts to demonstrate a pulsatile LH or FSH secretion in castrated males and females of *Rana catesbeiana* remained unsuccessful. All these data taken together suggest that amphibian oocyte maturation does not require a pulsatile stimulation with gonadotropins, contrary to the case of mammals, but rather necessitates, in order to take place, a continuous secretion of gonadotropins. With respect to the importance of the mode of stimulation by gonadotropins, it is worth stressing that the situation in amphibians appears to be similar to that in the fish, *Salmo gairdneri*. In this species, continuous rather than episodic elevated levels of gonadotropins were recorded during the periovulatory period (Zohar et al., 1986a). This, however, does not exclude the possibility that, in amphibians as well as in fish, a pulsatile secretion is needed during ovarian growth (Breton and Derrien-Guimard, 1983; Zohar et al., 1986b). Additional information will be needed in order to understand the mode of stimulation by gonadotropins, particularly by recording the events taking place at the level of the receptors.

3.2. Cellular and molecular events induced by gonadotropins

At the cellular and molecular levels, pituitary control of steroid secretion is poorly understood. No data are available on the regulation of the production and function of the gonadotropin receptors in the female amphibians. On the other hand, intracellular levels of cyclic AMP (cAMP) are known to play a key role in the regulation of progesterone levels in the follicle cells at the time of oocyte maturation. The specificity of amphibian LH in triggering oocyte maturation has been demonstrated by experiments in which *Rana* LH induced cAMP accumulation in ovaries of mature frogs (*Rana catesbeiana*), whereas *Rana* FSH induced cAMP accumulation only in ovaries from immature frogs but not in ovaries from mature frogs (Gavaud et al., 1979).

These results are in contrast with measurements of cAMP levels inside the oocyte, in which progesterone produces a rapid decline in cAMP concentration. Such a decrease in cAMP is a necessary and crucial event in the process of oocyte maturation (reviewed by Maller, 1985). When the intracellular level of cAMP in the *Xenopus* oocyte was artificially stabilized or increased by theophylline or forskolin, progesterone-induced oocyte maturation was prevented (O'Connor and Smith, 1976; Morrill et al., 1977; Schorderet-Slatkine and Baulieu, 1982). In contrast, similar treatments resulting in the stabilization or increase of oocyte cAMP levels were seen to have a marked synergistic effect on progesterone secretion by the follicle cells, in *Rana pipiens* (Kwon and Schuetz, 1985, 1986). Moreover, stimulation of oocyte cAMP synthesis by forskolin (Kwon and Schuetz, 1985), or inhibition of phosphodisterase by IMBX (Kwon and Schuetz, 1985) or by theophylline (Elzein et al., 1988) had only limited effects on the basal level of steroid secretion in the follicle cells. On the other hand, an inhibition of phosphodiesterase by IMBX and a stimulation of adenylate cyclase, by forskolin, produced an increase in the progesterone levels secreted by the follicle cells, thus mimicking the action of gonadotropins (Kwon and Schuetz, 1986). These experiments suggest that the two enzymes, phosphodiesterase and adenylate cyclase, which regulate the level of cAMP are both required to support the secretion of progesterone by the follicle cells.

In amphibians, the activation of steroidogenesis by gonadotropins requires protein synthesis (Hubbard and Licht, 1986b). Indeed, *in vitro* secretion of testosterone by ovaries was found to be reversibly blocked by cycloheximide, in *Rana catesbeiana* (Hubbard and Licht, 1986b) and in *Xenopus laevis* (Fig. 2). Extensive studies have been carried out by Petrino and Schuetz (1986, 1987) in order to determine which fractions of the gonadotropin-induced steroidogenesis process were dependent on protein synthesis. Thus, the activity of 3β-hydroxy steroid dehydrogenase was found to be independent from protein synthesis, whereas the cleavage of the cholesterol side-chain was partially dependent on protein synthesis (Petrino and Schuetz, 1986). Prior steps involving mobilization and/or transport of endogenous cholesterol might also be protein synthesis-depending processes (Petrino and Schuetz, 1987).

4. Steroid secretion during oocyte maturation

In the amphibian ovary, oocytes are enclosed in individual follicles and are surrounded by an inner layer of epithelial cells, the follicle cells, a layer of connective tissue containing blood vessels and an outer surface epithelium (Fig. 1). The organization of the follicles has been described in the anuran, *Xenopus laevis* (Dumont, 1972) and in the urodeles, *Salamandra salamandra* (Joly and Picheral, 1972) and *Pleurodeles waltlii* (Bonnanfant-Jaïs and Mentré, 1983). Biochemical and histochemical studies have established that these ovarian follicles secrete three major classes of sex steroids (Fig. 3) and are able to convert exogenous radiolabeled steroid precursors into estrogens, androgens and progestins, in *Xenopus laevis* (Redshaw and Nicholls, 1971; Fouchet et al., 1975), *Rana pipiens* (Reynouth and Smith, 1973; Sanyal and Sbire, 1973) and *Pleurodeles waltlii* (Fouchet et al., 1975).

A few studies have been undertaken in amphibians in order to determine the role of the different components of the follicle wall. Full maturation can be produced by gonadotropins in *Rana* oocytes surrounded by the follicle cells alone, indicating that these cells are able to synthesize all the steroids needed for oocyte maturation (Schuetz and Lessman, 1982). However, ovulation, which consists in the release of the maturing oocyte from its surrounding layers, cannot be obtained when the outer epithelium has been previously removed (Schuetz and Lessman, 1982).

A seasonal variation in the secretion of steroids has been recorded in various species of amphibians, including the anurans, *Rana esculenta* (d'Istria et al., 1974; Pierantoni et al., 1984), *Rana catesbeiana* (Licht et al., 1983b), *Bufo mauritanicus* (Siboulet, 1981) and *Pachymedusa dacnicolor* (Iela et al., 1986) and the urodele, *Pleurodeles waltlii* (Garnier, 1985). The majority of these studies was based on monthly samples and did not allow a detailed examination of the periovulatory changes in ovarian steroids. However,

Fig. 2: Role of protein synthesis in gonadotropin stimulation. Effect of cycloheximide on testosterone release from *Xenopus laevis* ovarian explants. Ⓐ Ovarian explants were perifused with (○——○) or without (●——●) cycloheximide (20 μg/ml) in the continuous presence of gonadotropin (0.5 μg/ml LHov provided by NIADDK). Ⓑ Recovery of ovarian testosterone secretion. Ovarian explants were perifused during five hours with (□——□) or without (○●——●○) cycloheximide (20 μg/ml) and then continuously stimulated by gonadotropin (0.5 μg/ml) in the absence (□——□; ●——●) or presence (○——○) of cycloheximide (unpublished results of perifusion experiments).

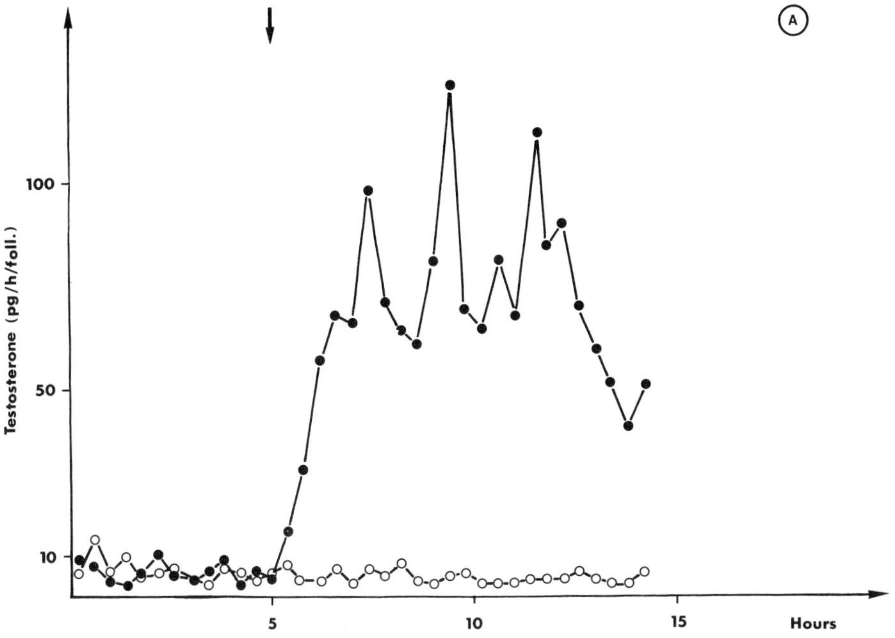
A
100
50
10
Testosterone (pg/h/foll.)
5
10
15
Hours

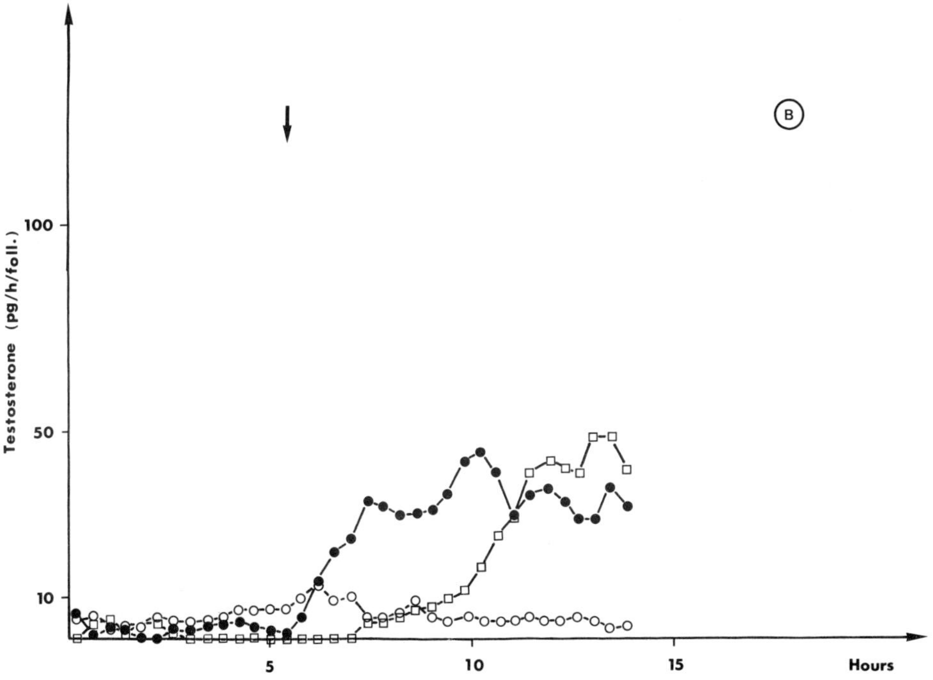
B
100
50
10
Testosterone (pg/h/foll.)
5
10
15
Hours

McCreery and Licht (1983a), in experiments using catheterized animals (*Rana catesbeiana*), could demonstrate that ovulation and egg laying were accompanied by a decrease in plasma testosterone followed by an increase in progesterone (Fig. 3). The same phenomenon has been observed in ovaries placed in a perifusion system, in *Rana pipiens* and *Rana catesbeiana* (Hubbard and Licht, 1986a) and in *Xenopus laevis* (Elzein et al., 1988, Fig. 4). In these experiments, gonadotropin induced an increase in testosterone secretion which persisted until the occurrence of a rise in progesterone secretion. This rise in progesterone secretion only appeared in experiments in which oocyte maturation took place. A decrease in androgen secretion preceding an increase in progesterone secretion seems to be a general feature in vertebrate ovaries. Using a technique of perifusion similar to that used to study amphibian ovary secretion, a pattern of steroid secretion similar to that described above has been observed in fish (Zohar et al., 1982) and mammals (d'Amato et al., 1981; Hedin et al., 1983).

In addition to the observed variations in testosterone levels during amphibian oocyte maturation, an increased secretion of androstenedione has been detected in *Xenopus* ovarian explants after stimulation with gonadotropins in a perifusion system (Elzein et al., 1988). A secretion of androstenedione had been previously detected, in *vivo*, in *Rana esculenta* ovaries (Pierantoni et al., 1984a). However, no precise role could be attributed to this secretion of androgen. In mammals, androstenedione is secreted by the inner theca

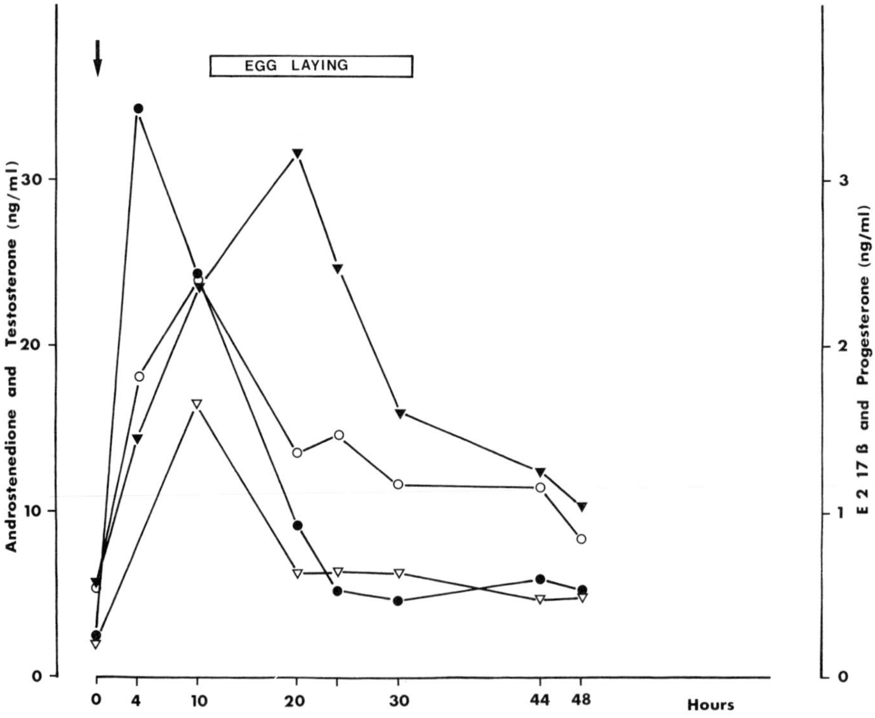

Fig. 3: Plasma levels of steroids during gonadotropin-induced maturation and ovulation in catheterized *Xenopus*. Typical profiles obtained after injection of hCG (500 I. U.) into the lymphatic dorsal sac. (●——●) testosterone; (▽——▽) androstenedione; (▼——▼) estradiol-17β; (○——○) progesterone (unpublished results).

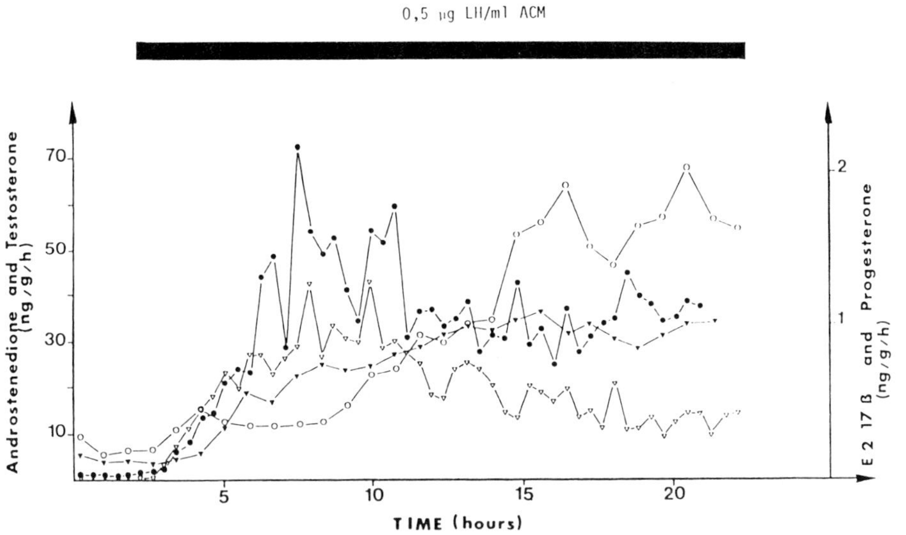

Fig. 4: In *vitro* study of the changes in steroid secretion occurring during the periovulatory period: steroidogenic response of perifused *Xenopus* ovarian explants continuously stimulated by gonadotropin (LHov, 0.5 µg/ml provided by NIADDK) (from Elzein et al., 1988). The line indicates the duration of the stimulation (●——●) testosterone; (▽——▽) androstenedione; (▼——▼) estradiol-17β; (○——○) progesterone.

before entering the granulosa cells by diffusion (McNatty et al., 1984). Such a mechanism has never been studied in amphibians.

Continuous stimulation of *Xenopus* ovarian explants in a perifusion system with gonadotropins induces a substantial fluctuation in testosterone secretion, fluctuation which shows a periodicity of about two hours (Elzein et al., 1988). It is not yet possible to decide whether or not such regular fluctuations are of physiological importance. However, since continuous stimulation with gonadotropins might represent a particular feature of the periovulatory period in amphibians, additional studies on the rythmicity of testosterone secretion might be of a great interest.

In contrast with the patterns of androgen and progesterone secretions which are similar among various amphibian species, estradiol secretion at the time of oocyte maturation varies according to the species. In *Xenopus laevis*, ovarian explants placed in a perifusion system secreted 17β estradiol at a constant rate whatever the rhythm of stimulation with gonadotropins (Elzein et al., 1988). Acute stimulations, as well as continuous stimulation, induced an increase in 17β estradiol during the first 6 hours, followed by a plateau which was maintained for at least 24 hours. Similar observations were made under static conditions of incubation, also in *Xenopus* (Fortune and Tsang, 1981). This would tend to indicate that 17β estradiol is not solely under the control of gonadotropins.

In vivo studies performed on catheterized females of *Xenopus* showed that stimulation with gonadotropins provoked an increase in estradiol levels which persisted during egg laying (Elzein et al., 1987) (Fig. 3, 4). On the other hand, McCreery and Licht (1983 a) demonstrated, in *Rana catesbeiana*, that a decrease in estradiol levels took place before oocyte maturation. As will be seen below, since estradiol is susceptible of interfering with oocyte maturation, the problem of knowing whether estradiol levels increase or decrease during oocyte maturation is of importance. A possible explanation for such a discrepancy can be provided by the examination of ovarian organization in various amphibian species. In temperate climate anurans, as well as in some urodeles, post-spawning ovaries are entirely depleted of all the late stages of oogenesis (the pigmented oocytes) and resemble ovaries from juvenile individuals; this is the case in the anurans, *Rana* and *Bufo* (Mizell, 1964; Jorgensen, 1973) and in the urodeles, *Taricha* and *Salamandra* (Millers and Robbins, 1952; Joly and Picheral, 1972). Amphibians living in rainy tropical regions are also characterized by an asynchronous process of oogenesis which allows full-grown oocytes to be present in the ovary throughout the year (Dumont, 1972). This is not true for *Discoglossus occipitalis* (Kühn et al., 1987). In *Xenopus laevis*, only one annual breeding period exists which extends over several months and is characterized by the existence of more than one egg laying (for references, see Callen et al., 1986). The population of vitellogenic oocytes in adult *Xenopus* ovaries has been estimated to represent about 4 times the number of eggs laid after one clutch deposit (Callen et al., 1986). After egg laying, only the largest oocytes were absent from the ovary, and were replaced within a few weeks (Callen et al., 1986). Moreover, in *Xenopus*, only the vitellogenic follicles were found to be able to secrete estradiol (Mulner et al., 1978; Fortune, 1983). This explains why in all amphibian species, estradiol decreases at the time of maturation, provided that one assumes that such a pattern of estradiol secretion by vitellogenic oocytes can be generalized to all amphibian species. In anurans from temperate climates, since all growing oocytes become post-vitellogenic within one sexual cycle, secretion of estradiol ceases as soon as the wave of growing oocytes has attained the post-vitellogenic stage. On the other hand, in *Xenopus laevis*, the decrease in estradiol secretion is limited to the fraction of the secretion corresponding to those oocytes which have reached the post-vitellogenic stage, that is only one part of the population of growing oocytes. The increase in gonadotropin levels accompanying oocyte maturation indirectly induces an increase in the secretion of estradiol by vitellogenic follicles, in order to support the following egg laying. The secretion of estradiol plays an important role in oocyte maturation, as will be seen later.

5. Role of steroids in oocyte maturation

In *Xenopus laevis*, full-grown oocytes, stage VI (Dumont, 1972), possess a plasma membrane steroid receptor (Sadler and Maller, 1982). Smaller oocytes (stage IV), which do not respond to progesterone but undergo maturation upon microinjection with MPF, were seen to possess less steroid receptors than stage VI oocytes (Sadler and Maller, 1983). Uncompetent stage IV oocytes could undergo meiotic maturation when they were previously injected with cytoplasm withdrawn from stage VI oocytes (Taylor and Smith, 1987). These experiments showed that a cytoplasmic factor appearing during late stage V is required for progesterone responsiveness.

In addition to progesterone, various steroids, as well as numerous drugs and substances have been shown to induce *Xenopus* oocyte maturation (Baulieu et al., 1978). In some cases, maturation can be triggered by agents that do not act directly on specific receptors. For instance, La^{3+} ions, which have been reported to induce *Xenopus* oocyte maturation, seem to act by displacing external membrane calcium, thus artificially altering Ca^{2+} distribution, a possible physiological step of oocyte maturation (Schorderet-Slatkine et al., 1976).

It is currently admitted that progesterone represents the physiological inducer of amphibian oocyte maturation, at least in *Xenopus* and *Rana*. However, a detailed examination of the situation reveals that other steroids, principally androgens, can facilitate or even induce oocyte maturation. In the females of amphibians, the plasma levels of androgens were always found to be higher than plasma levels of estradiol and progesterone, both in the anurans, *Rana esculenta* (d'Istria et al., 1974) and *Rana catesbeiana* (Licht et al., 1983) and in the urodeles, *Necturus maculosus* (Bolaffi and Callard, 1979) and *Pleurodeles waltlii* (Garnier, 1985). After stimulation with gonadotropins, testosterone represented, among steroid hormones, the most abundant hormone present in the plasma (Fortune and Tsang, 1981; McCreery and Licht, 1983 a). Recent experiments on *Xenopus* pointed out to the fact that testosterone was at least as efficient as progesterone in inducing oocyte maturation of defolliculated oocytes (Le Goascogne et al., 1985). This raised the question of whether or not progesterone represents the steroid physiologically involved in meiosis resumption. It should be noted, however, that *Rana catesbeiana* or *Rana pipiens* oocytes (Hubbard and Licht, 1986), as well as *Xenopus laevis* oocytes (Elzein et al., 1988), never underwent maturation without a prior increase in the level of progesterone secreted by the follicles. Although progesterone appears to be physiologically necessary to the induction of oocyte maturation, the variations in plasma testosterone occurring concomitantly with the variations in plasma progesterone seem to indicate a possible synergistic effect of the two steroids. The well-known «priming dose» effect reinforces the hypothesis of the existence of a synergism of the two steroids during oocyte maturation. Thus, maturation was found to be facilitated by a first subthreshold dose of gonadotropin, in *Xenopus laevis* (Reynouth et al., 1975). Similarly, the period of time comprised between progesterone action and the induction of meiosis resumption, in *Xenopus*, was shortened when oocytes were preincubated with subthreshold doses of progesterone (Marot et al., 1977) or of human chorionic gonadotropin (La Marca et al., 1985). Such low doses of hCG or LH have been seen to induce, in a perifusion system and *in vivo*, changes in testosterone but not in progesterone (Boujard, unpublished results). These results strengthen the idea that testosterone might play *in vivo* a role in the regulation of the hormonal levels leading to progesterone secretion.

Another class of steroids, the estrogens, are also thought to interfere with other hormones in the control of oocyte maturation. In the first experiments, not only were estrogens seen to be unable to induce oocyte maturation in *vitro* (Baulieu et al., 1978), but also to block gonadotropin-induced maturation (Schuetz, 1972; Spiegel et al., 1978). However, more recent studies suggested that estrogens might act by preventing the synthesis or the release of progesterone (Lin and Schuetz, 1983). It was also argued that the inhibitory effect of estrogens on maturation might be directed towards the oocyte itself, based on the observation that the estrogen blockade could be released by increasing the concentration of progesterone during oocyte stimulation (Lin and Schuetz, 1983). More recent studies proposed the existence of an estrogen-sensitive phase taking place in the follicle cells during the early phase of gonadotropin stimulation (Lin and Schuetz, 1985). When applied during later phases of the hormonal process, estrogens could not anymore inhibit progesterone secretion and the ensuing oocyte maturation (Lin and Schuetz, 1985). These experiments suggest for estrogens a determinant, but not yet well understood, role in the regulation of oocyte maturation.

Sex steroids have also been shown to exert a feed-back control on plasma gonadotropin secretion by acting on the hypothalamo-pituitary axis. Such mechanisms were discovered by examining histological preparations of pituitaries after ovariectomy followed or not by steroid therapy. Thus, in *Rana esculenta*, changes in the organization of the *pars distalis* cells induced by gonadoectomy could be prevented by simultaneous administration of estadiol benzoate (Rastogi and Chieffi, 1970). The observation of a compensatory hypertrophy of gonadotropic cells following unilateral oariectomy, in *Bufo bufo*, also indicated the existence of such a control of pituitary secretion by the gonads (Vijayakumar et al., 1971). More recently, McCreery and Licht (1983 b, 1984 a, b) and Licht et al. (1983 a, b), in *Rana catesbeiana*, have reported both an increase and a polymorphism variation in LH and FSH secretion following gonadoectomy. These experiments were the first to directly demonstrate the existence, in amphibians, of a negative feed-back control on the secretions of the hypothalamo-pituitary axis by the gonads. In addition, dihydrotestosterone (a non aromatizable androgen), but not estradiol, was shown to act directly at the pituitary level to increase the GnRH-induced release of gonadotropins (McCreery and Licht, 1984 a). These results lead to the hypothesis that androgens might be implicated in the onset of the LH surge occurring prior to oocyte maturation.

6. Role of non steroidal substances in oocyte maturation

Follicle cells are thought to be responsible for the physiological production of progesterone under gonadotropic stimulation. In *vitro*, manually or enzymatically defolliculated oocytes always undergo maturation following stimulation with progesterone, but not after gonadotropic stimulation (Smith and Ecker, 1970; Masui and Clarke, 1979). Progesterone effect can be mimicked by a number of substances apparently acting at the cell surface, such as lanthanum (Schorderet-Slatkine et al., 1976), local anesthetics and cationic drugs (Baulieu et al., 1975) and sulfhydril reagents (Brachet et al., 1975). Insulin has also been reported to mimic progesterone by inducing germinal vesicle breakdown (GVBD), an indicator of meiosis resumption taking place during oocyte maturation, through the insulin receptor (El-Etr et al., 1979). For some time these latter results were contested by other authors who argued that Zn^{2+} ions present in the insulin preparations constituted the real effector of oocyte maturation (Wallace and Misulovin, 1980) and that, in addition, insulin was acting on the follicle wall, thus stimulating the production of steroid (Lessman and Schuetz, 1981, 1982). Experiments designed to totally eliminate possible interferences by follicle cells, demonstrated that insulin and MSA (Multiplication Stimulation Activity) acted directly on oocytes deprived of their vitelline envelope and follicle cells and triggered oocyte maturation (Maller and Koontz, 1981; Hirai et al., 1983). Thus, it appeared that insulin represented a real inducer of GVBD and oocyte maturation acting through plasma membrane receptors, as it had been previously stated (El-Etr et al., 1979).

The observation of a synergistic effect of steroids((progesterone and testosterone) and insulin on meiosis resumption in *Xenopus* oocytes deprived of their follicle cells confirmed that insulin exerted a direct effect on the oocyte (Hirai et al., 1983; Le Goascogne et al., 1984, 1985). The fact that insulin directly acts on the oocyte membrane does not exclude the possibility that insulin might also act on follicle cells, for instance by increasing progesterone production (Lessman and Schuetz, 1981, 1982). The *Xenopus* oocyte membrane possesses a large number of high-affinity insulin binding sites (Maller and Koontz, 1981). However, insulin was seen to induce oocyte maturation only at concentrations 10 to 100-fold higher than the dissociation constant for binding to these high-affinity binding sites (Maller and Koontz, 1981). This observation, taken together with the fact that anti-insulin antibodies had no effect on the dose-response curve of insulin, led to the suggestion that insulin action was not mediated by the high-affinity component of the insulin receptors but possibly *via* other low-affinity components such as insulin-like growth factor receptors (Maller and Koontz, 1981). More recently, Deshpande and Kung (1987) have shown that insulin induced *Xenopus* oocyte maturation *via* a pathway different from that of steroids. When oocytes were microinjected with a monoclonal antibody directed against p 21 *ras* proteins (which induce oocyte maturation when microinjected), they subsequently failed to undergo maturation in response to insulin but not in response to progesterone (Deshpande and Kung, 1987). Although these two inducers, progesterone and insulin, seem to utilize two different modes of action, they were both seen to produce MPF, the factor responsible for the resumption of meiosis during oocyte maturation (Deshpande and Kung, 1987). These experiments indicate that the *ras* gene product, which induces oocyte maturation when microinjected (Birchmeier et al., 1985; Deshpande and Kung, 1987), is involved in insulin-induced oocyte maturation. It would be interesting to know why progesterone, the probable physiological inducer of oocyte maturation in *Xenopus*, apparently utilizes a pathway in which the plasma membrane *ras* proteins do not seem to be included.

References

Alonso-Bedate, M., Gancedo, B. Delgado, M.J. (1989): Gonadotropin releasing-hormone (GnRH) and oocyte maturation in Discoglossus pictus. Karlsruher Beiträge zur Zoophysiologie, Vol. *14*, p. 90.

Alpert, L.C., Brawer, J.R., Jackson, I.M.D., Reichlin, S. (1976): Localization of LHRH in neurons in frog brain (*Rana pipiens* and *Rana catesbeiana*). Endocrinol. *98*, 910–921.

Barry, J. (1979): Immunohistochemistry of luteinizing hormone-releasing hormone producing neurons of the vertebrates. Int. Rev. Cytol. *44*, 179–221.

Baulieu, E.E., Godeau, F., Schorderet, M., Schorderet-Slatkine, S. (1978): Steroid-induced meiotic division in Xenopus laevis oocytes: surface and calcium. Nature *275*, 593–598.

Birchmeier, C., Broek, D., Wigler, M. (1985): RAS proteins can induce meiosis in *Xenopus* oocytes. Cell *43*, 615–621.

Bollafi, J.L., Callard, I.P. (1979): Plasma steroid profiles in male and female mudpuppies *Necturus maculosus* (Rafinesque). Gen. Comp. Endocrinol. *37*, 443–450.

Bonnanfant-Jaïs, M.L., Mentré, P. (1983): Study of oogenesis in the newt *Pleurodeles waltlii* M.. I. Ultrastructural study of the different stages of oocyte development. J. Submicrosc. Cytol. *15*, 453–478.

Boujard, D., Elzein, G., Garnier, D.H., Joly, J. (1987): Sex steroid changes during perifusion of *Xenopus* ovarian follicles submitted to constant gonadotrope stimulation. Gen. Comp. Endocrinol. (abstract) *66*, 22–23.

Boujard, D., Joly, J. (1983): The dynamics of the steroidogenic response of perifused *Xenopus* testis explants to gonadotropins. Gen. Comp. Endocrinol. *51*, 406–413.

Brachet, J., Baltus, E., Pays-de-Schutter, A., Hanocq-Quertier, J., Hubert, E., Steinert, G. (1975): Induction of maturation (meiosis) in *Xenopus* laevis oocytes by three organomercurials. Proc. Natl. Acad. Sci. USA *72*, 1574–1578.

Breton, B., Derrien-Guimard, M.C. (1983): Action de stimulations gonadotropes pulsatiles sur l'incorporation de vitellogénine in vitro par des follicules de truites incubés dans un système de périfusion ouvert. C.R. Acad. Sci. (Paris) Ser. III *296*, 857–860.

Brinkley, H.J. (1981): Endocrine signaling and female reproduction. Biol. Reprod. *24*, 22–43.

Callen, J.C., Dennebouy, N., Mounolou, J.C. (1986): Early onset of a large pool of previtellogenic oocytes and cyclic escape by vitellogenesis: the pattern of ovarian activity of *Xenopus laevis* females and its physiological consequences. Reprod. Nutr. Dévelop. *26*, 13–30.

Crim, J.W. (1985): Immunocytochemistry of Luteinizing Hormone-Releasing Hormone and sexual maturation of the frog brain: Comparisons of juvenile and adult bullfrogs (*Rana catesbeiana*). Gen. Comp. Endocrinol. *59*, 424–433.

D'Amato, C., Calvo, F.O., Stockert, B., Bahr, J.M. (1981): Steroid secretion by perifused rabbit follicles: Effect of repeated gonadotropin challenges. Biol. Reprod. *25*, 843–850.

Daniels, E., Licht, P. (1980): Effects of gonadotropin-releasing hormone on the levels of plasma gonadotropins (FSH and LH) in the bullfrog *Rana catesbeiana*. Gen. Comp. Endocrinol. *42*, 455–463.

Denver, R. J. (1988): Several hypothalamic peptides stimulate *in vitro* hyrotropin secretion by pituitaries of anuran amphibians. Gen. Comp. Endocrinol. *72*, 383–393.
Deshpande, A. K., Kung. H. F. (1987): Insulin induction of *Xenopus* laevis oocyte maturation is inhibited by monoclonal antibody against p 21 ras proteins. Mol. Cell. Biol. *7*, 1285–1288.
D'Istria, M., Delrio, G., Botte, V., Chieffi, G. (1974): Radioimmunoassay of testosterone, 17β-oestradiol and oestrone in the male and female plasma of *Rana esculenta* during sexual cycle. Steroids Lipids Res. *5*, 42–48.
Doerr-Schott, J., Dubois, M. P. (1976): LHRH-like system in the brain of *Xenopus laevis* Daud. Immunohistochemical identification. Cell Tissue Res. *172*, 477–486.
Dumont, J. N. (1972): Oogenesis in *Xenopus laevis* (Daudin). I. Stages of oocytes development in laboratory maintened animals. J. Morphol. *136*, 153–180.
Eiden, L. E., Loumaye, E., Sherwood, N., Eskay, R. L. (1982): Two chemically and immunologically distinct forms of luteinizing hormone-releasing hormone are differentially expressed in frog neural tissues. Peptides. *3*, 323–327.
El-Etr, M., Schorderet-Slatkine, S., Baulieu, E. E. (1979): Meiotic maturation in *Xenopus laevis* oocytes initiated by insulin. Science *205*, 1397–1399.
Elzein, G., Boujard, D., Garnier, D. H., Joly, J. (1988): The dynamics of the steroidogenic response of perifused Xenopus ovarian explants to gonadotropins. Gen. Comp. Endocrinol. *71*, 132–140.
Elzein, G., Boujard, D., Delarue, C., Joly, J. (1987): Aortic arch catheterization in *Xenopus laevis* females: Its validity in the study of plasma steroid changes. Gen. Comp. Endocrinol. *66*, 22 (abstract).
Farmer, S. W., Licht, P., Papkoff, H., Daniels, E. L. (1977): Purification of gonadotropins in the leopard frog (*Rana pipiens*). Gen. Comp. Endocrinol. *32*, 158–162.
Fontaine, Y. A. (1980): Les hormones gonadotropes de l'hypophyse: Biochimie et biologie comparées; spécificité et évolution. Reprod. Nut. Develop. *20*, 381–418.
Fortune, J. E. (1983): Steroid production by *Xenopus* ovarian follicles at different developmental stages. Dev. Biol. *99*, 502–509.
Fortune, J. E., Tsang, P. C. (1981): Production of androgen and estradiol-17β by *Xenopus* ovaries treated with gonadotropin in vitro. Gen. Comp. Endocrinol. *43*, 234–242.
Fouchet, G., Serres, C., Bellé, R., Ozon, R. (1975): Mechanism of action of progesterone on amphibian oocyte: Uptake and metabolism of progesterone by isolated oocytes of Pleurodeles waltlii and of *Xenopus laevis*. Comp. Biochem. Physiol. *52 B*, 205–210.
Garnier, D. H. (1985): Androgen and estrogen levels in the plasma of *Pleurodeles waltl.* Michah., during the annual cycle. Gen. Comp. Endocrinol. *60*, 414–418.
Gavaud, J., Licht, P., Papkoff, H. (1979): In vitro stimulation of cyclic-AMP production in *Rana catesbeiana* ovaries by homologous gonadotropins. Gen. Comp. Endocrinol. *38*, 83–92.
Goos, H. J. T., Ligtenberg, P. J. M., van Oordt, P. G. W. J. (1976): Immunofluorescence studies on gonadotropin-releasing hormone (GNRH) in the forebrain and the neurohypophysis of the green frog, *Rana esculenta* L., Cell Tissue Res. *168*, 325–334.
Green, J. D. (1951): The comparative anatomy of the hypophysis, with special reference to its blood supply and innervation. Amer. J. Anat. *88*, 225–311.
Hedin, L., Ekholm, C., Hillensjö, T. (1983): Dose-related effects of luteinizing hormone on the pattern of steroidogenesis and cyclic adenosine monophosphate release in superfused preovulatory rat follicles. Biol. Reprod. *29*, 895–904.
Hirai, S., Le Goascogne, C. and Baulieu, E. E. (1983): Induction of Germinal Vesicle BreakDown in *Xenopus laevis* oocytes: Response of denuded oocytes to progesterone and insulin. Dev. Biol. *100*, 214–221.
Houssay, B. A. (1947): La fonction sexual del sapo *Bufo arenarum* Hensel. Ann. Acad. Rac. Cienc. B. Aires. *12*, 103–124.
Hubbard, G. M. and Licht, P. (1985): In vitro study of the direct ovarian effects of gonadotropin-releasing hormone (GnRH) in the frogs, *Rana pipiens* and *Rana catesbeiana*. Gen. Comp. Endocrinol. *60*, 154–161.
Hubbard, G. M. and Licht, P. (1986 a): In vitro ovarian responses to pulsatile and continuous gonadotrophin administration on steroid secretion and oocyte maturation in the frogs, *Rana pipiens* and *Rana catesbeiana*. Gen. Comp. Endocrinol. *61*, 417–423.

Hubbard, G. M., Licht, P. (1986b): Effects of cycloheximide on in vitro testosterone secretion from *Rana catesbeiana* ovaries. Comp. Biochem. Physiol. *84A*, 401–403.

Iela, L., Rastogi, R. K., Delrio, G. and Bagnara, J. T. (1986): Reproduction in the Mexican leaf frog, *Pachymedusa dacnicolor*. III. The female. Gen. Comp. Endocrinol. *63*, 381–392.

Joly, J., Picheral, B. (1972): Ultrastructure, histochimie et physiologie du follicule préovulatoire et du corps jaune de l'urodèle ovo-vivipare *Salamandra salamandra* (L.). Gen. Comp. Endocrinol. *18*, 235–259.

Jokura, Y., Urano, A. (1985): An immunohistochemical study of seasonal changes in luteinizing hormone-releasing hormone and vasotocin in the forebrain and the neurohypophysis of the toad, *Bufo japonicus*. Gen. Comp. Endocrinol. *59*, 238–245.

Jorgensen, C. B. (1973): Mechanisms regulating ovarian function in amphibians (toads). In «The development and maturation of the ovary and its function». H. Peters Ed. Excerpta med., Amsterdam, pp. 133–151.

Kiehm, D. J., Dunn, T. G., Murdoch, W. J., Kaltenbach, C. C. (1984): Effect of constant and pulsed administration of luteinizing hormone on ovarian secretion of estradiol-17β and ovulation in hypophysectomized proestrus ewes. Biol. Reprod. (abstract) *30*, 64.

King, J. A., Millar, R. P. (1979): Hypothalamic luteinizing hormone-releasing hormone content in relation to the seasonal reproductive cycle of *Xenopus laevis*. Gen. Comp. Endocrinol. *39*, 309–312.

King, J. A., Millar, R. P. (1986): Identification of His^5, Trp^7, Tyr^8-GnRH (Chicken GnRH II) in amphibian brain. Peptides, *7*, 827–834.

Kühn, E. R., Gevaerts, H., Jacobs, G., Vandorpe, G. (1987): Reproductive cycle thyroxine and corticosterone in females of the grass swamp frog (*Dicroglossus occipitalis*) at the equator. Gen. Comp. Endocrinol. *66*, 137–144.

Kwon, H. B., Schuetz, A. W. (1985): Dichotomous effects of forskolin on somatic and germ cell components of the ovarian folicle: evidence of cAMP involvement in steroid production and action. J. Exp. Zool. *236*, 219–228.

Kwon, H. B., Schuetz, A. W. (1986): Role of cAMP in modulating intrafollicular progesterone levels and oocyte maturation in amphibians (*Rana pipiens*). Dev. Biol. *117*, 354–364.

LaMarca, M. J., Westphal, L. M., Rein, D. A. (1985): Gonadotropins and the timing of progesterone-induced meiotic maturation of *Xenopus laevis* oocytes. Dev. Biol. *109*, 32–40.

Le Goascogne, C., Hirai, S., Baulieu, E. E. (1984): Induction of germinal vesicle breakdown in Xenopus laevis oocytes: synergistic action of progesterone and insulin. J. Endocr. *101*, 7–12.

Le Goascogne, C., Sananes, N., Gouezou, M., Baulieu, E. E. (1985): Testosterone induced meiotic maturation of *Xenopus laevis* oocytes: Evidence for an early effect in the synergistic action of insulin. Dev. Biol. *109*, 9–14.

Lessman, C. A., Schuetz, A. W. (1981): Role of follicle wall in meiosis reinitiation by insulin in *Rana pipiens* oocytes. Amer. J. Physiol. *241*, E51–E56.

Lessman, C. A., Schuetz, A. W. (1982): Insulin induction of meiosis of *Rana pipiens* oocytes: Relation to endogenous progesterone. Gamete Res. *6*, 95–106.

Licht, P. (1983): Evolutionary divergence in the structure and function of pituitary gonadotropins of tetrapod vertebrates. Amer. Zool. *23*, 673–683.

Licht, P. (1986): Suitability of the mammalian model in comparative reproductive endocrinology. In Comparative Endocrinology: Developments and Directions. C. L. Ralph Ed., A. R. Liss, Inc. pp. 95–114.

Licht, P., Crews, D. (1976): Gonadotropin stimulation of in vitro progesterone production in reptilian and amphibian ovaries. Gen. Comp. Endocrinol. *29*, 141–151.

Licht, P., Farmer, W., Papkoff, H. (1975): The nature of the pituitary gonadotropins and their role in ovulation in a urodele amphibian (*Ambystoma tigrinum*). Life Sci. *17*, 1049–1054.

Licht, P., McCreery, B. R., Barnes, R. (1983a): Relation between acute pituitary responsiveness to gonadotropin releasing hormone (GnRH) and the ovarian cycle in the Bullfrog *Rana catesbeiana*. Gen. Comp. Endocrinol. *51*, 148–153.

Licht, P., McCreery, B. R., Barnes, R., Pang, R. (1983b): Seasonal and stress related changes in plasma gonadotropins, sex steroid, and corticosterone in the bullfrog, *Rana catesbeiana*. Gen. Comp. Endocrinol. *50*, 124–145.

Licht, P., McCreery, B. R., Papkoff, H. (1983): Effects of gonadectomy on polymorphism in stored and circulating gonadotropins in the bullfrog, *Rana catesbeiana*. II Gel filtration chromatography. Biol. Reprod. *29*, 646–657.

Licht, P., Papkoff, H. (1974): Separation of two distinct gonadotropins from the pituitary gland of the bullfrog *Rana catesbeiana*. Endocrinol. *94*, 1587–1594.

Licht, P., Papkoff, H. (1976): Species specificity in the response of an in vitro amphibian (*Xenopus laevis*) ovulation assay to mammalian luteinizing hormones. Gen. Comp. Endocrinol. *29*, 552–555.

Licht, P., Papkoff, H., Farmer, S. W., Muller, C. H., Tsui, H. W., Crews, D. (1977): Evolution of gonadotropin structure and function. Recent Progr. Horm. Res. *33*, 169–248.

Lin, Y. W. P., Schuetz, A. W. (1983): In vitro estrogen modulation of pituitary and progesterone induced maturation in *Rana pipiens*. J. Exp. Zool. *226*, 281–291.

Lin, Y. W. P., Schuetz, A. W. (1985): Intrafollicular action of estrogen in regulating pituitary-induced ovarian progesterone synthesis and oocyte maturation in *Rana pipiens*: Temporal relationship and locus of action. Gen. Comp. Endocrinol. *58*, 421–435.

Lohka, M. J., Hayes, M. K., Maller, J. L. (1988): Purification of maturation-promoting factor, an intracellular regulator of early mitotic events. Proc. Natl. Acad. Sci. USA *85*, 3009–3013.

Maller, J. L. (1985): Regulation of amphibian oocyte maturation. Cell Differ. *16*, 211–221.

Maller, J. L., Koontz, J. W. (1981): A study of the induction of cell division in amphibian oocytes by insulin. Dev. Biol. *85*, 309–316.

Marot, J., Bellé, R., Ozon, R. (1977): In vitro facilitation of *Xenopus* oocyte maturation by sub-threshold doses of progesterone. Dev. Biol. *59*, 91–95.

Masui, Y. (1967): Relative roles of the pituitary follicle cells, and progesterone in the induction of oocyte maturation in *Rana pipiens*. J. Exp. Zool. *166*, 365–376.

Masui, Y., Clarke, H. J. (1979): Oocyte maturation. Int. Rev. Cytol. *57*, 185–282.

McCreery, R., Licht, P. (1983 a): Induced ovulation and changes in pituitary responsiveness to continuous infusion of gonadotropin-releasing hormone during the ovarian cycle in the Bullfrog, *Rana catesbeiana*. Biol. Reprod. *29*, 863–871.

McCreery, R., Licht, P. (1983 b): Effects of gonadectomy on polymorphism in stored and circulating gonadotropins in the Bullfrog, *Rana catesbeiana*. Biol. Reprod. *29*, 637–645.

McCreery, R., Licht, P. (1984 a): Effects of gonadectomy and sex steroids on pituitary gonadotropin release and response to gonadotropin-releasing hormone (GnRH) agonist in the Bullfrog *Rana catesbeiana*. Gen. Comp. Endocrinol. *54*, 283–296.

McCreery, R., Licht, P. (1984 b): The role of androgen in the development of sexual differences in pituitary responsiveness to gonadotropin-releasing hormone (GnRH) agonist in the Bullfrog *Rana catesbeiana*. Gen. Comp. Endocrinol. *54*, 350–359.

McNatty, K. P., Heath, D. A., Lun, S., Fannin, J. M., McDiarmid, J. M., Henderson, K. M. (1984): Steroidogenesis by bovine theca interna in an in vitro perifusion system. Biol. Reprod. *30*, 159–170.

Millers, M. R., Robbins, M. E. (1954): The reproductive cycle in *Taricha torosa* (*Triturus torosus*). J. Exp. Zool. *125*, 415–445.

Mizell, S. (1964): Seasonal differences in spermatogenesis and oogenesis in *Rana pipiens*. Nature *202*, 875–876.

Morrill, G. A., Schatz, F., Kostellow, A. B., Poupko, J. M. (1977): Changes in cyclic AMP levels in the amphibian follicle following progesterone induction of meiotic maturation. Differentiation. *8*, 97–104.

Mulner, O., Thibier, C., Ozon, R. (1978): Steroid biosynthesis by ovarian follicles of *Xenopus laevis* in vitro during oogenesis. Gen. Comp. Endocrinol. *34*, 287–295.

O'Connor, C. M., Smith, L. D. (1976): Inhibition of oocyte maturation by theophylline: Possible mechanism of action. Dev. Biol. *52*, 318–322.

Petrino, T. R., Schuetz, A. W. (1986): Protein synthesis and steroidogenesis in amphibian (*Rana pipiens*) ovarian follicles: Studies on the conversion of pregnenolone to progesterone. Gen. Comp. Endocrinol. *63*, 441–450.

Petrino, T. R., Schuetz, A. W. (1987): Cholesterol mediation of progesterone production and oocyte maturation in cultured amphibian (*Rana pipiens*) ovarian follicles. Biol. Reprod. *36*, 1219–1228.

Pierantoni, R., Fasano, S., Minucci, S., Di Matteo, L., Chieffi, G. (1988): GnRH-like substances in hypothalamus and testis of the frog *Rana esculenta*. 14th Conference of European Comparative Endocrinologists. Salzburg, Abstract p. 67.

Pierantoni, R., Iela, I., Delrio, G., Rastogi, R. K. (1984): Seasonal plasma sex steroid levels in the female *Rana esculenta*. Gen. Comp. Endocrinol. *53*, 126–134.

Pierantoni, R., Iela, L., d'Istria, M., Fasano, S., Rastogi, R. K., Delrio, G. (1984): Seasonal testosterone profile and testicular responsiveness to pituitary factors and gonadotrophin releasing hormone during two different phases of the sexual cycle of the frog (*Rana esculenta*). J. Endocrinol. *102*, 387–392.

Pilone, G. B., Humphries, A. A. (1975): Progesterone-induced in vitro maturation in oocytes of *Notophtalmus viridescens* (Amphibia, Urodela) and some observation on cytological aspects of maturation. J. Embryol. Exp. Morphol. *34*, 451–466.

Porter, D. A., Licht, P. (1985): Pituitary responsiveness to superfused GnRH in two species of ranid frogs. Gen. Comp. Endocrinol. *59*, 308–315.

Rastogi, R. K., Chieffi, G. (1970): A cytological study of the pars distalis of pituitary gland of normal, gonadectomized and gonadectomized steroid hormone-treated green frog *Rana esculenta* L. Gen. Comp. Endocrinol. *15*, 247–263.

Redschaw, M. R., Nicholls, T. J. (1971): Oestrogen biosynthesis by ovarian tissue of the south african clawed toad, *Xenopus laevis* Daudin. Gen. Comp. Endocrinol. *16*, 85–96.

Reynouth, J. K., Smith, L. D. (1973): Evidence for steroid metabolism during the in vitro induction of maturation in oocytes of *Rana pipiens*. Dev. Biol. *30*, 392–402.

Reynouth, J. K., Taddei, C., Smith, L. D., LaMarca, M. J. (1975): Response of large oocytes of Xenopus laevis to progesterone in vitro in relation to oocyte size and time after previous hCG-induced ovulation. Dev. Biol. *44*, 375–379.

Sadler, S. E., Maller, J. L. (1982): Identification of a steroid receptor on the surface of *Xenopus* oocytes by photoaffinity labeling. J. Biol. Chem. *257*, 355–361.

Sadler, S. E., Maller, J. L. (1983): The development of competence for meiotic maturation during oogenesis in *Xenopus laevis*. Dev. Biol. *98*, 165–172.

Sanyal, M. K., Sibre, E. R. (1973): Breakdown of germinal vesicle of frog oocytes with 5α-reduced products of progesterone *in vitro*. Proc. Soc. Exp. Biol. Med. *144*, 483–486.

Schorderet-Slatkine, S., Baulieu, E. E. (1982): Forskolin increases cAMP and inhibits progesterone induced meiosis reinitiation in *Xenopus laevis* oocytes. Endocrinol. *111*, 1385–1387.

Schorderet-Slatkine, S., Schorderet, M., Baulieu, E. E. (1976): Initiation of meiotic maturation in *Xenopus laevis* oocytes by lanthanum. Nature *262*, 289–290.

Schuetz, A. W. (1967): Action of hormones on germinal vesicle breakdown in frog (*Rana pipiens*) oocytes. J. Exp. Zool. *166*, 347–354.

Schuetz, A. W. (1972): Estrogens and ovarian follicular function in *Rana pipiens*. Gen. Comp. Endocrinol. *18*, 32–36.

Schuetz, A. W., Lessman, C. A. (1982): Evidence for follicle wall involvement in ovulation and progesterone production by frog (*Rana pipiens*) follicles in vitro. Differentiation *22*, 79–84.

Sherwood, N. M. (1987): The GnRH family of peptides. Trends In Neurosci. *10*, 129–132.

Sherwood, N. M., Zoeller, R. T. and Moore, F. L. (1986): Multiple forms of Gonadotropin-releasing hormone in amphibian brains. Gen. Comp. Endocrinol. *61*, 313–322.

Siboulet, R. (1981): Variations saisonnières de la teneur plasmatique en testostérone et dihydrotestostérone chez le crapaud de Mauritanie (*Bufo mauritanicus*). Gen. Comp. Endocrinol. *43*, 71–75.

Smith, L. D., Ecker, R. E. (1970): Regulatory processes in the maturation and early cleavage of amphibian eggs. Curr. Top. Dev. Biol. *5*, 1–38.

Smith, L. D., Ecker, R. E., Subtelny, S. (1968): In vitro induction of physiological maturation in *Rana pipiens* oocytes removed from their ovarian follicles. Dev. Biol. *17*, 627–643.

Spiegel, J., Jones, E., Snyder, B. W. (1978): Estradiol 17β interference with meiotic maturation in Rana pipiens ovarian follicles: Evidence for inhibition of 3β-hydroxy-steroid dehydrogenase. J. Exp. Zool. *204*, 187–192.

Suzuki, K., Kawauchi, H., Nagahama, Y. (1988 a): Isolation and characterization of two distinct gonadotropins from chum salmon pituitary glands. Gen. Comp. Endocrinol. *71*, 292–301.

Suzuki, K., Kawauchi, H., Nagahama, Y. (1988 b): Isolation and characterization of subunits from two distinct salmon gonadotropins. Gen. Comp. Endocrinol. *71*, 302–306.

Taylor, M. A., Smith, L. D. (1987): Induction of maturation in small *Xenopus laevis* oocytes. Dev. Biol. *121*, 111–118.

Thornton, V. F., Geschwind, I. I. (1974): Hypothalamic control of gonadotropin release in amphibia: evidence from studies of gonadotropin release *in vitro* and *in vivo*. Gen. Comp. Endocrinol. *23*, 294–301.

Vellano, C., Bona, A., Mazzi, V., Colucci, D. (1974): The effect of synthetic luteinizing hormone-releasing hormone on ovulation in the crested newt. Gen. Comp. Endocrinol. *24*, 338–347.

Vijayakumar, S., Jorgensen, C. B., Kjaer, K. (1971): Regulation of ovarian cycle in the toad *Bufo bufo* bufo (L.): Effects of autografting pars distalis of the hypophysis, of extirpating gonadotropic hypothalamic region and of partial ovariectomy. Gen. Comp. Endocrinol. *17*, 432–443.

Wallace, R. A., Misulovin, Z. (1980): The role of zinc and follicle cells in insulin-initiated meiotic maturation of *Xenopus laevis* oocytes. Science *210*, 928–929.

Ying, S.-Y., Ling, N., Bohlen, P., Guillemin, R. (1981): Gonadocrinins: Peptides in ovarian follicular fluid stimulating the secretion of pituitary gonadotropins. Endocrinol. *108*, 1206–1215.

Zohar, Y., Breton, B., Fostier, A. (1986a): Short-term profiles of plasma gonadotropin and 17α-hydroxy-20β-dihydroprogesterone levels in the female rainbow trout at the periovulatory period. Gen. Comp. Endocrinol. *64*, 189–198.

Zohar, Y., Breton, B., Fostier, A. (1986b): Short-term profiles of plasma gonadotropin and estradiol-17β levels in the female rainbow trout, from early ovarian recrudescence and throughout vitellogenesis. Gen. Comp. Endocrinol. *64*, 172–188.

Zohar, Y., Breton, B., Fostier, A. (1982): Gonadotropic function during the reproductive cycle of the female rainbow trout, Salmo gairdneri, in relation of ovarian steroid secretion: *in vivo* and *in vitro* studies. In: Reproductive Physiology of Fish (C. J. J. Ritcher, H. J. Th. Goos, Eds.) pp. 14–18, Pudoc, Wageningen.

Fortschritte der Zoologie, Band/Vol. 38 · Hanke, W. (Hrsg.), Biology and Physiology of Amphibians
Gustav Fischer Verlag · Stuttgart · New York · 1990

A direct effect of gonadotropin-releasing hormone on steroid secretion and oocyte maturation in amphibians

M. Alonso-Bedate, B. Gancedo and M. J. Delgado

Facultad de Biologia, Departamento de Fisiologia Animal, Universidad Complutense, E-28040 Madrid, Spain

1. Introduction

In mammals, granulosa cells under a pituitary control are responsible for producing the two most important ovarian steroids, estradiol and progesterone. Although granulosa cells are capable of producing progesterone independent of other ovarian cell types, the biosynthesis of estradiol needs the interaction of granulosa and theca cells. It was difficult to understand the mammalian ovarian function in detail only by the action of pituitary hormones. Therefore, some local factors were suggested that may modulate the actions of gonadotropins on the ovarian function. Thus, besides the endocrine pituitary control of the ovary a paracrine regulation has been suggested. A given cell may secrete a substance which may regulate, within the ovary, the functions of its neighbouring cells. It is now widely accepted that in addition to steroids, some ovarian cells also secrete mitogenic and growth factors (Hammond, 1981; Hsueh et al., 1984), Gonadotropin-binding inhibitors (Reichert et al., 1984; Ward et al., 1983), Oocyte Maturation Inhibitor, OMI (Tsafriri 1977; Tsafriri and Pomerantz, 1986; Tsafriri, 1988), and some other substances. There is also strong evidence for the existence of an intragonadal GnRH-like peptide in rat, bovine, ovine and human ovaries (Aten et al., 1987) that probably plays a physiological role in regulating ovarian steroidogenesis capacity through a paracrine control mechanism. The existence of receptors for GnRH in the granulosa, theca and lutheal cells has been shown (Gore-Langton and Armstrong, 1988; Hsueh et al., 1984).

GnRH administration to hypophysectomized rats or *in vitro* granulosa cells exerts both stimulatory and inhibitory actions. Given alone GnRH stimulates granulosa cell production of estrogen, progesterone, 20α hydroxyprogesterone associated with increases in aromatase, 3β and 20α hydroxysteroid dehydrogenase activities in mammals (Tsafriri, 1988). In addition, GnRH induces maturation of follicle-enclosed rat oocytes *in vitro* (Dekel et al., 1983; Eckholm et al., 1981; Erickson et al., 1983; Hillensjö and Le Maire, 1980) and ovulation in hypophysectomized rats (Corbin and Bex, 1981; Dekel et al. 1983; Ekholm et al., 1981; Naor et al., 1983). The ovulation is presumably mediated by a stimulatory effect of GnRH on prostaglandin production which promotes the production of a plasminogen activator by granulosa cells. The action of plasminogen activator on plasminogen produces plasmin that in turn decreases follicle wall strength and provoques ovulation. The action of GnRH on ovulation is not mediated by cAMP (Dekel et al., 1985). On the other hand studies by Aberdan and Dekel (1985) indicate that the effect of GnRH on oocyte maturation implicates a protein kinase C.

A direct inhibitory effect of GnRH was observed in hypophysectomized rats *in vivo* and in cultures of granulosa cells *in vitro*. This peptide decreased the ovarian weight increased by HCG and inhibited ovarian steroidogenesis stimulated by FSH (Hsueh and Jones, 1981). Both inhibitory and stimulatory actions seem to be associated with the regulation of follicular development and follicle selection in rats.

In anuran amphibians oocyte growth and maturation are stimulated by steroid hormones synthesized and secreted by the follicle cells surrounding each oocyte. Estradiol regulates synthesis and secretion of vitellogenin by the liver that is taken up by the growing oocytes to produce yolk proteins. On the other hand progesterone is responsible for oocyte resumption of meiosis (Germinal Vesicle Breakdown, GVBD) known as oocyte maturation (Chieffi and Pierantoni, 1987; Maller, 1985; Schuetz, 1985; Shukmei-Ho, 1987; Wallace, 1985). It is now widely accepted that the ovary of amphibians is mainly regulated by pituitary gonadotropins (GtHs) which are under the hypothalamic control of gonadotropin releasing hormone (GnRH) (Licht and Porter, 1987).

Few studies have been done to elucidate the potential extrapituitary action of GnRH in nonmammalian vertebrates. GnRH enhanced progesterone production stimulated by LH in isolated granulosa cells of *Gallus domesticus* (Hertelendy et al., 1982). The first studies about the direct influence of GnRH on steroidogenesis and oocyte maturation in amphibians were performed by Hubbard and Licht (1985) in *Rana pipiens* and *Rana catesbeiana* ovaries *in vitro*. This study demonstrated that GnRH had no effect on basal or LH-stimulated testosterone or progesterone secretion. Maturation (GVBD) was observed in LH-stimulated fragments but GnRH did not have any effect. Studies by Zerani et al. (1987) in *Rana esculenta* made clear that GnRH did not alter significantly the basal titers of testosterone, progesterone and estradiol but in combination with homologous pituitary gland, estradiol secretion was increased. No modifications in androgens and progesterone titers were found.

The male gonads of vertebrates have the dual function of producing and secreting androgens and generating new spermatozoa for animal reproduction. The primordial regulatory mechanisms for these testicular functions is based on secretion of gonadotropins by the adenohypophysis which is under the control of the hypothalamic factor GnRH. Although the main mechanism controlling the gonadal function is based on pituitary gonadotropins other local factors as GnRH-like peptides or prostaglandins have been proposed. The presence of receptors to LHRH has been demonstrated in testicular interstitial tissue in the rat (Dalkin et al., 1981) and GnRH has been measured in rat testis (Hedger et al. 1985). Moreover, it has been shown that LHRH can directly modify steroidogenesis in the rat testis (Sharpe and Cooper, 1982; Sharpe et al., 1983). It has been proposed that the factor does not operate through adenylate cyclase and may be related with local interactions between Sertoli cells and Leydig cells (Sharpe and Cooper, 1982).

Studies *in vivo* and *in vitro* demonstrated that GnRH or GnRH analogs are able to increase androgen production in *Rana pipiens* (Segal and Adejuwon, 1979) and *Rana esculenta* (Pierantoni et al., 1984a, 1984b). A GnRH analog (HOE 766) enhances also spermatogonial multiplication in *R. esculenta* (Minucci et al., 1986). Recently, Fasano et al. (1988) measured testicular GnRH in *Rana esculenta* and observed that irGnRH reached high levels in autumn and spring. In *R. esculenta*, a gonadotropin-releasing hormone antagonist decreases androgen production and spermatogonial multiplication whereas the existence of GnRH or GnRH-like material receptors in the hypophysis and testis has been observed.

The present work was performed in order to study the influence of GnRH on oocyte maturation (GVBD) and estradiol secretion by the ovaries as well as on testosterone production by the testis in the anuran amphibians, *Discoglossus pictus* and *Rana perezi in vitro*.

2. Materials and methods

2.1. Animals

Discoglossus pictus females (body weight about 15–20 g) were collected from nature in the outskirts of Madrid in December and early February. Animals were kept in small aquaria on a 12 h light: 12 h darkness cycle at laboratory temperature (21 °C ± 2 °C) for two weeks. Before use frogs were force-fed pieces of fresh beef liver twice a week.

Rana perezi males (body weight 20–22 g) and females (body weight 35–40 g) were collected from the nature by a commercial supplier (North-West of Spain, Galicia) and kept at the same conditions as *D. pictus*.

2.2. Estradiol pretreatment of female frog

At the beginning of the experiment (December) a small part of the ovaries of *Discoglossus* (n = 4) and *Rana perezi* (n = 6) was removed surgically through a small lateral incision of the abdomen. The wound was subsequently closed with a silk thread, and the animals were allowed to recover. To verify that progesterone does not produce oocyte maturation (Germinal vesicle breakdown, GVBD) at that time of the year, the oocytes were treated with progesterone (20 μg/ml culture medium) as described below. To compare the responsiveness of oocytes from untreated females with that after estradiol stimulation, frogs were injected with estradiol (20 μg) in the lateral lymph sac three times a week for 1 week in *D. pictus* and 50 μg every other day for two weeks in *R. perezi* before the ovaries were examined again. These doses allowed oocyte growth in both species and therefore to maturate after progesterone treatment. The results of these experiments are not reported in this paper.

2.3. Follicle preparation and in vitro culture

It is well known that the GVBD response of oocytes varies from one animal to another, and experiments have to be performed with the same animal to study the response to different kind of substances (Alonso Bedate et al., 1974). After estradiol pretreatment only ovaries with a percentage of oocytes that maturate when progesterone (20 μg/ml culture medium) was added to the incubation medium were selected for these experiments (full grown oocytes about 1.6–1.8 mm diameter for *D. pictus* or 1.3–1.6 mm for *R. perezi*).

The ovarian tissue was removed from the animals anaesthesized with MS 222 (Sandoz, Switzerland. 1 g/l) and quickly transferred into Petri dishes containing Dulbecco's modified Eagle's medium (DME) (Hubbard and Licht, 1985). After rinsing, ovarian tissue was cut into small pieces. The oocytes were selected using a watch-maker's forceps under a stereo dissecting microscope. Four oocytes were incubated in 1 ml of culture medium in sterile plastic multiwell culture dishes (Nunclon, interMed. Ref. 146485, Denmark) at 26 °C in a shaking thermostatically controlled incubator.

Lyophylized progesterone was purchased from Sigma (U.S.A.) dissolved in 0.1 ml of ethanol-propylene glycol (1:1) and diluted in DME at the appropriate concentration just before use. Progesterone was employed at 10 and 20 μg/ml.

Synthetic mammalian Gonadotropin releasing hormone (GnRH) was obtained from Serono (Italy) and dissolved in culture medium at the appropriate concentration just before use. It was used at 1 μg/ml DME.

For testing oocyte maturation four oocytes per well in 5 or more replicates were used. They were maintained for 24 hours and then the medium was thrown away.

To measure estradiol, after GnRH treatment (0.1 μg or 1 μg/ml DME) four oocytes per well for quintuplicates were used. Culture medium was taken at 1,4 and 19 hours and frozen at −20 °C until used for assay. It was completely renewed at 1 and 4 hours.

2.4. Assay for oocyte maturation

Germinal vesicle breakdown was monitored by manual dissection of oocytes after boiling slightly looking for the disappearance of the germinal vesicle.

2.5. Estradiol radioimmunoassay

Ovarian culture medium samples were assayed for estradiol using an estradiol direct kit (Serono, MAIA, Italy). The coefficient of variation between and within assays was 9.5% and 7.4% respectively. Sensitivity was 10 pg/ml. The percentage of cross-reactions shows that the specificity of the antiserum used is 100% for estradiol, 0,87% for estrone and 0.17% for estriol. Final values were expressed as pg of steroid per milliliter of medium per follicle.

Dilutions of the medium were parallel to the standard curve. Radioactivity was measured by a Gammachem 2400 (Labs Clinics) apparatus equipped with a microcomputer.

2.6. Preparation and incubation of testis

Males of *R. perezi* were anaesthesized with MS 222 and testes were quickly excised and placed into incubation medium. Pieces of testis were prepared by transversely cutting the testis with a razor blade. Each testis yielded 8 pieces. In most of the experiments, testis pieces from the same frog were used. One piece of the testis was incubated in 1 ml of incubation medium in sterile plastic multiwell culture dishes for quadruplicate at 26 °C in a shaking thermostatically controlled incubator. The incubation medium was renewed at 2, 4 and 19 hours and frozen at −20 °C until use. Pieces of testes were finally analysed for protein (Lowry et al., 1951). These experiments were carried out in autumn (November), winter (February), spring (May) and summer (July). GnRH (0.1 μg/ml, 1 μg/ml or 10 μg/ml DME) was added directly into the culture dish. The medium was assayed for testosterone.

2.7. Testosterone radioimmunoassay

Incubation medium samples from testes tissues were assayed for testosterone using a testosterone direct kit (Sorin, Italy). The coefficient of variation inter and intraassays was 10% and 9.4% respectively. Sensitivity was 80 μg/ml. The percentage of crossreactions shows that the specificity of the antiserum used is 100% for testosterone, 9.2% for dihydrotestosterone and 0.01% for other steroids. Final values were expressed as nanograms of steroid per milliliter of medium per milligram of protein.

Dilutions of the medium were parallel to the standard curve. Radioactivity was measured by a Gammachem 2400 (Labs Clinics) apparatus equipped with a microcomputer.

2.8. Statistical analysis

The significance of differences was evaluated by using a one-way analysis of variance (ANOVA) and Duncan's multiple range test (at $P < 0.05$ and $P < 0.01$) for multigroup comparisons.

3. In vitro effects of progesterone, GnRH or progesterone plus GnRH on GVBD

The effect of progesterone, GnRH or both on oocyte maturation in *R. perezi* can be seen in table 1. There was no spontaneous maturation in untreated control. A progesterone concentration of 10 μg/ml and 20 μg/ml was able to promote oocyte maturation of 65% and 80% respectively in 24 hours. On the other hand all germinal vesicles were found intact when oocytes were treated with GnRH alone (1 μg/ml). In addition, GnRH was unable to modify the percentage of GVBD obtained by progesterone treatment.

The effect of progesterone, GnRH or both on GVBD in *D. pictus* is shown in table 2. Progesterone (10 μg/ml and 20 μg/ml) induced the GVBD in almost all the oocytes treated

Table 1: Effect of mammalian gonadotropin releasing hormone (GnRH), on germinal vesicle breakdown (GVBD) in *Rana perezi in vitro*.

Treatment	Doses (μg/ml)	Oocytes (Total n°)	GVBD (n°)	Maturation (%)
Control	—	40	0	0
Progesterone	10	26	17	65
Progesterone	20	18	16	89
GnRH	1	38	0	0
Progesterone + GnRH	10 1	33	21	64

Table 2: Effect of mammalian gonadotropin releasing hormone (GnRH), on germinal vesicle breakdown (GVBD) in *Discoglossus pictus in vitro*.

Treatment	Doses (μg/ml)	Oocytes (Total n°)	GVBD (n°)	Maturation (%)
Control	—	65	0	0
Progesterone	10	22	20	91
Progesterone	20	45	40	89
GnRH	1	65	0	0
Progesterone + GnRH	10 1	20	18	90
Progesterone + GnRH	20 1	45	43	95

after 24 hours of incubation (Alonso-Bedate et al., 1971). As in *R. perezi*, GnRH alone did not induce the dissolution of germinal vesicle and was not able to modify the percentage of GVBD observed with progesterone treatment.

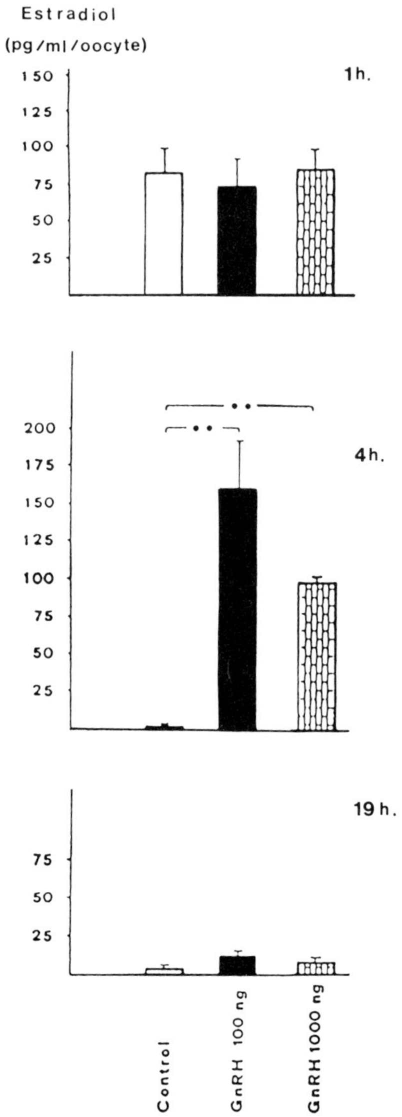

Fig. 1: *In vitro* effects of mammalian GnRH (100 ng/ml, 1000 ng/ml) on estradiol levels in the incubation medium of *Discoglossus pictus* oocytes after 1 h, 4 h, and 19 h of incubation. Data are expressed as mean ± SEM. Statistical differences: ; * $p < 0.05$ ** $p < 0.01$.

4. In vitro effect of GnRH on estradiol levels in the incubation medium of *D. pictus* oocytes

The effect of GnRH (0.1 μg/ml and 1 μg/ml) on estradiol levels is shown in Fig. 1. At 1 hour, GnRH did not modify the secretion of estradiol when compared with untreated controls, but 3 hours later (4 hours after the beginning of the treatment) the levels of estradiol significantly increased.

5. Effect of GnRH on testosterone levels in the incubation medium of *R. perezi* testis

The studies about the effect of GnRH in *R. perezi* males were performed in November, early February, May and July. GnRH (0.1 μg/ml and 1 μg/ml) enhanced the level of testosterone 2 h following the addition of the hormone in November (Fig. 2). In early February

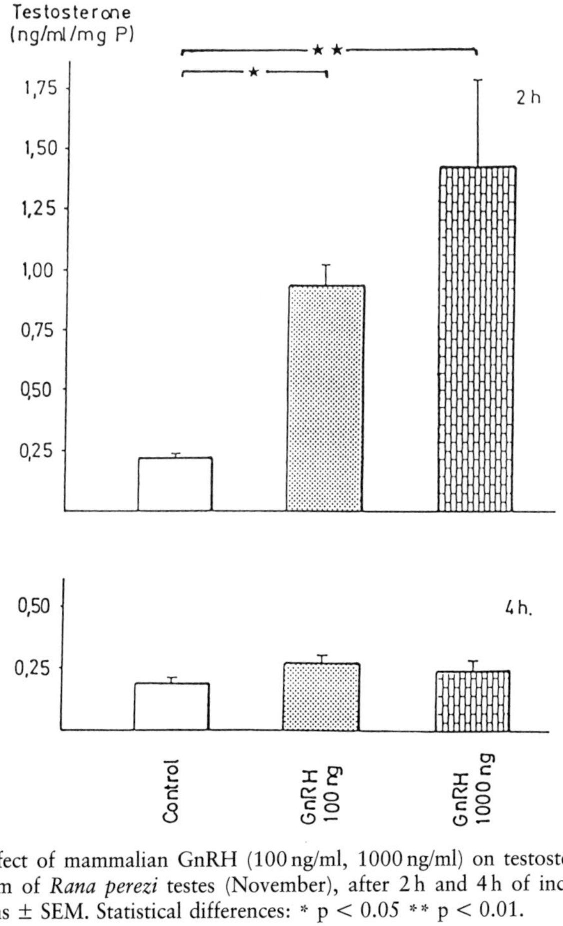

Fig. 2: *In vitro* effect of mammalian GnRH (100 ng/ml, 1000 ng/ml) on testosterone levels in the incubation medium of *Rana perezi* testes (November), after 2 h and 4 h of incubation. Data are expressed as means ± SEM. Statistical differences: * $p < 0.05$ ** $p < 0.01$.

only a dosis of 1 μg/ml increased testosterone 2 h later the addition of the hormone (Fig. 3). Finally, it was not possible to observe any effect when measured in spring or during the summer (Fig. 4 and Fig. 5). The spontaneous release of testosterone into the medium varied with the season. Thus, values comparable to those after GnRH stimulation were reached.

6. Discussion

Although a GnRH-like peptide induces maturation of follicle-enclosed rat oocytes *in vitro*, the results reported in other species of mammals are not so clear. The data presented here demonstrate that synthetic mammalian GnRH do not have any effect on germinal vesicle dissolution in *Rana perezi* and *Discoglossus pictus*.

Our results are in accordance with those obtained by Hubbard and Licht (1985) in *Rana pipiens*. They did not find any significant differences between control oocytes and

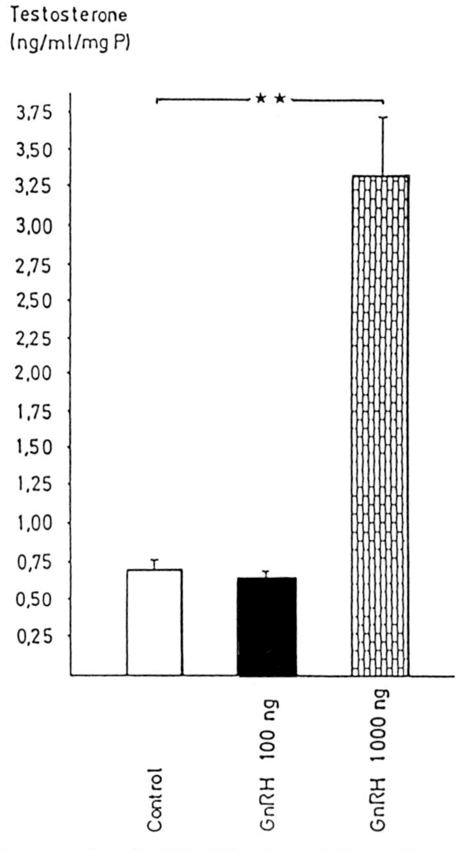

Fig. 3: *In vitro* effect of mammalian GnRH (100 ng/ml, 1000 ng/ml) on testosterone levels in the incubation medium of *Rana perezi* testis (February) after 2 h of incubations. Data are expressed as means ± SEM. Statistical differences: ** $p < 0.01$.

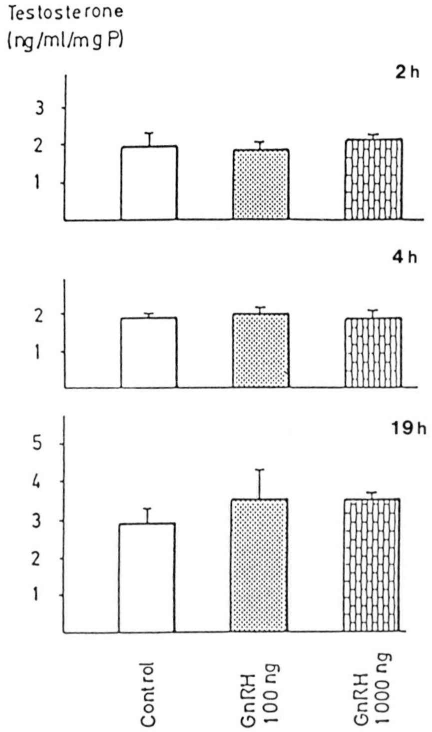

Fig. 4: *In vitro* effect of mammalian GnRH (100 ng/ml, 1000 ng/ml) on testosterone levels in the incubation medium of Rana perezi testis (May) after 2 h, 4 h, and 19 h of incubations. Data are expressed as mean ± SEM. No statistical differences were observed.

those treated with GnRH. The percentage of GVBD was unaffected by GnRH in the presence of pituitary homogenates or LH. Without gonadotropins or pituitary homogenates GVBD was absent both in control and GnRH-treated.

In addition, it has been reported (Hubbard and Licht, 1985) in *R. pipiens* and *R. catesbeiana* oocytes *in vitro* that the level of progesterone did not change when GnRH was added into the culture medium. Since progesterone is one of the most effective steroids that stimulates oocyte maturation in *R. perezi* and *D. pictus* (Alonso Bedate et al., 1971; Alonso Bedate et al., 1974) we can conclude that progesterone in our experimental conditions was not enhanced by GnRH at least in enough amount for triggering maturation in these species. The discrepant response to GnRH in rats and frogs is not surprising and support the hypothesis that the endocrine regulation of maturation and ovulation in these animals could be accomplished by different ways.

In contrast with the results obtained on maturation, an increased level of estradiol was observed when GnRH was present in the incubation medium of *D. pictus* ovaries. A change in estradiol level has also been suggested by Zerani et al. (1987) when GnRH and pituitary extract were present in the incubation medium of *Rana esculenta* oocytes *in vitro* as compared to those with pituitary extract only. Ovarian fragments superfused by GnRH alone did not alter the secretion of androgens, estradiol and progesterone. Hubbard and Licht (1985) also obtained negative results by using GnRH alone as stimulator for altered

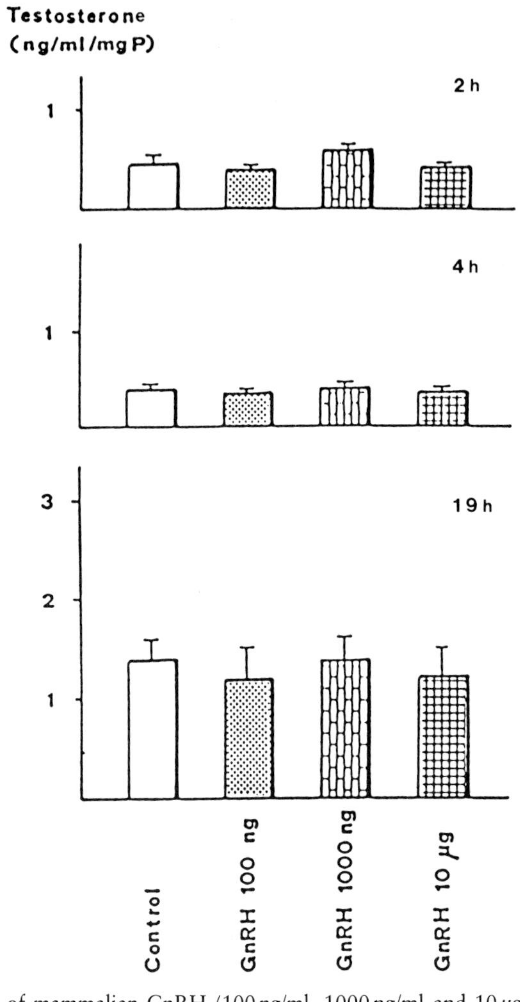

Fig. 5: *In vitro* effect of mammalian GnRH (100 ng/ml, 1000 ng/ml and 10 μg/ml) on testosterone levels in the incubation medium of *Rana perezi* testis (July) after 2 h, 4 h, 19 h. Data are expressed as mean ± SEM. No statistical differences were observed.

steroid secretion from ovaries *in vitro*. There was also no effect on LH-stimulated *in vitro* steroid secretion (or oocyte maturation in ovaries).

Much more studies are necessary to understand the potential physiological role of GnRH on steroidogenesis and oogenesis in amphibian females. It is possible that as in rat some local factors like GnRH are indispensable to modulate oocyte growth or follicular atresia during the seasonal cycle.

Seasonal testicular cycles of spermatogenesis and steroidogenesis have been studied in our laboratory in *R. perezi* (Delgado et al., 1989). Testis weight did not change significantly through the year and this was not a good parameter for testing testicular function in *R. perezi*. On the contrary significant differences in plasma testosterone were evident among seasons. Our previous reports reveal a single annual peak in plasma testosterone at the end of the winter or early spring depending on the year followed by a rapid fall in the early summer. During the summer the levels of testosterone are the lowest.

Rana perezi has a potentially continuous testis cycle. During the year, seminiferous tubules have all types of germinal cells from gonias to spermatozoa. Spermatogenesis begins in summer and continues through the autumn to the final formation of spermatozoa. In winter, the number of spermatogenetic cysts decrease except for spermatids and spermatozoa which will be released during the breeding season in the spring time.

Our present studies were performed to know the effect of GnRH on steroidogenesis in *R. perezi* testes. Two hours after the addition of GnRH, testosterone concentration increased in the incubation medium of testes taken from the autumn and winter frogs but did not change in the medium from testes taken from spring and summer frogs. There is a clear correlation between the levels of testosterone during the testicular cycle and the effect of GnRH on testis in *R. perezi*. These results are partially in accordance with those obtained by Pierantoni et al. (1984 a, 1984 b). They also observed testosterone stimulation in testes homogenates taken from males in winter and not in homogenates of testes taken from males in summer, but they only were able to evaluate changes in the incubation medium 6 hours after incubation. The differences between their and our results might probably be explained by using different GnRH and different media (Dulbecco's modified Eagles mediums instead of Krebs-Ringer bicarbonate buffer etc.)

Fasano et al. (1988) measured testicular GnRH in *R. esculenta* and found that irGnRH reached high levels in autumn and winter. There was a clear correlation between these levels and the wave of spermatogenesis. It seems interesting that it was also in winter when GnRH increased production of androgens by the testes in *R. esculenta* (Pierantoni et al., 1984 b).

In contrast with the high levels of GnRH and GnRH analogs needed to obtain an stimulatory effect on steroidogenesis or spermatogenesis in *R. esculenta* the amount of irGnRH measured in the testes was very low. It is possible that GnRH and GnRH analogs are poorly ligands compared to endogenous factors (Fasano et al., 1988).

An endogenous circanual rhythm regulating testicular functions in *R. esculenta* can exist as suggested by Pierantoni et al. (1984 a, b). They also put forward for consideration the possibility that there may be cyclic changes in testicular responsiveness to GnRH-like substances in the frog.

Much more experiments using different experimental conditions have to be done to clarify the mechanisms and the potential physiological role of GnRH-like peptides in anuran amphibians.

Summary

The effect of synthetic mammalian gonadotropin-releasing hormone (GnRH) has been studied in ovaries and testes in the amphibians *Rana perezi* and *Discoglossus pictus in vitro*. GnRH alone (1 μg/ml) did not stimulate the germinal vesicle breakdown (GVBD) or maturation and did not modify the percentage of GVBD obtained by progesterone treatment (10 μg/ml and 20 μg/ml) in *R. perezi* and *D. pictus*. On the contrary, GnRH stimulated estradiol secretion by the *D. pictus* ovaries *in vitro*. On the other hand, in *R. perezi*, testosterone release in culture medium where fragments of testes from autumn and winter frogs have been incubated was stimulated by GnRH. No effect was detectable in testes from spring and summer frogs. These results suggest that mammalian GnRH directly stimulates steroidogenesis in *R. perezi* and *D. pictus*.

References

Aberdan, E., Dekel, N. (1985): Activators of protein kinase C stimulate meiotic maturation of rat oocyte. Biochem. Biophys. Res. Commun. *132*, 570–574.

Alonso-Bedate, M., Fraile, A., Lopez Gordo, J. L., Calle, C. (1971): Action of progesterone on maturation and ovulation of *Discoglossus pictus* oocytes: Results obtained in vivo and in vitro. Acta Embryol. Exp. *3*, 177–186.

Alonso-Bedate, M., Lopez Gordo, J. L., Calle, C. (1974): Control endocrino de la maduración del ovocito de *Rana perezi*. Bol. R. Soc. Esp. Hist. Nat. *70*, 3–9.

Aten, R. F., Poland, M. L., Bayless, R., Behrman, H. R. (1987): A gonadotropin-releasing hormone (GnRH)-like protein in human ovaries: Similarity to the GnRH-like ovarian protein of the rat. J. Clin. Endocrinol. Metab. *64*, 1288–1293.

Corbin, A., Bex, F. J. (1981): Luteinizing hormone releasing hormone agonists induce ovulation in hypophysectomized proestrous rat: direct ovarian effect. Life Sci. *29*, 185–192.

Chieffi, G., Pierantoni, R. (1987): Regulation of ovarian steroidogenesis. In: Hormones and reproduction in fishes, amphibians and reptiles (D. O. Norris, R. E. Jones, eds.) pp. 117–144. Plenum Press, New York.

Dalkin, A. C., Bourne, G. A., Pieper, D. R., Regiani, S., Marshall, J. C. (1981): Pituitary and gonadal gonadotropin releasing hormone receptors during sexual maturation in the rat. Endocrinology, *108*, 1658–1664.

Delgado, M. J., Gutierrez, P., Alonso-Bedate, M. (1989): Seasonal cycles in testicular activity in the frog *Rana perezi*. Gen. Comp. Endocrinol. *73*, 1–11.

Dekel, W., Sherizly, I., Phillips, D. M., Nimrod, A., Zilberstein, M., Naor, Z. (1985): Characterization of the maturational changes induced by a GnRH analogue in the rat ovarian follicle. J. Reprod. Fert. *75*, 461–466.

Dekel, N., Sherizly, I., Tsafriri, A., Naor, Z. (1983): A comparative study of the mechanism of action of luteinizing hormone and gonadotropin releasing hormone analog on the ovary. Biol. Reprod. *28*, 161–166.

Di Matteo, L., Minucci, S., Fasano, S., Pierantoni, R., Varriale, B., Chieffi, G. (1988): A gonadotropin-releasing hormone (GnRH) antagonist decreases androgen production and spermatogonial multiplication in frog (*Rana esculenta*): Indirect evidence for the existence of GnRH or GnRH-like material receptors in the hypophysis and testis. Endocrinology. *122*, 62–67.

Eckholm, C., Hillensjö, T., Isaksson, O. (1981): Gonadotropin releasing hormone agonists stimulate oocyte meiosis and ovulation in hypophysectomized rats. Endocrinology. *108*, 2022–2024.

Erickson, G. F., Hofeditz, C., Hsueh, A. J. W. (1983): GnRH stimulates meiotic maturation in preantral follicles of hypophysectomized rats. In: Factors Regulating Ovarian Function. (G. S. Greenwald, P. F. Terranova, eds.) pp. 257–261. Raven Press, New York.

Fasano, S., Minucci, S., Pierantoni, R., Fasolo, A., Di Matteo, L., Basile, C., Varriale, B., Chieffi, G. (1988): Hypothalamus-hypophysis and testicular GnRH control of gonadal activity in the frog, *Rana esculenta*: seasonal GnRH profile and annual variations of in vitro androgen output by pituitary-stimulated testes. Gen. Comp. Endocrinol. *70*, 31–40.

Gore-Langton, R., Armstrong, D. T. (1988): Follicular steroidogenesis and its control. In: The Physiology of Reproduction. (E. Nobil, J. Neill, eds.) pp. 331–385. Raven Press, New York.

Hammond, J. M. (1981): Peptide regulators in the ovarian follicle. Aust. J. Biol. Sci. *34*, 491–504.

Hedger, M. P., Robertson, U. M., Browne, C. A., Krester, D. M. (1985): The isolation and measurement of luteinizing hormone-releasing hormone (LHRH) from the rat testis. Mol. Cell. Endocrinol. *42*, 163–170.

Hertelendy, F., Lintner, F., Asem, E. K., Raab, B. (1982): Synergistic effect of gonadotropin releasing hormone on LH-stimulated progesterone production in granulosa cells of the domestic fowl (*Gallus domesticus*). Gen. Comp. Endocrinol. *48*, 117–122.

Hillensjö, T., Le Maire, W. J. (1980): Gonadotropin releasing hormone agonists stimulate meiotic maturation of follicle-enclosed rat oocytes in vitro. Nature. London. *287*, 145–146.

Hsueh, A. J. W., Adashi, E. Y., Jones, P. B. C., Welsh, T. H. (1984): Hormonal regulation of the differentiation of cultured granulosa cells. Endocr. Rev. *5*, 76–127.

Hsueh, A. J. W., Jones, P. B. C. (1981): Extrapituitary actions of gonadotropin releasing hormone. Endocr. Rev. *2*, 437–461.

Hubbard, G. M., Licht, P. (1985): In vitro study of the direct ovarian effect of gonadotropin-releasing hormone (GnRH) in the frogs, *Rana pipiens* and *Rana catesbeiana*. Gen. Comp. Endocrinol. *60*, 154–165.

Licht, P., Porter, D. (1987): Role of gonadotropin-releasing hormone in regulation of gonadotropin secretion from amphibian and reptilian pituitaries. In: Hormone and Reproduction in Fishes Amphibians and Reptiles. (D. O. Norris, R. E. Jones, eds.) pp. 68–85. Plenum Press, New York.

Lowry, O. H., Rosebrough, N. J., Farr, A. L., Randall, R. J. (1951): Protein measurement with the Folin phenol reagent. J. Biol. Chem. *193*, 265–275.

Maller, J. L. (1985): Oocyte maturation in Amphibians. In: Development Biology. A comprehensive synthesis. (L. W. Brawder, ed.). Vol. I, pp. 289–311. Plenum Press. New York.

Minucci, S., Di Matteo, L., Pierantoni, R., Varriale, B., Rastogi, R., Chieffi, G. (1986): In vivo and in vitro stimulatory effect of a Gonadotropin-releasing hormone analog (HOE 766) on spermatogonial multiplication in the frog, *Rana esculenta*. Endocrinology. *119*, 731–736.

Naor, Z., Zilberstein, M., Zakut, H., Lindner, H. R., Dekel, N. (1983): Dissociation between the direct stimulatory and inhibitory effect of gonadotropin releasing hormone analog on ovarian function. Moll. Cell, Endocr. *31*, 261–270.

Pierantoni, R., Fasano, S., Di Mateo, L., Minucci, S., Varriale, B., Chieffi, G. (1984a): Stimulatory effect of a GnRH agonist (Buserelin) in in vitro and in vivo testosterone production by the frog (*Rana esculenta*) testis. Moll. Cell. Endocr. *38*, 215–219.

Pierantoni, R., Iela, L., d'Istria, M., Fasano, S., Rastogi, R. K., Delrio, G. (1984b): Seasonal testosterone profile and testicular responsiveness to pituitary factors and gonadotropin releasing hormone during two different phases of the sexual cycle of the frog (*Rana esculenta*). J. Endocrinol. *102*, 387–392.

Reichert, L. E., Andersen, T. T., Branca, A. A., Fletcher, P. W., Sluss, P. M. (1984): FSH binding inhibitors of follicular fluid. In: Gonadal Proteins and Peptides and their Biological Significance. (M. R. Sairam, L. E. Atkinson, eds.) pp. 153–160. World Scientific Publishing Co., Singapore.

Schuetz, A. W. (1985): Local controls mechanisms during oogenesis and folliculogenesis. In: Developmental Biology: A comprehensive synthesis. Vol. 1, Oogenesis. (L. W. Browder, ed.) pp. 3–83. Plenum Press, New York.

Segal, S. J., Adejuwon, C. A. (1979): Direct effect of LHRH on Leydig cell steroidogenesis in *Rana pipiens*. Biol. Bull. *157*, 393–394.

Sharpe, R. M., Cooper, I. (1982): Stimulatory effect of LHRH and its agonist on Leydig cell steroidogenesis in vitro. Mol. Cell. Endocrinol. *26*, 141–150.

Sharpe, R. M., Dogan, D. G., Cooper, I. (1983): Factors determining whether the direct effects of an LHRH agonist on Leydig cell function in vivo are stimulatory or inhibitory. Mol. Cell. Endocrinol. *32*, 57–71.

Sharpe, R. M., Fraser, H. M., Cooper, I., Rommerts, F. F. G. (1981): Sertoli cell-Leydig cell communication via an LHRH like factor. Nature. *290*, 785–787.

Shukmei-Ho (1987): Endocrinology of vitellogenesis. In: Hormones and Reproduction in Fishes, Amphibians, and Reptiles. (D. O. Norris, R. E. Jones, eds.) pp. 145–169. Plenum Press, New York.

Tsafriri, A. (1988): Local nonsteroidal Regulators of Ovarian Function. In: The Physiology of Reproduction. (E. Knobil, J. Neill et al., eds.) pp. 227–265. Raven Press, New York.

Tsafriri, A., Channing, C. P., Pomeranz, S. H., Lidner, H. R. (1977): Inhibition of maturation of isolated rat oocytes by porcine follicular fluid. J. Endocrinol. *75*, 285–291.

Tsafriri, A., Pomerantz, S. M. (1986): Oocyte maturation inhibitor. Clin. Endocrinol. Metab. *15*, 157–170.

Wallace, R. A. (1985): Vitellogenesis and oocyte growth in mammalian vertebrates. In: Development biology. A comprehensive synthesis. (Brawder, L. W., ed.) Vol. I. pp. 127–177. Plenum Press, New York.

Ward, D. N., Glen, S. D., Lin, W. K., Gordon, W. L. (1983): Chemistry and Physiology of gonadal peptides. In: Factors Regulating Ovarian Functions. (G. S. Greenwald, P. F. Terranova, eds.) pp. 141–156. Raven Press, New York.

Zerani, M., Gobbetti, A., Carnevali, O., Polzonetti-Magni, A., Botte, V. (1987): In vivo and in vitro study of direct ovarian effects of gonadotropin releasing hormone (GnRH) in the frog, *Rana esculenta*. Gen. Comp. Endocrinol. 66, 8–9.

Fortschritte der Zoologie, Band/Vol. 38 · Hanke, W. (Hrsg.), Biology and Physiology of Amphibians
Gustav Fischer Verlag · Stuttgart · New York · 1990

Differential histochemical demonstration of Ca^{2+}-ATPase and Mg^{2+}-ATPase in the frog testis during an annual cycle

S. G. Haider, D. Passia[1]

Department of Anatomy II, University of Düsseldorf, D-4000 Düsseldorf 1, FRG

1. Introduction

There are only few reports on the histochemical demonstration of testicular enzymes in the frog (van Oordt and Brands, 1970; Lofts, 1974; Jülich et al., 1982; Haider and Passia, 1981, 1985). These studies show that the changes in the pattern of enzymatic distribution depend upon the phases of the annual reproductive cycle. Jülich et al. (1982) and Haider and Passia (1985) provided a detailed description of the enzymatic changes in frog Sertoli cells. The aim of the present report is to study the histochemical behaviour of Ca^{2+}-ATPase and Mg^{2+}-ATPase in the testis of the frog *Rana temporaria* during an annual cycle.

2. Material and methods

Seven male frogs of the species *Rana temporaria* (body weight: 35–45 g) were caught in the third week of each month by an animal supplier and were transported immediately to the University Animal House. The frogs were killed by decapitation and destruction of the spinal cord. The testes were removed and rapidly frozen in liquid nitrogen and further processed for enzyme histochemical reactions. The following enzymes were demonstrated in 8–10 μm thick cryostat sections:

1. Mg^{2+}-ATPase (according to the method of Meijer and Vloedman, 1980). The incubation medium contained 0.83 mM ATP (disodium salt), 0.2 M Tris maleate buffer pH 7.2, 1 mM 2,4-dinitrophenol, 0.06 M Pb $(NO_3)_2$, 0.04 M $MgSO_4$, 1 mM levamisole. Incubation lasted for 25 minutes at 37 °C.
2. Ca^{2+}-ATPase (according to the method of Padykula and Herman, 1955 a, b). The incubation medium contained 0.83 mM ATP (disodium salt), 0.1 M sodium barbiturate buffer, 0.0025 M L-(+)-cysteine. Incubation was for 2 hours at 37 °C at pH 9.4.

Alternate sections were counterstained with hematoxylin.

3. Seasonal changes of the enzyme activity of the testis tissue

Table 1 shows the distribution of various phases of the annual reproductive cycle in the testis of the frogs, studied here.

---

[1] Dedicated to Prof. H. G. Goslar on the occasion of his 70th birthday.

Table 1: Phases of reproductive cycle

month		phase	GSI*
1	mid-Sept. till mid-Feb.	hibernation	0,8
2	end-Feb. till end March	spawn + spermiation	0,3
3	April	involution	0,2
4	May-June	germinal cyst	0,4
5	July-Aug.	maturation	1,1

* GSI = gonadosomatic index = $\frac{100x\ (wt\ of\ one\ testis)}{body\ wt}$ mean of n = 7 per month

3.1. Ca^{2+}-ATPase-activity

The enzymatic reaction is localized in the walls of interstitial blood capillaries, in the myoid cells of the lamina propria, in the follicular cells of the germinal cyst, and in the cytoplasm of the Sertoli cells (Fig. 1).

A strong reaction was present in the cytoplasm of Sertoli cells during hibernation; the activity became moderate at the time of sperm release. An increased activity was found in the cytoplasm of follicle cells during proliferation (March to May). After a short period of decreased activity in July, the activity increased during the maturation phase (Aug.).

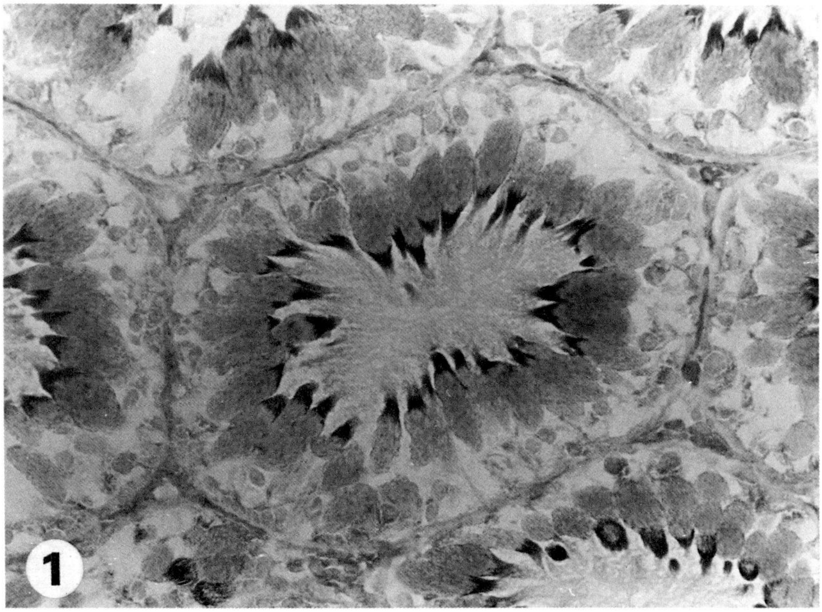

Fig. 1: Histochemical demonstration of Ca^{2+}-ATPase in the testis of the frog. October.
The reaction is localized in the walls of the interstitial blood capillaries, in the myoid cells of the lamina propria and in the apical portions of the Sertoli cells bearing the bundles of spermatozoa. × 220

3.2. Mg^{2+}-ATPase activity

The enzymatic reaction can be demonstrated histochemically mainly in the mid piece and flagellum of the matured spermatozoa (Fig. 2). The maximum reaction was observed during hibernation. The matured spermatozoa were arranged in the form of bundles in the lumen of the seminiferous tubules (Fig. 3).

4. Discussion

In order to achieve a specific histochemical reaction for Ca^{2+}-ATPase and Mg^{2+}-ATPase separately, it is necessary to perform various pretests to find out the optimal prefixation of the cryostat sections, substrate concentration, pH of the incubation medium and the inhibition of interfering enzymes, e.g. alkaline phosphatases. Both reactions should also be carried out along with various controls. Another important condition is to use consecutive tissue sections for both of the reactions and the corresponding controls. The fullfillment of these conditions allows a clear comparison of the pattern of Ca^{2+}-ATPase with that of Mg^{2+}-ATPase.

Ca^{2+}-ATPase, demonstrated according to the method of Padykula and Herman (1955 a, b), shows mainly the reaction of myosin ATPase, which is required for the contractility of filaments. The weak activity in follicle cells in the month of February increases to a moderate degree in the month of August during maturation phase. As the germ cells within the cyst multiply and the number of follicle cells remains constant it can be assumed that the follicle cells possess contractile elements which allow the expansion of the cyst size, caused by probably the multiplication of the spermatogonia and spermatocytes. These contractile elements of follicle cells show the Ca^{2+}-ATPase, as reported here. The enzymatic activity increases in the month of August, when the process of spermatogenesis is at its peak; this activity, which is required for the energy-dependent metabolic process, exhibits the nutritive function of the follicle cells. In August the Sertoli cells, arising from the follicle cells and attaching with the lamina propria, show an increased activity of Ca^{2+}-ATPase. In the hibernation period, when the Sertoli cells perform nutritive, supportive and contractile functions for the sperm the Sertoli cell cytoplasm shows a maximum reaction. Lofts (1974) pointed out that the contractility of Sertoli cell is of immense importance for the nutrition and spermiation of the spermatozoa.

The Mg^{2+}-ATPase, demonstrated according to the method of Meijer and Vloedman (1980), involves mainly the mitochondrial ATPase and provides information on the capacity of energy production. The histochemical reaction for this enzyme was observed chiefly in the midpiece and the flagellum of the matured spermatozoa. The reaction is probably localized in the mitochondria of the sperm. The enzyme is required for the motility of the sperm in order to accomplish the process of spermiation at the end of February. As the consecutive cryostat sections, processed for the demonstration of Ca^{2+}-ATPase, showed no reaction in the midpiece and flagellum of the sperm, it can be concluded that the methods employed here for the differential histochemical reactions for Ca^{2+}-ATPase and Mg^{2+}-ATPase are specific.

Acknowledgements

The authors wish to express their thanks to Ms. G. Berthold for her expert technical assistance in the laboratory.

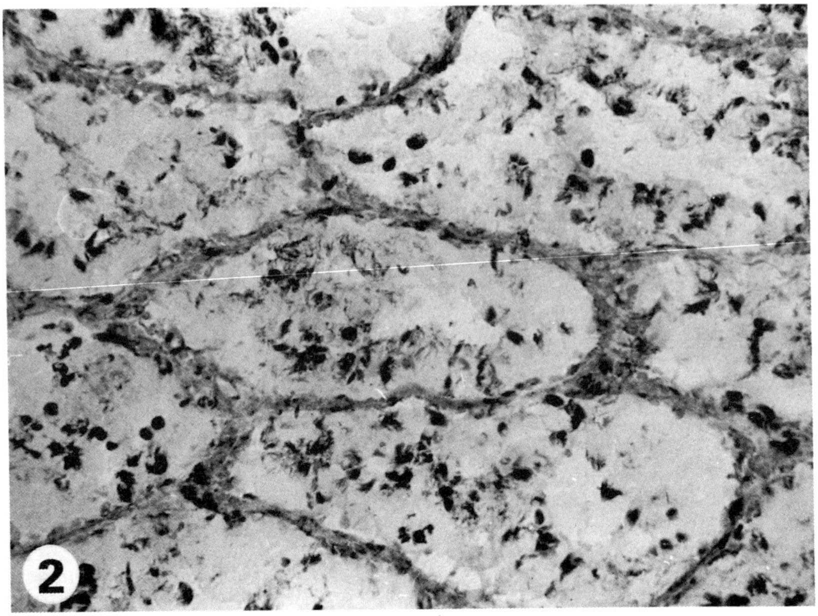

Fig. 2: Histochemical reaction of Mg^{2+}-ATPase in the testis of the frog. October.
The reaction is localized in the lamina propria and mainly in the bundles of spermatozoa. × 130

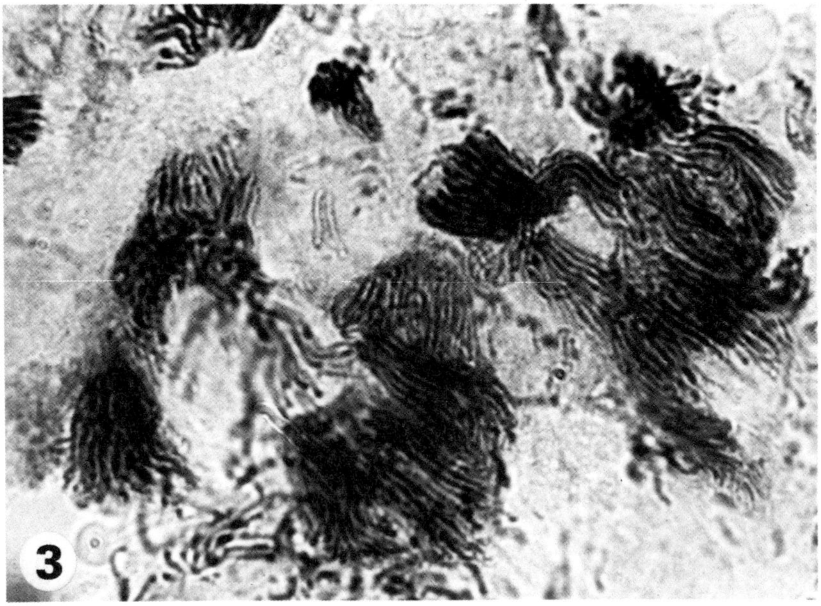

Fig. 3: A magnification of a portion of Fig. 2. The reaction is localized in the midpiece and flagellum of spermatozoa. × 1300

References

Haider, S. G., Passia, D. (1981): Enzymhistochemical localization of alkaline phosphatases in germinal cysts of the testis of the frog *Rana temporaria* (Anura). Acta Zool. *62*, 215–218.

Haider, S. G., Passia, D. (1985): Seasonal changes in the activity of phosphatases in Sertoli cells in the frog *Rana temporaria*. Acta histochem. Suppl. XXXI, 145– 149.

Jülich, G., Haider, S. G., Passia, D., Goslar, H. G. (1982): Jahreszeitliche Veränderungen der Adenosintriphosphatase-Aktivität in den Germinalcysten des Testis vom Grasfrosch *Rana temporaria*. Eine enzymhistochemische Studie. Acta histochem. *71*, 191–200.

Lofts, B. (1974): Reproduction. In: Physiology of Amphibia. Vol. 2 (B. Lofts, ed.) Academic Press, New York.

Meijer, A. E. F. H., Vloedman, A. H. T. (1980): The histochemical characterization of the coupling state of skeletal muscle mitochondria. Histochemistry *69*, 217–232.

van Oordt, P. G. W. J., Brands, F. (1970): The Sertoli cells in the testis of the common frog *Rana temporaria*. J. Endocrinol. *48*, 1 (Abstract).

Padykula, H., Herman, E. (1955 a): Factors affecting the activity of adenosine triphosphatase and other phosphatases as measured by histochemical techniques. J. Histochem. Cytochem. *3*, 161–169.

Padykula, H., Herman, E. (1955 b): The specificity of the histochemical method for adenosine triphosphatase. J. Histochem. Cytochem. *3*, 176–195.

II. Metamorphosis

Fortschritte der Zoologie, Band/Vol. 38 · Hanke, W. (Hrsg.), Biology and Physiology of Amphibians
Gustav Fischer Verlag · Stuttgart · New York · 1990

Regulation of metamorphosis

PER ROSENKILDE[1] and ANNE PHAFF USSING[1&2]

[1] Zoophysiological Laboratory A, August Krogh Institute, University of Copenhagen, DK-2100 Copenhagen.
[2] Immunological Laboratory, Statens Seruminstitut, DK-2300 Copenhagen, Denmark.

1. Introduction

Amphibian metamorphosis is a natural fairy-tale, especially in the typical anuran form: The beast changes before your eyes (into another beast). The tail disappears, legs appear. The rounded body becomes broad-backed, profiled, the eyes bulge out from the head, and the skin changes from soft and smudging into a strong slough. The previous gill-breathing larva gets lungs and leaves the water.

Urodeles and a number of anuran species lack some of these features. On the other hand metamorphosis comprises so many more changes than those that meet the naked eye that even a less complete transformation is a complex of many series of changes taking place simultaneously in a very well-defined pattern.

Many, local as well as comprehensive regulating systems, are involved in the correct progress of metamorphic change.

The thyroid axis gives a beautiful demonstration of the common pattern of ontogenic organization in vertebrates. It has been studied through long periods with the techniques available and has become the best understood part of the many systems involved in the regulation of amphibian ontogenesis (and maybe in vertebrate ontogenesis as a whole). There is a natural tendency in each period, to concentrate upon the knowledge that can be added to the existing by newly adopted techniques. However, in a regulating system acting on several levels and with an intricate network of interrelations, it is strikingly necessary to involve also older methods, e.g. to supplement chemical analyses of cellular receptors or small amounts of hormones in free solution with classical structural analysis. It may actually turn out that the most informative and dynamic picture arises from these older studies.

2. The thyroid axis

2.1. The Pituitary and hypothalamic level

Pehlemann's (1974) meticulous analysis, at the electron microscope level, of structural development of the thyroid system in *Xenopus* larvae, is a good illustration of the above statement. He identified secretory granules in the thyrotropic cells and described stages in their morphology corresponding to hormone synthesis and secretion. He further showed that the distribution of functional stages in the secretory granules reflected the development of synthetic and secretory capacity in the thyrotropic cells.

The basophilic TSH-cells could be identified from the premetamorphic stage 47 (Nieuwkoop & Faber, 1956). In these early stages, the secretory granules were predominantly of the smallest type, 140 nm in diameter. During the whole metamorphosis, these small rounded granules were found near to the Golgi zone and apparently represented hormone granules newly formed in the ribosomes and Golgi region. The small granules presumably merge to form larger granules as a part of maturation for secretion.

Fig. 1 shows the size of TSH granules through metamorphosis. To assist analysis of the course of events, plasma thyroxine concentrations in stages 54–66 have been included in Fig. 1a as a further parameter of TSH and thyroid hormone secretion. Thyroxine is the hormone molecule secreted by the thyroid, and even though there is some change in the rate of excretion, primarily due to an increased hormone retention in the organism in midclimax (Buscaglia et al., 1985), the hormone concentration gives a fair picture of thyroid secretion rate for the present purpose.

The period from stage 47 to 54 is apparently a storage phase. The accumulation continues even after the increase in thyroid secretion rate is initiated, with a practically undisturbed rate of increase even in the mean granule diameter, i.e. increase in number of large granules. However, in the peripheral part of the cytoplasm where the granules are stored in the final phase before exocytosis, there is a distinct fall in granule diameter immediately preceding the thyroxine increase.

The release of granules from the storage zone probably corresponds to a gradual increase in thyroxine secretion beginning around stage 55. Larvae under goitrogen treatment will not pass st. 55 (Goos, 1968). Although the morphological changes are less than striking, this is the period of limb growth and differentiation, and the adult type skin begins to take over. Further, key processes in the hypothalamus must take place during this period (see below).

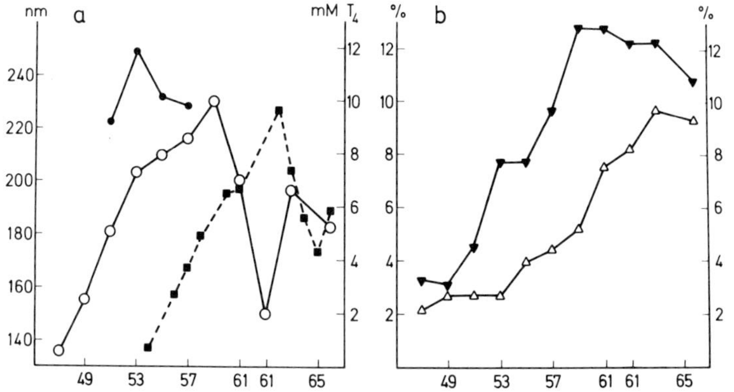

Fig. 1: Activity in the pituitary TSH cells during metamorphosis in Xenopus laevis. Material from Pehlemann (1974). Abscissa: Nieuwkoop and Faber stages. a) Mean diameter (nm) of secretion granules.
○: In the cytoplasm as a whole. ●: In the peripheral storage zone. ■: Plasma thyroxine concentrations, nM (same as in Fig. 2).
b) Amount of secretion granules per unit of cell cytoplasm.
△: Number of granules/area of cytoplasm.
▼: Area covered by granules/area of cytoplasm.

The steep decrease in the number of large granules, beginning after st. 59 and motivating a subdivision of st. 61, is not reflected in a changed rate of increase in circulating thyroxine. The number of secretory granules continues to increase at such a rate that the area covered by granules remains constant, signifying that synthesis equals secretion, up to st. 63. Thereafter, TSH activity seems to decrease slightly, perhaps a reaction to decreased excretion rate of thyroid hormone.

The major morphological changes are approaching their end at st. 63, but intense differentiation goes on till the end of metamorphosis (st. 66).

The abrupt activity increase in the TSH cells is best explained by a hypothalamic stimulation. By analogy with higher vertebrates, the tripeptide TRH (Pyr-His-Pro-NH_2) would be the probable mediator. The demonstration of this has met difficulties, aggravated by the presence of the tripeptide in many parts of the nervous system and in the skin, and, sometimes in high concentrations, in circulation. For a long period, the general opinion was that TRH in the sense of the mammalian tripeptide was not a TSH releaser in amphibians (For a survey of negative results, see, e.g.: Jackson, 1979).

It was not doubted that a hypothalamic stimulation must exist, on background of the hormonal secretory pattern in metamorphic climax. Further, it had been shown early by Etkin and Sussman (1961) that metamorphosis in *Ambystoma maculatum* was blocked by hypothalamic transection and prevention of nerve regeneration by a plastic membrane.

However, an effect on metamorphosis was shown by Shiomi et al. (1972) with the use of high doses of the tripeptide, and effect in adult amphibians was demonstrated with reasonable amounts of TRH by Darras and Kühn (1982), and Rosenkilde (1979).

Etkin and Kim (1971) measured metamorphic change in vitro: In a preparation containing pituitary, thyroid, and a tail fragment, TRH addition caused shrinking of the latter.

Further, TRH appears in the brain of *Xenopus* larvae at the right time. Balls et al. (1985) found an increase from 90 pg/brain in NF stage 51/52, over 990 pg/brain in st. 56/57 to 25 ng in st. 65. The latter is of the same size of order as the amount found in adult *Xenopus*, 39 ng. This increase may reflect that TRH mediates the activation of the thyroid axis, but it may also reflect the general maturation of the brain in the metamorphic period.

There may be several reasons to the scarceness of successful attempts to demonstrate TSH-releasing effects of TRH. The primary reason is probably that the effect of TRH is short-lived, and most of the techniques that were used in attempts to demonstrate TRH-effects measured delayed changes, such as thyroidal iodine uptake, or metamorphic change in vivo. Contributing to this is the fact that the tripeptide was extremely expensive at the time when the interest to demonstrate effects (especially on metamorphosis) was highest. The positive results have generally been obtained with acute effects as increased thyroid hormone secretion rate, measured as I-125 release from the thyroid (Rosenkilde 1979) or as increase of circulating hormone (Darras and Kühn 1982; Jacobs et al. 1988 a).

In vitro technique has recently been used by Denver (1988) who got positive results with pituitaries of adult *Rana pipiens*, *Hyla regilla*, and *Xenopus laevis*, and with TRH concentrations comparable to those effective in mammals.

The disappointments with TRH led to search for other hypothalamic factors with TSH-releasing properties. Among the known releasing hormones, some had already been shown to have effect on more than one pars distalis hormone in mammals. Such a TSH-releasing activity has recently been demonstrated also in amphibians. Jacobs et al. (1988 b) found that synthetic LHRH can increase the level of thyroid hormone in three *Rana* species, and that the effect is absent in hypophysectomized frogs. Denver (1988) in the above-cited study showed that synthetic LHRH and ovine CRH both stimulate pituitaries in vitro to secrete TSH, and that the activity in this preparation is CRH > TRH > LHRH. (See also: Gracia-Navarro et al., this volume.)

2.2. The thyroid level

The activity of the thyroid gland has been studied with classical as well as modern methods. The classical structural analysis shows generally a strong increase up to climax, reaching a level not found in any other life stage. (See, e.g., Coleman et al. 1968). The thyroid epithelium increases in mass, the cell height increases, and ultrastructural analysis reveals that the increase is due to increased amounts of synthetic organelles: Golgi apparatus and rough endoplasmic reticulum. The follicular colloid which is stored prohormone, thyroglobulin, increases to maximal amounts in prometamorphosis, and decreases in climax at the end of metamorphosis leaving the follicles flat, collapsed, demonstrating the termination of a period of heavy synthetic and secretory activity.

2.3. The thyroid hormone in blood

Measurements of thyroid hormone in blood depict almost the same situation. A number of published analyses are illustrated graphically in Fig. 2 and 3. It is seen that neither methodological differences nor species variation have led to striking differences. Fig. 2 shows that blood content of thyroxine (T_4) is low, with most methods actually undemonstrable until some time in prometamorphosis. The concentration cannot be zero, since effects of endogenous hormone can be demonstrated in these early stages (see below). The picture of activity increase in the three series of determinations in *Rana catesbeiana* shows variation between the populations or groups both with respect to stage when the increase begins and to the level achieved. As the stages are defined by morphological criteria, the increases can be characterized as coming just before, coincident with, or after the breakthrough of forelimbs, at stages when the processes with a large element of growth are far advanced, and in the beginning of the phase with extensive reallocation. One difference between the series may be of a more qualitative nature than the others. Mondou and Kaltenbach (1979) report that they always found some values below detection level (d.l.) even in the climax stages with the remarkably high mean values. In contrast, the two other series had only values below d.l. outside the climax stages and rather modest variation between the values within the respective climax stages (cf. urodeles, below).

The T_4 increase in *X. laevis* apparently begins at an earlier stage than in *R. catesbeiana*. However, a comparison between the anatomical development of distantly related anurans can of course only be approximate but it may be noted that the increase in both species comes at the stage when the forelegs break through.

To the above may be added that the hormone determination in *X. laevis* has been extended by Buscaglia et al. (1985) with measurements in three other *Xenopus* species. The most remarkable difference with respect to T_4 may be the duration of the hormone maxima. They are narrow and high in *X. clivii* and *X. borealis* (T_4 appr. 11nM in NF st. 60–61), while *X. muelleri* and *X. laevis* show more extended duration of activity (T_4 appr. 8 nM, duration as in Fig. 2a).

Fig. 2b compares the T_3 concentrations in *R. catesbeiana* and *X. laevis*. The increase seems slightly delayed compared to that of T_4, and the concentration is lower, although T_3 may still carry the larger part of the hormonal activity, owing to its more efficient receptor binding. The T_3 is primarily of extrathyroidal origin, as the T_3 in the thyroid secretion is low or negligible (Suzuki and Suzuki, 1981; Rosenkilde, 1978, and unpubl.) The concentrations in the above-mentioned four *Xenopus* species show durations of the maximal T_3 activity which compare to the T_4 maxima, but the maximal concentrations show remarkably little consistency with the T_4 concentrations. They are, respectively, appr. 3 nM in *X. clivii*, 5–6 nM in *X. borealis*, and 7 nM in *X. muelleri* and *X. laevis*.

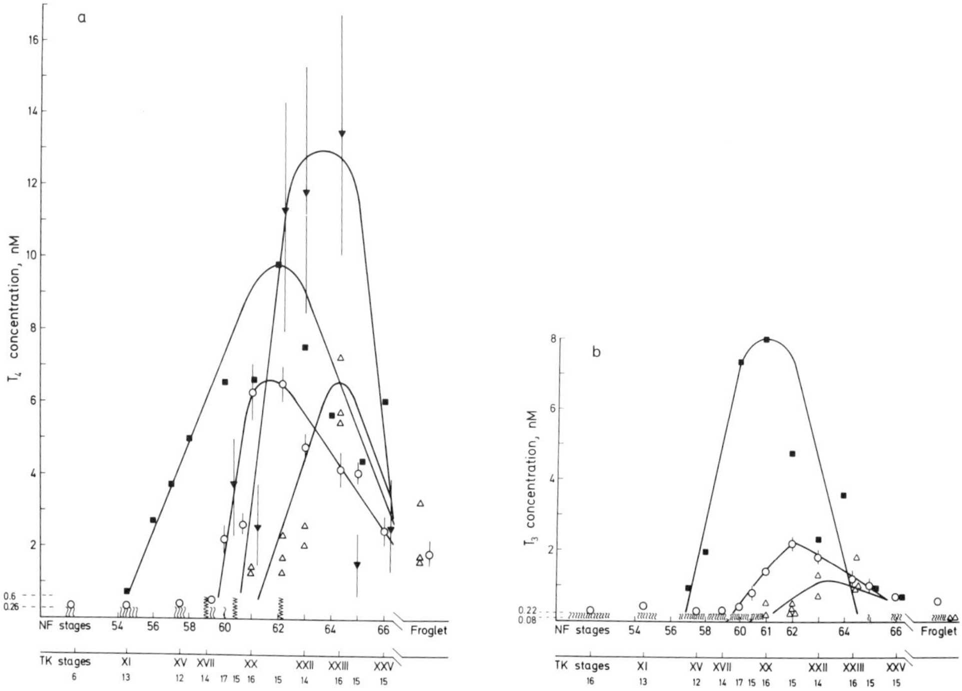

Fig. 2: Thyroid hormone concentrations in metamorphosing anurans (nM). Concentrations below detection level (d.l.) are shown by signatures ranging from zero to d.l. a) T_4. ○: *Rana catesbeiana* (Suzuki and Suzuki, 1981, d.l. 0.26 nM). Mean values +/− s.e. Number of determinations at the base of the figure. △: *R. catesbeiana* (Regard et al., 1978, d.l 0.6 nM). ▼: *R. catesbeiana* (Mondou and Kaltenbach, 1979, d.l. 2.6 nM). Concentrations below d.l. were found in all stages, including climax stages. They are not given separately, but included in s.e. as zero values. Up to Taylor-Kollros st. XVIII, all samples were below d.l. ■: *X. laevis* (Leloup and Buscaglia, 1977, d.l. not given).
b) T_3. ○: *R. catesbeiana* (Suzuki and Suzuki, 1981, d.l. 0.23 nM). △: *R. catesbeiana* (Regard et al., 1978, d.l. 0.08 nM). ■: *X. laevis* (Leloup and Buscaglia, 1977, d.l. not given).
The lines are loosely hand-fitted and only meant to help the eye follow the trend in the point series, not to mark a specific course.

Fig. 3a and b show thyroid hormone concentrations during metamorphosis in two urodele species. They are strikingly different from the general anuran picture. Both species have concentrations below detection level in all stages, but they also have climax values that are exceptionally high.

There is no sense in defining mean values. The picture points to rocket-like bursts of T_4-secretion. Some of the T_4 is deiodinated to T_3 (Fig. 3b). (The thyroid in axolotls produces only negligible amounts of T_3, Rosenkilde, unpubl.)

Following a secretory burst circulating T_4 appears to fall to almost complete depletion, before a new burst occurs. The distribution of T_3 values in Fig. 3b suggests that when concentrations of circulating T_4 are low, most is converted to T_3 rather than excreted. Thus, even though the concentration of circulating T_4 varies widely in metamorphosing urodeles and includes periods with very low titers, the metamorphic processes will only need to run unstimulated (or slow down) for shorter periods.

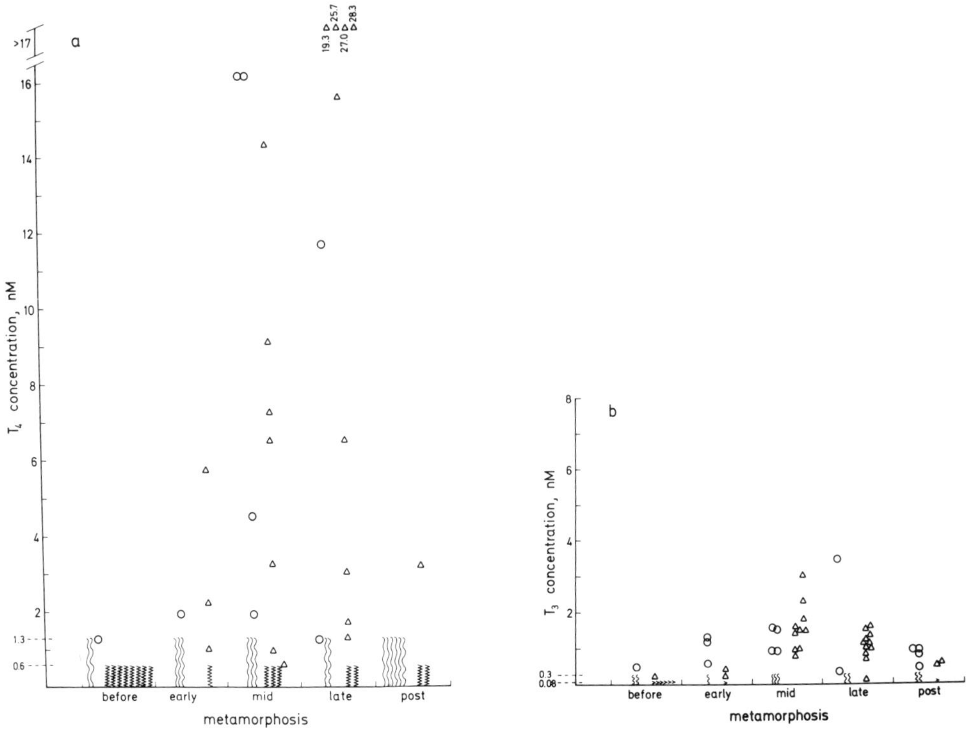

Fig. 3: Thyroid hormone concentrations in metamorphosing urodeles. a) T_4. ○: *Eurycea bislineata* (Alberch et al., 1986, d.l. 1.3 nM). △: *Ambystoma tigrinum* (Larras-Regard 1981, d.l. 0.64 nM). b) T_3. ○: *E. bislineata* (Alberch et al., 1986, d.l. 0.26 nM). △: *A. tigrinum* (Larras-Regard et al., 1981, d.l. 0.08 nM).

Even though this picture deviates from the typical anuran pattern (based on measurements in *Xenopus* species and *R. catesbeiana*), it may find some resemblance in the *R. catesbeiana* measured by Mondou and Kaltenbach (1979). It is striking that this series differs from the other anuran series by both concentrations below detection level, and extremely high values.

2.4. Hormone effects on cells

It is established but perhaps not always recognized that not only must adequate amounts of hormone be secreted, the tissues must be responsive to thyroid hormone. They must of course possess receptors to the hormone, as well as the cellular apparatus to promote the message received with the hormone signal. How this is brought about is poorly understood. In general terms it could be said that the cell must be mature to perform the proper reaction to the message. The maturation is often brought about by (a.o.?) low concentrations of thyroid hormone itself. A notable example of this is the maturation and activation of the hypothalamic TRH-producing cells. The attention was first drawn to this fact by Goos (1968, 1969, Goos et al., 1968 a and b) demonstration of cellular differentiation in pars magnocellularis of the nucleus preopticus in *Xenopus* larvae. The cells that Goos saw may not have been TRH cells, but other neurons, possibly leading to the neurohypophysis, but this actually underlines the importance of the observation, since it emphasizes that the development of the TRH cells is part of a general structural and functional maturation of the brain.

Another demonstration of the importance of the cell's inherent potential is the fact that one hormone in the same body induces changes as varied as 1) disappearance in some tissues, 2) growth and differentiation in other tissues, and 3) changes in synthetic potential in again other tissues. The background to such varied reactions in cells with the same genes must lie in the ontogenetic history of the tissue in question, the influence from the surrounding cells and from the part of ovoplasm where the cells of that tissue originated.

Until now, the nature of the secreted and circulating thyroid hormone has only been mentioned vaguely. However, it has been amply demonstrated that of the two molecular forms, triiodothyronine is by far more potent than thyroxine. Measured by their affinity to the hormone receptors, T_3 binds 10–20 times as avidly as T_4, and this difference is inversely reflected in the amounts necessary to elicit given effects in short-time experiments. Induction of metamorphosis in axolotls by immersion in hormone solutions has shown that the two molecules are about equally efficient in long-term experiments, but that metamorphic change induced by T_4 occurs 3–4 days later than with T_3 (Prahlad and DeLanney, 1965).

This can be explained by a T_4-induced maturation of the capacity to deiodinate T_4 to T_3. Such a maturation was induced in premetamorphic bullfrog larvae by T_4 treatment (Galton et al., 1982).

2.5. Summary of knowledge and problems concerning the development of the thyroid axis and amphibian metamorphosis

Larval development takes place with concentrations of thyroid hormone which possibly increase in the course of development but continues to be low compared with climactic values (but possibly not very low compared to adult values!). Some parts of larval development are independent of thyroid hormone, as seen by the development of thyroidectomized larvae, while these comparatively low hormone concentrations are vital for the development of other features. The latter include central steps in the development of the thyroid axis itself: The TRH producing cells, the T_4->T_3 enzyme system, cellular receptors. Prometamorphosis and climax are set moving by a strong increase in TSH and TH secretory activity, possibly as (a) burst(s).

3. Prolactin

Prolactin undoubtedly has a role in metamorphosis, but there is doubt as to what the role can be. There is a large experimental experience of growth-promoting and metamorphosis-inhibiting actions in amphibian larvae (see, e.g. Dodd an Dodd, 1976; White and Nicoll, 1981; Rosenkilde, 1985b).

The classical hypothetical model for the role of prolactin in metamorphosis (see: Etkin, 1968) fitted well with this experience and the classical knowledge of the control of prolactin secretion. Prolactin seems in contrast to the other pars distalis hormones to be primarily controlled by an inhibition from the hypothalamus.

The metamorphosis-inhibiting action is an antagonism between prolactin and thyroid hormone, and it changes with time. In vitro experiments (incorporation of labelled proline in thigh bone of *R. catesbeiana* larvae, Yamaguchi and Yasumasu, 1977) showed that prolactin promotes growth and delays and prevents metamorphic change only up to climax or with low doses of thyroid hormone present, while there were no visible effect with high thyroxine concentration in the medium or with tissues from midclimax (TK st. XXII) larvae. It would thus be logical to have a high prolactin activity in premetamorphosis, and a decrease towards climax.

However, as determination with radioimmunoassay became possible, it was found, first with reluctance (Clemons & Nicoll, 1977), but later confirmed beyond denial (Yamamoto and Kikuyama, 1982b) that PRL increases from indeterminable values in prometamorphosis to high concentrations in late climax (Fig. 4a).

In view of Yamaguchi and Yasumasu's results it might be expected that prolactin has lost its metamorphosis-delaying effect in the stages where the high amounts are secreted. However, Yamamoto and Kikuyama (1982a) found that injection of prolactin antiserum to *R. catesbeiana* larvae immersed in thyroxine accelerated tail shrinking. Contrary to general experience, the prolactin increase in metamorphosis is caused by a hypothalamic stimulation (Kawamura et al., 1986). Bullfrog larvae in TK st. XVI–XVIII, thyroidectomized and treated with thyroxine, had increased plasma prolactin in st. XXIV, while those not treated with thyroxine had no increase. Further, larvae with the pituitary grafted, or the stalk transected in early climax, would complete morphological metamorphosis, but without increase in prolactin concentration. The hypothalamic stimulation thus seems to rely upon maturation processes which require thyroid hormone. The releaser(s) could be one or more of the known hypothalamic factors. Vasoactive intestinal peptide (VIP), and peptide histidine isoleucine (PHI) stimulate prolactin synthesis and release from bullfrog pituitaries in vitro (Koiwai et al., 1986). TRH can elicit TSH release from isolated bullfrog pituitary, but maybe not synthesis (Seki and Kikuyama, 1986), but the prolactin increase in vivo comes at a stage that makes TRH less obvious.

The above-mentioned prolactin effect on tail shrinking in the bullfrog points to a role for prolactin in metamorphic climax, but it is not known whether the animal's survival and fitness is influenced by a moderation of metamorphic progress. It is still possible that the prolactin surge is a mere reflection of hectic maturation activity in hypothalamus.

4. Corticoid hormones

Adrenocortical hormones are also involved in metamorphosis, and their roles, too, are unclarified.

Corticoids might be active in the regulation of carbohydrates and proteins in the anabolic and catabolic processes in metamorphosis. They cause blood sugar increase in *Xenopus* larvae, but it is doubtful whether they are gluconeogenetic (see: Hanke, 1974, for discussion).

The increase in corticoid level might be secondary to stress effects of metamorphosis. A similar reaction is seen in other situations of natural stress in vertebrates, e.g. salmonid fishes (Pickering and Pottinger, 1987).

The corticoid activity might contribute to the promotion of metamorphic change. Amphibian larvae close to metamorphosis are prone to undergo premature metamorphosis if they are subjected to adverse conditions, such as hunger (D'Angelo et al., 1941) or handling (Rosenkilde, 1985a). A similar effect was induced in *Rana pipiens* tail fins by Kaltenbach (1958) with glucocorticoid enrichment of subthreshold thyroxine implants.

Yet another role for corticoid hormones might lie in their suppressing effect on the immune system. In mammals, glucocorticoids impair the function of macrophages by stabilizing their membranes and inhibiting antigen modification and presentation. In amphibians, effect has been seen in adult *Xenopus laevis*, where hydrocortisone injection impaired the sheep red blood cell response (see: Ruben et al. 1985). The increased corticoid level in spawning fish is followed by immune suppression (Pickering and Pottinger, 1987). Immune suppression seems to occur in metamorphosis (see below), but it is not known whether the corticoid hormones are involved.

The above-mentioned effects refer to glucocorticoids, but also aldosterone has metamorphosis-promoting effect synergistically with thyroid hormone. It increases nuclear binding of T_3 (Niki et al., 1981), and causes increased shrinking of tail segments of toad and bullfrog (Kikuyama et al., 1983a, b). Also, T_4 potentiates ACTH stimulated release of aldosterone (Jaffe, 1981; Kikuyama et al., 1986).

Plasma concentrations of cortisol, corticosterone, and aldosterone have been determined with radioimmunoassay in *R. catesbeiana* in a number of laboratories (Fig. 4b), with somewhat different results. Krug et al. (1983) suggest that part of the differences between the results may be caused by different methods of sampling and determination, but they do not go further in the discussion, and they do not give the information necessary to an evaluation. Kikuyama et al. (1986) state that their blood samples were taken between 1300 and 1600 in the afternoon. Krug et al. (1983) do not mention sampling

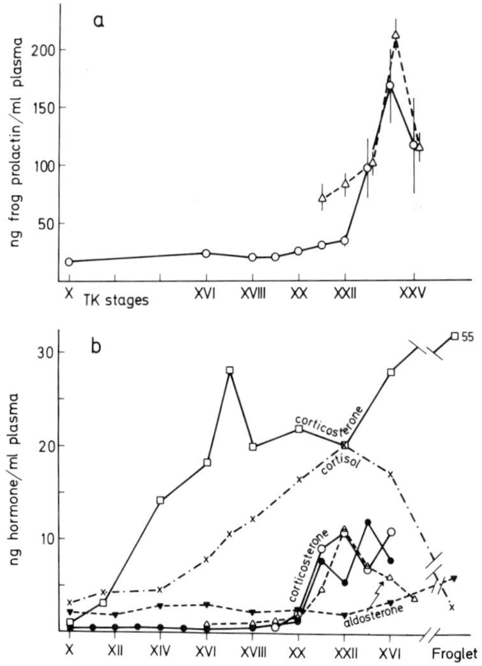

Fig. 4: Circulating prolactin and corticosteroids in metamorphosing R. catesbeiana. a) Prolactin. △: Material from Clemons and Nicoll (1977). ○: Material from Yamamoto and Kikuyama (1982).
b) Corticosteroids. Material from ▼: Krug et al. (1983); d.l. aldosterone 19 pg/ml plasma).
□ corticosterone 39 pg/ml plasma
X cortisol 39 pg/ml plasma
○● }: Jaffe (1981); corticosterone, d.l. 0.3 ng/ml plasma)
△: Kikuyama et al. (1986); aldosterone, d.l. 20 pg/ml)

times for their larvae, but the adults (one point in the figures) were taken in the morning. Jaffe (1981) do not state sampling time. Sampling stress is hardly probable as sampling seems to have been done quickly in all experiments. Kikuyama et al. (1986) state that the animals had gone for six days in the laboratory before sampling. In the other experiments, the larvae had gone for some time in the laboratory after purchase, and had been fed.

The corticosterone and the aldosterone in Jaffe's and Kikuyama et al's determination series, respectively, both increased after TK stage XX, i.e. at a time when the thyroid level was high and able to influence their release.

It is not easy to explain the increase in the early stages of Krug et al.'s larvae, but the general level may be another illustration of the experience from thyroid hormone concentrations: That there is an enormous potential for variation between populations or groups of the same species. The increase in corticosterone and aldosterone after stage XXII may correspond to the increase found in corticosterone and aldosterone by the other authors.

The cortisol concentrations have no other determinations to be compared with. Hopefully they will appear. Its presence in metamorphosing larvae is the more interesting as cortisol is seldom found in appreciable concentrations in amphibians. The authors mention cross-reaction in the immunoassay which opens the possibility of confusion with other (rare) corticoids.

5. Development of the immune system

The development of the immune system is closely linked with other larval development and metamorphosis.

The larvae are immunocompetent, able to resist invasion by microorganisms, in accordance with their free-living existence. The antibody repertoire is less heterogenous in the larvae than in postmetamorphic animals (DuPasquier et al., 1979). This correlates with the organization of the immune system, in that the cell-mediated branch of the immune system is the more developed in this period. Natural killer cells (not of lymphocyte origin) are presumably important in the defence of the organism against foreign antigens in the larval period (Reynolds and Ortaldo, 1987). In the metamorphosed animal, cytotoxic lymphocytes will take over part of this role.

The humoral branch of the immune system goes through a rapid development, which begins in early prometamorphosis and is completed in late climax or shortly after the end of the climax period (Flajnik et al., 1987).

In metamorphosis, a high number of new antigenic compounds appear, structural proteins, enzymes etc., and a somewhat lower, but still high number of larval antigens disappear. In this period, antigens of larval and adult type will be present in the animal simultaneously. The antigen change is correlated with changes in the immune system.

Lymphocytes of larval type are tolerant to larval antigens, but both disappear in the course of metamorphosis. The adult type lymphocytes become tolerant to the new antigens but not to the larval ones. The mechanism of tolerization is not clarified but requires co-existence of antigen and the responsive elements of the immune system for a certain period. The larval antigens are probably not present together with the new lymphocytes long enough for them to become tolerized (Flajnik et al., 1986).

Cloned frogs, especially *Xenopus* (Kobel and DuPasquier, 1975) have proved very helpful in studies of histocompatibility. The clones are obtained e.g. by interspecies hybridization. Hybrid *Xenopus laevis* × *X. gilli* females produced some tetraploid oocytes which by meiosis generate diploid eggs containing the genome of both parents. By means of UV-irradiated sperm they can be induced to gynogenetic development, and such cloned animals should hence produce identical antigens. Grafts from adult to adult or from larva to larva of the same clone are accepted to a high degree. However, grafts exchanged between larvae and adults of the same clone are rejected.

An important link in the pattern of change seems to be an immune suppression which obviously does not affect the resistance to infections (antibody production in general is not depressed during metamorphosis) but may be essential to the co-existence during climax of larval and adult tissue.

The immune suppression which appears to be caused by suppression of the activity of thymus- derived cells (Cohen et al., 1985) has been elucidated by experiments with skin grafting. Grafts exchanged between animals are generally rejected (Host Versus Graft reaction). However, grafts to larvae during or shortly after metamorphosis turned out to be tolerated or have a much longer survival time, 20–80 days instead of 10–20 days (Bernardini et al., 1969; Chardonnens and DuPasquier, 1973).

Other authors have found tolerance to grafting during a period of metamorphosis, to the extent that rejection was less acute when grafting was done during this period. Most grafts were eventually rejected, but second set grafts persisted longer or were tolerized, when first grafting was performed during the «tolerance period» of metamorphosis (DiMarzo and Cohen, 1982).

If a suppression of the response to tissue antigens has a function, it might be sought in climax when larval and adult type antigens are present at the same time. It could be imagined that the larval immune system could damage the first cells carrying antigens of adult type. This would require that the immune reaction to the new antigens could run to completion before the cells of the larval immune system disappear. The duration of the rejection process is short compared to both suppression period and climax. A skin graft becomes vascularized in 2–3 days, and the vascularization is destroyed as a visible part of the rejection in 10–20 days. In *Xenopus*, the period from NF stage 58 when atrophy of larval tissues is first visible, to completion of metamorphosis, takes about two weeks at 20–25 °C.

This suggests that larval and adult tissues coexist long enough to need a suppression of reactions to tissue antigens.

References

Alberch, P., Gale, E. A., Larsen, P. R. (1986): Plasma T_4 and T_3 levels in naturally metamorphosing *Eurycea bislineata*. Gen. Comp. Endocrinol. *61*, 153–163.

Balls, M., Clothier, R. H., Rowles, J. M., Kiteley, N. A., Bennett, G. W. (1985): TRH distribution, levels and significance during the development of *Xenopus laevis*. In: Metamorphosis (M. Balls, M. Bownes, eds.) pp. 260–272. Clarendon Press, Oxford.

Bernardini, N., Chardonnens, X., Simon, D. (1969): Développement après la métamorphose de compétence immunologique envers les homogreffes cutanées chez *Xenopus laevis* (Daudin). C. R. Acad. Sci. Paris *269 D*, 1011–1014.

Buscaglia, M., Leloup, J., de Luze, A. (1985): The role and regulation of monodeiodination of thyroxine to 3,5,3'-triiodothyronine during amphibian metamorphosis. In: Metamorphosis (M. Balls, M. Bownes, eds.) pp. 273–293. Oxford, Clarendon Press.

Chardonnens, X., Du Pasquier, L. (1973): Induction of skin allograft tolerance during metamorphosis of the toad, *Xenopus laevis* (Daudin). Eur. J. Immunol. *3*, 569–573.

Clemons, G. K., Nicoll, C. S. (1977): Development and preliminary application of a homologous radioimmunoassay for bullfrog prolactin. Gen. Comp. Endocrinol. *32*, 531–535.

Cohen, N., DiMarzo, S., Rollins-Smith, L., Barlow, E., Vanderschmidt-Parsons, S. (1985): The ontogeny of allo-tolerance and self-tolerance in larval *Xenopus laevis*. In: Metamorphosis (M. Balls, M. Bownes, eds.) pp. 388–419. Clarendon Press, Oxford.

Coleman, R., Evennett, P. J., Dodd, J. M. (1968): Ultrastructural observations on the thyroid gland of *Xenopus laevis* Daudin throughout metamorphosis. Gen. Comp. Endocrinol. *10*, 34–46.

D'Angelo, S. A., Gordon, A. S., Charipper, H. A. (1941): The role of the thyroid and pituitary glands in the anomalous effect of inanition on amphibian metamorphosis. J. exp. Zool. *87*, 259–278.

Darras, V. M., Kühn, E. R. (1982): Increased plasma levels of thyroid hormones in a frog *Rana ridibunda* following intravenous administration of TRH. Gen. Comp. Endocrinol. *56*, 321–325.

Denver, R. J. (1988): Several hypothalamic peptides stimulate in vitro thyrotropin secretion by pituitaries of anuran amphibians. Gen. Comp. Endocrinol. *72*, 383–393.

DiMarzo, S. J., Cohen, N. (1982): Immunogenetic aspects of in vivo allotolerance induction during the ontogeny of *Xenopus laevis*. Immunogenetics *16*, 103–116.

Dodd, M. H. I., Dodd, J. M. (1976): The biology of metamorphosis. In: Physiology of the Amphibia, Vol. III (B. Lofts, ed.), 467–599. Academic Press, New York.

DuPasquier, L., Blomberg, B., Bernard, C. C. A. (1979): Ontogeny of immunity in amphibians: Changes in antibody repertoires and appearance of adult major histocompatibility antigens in *Xenopus*. Eur. J. Immunol. *9*, 900–906.

Etkin, W. (1968): Hormonal control of amphibian metamorphosis. In: Metamorphosis, A Problem in Developmental Biology (W. Etkin, L. I. Gilbert, eds.) pp. 313–348. Appleton-Century-Crofts, New York.

Etkin, W., Kim, Y. S. (1971): Effects of TRH on tadpole tissue. Amer. Zool. *11*, 654.

Etkin, W., Sussman, W. (1961): Hypothalamo-pituitary relations in metamorphosis of *Ambystoma*. Gen. Comp. Endocrinol. *1*, 70–79.

Flajnik, M. F., Kaufmann, J. F., Hsu, E., Manes, M., Parisot, R., DuPasquier, L. (1986): Major histocompatibility antigens are absent in immunologically competent *Xenopus* before metamorphosis. J. Immunol. *137*, 3891–3899.

Flajnik, M., Hsu, E., Kaufman, J. F., DuPasquier, L. (1987): Changes in the immune system during metamorphosis of *Xenopus*. Immunol. Today *8*, 58–64.

Galton, V. A., Cohen, J. S., Munck, K. (1982): T_4 5′-monodeiodinase: the acquisition and significance of this enzyme system in the developing *Rana catesbeiana* tadpole. In: Phylogenetic Aspects of Thyroid Hormones, S. Suzuki, ed., 75–90. Center Acad. Publ. Japan, Tokyo.

Goos, H. J. Th. (1968): Hypothalamic neurosecretion and metamorphosis in *Xenopus laevis*. III. The effect of an interruption of thyroid hormone synthesis. Z. Zellforsch. *92*, 585–587.

Goos, H. J. Th. (1969): Hypothalamic neurosecretion and metamorphosis in *Xenopus laevis*. IV. The effect of extirpation of the presumed TRF cells and of a subsequent PTU treatment. Z. Zellforsch. *97*, 449–458.

Goos, H. J. Th., deKnecht, A. M., de Vries, J. (1968a): Hypothalamic neurosecretion and metamorphosis in *Xenopus laevis*. I. The effect of propylthiouracil. Z. Zellforsch. *86*, 384–392.

Goos, H. J. Th., Zwanenbeek, H. C. M., van Oordt, P. G. W. J. (1968b): Hypothalamic neurosecretion and metamorphosis in *Xenopus laevis*. II. The effect of thyroxine following treatment with propylthiouracil. Arch. Anat. Histol. Embryol. *51*, 269–274.

Hanke, W. (1974): Die hormonale Regulation des Stoffwechsels bei Amphibien. Fortschritte der Zoologie *22*, Hefte 2/3, 431–455, Fischer, Stuttgart.

Jackson, I. M. D. (1979): The releasing factors of the hypothalamus. In: Hormones and Evolution (E. J. W. Barrington, ed.) pp. 723–790. Academic Press, London.

Jacobs, G. F. M., Michielsen, R. P. A., Kühn, E. R. (1988a): Thyroxine and triiodothyronine in plasma and thyroids of the neotenic and metamorphosed axolotl, *Ambystoma mexicanum*: Influence of TRH injections. Gen. Comp. Endocrinol. *70*, 145–151.

Jacobs, G. F. M., Goyvaerts, M. P., Vandorpe, G., Quaghebeur, A. M. L., Kühn, E. R. (1988b): Luteinizing hormone-releasing hormone as a potent stimulator of the thyroidal axis in ranid frogs. Gen. Comp. Endocrinol. *70*, 274–283.

Jaffe, R. C. (1981): Plasma concentration of corticosterone during *Rana catesbeiana* tadpole metamorphosis. Gen. Comp. Endocrinol. *44*, 314–318.

Kaltenbach, J. C. (1958): Direct steroid enhancement of induced metamorphosis in peripheral tissues. Anat. Rec. *131*, 569–570.

Kawamura, K., Yamamoto, K., Kikuyama, S. (1986): Effects of thyroid hormone, stalk section, and transplantation of the pituitary gland on plasma prolactin levels at metamorphic climax in *Rana catesbeiana*. Gen. Comp. Endocrinol. *64*, 129–135.
Kikuyama, S., Niki, K., Mayumi, M., Shibayama, R., Nishikawa, M., Shintake, N. (1983 a): Studies on corticoid action on the toad tadpole tail in vitro. Gen. Comp. Endocrinol. *52*, 395–399.
Kikuyama, S., Suzuki, M. R., Niki, K., Yoshizato, K. (1983 b): Thyroid hormone-adrenal corticoid interaction in the tadpole tail. In: Current Problems in Thyroid Research (N. Ui, K. Torizuka, S. Nagataki, K. Miyai, eds.) pp. 202–205. Amsterdam, Excerpta Medica.
Kikuyama, S., Suzuki, M. R., Iwamuro, S. (1986): Elevation of plasma aldosterone levels of tadpoles at metamorphic climax. Gen. Comp. Endocrinol. *63*, 186–190.
Kobel, H. R., DuPasquier, L. (1975): Production of large clones of histocompatible fully identical clawed toads (*Xenopus*). Immunogenetics *2*, 87–91.
Koiwai, K., Kikuyama, S., Seki, T., Yanaihara, N. (1986): In vitro effect of vasoactive intestinal polypeptide and peptide histidine isoleucine on prolactin secretion by the bullfrog pituitary gland. Gen. Comp. Endocrinol. *64*, 254–259.
Krug, E. C., Honn, K. V., Battista, J., Nicoll, C. S. (1983): Corticoids in serum of *Rana catesbeiana* during development and metamorphosis. Gen. Comp. Endocrinol. *52*, 232–241.
Larras-Regard, E., Taurog, A., Dorris, M. (1981): Plasma thyroxine and triiodothyronine levels in *Ambystoma tigrinum* at various stages of metamorphosis Gen. Comp. Endocrinol. *43*, 443–450.
Leloup, J., Buscaglia, M. (1977): La triiodothyronine, hormone de la métamorphose des amphibiens. C. R. Acad. Sci. *284 D*, 2261–2263.
Mondou, P. M., Kaltenbach, J. C. (1979): Thyroxine concentrations in blood serum and pericardial fluid of metamorphosing tadpoles and of adult frogs. Gen. Comp. Endocrinol. *39*, 343–349.
Nieuwkoop, P. D., Faber, J. (1956): Normal Table of *Xenopus laevis* Daudin. Amsterdam, North-Holland.
Niki, K., Yoshizato, K., Kikuyama, S. (1981): Augmentation of nuclear binding capacity for triiodothyronine by aldosterone in tadpole tail. Proc. Japan. Acad. Ser. B *57*, 271–275.
Pehlemann, F.-W. (1974): Funktionsmorphologie der Adenohypophyse von Anuren. Fortschritte der Zoologie *22*, Hefte 2/3, 204–227, Stuttgart, Fischer.
Pickering, A. D., Pottinger, T. G. (1987): Lymphocytopenia and interrenal activity during sexual maturation in the brown trout, *Salmo trutta* L. J. Fish Biol. *30*, 41–50.
Prahlad, K. V., DeLanney, L. E. (1965): A study of induced metamorphosis in the axolotl. J. Exp. Zool. *160*, 137–146.
Regard, E., Taurog, A., Nakashima, T. (1978): Plasma thyroxine and triiodothyronine levels in spontaneously metamorphosing *Rana catesbeiana* tadpoles and in adult anuran amphibia. Endocrinology *102*, 674–684.
Reynolds, C. W., Ortaldo, J. R. (1987): Natural killer activity: The definition of a function rather than a cell type. Immunology Today *8*, 6, 172–174.
Rosenkilde, P. (1978): Thyroid hormone synthesis in metamorphosing and adult *Xenopus laevis*. Gen. Comp. Endocrinol. *34*, abstr. 87.
Rosenkilde, P. (1979): The thyroid hormones in amphibia. In: Hormones and Evolution (E. J. W. Barrington, ed.) pp. 437–491. Academic Press, London.
Rosenkilde, P. (1985 a): The role of hormones in the regulation of amphibian metamorphosis. In: Metamorphosis (M. Balls, M. Bownes, eds.) pp. 221–259. Clarendon Press, Oxford.
Rosenkilde, P. (1985 b): Control of amphibian development. In: Current Trends in Comparative Endocrinology (B. Lofts, W. N. Holmes, eds.) pp. 547–550. Hong Kong University Press, Hong Kong.
Ruben, L. N., Clothier, R. H., Jones, S. E., Bonyhadi, M. L. (1985): The effects of metamorphosis on the regulation of humoral immunity in *Xenopus laevis*, the South African clawed toad. In: Metamorphosis (M. Balls, M. Bownes, eds.) pp. 360–387. Clarendon Press, Oxford.
Seki, T., Kikuyama, S. (1986): Effect of thyrotropin-releasing hormone and dopamine on the in vitro secretion of prolactin by the bullfrog pituitary gland. Gen. Comp. Endocrinol. *61*, 197–202.
Shiomi, K., Hachiya, T., Yoshimura, M., Miyazaki, T., Ochi, Y. (1972): Effect of synthetic TRH on tadpole metamorphosis. Folia Endocrinol. Jap. *48*, 632 (abstr.), 670–673.
Suzuki, S., Suzuki, M. (1981): Changes in thyroidal and plasma iodine compounds during and after metamorphosis of the bullfrog, *Rana catesbeiana*. Gen. Comp. Endocrinol. *45*, 74–81.

White, B. A., Nicoll, C. S. (1981): Hormonal control of amphibian metamorphosis. In: Metamorphosis, A Problem in Developmental Biology (L. I. Gilbert, E. Frieden, eds.) pp. 363–396. Plenum Press, New York.
Yamaguchi, K. Yasumasu, I. (1977): Hormones controlling collagen synthesis during metamorphosis in the thigh bone of the tadpole of *Rana catesbeiana*. Devel. Growth Differ. *19*, 149–159.
Yamamoto, K., Kikuyama, S. (1982a): Effect of prolactin antiserum on growth and resorption of tadpole tail. Endocrinol. Japon. *29*, 81–85.
Yamamoto, K., Kikuyama, S. (1982b): Radioimmunoassay of prolactin in plasma of bullfrog tadpoles. Endocrinol. Japon. *29*, 159–167.

Fortschritte der Zoologie, Band/Vol. 38 · Hanke, W. (Hrsg.), Biology and Physiology of Amphibians
Gustav Fischer Verlag · Stuttgart · New York · 1990

Interrenal function during the metamorphosis in anuran amphibia

JEANINE LELOUP-HATEY, MARINO BUSCAGLIA, GENEVIÈVE JOLIVET-JAUDET and JACQUES LELOUP

Laboratoire de Physiologie générale et comparée, Muséum National d'Histoire Naturelle et Unité d'Endocrinologie Comparée associée au CNRS 90,71 rue Cuvier, 75231 Paris Cedex 05, France

1. Introduction

The thyroid is essential to the amphibian metamorphosis. But other components from the neuro-endocrine system appear required to achieve a complete metamorphosis. Concerning the interrenal gland, the first interrenal cells can be identified in *Xenopus laevis* before the hindleg buds have appeared. A cell proliferation occurs during the premetamorphosis, which intensifies as the metamorphosis progresses. The cytological and cytochemical pictures, both show a peak in the interrenal cell activity during the climax of the metamorphosis (Rapola, 1962, Leist et al., 1969, Hsu et al., 1980).

These data suggest interrenal secretion could have an important function during the amphibian metamorphosis. In the present paper, we provide biochemical data, mainly in *Xenopus laevis*, supporting this interpretation.

2. Material and methods

Animals – Adults of *Xenopus laevis* Daudin were obtained from the Department of Biology of Geneva (Switzerland) and from «Service régional d'élevage d'amphibiens» (S.E.R.E.A., Argenton l'Eglise, France). They were maintained at 24 °C in aquaria (20 animals in 70 liters of tap water) and were fed every other days with chopped beef liver. Spawning was induced through injection of human chorionic gonadotropin in previously isolated males and females according to Oschsé's method (Nieuwkoop and Faber, 1975). The larvae were kept at 24 °C (100 animals in 70 liters of oxygenated spring water) and fed twice a day with nettle powder. All the animals were maintained under a 12 L:12 D photoperiod in autumn and winter and a natural photoperiod in spring and summer.

The developmental stages (St) of the tadpoles were determined according to Nieuwkoop and Faber (1975).

Treatments – Some prometamorphic tadpoles (St 57) received a steroid implant (20 to 50 μg), every 5 days. The implant was inserted under the forehead skin with ophthalmic forceps. Sham-implanted tadpoles underwent in the same handling.

The influence of the treatments on the tadpole development was followed daily. Kinetics of metamorphosis were obtained. Stages (X) (expressed in arbitrary units taking X = 1 for the St 57) were plotted in terms of the mean time (Y) necessary to reach the next stage. The sample regression of Y on X was tested by a variance analysis. The slope gave the metamorphosis rate. The regression data of the different experimental groups were compared by a covariance analysis.

Sampling – The blood was collected by direct heart puncture, using a heparinized tapered capillary tube for tadpoles. Samples from 6 to 10 tadpoles were pooled for each assay.

Tissues from forelegs, hindlegs, liver, tail, skin and intestine were taken from 8 to 14 tadpoles at different developmental stages.

Radioimmunoassays – Corticosteroid levels were determined in dichloromethane-extractable fractions of plasma or tissue homogenates as previously described (Jolivet-Jaudet et al., 1984 for aldosterone, Jolivet-Jaudet and Leloup-Hâtey, 1984a for corticosterone).

Plasma thyroxine and triiodothyronine were estimated according to Leloup and Buscaglia (1977).

3. Interrenal function during the metamorphosis of amphibia

In adult *Xenopus laevis* (Chan and Edwards, 1970), as in other adult amphibia (Sandor, 1972; Hanke, 1978), interrenal cells synthesize more corticosterone than aldosterone. In *Xenopus laevis* tadpoles, biosynthetic pathways of corticosteroidogenesis appear when the interrenal cells differentiate. Corticosterone, aldosterone, but no cortisol, were identified in the incubation medium of interrenal tissue from *Xenopus laevis* tadpole or adult (Jolivet-Jaudet and Leloup-Hâtey, 1984b).

3.1. Plasma levels of corticosteroids

Corticosterone and aldosterone were detected in *Xenopus laevis* plasma from stage 54 to adult. Important changes in their level were noticed during the metamorphosis (Jolivet-Jaudet and Leloup-Hâtey, 1984a) (Fig. 1).

The aldosterone plasma level showed a bimodal pattern. The first significant increase was observed during the prometamorphosis (St. 57–58), and was followed by a sharp significant decrease. A second peak occurred afterwards at the mid-climax (St. 62). Finally, the level reached up a value presenting no significant difference compared to the level in adult.

The corticosterone plasma level was at its lowest during the prometamorphosis (St 55 to 58). From the beginning of the climax (St 59 to 61), it was significantly higher. At the mid-climax (St 62–63), the level was sharply increased before being reduced, at the end of the metamorphosis, to its value of the beginning of climax.

Prominent peaks of aldosterone and corticosterone plasma levels around the mid-climax were synchronized with an increase in the synthetic activity (Jolivet-Jaudet, 1982) and a large proliferation of the interrenal cells (Rapola, 1962). In other species of anura such as *Rana catesbeiana* (Jaffe, 1981; Krug et al., 1983; Kikuyama et al., 1986) or *Bufo bufo* (Jolivet-Jaudet, 1982), and also in urodela such as *Ambystoma tigrina* (Carr and Norris, 1988), the maximal values of corticosteroid plasma levels were also reached at the mid-climax. However, before concluding to a true hypercorticism, the presence of a corticosteroid-binding system and its changes during the metamorphosis must be considered, as only the free fraction of the corticosteroid is postulated biologically active.

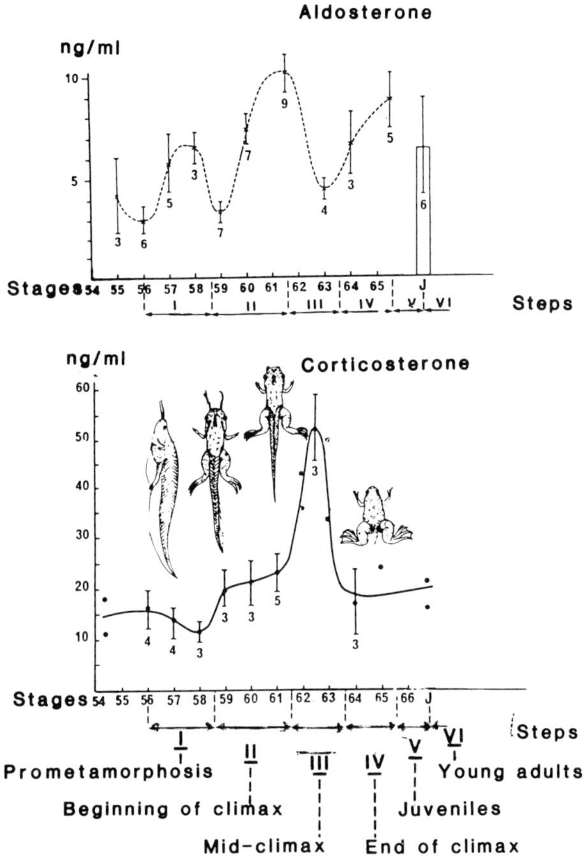

Fig. 1: Plasma levels in aldosterone and corticosterone during the metamorphosis of *Xenopus laevis*. Values are means ± S.E.M. The number of plasma pools at each stage is indicated.

3.2. Corticosteroid-binding proteins in plasma

In adult as in tadpole, a specific aldosterone-binding system was not present in *Xenopus laevis*, whereas a system is present for corticosterone (Jolivet-Jaudet and Leloup-Hâtey, 1986). The plot of equilibrium dialysis data according to Scatchard (Fig. 2) showed, in tadpole plasma, a single component of high affinity and low binding capacity, specific for the corticosterone (Table 1). In adult plasma, the presence of a two component binding system was found (Fig. 2). A first component with a high affinity and low capacity, a second with a low affinity and high capacity (Table 1). A polyacrylamide gel electrophoresis has shown that the migration of the high affinity protein was the same for all the studied stages (Fig. 3A), though different from the mammalian corticosteroid-binding globulin (Fig. 3B). The migration of the low affinity protein only found in adult was similar to that of bovine serum albumin.

The binding affinity (K_a) of the high affinity protein (1.8 to 4.10^8M) was similar to those of other adult amphibia (Martin and Ozon, 1975). No dependence on the developmental stage of *Xenopus laevis* was found (Table 1). The maximum binding capacity was

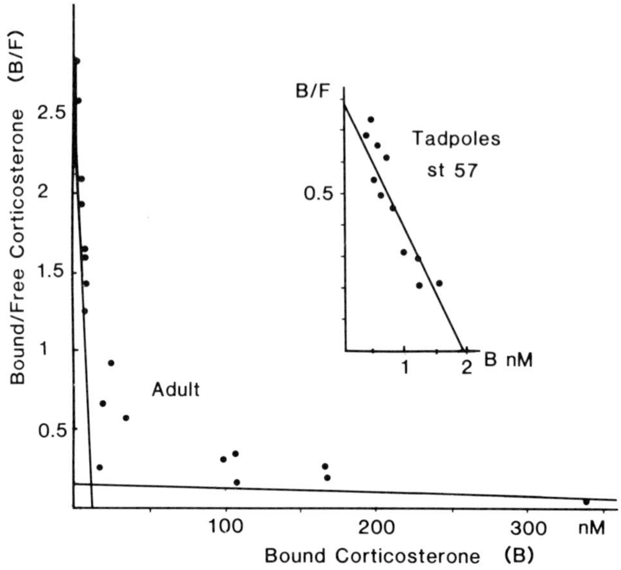

Fig. 2: Scatchard plot of the corticosterone binding to plasma proteins in adult and prometamorphic tadpoles of *Xenopus laevis*.

Equilibrium dialyses were performed on diluted plasma (adult: 1:20 and tadpole: 1:40 v/v) with (^{3}H'corticosterone (0,5 nM) and increasing amounts of corticosterone (0 to 72,4 μM). Dialyses were stopped after 20 hour incubation at 4 °C.

Table 1: Characteristics of corticosterone binding to plasma proteins of *Xenopus laevis* determined from Scatchard analysis of binding data in equilibrium dialysis at 4 °C.

		First component		Second component	
Stages	Plasma Proteins (mg·ml^{-1})	K_a ($10^8 M^{-1}$)	Maximum binding capacity nM	K_a ($10^5 M^{-1}$)	Maximum binding capacity μM
Prometamorphosis (Stage 57)	7.3 ± 1.2	3.2 ± 0.67	66.7 ± 16.8	ND	ND
Climax (Stage 63)	8.8 ± 0.6	1.8 & 2.4	73.3 & 76.6	ND	ND
Juveniles (2 months)	11.4 & 9.6	2.2	132.7	ND	Nd
Adults	46.9 ± 3.9* (8)	3.1 ± 0.35 (5)	173.0 ± 19.4* (5)	2.0 ± 0.28 (5)	18.3 ± 3.09 (5)

ND ⟶ No detectable

Proteins were estimated according to Bradford (1976)

Values are means ± S.E.M. In brackets, number of determinations

(*) $P < 0.05$ compared with tadpoles at St 57 or at St 57 + 63 (U test of Mann and Whitney)

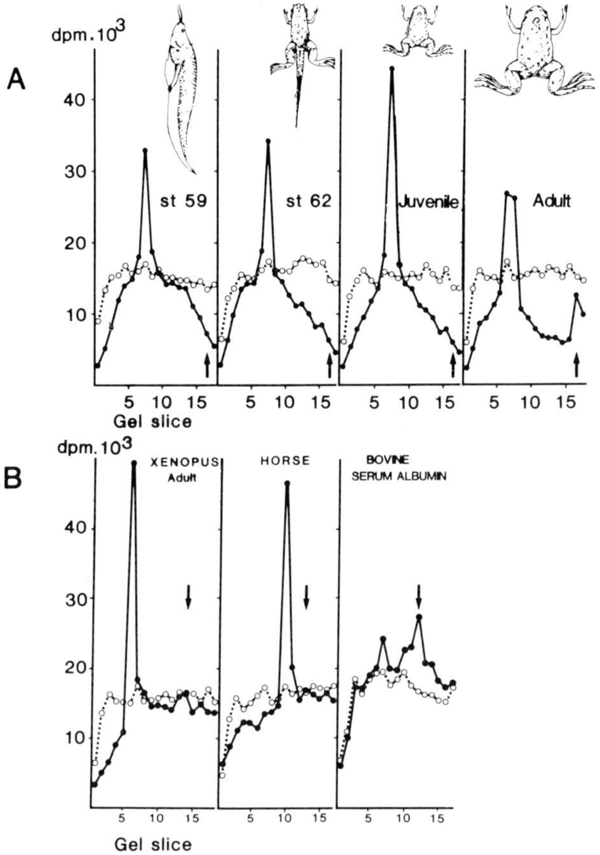

Fig. 3: Corticosterone-binding system studied by polyacrylamide gel electrophoresis in steady state conditions according to Ritzen et al. (1974). – A. Comparison of *Xenopus laevis* at 4 different stages. Plasma sample, 20 µl. Duration of the electrophoresis, 4 hours. – B. Comparison of adult *Xenopus laevis* plasma (10 µl, 940 µg proteins), horse serum (5 µl, 290 µg proteins) and bovine serum albumin 1750 µg). Duration of the electrophoresis 3 hours.

Tritiated corticosterone (0.78 nM) with (○– – –○) or without (●——●) excess cold corticosterone (0,78 µM) were incorporated in gel. The arrows indicated the front of migration of proteins. Four mm gel slices were incubated 4 hours in scintillation liquid before counting.

constant and always low in tadpoles; it increased in juveniles and in adults. The increase coincided with an increase in plasma proteins. The development of the low affinity protein was synchronous with the one of serum albumin and its K_a, about 10^5M, was characteristic for albumins.

As a consequence of the steady characteristics of the binding system during the metamorphosis, the free corticosterone (Table 2), which represented from 10 to 17 per 100 of total circulating corticosterone in prometamorphosis and at the beginning of climax, increased dramatically to 50 per 100 at the mid-climax, and came back to 13 per 100 at the end of climax.

Table 2: Concentrations of total and free corticosterone in the *Xenopus laevis* plasma.

Stages	Total corticosterone $ng.ml^{-1}$	Free corticosterone* $ng.ml^{-1}$	Per 100 of total corticosterone
Prometamorphosis (St 54 to 58)	14.2 ± 1.44 (11)	1.5	10.6
Beginning of the climax (St 59 to 61)	21.3 ± 1.80 (11)	3.6	16.9
Middle of the climax (St 62 and 63)	45.8 ± 3.96 (5)	23.1	50.4
End of the climax (St 64 and 65)	17.1 ± 3.11 (4)	2.25	13.1
Adults	4.6 ± 1.47 (4)	0.1	2.2

Values are means ± S.E.M. In brackets, number of determinations

* – Calculated according to Labrie (1967) and Dalle (1982) from equilibrium dialysis data (4 °C)

Thus, at the mid-climax, the binding sites were saturated by the important endogenous supply of the corticosterone. The free fraction was about 15 times higher than during the prometamorphosis and 230 times higher than in adult. The hypercorticism is of higher severity than it can be inferred from the 2 to 3 times increase in total circulating corticosteroids.

3.3. Corticosteroid levels in tissues

At the mid-climax, the increase in free circulating corticosteroids did not bring similar changes in all the different tissues (Leloup-Hâtey et al., 1988) (Fig. 4).

Corticosterone and aldosterone did not change significantly in hindlegs and forelegs, but increased significantly in liver, tail, intestine and skin. Highest levels observed in tissues at the mid-climax were maintained at least until the end of the metamorphosis, although the corticosteroid plasma concentrations were then falling down (Fig. 1). As the corticosteroid retention is a characteristic property of steroid target tissues in higher vertebrates (Jensen and Jacobson, 1962), tail, liver, skin and intestine could be consider as possible target tissues, especially when they undergo morphological and biochemical changes during the hypercorticism part of the metamorphosis.

4. Effects of corticosteroids during the metamorphosis of amphibia

4.1. Energetic metabolism

Aldosterone does not strongly act on carbohydrate, lipid and protein metabolisms and does not take part in the regulation of water exchanges in *Xenopus laevis* tadpoles (Hanke, 1978). ACTH, corticosterone or cortisol can stimulate the gluconeogenesis (Hanke and Leist, 1971), and increase the nitrogen plasma levels and the production of urea (Balinsky et al., 1967; Leist, 1970). They can also cause the tissue dehydration (Leist,

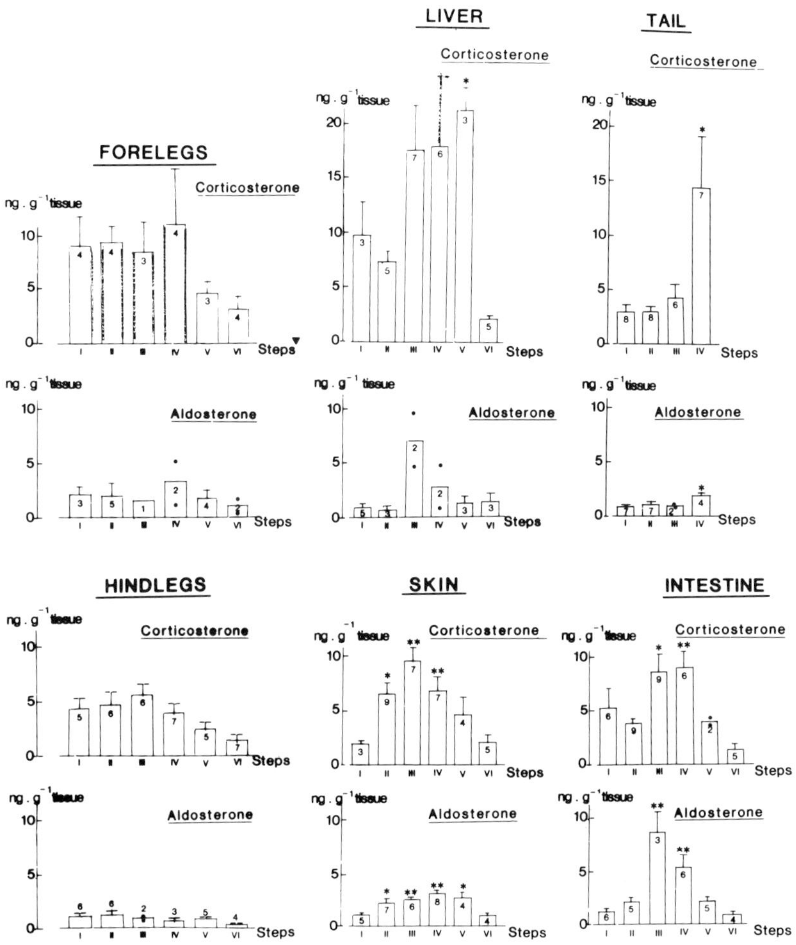

Fig. 4: Tissue levels in corticosterone and aldosterone in *Xenopus laevis* tadpoles at diverse developmental stages.

(I – Prometamorphosis, II – Beginning of the climax, III – Mid-climax, IV – End of the climax, V and VI – Juveniles 1 week and 2 months post metamorphosis. Vertical bars = S.E.M. Number of determinations is indicated in each column. $P < 0.05$ (*) or $P < 0.01$ (**) compared with developmental stages I and VI (U test of Mann and Whitney).

1970). These effects seem similar to those found in higher vertebrates (Dodd and Dodd, 1976; Hanke, 1978, Hourdry and Beaumont, 1985).

During the climax, the increase in interrenal activity could provide the energetic metabolites necessary to the achievement of the tissue rehandling from the stores of fasting tadpoles.

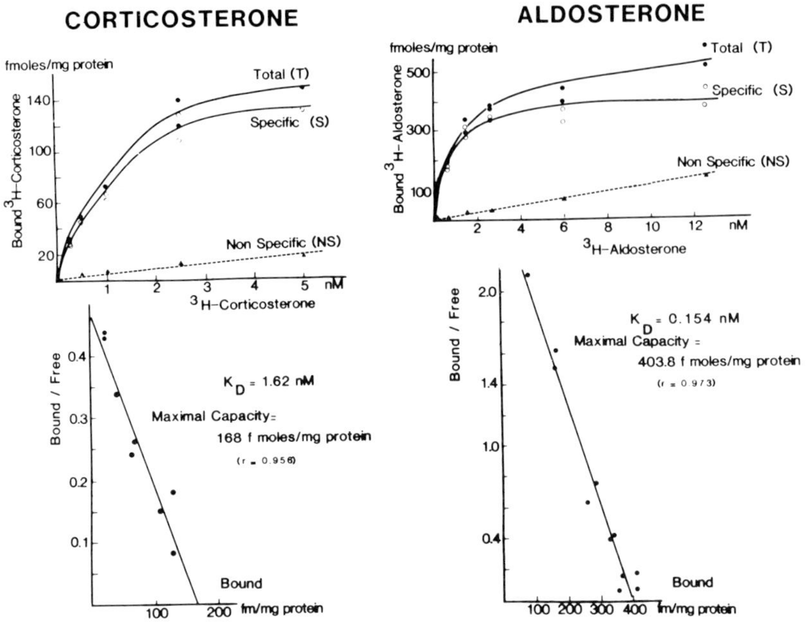

Fig. 5: Binding of (^{3}H)-corticosteroids by the skin cytosol of adult *Rana esculenta*. Steroid-free cytosol (charcoal-dextran T70 treatment) (150 μl) was incubated with (^{3}H)-corticosteroid (0.25 to 12 nM) in absence or in presence of an excess of stable corticosteroid (100 times) for 20 hours at 4 °C (final volume: 300 μl). Bound and free hormone fractions were separated by charcoal dextran T70 treatment and specific bindings (S) (○——○) calculated as the difference between total (T) (●——●) and non specific (NS) (▲- - -▲) bindings. *Upper part* – Representative saturation curve in the cytosol. *Lower part* – Scatchard analysis of specific binding.

4.2. Morphogenic changes

A complete metamorphosis was not obtained in thyroxine-treated hypophysectomized *Alytes obstetricans* tadpoles (Remy and Bounhiol, 1971) and in *Rana catesbeiana* tadpoles which interrenal secretion was inhibited by amphenone (Kikuyama et al., 1982). Without, either ACTH or corticosteroid treatment, which mimicked the spontaneous hypercorticism, the tail did not disappear totally at the mid-climax and the animal did not leave the water. The new cutaneous and intestinal mechanisms involved in the osmoregulation in terrestrial environment were probably not differentiated in absence of corticosteroids. On the other hand, in absence of thyroxine, the cortisol increased the hydrolase activities in intestinal explants of *Alytes obstetricans* tadpoles at the beginning of the climax (Pouyet and Hourdry, 1988). This increase is similar to the one observed *in vivo* during the climax (El Maraghi-Ater et al., 1986). As the tail, the skin or the intestine start retaining the corticosteroids from the mid-climax, the presence of large amounts of these hormones could be required in the processes responsible for these morphogenic and biochemical changes.

Other arguments were given in our study of corticosteroid binding in the skin. High affinity, low capacity binding sites for corticosterone and aldosterone were detected in the skin cytosol fraction of adult *Rana esculenta* (Jolivet-Jaudet and Leloup-Hâtey, 1985 and unpublished data) (Fig. 5). The K_D was 1.62×10^{-9}M for corticosterone and 0.15×10^{-9}M for aldosterone. Corticosterone and aldosterone competed with each other suggesting that the same sites could bind any of two hormones. In tadpoles, at the mid-climax, saturable binding sites for aldosterone (only steroid studied) were found in the skin cytosol (Fig. 6) with maximum binding capacity about 20 times lower than in adult skin. At this stage of development, their presence can be correlated with the appearance, in the skin, of a transepithelial potential difference (Taylor and Barker, 1965) and a new physiological mechanism, the aldosterone-dependent active sodium transport (Yorio and Bentley, 1978 a). Furthermore, the rise in the number of sites from the climax to adult stage was concomitant with an increase in the skin sodium transport capacity in terrestrial environment (Alvaredo and Moody, 1970).

In contrary to *Rana esculenta*, *Xenopus laevis* remains in aquatic environment after the metamorphosis. In this last species, we identified no high affinity sites for aldosterone in the skin cytosol fraction from tadpoles, juveniles and adults (Data on juveniles shown in fig. 6). This lack can be correlated with the quite low active sodium transport and the inefficacy of aldosterone to stimulate this former (Yorio and Bentley, 1978 b). On the other hand, just as the amphibian adult moult is a corticosterone dependent process (Barker-Jørgensen and Larsen, 1970), the corticosterone appears also involved in the sloughing mechanisms which take place at climax. Alterations at the surface of the *Xenopus laevis* was shown by scanning electron microscopy (Wüest et al., 1987 and unpublished data). Microzones of desquamation appeared in the first part of the climax. At the mid-climax, the cell surface is modified by many foldings which then disappear in the second part of the climax. The underlying cells exhibit adult surface characteristics.

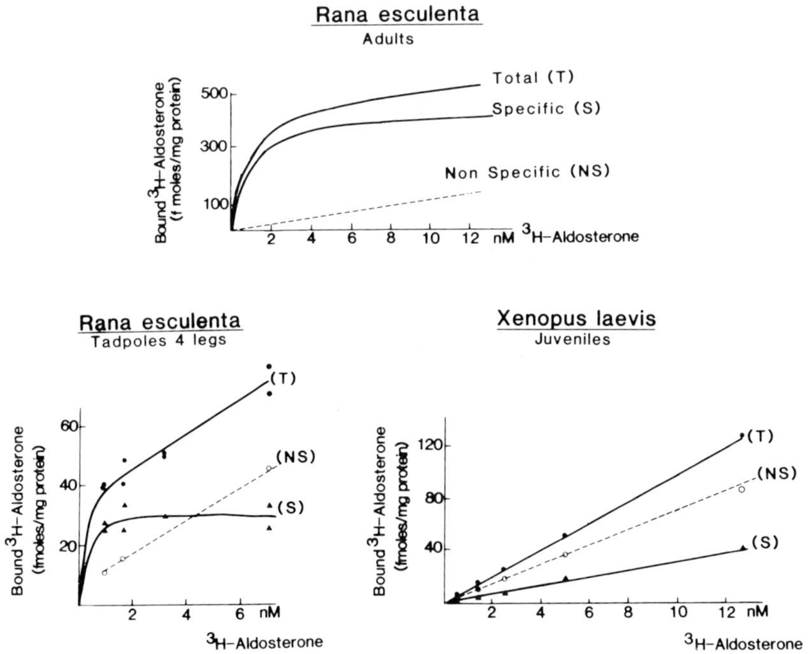

Fig. 6: Representative saturation curve of (^{3}H)-aldosterone in the skin cytosol of amphibia, *Rana esculenta* and *Xenopus laevis*. Experimental conditions were similar to these indicated in Fig. 5.

The first typical moult in *Xenopus laevis* (Dodd and Dodd, 1976) coincides with an increase in skin corticosteroid concentrations, especially corticosterone, reaching the highest at the mid-climax (Fig. 4). A study of the corticosterone binding sites, before and after the shedding, would be particularly interesting.

Thus, corticosteroids are involved in the metamorphosis, principally from the climax onwards. Large amounts of corticosteroids seems necessary to achieve the morphological and physiological changes.

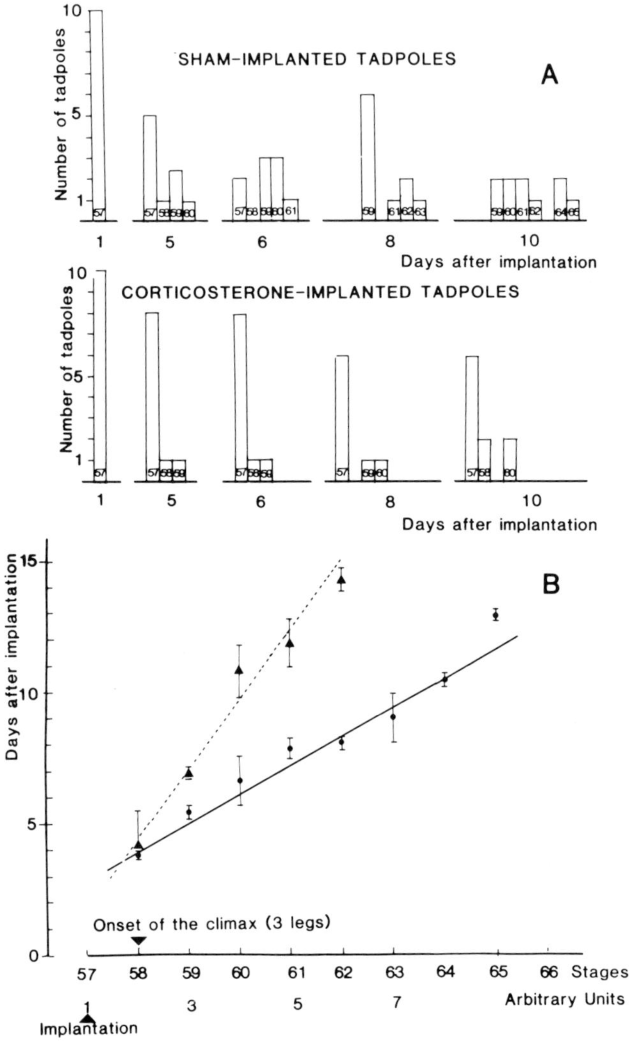

Fig. 7: Influence of corticosterone implantation at prometamorphosis on the evolution of the *Xenopus laevis* metamorphosis.

A. Histograms of the stage frequency distribution as a function of time. Stages are indicated in each column. – B. Kinetics of metamorphosis in untreated tadpoles (n = 51) (●——●) and in corticosterone-implanted tadpoles (n = 19) (▲– – –▲).

5. Relationships between thyroid and interrenal functions during the metamorphosis

Owing to the essential role of thyroid hormones in the induction of this process, relationships between thyroid hormones and corticosteroids are now considered.

5.1. Relationships during the prometamorphosis

Desoxycorticosterone acetate (Kobayashi, 1958) or cortisol treatments (Rapola, 1962) inhibit the metamorphosis when they were given during the premetamorphosis. In *Xenopus laevis*, metamorphosis did not take place in about 70 per 100 of tadpoles when a corticosterone implant was inserted during the prometamorphosis (St 57), and so long as implantations were repeated every 5 days (Buscaglia et al., 1981 and unpublished data) (Fig. 7 A). In these tadpoles, neither the foreleg emergence, nor the reduction of the tail size were observed 28 days after the implantation (Fig. 8), whereas in untreated tadpoles, the metamorphosis was finished within 12 days. Nevertheless, a narrowing of the head was already noticeable suggesting that some morphological events of small importance have already started. The corticosterone inhibitory effect was specific. None other treatment, sham-implantation, cholesterol, progesterone or even aldosterone-implantation, were able to suppress the induction of the metamorphosis.

The inhibition of metamorphosis was associated with alterations in the thyroid function. While thyroxine (T_4) and triiodothyronine (T_3) plasma levels rose rapidly from St 57 in untreated tadpoles (Leloup and Buscaglia, 1977), T_4 and T_3 decreased progressively, in the corticosterone-implanted tadpoles (Fig. 9 A). However, the metabolism of circulating T_4 and its peripheral deiodination in T_3 did not seem modified as shown by the similar

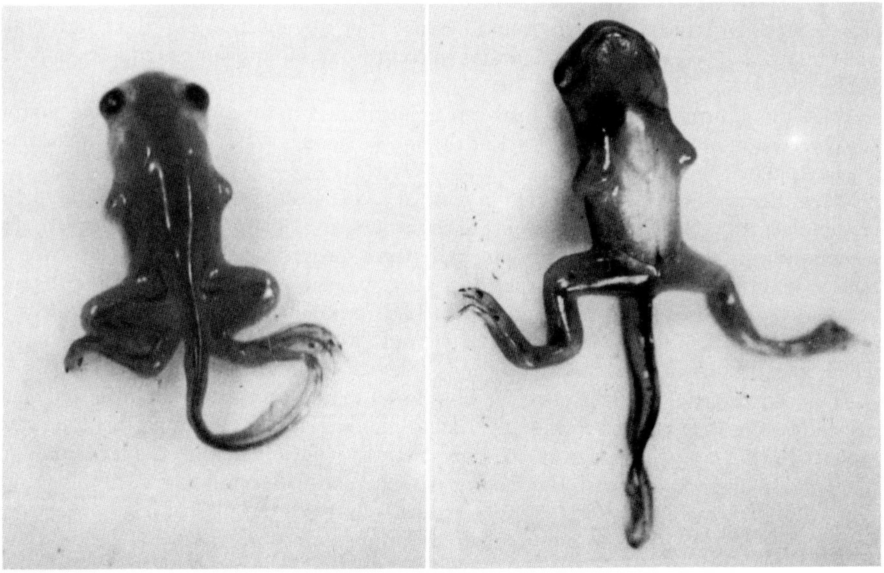

Fig. 8: Corticosterone-implanted tadpole of *Xenopus laevis* 28 days after the first implantation at stage 57.

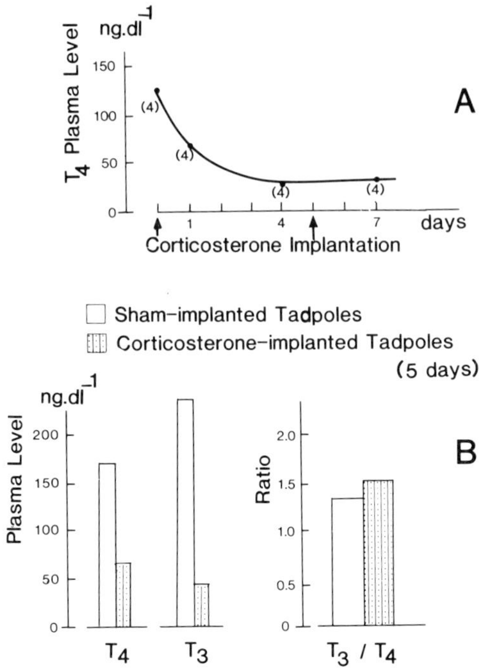

Fig. 9: Effect of corticosterone implantation on circulating thyroid hormones in *Xenopus laevis* tadpoles. First implantation at stage 57.

plasma levels of labeled T_4 or T_3 found 6 hours after the injection of ^{125}I-T_4 and by the constancy of labeled and cold T_3/T_4 ratios in controls and in implanted tadpoles (Fig. 9B, Table 3).

Thus, the failure of metamorphosis can be attributed to an inhibition of the thyroid activity. The inductive threshold level of thyroid hormones was not reached in corticosterone-implanted tadpoles.

When the metamorphosis occurred in spite of a corticosterone implantation (30 p.100 of tadpoles), all the characteristic events of the process took place but at a slower rate. The metamorphosis, expressed in developmental stages, progresses linearly as a function of time. A retardation of the metamorphosis process was shown by the significant difference between the slopes of the regressions depicting its kinetics for treated and untreated tadpoles (Fig. 7B, Table 4). Other tested steroids were ineffective except progesterone which was less active than corticosterone (Table 4).

The corticosterone distinct effect, inhibition or retardation of metamorphosis, could depend on the time elapsed in the St 57 before the implantation. During this long stage (about 3 days), appreciated from external criteria, some metabolic changes could be induced as suggested by the study of corticosterone plasma levels 10 days after implantation. When the metamorphosis events were not observed, the plasma level of corticosterone was about 10 times higher than in prometamorphic tadpoles (143.4 versus 14.2 ng.ml^{-1} at St 57). When the metamorphosis proceeded, the plasma level in corticosterone was only about twice the normal level (26.1 versus 12.1 ng.ml^{-1} at St 58; 35.4 versus 21.5 at St 60). An increase in the metabolic clearance rate of corticosterone released

Table 3: Effect of corticosterone implantation on thyroxine metabolism in prometamorphic tadpoles of *Xenopus laevis*.

	Control	Corticosterone	Significance of the difference
T_4*	19.0 ± 1.9	27.4 ± 3.6	P > 0.05
T_3*	8.2 ± 1.6	12.9 ± 1.7	P > 0.05
T_3*/T_4*	0.43	0.45	

Values are means ± S.E.M.

Tadpoles received, 5 days after the implantation, one injection of 0.25 μCi of $^{125}I-T_4$ (Specific activity : 1600 μCi/μg) and were sacrified 6 hours later. Labeled thyroxine (T_4*) and triiodothyronine (T_3*) were expressed as per cent of plasma total radioactivity.

Table 4: Influence of corticosteroid implantation on the kinetics of the metamorphosis process.

Treatment	Number of tadpoles	Equation of linear regression
None	51	Y = 1.08 X + 1.76
Sham-implanted	6	Y = 1.03 X + 2.63
Corticosterone	19	Y = 2.56*X − 0.69
Aldosterone	13	Y = 1.04 X + 5.33
Progesterone	5	Y = 1.66*X + 1.22
Cholesterol	5	Y = 1.28 X + 1.88

X = 1 for tadpoles at the stage 57 and one arbitrary unity correspond to each developmental stage
Y = number of days after the tadpole selection

The linearity of the regression curves are tested by analysis of variance. P < 0.01 (*) compared with the slope of untreated tadpoles by analysis of covariance.

by the implant was probably lately induced in the St 57. In this case, circulating corticosterone did not reach the high levels which inhibit the induction of metamorphosis by thyroid hormones.

Finally, the experimental inhibition of metamorphosis by corticosterone can be compared to the well known delayed metamorphosis observed in stress conditions (e.g., temperature, excess population) (Hourdry and Beaumont, 1985). Indeed, in such conditions, an increase in circulating corticosterone was found as shown in adult amphibian (Hanke, 1978). Thus, the modulation of the equilibrium between thyroid hormones and corticosterone may represent a control mechanism for the induction of the metamorphosis only takes place in the best environmental conditions.

5.2. Relationships during the climax

In *Xenopus laevis*, metamorphosis proceeded when corticosterone was implanted during the first part of climax (St 61) (Buscaglia et al., 1981 and unpublished data), in agreement with previous observations. A more and less accelerating effect of corticosteroids were shown (cf. Kaltenbach, 1968). In this respect, corticosterone and aldosterone potentiate the *in vitro* action of thyroid hormones on the tail shrinkage in *Bufo bufo japonicus* tadpoles (Kikuyama et al., 1983), in relation to an increase in the number of T_3 nuclear receptors (Niki et al., 1981). Furthermore, the interrenal were stimulated by thyroid hormones. In *Rana catesbeiana* tadpoles, thyroid hormones increased the interrenal activity (Hsu et al., 1984), the corticosteroid plasma levels (Jaffe, 1981; Krug et al., 1983; Kikuyama et al., 1986) and sensibilized the interrenal cells to ACTH (Hsu et al., 1984; Jaffe, 1981; Krug et al., 1983; Kikuyama et al., 1986). The interrenal response was also found in hypophysectomized tadpoles (Hsu et al., 1984; Kikuyama et al., 1986).

Consequently, during the climax, the thyroid hormones directly stimulate the interrenal activity; then, the released corticosteroids may amplify the effect of thyroid hormones on the tissues.

6. Conclusions

In *Xenopus laevis* tadpoles, prominent peaks of aldosterone and corticosterone plasma levels were found around the mid-climax. Circulating corticosterone, but not aldosterone, was specifically bound to high affinity sites of plasma proteins. As the maximum binding capacity did not change during the metamorphosis, the biologically active «free corticosterone» rose sharply pointing out a true hypercorticism at the mid-climax.

Simultaneously, corticosterone and aldosterone concentrations increased in some largely rehandled tissues (tail, liver, intestine, skin) and remained high when plasma levels were reduced in the second part of climax. Thus, corticosterone and aldosterone appears involved in the setting of these morphological and physiological changes appearing after the mid-climax. Furthermore, corticosterone acts on the tissue metabolism to provide the energy required by the tissue reorganization.

The normal evolution of metamorphosis appears dependent on a adequate equilibrium between corticosterone and thyroid hormones. In prometamorphosis, a relative excess of corticosterone determined a specific inhibition of the metamorphosis consecutive to a decrease in the plasma levels of thyroid hormones. The delayed metamorphosis observed under stressful conditions could result from a same mechanism. During the climax, thyroid hormones induce the stimulation of interrenal cells allowing the release of high amounts of corticosterone and aldosterone necessary to the achievement of the metamorphosis.

References

Alvaredo, R. H., Moody, A. (1970): Sodium and chloride transport in tadpoles of the bullfrog *Rana catesbeiana*. Am. J. Physiol. *218*, 1510–1516.

Balinsky, J. B., Choritz, E. L., Coe, C. G. L., van der Schans, G. S. (1967): Urea cycle enzymes and urea excretion during the development and metamorphosis of *Xenopus laevis*. Comp. Biochem. Physiol. 22, 53–57.

Barker Jørgensen, C., Larsen, L. O. (1961): Molting and its hormonal control in toads. Gen. comp. Endocrinol. *1*, 145–153.

Bradford, M. M. (1976): A rapid and sensitive method for the quantitation of microgram quantities of protein utilizing the principle of protein-dye binding. Analyt. Biochem. 72, 248–254.

Buscaglia, M., Leloup-Hâtey, J., Jaudet, G., Leloup, J. (1981): Effets de la corticostérone sur la métamorphose d'un amphibien anoure, *Xenopus laevis*. Ann. Endocrinol. *42*, 80C.

Carr, J. A., Norris, D. O. (1988): Interrenal activity during the metamorphosis of the tiger salamander *Ambystoma tigrinum*. Gen. comp. Endocrinol. *71*, 63–69.

Chan, S. T. H., Edwards, B. R. (1970): Kinetic studies on the biosynthesis of corticosteroids *in vitro* from exogenous precursors by the interrenal glands of the normal, corticotrophin-treated and adenohypophysectomized *Xenopus laevis* DAUDIN. J. Endocrinol. *47*, 183–195.

Dalle, M. (1982): La fonction glucocorticoïde au cours des périodes pré-natales et post-natales chez la mère et le nouveau-né de cobaye. Thèse de Doctorat d'Etat, Université de Clermont-Ferrand II, France.

Dodd, M. H. I., Dodd, J. M. (1976): The biology of metamorphosis. In: Physiology of the Amphibia, Vol. *3*, (B. Lofts, ed.) 467–599. Acad. Press, New York.

El Maraghi-Ater, H., Mesnard, J., Hourdry, J. (1986): Hormonal control of the intestinal brush border enzyme activities in developing anuran amphibians. I. Effects of hydrocortisone and insulin during and after spontaneous metamorphosis. Gen. comp. Endocrinol. *61*, 53–63.

Hanke, W. (1978): The adrenal cortex of amphibia. In: General, comparative and clinical endocrinology of the adrenal cortex. Vol. 2 (I. Chester Jones, I. W. Henderson, eds.) pp. 419–495. Acad. Press, New York.

Hanke, W., Leist, K. H. (1971): The effect of ACTH and corticosteroids on carbohydrate metabolism during the metamorphosis of *Xenopus laevis*. Gen. comp. Endocrinol. *16*, 137–148.

Hourdry, J., Beaumont, A. (1985): Les métamorphoses des amphibiens. Masson, Paris.

Hsu, C. Y., Yu, N. W., Chen, S. J. (1980): Development of Δ_5-3β-hydroxysteroid dehydrogenase activity in the interrenal gland of *Rana catesbeiana*. Gen. comp. Endocrinol. *42*, 167–170.

Hsu, C. Y., Yu, N. W., Pi, C. M., Chen, S. J., Ruan, C. C. (1984): Hormonal regulation of development of the interrenal activity of Δ_5-3β-hydroxysteroid dehydrogenase in bullfrog tadpoles. J. exp. Zool. *232*, 73–78.

Jaffe, R. C. (1981): Plasma concentration of corticosterone during *Rana catesbeiana* tadpole metamorphosis. Gen. comp. Endocrinol. *44*, 314–318.

Jensen, E. V., Jacobson, H. I. (1962): Basic guides to the mechanism of estrogen action. Rec. Progr. Horm. Res. *18*, 387–414.

Jolivet-Jaudet, G. (1982): Etude de la fonction interrénalienne pendant la métamorphose du têtard de *Xenopus laevis*. Thèse de Doctorat de 3ème cycle, Université Paris 6.

Jolivet-Jaudet, G., Inoue, M., Takada, K., Ishii, S. (1984): Circannual changes in plasma aldosterone levels in *Bufo japonicus formosus*. Gen. comp. Endocrinol. *53*, 163–167.

Jolivet-Jaudet, G., Leloup-Hâtey, J. (1984a): Variations in aldosterone and corticosterone plasma levels during metamorphosis in *Xenopus laevis* tadpoles. Gen. comp. Endocrinol. *56*, 59–65.

Jolivet-Jaudet, G., Leloup-Hâtey, J. (1984b): Interrenal function during amphibian metamorphosis: *in vitro* biosynthesis of radioactive corticosteroids from ($4C^{14}$)-progesterone by interrenal in *Xenopus laevis* tadpoles. Comp. Biochem. Physiol. *79 B*, 239–244.

Jolivet-Jaudet, G., Leloup-Hâtey, J. (1985): Mise en évidence de récepteurs des corticostéroïdes dans la peau de grenouille. J. Physiol. Paris *80*, 12 A.

Jolivet-Jaudet, G., Leloup-Hâtey, J. (1986): Corticosteroid binding in plasma of *Xenopus laevis*. Modifications during metamorphosis and growth. J. Steroid Biochem. *25*, 343–350.

Kaltenbach, J. C. (1968): Nature of hormone action in amphibian metamorphosis. In: Metamorphosis. (W. Etkin, L. I. Gilbert, eds.) pp. 399–441. Appleton-Century-Crofts, New York.

Kikuyama, S., Niki, K., Mayumi, M., Kawamura, K. (1982): Retardation of thyroxine-induced metamorphosis by amphenone B in toad tadpoles. Endocrinol. Japon. *29*, 659–662.

Kikuyama, S., Niki, K., Mayumi, M., Shibayama, R., Nishikawa, M., Shintake, N. (1983): Studies on corticosteroid action on the toad tadpole tail *in vitro*. Gen. comp. Endocrinol. *52*, 395–399.

Kikuyama, S., Suzuki, M. R., Iwamuro, S. (1986): Elevation of plasma aldosterone levels of tadpoles at metamorphic climax. Gen. comp. Endocrinol. *63*, 186–190.

Kobayashi, H. (1958): Effect of desoxycorticosterone acetate on metamorphosis induced by thyroxine in anuran tadpoles. Endocrinology 62, 371–377.

Krug, E. C., Honn, K. V., Battista, J., Nicoll, C. S. (1983): Corticosteroids in serum of *Rana catesbeiana* during development and metamorphosis. Gen. comp. Endocrinol. *52*, 232–241.

Labrie, F. (1967): Interactions hormonales et rôle de la transcortine dans l'ajustement de l'activité hypophyso-surrénalienne. Thèse de Doctorat d'Etat, Université Laval, Québec.

Leist, K. H. (1970): Die Bedeutung des Adenohypophysen-Interrenal-Systems für den Osmomineral-Haushalt des Krallenfrosches (*Xenopus laevis* DAUDIN) im Verlauf der Metamorphose. Zool. Jb. Physiol. *75*, 375–401.

Leist, K. H., Bergerhoff, K., Pehlemann, F. W., Hanke, W. (1969): Histophysiologische Untersuchungen der Entwicklung des Interrenalorgans beim Krallenfrosch (*Xenopus laevis* DAUDIN). Z. Zellforsch. *93*, 105–125.

Leloup, J., Buscaglia, M. (1977): La triiodothyronine, hormone de la métamorphose des Amphibiens. C. R. Acad. Sci., Sér. D., *284*, 2261–2263.

Leloup-Hâtey, J., Baloche, S., Jolivet-Jaudet, G. (1988): Variations des concentrations en corticostérone et en aldostérone dans divers tissus du têtard de *Xenopus laevis* pendant la métamorphose. C. R. Soc. Biol. *182*, 354–360.

Martin, B., Ozon, R. (1975): Steroid-protein interactions in nonmammalian vertebrates. II – Steroids binding proteins in the serum of amphibians; a physiological approach. Biol. Reprod. *13*, 371–380.

Nieuwkoop, P. D., Faber, J. (1975): Normal table of *Xenopus laevis* (DAUDIN). A systematical and chronological survey of the development from the fertilized egg till the end of metamorphosis. Amsterdam: North Holland Publishing Comp.

Niki, K., Yoshizato, K., Kikuyama, S. (1981): Augmentation of nuclear binding capacity for triiodothyronine by aldosterone in tadpole tail. Proc. Jap. Acad. *57B*, 271–275.

Pouyet, J. C., Hourdry, J. (1988): *In vitro* study of the intestinal brush border enzyme activities in developing anuran amphibian: effects of thyroxine, cortisol and insulin. J. exp. Zool. *245*, 200–205.

Rapola, J. (1962): Development of the amphibian adrenal cortex. Morphological and physiological studies on *Xenopus laevis* DAUDIN. Ann. Acad. Sci. Fenn. *64A*, 1–81.

Rémy, C., Bounhiol, J. J. (1971): Métamorphoses normalisées obtenues par l'hormone adrénocorticotrope chez des têtards d'*Alytes* hypophysectomisés et thyroxinés. C. R. Acad. Sci., Paris, Sér. D *272*, 455–458.

Ritzen, E. M., French, F. S., Weddington, S. C., Nayfen, S. N., Hansson, V. (1974): Steroid binding in polyacrilamide gels. Quantitation at steady state conditions. J. biol. Chem. *249*, 6597–6604.

Sandor, T. (1972): Corticosteroids in amphibia, reptilia and aves. In: Steroids in nonmammalian Vertebrates. (D.. Idler, ed.) pp. 253–327. Acad Press, New York.

Scatchard, G. (1949): The attraction of proteins for small molecules and ions. Ann. N. Y. Acad. Sci. *51*, 660–672.

Taylor, R. E. Jr., Barker, S. B. (1965): Transepithelial potential difference: development in anuran larvae. Science *148*, 1612–1613.

Wüest, J., Jolivet-Jaudet, G., Leloup-Hâtey, J., Buscaglia, M. (1987): Skin surface pattern evolution and skin corticosteroid content during the metamorphosis of *Xenopus laevis* tadpoles. Gen. comp. Endocrinol. *66*, 30–31.

Yorio, T., Bentley, P. J. (1978 a): Stimulation of the short-circuit current (sodium transport) across the skin of the frog (*Rana pipiens*) by corticosteroids: structure-activity relationships. *J. Endocrinol.* *79*, 283–290.

Yorio, T., Bentley, P. J. (1978 b): The permeability of the skin of the aquatic anuran *Xenopus laevis* (Pipidae). J. exp. Biol. *72*, 285–289.

Fortschritte der Zoologie, Band/Vol. 38 · Hanke, W. (Hrsg.), Biology and Physiology of Amphibians
Gustav Fischer Verlag · Stuttgart · New York · 1990

Differentiation of PRL, GH and ACTH cells during *Rana dalmatina* larval development

A. Guastalla and E. Campantico

Dipartimento di Biologia animale, Via Accademia Albertina 17, I-10123 Torino, Italy

1. Introduction

For a long time the morphogenetic features of amphibian adenohypophysis have been the subject of several studies (Copeland, 1943; Pasteels, 1957; Kerr, 1966; Nieuwkoop and Faber, 1967; Doerr-Schott, 1968; Zuber-Vogeli and Bihoues-Louis, 1971; Mira-Moser, 1972; Nyholm, 1977). The bulk of results obtained showed the morphogenesis of the adenohypophysis to be similar in the different amphibian species during the embryonic and larval stages.

An interesting developmental aspect of the amphibian pituitary is the early appearance and evolution of specific functional activities displayed by the different types of hypophysial cells. This topic, indeed, is strictly linked to the functional significance of various hypophysial hormones in the earlier developmental stages and to the settling on of the endocrine control mechanism (see Garcia-Navarro et al., 1988 a).

While studying the pituitary cell differentiation, the appearance of either the typical morphologic characters or, when possible, of the specific immunoreactivity, is considered to classify the different cell types.

The staining techniques used in the cytophysiological approach only reveal the piling up of secretion material in an amount higher than their limit of sensitivity. Thus, they do not allow to detect the starting of the synthesis or the early secreting activity of the differentiating cells.

At the electron microscope, the criterion of functional differentiation is the appearance of the first secretory granules, that can be noted earlier than at the light one (Dent and Gupta, 1967; Doerr-Schott, 1968; Mira-Moser, 1972). However morphologic data does not elucidate the kind of the synthesized molecule, at least before the cell will assume the look typical of the full differentiation.

Beside the specificity, immunocytochemical methods have the advantage to be much more sensitive than staining methods. Thus, they allow a secure identification also with minimum amount of specific differentiation products (as hormones, in this case).

In parallel with electron microscopy they are essential for the identification of the otherwise anonimous nature of the secretory granules. They are by then much more preferable for differentiation studies at both the light microscope and the ultrastructural level.

Unfortunately, relatively few works have been carried out on adenohypophysial cell differentiation by applying cytoimmunological techniques. Antisera raised against mammalian pituitary hormones have revealed the ontogenesis of some adenohypophysial cells in certain amphibian species (Doerr-Schott and Dubois, 1973; Rémy and Dubois, 1973, 1974; Nyholm and Doerr-Schott, 1977; Guyetant et al., 1977; Eagleson and McKeown, 1978; Moriceau-Hay et al., 1979, 1982; Zuber-Vogeli and Doerr-Schott, 1984; Garcia-Navarro et al., 1988 a, b).

However, these studies were undertaken in a minority of amphibian species and focused exclusively on some immunoreactive cells in a given species, remaining largely incomplete.

Only in *Bufo melanostictus* comprehensive study on cytodifferentiation, immunoreactivity and topographical distribution have been performed for all kinds of hormone secreting cells in embryonic, larval as well as adult pituitary gland (Kar and Naik, 1986).

The present report provides informations regarding cytodifferentiation, immunocharacteristics and topographical distribution of PRL-, GH- and ACTH-secreting cells in the larval pituitary of *Rana dalmatina*, employing indirect immunofluorescence and unlabelled antibody enzyme methods. PRL-immunoreactive cells have been revealed by using antiserum raised against the amphibian hormone; GH-immunoreactive cells have been revealed by means of antisera raised against the hormone from two mammalian species.

2. Material and methods

Spawns of *Rana dalmatina* were collected in March and embryos/larvae were reared in the laboratory under normal environmental conditions until metamorphosis. The staging of the larvae was done according to Cambar and Marrot (1954) developmental tables. At least 5 animals of each stage (from stage 28, i.e. twelve hours after hatching, to stage 53, i.e. climax) were fixed in Bouin-Hollande fluid and paraffin embedded. Serial sagittal sections 5 μm thick were used for immunochemical reactions.

The following primary antisera were used: rabbit anti-*Rana catesbeiana* PRL (anti-fPRL) 1/2500, 1/5000; rabbit anti-ovine GH (anti-oGH) 1/500; monkey anti-rat GH (anti-rGH) 1/400; rabbit anti-synthetic (1–24) ACTH (Miles) 1/1000. Anti-fPRL was generously provided by prof. S. Kikuyama and K. Yamamoto (Waseda University, Tokio). Anti-oPRL, anti-oGH and anti-rGH were gifts from NIADDK, Bethesda, U.S.A.

The avidin-biotin-peroxidase complex (ABC) method was applied for single staining. The sections were dewaxed, gradually hydrated, treated with 7,5% H_2O_2, 2.28% HIO_4 and then normal goat serum (1/50, 20 min at room temperature). They were then incubated with the primary antisera in a moist chamber at 8 °C for 22 hr, exposed to biotynilated goat anti-rabbit IgG, and to avidin-biotinylated horseradish peroxidase complexes. The immunoreactive sites were visualized by using 3-3′-diaminobenzidine tetrahydrocloride (30 mg in 250 ml 0.05M pH 7.6 Tris-HCl buffer containing 40 μl of 30% H_2O_2). Subsequently, sections were dehydrated and mounted in DPX.

In the double sequential staining, the ABC method (used to point out the rabbit anti-fPRL binding sites) was followed by the indirect immunofluorescence technique; sections were incubated with the second primary antibody (monkey anti-rGH) in a moist chamber at 8 °C for 22 hr, washed thoroughly in phosphate saline buffer (0.01M PBS, pH 7.4), then incubated with 1/50 FITC conjugated rabbit anti-monkey IgG (USB) for 1 hr.

The specificity tests included incubation of adjacent paraffin sections with normal rabbit serum (or normal monkey serum) or with solid-phase adsorbed primary antibodies.

3. Stage-dependent development of PRL-, GH- and ACTH-secreting cells

No reaction was observed when sections were incubated with normal rabbit or monkey serum instead of the primary antibody. Immunostaining was abolished when sections were incubated with primary antisera preadsorbed with corresponding antigens. Anti-fPRL antiserum specifically reacts at pretty high dilution (1/5000); a lower dilution (1/2500) is useful when lower antigen concentrations are present, as in earlier stages. Anti-mammalian GH antisera need 5 to 10 times lower dilutions to give very good results.

The cytodifferentiation, immunocharacteristics and topographical distribution of PRL, GH and ACTH cells revealed by immunohistochemical techniques in the larval adenohypophysis of *Rana dalmatina* are described stage by stage.

3.1. Stage 28

Twelve hours after hatching, the tadpole is 7–8 mm long; the eye is evident and the external gills are still visible. The pituitary anlage is migrating and not yet differentiated. In medial sagittal sections, it looks like a crescent, open forward, adhering to the infundibulum floor, oriented almost perpendicularly to the cephalo-caudal axis: the posterior part is blunt and in contact ventrally with the anterior tip of the notochord.

At this stage the first signals of cell differentiation show up. In the central part a group of 3 to 5 cells with large nucleus and thin cytoplasm faintly but clearly reacts to both anti-GH and anti-PRL antibodies. Comparison of adjacent sections stained with single labeling technique does not allow to understand whether they are the same cells or not. Double immunostaining of the same section clearly shows that the very same cell population reacts to both antisera (Fig. 1). Melanine granules and vitelline platelets also are particularly abundant in the pituitary anlage cells.

3.2. Stage 32

At stage 32, two days after the hatching, the tadpole is 9 mm long. The right side gills are completely covered by the operculum. The hypophysial anlage completed its migration and became thicker along its dorso-ventral axis.

Single stained sections show 5–6 rather large cells in the anlage central region, reacting strongly with anti-PRL and as many cells reacting with anti-GH in the same region. With double immunostaining the two antigens are colocalized in most of the cells. From this stage on, however, few rare cells bind either anti-PRL or anti-GH only (Fig. 1).

3.3. Stage 33

Stage 33 is regarded as the beginning of the larval life. Left side gills are almost fully covered, and the rectum is delimited.

The adenohypophysial anlage, thickened further, became claviform. The posterior region is blunt and the major axis is still almost perpendicular to the cephalo-caudal axis of the larva.

PRL- and GH-secreting cells increase in number, while the reactivity becomes stronger. Double immunostaining shows the number of cells reacting to only one of the sera to increase along the development (Fig. 1). On a median parasagittal section, preliminary quantitative data show a little more than half of each cell population to be reactive to both antisera.

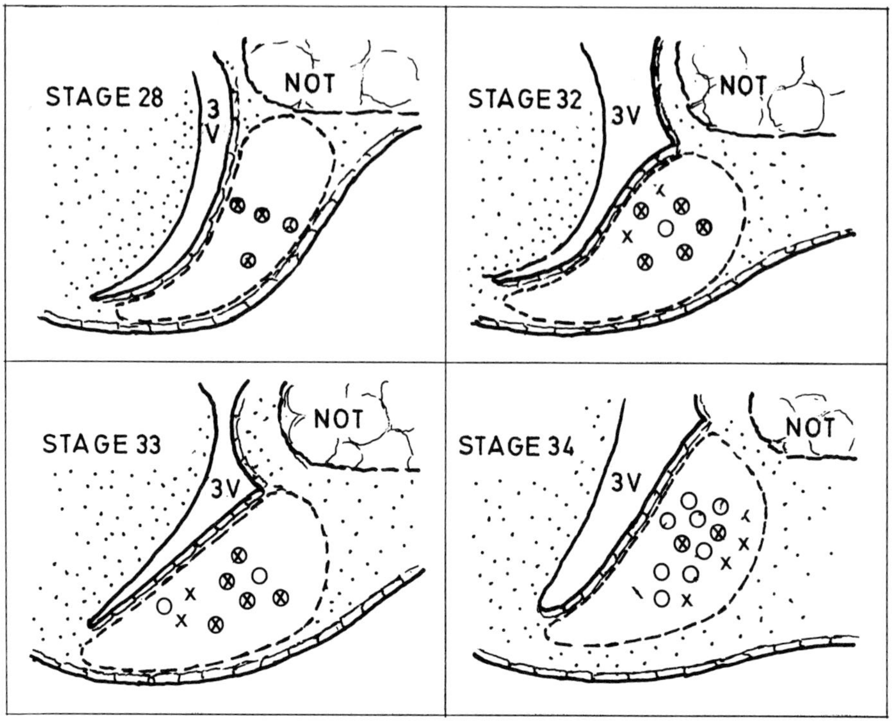

Fig. 1: Diagrams of midsagittal sections of pituitary anlage at different developmental stages showing the topographical distribution of various cell types. ○ PRL cells; X GH cells; ▲ ACTH cells; ⊗ colocalization. NOT, notochord; 3V, third ventricle.

3.4. Stage 34

At stage 34 the larva is about 10 mm long. Left side gills completely disappeared and the first intestinal loop is outlining. Adenohypophysial primordium is not yet divided in *pars intermedia* and *pars distalis*.

Immunoreacting cells are rather large, increased in number and are very clearly stained by the antisera (Fig. 1). Pigment has decreased and vitelline platelets are still present though in a very smaller amount than in earlier stages.

3.5. Stage 41

Twenty days after the hatching, the larva has reached 14 mm length. The primordia of the limbs are evident; in particular the hindlimb is as large as broad. The feature of the adenohypophysial primordium has changed as its size is bigger and its long axis is now horizontal, parallel to the cephalo-caudal axis of the larva. The infundibulum floor is V-shaped, open forward while in the dorsal region the nervous lobe begins to differentiate.

The PRL cells are large, numerous and intensely reacting as well as the GH cells. A smaller fraction of immunoreactive cells shows the colocalization of the two hormones.

At this stage, the first ACTH cells appear as 2 to 6 small elements scattered in the anterior region under the future median eminence (Fig. 2). No immunoreactivity is seen in the intermediate lobe.

3.6. Stage 45

At stage 45, which marks the end of premetamorphosis, the hindlimb is in paddle stage and already shows four fingers. The larva's total length is about 20 mm. The nervous and the intermediate lobe are now well evident. In the distal lobe the PRL and GH cells begin to segregate. PRL cells occupy most of the anterior region while GH cells are more present in the caudal region. Instead the two cell types are equally frequent and largely mixed in the central area of the lobe. At this stage the two cell populations appear actually to be almost completely separated at the double immunostaining method (Fig. 2).

ACTH cells are now more numerous, up to ten, in sagittal sections, dispersed in all the anterior region until the middle of the distal lobe (Fig. 2). They are spindle or irregular shaped. No anti-(l-24)ACTH reaction is seen in the intermediate lobe.

3.7. Stage 48

In the middle of prometamorphosis, the tadpole's hindlimbs are well developed. Their length is about one third of the tail. The pituitary gland feature is approaching the adult one: the nervous lobe, the median eminence and the intermediate lobe are completely developed.

PRL cells clearly prevail in the anterior region of the distal lobe while GH cells are almost exclusively located in the posterior third. From this stage on, the two cell populations are complety separated, as shown by the double immunostaining method. This becomes more and more evident in parallel with the establishment of the different topographical distribution (Fig. 2).

ACTH cells, up to 15 per section, are arranged like a cap at the edge of the rostral part. Few scattered cells are found in the central region (Fig. 2). There is no reactivity in the intermediate lobe cells.

3.8. Stage 49

Stage 49 marks the end of prometamorphosis. The hindlimb is fully developed and has assumed the characteristic bending with a 60 °C angle between thigh and leg. At almost 50 days after hatching the tadpole reaches the maximum size of about 33 mm. The pituitary gland feature is by now the typical adult one. Immunocytochemical characters are not different from the preceding stage and will be kept during the climax (stages 51, 52, 53).

4. Comparison of the functional development of different amphibian hypophysis

The antibody against *Rana catesbeiana* PRL allowed to evidence the immunoreacting cells at higher dilutions than those used with the antisera raised against mammalian hormones (Kar and Naik, 1986; Garcia-Navarro et al., 1988 a), probably due to their higher affinity.

The use of antibodies specific to mammalian hormones (sheep and rat GH) demonstrated to be useful in locating *Rana dalmatina* GH as it was for the same hormone in other

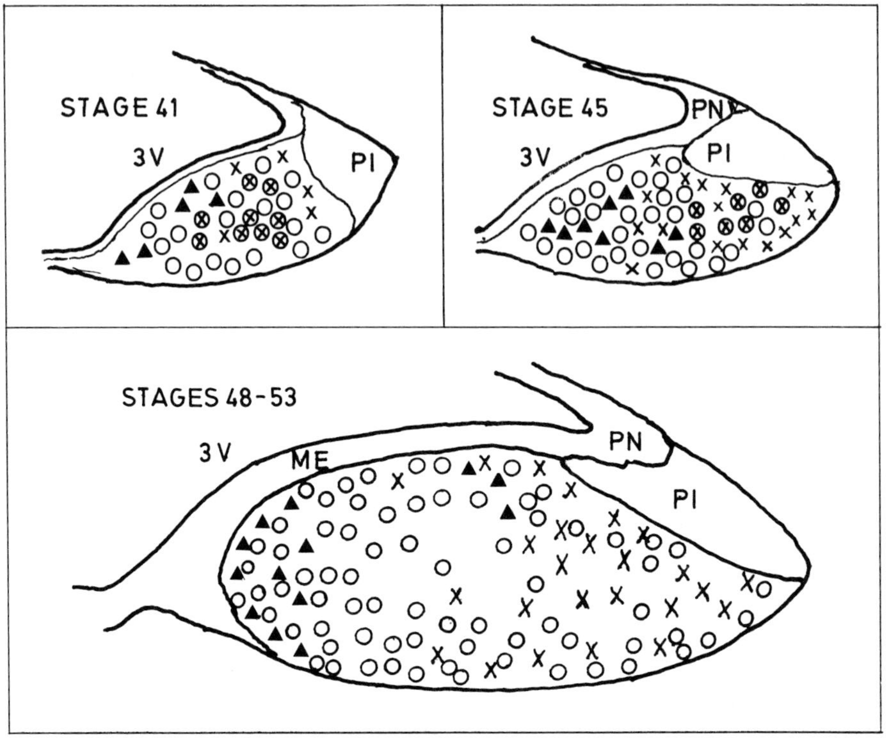

Fig. 2: Diagrams of midsagittal sections of pituitary gland at different developmental stages showing the topographical distribution of various cell types. ○ PRL cells; X GH cells; ▲ ACTH cells; ⊗ colocalization. 3V, third ventricle; ME, median eminence; PI, *pars intermedia*; PN, *pars nervosa.*

amphibian species (Campantico et al., 1985 a; Kar and Naik, 1986), confirming the existence of an immunological relationship between mammalian and amphibian hormone.

Once more, immunocytochemistry is shown to be particularly suitable to study cell differentiation of the adenohypophysial anlage during larval development, as its elevated specificity and sensitivity allowed to follow the differentiation from extremely early stages (stage 28 is just subsequent to the hatching).

Our results about *Rana dalmatina* will be compared with those obtained in other species by means of immunocytochemical methods, due to the poor reliability of data about the differentiation and ontogenesis of various endocrine cells of amphibian hypophysis obtained through traditional cytological techniques and electron microscopy. However, a comparative analysis of results obtained in different amphibian species is rather difficult, because the investigators have followed different criteria in defining larval developmental stages. We tried, as far as possible, to establish a correspondence, based on the descriptions given by the authors, between the normal tables of *Rana dalmatina* development (Cambar and Marrot, 1954) and the simplified tables of Gosner (1960), similarly to what Nieuwkoop and Faber (1967) did for the normal tables of *Rana dalmatina* and *Xenopus laevis*. Of course, this comparison could only be an approximate one, but allowed us to fix useful criteria in comparing the different species.

The developmental course of the pituitary of *Rana dalmatina* closely follows the general one described in other anura, particularly *Xenopus laevis* (Nieuwkoop and Faber, 1967; Nyholm, 1977) and *Bufo melanostictus* (Kar and Naik, 1986). The adenohypophysial primordium is already separated from the stomodeal epithelium right after hatching (stage 28) as it happens in *Xenopus laevis* and differing from *Rana temporaria*, where the segregation is delayed (Doerr-Schott, 1968).

The differentiation of hypophysial anlage into *pars intermedia* and *pars distalis* begins to be evident at stage 41 and it accomplishes at stage 45 in *Rana dalmatina*, may be just a little later than in *Xenopus laevis*. It is then followed, as in *Xenopus laevis*, by the differentiation of the *pars nervosa*. The three pituitary parts are differentiated before the end of the premetamorphosis.

4.1. PRL cells

Some 3–5 cells immunoreactive to anti-fPRL first appear at stage 28 in the central region of the primordium. Both the location and the appearance time are in agreement with the observations in *Xenopus laevis* (Moriceau-Hay et al., 1979) and in *Bufo melanostictus* (Kar and Naik, 1986). PRL cells appear early in *Ambystoma gracile* also (Eagleson and McKeown, 1978) but no precise correspondence can be made for this species with *Rana dalmatina*. A later differentiation for this cell type is observed in *Alytes obstetricans* (Rémy and Dubois, 1973; Guyetant et al., 1977) and in *Nectophrynoides occidentalis* (Zuber-Vogeli and Doerr-Schott, 1984). According to Garcia-Navarro et al. (1988 a), PRL cells appear at stages corresponding to 35–40 of *Rana dalmatina* in *Bufo calamita*, *Hyla meridionalis*, *Alytes cisternasi*, *Pelobates cultripes* and *Rana perezi*. These discrepancies may be attributed to species differences as well as to both specificity and affinity variations of the antisera employed.

The topographical distribution of immunoreactive PRL cells in the larval *pars distalis* remains scattered until stage 41, then, at stage 45, they are preferentially located in the anterior part, as in *Xenopus laevis* (Moriceau-Hay et al., 1979) and in *Alytes obstetricans* (Rémy and Dubois, 1973; Guyetant et al., 1977). This location likely announces the adult one, as it becomes more evident from stage 48 on. In *Bufo melanostictus*, PRL cells remain scattered through the whole *pars distalis* (Kar and Naik, 1986) as well as in *Nectophrynoides occidentalis* (Zuber-Vogeli and Doerr-Schott, 1984), *Pelobates cultripes* and *Rana perezi* (Garcia-Navarro et al., 1988 a). In *Bufo calamita*, *Hyla meridionalis* and *Alytes cisternasi*, instead, the PRL cells are located in the posterior two thirds of the *pars distalis* midsagittal sections since their appearance (Garcia-Navarro et al., 1988 a). These data point out considerable species differences.

4.2. GH cells

GH cells appear at stage 28 in *Rana dalmatina*, that is at an earlier developmental stage than in all other species, contemporarily with the PRL cells, and not subsequently, as it happens in *Xenopus laevis* (Moriceau-Hay et al., 1979) and in *Bufo melanostictus* (Kar and Naik, 1986).

In late larval stages of *Rana dalmatina*, that is from stage 45, GH cells are topographically separated from PRL cells. Their location is the same observed in both the species where they differentiate in early stages but after the PRL cells (Kar and Naik, 1986, in *Bufo melanostictus*, Moriceau-Hay et al., 1979, in *Xenopus laevis*) and the ones where they differentiate in parallel with PRL cells though in later stages (Guyetant et al., 1977, in *Alytes obstetricans*; Zuber-Vogeli and Doerr-Schott, 1984, in *Nectophrynoides occidentalis*).

There is no evidence of even a partial coincidence of the two cell populations in any of the amphibian species examined. The double immunocytochemical staining for PRL and GH excluded the location of the hormones in a unique cell type in *Bufo melanostictus* (Kar and Naik, 1986). Therefore, it may seem surprising that the first cells differentiating in the early larval stages (stage 28) are immunoreactive to both the anti-fPRL and the anti-mammalian GH antisera. However this is strongly suggested by both the results of the single immunostaining of adjacent sections and those obtained with the double staining on the same section. At stage 32, some of the cells begin to be reactive to only one antibody and at stage 33, a little more than half of each cell population shows a colocalization of both the hormones.

Theoretically, the double method we used could seem to be unsuitable to observe the presence of different antigens within the same cell, for the product of the reaction catalyzed by peroxidase could hide or empair the following immunofluorescence reaction for the second antigen. This did not happen, except may be very partially, because we used two antisera from different species (rabbit anti-fPRL and monkey anti-rGH) and thanks to the very high reactivity of the anti-fPRL antiserum which allowed to perform a mild peroxidase reaction, so to avoid the chance to interfere with the second reaction.

In our opinion, these results need to be further investigated at an ultrastructural immunocytochemical level. However, it can be hypothesized that a unique cell population capable of a double hormonal secretion appears at the start of the pituitary differentiation. Then, from this primitive GH/PRL cells, the two distinct populations gradually differentiate and assume different topographycal location. In fact, our still unpublished observations about immunocytochemical ultrastructural characters of the adenophyophysial cells seem to exclude a PRL and GH colocalization in *Xenopus laevis, Hyla arborea* and *Triturus cristatus* adult specimens.

We think it is interesting on an evolutionary and a comparative standpoint, to remember that immunocytochemical techniques at the electron microscope demonstrated PRL and GH to be present in the same cell type in cow (Fumagalli and Zanini, 1985) and rat (Papka et al., 1986; Nikitovitch-Winer et al., 1987) pituitary and in the normal and neoplastic human adenohypophysis (Zurschmiede and Landolt, 1987). Moreover, Hoeffler et al. (1985) described the early appearance of adenohypophysial cells secreting both GH and PRL in neonatal development of rats, and have raised the possibility that PRL-secreting cells arise from GH-secreting cells. In the human fetal adenohypophysis, Asa et al. (1988) have documented the existence of bihormonal mammosomatotrophs: these results suggest that the two cell types may have a common embryologic stem cell. On the other hand, the gene encoding for GH and PRL share a common tissue specific transcription factor in rat anterior pituitary gland (Nelson et al., 1988) and may have evolved from a common ancestral gene (Specker et al., 1984).

The fact that this situation is only seen in *Rana dalmatina* could be explained by the later identification of the immunoreacting cells, when the two cell populations already differentiated, in other species. However this is surely not the case in *Bufo melanostictus* in which no colocalization has been observed in stages as early as those described in *Rana dalmatina* (Kar and Naik, 1986).

4.3. ACTH cells

In adenohypophysial anlage from *Rana dalmatina*, cells immunoreactive to (1–24)ACTH antiserum first appear at stage 41, later than PRL and GH cells, in a stage corresponding to the one observed in *Alytes obstetricans* (Disclos and Surleve-Bazeille, 1974) and in *Nectophrynoides occidentalis* (Zuber-Vogeli and Doerr-Schott, 1984). The differentiation would be delayed in *Bufo bufo*, according to Mira-Moser (1972). In *Xenopus laevis*, immunoreactive cells to anti-ACTH antiserum appear earlier than in *Rana dalmatina* but these are probably the MSH cells of the future *pars intermedia*; the true ACTH cells of the rostral region of the distal lobe (Nyholm and Doerr-Schott, 1977; Moriceau-Hay et al., 1982) differentiate at a stage just before the one shown in *Rana dalmatina*; this also happens in *Rana temporaria* (Doerr-Schott and Dubois, 1973). In *Bufo melanostictus*, the appearance of ACTH cells distinct from the cells of the *pars intermedia* occurs much earlier (Kar and Naik, 1986).

Nothwithstanding the difference in the developmental stages, the topographic distribution at the first appearance and the successive gradual location in the rostral region of the *pars distalis*, observed in midsagittal sections of *Rana dalmatina* adenohypophysis, are in good agreement with those described for *Bufo melanostictus* (Kar and Naik, 1986) and in most of the other amphibians.

The cells of the larval *pars intermedia* of *Rana dalmatina* never exhibited immunoreactivity to anti-(1–24)ACTH antiserum in our preparations. In our opinion, this is due to the peculiar characters of the serum used, because we repeatedly obtained the same result on the *pars intermedia* of adult specimens of *Hyla arborea, Xenopus laevis* and *Triturus cristatus*, which showed a positive reaction with antisera of different origin (Gaudino et al., 1983; Campantico et al., 1985 b). Therefore, the cells reacting to anti-(1–24)ACTH antiserum we identified in *Rana dalmatina* pituitary primordium should be regarded as true ACTH-secreting cells.

References

Asa, S. L., Kovacs, K., Horvath, E., Losinski, N. E., Laszlo, F. A., Domokos, I., Halliday, W. C. (1988): Human fetal adenohypophysis. Electron microscopic and ultrastructural immunocytochemical analysis. Neuroendocrinology *48*, 423–431.

Cambar, R., Marrot, B. (1954): Table chronologique du développement de la grenouille agile (*Rana dalmatina* Bon.). Bull. Biol. *88*, 168–174.

Campantico, E., Guastalla, A., Patriarca, E. (1985 a): Identification by immunofluorescence of prolactin and somatotrophin producing cells in the pituitary gland of the tree frog *Hyla arborea*. Gen. Comp. Endocrinol. *57*, 110–116.

– (1985 b): Identification by immunofluorescence of ACTH-producing cells in the pituitary gland of the tree frog *Hyla arborea*. Gen. Comp. Endocrinol. *59*, 192–198.

Copeland, D. E. (1943): Cytology of the pituitary gland in developing and adult *Triturus viridescens*. J. Morphol. *72*, 379–409.

Dent, J., Gupta, B. (1967): Ultrastructural observations on the developmental cytology of the pituitary gland in the spotted newt. Gen. Comp. Endocrinol. 8, 273–288.

Disclos, P., Surlève-Bazeille, J. E. (1974): L'adenohypophyse du têtard d'*Alytes obstetricans* (Laur.). Ultrastructure avec description du troisième type de cellule acidophile. C. R. Soc. Biol. *168*, 277–281.

Doerr-Schott, J. (1968): Développement de l'hypophyse de *Rana temporaria* L.. Etude au microscope éléctronique. Z. Zellforsch. *90*, 616–645.

Doerr-Schott, J., Dubois, M. P. (1973): Detection par immunofluorescence des cellules corticotropes et mélanotropes dans l'hypophyse de la grenouille, *Rana temporaria* L., au cours du développement. Z. Zellforsch. *142*, 571–580.

Eagleson, G. W., McKeown, B. A. (1978): Localization of the pituitary lactotropes and thyreotropes within *Ambystoma gracile* by histochemical and immunochemical methods. A developmental study of two populations. Cell Tissue Res. *189*, 53–66.

Fumagalli, G., Zanini, A. (1985): In cow anterior pituitary, growth hormone and prolactin can be packed in separate granules of the same cell. J. Cell. Biol. *100*, 2019–2024.

Garcia-Navarro, S., Malagon, M. M., Garcia-Herdugo, G., Gracia-Navarro, F. (1988a): Immunocytochemical and morphometric study of prolactin cells during amphibian morphogenesis. Gen. Comp. Endocrinol. *69*, 188–196.

Garcia-Navarro, S., Malagon, M. M., Garcia-Navarro, F. (1988b): Immunohistochemical localization of thyrotropic cells during amphibian morphogenesis: a stereological study. Gen. Comp. Endocrinol. *71*, 116–123.

Gaudino, G., Mazzi, V., Fasolo, A. (1983): Immunocytochemical identification of ACTH containing cells in the hypophysis of the crested newt. Monitore Zool. Ital. *17*, 409–413.

Gosner, K. L. (1960): A simplified table for staging anuran embryos and larvae with notes on identification. Herpetologica *16*, 183–190.

Guyetant, R., Bugnon, C., Fellmann, D., Bloch, B. (1977): Étude cytoimmunologique comparative des cellules à prolactine et des cellules à somatohormone chez des têtards d'*Alytes obstetricans* (Laur.) élévés en groupe ou isolés. C. R. Acad. Sci. (Paris) *285*, 559–562.

Hoeffler, J. P., Bookfor, F. R., Frawley, L. S. (1985): Ontogeny of prolactin cells in neonatal rats: initial prolactin secretors also release growth hormone. Endocrinology *117*, 187–195.

Kar, S., Naik, D. R. (1986): Cytodifferentiation and immunocharacteristics of adenohypophysial cells in the toad, *Bufo melanostictus*. Anat. Embryol. *175*, 137–146.

Kerr, T. (1966): The development of the pituitary in *Xenopus laevis* Daudin. Gen. Comp. Endocrinol. 6, 303–311.

Mira-Moser, F. (1972): L'ultrastructure de l'adénohypophyse du crapaud *Bufo bufo* L.. III. Différenciation des cellules de la *pars distalis* au cours du développement larvaire. Z. Zellforsch. *125*, 88–107.

Moriceau-Hay, D., Doerr-Schott, J., Dubois, M. P. (1979): Mise en évidence par immunofluorescence des cellules à prolactine et des cellules somatotropes dans l'hypophyse du têtard de Xénope (*Xenopus laevis* D.). Gen. Comp. Endocrinol. *39*, 322–326.

– (1982): Immunohistochemical demonstration of TSH-, LH- and ACTH-cells in the hypophysis of tadpoles of *Xenopus laevis* D.. Cell Tissue Res. *225*, 57–64.

Nelson, C., Albert, V. R., Elsholtz, H. P., Lu, L. I. W., Rosenfeld, M. G. (1988): Activation of cell-specific expression of rat growth hormone and prolactin genes by a common transcription factor. Science *239*, 1400–1405.

Nieuwkoop, P. D., Faber, J. (1967): Normal table of *Xenopus laevis* (Daudin). North Holland, Amsterdam.

Nikitovitch-Winer, M. B., Atkin, J., Maley, B. E. (1987): Colocalization of prolactin and growth hormone within specific adenohypophysial cells in male, female and lactating female rats. Endocrinology *121*, 625–630.

Nyholm, N. E. I. (1977): Some morphogenetic features of the adenohypophysial primordium of early *Xenopus laevis* tadpoles. Cell Tissue Res. *180*, 223–230.

Nyholm, N. E. I., Doerr-Schott, J. (1977): Developmental immunohystology of melanotrophs in *Xenopus laevis* tadpoles. Cell Tissue Res. *180*, 231–239.

Papka, R. E., Yu, S. M., Nikitovitch-Winer, M. B. (1986): Use of immunoperoxidase and immunogold method in studying prolactin secretion and application of immunogold labelling for pituitary hormones and neuropeptides. Am. J. Anat. *175*, 289–306.

Pasteels, J. L. (1957): Recherches expérimentales sur le rôle de l'hypothalamus dans la differenciation cytologique de l'hypophyse, chez *Pleurodeles waltlii*. Arch. Biol. *68*, 65–114.

Rémy, C., Dubois, M. P. (1973): Les cellules somatotropes et les cellules à prolactine de l'hypophyse du têtard d'*Alytes obstetricans* Laur. Identification par immunofluorescence C. R. Soc. Biol. *167*, 1581–1584.

– (1974): Identification par immunofluorescence des cellules corticotropes et melanotropes de l'hypophyse d'*Alytes obstetricans* (Laur.) larvaire. C. R. Soc. Biol. *168*, 1275–1279.

Specker, J. L., Ingleton, P. M., Bern, H. A. (1984): Comparative physiology of the prolactin cell. In: Prolactin secretion: a multidisciplinary approach. (F. Mena, R. C. M. Valverde, eds.), Academic Press, New York.)

Zuber-Vogeli, M., Bihouès-Louis, M. A. (1971): L'hypophyse de *Nectophrynoides occidentalis* au cours du développement embryonnaire. Gen. Comp. Endocrinol. *16*, 200–216.

Zuber-Vogeli, M., Doerr-Schott, J. (1984): Localisation par immunofluorescence de différents principes hormonaux de l'hypophyse de *Nectophrynoides occidentalis* Angel, au cours du développement embryonnaire. Gen. Comp. Endocrinol. *53*, 264–271.

Zurschmiede, C., Landolt, A. M. (1987): Distribution of growth hormone and prolactin in secretory granules of the normal and neoplastic human adenohypophysis. Virchows Arch. B. *53*, 308–315.

Fortschritte der Zoologie, Band/Vol. 38 · Hanke, W. (Hrsg.), Biology and Physiology of Amphibians
Gustav Fischer Verlag · Stuttgart · New York · 1990

The metabolic situation of the liver during development in respect to corticosteroid function

WILFRIED HANKE, CARMEN LANGE and KURT WEINDEL

Department of Zoology, University of Karlsruhe, D-7500 Karlsruhe, FRG

The metabolic pathways which operate in the liver during development of Amphibia change extremely with the developmental stage. Two aspects are especially important, the change from ammoniotelism to ureotelism and the shift from lipid to carbohydrate storage. The first event is necessary for the transition from aquatic to terrestrial life and is therefore important in those groups living out of the water after metamorphosis. The second process is not clearly limited to adaptational types of life. It occurs in all groups of Amphibia as far as it is known. There is no clear evidence to expect that it is linked to the shift from herbivorous to carnivorous type of nutrition. It might just be that storing lipids instead of carbohydrates has advantage for the larva to limit space and weight (Weber, 1967; Dodd and Dodd, 1976).

The activity of enzymes must certainly depend on the type of metabolism. It has to be analyzed whether enzymes linked with lipid metabolism have a stage-dependent activity profile different from that of the enzymes of carbohydrate metabolism.

A parallel analysis of all these metabolic changes during metamorphosis has not been done. Nevertheless, the main course of the changes is quite well known. This report deals with variations which depend on developmental stages of *Xenopus laevis*, the clawed toad. The developmental stages are determined according to the Normal Table of Nieuwkoop and Faber (1975). The stage dependent changes of the amount of lipids and carbohydrates in the liver has been studied and suggestions for the regulation of the variations are made. The activities of some metabolic enzymes are measured. All this should explain the shift and regulation of the metabolic situation of the liver during development. Additionally, the influence of corticosteroids on liver compounds and enzymes has been analyzed.

1. Changes of the liver composition during development

The weight of the liver of the clawed toad changes characteristically during development. It increases during prometamorphosis congruently with the increase of body weight. The liver weight also increases from stage 60 to 62 while the body weight starts decreasing. This means that the liver-somatic-index is enlarged during this period. A reduction of the liver weight is found from stage 62 to 64 parallelly with the stop of food intake. Afterwards a rapid augmentation of the liver weight occurs (Fig. 1).

The amount of all lipids (total lipid fraction, TLF) present in the body of the tadpole or juveniles of the clawed toad decreases during the last stages of metamorphosis, if the value is related to the dry weight of the body. Values found by Meißl (1975) were about 12 mg

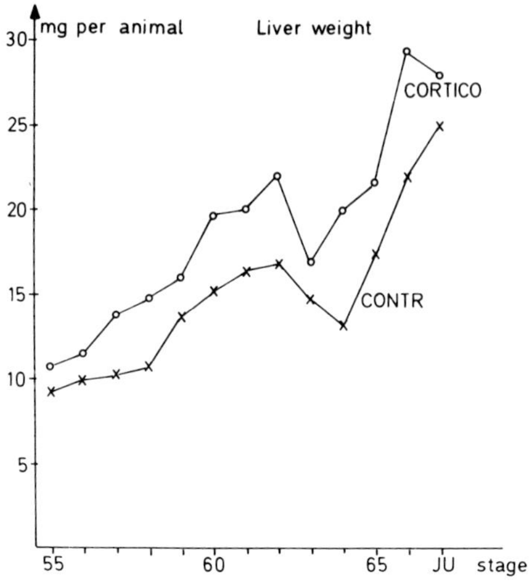

Fig. 1: Weight of the liver of *Xenopus* stages and changes after treatment with twice 1 g corticosterone per animal. All differences between controls and corticosterone treated animals are statistical significant ($p < 0.05$). Aldosterone treatment has no effect. JU = juveniles, n = 10 (Hanke and Leist, 1971).

TLF/100 mg DW for prometamorphic stages (stage 54–58) which decrease to 10 mg/100 mg during metamorphic climax and 8 mg/100 mg in juveniles. These values depend on the food. If the values are related to fresh weight maximal values are found at metamorphic climax when the water content of the animal is going to be reduced.

The lipid content of the whole body depends strongly on hormones. Hypophysial hormones like ACTH (and presumably prolactin) reduce the lipid content. Other metabolic hormones like insulin increase the lipid content (Gunesch, 1973; Fig. 2).

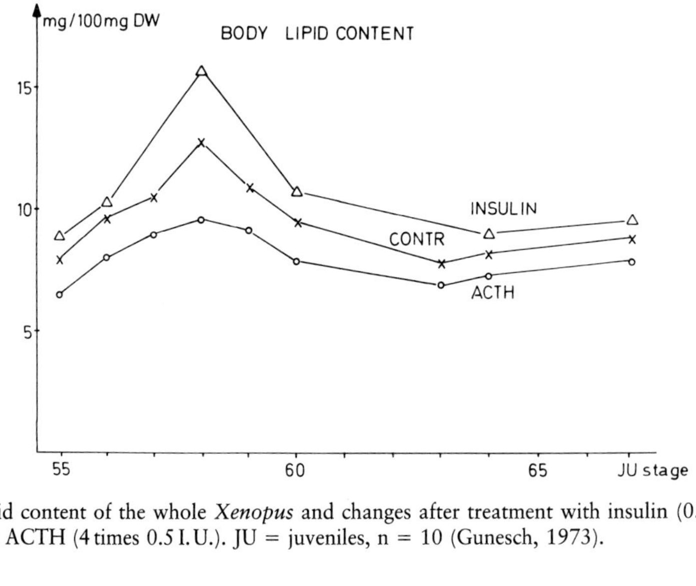

Fig. 2: Lipid content of the whole *Xenopus* and changes after treatment with insulin (0.05 I.U. per animal) or ACTH (4 times 0.5 I.U.). JU = juveniles, n = 10 (Gunesch, 1973).

The colour of the liver indicates the changes of the lipid content which occurs. The liver appears yellowish pale during prometamorphosis and gets deep red-brown at metamorphic climax and in juveniles. This is congruent with the transition from lipid to carbohydrate storage.

The lipid content (TLF) of the liver declines sharply from stage 64 onwards in connection with the last morphological changes of metamorphosis (Fig. 3).

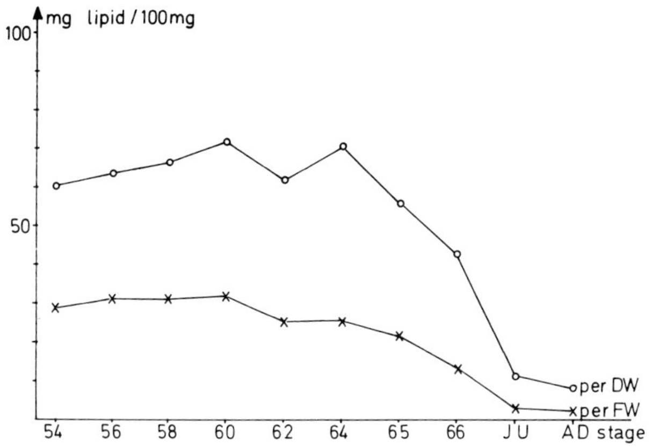

Fig. 3: Lipid content of the liver of *Xenopus* stages (JU = juveniles, AD = adults) related to dry weight (DW) or fresh weight (FW), n = 10 (Meißl, 1975).

Triglyzerids are found to be the most frequent fraction of lipids in tadpoles (about 80%). Their portion is reduced in juveniles where they account to about 30% of the TLF (Meißl, 1975).

The amount of lipids of the tadpole body of the clawed toad is also dependent on a well developed fat body near the gonadal anlage. The weight of this tissue increases till stage 60 and can reach about 10 mg per tadpole. Afterwards, the weight is reduced to just 3–4 mg per juvenile tadpole. Several effectors are known to influence the size of the fat body, the season (Smith, 1950 and 1954 for *Rana temporaria*; Mizell, 1965 for *R. pipiens*), the developmental stage (Sawant and Varute, 1973 for *R. tigrina*), the presence or absence of the pituitary, etc. The regulation seems to depend mainly on pituitary hormones, since hypophysectomy enlarges the fat body significantly.

The glycogen content of the liver of the clawed toad increases from stage 57 onwards. It is about 0.4% of the fresh weight during prometamorphosis and increases to more than 10% in the juvenile liver dependent on the food. Similar changes are known for *Rana temporaria* (Urbani, 1956). The tadpole of *Xenopus* cannot take up food at several stages of metamorphic climax. Therefore, the increase of the glycogen content has a depression at stage 62–64 (Fig. 4).

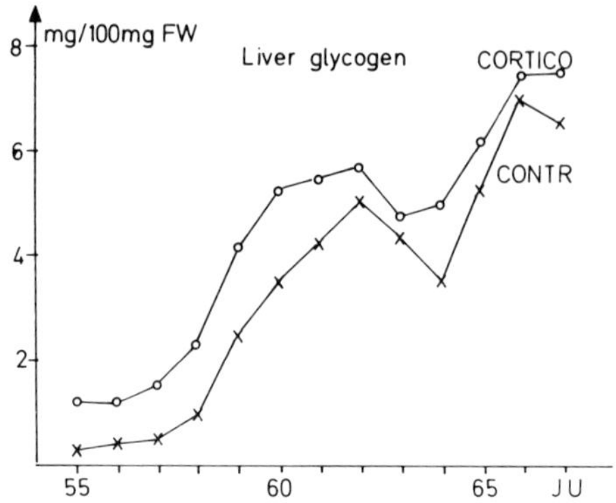

Fig. 4: Glycogen content of the liver of *Xenopus* stages and changes after treatment with twice 1 g corticosterone per animal. All differences between controls and corticosterone treated animals are statistical significant ($p < 0.05$). Aldosterone treatment has no effect. JU = juveniles, n = 10 (Hanke and Leist, 1971).

2. Influence of corticosteroids on the liver during development

It is well known that the activity of the interrenal tissue of clawed toads is quite low during prometamorphosis and increases at the end of this period. The changes in the liver which occur during the first stages (58–62) of metamorphic climax are influenced apparently by the interrenal secretion. An increase of the liver weight and the amount of glycogen can be induced by injection of corticosterone (Fig. 1, 4). This suggests that the normal interrenal secretion is responsible for the changes which occur during the normal development.

3. Changes of the activity of liver enzymes during development

This chapter deals with the activity of several enzymes of carbohydrate metabolism at different stages of development. The activity of the following enzymes has been determined:
Pyruvate kinase (enzyme of glycolysis),
glucose-6-phosphate dehydrogenase/6-phosphogluconate dehydrogenase (enzyme system of pentosephosphate shunt),
fructose-1,6-diphosphatase (enzyme of gluconeogenesis),
phosphorylase a (enzyme of glycogenolysis),
uridinediphosphoglucose pyrophosphorylase (enzyme of glycogen production).

Pyruvate kinase provides ATP under anaerobic conditions. The enzyme system of the pentose shunt delivers NADPH for lipogenesis using glucose-6-phosphate. Fructose-1,6-diphosphatase is important for the synthesis of glycogen to increase the stores and plasma glucose levels. Phosphorylase a is the active form of the enzyme which splits off glucose phosphate from glycogen and uridinediphosphoglucose pyrophosphorylase (glycogen synthase) is the enzyme which catalyzes the step from glucose-1-phosphat to glycogen.

The stages of development which have been studied are stage 53/54, the start of prometamorphosis, stage 57, near the end of prometamorphosis, and juveniles shortly after metamorphic climax. The stages of metamorphic climax during which dramatic changes may occur are not investigated, till now.

The specific activity of the enzymes is the value related to the protein content. The amount of water present in the liver tissue and, therefore, also the protein content change significantly between prometamorphosis and juveniles. The protein content increases from stage 53/54 to 57 indicating water loss. It decreases from stage 57 to juveniles for more than 20% due to an augmentation of water but also to an increase of glycogen. The liver gains water during metamorphic climax, while the other tissues lose water (Fig. 5).

The profile of the activity of the enzymes calculated for the 3 stages is much different when related to fresh weight (FW) than to mg protein. To demonstrate clearly the changes between the 3 stages both types of relations are given in the figures.

The activity of pyruvate kinase increases with the development (Fig. 6). An enormous increase is seen from stage 7 to juveniles when the specific activity is calculated. This points to a strong increase of carbohydrate metabolism at the end of metamorphosis.

The same profile is found for the activity of the enzymes of the pentose shunt (Fig. 7). This suggests an increase of glucose degradation, too. But, this enzyme also provides NADPH which is necessary for lipogenesis. The changes of this enzyme system do not give clear evidence what metabolic pathway is prefered.

The activity of fructose-diphosphatase decreases in juveniles when the activity is related to fresh weight, but it is constant when related to protein content (Fig. 8). This is surprising because one would expect an increase of the activity when more glycogen is produced.

The phosphorylase activity again is much higher in juvenile livers than in those of premetamorphic larvae (Fig. 9). This result explains the preference of glycogen utilization after metamorphosis compared with larvae.

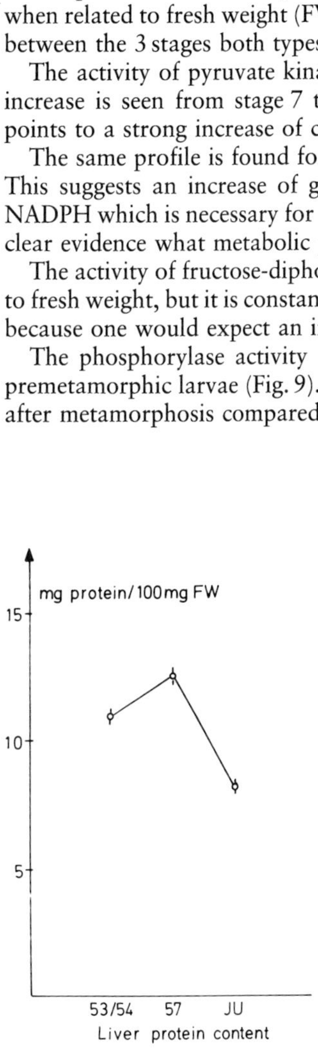

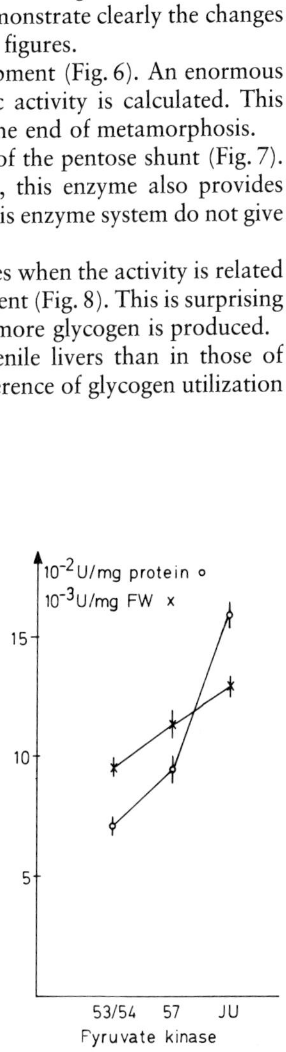

Fig. 5 (left): Liver protein content of different stages of *Xenopus laevis*. n = 10.

Fig. 6 (right): Activity of pyruvate kinase of the liver of *Xenopus laevis* of different stages related to protein content or fresh weight (FW). n = 10.

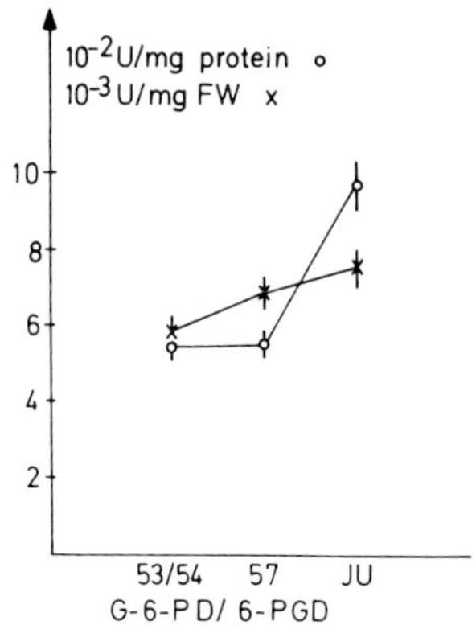

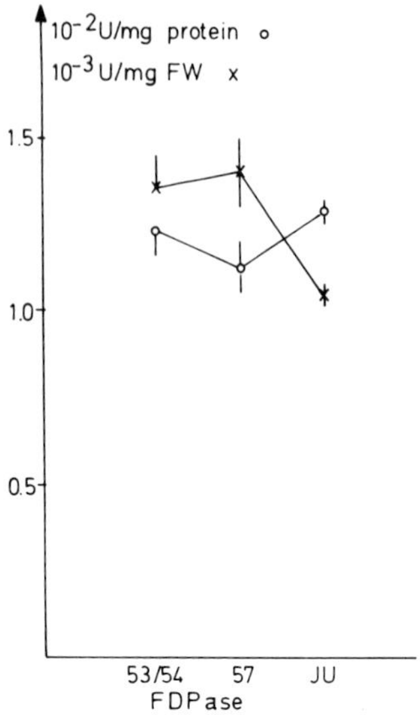

Fig. 7 (left): Activity of glucose-6-phosphate dehydrogenase/6-phosphogluconate dehydrogenase of the liver of *Xenopus laevis* of different stages related to protein content or fresh weight (FW). n = 10.

Fig. 8 (right): Activity of fructose-diphosphatase of the liver of *Xenopus laevis* of different stage related to protein content or fresh weight (FW). n = 10.

The activity of the enzyme which is important for the synthesis of glycogen, the uridinephosphoglucose pyrophosphorylase, increases strongly after metamorphosis, too. This is demonstrated in both relations, to fresh weight or to protein content (Fig. 10).

These changes of enzyme activity during metamorphosis reflect the energetic demands and the metabolic pathways. The higher activity of pyruvate kinase is necessary because of the higher activity of the protein synthesis in the liver of postmetamorphic animals. The activity of the pentose shunt is needed for the production of pentose-phosphate and NADPH. The first product is important for protein synthesis, too. NADPH may be needed for the increased production of structural lipids after metamorphosis.

The activity of fructose-diphosphatase does not change statistically significant. This can be explained by the fact that it is not a rate-limiting enzyme of gluconeogenesis. The first evidence for gluconeogenesis occurs after prometamorphosis in stage 58–61 (Hanke and Leist, 1971; Leist, 1970; Hanke, 1974 and 1978). The indications for gluconeogenesis at these stages are an increase of the glucose level in the body fluid, of the liver and muscle glycogen content. If the fructose-diphosphatase would be rate-limiting an increase of the activity at metamorphic climax and in juveniles must be expected.

The comparison of the activity of phosphorylase and glycogen synthase between stage 53/54 and stage 57 shows that the breakdown of glycogen is reduced and the synthesis is enhanced at stage 57. This could result in an increase of glycogen concentration. Both enzyme systems are more active in juveniles. At this time the breakdown and the synthesis is balanced on a higher level.

Nothing is known about the activity of a key enzyme for turnover of triglyzerides in larvae of *Xenopus*. It is, therefore, not possible to discuss changes of triglyceride production or breakdown in the liver of the clawed toad.

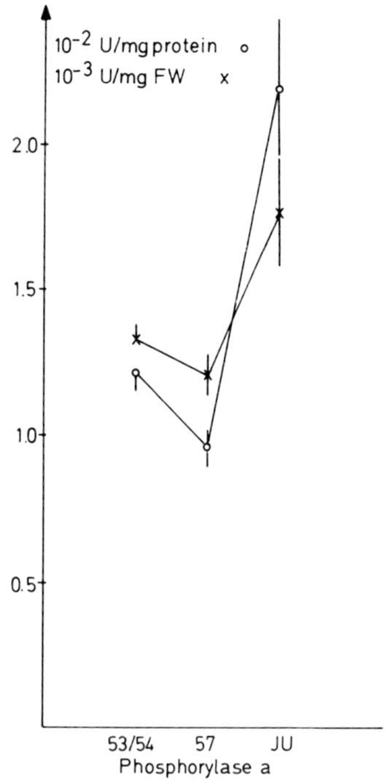

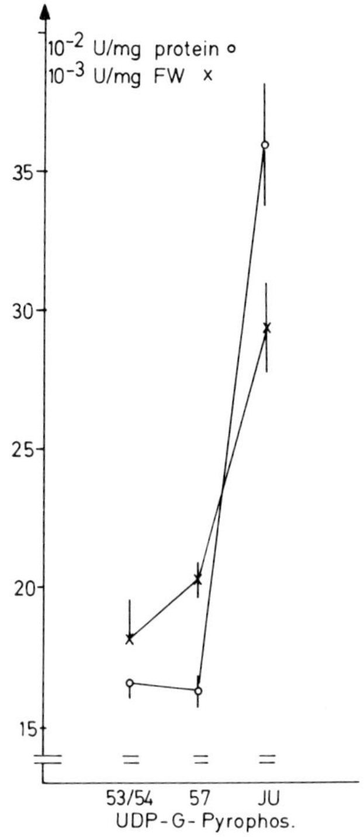

Fig. 9 (left): Activity of phosphorylase a of the liver of *Xenopus laevis* of different stages related to protein content or fresh weight (FW). n = 10.

Fig. 10 (right): Activity of uridine-diphosphate-glucose pyrophosphatase of the liver of *Xenopus laevis* of different stages related to protein content of fresh weight (FW). n = 10.

4. Changes of the activity of liver enzymes by corticosteroids

This chapter reports effects of corticosteroids on several enzymes in juveniles of the clawed toad. The study was done to answer the question whether enzymatic variations at the end of metamorphosis can be due to changes of the activity of the interrenal tissue.

The activity of the pentose shunt enzyme system and of the malate enzyme were determined. The malate enzyme catalyzes the conversion of malate to pyruvate by splitting off CO_2 and reduction of $NADP^+$ to NADPH. Both systems provide NADPH for the reductive synthesis of triglycerides. Besides the activity of these enzymes, the correlated lipid content of the liver and the blood plasma were determined. Despite of using juvenile toads (10–15 g) clear sexual differences were seen in these animals. Therefore the response of males and females must be indicated separately.

The activity of the pentose shunt enzymes increases after treatment with corticosterone in both sexes. The activity was measured 4 hrs after the injection because short term effects were expected (Fig. 11).

The same response was found for the malate enzyme (Fig. 12). The activities for both enzymes were higher in females than in males which points to a specific role in vitellogenesis via NADPH generation.

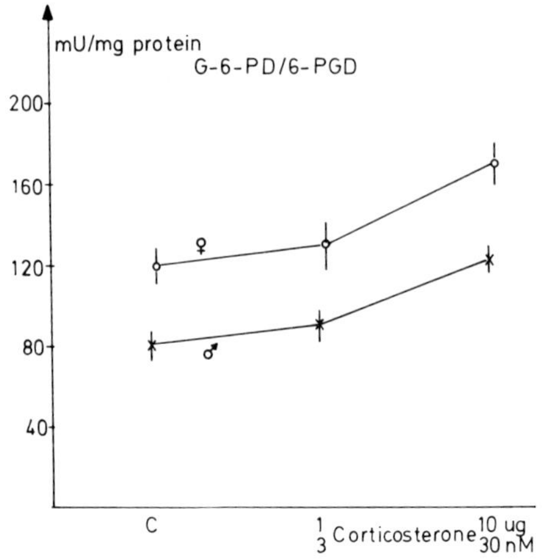

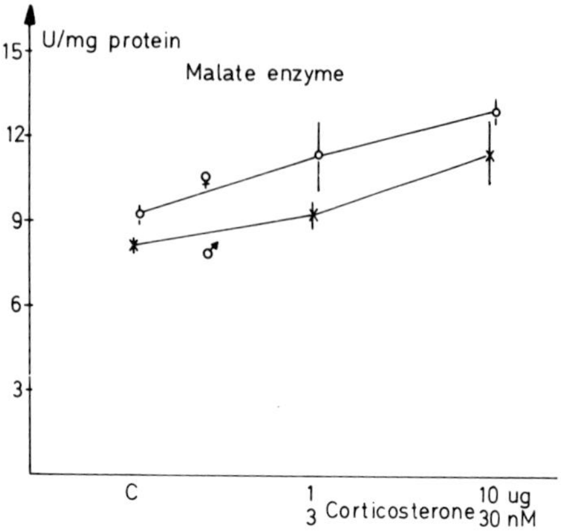

Fig. 11 (left): Changes of the activity of glucose-6-phosphate dehydrogenase/6-phosphogluconate dehydrogenase of the liver of juvenile *Xenopus laevis* (males and females) after treatment with 1 or 10 g corticosterone (4 hrs after injection). n = 6–8.

Fig. 12 (right): Changes of the activity of malate enzyme of the liver of juvenile *Xenopus laevis* (males and females) after treatment with 1 or 10 g corticosterone (4 hrs after injection). n = 6–8.

The lipid content of the liver was higher in males than in females. In both sexes, corticosterone increased significantly the lipid content of the liver. Treatment with aldosterone has less effect than that with corticosterone. Corticosterone influenced also the lipid content of the plasma. A clear increase was found after treatment (Fig. 13).

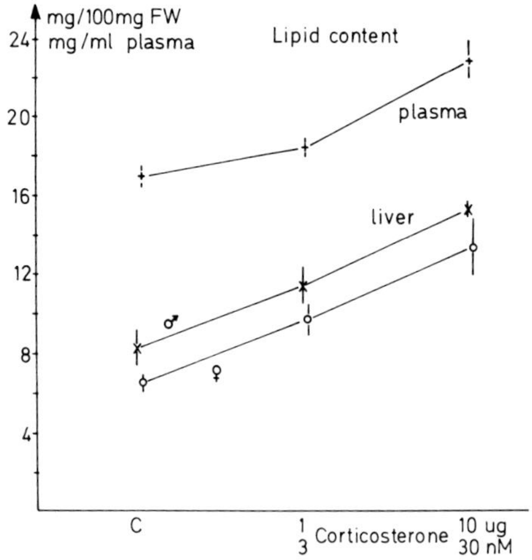

Fig. 13: Changes of the lipid content of the plasma and the liver of juvenile *Xenopus laevis* (males and females) after treatment with 1 or 10 g corticosterone (4 hrs. after injection). n = 6–8.

It is difficult to get a homogenous picture from all these results. Interrenal secretion increases at the end of prometamorphosis and is quite high in metamorphic climax. This explains the elevation of liver glycogen and blood glucose at this stage. This is supported by some of the enzyme studies, e. g. high activity of glycogen synthase and pyruvate kinase and presumably also phosphorylase. The increase of liver lipid content in juveniles by corticosterone is contradictory. But the elevation of plasma lipids by this treatment support again the idea of lipid mobilization by corticosteroids.

It is evident, that NADPH generation is enhanced at the end of metamorphosis and under corticosterone treatment in juveniles. This suggests a moderate and special support of lipid synthesis.

References

Dodd, M. H. J., Dodd, J. M. (1976): The biology of metamorphosis, In: Physiology of the Amphibia (B. Lofts, ed.), vol. 3, pp. 467–599, Academic Press. New York, London.

Gunesch, K. D. (1973): Beeinflussung des Fettstoffwechsels beim Krallenfrosch (*Xenopus laevis* Daudin) durch ACTH, Corticosteroide und Insulin, Zool. Jb. Physiol. *78*, 108–127.

Hanke, W. (1974): Die hormonale Regulation des Stoffwechsels bei Amphibien, Fortschritte der Zoologie *22*, 431–455.

Hanke, W. (1978): The adrenal cortex of Amphibia. In: General and comparative endocrinology of the adrenal cortex (I. Chester Jones and I. W. Henderson, eds.), vol. 2, p. 419–495, Acad. Press, New York, London.

Hanke, W., Leist, K. H. (1971): The effect of ACTH and corticosteroids on carbohydrate metabolism during the metamorphosis of *Xenopus laevis*. Gen. Comp. Endocrinol. *16*, 137–148.

Leist, K. H. (1970): Die Bedeutung des Adenohypophysen-Interrenal-Systems für den Osmomineral-Haushalt des Krallenfrosches (*Xenopus laevis* Daudin) im Verlauf der Metamorphose, Zool. Jb. Physiol. *75*, 375–401.

Meißl, H. (1975): Der Einfluß von Prolaktin und Somatotropin auf den Lipidstoffwechsel während der Metamorphose des Krallenfrosches *Xenopus laevis* Daudin. Thesis University of Karlsruhe FRG.

Mizell, S. (1965): Seasonal changes in energy reserves in the common frog, *Rana pipiens*. J. cell. comp. Physiol. *66*, 252–258.

Nieuwkoop, P. D., Farber, J. (1975): Normal tables of *Xenopus laevis* Daudin, North Holland Publ. Co., Amsterdam.

Sawant, V. A., Varute, A. T. (1973): Lipid changes in the tadpoles of *Rana tigrina* during growth and metamorphosis. Comp. Biochem. Physiol. *44*, 729–750.

Smith, C. L. (1950): Seasonal changes in blood sugar, fat body, liver glycogen and gonads in the common frog, *Rana temporaria* L. J. Exp. Biol. *26*, 412–429.

Smith, C. L. (1954): The relation between seasonal hyperglycemia and thyroid activity in the frog (*Rana temporaria*). J. Endocrinol. *10*, 184–191.

Urbani, E. (1956): Lipases and lipids in the embryonic and larval developments of *Bufo vulgaris* and *Rana esculenta*. Atti Acad. Nazl. Lincei *21*, 598–503.

Weber, R. (1967): Biochemistry and amphibian development. In: The biochemistry of animal development (Weber, R., ed.), vol. II: Biochemical control mechanisms and adaptations in development, Academic Press, New York and London, pp. 267–301.

Fortschritte der Zoologie, Band/Vol. 38 · Hanke, W. (Hrsg.), Biology and Physiology of Amphibians
Gustav Fischer Verlag · Stuttgart · New York · 1990

Anatomy and development of the inner ear in amphibians*

IRIS HERTWIG[1] and JOACHIM HENTSCHEL[2]

[1] Zoologisches Institut der Universität, Poppelsdorfer Schloß, 5300 Bonn 1, FRG
[2] Max-Planck-Institut für Systemphysiologie, Rheinlanddamm 201, 4600 Dortmund 1, FRG

1. Introduction

Development and function of sensory organs are always closely related to animal's habitat and way of life. Investigating structure and physiology of such organs, amphibians become the matter of interest because they are living in two totally different biotopes – water and land – during their ontogenesis. Especially the inner ear which possess various functions, detection of gravity and rotation as well as perception of acoustic signals, undergoes far reaching changes. Therefore great emphasis was laid on the physiological aspects (Brzoska et al. 1977, Hubl & Schneider, 1979, Mohneke & Schneider, 1979, Mohneke 1983, Walkowiak 1980, Joermann & Schneider 1986, Diekamp & Schneider 1988, Schneichel & Schneider 1988) and on morphology (Larsell 1933, Anson 1934, Evans 1936, Witschi 1949, Heywood et al. 1975, Thorn 1976, Van de Water et al. 1977, Li et al. 1978, Cohen & Fermin 1979, Favre & Sans 1979) in inner ear research in the last decades. Unfortunately these investigations deal mainly with the adult organ or consider rather limited aspects in the developing inner ear.

This paper is to give a short survey of organogenesis beginning with the first developmental steps up to transition of amphibians from water to land taking into account most recent results including our own findings.

2. Materials and methods

The material used was the inner ear of *Rana temporaria*, *Xenopus laevis* and *Salamandra salamandra*. In order to investigate morphology, cytology and development of the labyrinth and to visualize details of two dimensional LM- and TEM-micrographs in their three dimensional organization by SEM views the method of choice was a combined light, transmission and scanning electron microscopical technique on one and the same sample (for details see Hertwig & Schneider 1986, Hertwig 1987a and Hertwig & Hentschel 1989).

---

* Dedicated to Prof. Dr. H. Schneider on the occasion of his 60th year of birth

3. Development of morphology and cytology of the inner ear of amphibians

The inner ear of vertebrates is a complex organ with various functions such as detection of attitude in space, rotation and acoustic signals (Hertwig & Schneider 1986; Hertwig 1987 a). For this purpose different sensory structures have been developed. In anurans for example the utricle, the saccule and the lagena are responsible for orientation in space, rotation is detected by the three ampullar cristae. Acoustic signals are distinguished by the basilar and – typical for amphibians – the amphibian papillae (Fig. 1 a). Each gravity-sensing organ contains an otolith while the ampullar cristae lie below a cupula. The two sound-detecting papillae are equipped with tectorial membranes (Geißler & van Bergeijk 1964, Frishkopf & Flock 1966, Alfs & Schneider 1973, Wever 1973, Alfs 1978, Hertwig & Schneider 1986, Hertwig 1987 a, Hertwig & Hentschel 1989). In all of these structures the sensory epithelium is made up of hair (sensory) cells and supporting cells (Wersäll 1956, Wersäll & Bagger-Sjöbäck 1974, Anniko 1983). A very interesting aspect is the development of the inner ear during ontogenesis because different sensory efforts have to be made in water and on land.

3.1. General morphology

Development of the inner ear begins early during the intermediate neurula stage by invagination on the auditory placode to form the otocyst (Fig. 2), the anlage of the labyrinth (Huschke 1845, van der Sticht 1908, Hertwig 1987 a). Typical for the developing otocyst is only one primordial sensory epithelium, the macula communis. Overlying the macula is a densely structured network of organic material (Fig. 2). It was often stated out, that the rhombencephalon has inductive influence on otocyst formation and differentiation in vertebrates (Sharp 1885, Detwiler 1948, 1951, Detwiler & Van Dyke 1950, Waddington 1937, Li et al. 1978). This conclusion must be questioned at least for the amphibians because otocyst formation occurs completely separate from the developing brain (Hertwig 1987 a). Not until the macula communis is complete, the semicircular canals take shape during the transition from the young larval stage to tadpoles. First two dorsal pockets are formed as protrusions from the otocyst representing the two vertical canals, soon followed by a lateral pocket, the anlage of the horizontal canal. Thereafter in the central regions of opposite walls of all three pockets, depressions appear in the epithelia (Fig. 1 b) and in the pocket the lumen epithelia fuse, separating the three canals from the common lumen of the otocyst. At the same time the ampullar cristae develop separate from the macula communis and even their developing cupulae can be recognized (Fig. 3).

In the young tadpole stage the formation of the utricle and the saccule occurs by constriction between the superior and inferior part of the otocyst, dividing the macula communis into two parts. That this dividing process is not only a local event – as it looks like in the phasecontrast micrograph (Fig. 4 b) – but is a concentric constriction of the whole otocyst is revealed by scanning electron micrographs (Fig. 4 a). The region dorsal to the constriction is already identifiable as the utricle and the ventral part as the saccule. When utricle and semicircular canals have completely differentiated, the saccule region is still undergoing morphological development: both the basilar and amphibian papilla as well as the lagena are formed by invagination of the saccule (Fig. 5) in stages of early tadpolews, i. e. before metamorphosis (Hertwig & Schneider, 1986, Hertwig 1987 a, Hertwig & Hentschel 1989).

Thus all sensory epithelia are formed before the animal takes up life on land. Development of the inner ear already starts during the intermediate neurula stage and the first

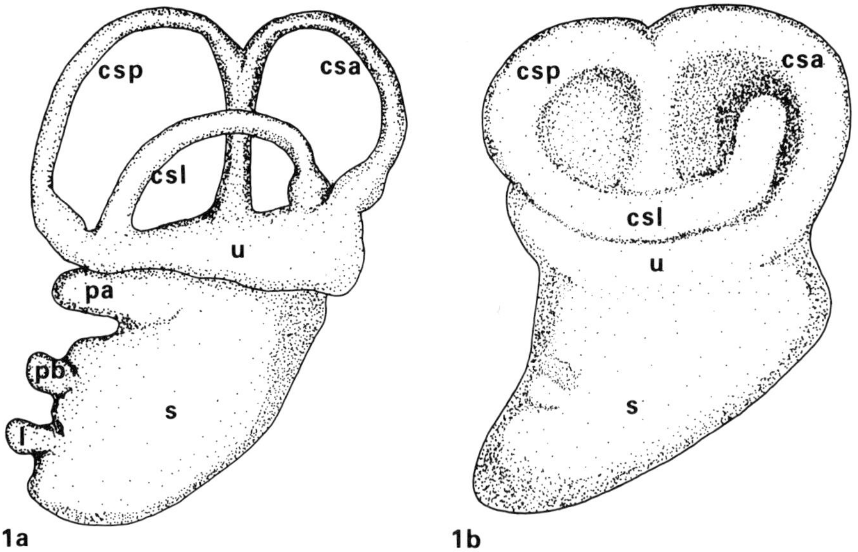

Fig. 1: Schematically drawings of the fully differentiated (1 a) and developing inner ear (1 b) with the tree gravity organs utricle (u), saccule (s), lagena (1), the auditory papilla amphibiorum (pa) and papilla basilaris (pb) and the semicircular canals canalis semicircularis anterior (csa), lateralis (csl) and posterior (csp)
Abbreviations: c cilium – ca crista ampullaris – cc crus commune – csa canalis semicircularis anterior – csl canalis semicircularis lateralis – csp canalis semicircularis posterior – cu cupula – ed epidermis – fus foramen utriculo-sacculare – g ganglion – kc kinocilium – l lagena – ma main axis – mc macula communis – ms macula of the saccule – mv microvilli – o otolith – om otolith membrane – on organic network – pa papilla amphibiorum – pb papilla basilaris – po preotoconia – s saccule – sc supporting cell – stc stereocilia – u utricle

perception of gravity detection by the otocyste is possible in young larval stages. At that time even the semicircular canals responsible for rotation have developed. In the early tadpole stages these structures are refined by dividing the otocyst into utricle, possessing a horizontal oriented sensory epithelium, and the saccule with a vertical situated epithelium. The early completion of gravity receptors makes sense because of the priority of orientation in space for animals living in water. In context with the lateral line system the animal is optimal equipped for orienting in space and capturing prey.

The auditory papilla basilaris and papilla amphibiorum are developed later during late tadpole stages shortly before metamorphosis. The same applies to the lagena, which is a very unimportant epithelium for gravity perception in amphibians. At the same time the nucleus dorsolateralis nervi octavii for handling acoustic signals is developed in the medulla (Hertwig 1987b). This sequence of development is reasonable because with beginning their life on land the amphibians require acoustic organs for instance to recognize enemies and the characteristic sounds of the species.

3.2. Cytology

All sensory epithelia of the inner ear show two characteristic cell types, the hair or sensory cell and the supporting cell (Wersäll 1956, Ginzberg & Gilula 1977, 1979, Yokoh

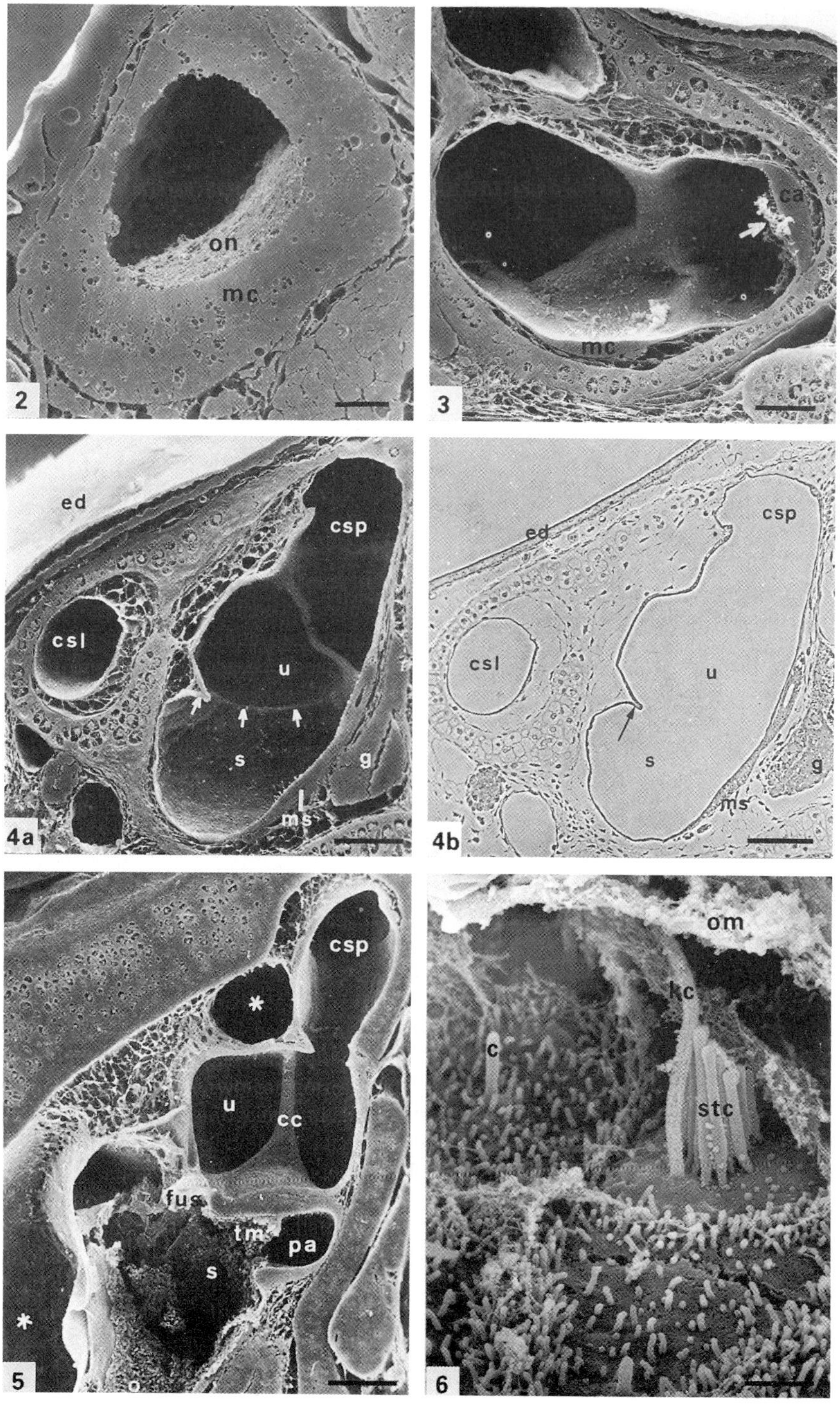
on
mc
2
ca
mc
3
ed
csp
csl
u
s
g
ms
4a
ed
csp
csl
u
s
g
ms
4b
csp
*
u
cc
fus
tm
pa
s
*
5
om
kc
c
stc
6

1971, Anniko 1983). In different epithelia, however, these cell types possess slightly morphological and cytological variations depending on their function. That a sensory epithelium is being formed first becomes evident with the appearance of two cell layers (Hertwig & Schneider 1986). The mechanism by which embryonic cells differentiate into sensory or supporting cells still is unknown and investigations of several authors have led to different results. On the one hand cytogenesis is supposed to be induced by the entry of nerve fibers into the developing neuroepithelium (Ginsberg & Gilula 1977, 1979, Yokoh 1971). On the other hand it has been demonstrated, that the sensory and supporting cells develop prior to innervation (Evans 1943, Anniko et al. 1979, Hertwig & Schneider 1986).

3.2.1. Hair cells

When fully differentiated each hair cell of every sensing epithelium bears one large kinocilium and several stereocilia while each supporting cell possesses only a short cilium but mass of microvilli (Fig. 6). However, the hair cells can vary in length of the kinocilium and number of stereocilia in different sensory epithelia of one species as well as in the same epithelia of different species. Additionally the connection of the cilia to the respective organic matrix of each epithelium is different. This is clearly to be seen in the following examples:

a) In utricle and saccule of amphibians kinocilia of hair cells attach to an organic matrix, the otolith membrane (Fig. 6). They don't reach the otoliths directly. The organ-pipe like stereocilia of each hair cell have different length. It is obviously, however, that in *Salamandra* the stereocilia are much shorter than the kinocilia (Fig. 7).

b) The kinocilia of the auditory papillae in *Rana* and *Xenopus* are three times longer (8–12 μm) than that of *Salamandra* (3–4 μm). The organic material of the tectorial membrane is in contact only with the microvilli of the supporting cells, forming dome-like cavities over the apical surface of the receptor cells. The kino- and stereocilia of the latter extend through these spaces and don't touch the tectorial membrane. The organic network is different in the amphibian and basilar papilla leading to detection of different frequencies. The papilla amphibiorum perceives deep and middle frequencies between 300–700 Hertz (Frishkopf & Goldstein 1963), while the papilla basilaris distinguishes high frequencies of 1300 Hertz and more (Frishkopf et al. 1967, Feng et al. 1975). Additionally the sense cells of sound detecting papillae and of the saccule possess a special structure, a bulbus on the distal end of the kinocilium. This fact, together with the type of innervation, led to the conclusion, that even the saccule has hearing capacity (Alfs 1978). Between the distal ends of the kinocilium and stereocilia as well as between the stereocilia themselves filamentous material could be demonstrated (Fig. 9), connecting all cilia. This is senseful because the distal ends of the cilia underlie great mechanical stress. In addition to that morphological (Thurm 1984, Schmidt & Thurm 1984) and physiological investigations (Hudspeth 1983) showed, that the distal area of the hair bundle is very important

---

Fig. 2–6: Development of the inner ear in *Rana temporaria*. Fig. 2: SEM view of the otocyst and macula communis (mc) with organic network (on). Bar 20 μm. Fig. 3: SEM-micrograph of the macula communis, developing crista ampullaris (ca) and cupula (arrow). Bar 100 μm. Fig. 4a, b: Matching SEM (4a) and LM (4b) views of the concentric constriction (arrows) dividing the otocyst into utricle (u) and saccule (s). Bar 100 μm. Fig. 5: Fully differentiated inner ear (asterisks marking the perilymphatic space). Bar 200 μm. Fig. 6: SEM-micrograph of a sense cell and supporting cells of the utricle. Note the stereocilia (stc) and the long kinocilium of the sense cell in opposite to the normal cilium (c) of the supporting cell. Bar 1 μm. (Fig. 2–5 taken from Hertwig 1987a, Springer Verlag) for conductive changes. In other vertebrate species, for example in fish, one can detect various connecting structures (Neugebauer & Thurm 1984, 1985). This may depend on adaptation to different requirements caused by different way of life.

c) The kinocilia of the cristae ampullares are extremely long with a maximum of 40 μm linking directly the sensing epithelium with the cupula only in the peripheral regions (Fig. 9), whereas the kinocilia of sense cells located more centrally extend through cavities formed by the cupula. This construction amplifies the stimuli caused by rotation.

These divergent findings in different epithelia of one species have their causality in perceptinig various signals. The exact physiological events still remain to be clarified but it is obviously that – because of the similar morphology of sense cells in each epithelium – the transducing system for various signals such as gravity, rotation and sound must be different. The diverging morphology of the percepting apparatus of sense cells in same epithelia of different species – for example in *Rana* and *Xenopus* on the one hand and *Salamandra* on the other hand – might be due to the varying development – *Salamandra* is a viviparous species – or even caused by different habitats and habits.

3.2.2. Supporting cells and structures derived from them

When fully differentiated the supporting cells – the second cell type of the sensory epithelia of the inner ear – are pentagonal to hexagonal in cross-section. At the apico-lateral pole each cell is surrounded by a compact band of strongly osmiophilic material (Hertwig & Schneider 1986), which is of the cytoceratine type and stabilizes the form of the cells and that means of the whole epithelium. Directly below this zone lies a band of spot desmosomes. The process of supporting-cell-differentiation (from embryonic to the final form) is the same in all sensory epithelia of the inner ear. As these epithelia develop, however, cytological differences appear at various times when specialized structures are being derived from the supporting cells. These structures are on one hand the otoliths in the utricle, saccule and lagena, and on the other hand the cupula in the ampullae and the tectorial membranes in the papillae.

In adult frogs the otoliths are composed of a large number of otoconia. Early in development blister-like evaginations with non-homogeneous content appear at the apical pole of supporting cells in the macula communis (Fig. 10). These structures are separated from the cells by constriction and then fuse to form larger trior polygonal vesicles (Fig. 11), called preotoconia (Hertzog 1925, Carlström & Engström 1955, Igarishi & Kanda 1969, Kellerhals et al. 1970, Lim 1973, Anniko 1980, 1983, Salamat et al. 1980). They continue to enlarge to otoconia (Fig. 12) by incorporating other vesicles and additionally by progressive incorporation and superficial accumulation of inorganic material. A further interesting question is the composition the otoliths. It is already known that calcium plays a crucial role in forming otoconia (Harada 1979, Anniko 1983). And indeed it was shown

---

Fig. 7–9: SEM views of sense cells of different input structures in the inner ear of amphibians. Fig. 7: Sense cell of the utricle in Salamandra with long kinocilium (kc) and short stereocilia (stc). Bar 1 μm. Fig. 8: Kinocilium and stereocilia of the auditory papillae in Salamandra extend in cavities of the tectorial membrane, which is connected with microvilli (mv) of the supporting cells. Bar 1 μm. Fig. 9: Long kinocilia of the sense cells of a crista ampullaris in Rana. Bar 1 μm.

Fig. 10–12: Forming of the otoconia. Fig. 10: TEM-micrograph of an early preotoconia (arrrowheads), formed by secreting supporting cells (sc). Bar 1 μm. Fig. 11: TEM view of a late preotoconia (po) with three main axis (ma). Bar 1 μm. Fig. 12: SEM-micrograph of otoconia of the saccule in an adult frog. Bar 15 μm. (Fig. 10, 11 taken from Hertwig & Schneider 1986, Springer Verlag)

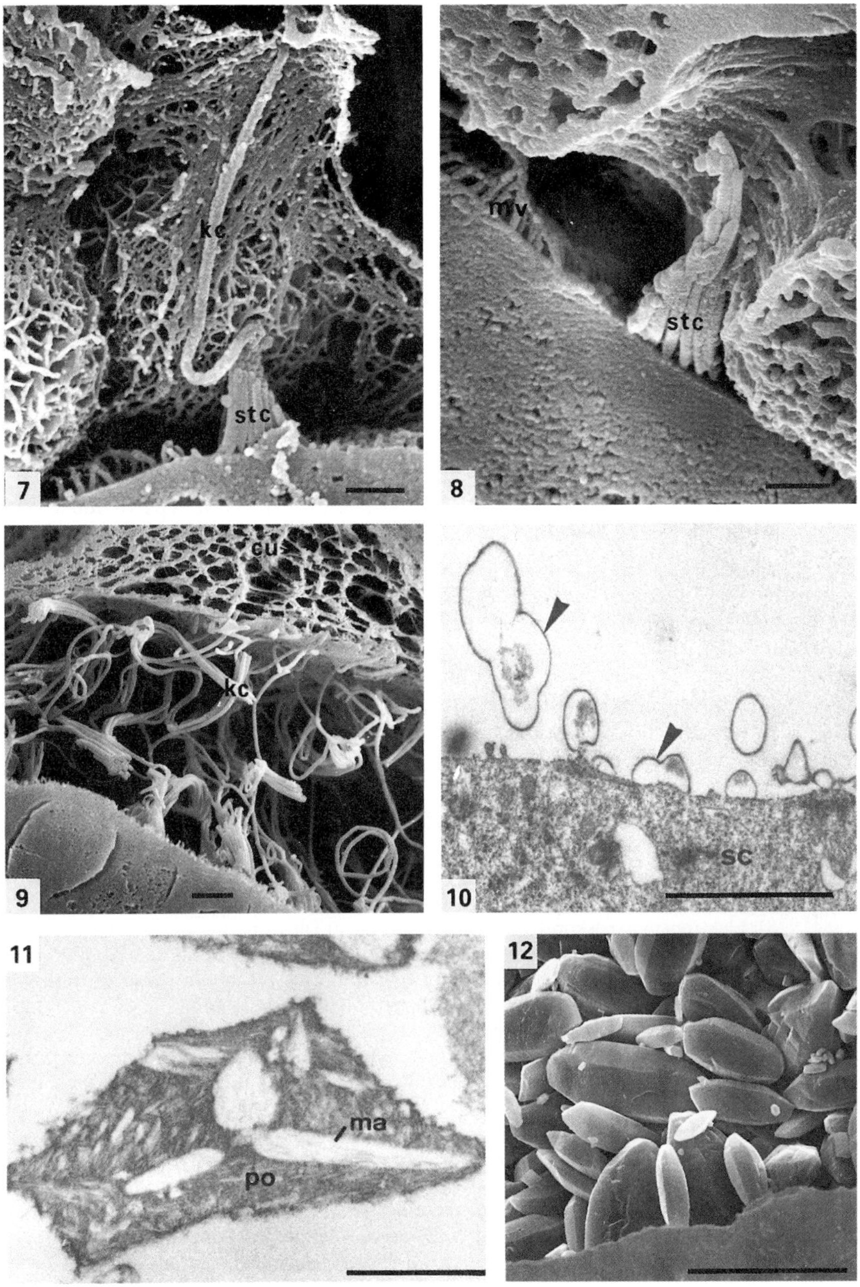
kc
stc
7
mv
stc
8
cu
kc
9
sc
10
11
ma
po
12

by x-ray-microanalysis that for example in *Rana* calcium is a main component of these structures (Hertwig & Schneider 1986). Often it is believed that the compound of the detected calcium is carbonate. However, with a refined analytical procedure a lot of other calcium salts can be proved. In *Xenopus* we found a mixture of at least three calcium compounds: carbonate, apatite and sulphate (Hertwig & Hentschel 1989). The otoconia of mammals, reptiles and birds mainly contain calcite, whereas in fish other calcium salts have been found, e.g. apatite, aragonite and valerite (Carlström et al. 1953, Parsons & Cardell 1965, Ross 1979, Salamat et al. 1980, Anniko 1983, Hertwig & Schneider 1986, Hertwig & Hentschel 1989).

The supporting cells in the cristae ampullares and auditory papillae only produce pure organic substances, which are released by exocytosis (Hertwig & Schneider 1986) and form the ampullar cupula and the tectorial membranes of the papillae. Typical for such cells in the productive phase is a high amount of dictyosomes and rough endoplasmic reticulum.

4. Concluding remarks

In conclusion, morphogenesis of the amphibian inner ear is a very rational process in which various structures develop in the order in which they are required by the maturing animal. Therefore the sequence of developing epithelia is precisely adjusted to the amphibian life cycle. Both in water and on land the animals rely heavily on their sense of equilibrium, therefore development of gravity and equilibrium sensory organs has priority. As soon as the animal takes up life on land, identification of sounds becomes important. So it is of positive selective value for the auditory papillae to develop before metamorphosis excluding any deficit of information about environmental conditions at any time during the life cycle.

References

Alfs, B. (1978): Elektronenmikroskopische Untersuchungen zur Ultrastruktur der Sinnesendstellen im Labyrinth des Laubfrosches *Hyla arborea savignyi* (Audouin). Zool. Anz. *200*, 145–172.

Alfs, B., Schneider, H. (1973): Vergleichende Anatomische Untersuchungen am Labyrinth zentraleuropäischer Froschlurcharten (Anura). Z. Morph. Tiere *76*, 129–143.

Anniko, M. (1980): Development of otoconia. Am. J. Otolaryngol *1*, 400–410.

Anniko, M. (1983): Embryonic development of vestibular sense organs and their innervation. In; Development of auditory and vestibular systems. Romand, R. ed. pp. 375–424, Academic Press, New York/London.

Anniko, M., Nordemar, H., van de Water, T. R. (1979): Embryogenesis of the inner ear. 1. Development and differentiation of the mammalian crista ampullaris in vivo and in vitro. Arch Oto-Rino-Laryngol *224*, 285–299.

Anson, B. J. (1934): The early development of the membranous labyrinth in mammalian embryos, with special reference to the endolymphatic duct and the utriculoendolymphatic duct. Anat. Rec. Suppl. *59*, 15–25.

Brzoska, J., Walkowiak, W., Schneider, H. (1977): Acoustic communication in the grass frog *Rana t. temporaria* L.: Calls, auditory thresholds and behavioral responses. J. Comp. Physiol. *118*, 173–186.

Carlström, B., Engström, H. (1955): The ultrastructure of statoconia. Acta Oto-Laryngol *45*, 14–18.

Carlström, B., Engström, H., Hjorth, S. (1953): Electronmicroscopic and X-ray diffraction studies of statoconia. Laryngoscope *63*, 1052–1057.

Cohen, -G. M., Fermin, C. D. (1979): The development of hair cells in the embryonic chick's basilar papilla. Acta Otolaryngol. *86*, 324–358.

Detwiler, S. R. (1948): Further quantitative studies on locomotor capacity of larval *Amblystoma* following surgical procedures upon the embryonic brain. J. Exp. Zool. *108*, 45–74.

Detwiler, S. R. (1951): Recent experiments on the differentiation of the labyrinth in *Amblystoma*. J. Exp. Zool. *118*, 187–201.

Detwiler, S. R., van Dyke, R. H. (1950): The role of the medulla in the differentiation of the otic vesicle. J. Exp. Zool. *113*, 197–199.

Diekamp, B., Schneider, H. (1988): Neuronal processing of conspecific and related calls in the torus semicircularis of *Rana r. ridibunda* Pall. (Anura): Single-unit recordings. J. Comp. Physiol. A. *163*, 301–315.

Evans, L. T. (1936): The development of the cochlea in the gecko, with special reference to the cochlea-lagena ratio and its bearing on vocality and social behaviour. Anat. Rec. *64*, 187–201.

Evans, L. T. (1943): The independent differentiation of the sensory areas of the avian inner ear. The biological Bulletin *84* (3), 252–262.

Favre, D., Sans, A. (1979): Embryonic and postnatal development of afferent innervation in cat vestibular receptors. Acta Oto-Laryngol. 87, 97–107.

Feng, A. S., Narins, P. N., Capranica, R. R. (1975): Three populations of primary auditory fibers in the bullfrog (Rana catesbeiana): their peripheral origins and frequency sensivities. J. Comp. Physiol. *100*, 221–229.

Frishkopf, L. S., Capranica, R. R., Goldstein, M. H. (1967): Neural coding in the bullfrog's auditory system – a teleological approach. Proc. IEEE *56*, 969–980.

Frishkopf, L. S., Flock, A. (1966): Ultrastructure of the basilar papilla in the bullfrog. J. Acoust. Soc. Amer. *40*, 1262.

Frishkopf, L. S., Goldstein, M. H. (1963): Responses to acoustic stimuli from single units in the eight nerve of the bullfrog. J. acoust. Soc. Amer. *35*, 1219–1228.

Geisler, C. D., van Bergeijk, S. (1964): The inner ear of the bullfrog. J. Morphol. *114*, 53–58.

Ginzberg, R. D., Gilula, N. B. (1977): A correlation between gap-junctions and synaptogenesis in the developing chicken otocyst. J. Cell. Biol. *75*, 38 a.

Ginzberg, R. D., Gilula, N. B. (1979): Modulation of cell junctions during differentiation of the chicken otocyst sensory epithelium. J. Cell. Biol. *75*, 110–129.

Harada, Y. (1979): Formation area of statoconia. In: Scanning electron microscopy 3, R. P. Becker, O. Johari, eds. pp. 963–966, Inc. O'Hara Illinois.

Hertwig, I. (1987a): Morphogenesis of the inner ear of *Rana temporaria* (Amphibia, Anura). Zoomorphology 107, 103–114.

Hertwig, I. (1987b): Die Entwicklung der peripheren Hörbahn beim Grasfrosch, *Rana t. temporaria* L. (Amphibia, Anura) Verh Dtsch Zool Ges 80, 147.

Hertwig, I., Hentschel, J. (1989): Vestibular Morphology of *Xenopus laevis* (Amphibia, Anura) following Larval Development in Zero Gravity. Zool. Jahrb. Anat. Onto. Tiere *118*, 463–472.

Hertwig, I., Schneider, H. (1986): Development of the supporting cells and structures derived from them in the inner ear of the grass frog, *Rana temporaria* (Amphibia, Anura). Zoomorphology *106*, 137–146.

Hertzog, E. (1925): Über die Entstehung der Otolithen. Z. Hals-Nasen-Ohrenheilk. *12*, 413–416.

Heywood, P., van de Water, T. R., Hilding, D. A., Ruben, R. J. (1975): Distributions of mikrotubules and microfilaments in developing vestibular sensory epithelium in mouse otocysts grown in vitro. J. Cell. Sci. *17*, 171–189.

Hubl, L., Schneider, H. (1979): Temperature and auditory thresholds: Bioacoustic studies of the frogs *Rana r. ridibunda*, *Hyla a. arborea* and *Hyla a. savignyi* (Anura, Amphibia). J. Comp. Physiol. *130*, 17–27.

Hudspeth, A. J. (1983): Mechanoelectrical transduction by hair cells in the acousticolateralis sensory system. Ann. Rev. Neurosci. *6*, 187–215.

Huschke, E. (1845): Traite de Splanchnologie et des Organes of Sense. Bailiere, Paris.

Igarashi, M., Kanda, T. (1969): Fine structure of the otolithic membrane in squirrel monkey. Acta Oto-Laryngol. *63*, 43–52.

Joermann, G., Schneider, H. (1986): The influence of white noise on the auditory evoked potential in the midbrain of the frog *Rana ridibunda*. Zool. Jb. Physiol. *90*, 329–338.

Kellerhals, H., Martine, E., Villinger, W. (1970): Surface view of the guinea pig otolith membrane. Pract. Oto Rhino Laryngol. *32*, 65–73.
Larsell, G. (1933): The differentiation of the peripheral and central acoustic apparatus in the frog. J. Comp. Neurol. *60*, 473–527.
Li, C. W., van de Water, T. R., Ruben, R. J., Shea, C. A. (1978): Rhombencephalic induction of the differentation of the tenth gestation day mouse otocyst. Ass. Res. Otolaryngol. Midwinter Meeting, Clearwater, Florida 1978.
Lim, D. J. (1973): Formation and fate of otoconia. Ann. Otol. Rhinol. Laryngol. *82*, 23–35.
Mohneke, R. (1983): Tonotopic organisation of the auditory midbrain nuclei of the midwife toad (*Alytes obstetricans*). Hearing Res. 9, 91–102.
Mohneke, R., Schneider, H. (1979): Effect of temperature upon auditory thresholds in two anuran species, *Bombina v. variegata* and *Alytes o. obstetricans* (Amphibia, Discoglossidae). J. Comp. Physiol. *130*, 9–16.
Neugebauer, D. Ch., Thurm, U. (1984): Chemical dissection of stereovilli from fish inner ear reveals differences from intestinal microvilli. J. Neurocytol. *13*, 797–808.
Neugebauer, D. Ch., Thurm, U. (1985): Interconnections between the stereovilli of the fish inner ear. Cell Tissue Res. *240*, 449–453.
Parsons, J., Cardell, R. R. (1965): Analysis of statoliths by X-ray diffraction and emission spectroscopy. Trans. Am. Soc. *84*, 415–421.
Ross, M. D. (1979): Calcium ion uptake and excange in otoconia. Adv Oto Rhino Laryngol. *25*, 26–33.
Salamat, M. S., Ross, M. D., Peacor, D. R. (1980): Otoconial formation in the fetal rat. Ann. Otol. Rhinol. Laryngol. *89*, 229–238.
Schmidt, B., Thurm, U. (1984): Structures transmitting stimulatory force to the sensory hairs (stereovilli) of the frog sacculus. Verh. Dtsch. Zool. Ges. *77*, 326.
Schneichel, W., Schneider, H. (1988): Hearing and calls of the banana frog, *Afrixalus fornasinii* (Bianconi) (Anura: Rhacophoridae). Amphibia/Reptilia 9, 251–263.
Sharp, B. (1885): Homologies of the vertebrate crystalline lens. Proc. Acad. Nat. Sci. Philadelphia, 300–310.
Sticht, N., van der (1908): L'istogenese des parties constituants du neuroepithelium acoustique. Arch. Biol. 23, 541–693.
Thorn, L. (1976): Die Entwicklung des Cortischen Organs beim Meerschweinchen. Georg Thieme Verlag, Stuttgart.
Thurm, U. (1984): Beiträge der Ultrastrukturforschung zur Aufklärung sensorischer Mechanismen. Verh. Dtsch. Zool. Ges. *77*, 89–103.
Waddington, C. H. (1937): The determination of the auditory placode in the chicken. DLV Biol. *14*, 232–239.
Walkowiak, W. (1980): Sensitivity, range and temperature dependence of hearing in the grass frog and fire-bellied toad. Behav. Processes *5*, 363–372.
Water, T. R., van de, Anniko, M., Nordemar, H., Wersäll, J. (1977): Embryonic development of the sensory cells in macula utriculae of mouse. In: Inner ear biology. J. M. Aran, eds. pp. 25–35. Inserm. Paris.
Wersäll, J. (1956): Studies on the structure and innervation of the sensory epithelium of the cristae ampullares in the guinea pig. Acta Oto Laryngol. *126*, 1–85.
Wersäll, J., Bagger-Sjöbäck, D. (1974): Morphology of the vestibular sense organ. In: Handbook of sensory physiology 6: H. H. Korn-Huber ed., pp. 123–170, Springer Verlag, New York.
Wever, E. G. (1973): The ear and hearing in the frog, *Rana pipiens*. J. Morph. *141*: 461–478.
Witschi, E. (1949): The larval ear of the frog and its transformation during metamorphosis. Z. Naturforsch. *4b*, 320–342.
Yokoh, Y. (1971): Early formation of nerve fibers in the human otocyst. Acta Anat. *80*, 90–106.

III. Neural and Endocrine Regulation

Fortschritte der Zoologie, Band/Vol. 38 · Hanke, W. (Hrsg.), Biology and Physiology of Amphibians
Gustav Fischer Verlag · Stuttgart · New York · 1990

ACTH-like activity of the brain

William Thurmond[1] and Wilfried Hanke[2]

[1] Biological Sciences Department, California Polytechnic State University, San Luis Obispo, CA 93407, USA
[2] Department of Zoology, The University, D-7500 Karlsruhe, FRG

Adrenocorticotropin (ACTH) has been identified (Krieger et al., 1977a, b) and localized in the arcuate nucleus of the hypothalamus of mammals (Watson et al., 1978; Pelletier and Leclerc, 1979). However, the presence of this hormone in the brain of amphibians is in doubt.

Only small amounts of immunoreactive ACTH have been identified in hypothalamic extracts of adult *Rana ridibunda* (Jégou et al., 1983) and none has been found in extracts or in perikarya of the hypothalamus of adult *Rana esculenta* (Vaudry et al., 1978; Vallarino, 1987). On the other hand, strong ACTH-like activity has been found in the hypothalamus of *Xenopus laevis*. The ACTH-like activity was determined by measuring the increase of steroiddehydrogenase activity and the production of corticosteroids from hypothalamic stimulated interrenal glands of larval and juvenile *Xenopus* respectively (Thurmond and Hanke, 1971; Horn-Ebert et al., 1974; Horn, 1976; Thurmond et al., 1986).

Pro-opiomelanocortin (POMC), the common precursor molecule for pituitary ACTH and α-MSH in both *Xenopus laevis* (Loh et al., 1982; Martens et al., 1982) and *Rana ridibunda* (Vaudry et al., 1984), has been found in low levels in the brain of *Xenopus laevis* (Martens et al., 1985). Thus one might expect to find low levels of ACTH and α-MSH in the amphibian brain. Bioactive α-MSH has been demonstrated in the hypothalamus of hypophysectomized *Rana pipiens* (Ralph and Peyton, 1966), *Hyla regilla* and *Ambystoma tigrinum* (Thurmond, 1960, 1961, 1967). In addition, immunoreactive α-MSH has been identified in brain extracts of *Rana esculenta* (Vaudry et al., 1978) and has been localized in the hypothalamic perikarya of both *Rana ridibunda* (Benyamina et al., 1986) and *Rana esculenta* (Vallarino, 1987).

Both the hypothalamus and the pars intermedia of the pituitary gland display MSH bioactivity and immunoreactivity as well as ACTH bioactivity and possibly an absence of ACTH immunoreactivity. An early study reported that immunoreactive ACTH was present in pars intermedia extracts of *Rana esculenta* (Vaudry et al., 1974) and this appeared to be confirmed with bioassays for ACTH-like activity in *Rana ridibunda* (Leboulenger et al., 1978, Delarue et al. 1979). However, a more recent study using indirect immunofluorescence has found that the cells of the pars intermedia of *Rana esculenta* were unreactive with antiserum to $ACTH_{1-39}$ and $ACTH_{1-24}$ (Vallarino, 1987).

The similarity of the presence of bioactive and immunoreactive α-MSH and bioactive ACTH but absence of immunoreactive ACTH within the hypothalamus and pars intermedia suggests that POMC is processed in the two tissues in the same manner. Vaudry et al. (1984) have proposed that once POMC is formed in the frog pars intermedia, the processing enzymes, or enzyme complex, begin to rapidly cleave the molecule to yield α-MSH, corticotropin-like peptide and endorphin-like peptide. Since ACTH is a temporary intermediate in the processing, only small amounts, if any, would be detectable. This could explain the absence of immunoreactive $ACTH_{1-39}$ in the hypothalamus and pars intermedia, but it would not account for the strong ACTH bioactivity exhibited by these tissues.

A possible explanation for the strong ACTH bioactivity is found in the stimulation of corticosteroid biosynthesis by α-MSH. Although steroidogenic activity of α-MSH in adult frogs is almost four orders of magnitude lower than that of ACTH (Leboulenger et al., 1986), the abundance of α-MSH in the pars intermedia (Doerr-Schott and Dubois, 1972) and substantial amounts in the hypothalamus (Vaudry et al., 1978) may account for the strong corticotropic response exhibited by these tissues.

ACTH bioactivity of hypothalamic tissue has been measured only with interrenals of larval and juvenile *Xenopus laevis* (Thurmond and Hanke, 1971; Horn-Ebert et al., 1974; Horn, 1976; Thurmond et al., 1986). If the interrenals of young *Xenopus* are as sensitive to α-MSH as are the adrenals of fetal and new born mammals (Challis et al., 1977; Glickman et al., 1979; Llannos et al., 1979; Sugihara et al., 1982), then hypothalamic α-MSH may in fact stimulate a strong corticotropin-like response.

Still another explanation for the strong bioactivity and weak immunoreactivity of hypothalamic ACTH may lie in alternate forms of ACTH. Argiolas et al. (1986) reported that large amounts of ACTH bioactivity in the hypothalamus of rats could not be accounted for by the small amount of $ACTH_{1-39}$ plus α-MSH found by radioimmunoassay. They extracted ACTH from the hypothalamus of hypophysectomized rats, fractionated it by high pressure liquid chromatography and analyzed the fractions for ACTH bioactivity. They found several peaks of ACTH bioactivity and concluded that a heterogeneous population of peptides exist in the hypothalamus rather than the single peptide, $ACTH_{1-39}$.

Several neuropeptides found in the hypothalamus have been shown to stimulate the interrenal gland directly. Arginine vasotocin (Maser and Hanke, 1982), vasoactive intestinal peptide (Leboulenger et al., 1983), angiotensin II (Hanke, 1984), acetylcholine (Benyamina et al., 1987), serotonin (Delarue et al., 1988), corticotropin releasing factor, endorphin and met-enkephalin (Thurmond et al., unpublished data) are all capable of stimulating *in vitro* corticosteroid biosynthesis. Some species specificity may exist, because Hanke and Yousri (1985, 1988) found only a slight direct stimulation of *in vitro* steroidogenesis of *Rana temporaria* tissue by CRF, no significant change after addition of met-enkephalin and a stimulation only for aldosterone release by endorphin. Further studies are needed to determine whether sufficient amounts of these peptides are produced and released from the hypothalamic tissue to cause a strong corticotropin-like response.

In conclusion, studies which indicate an absence or only a small amount of immunoreactive ACTH in hypothalamic tissue have been conducted on adult *Rana esculenta* and adult *Rana ridibunda*, whereas, studies which indicate a strong ACTH bioactivity in hypothalamic tissue have utilized interrenals of larval and juvenile *Xenopus laevis* in the bioassay procedure. Only future studies will determine whether the difference in hypothalamic ACTH immunoreactivity and bioactivity is a result of differences between species, the responsiveness of larval and adult interrenal tissues or the actions of several hypothalamic neuropeptides including α-MSH and possible alternate forms of ACTH.

At present, the prime candidate for the ACTH-like activity found in hypothalamic tissue of the amphibian is α-MSH.

References

Argiolas, A., Melis, M. R., Fratta, W., Gessa, G. L. (1986): Existence of different forms of adrenocorticotropin in rat hypothalamus. Peptides *7*, 591–596.

Benyamina, M., Delbende, C., Jégou, S., Leroux, P., Leboulenger, F., Tonon, M. C., Guy, J., Pelletier, G., Vaudry, H. (1986): Localization and identification of α-melanocyte-stimulating hormone (α-MSH) in the frog brain. Brain Res. *366*, 230–237.

Benyamina, M., Leboulenger, F., Lirhmann, I., Delarue, C., Feuilloley, M., Vaudry, H. (1987): Acetylcholine stimulates steroidogenesis in isolated frog adrenal gland through muscarinic receptors: evidence for a desensitization mechanism. J. Endocrinol. *113*, 339–348.

Challis, J. R. G., Torosis, J. D. (1977): Is α-MSH tropic to adrenal function in the fetus? Nature (London) *269*, 818–819.

Delarue, C., Tonon, M. C., Leboulenger, F., Jégou, S., Leroux, P., Vaudry, H. (1979): *In vitro* study of frog (*Rana ridibunda* Pallas) interrenal function by use of a simplified perifusion system. II. Influence of adrenocorticotropin upon aldosterone production. Gen. Comp. Endocrinol. *38*, 399–409.

Delarue, C., Lefebvre, H., Idres, S., Leboulenger, F., Homo-Delarche, G., Lihrmann, I., Feuilloley, M., Vaudry, H. (1988): Serotonin stimulates corticosteroid secretion by frog adrenocortical tissue *in vitro*. J. Steroid Biochem. *29*, 519–525.

Doerr-Schott, J., Dubois, M. P. (1972): Identification par cytoimmunofluorescence des cellules corticotropes et mélanotropes de l'adénohypophyse des Amphibiens. Z. Zellforsch. 132, 323–331.

Glickman, J. A., Carson, G. D., Challis, J. R. G. (1979): Differential effects of synthetic adrenocorticotropin 1–24 and α-melanocyte stimulating hormone on adrenal function in human and sheep fetuses. Endocrinology *104*, 34–39.

Hanke, W. (1984): Changes of the biology of the adrenal cortex in the vertebrate evolution. In «Nova Acta Leopoldina, The evolution of hormonal systems» (M. Gersch and P. Karlson, eds.), N. F. 56, No. *255*, 363–378.

Hanke, W., Yousri, R. (1985): Neuroendocrine regulation of ACTH release from the pituitary of frogs. Acta endocrinologica, *108*, suppl. *267*, 160.

Hanke, W., Yousri, R. (1988): Regulation of the pituitary interrenal axis of *Rana temporaria*. Zool. Jb. Physiol. *92*, 429–445.

Horn, I. (1976): The stimulatory effect of hypothalamic and mesencephalic tissue on the interrenal of tadpoles of *Xenopus laevis* Daudin. Gen. Comp. Endocrinol. *29*, 175–186.

Horn-Ebert, I., Thurmond, W., Hanke, W. (1974): ACTH-like activity in the brain of *Xenopus laevis* Daudin. Zool. Jahrb. Physiol. *78*, 333–343.

Jégou, S., Tonon, M. C., Leroux, P., Delarue, C., Leboulenger, F., Pelletier, G., Côté, J., Ling, N., Vaudry, H. (1983): Immunological characterization of endorphins, adrenocorticotropin, and melanotropins in frog hypothalamus. Gen. Comp. Endocrinol. *51*, 246–254.

Krieger, D. T., Liotta, A., Brownstein, M. J. (1977a): Presence of corticotropin in brain of normal and hypophysectomized rats. Proc. Natl. Acad. Sci. USA *74*, 648–652.

Krieger, D. T., Liotta, A., Brownstein, M. J. (1977b): Presence of corticotropin in limbic system of normal and hypophysectomized rats. Brain Res. *128*, 575–579.

Leboulenger, F., Delarue, C., Tonon, M. C., Jégou, S., Vaudry, H. (1978): In *vitro* study of frog (*Rana ridibunda* Pallas) interrenal function by use of a simplified perifusion system. I. Influence of adrenocorticotropin upon corticosterone release. Gen. Comp. Endocrinol. *36*, 327–338.

Leboulenger, F., Leroux, P., Delarue, C., Tonon, M., Charna, Y., Dubois, P., Coy, D., Vaudry, H. (1983): Co-localization of vasoactive intestinal peptide (VIP) and enkephalins in chromaffin cells of the adrenal gland of amphibia. Stimulation of corticosteroid production by VIP. Life Sci. *32*, 375–383.

Leboulenger, F., Lihrmann, I., Netchitailo, P., Delarue, C., Perroteau, I., Ling, N., Vaudry, N. (1986): In *vitro* study of frog (*Rana ridibunda* Pallas) interrenal function by use of a simplified perifusion system. VIII. Structure-activity relationship of synthetic ACTH fragments and γ-MSH. Gen. Comp. Endocrinol. *61*, 187–196.

Llannos, A. J., Ramachandran, J., Creasy, R. K., Rudolph, A. M., Serón-Ferré, M. (1979): α-Melanocyte-stimulating hormone and adrenocorticotropin in the regulation of glucocorticoid secretion during the perinatal period in sheep. Endocrinology *105*, 613–617.

Loh, Y. P., Gritsch, A., Chang, T.-L. (1982): Pro-opiocortin processing in the pituitary: A model for neuropeptide biosynthesis. Peptides *3*, 397–404.

Martens, G. J. M., Cirelli, O., Herbert, E. (1985): Nucleotide sequence of cloned cDNA for pro-opiomelanocortin in the amphibian *Xenopus laevis*. J. Biol. Chem. *260*, 13685–13689.

Martens, G. J. M., Jenks, B. G., Van Overbeeke, A. P. (1982): Biosynthesivs of pairs of peptides related to melanotropin, corticotropin and endorphin in the pars intermedia of the amphibian pituitary gland. Eur. J. Biochem. *122*, 1–10.

Maser, C., Hanke, W. (1982): Regulation of interrenal secretion in amphibia. Gen. Comp. Endocrinol. *46*, 411.

Pelletier, G., Leclerc, R. (1979): Immunohistochemical localization of adrenocorticotropin in the rat brain. Endocrinology *104*, 1426–1433.

Ralph, C. L., Peyton, S. C. (1966): MSH-like substance in the brain of the frog *Rana pipiens*. Gen. Comp. Endocrinol. *7*, 363–369.

Sugihara, H., Miyabara, S., Yun, K., Ohta, K., Yonemitsu, N. (1982): The effect of α-melanocyte-stimulating hormone on the adrenal cortex of the fetal rat. Endocrinologie *79*, 415–422.

Thurmond, M. (1960): Evidence of a melanophore-stimulating substance of neural origin. Anat. Rec. *137*, 398.

Thurmond, W. (1961): A melanophore-stimulating substance in the hypothalamus of the tadpole and adult tree frog, *Hyla regilla*. Amer. Zool. *1*, 472.

Thurmond, W. (1967): Hypothalamic chromatophore-stimulating activity in the amphibian *Hyla regilla* and *Ambystoma tigrinum*. Gen. Comp. Endocrinol. *8*, 245–251.

Thurmond, W., Hanke, W., (1971): Effect of hypophysial and hypothalamic grafts on the interrenal tissue of larvae of *Xenopus laevis* (Daudin). Amer. Zool. *11*, 654.

Thurmond, W., Kloas, W., Hanke, W. (1986): The distribution of interrenal stimulating activity in the brain of *Xenopus laevis*. Gen. Comp. Endocrinol. *63*, 117–124.

Vallarino, M. (1987): Immunocytochemical evidence for α-melanocyte-stimulation hormone in the hypothalamus of the frog *Rana esculenta*. Cell Tissue Res. *248*, 559–563.

Vaudry, H., Leboulenger, F., Dupont, W., Vaillant, R. (1974): Estimation du taux d'hormone corticotrope hypophysaire chez la grenouille verte *Rana esculenta* L. par une méthode radioimmunologique. C. R. Soc. Biol. *168*, 801–806.

Vaudry, H., Oliver, C., Jégou, S., Leboulenger, F., Tonon, M. C., Delarue, C., Morin, J.-P., Vaillant, R. (1978): Immunoreactive melanocyte-stimulating hormone (α-MSH) in the brain of the frog (*Rana esculenta* L.). Gen. Comp. Endocrinol. *34*, 391–401.

Vaudry, H., Jenks, B. G., Van Overbeeke, A. P. (1984): Biosynthesis, processing and release of pro-opiomelanocortin related peptides in the intermediate lobe of the pituitary gland of the frog (*Rana ridibunda]. Peptides 5*, 905–912.

Watson, S. J., Richard III., C. W., Barchas, J. D. (1978): Adrenocorticotropin in rat brain: Immunocytochemical localization in cells and axons. Science *200*, 1180–1181.

Fortschritte der Zoologie, Band/Vol. 38 · Hanke, W. (Hrsg.), Biology and Physiology of Amphibians
Gustav Fischer Verlag · Stuttgart · New York · 1990

Neuroendocrine regulation of adrenocortical cells in amphibians

C. Delarue, F. Leboulenger, P. Netchitaïlo, I. Lihrmann, M. Feuilloley, S. Idres, A. Larcher, M. Morra, H. Lefebvre, G. Pelletier* and H. Vaudry

Groupe de Recherche en Endocrinologie Moléculaire, URA CNRS 650, Unité Alliée à l'INSERM, Université de Rouen, F-76130 Mont-Saint Aignan, France
* Centre de Recherche en Endocrinologie Moléculaire, Le Centre Hospitalier de L'Université Laval, Québec, Canada.

1. Introduction

Although the adrenal cortex and medulla both play pivotal roles in the response to stress, little is known concerning the regulation of adrenocortical cells by the secretory signals produced by chromaffin cells of the adrenal medulla. In mammals, the adrenal medulla synthesizes both catecholamines (mainly epinephrine) and a variety of bioactive substances including classical neurotransmitters and neuropeptides. Immunocytochemical and biochemical studies have shown that chromaffin cells produce serotonin (Verhofstad and Jonsson, 1983; Holzwarth et al., 1984) and dopamine (McKenna et al., 1979). Besides chromogranins, which have the potential activity to generate a number of biologically active peptides (Simon et al., 1988), the most abundant signals appear to be proenkephalin A-derived peptides (Varndell et al., 1982; Lewis and Stern, 1983; Udenfriend and Kilpatrick, 1983). In addition, adrenal medullary cells are able to synthesize neuropeptide Y (Allen et al., 1983; Emson et al., 1984; Kuramoto et al., 1986), vasoactive intestinal peptide (VIP) (Eiden et al., 1983; Holzwarth, 1984; Siegel et al., 1985), neurotensin (Lee et al., 1981; Terenghi et al., 1983; Rökaeus et al., 1984) and somatostatin (Aguilera et al., 1981; Srikant and Patel, 1985; Maurer and Reubi, 1986).

In mammals, the blood flow is directed from the outer cortex to the inner medulla and there is little possibility that the bioactive signals secreted by chromaffin cells participate to the regulation of adrenocortical cells. In contrast the interrenal gland of amphibians is an interesting model to study the interactions between the two categories of adrenal cells in that it consists of intermingled networks of corticosteroidogenic and chromaffin tissues, a situation which facilitates cross-talks between the two cell types. In fact, it has been shown that hypophysectomy does not completely suppress corticosteroid production by frog interrenal tissue, indicating that the adrenocortical activity does not totally depend on pituitary ACTH (Leboulenger et al., 1980). Due to the peculiar anatomy of the interrenal gland, corticosteroid secretion in amphibians is likely to be regulated by two additional categories of hormones and/or neurotransmitters. First, the interrenal gland is located on the ventral surface of the kidney and this anatomical situation favours interactions between renal and interrenal tissues. Second, the interrenal gland is innervated by splanchnic nerve fibers which release acetylcholine and possibly various regulatory peptides. These biologically active substances might also participate in the multifactorial control of corticosteroid production. In addition, the interrenal tissue represents an interesting model in that it consists of only one type of adrenocortical cells which produce both corticosterone and aldosterone. Since these endocrine cells are highly sensitive to adrenocorticotropin (ACTH) and angiotensin II, they are generally regarded as the homologous of mammalian glomerulosa cells.

2. Development of an in vitro perifusion model

Static incubation systems are obviously inadequate to study the dynamic aspects of the response to various factors implicated in the control of corticosteroid secretion. A perifusion system which makes it possible to investigate kinetics of the response of adrenocortical cells to regulatory signals has been developed by Tait et al. (1967). Using this technique a few studies have been carried out either with perifused rat adrenal quarters (Tait et al., 1970; Feuilloley et al., 1986) or rat adrenal cells (Schulster, 1973; Lowry and McMartin, 1974). This system has been further extended to the study of fish adrenal function (Ilan and Yaron, 1976). In 1978, we have described a perifusion technique for frog interrenal tissue which soon appeared to be a powerful method to investigate the regulation of adrenocortical cell activity in amphibians. The perifusion system used in our laboratory has previously been described in detail (Leboulenger et al., 1978). Briefly, male frogs (*Rana ridibunda* Pallas) are maintained in tanks in natural conditions of light and temperature. Animals are sacrificed by decapitation, the kidneys are quickly removed, and the interrenal tissue is carefully dissected free of kidney. The glands are sliced and incubated for 15 min in perifusion medium gassed with 95% O_2 and 5% CO_2. The interrenal slices are rinsed with fresh medium and transferred into perifusion chambers. The interrenal fragments are layered in preswollen Bio-Gel P2 and continuously supplied with appropriate medium by means of a peristaltic pump. The medium consists of either amphibian culture medium prepared according to Wolf and Quimby (1964) or Ringer HEPES buffer (Lihrmann et al., 1985; 1986). Flow rate (200 μl/min), pH (7.35) and temperature (24 °C) are kept constant throughout the experiments. Effluent fractions are collected at 5 min intervals and immediately chilled on ice. Corticosterone and aldosterone, the two major steroids produced by the frog adrenal gland, are radioimmunoassayed in the fractions using antisera developed in our laboratory (Leroux et al., 1980; Leboulenger et al., 1982). Experiments have been conducted where the effluent medium was submitted to Sephadex LH-20 and reverse phase high performance liquid chromatography before radioimmunoassay quantification. These studies have shown that only corticosterone and aldosterone are measured in the respective assays; the two steroids can thus be directly assayed in the effluent perifusate without prior extraction (Delarue et al., 1981).

3. Regulation of adrenocortical cells by hypophyseal factors

Administration of frog adenohypophyseal (distal lobe) extracts induces a dose-related stimulation of corticosterone and aldosterone secretion (Fig. 1) by perifused interrenal tissue (Leboulenger et al., 1978; Delarue et al., 1979). The perifusion model can thus be used as a semi-quantitative system to assess the concentration of biologically active ACTH in frog pars distalis. The stimulatory effect of pituitary extracts can be mimicked by synthetic human ACTH 1–39. We have observed that frog neurointermediate lobe (NIL) extracts, also stimulate corticosteroid release (Leboulenger et al., 1978, Delarue et al., 1979).

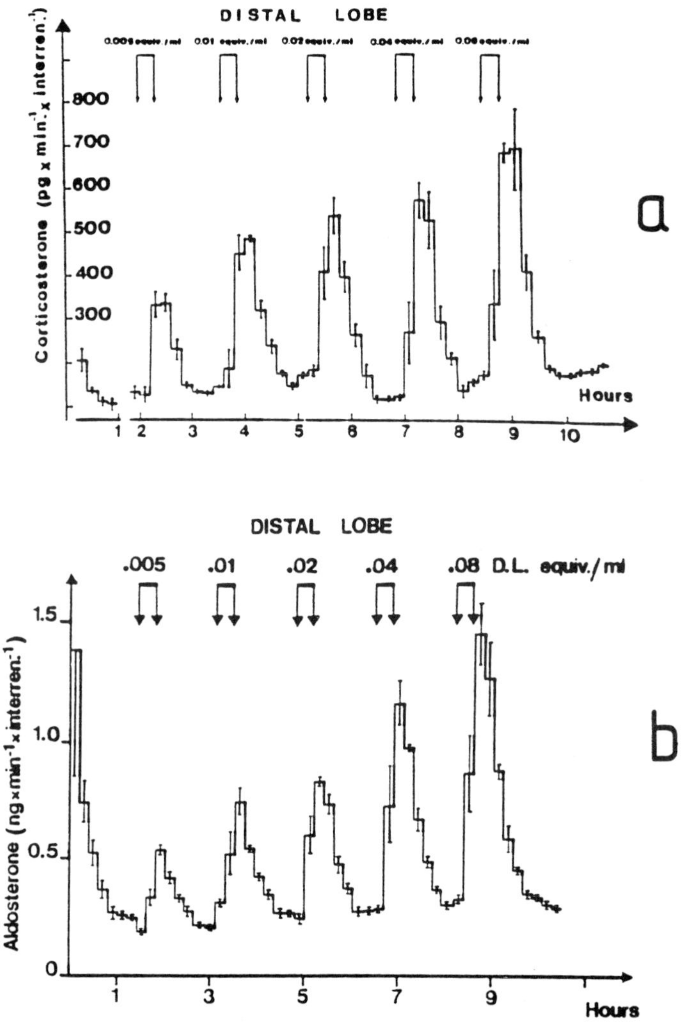

Fig. 1: Effect of crude frog adenohypophyseal extracts on corticosterone (a) and aldosterone (b) production. The interrenal slices were perifused with increasing concentrations of distal lobe extracts (dilutions ranging from 0.005 to 0.08 distal lobe equivalent/ml). Two consecutive infusions of secretagogue were separated by 80-min stabilization periods. (From Leboulenger et al., 1978, and Delarue et al., 1979).

Biosynthetic studies indicate that, in the frog pars intermedia, the high molecular weight precursor proopiomelanocortin (POMC) generates α-melanotropin-stimulating hormone (α-MSH), γ-melanotropin-stimulating hormone (γ-MSH), corticotropin-like intermediate lobe peptide (CLIP) and endorphins (Vaudry et al., 1984, 1986). In contrast, we do not observe the formation of ACTH in frog pituitary melanotrophs, indicating that the corticotropic activity of NIL extracts cannot be accounted for by the presence of ACTH. We have thus investigated the potential activity of various proopiomelanocortin-derived peptides on steroidogenesis. Synthetic α-MSH and γ-MSH induce a weak but significant increase in corticosteroid secretion (Fig. 2).

The potency of γ-MSH is approximately 10 fold lower than that of α-MSH (Leboulenger et al., 1986b). These results suggest that, in amphibians, several peptides of the POMC family, other than ACTH, may also participate in the control of steroidogenesis. Other synthetic peptides such as somatostatin-14 (Delarue et al., 1984) are totally devoid of an effect on corticosteroid production.

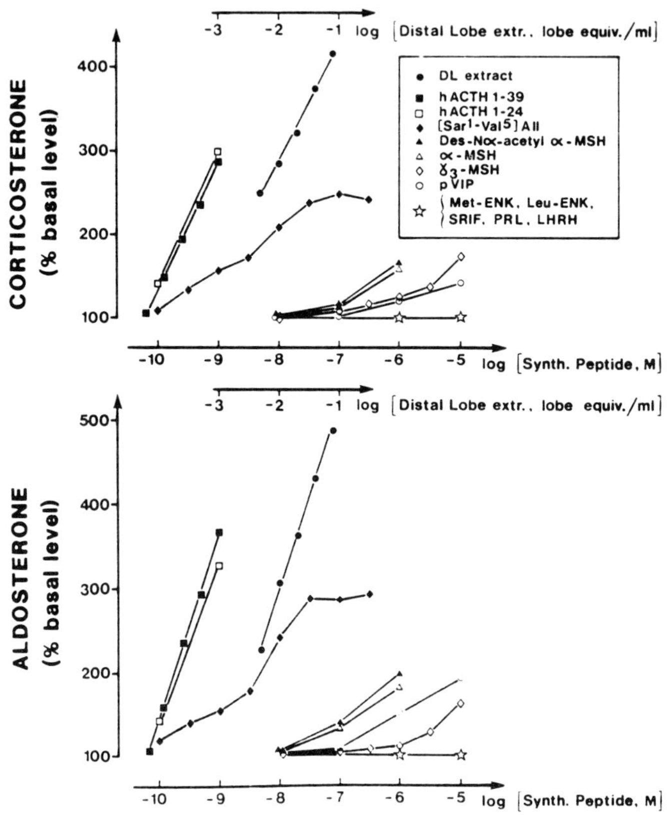

Fig. 2: Dose-response curves comparing the corticotropic activities of frog distal lobe extracts with those of various synthetic peptides on perifused frog interrenal slices. Perifusion experiments similar to those presented in Fig. 1 were conducted with each secretagogue (pituitary extracts or synthetic peptides) using various concentrations of test substances. Responses are expressed in percentages of spontaneous secretory levels. DL: distal lobe; ENK: enkephalin; SRIF: somatostatin 14.

4. Regulation of adrenocortical cells by non-hypophyseal circulating factors

The angiotensin II agonist (Sar^1-Val^5) AII is also a potent stimulator of steroidogenesis in the frog (Perroteau et al., 1984). Fig. 3 shows that the kinetics of the effect of the angiotensin II analogue are almost identical to those previously reported for ACTH

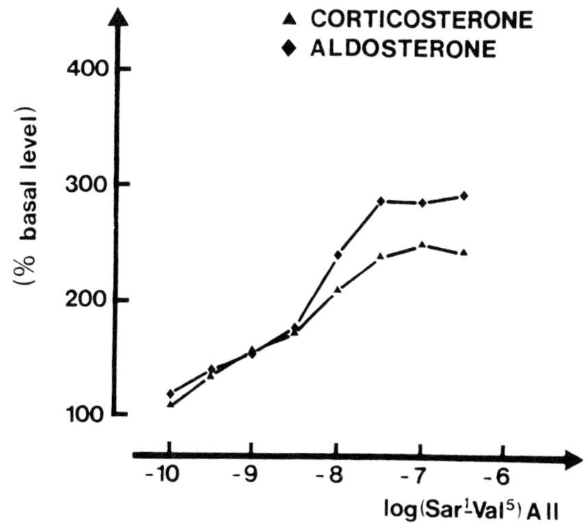

Fig. 3: Dose-response curves comparing the effect of the angiotensin II agonist (Sar^1-Val^5) AII on the secretion of corticosterone and aldosterone by perifused frog interrenal slices. See legend to Fig. 2 for other designations.

(Fig. 2). The peculiar anatomical localization and morphological organization of the amphibian adrenal gland favour functional interactions between corticosteroidogenic and renal tissues and suggest that angiotensin II produced locally may act as a paracrine factor to stimulate steroidogenesis.

Recently, using the indirect immunofluorescence technique, we have shown the presence of atrial natriuretic factor (ANF) in the heart of the frog (Netchitaïlo et al., 1986; 1988). ANF-like immunoreactivity is localized in most atrial cardiocytes and in a few ventricular cells. At the electron microscopic level, the immunogold technique revealed that all secretory granules present in cardiocytes contain ANF-like immunoreactive material (Netchitaïlo et al., 1986). The immunoreactive peptide has been characterized using various analytical approaches combined with radioimmunological detection (Netchitaïlo et al., 1986). Sephadex G-50 Gel chromatography shows that the majority of the immunoreactive substance corresponds to a high molecular weight precursor material (PM > 10000 daltons) and that only a small proportion of the peptide is processed to give mature forms within cardiocytes. High performance liquid chromatography analysis indicates that another compound co-elutes with synthetic rat ANF (Arg 101-Tyr 126) (Netchitaïlo et al., 1986). Recently, the primary sequence of the C-terminal (biologically active) portion of frog ANF has been determined (Lazure et al., 1988). In order to investigate a possible role of atrial natriuretic factor in the control of corticosteroid biosynthesis in amphibians, we have examined the effect of synthetic ANF on perifused frog interrenal slices (Lihrmann et al., 1988). ANF does not affect the spontaneous secretion of corticosterone and aldosterone. In contrast ANF (10^{-6} M) inhibits ACTH- and angiotensin II-stimulated corticosteroid production. It can be noted that ANF is more potent in suppressing aldosterone than corticosterone secretion (Fig. 4a and b). We have recently shown the presence of ANF-immunoreactive nerve fibers among the interrenal gland of the frog (Lihrmann et al., 1988). We thus assume that both hormonal ANF (from cardiac origin) and neuronal ANF (released by nerve terminals) may participate to the regulation of adrenocortical activity. But, the release of ANF by nerve terminals is not clearly proved.

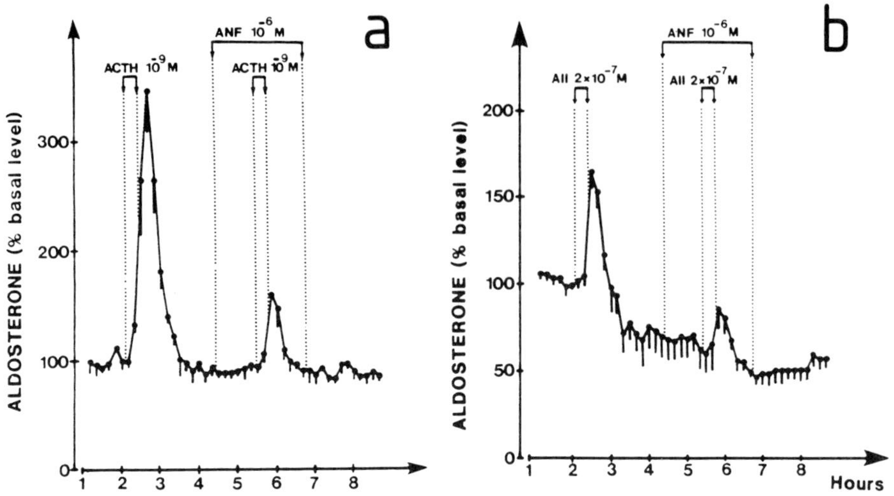

Fig. 4: Effect of ACTH (10^{-9} M; a) and angiotensin II (2×10^{-7} M; b) alone or during prolonged administration of ANF (10^{-6} M) on the secretion of aldosterone by perifused frog interrenal slices. The profiles represent the mean (± SEM) secretion pattern of three independent perifusion experiments. Each point is the mean corticosteroid production (expressed as a percentage of spontaneous steroid output) of two consecutive fractions collected during 5 min. The mean secretion rate of aldosterone in these experiments was 23.8 ± 9.1 (a) and 15.5 ± 7.7 (b) pg/interrenal/min. (From Lihrmann et al., 1988).

Increasing concentrations of calcium (2.5 to 15 mM) cause a dose-dependent stimulation of corticosterone and aldosterone secretion (Lihrmann et al., 1985) whereas incrément of sodium (114 to 130 mM) or potassium (5 to 15 mM) does not affect steroid production. Since plasma calcium concentrations vary in physiological conditions, from 1.19 to 2.18 mM in *Rana ridibunda*, our results suggest that circulating calcium may directly influence steroid secretion *in vivo*. In amphibians, extracellular calcium ions are required for basal production of corticosteroids (Lihrmann et al., 1985) and for the action of ACTH (Lihrmann et al., 1986) while the mechanism of action of angiotensin II does not involve Ca^{++} uptake from the extracellular space but is strickly dependent on mobilization of Ca^{++} from an intracellular pool which probably originates from the endoplasmic reticulum.

5. Regulation of adrenocortical cells by local factors

Using conventional immunocytochemical methods, we have demonstrated that amphibian adrenochromaffin cells contain several peptidergic neurotransmitters. The presence of met-enkephalin Arg^6-Phe^7 has been detected in *Rana ridibunda* (Leboulenger et al., 1983; 1986a) and in *Rana catesbeiana* (Kondo and Yui, 1984). Conversely, Leu-enkephalin is virtually absent from the adrenal tissue (Leboulenger et al., 1986a). Using a specific antiserum against porcine vasoactive intestinal peptide (VIP), we have shown the presence of VIP-like immunoreactive material in most chromaffin cells (tyrosine hydroxylase positive cells) of frog interrenal gland (Leboulenger et al., 1983). Similarly, we have demonstrated that chromaffin cells contain 5-HT-like immunoreactivity as revealed by the indi-

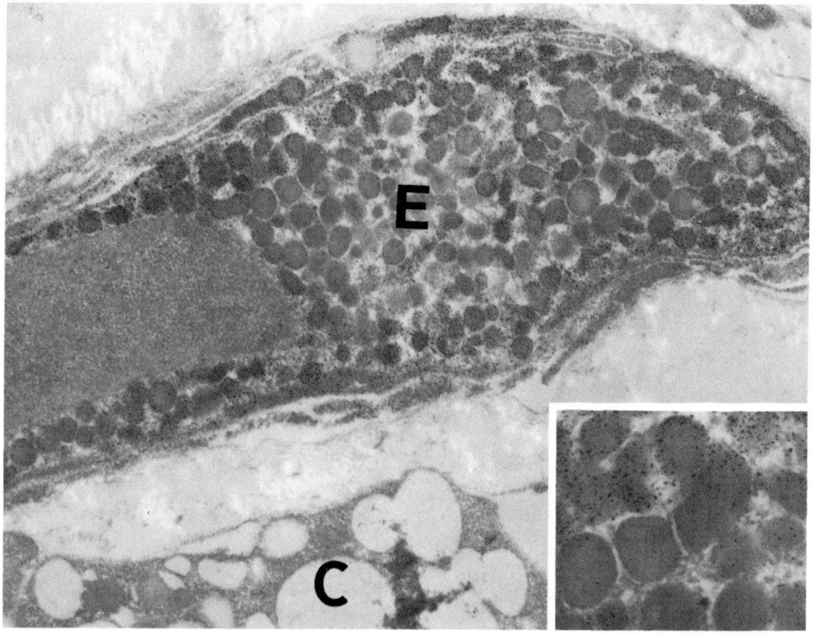

Fig. 5: Subcellular localization of 5-HT immunoreactivity in epinephrine (E) cells (x 6000). C, corticosteroid-producing cell. The inset shows a higher magnification (× 20000) of gold-labelled secretory granules. (From Delarue et al., 1988 a.)

rect immunofluorescence technique (Delarue et al., 1988 a). At the electron microscopic level, VIP, Met-enkephalin and 5-HT immunoreactivities appear to be co-localized in chromaffin granules suggesting that catecholamines, 5-HT (Fig. 5) and various neuropeptides can be simultaneously released under splanchnic nerve stimulation (Leboulenger et al., 1983; Delarue et al., 1988 a).

Owing to the close contacts which exist between chromaffin and adrenocortical cells in the frog interrenal gland, we have investigated the possible effects of the neuroendocrine signals contained in chromaffin cells on the secretory activity of adrenocortical cells located in the neighbourhood. *In vitro*, using perifused frog interrenal fragments, we have shown that VIP (Leboulenger et al., 1983; 1984) and 5-HT (Delarue et al., 1988 b) induce a dose-related stimulation of corticosteroid secretion (Fig. 6). In contrast Met-or Leu-enkephalins do not modify basal corticosteroidogenesis (Leboulenger et al., 1983). From these studies, it emerges that neuropeptides such as VIP and classical neurotransmitters such as 5-HT, produced by chromaffin cells, are likely to exert a paracrine action on steroidogenesis.

6. Regulation of adrenocortical cells by acetylcholine

The existence of cholinergic nerve terminals in the adrenal cortex has been reported in various species including sheep (Robinson et al., 1977), hamster (Unsicker, 1969), birds (Unsicker, 1973) and reptiles (Unsicker, 1974). In addition, Hadjian et al. (1982) have

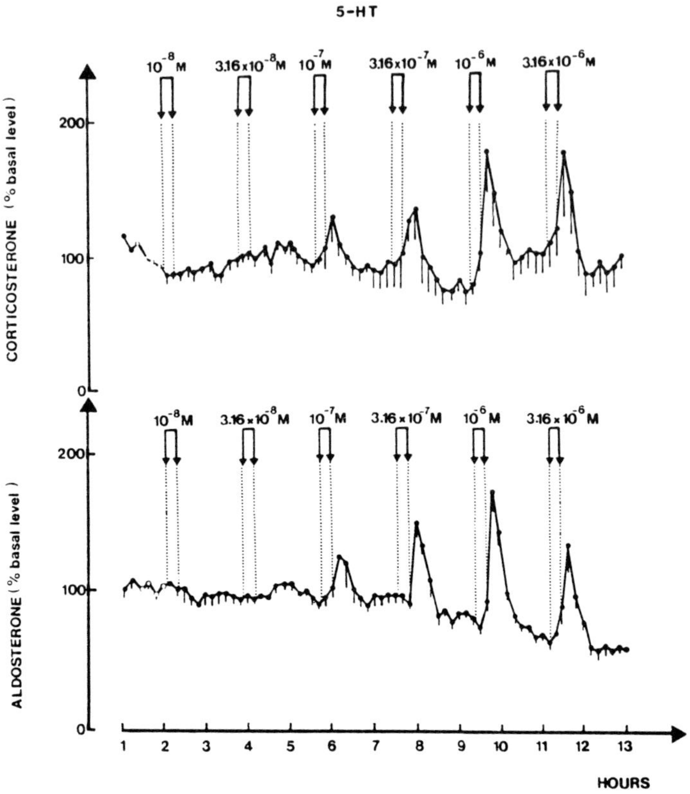

Fig. 6: Effect of graded concentrations of 5-HT (from 10^{-8} M to 3.16×10^{-6} M) on the production of corticosterone (a) and aldosterone (b) by frog interrenal slices. The mean secretion rates of corticosterone and aldosterone in these experiments were 49.4 ± 17.4 and 34.5 ± 13.0 pg / interrenal gland per min, respectively. See legend to Fig. 4 for other designations. (From Delarue et al., 1988b).

shown that acetylcholine is a powerful stimulator of cortisol production by isolated cells from the bovine zona fasciculata. It was thus of interest to examine the effect of cholinergic agonists on glucocorticoid and mineralocorticoid production by frog interrenal tissue using our perifusion model. Acetylcholine (ACh), at doses ranging from 10^{-6} M to 10^{-4} M, stimulates both corticosterone and aldosterone secretion in a dose-dependent manner (Benyamina et al., 1987). Repeated pulses of acetylcholine result in a marked reduction of the secretory response subsequently to the second pulse (Fig. 7). In contrast, none of the other corticotropic factors (ACTH, angiotensin II or 5-HT) induce a desensitization.

Using various cholinergic agonists and antagonists we have observed that ACh stimulates corticosteroid secretion through typical muscarinic receptors. Muscarine (10^{-5} M) mimicks the effect of ACh while nicotine (10^{-6} M to 10^{-4} M) is totally devoid of an effect on steroidogenesis (Benyamina et al., 1987). Simultaneous infusion of submaximal doses of VIP (10^{-5} M) and ACh (5×10^{-5} M) induces stimulation of corticosteroids which are strictly additive. When VIP (10^{-5} M) and serotonin (5×10^{-6} M) are infused

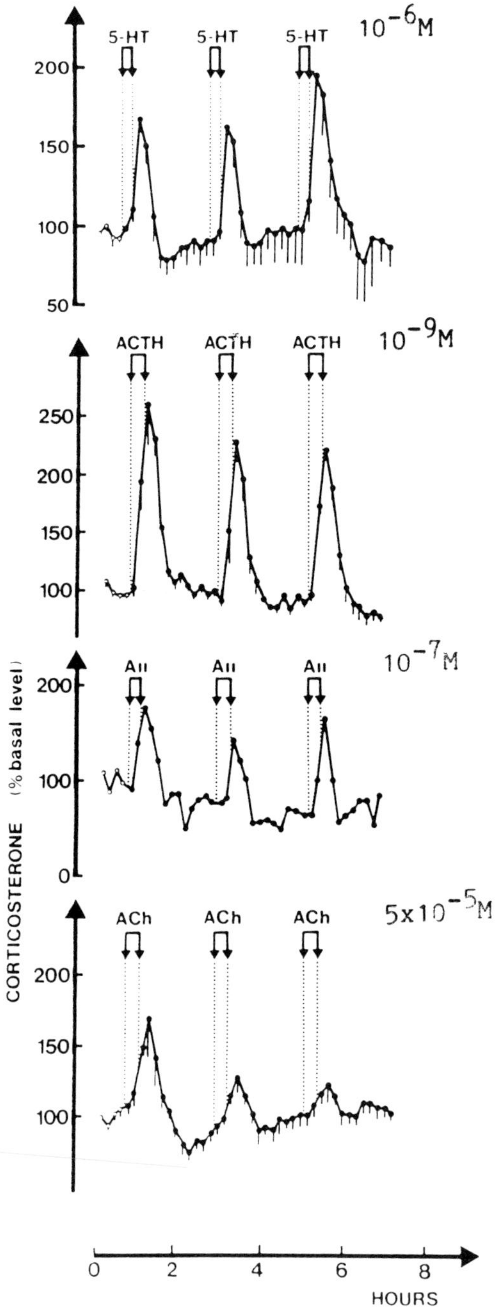

Fig. 7: Effect of administration of three iterative doses of 5-HT (10^{-6} M), ACTH (10^{-9} M), AII (10^{-7} M) and ACh (5×10^{-5} M) on corticosterone production by perifused frog interrenal slices. Note that ACh is the only secretagogue which causes a desensitization phenomenon. See legend to Fig. 4 for other designations.

together, a potentiation of the individual responses is observed. In contrast, concomitant infusion of ACh (5×10^{-5} M) and serotonin (5×10^{-6} M) causes a total blockage of the stimulatory effect of serotonin (Leboulenger et al., 1988).

7. Regulation of adrenocortical cells by prostaglandins

The stimulatory effect of the corticotropic peptides, ACTH and AII, is probably initiated through binding to specific receptors. Our main contribution to the investigation of stimulus-secretion coupling in adrenocortical cells has been to demonstrate the role of arachidonic acid metabolites in the mechanism of action of these corticotropic factors. The role of prostaglandins (PGs), the major metabolites of the cyclooxygenase pathway, in the regulation of corticosteroid production by the frog interrenal gland was studied *in vitro* by means of the perifusion technique (Fig. 8). No change in corticosteroid production is observed upon perifusion with PGA_1 or PGA_2 (up to 10^{-6} M) (Perroteau et al., 1984). Conversely, six other primary PGs and the prostacyclin (PGI_2) significantly stimulate corticosteroidogenesis; the order of potency being $PGE_1 > PGI_2 > PGE_2 > PGB_2 > PGB_1 > PGF_{2\alpha} > PGF_{1\alpha}$ (Perroteau et al., 1984; Delarue et al., 1981; 1986 a). In contrast, leukotrienes B_4 and C_4, the major metabolites of the lipoxygenase pathway, do not modify the spontaneous production of corticosteroids (Delarue et al., 1988 c). The ability of PGs to stimulate corticosterone and aldosterone production indicates that PGs may contribute to the regulation of corticosteroid biosynthesis. These data also suggest that endogenous PGs may act as mediators for certain corticosteroid stimulating factors.

Indomethacin (IDM) and meclofenamic acid, tow specific inhibitors of the cyclooxygenase pathway, which blocked the release of 6-keto-$PGF_{1\alpha}$ (the stable metabolite of PGI_2) induced also a marked reduction of the spontaneous secretion of corticosteroid which confirmed the involvement of endogenous PGs in the process of corticosteroid biosynthesis (Delarue et al., 1981; Perroteau et al., 1984). A direct stimulatory effect of angioten-

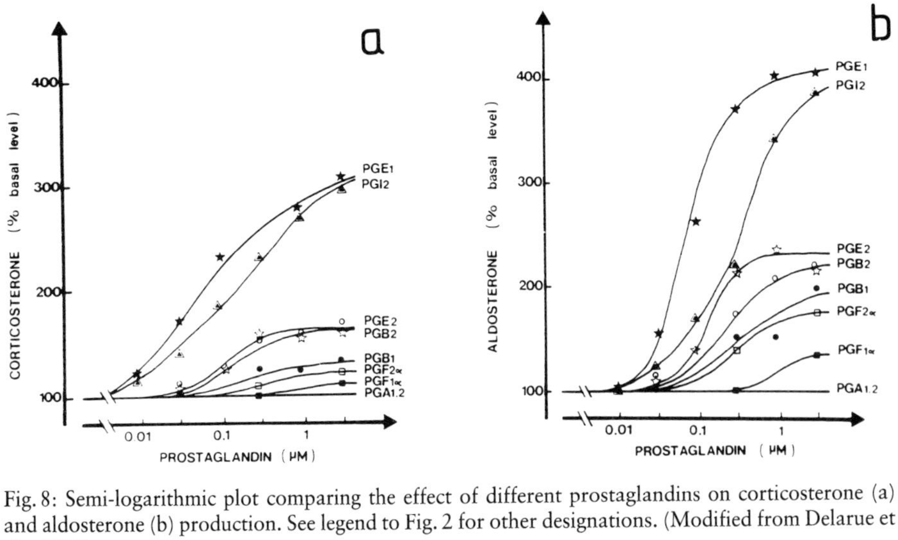

Fig. 8: Semi-logarithmic plot comparing the effect of different prostaglandins on corticosterone (a) and aldosterone (b) production. See legend to Fig. 2 for other designations. (Modified from Delarue et al., 1981).

sin II and acetylcholine on prostanoid biosynthesis is demonstrated by measuring the release of PGE_2 and 6-keto-$PGF_{1\alpha}$ by perifused frog interrenal slices (Perroteau et al., 1984; Delarue et al., 1986b). These results are confirmed by the reduction of the stimulatory effect of AII (Perroteau et al., 1984) and ACh (Delarue et al., 1986b) in the presence of IDM (Fig. 9). In contrast, neither ACTH (Perroteau et al., 1984) nor 5-HT (Delarue et al., 1988b) modified the production of PGs by the interrenal tissue. In addition, stimulation of ACTH, 5-HT and VIP is not affected by IDM (Fig. 9; Perroteau et al., 1984; Leboulenger et al., 1984; Delarue et al., 1988b).

These results show that exogenous and endogenous PGs are involved in the regulation of corticosteroid secretion in frog. Since in amphibians, the adrenocortical tissue makes close contacts with the kidney (a major source of PGEs), these results suggest a physiological relationship between the kidney and the interrenal gland in lower vertebrates. Our data demonstrate that the action of AII and ACh on corticosteroidogenesis is mediated by PGs whereas ACTH, 5-HT and VIP stimulate corticosteroid production through another pathway, presumably through stimulation of adenylate cyclase activity.

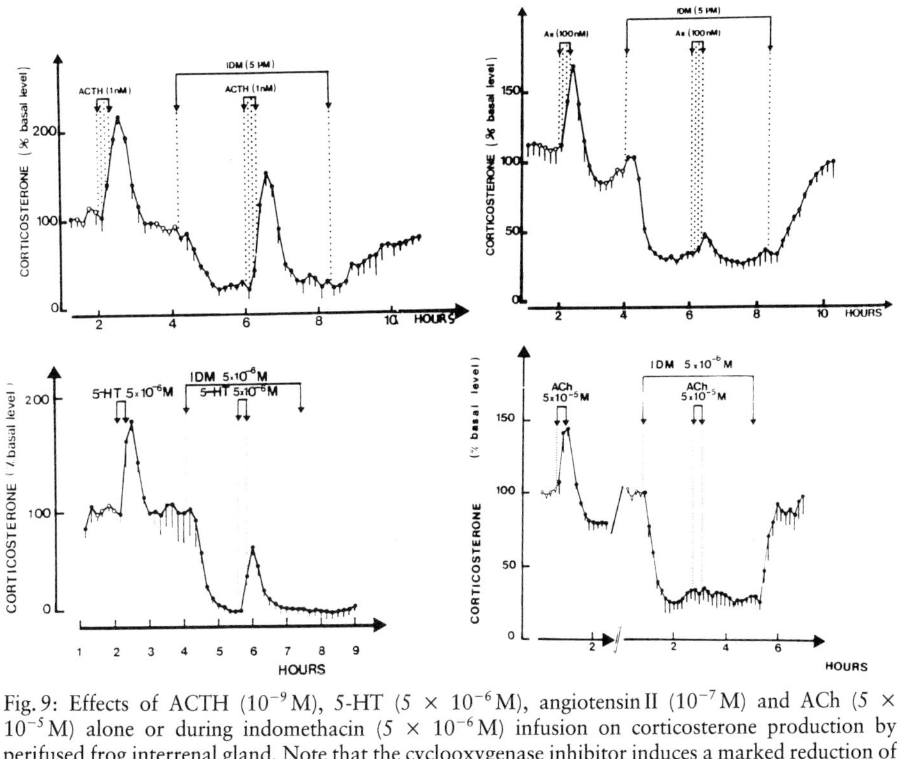

Fig. 9: Effects of ACTH (10^{-9} M), 5-HT (5×10^{-6} M), angiotensin II (10^{-7} M) and ACh (5×10^{-5} M) alone or during indomethacin (5×10^{-6} M) infusion on corticosterone production by perifused frog interrenal gland. Note that the cyclooxygenase inhibitor induces a marked reduction of angiotensin II- and ACh-induced corticosterone release. In contrast, indomethacin does not affect the steroidogenic activity of ACTH and 5-HT. See legend to Fig. 4 for other designations. (From Perroteau et al., 1984; Delarue et al., 1986; Delarue et al., 1988b).

8. Conclusion

During stress, an increase in plasma concentrations of both epinephrine and glucocorticoids is observed. In mammals, the response of the adrenal medulla to stress is secondary to splanchnic nerve stimulation and the response of the adrenal cortex is generally attributed to a burst of ACTH. Although these two phenomena take place early and occur concomitantly in all types of stress, there is little information regarding possible interactions between chromaffin and adrenocortical cells. The peculiar arrangement of the adrenal gland of amphibians, consisting of intermingled chromaffin and corticosteroidogenic cells, favours interactions between the two types of tissues. Our results demonstrate that the adrenocortical cells of the frog are under multifactorial control. Beside conventional steroidogenic hormones (ACTH and angiotensin II), different factors released from chromaffin cells, can influence corticosteroidogenesis. These paracrine factors, which include both neuropeptides, such as VIP, and amines, such as 5-HT, allow partial independence of the interrenal gland from the hypothalamo-hypophyseal axis. In addition to this paracrine mode of communication, endings from the splanchnic nerve may also influence corticosteroid production. We have observed the presence of ANF immunoreactive nerve fibers among the interrenal gland. Furthermore, both acetylcholine and ANF modulate the secretion of corticosteroids in our *in vitro* perifusion system. Besides the hormonal regulation by circulating ACTH, several substances, including paracrine factors, released locally by chromaffin cells, and neurotransmitters issued from nerve endings, may participate to a cell-to-cell synchronization of the response of chromaffin and adrenocortical tissues in stress conditions.

Acknowledgements

This research was supported in part by grants from URA CNRS 650, Fondation de Recherche en Hormonologie (76-85-009), DRET (87–135), ANVAR (A-83-07-017-PO1150) and France-Quebec Exchange Programs. The authors would like to thank Ms. S. Moreau for typing the manuscript.

References

Aguilera, G., Harwood, J. P., Catt, K. J. (1981): Somatostatin modulates the effects of angiotensin II in adrenal glomerulosa zone. Nature (London) *292*, 262–263.

Allen, J. M., Adrian, T. E., Polak, J. M., Bloom, S. R. (1983): Neuropeptide Y (NPY) in the adrenal gland. J. Auton. Nerv. Syst. *9*, 559–563.

Benyamina, M., Leboulenger, F., Lihrmann, I., Delarue, C., Feuilloley, M., Vaudry, H. (1987): Acetylcholine stimulates steroidogenesis in isolated frog adrenal gland through muscarinic receptors: evidence for a desensitization mechanism. J. Endocr. *113*, 339–348.

Delarue, C., Tonon, M. C., Leboulenger, F., Jégou, S., Leroux, P., Vaudry, H. (1979): In vitro study of frog (*Rana ridibunda* Pallas) interrenal function by use of a simplified perifusion system. II. Influence of adrenocorticotropin upon aldosterone production. Gen. Comp. Endocrinol. *38*, 399–409.

Delarue, C., Perroteau, I., Leboulenger, F., Netchitaïlo, P., Leroux, P., Jégou, S., Bélanger, A., Tonon, M. C., Vaudry, H. (1981): In vitro effect of prostaglandins on corticosterone and aldosterone production by frog interrenal gland. Biochem. Biophys. Res. Commun. *100*, 769–777.

Delarue, C., Netchitailo, P., Leboulenger, F., Perroteau, I., Escher, E., Vaudry, H. (1984): *In vitro* study of frog (*Rana ridibunda* Pallas) interrenal function by use of simplified perifusion system. VII. Lack of effect of somatostatin on angiotensin-induced corticosteroid production. Gen. Comp. Endocrinol. *54*, 333–338.

Delarue, C., Perroteau, I., Lihrmann, I., Netchitaïlo, P., Homo-Delarche, F., Vaudry, H. (1986a): Role of prostacyclin on steroidogenesis by frog interrenal gland *in vitro*. Prostaglandins *31*, 5–17.

Delarue, C., Leboulenger, F., Homo-Delarche, F., Benyamina, M., Lihrmann, I., Perroteau, I., Vaudry, H. (1986b): Involvement of prostaglandins in the response of frog adrenocortical cells to muscarinic receptor activation. Prostaglandins *32*, 87–91.

Delarue, C., Leboulenger, F., Morra, M., Héry, F., Verhofstad, A. J., Bérod, A., Denoroy, L., Pelletier, G., Vaudry, H. (1988a): Immunohistochemical and biochemical evidence for the presence of serotonin in amphibian adrenal chromaffin cells. Brain Research *459*, 17–26.

Delarue, C., Lefebvre, H., Idres, S., Leboulenger, F., Homo-Delarche, F., Lihrmann, I., Feuilloley, M., Vaudry, H. (1988b): Serotonin stimulates corticosteroid secretion by frog adrenocortical tissue *in vitro*. J. Steroid Biochem. *29*, 519–525.

Delarue, C., Lihrmann, I., Feuilloley, M., Netchitaïlo, P., Idres, S., Leboulenger, F., Bélanger, A., Perroteau, I., Vaudry, H. (1988c): *In vitro* study of frog adrenal function – IX. Evidence against the involvement of lipoxygenase metabolites in the control of steroid production. J. Steroid Biochem. *30*, 461–464.

Eiden, L. E., Eskay, R. L., Scott, J., Pollard, H., Hotchkiss, A. J. (1983): Primary cultures of bovine chromaffin cells synthesize and secrete vasoactive intestinal polypeptide (VIP). Life Sci. *33*, 687–693.

Emson, P. C., Corder, R., Lowry, P. J. (1984): Demonstration of a neuropeptide Y-like immunoreactivity in human phaechromocytoma extracts. Regul. Pept. *8*, 89–94.

Feuilloley, M., Netchitaïlo, P., Lihrmann, I., Delarue, C., Vaudry, H. (1986): Development of a simplified perifusion system of rat zona glomerulosa. Effect of cytochalasin B on spontaneous and ACTH-stimulated corticosteroidogenesis. J. Steroid Biochem. *24*, 331–334.

Hadjian, A. J., Guidicelli, C., Chambaz, E. M. (1982): Cholinergic muscarinic stimulation of steroidogenesis in bovine adrenal cortex fasciculata cell suspensions. Biochem. Biophys. Acta *714*, 157–163.

Holzwarth, M. A. (1984): The distribution of vasoactive intestinal peptide in the rat adrenal cortex and medulla. J. Auton. Nerv. Syst. *11*, 269–289.

Holzwarth, M. A., Sawetan, C., Brownfield, M. S. (1984): Serotonin-immunoreactivity in the adrenal medulla: distribution and response to pharmacological manipulation. Brain Res. Bull. *13*, 299–308.

Ilan, Z., Yaron, Z. (1976): Stimulation of carps interrenal function by adrenocorticotrophin. J. Endocr. *68*, 13–20.

Kondo, H., Yui, R. (1984): Co-existence of enkephalin and adrenalin in the frog adrenal gland. Histochemistry *80*, 243–246.

Kuramoto, H., Kondo, H., Fujita, T. (1986): Neuropeptide tyrosine (NPY)-like immunoreactivity in adrenal chromaffin cells and intraadrenal nerve fibers of rats. Anat. Rec. *214*, 321–328.

Lazure, C., Ong, H., McNicoll, N., Netchitaïlo, P., Chrétien, M., De Léan, A., Vaudry, H. (1988): The amino acid sequences of frog heart atrial natriuretic-like peptide and mammalian ANF are closely related. FEBS Letters *238*, 300–306.

Leboulenger, F., Delarue, C., Tonon, M. C., Jégou, S., Vaudry, H. (1978): *In vitro* study of frog (*Rana ridibunda* Pallas) interrenal function by use of a simplified perifusion system. I. Influence of adrenocorticotropin upon corticosterone release. Gen. Comp. Endocrinol. *36*, 327–338.

Leboulenger, F., Delarue, C., Jégou, S., Netchitaïlo, P., Leroux, P., Tonon, M. C., Vaudry, H. (1980): *In vitro* study of frog (*Rana ridibunda* Pallas) interrenal function by use of a simplified perifusion system. III. Influence of previous hypophysectomy or dexamethasone treatment of donors upon corticosterone and aldosterone production. Gen. Comp. Endocrinol. *42*, 389–400.

Leboulenger, F., Delarue, C., Bélanger, A., Perroteau, I., Netchitaïlo, P., Leroux, P., Jégou, S., Tonon, M. C., Vaudry, H. (1982): Direct radioimmunoassays for plasma corticosterone and aldosterone in frog: I. Validation of the methods and evidence for daily rhythms in a natural environment. Gen. Comp. Endocrinol. *46*, 521–532.

Leboulenger, F., Leroux, P., Delarue, C., Tonon, M.C., Charney, Y., Dubois, P.M., Coy, D.H., Vaudry, H. (1983): Co-localization of vasoactive intestinal peptide (VIP) and enkephalins in chromaffin cells of the adrenal gland of amphibia. Stimulation of corticosteroid production by VIP. Life Sci. *32*, 375–383.
Leboulenger, F., Perroteau, I., Netchitaïlo, P., Lihrmann, I., Leroux, P., Delarue, C., Coy, D.H. and Vaudry, H. (1984): Action of vasoactive intestinal peptide (VIP) on amphibian adrenocortical function, *in vitro*. Peptides *4*, 299–303.
Leboulenger, F., Cupo, A., Castenas, E., Benyamina, M., Pelletier, G., Vaudry, H. (1986a): Immunohistochemical and biochemical evidence for the presence of the pentapeptide met-enkephalin and the heptapeptide met-enkephalin-Arg^6-Phe^7 but not the octapeptide met-enkephalin-Arg^6 -Gly^7 -Leu^8 in amphibian chromaffin cells. Neurochem. Intern. *8*, 303–309.
Leboulenger, F., Lihrmann, I., Netchitaïlo, P., Delarue, C., Perroteau, I., Ling, N., Vaudry, H. (1986b): *In vitro* study of frog (*Rana ridibunda* Pallas) interrenal function by use of a simplified perifusion system. VIII. Structure-activity relationship of synthetic ACTH fragments and γ-MSH. Gen. Comp. Endocrinol. *61*, 187–196.
Leboulenger, F., Benyamina, M., Delarue, C., Netchitaïlo, P., Saint-Pierre, S., Vaudry, H. (1988): Neuronal and paracrine regulation of adrenal steroidogenesis: interactions between acetylcholine, serotonin and vasoactive intestinal peptide (VIP) on corticosteroid production by frog interrenal tissue. Brain Res. *453*, 103–109.
Lee, Y.C., Terenghi, G., Polak, J.M., Bloom, S.R. (1981): Neurotensin in the adrenal medulla of the cat. Acta Endocrinol. *97* suppl. 243, 84.
Leroux, P., Delarue, C., Leboulenger, F., Jégou, S., Tonon, M.C., Vaillant, R., Corvol, P., Vaudry, H. (1980): Development and characterization of radioimmunoassay technique for aldosterone output from perifused frog interrenal tissue. J. steroid Biochem. *12*, 473–478.
Lewis, R.V., Stern, A.S. (1983): Biosynthesis of the enkephalin and enkephalin-containing polypeptides. Ann. Rev. Pharmacol. Toxicol. *23*, 353–372.
Lihrmann, I., Netchitaïlo, P., Leboulenger, F., Delarue, C., Vaudry, H. (1985): Effect of calcium on corticosteroid secretion by isolated frog interrenal gland. J. Steroid Biochem. *23*, 169–175.
Lihrmann, I., Delarue, C., Feuilloley, M., Escher, E., Netchitaïlo, P., Leboulenger, F., Vaudry, H. (1986): Role of calcium in stimulus-secretion coupling on isolated frog interrenal gland. J. Steroid Biochem. *24*, 731–738.
Lihrmann, I., Netchitaïlo, P., Feuilloley, M., Cantin, M., Delarue, C., Leboulenger, F., De Léan, A., Vaudry, H. (1988): Effect of atrial natriuretic factor on corticosteroid production by perifused frog interrenal slices. Gen. Comp. Endocrinol. *71*, 55–62.
Lowry, P.J., McMartin, C. (1974): Measurement of the dynamics of stimulation and inhibition of steroidogenesis in isolated rat adrenal cells by using column perfusion. Biochem. J. *142*, 287–294.
Maurer, R., Reubi, J.C. (1986): Somatostatin receptors in the adrenal. Mol. Cell. Endocrinol. *45*, 81–90.
McKenna, T.J., Island, D.P., Nicholson, W.E., Liddle, G.W. (1979): Dopamine inhibits angiotensin-stimulated aldosterone biosynthesis in bovine adrenal cells. J. Clin. Invest. *64*, 287–291.
Netchitaïlo, P., Feuilloley, M., Pelletier, G., Cantin, M., De Léan, A., Leboulenger, F., Vaudry, H. (1986): Localization and characterization of atrial natriuretic factor (ANF)-like peptide in the frog atrium. Peptides *7*, 573–579.
Netchitaïlo, P., Feuilloley, M., Pelletier, G., Cantin, M., De Léan, A., Leboulenger, F., Vaudry, H. (1988): Localization and identification of immunoreactive atrial natriuretic factor (ANF) in the frog ventricle. Peptides *9*, 1–6.
Perroteau, I., Netchitaïlo, P., Homo-Delarche, F., Delarue, C., Lihrmann, I., Leboulenger, F., Vaudry, H. (1984): Role of exogenous and endogenous prostaglandins in steroidogenesis by isolated frog interrenal gland: Evidence for dissociation in adrenocorticotropin and angiotensin action. Endocrinology *115*, 1765–1773.
Robinson, P.M., Perry, R.A., Hardy, K.J., Coghlan, J.P., Scoggins, B.A. (1977): The innervation of the adrenal cortex in the sheep *Ovis ovis*. J. Anat. *124*, 117–129.
Rökaeus, A., Fried, G., Lundberg, J.M. (1984): Occurrence storage and release of neurotensin-like immunoreactivity from the adrenal gland. Acta Physiol. Scand. *120*, 373–380.
Schulster, D. (1973): Regulation of steroidogenesis by ACTH in a superfusion system for isolated adrenal cells. Endocrinology *93*, 700–704.

Siegel, R. E., Eiden, L. E., Pruss, R. M. (1985): Multiple populations of neuropeptide-containing cells in cultures of the bovine adrenal medulla. Dev. Brain Res. *17*, 267–270.

Simon, J. P., Bader, M. F., Aunis, D. (1988): Secretion from chromaffin cells is controlled by chromogranin A-derived peptides. Proc. Natl. Acad. Sci. *85*, 1712–1716.

Srikant, C. B., Patel, Y. C. (1985): Somatostatin receptors in the rat adrenal cortex: characterization and comparison with brain and pituitary receptors. Endocrinology *116*, 1717–1723.

Tait, S. A. S., Tait, J. F., Okamoto, M., Flood, C. (1967): Production of steroids by *in vitro* superfusion of endocrine tissue. I. Apparatus and a suitable analytical method for adrenal steroid output. Endocrinology *21*, 1213–1225.

Tait, S. A. S., Schulster, D., Okamoto, M., Flood, C., Tait, J. F. (1970): Production of steroids by in vitro superfusion of endocrine tissue. II. Steroid output from bisected whole, capsular and decapsulated adrenals of normal, intact hypophysectomized-nephrectomized rats as a function of time of superfusion. Endocrinology *86*, 360–382.

Terenghi, G., Polak, J. M., Varndell, I. M., Lee, Y. C., Wharton, J., Bloom, S. R. (1983): Neurotensin-like immunoreactivity in a subpopulation of noradrenaline-containing cells of the cat adrenal gland. Endocrinology *112*, 226–233.

Udenfriend, S., Kilpatrick, D. L. (1983): Biochemistry of the enkephalins and enkephalin-containing peptides. Arch. Biochem. Biophys. *221*, 309–323.

Unsicker, K. (1969): Zur Innervation der Nebennierenrinde vom Goldhamster. Z. Zellforsch. *95*, 608–619.

Unsicker, K. (1973): Fine structure and innervation of the avian adrenal gland. V. Innervation of interrenal cells. Z. Zellforsch. *146*, 403–416.

Unsicker, K. (1974): Innervation of adrenal cells in the lizards *Lacerta dugesi* and *Lacerta pityusensis*. Gen. Comp. Endocrinol. *24*, 409–412.

Varndell, I. M., Tapia, F. J., DeMey, J., Rush, R. A., Bloom, S. R., Polak, J. M. (1982): Electron immunocytochemical localization of enkephalin-like material in catecholamine-containing cells of the carotid body, the adrenal medulla, and pheochromocytomas of man and other mammals. J. Histochem. Cytochem. *30*, 682–690.

Vaudry, H., Jenks, B. G., an Overbeeke, A. P. (1984): Biosynthesis, processing and release of proopiomelanocortin related peptides in the intermediate lobe of the pituitary gland of the frog *Rana ridibunda*. Peptides *5*, 905–912.

Vaudry, H., Jenks, B. G., Verburg-van Kemenade, B. M. L., Tonon, M. C. (1986): Effect of tunicamycin on biosynthesis, processing and release of proopiomelanocortin-derived peptides in the intermediate lobe of the frog *Rana ridibunda*. Peptides *7*, 163–169.

Verhofstad, A. A. J., Jonsson, G. (1983): Immunohistochemical and neurochemical evidence for the presence of serotonin in the adrenal medulla of the rat. Neuroscience *10*, 1443–1453.

Wolf, F., Quimby, K. (1964): Amphibian cell culture: permanent cell line from the bullfrog (*Rana catesbeiana*). Science *144*, 1578–1580.

Fortschritte der Zoologie, Band/Vol. 38 · Hanke, W. (Hrsg.), Biology and Physiology of Amphibians
Gustav Fischer Verlag · Stuttgart · New York · 1990

Response of amphibian pituitary cells to thyrotropin-releasing hormone (TRH) stimulation

Francisco Gracia-Navarro, Maria M. Malagon, Socorro Garcia-Navarro, Antonio Ruiz-Navarro, Justo Castaño

Department of Cell Biology, University of Córdoba, C/San Alberto Magno s/n. E-14004 Cordoba, Spain

1. Introduction

Little is known about the hypothalamic control of the amphibian pituitary, particularly about cellular control in the different pituitary cell types. The present study was aimed at elucidating the role played by thyrotropin-releasing hormone (TRH) in the cellular control of some amphibian pituitary cell types.

Thyrotropin-releasing hormone induces the release of the thyroid-stimulating hormone (TSH) and prolactin (PRL) in a wide variety of mammalian species, both *in vivo* and *in vitro* (Bowers et al., 1965; Labella and Vivian, 1971; Vale et al., 1977; Horrobin, 1977). TRH has also been shown to induce the release of growth hormone (GH) in some mammalian species (Hall et al., 1986b).

In amphibians, TRH has been shown to occur at high concentrations in the hypothalamus (Jackson and Reichlin, 1974; Taurog et al., 1974; Giraud et al., 1979; Seki et al., 1983; Mimnagh et al., 1987), and in other tissues (Jackson and Reichlin, 1974, 1977, 1979). Nevertheless, its effect on the amphibian pituitary is a controversial subject. TRH has proved to be generally ineffective as a TSH-releasing factor (Etkin and Gona, 1968; Gona and Gona, 1974; Taurog et al., 1974; Vandesande and Aspeslagh, 1974; Sawin et al., 1978), although more recent reports suggest a TSH-releasing activity for this peptide (Rosenkilde, 1979; Darras and Kühn, 1982; Malagón et al., 1989).

With respect to the other hypophyseotropic releasing activities found in mammals, it has been clearly established that the administration of TRH stimulates the release of PRL from the amphibian pituitary gland, both *in vivo* and *in vitro* (Kühn and Engelen, 1976; Clemons et al., 1979; Seki and Kikuyama, 1982, 1984, 1986; Hall and Chadwick, 1984; Kühn et al., 1985; Malagón et al., 1989). In addition, TRH stimulates the *in vitro* release of GH as reported by Hall and Chadwick (1984).

Physiological reports suggest that TRH acts on the amphibian pituitary gland like in mammals, although no information is available about the dynamics of its action on amphibian pituitary cells. On the other hand, the lack of radioimmunoassays for some amphibian hormones (i.e. TSH) makes the morphometric measurement of immunocytochemically-identified cells a valuable method for evaluating pituitary responsiveness to specific hypothalamic factors. In addition, morphometric methods allow an evaluation of the physiological status of all the cell types of pars distalis under different experimental conditions.

This paper reports our recent research on the action of TRH on the amphibian pituitary, both *in vivo* and *in vitro*, based on the morphological changes observed in TSH, PRL and GH cells identified by immunocytochemistry.

2. Pituitary cell types in intact animals

The first goal of this work was to identify the pituitary cell types presumably involved in the action of TRH, namely PRL, TSH and GH cells in intact frogs, as a preliminary study aimed at identifying the morphological changes induced by the secretagogue. For this purpose, pituitary glands of *Rana perezi* were fixed in a 1:1 mixture of 1% glutaraldehyde and 2% paraformaldehyde in 0.1 M cacodylate buffer (pH 7.4) and postfixed in osmium tetroxide, after which the tissues were dehydrated and embedded in Araldite. Ultrathin sections were immunostained according to Roth (1983) by using anti-human-β-TSH 1:800, anti-human-PRL 1:1000, and anti-ovine-GH 1:1000 as first antisera for the identification of the cell types which synthesize and store each hormone. Specific control incubations were carried out as follows: (i) omission of the specific antiserum; (ii) substitution of rabbit pre-immune serum for the specific antiserum; (iii) adsorption of the specific antiserum with its corresponding homologous hormone.

Under the electron microscope, thyrotropic cells in *Rana perezi* show irregular morphology, pleomorphic secretory granules with diameters ranging between 120 and 375 nm, and poorly developed rough endoplasmic reticulum (RER) and Golgi complex (GC; Fig. 1a). They are usually polarized to capillaries (Malagón et al., 1988a).

On the other hand, prolactin cells show a polyhedral or ovoid shape, with spherical secretory granules ranging between 90 and 400 nm in diameter (Fig. 2a); RER and GC are not well developed. They are usually polarized to capillaries (Malagón et al., 1988b).

GH cells have morphologic features similar to those of PRL cells, although their secretory granules are bigger (200 to 650 nm in diameter) and their Golgi complex is better developed (Fig. 3a).

3. In vivo action of TRH on amphibian pituitary cells

For this study, adult male frogs (*Rana perezi*) were injected daily with 7.5 μg synthetic TRH/20 g b.w. into the dorsal lymph sac. Pituitary glands were collected at 8 h, 48 h and 6 days after the first injection. Control animals were injected the vehicle alone and sacrificed immediately after the first injection. Pituitaries were studied immunocytochemically under the electron microscope as described above. Point-analysis morphometry (Weibel, 1979) was used to evaluate the volume density (Vv) of rough endoplasmic reticulum, Golgi complex and secretory granules (SG).

3.1. TSH cells

After 8 h of *in vivo* TRH treatment, TSH cells showed morphological signs of activation (Table 1) with hypertrophied GC and RER. These effects were more marked after 48 h of TRH treatment and were accompanied by significant degranulation. Some TSH cells were almost completely degranulated with only a few remaining immunoreactive secretory granules (Fig. 1b). After 6 days of TRH treatment, the development of the biosynthetic

Table 1: Effect of TRH on the relative volume(1) of subcellular organelles of TSH and PRL cells *in vivo*.

	control	8 h	48 h	6 days
TSH cells				
RER(2)	6.21 ± 0.33	8.48 ± 0.51*	13.22 ± 1.06*	6.36 ± 0.29*
GC(3)	2.10 ± 0.34	3.44 ± 0.59*	4.63 ± 1.18	1.98 ± 0.49*
Mit.(4)	1.75 ± 0.17	3.20 ± 0.30*	2.59 ± 0.28	2.54 ± 0.22
SG(5)	34.42 ± 1.35	22.60 ± 1.37*	17.10 ± 1.67*	28.87 ± 1.42*
PRL cells				
RER(2)	5.42 ± 0.52	7.50 ± 0.58*	4.99 ± 0.33*	5.97 ± 0.34*
GC(3)	1.75 ± 0.32	3.02 ± 0.30*	2.74 ± 0.48	2.50 ± 0.36
Mit.(4)	2.83 ± 0.32	2.31 ± 0.17	2.12 ± 0.20	2.60 ± 0.20
SG(5)	33.03 ± 1.64	25.74 ± 1.44*	40.46 ± 1.29*	38.36 ± 1.12

All values means ± S.E., significantly different from the preceding group at $^*P > 0.05$ by U-test ($n = 3$ animals for each treatment group).
(1) Volume density of organelle in μm^3 per 100 μ^3 of cytoplasm.
(2) Rough Endoplasmic Reticulum.
(3) Golgi complex.
(4) Mitochondria.
(5) Secretory Granules.

machinery (RER and GC) was not significantly different from that found in control animals, although the cells still remained degranulated.

The morphometric data obtained show that TRH induces the *in vivo* hypertrophy of RER and GC, as well as the degranulation of TSH pituitary cells. These results suggest that TRH stimulates the synthesis and release of TSH and agree with the increased thyroid hormone levels observed in *Rana ridibunda* after an intravenous injection of TRH, as reported by Darras and Kühn (1982). Furthermore, TRH seems to have a long-term effect on TSH cells, since the hypertrophy of the RER and GC and degranulation are still significant after 48 h of TRH treatment.

3.2. PRL cells

After 8 h of TRH treatment, PRL cells were markedly activated and featured significantly expanded RER and GC, as well as decreased Vv of SG (Table 1, Fig. 2b). In 48 h-treated animals, the cytoplasm of PRL cells contained abundant SG and the extent of hypertrophy of RER and GC was smaller than that of 8 h-treated animals. These features remained similar in the 6 days-treatment group.

These morphological results show that TRH induces degranulation and hypertrophy of the biosynthetic machinery of PRL cells, probably resulting in increased synthesis and release of prolactin, which is consistent with the results reported for *Rana ridibunda in vivo* (Kühn et al., 1985).

Comparison of the time courses of the ultrastructural changes in both cell types shows that the action of TRH on TSH cells is longer-lasting and more intense than that on PRL cells. This suggests that the secretion of PRL and TSH are controlled by different hypothalamic mechanics. The increased Vv of SG, as well as the scant development of

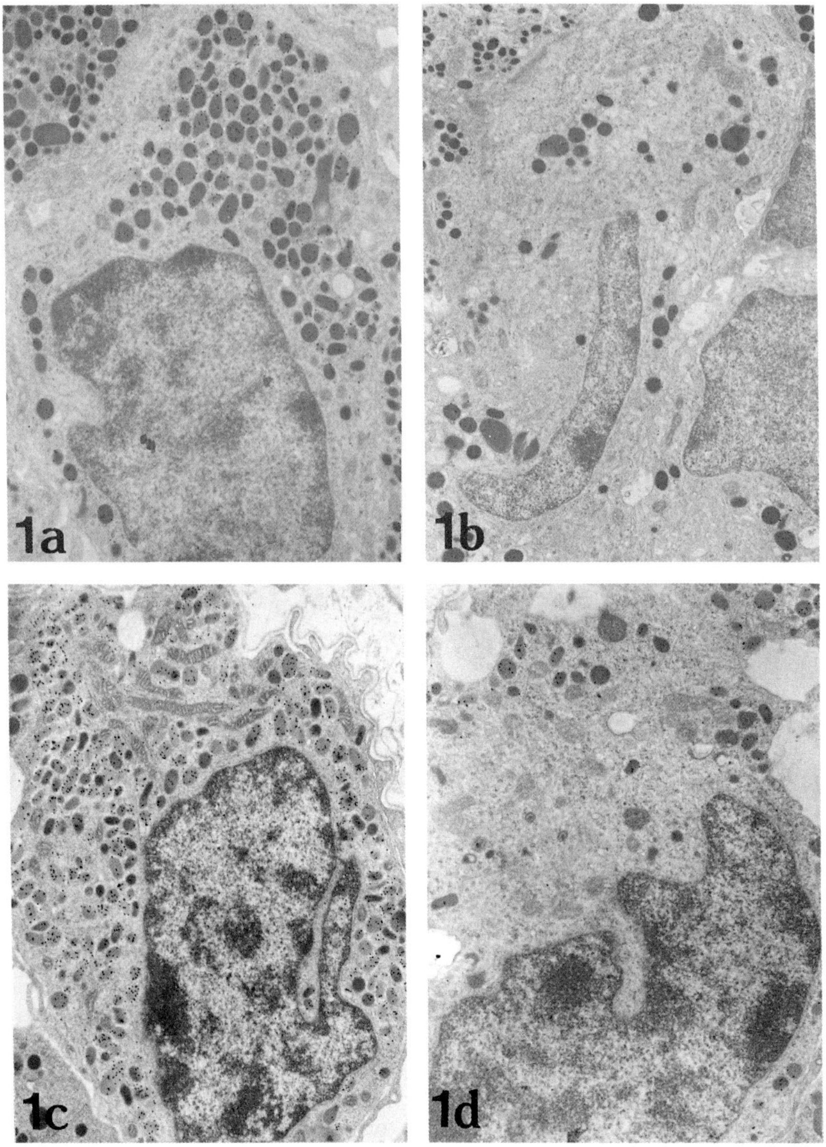

Fig. 1: TSH immunoreactive cells in the pituitary gland of *Rana perezi*. (a) In intact frog X11.900. (b) After 48 h of TRH treatment in vivo X9.900. (c) In hemipituitary superfused for 24 h with DME X9.900. (d) In hemipituitary superfused for 24 h with TRH X11.900.

RER and GC observed after 48 h, are indicative of decreased hormone release and diminished synthetic activity of PRL cells, which in turn suggests inhibition of the TRH-induced PRL cell activation. In amphibians, dopamine has been shown to counteract TRH

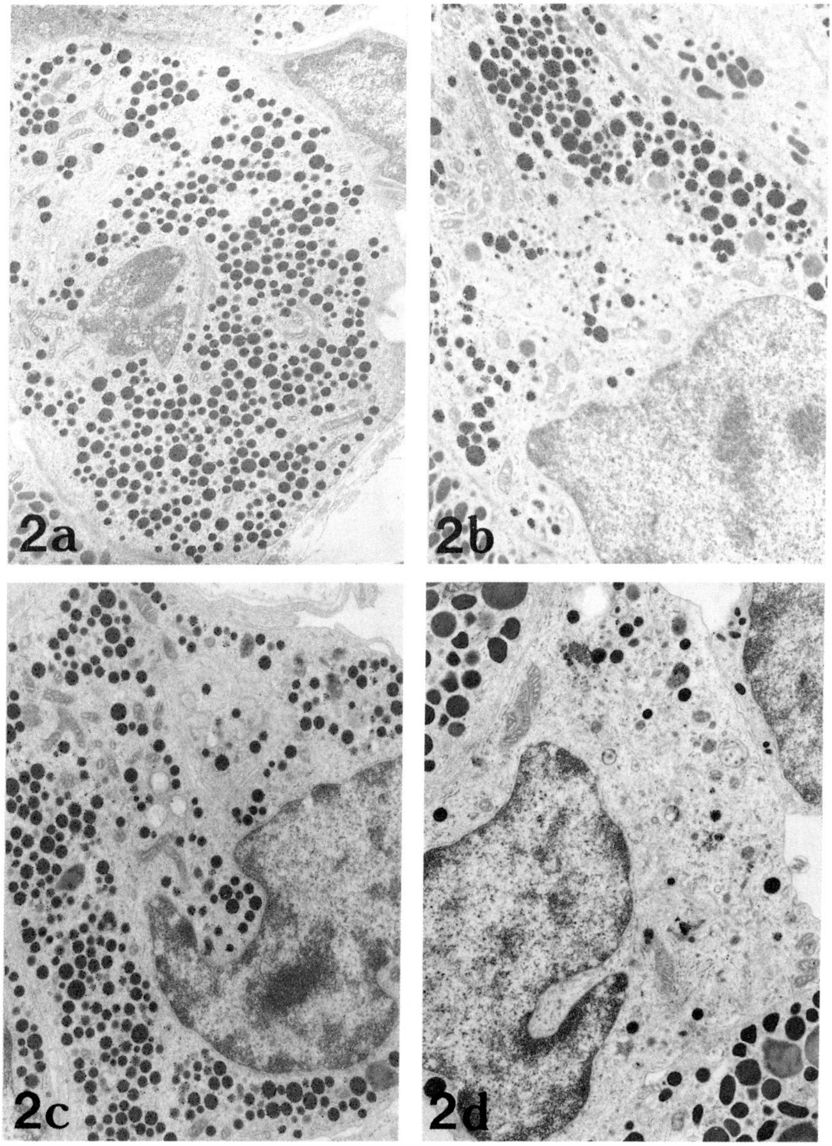

Fig. 2: PRL immunoreactive cells in the pituitary gland of *Rana perezi*. (a) In intact frog X9.900. (b) After 8 h of TRH treatment in vivo X7.800. (c) In hemipituitary superfused for 24 h with DME X11.900. (d) In hemipituitary superfused for 24 h with TRH X11.900.

in the suppression of TRH-induced prolactin release in vitro (Seki and Kikuyama, 1986). The inhibition of PRL release suggested by our results may have been the result of an increased hypothalamic dopamine release due to the elevated PRL levels induced by TRH.

3.3. GH cells

Although the stereological parameters have not been yet evaluated, we have found TRH to induce the *in vivo* degranulation of GH cells both in 8 h- and in 48 h-treated animals (Fig. 3 b). As with TSH and PRL cells, the morphological features of GH cells tend to revert to control conditions after lengthy treatment. These morphological results suggest that TRH induces an *in vivo* release of GH and indicate a long-term response of this cell type to TRH treatment. The reported recovery of the control morphology after 6 days may be explained on the basis of the inhibitory effects exerted by somatostatin (SRIF), as suggested by Hall and Chadwick (1986) in some amphibians and reptiles.

4. In vitro action of TRH on amphibian pituitary cells

In order to avoid the influence of the hypothalamus on the pituitary gland and to study the direct effect of TRH on *Rana perezi* pituitary cell types, we used a superfusion system reported elsewhere by Porter and Licht (1985). In short, anterior pituitaries were bisected midsagitally and each hemipituitary was immediately placed in the superfusion chamber. After a 3 h preincubation period with Dulbecco's modified Eagle's medium (DME) alone to stabilize the basal secretory levels (Porter and Licht, 1985), one hemipituitary from each animal was superfused with DME alone for 24 h at a rate of 5 ml/h, while the other was superfused for 24 h with DME containing 100 ng synthetic TRH/ml at the same rate. After 4 h, 14 h and 24 h of superfusion with or without the secretagogue, hemipituitaries were immediately immersed in the fixative and processed for their ultrastructural study as described above.

4.1. TSH cells

The avoidance of the influence of the hypothalamus on the pituitary gland induced no changes in TSH cells. They preserved the morphology found in intact control animals after 27 h of superfusion with DME alone (Fig. 1 c). These results agree with those reported by Denver (1988) in *Rana pipiens*, in which the basal secretion of TSH by pituitaries cultured *in vitro* does not induce the release of T_4 by the thyroid of the same animal in culture.

These results show that, when removed from their organic control, TSH cells do not change their biosynthetic and releasing activities and suggest that the TSH cells are not under inhibitory control or at least this control is very weak.

In the hemipituitaries superfused with TRH, TSH cells seem to be degranulated and with hypertrophied RER and GC, especially after 24 h of TRH superfusion (Fig. 1 d). These morphological results strongly suggest that TRH stimulates the *in vitro* release and synthesis of thyrotropin. This is consistent with the *in vitro* release of T_3 and T_4 by thyroids induced by the culture medium from *Rana pipiens* pituitaries stimulated with TRH (Denver, 1988). This, together with the *in vivo* results, clearly show that TRH has TSH-releasing activity in amphibians.

4.2. PRL cells

In the hemipituitaries cultured with the medium alone for 14 h and 24 h, PRL cells were degranulated and the GC hypertrophied in relation to intact animals (Fig. 2 c), thus indicating that PRL cells *in vivo* are under inhibitory control, probably exerted by dopamine as suggested by several authors (Hall and Chadwick, 1984; Seki and Kikuyama, 1986).

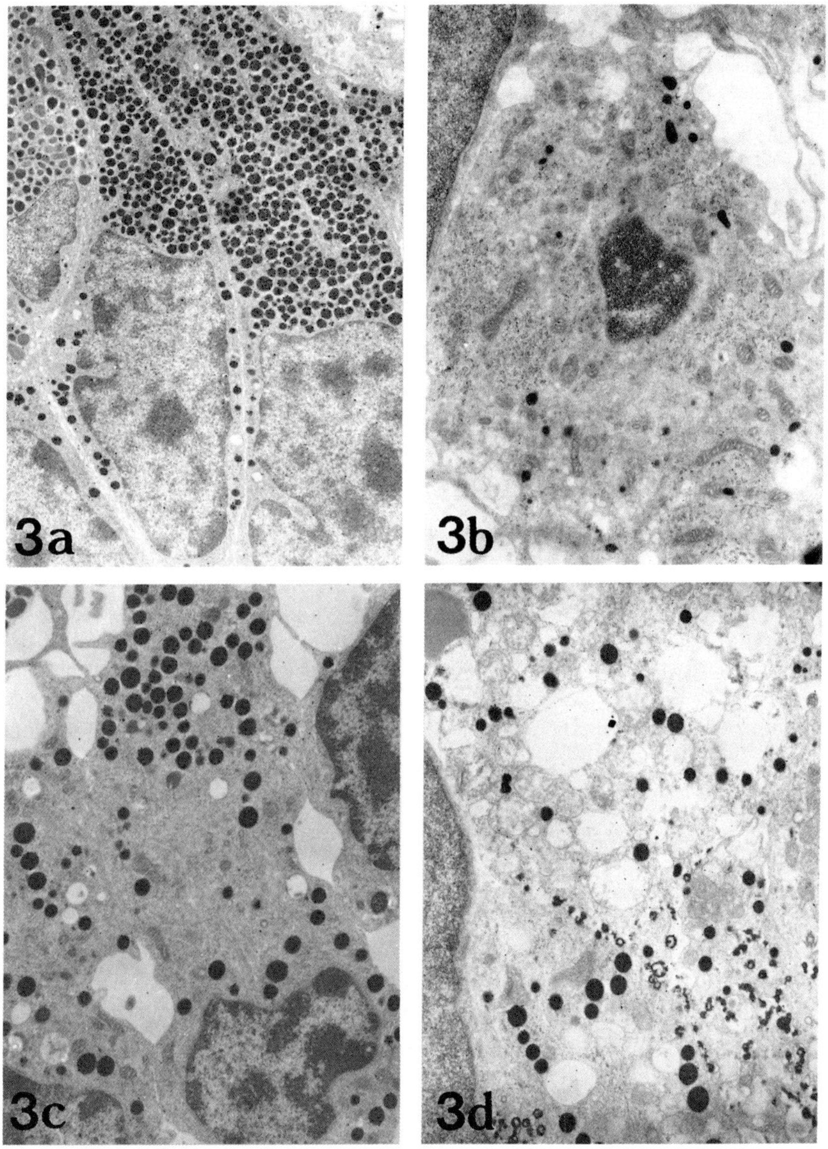

Fig. 3: GH immunoreactive cells in the pituitary gland of *Rana perezi.* (a) In intact frog X5.400. (b) After 48 h of TRH treatment in vivo X11.600. (c) In hemipituitary superfused for 24 h with DME X11.200. (d) In hemipituitary superfused for 24 h with TRH X9.900.

This mechanism seems to be common to mammals (Norris, 1980), birds (Hall et al., 1986 a), reptiles (Hall and Chadwick, 1984) and fish (Ball, 1981), in which dopamine has been shown to inhibit the release of PRL.

The morphological modifications of PRL cells were much more evident in the hemipituitaries superfused with TRH, in which PRL cells showed hypertrophied RER and an expanded GC with numerous condensing vesicles (Fig. 2 d). Secretory granules were few in number and images of discharging granules were frequently observed. This morphological activation of PRL cells increased as the stimulation with the peptide progressed, so that after 24 h the changes were much more ostensible than after 14 h of TRH treatment.

The morphological activation of PRL cells after TRH treatment, both *in vivo* and *in vitro*, agrees with previous physiological results in amphibians (Clemons et al., 1979; Hall and Chadwick, 1984; Kühn et al., 1985; Seki and Kikuyama, 1982; 1986) and clearly demonstrates the PRL-releasing activity of TRH. Compared with the *in vivo* experiment, the ultrastructural modifications induced by TRH are much more significant in the pituitaries cultured *in vitro*, probably due to the removal of the inhibitory hypothalamic influence.

4.3. GH cells

After culture incubation with DME alone, GH cells showed degranulation and hypertrophy of RER and GC (Fig. 3 c), thus indicating that, like PRL cells, GH cells are under primary inhibitory control in intact frogs, probably exerted by somatostatin (Hall and Chadwick, 1984).

In the hemipituitaries incubated with TRH, the morphological modifications were much more intense than in the hemipituitaries cultured with the medium alone. After 24 h of TRH stimulation, GH cells showed vacuolated cytoplasms with few granules, hypertrophied RER and numerous tonofilaments (Fig. 3 d). Exocytotic figures of SG were often observed. This was also evident in some GH cells after 14 h, thus indicating a quick response of GH cells to TRH stimulation. These results agree with the increased GH secretion observed by Hall and Chadwick (1984) after incubation of the pituitary gland with TRH *in vitro*.

On the other hand, GH cells were much more activated as compared not only to GH cells in the *in vivo* experiment, but also to the other cell types studied *in vitro*.

5. Conclusions

The morphological results reported herein show the ability of TRH to stimulate the synthesis and release of TSH, PRL and GH from the amphibian pituitary gland. However, each cell type shows different reaction pattern with respect to both time and sensitivity. While TSH cells are the most strongly activated cell type *in vivo*, the action of TRH in the *in vitro* experiment appears to be more intense on GH cells. This different reaction pattern of the cell types could be accounted for by the different type and strength of the primary control exerted by the hypothalamus and the interactions of the target organs with the hypothalamus or the pituitary.

In addition, these cell types show different time course responses. *In vivo*, PRL cells show short-term response while TSH and GH cells show a long-term response. Although no morphometric results about the differential response of the cell types to *in vitro* TRH stimulation are available, the preliminary results reported here suggest that GH cells are activated before PRL cells, and these before TSH cells. This suggests that the cells are pre-influenced by their previous hormonal control in the intact animal. Further study is needed to elucidate the cellular basis of the different sensitivity of each cell type to TRH.

Acknowledgements

This work has been supported by Comisión Interministerial de Ciencia y Tecnologia (Grant No. PB 86–0095).

References

Ball, J. N. (1981): Hypothalamic control of the pars distalis in fishes, amphibians and reptiles. Gen. Comp. Endocrinol. *44*, 135–170.

Bowers, C. Y., Redding, T. W., Schally, A. V. (1965): Effect of thyrotropin-releasing factor (TRF) of ovine, bovine, porcine and human origin on thyrotropin releasing *in vitro* and *in vivo*. Endocrinology *77*, 609–616.

Clemons, G. K., Russell, S. M., Nicoll, C. S. (1979): Effect of mammalian thyrotropin-releasing hormone on prolactin secretion by bullfrog adenohypophyses *in vitro*. Gen. Comp. Endocrinol. *38*, 62–67.

Darras, V. M., Kühn, E. R. (1982): Increased plasma levels of thyroid hormones in a frog *Rana ridibunda* following intravenous administration of TRH. Gen. Comp. Endocrinol. *48*, 469–475.

Denver, R. J. (1988): Several hypothalamic peptides stimulate *in vitro* thyrotropin secretion by pituitaries of anuran amphibians. Gen. Comp. Endocrinol. *72*, 383–393.

Etkin, W., Gona, A. G. (1968): Failure of mammalian thyrotropin-releasing factor preparation to elicit metamorphic responses in tadpoles. Endocrinology *82*, 1067–1068.

Giraud, P., Gillioz, P., Conte-Delvolx, B., Oliver, C. (1979): Distribution de thyroliberin (TRH), α-melanocitestimulating hormone (α-MSH) et somatostatine dans les tissus de la Grenouille verte (*Rana esculenta*). C. R. Acad. Sci. Paris Ser. D. *288*, 127–129.

Gona, A. G., Gona, O. (1974): Failure of synthetic TRF to elicit metamorphosis in frog tadpoles or red-spotted newts. Gen. Comp. Endocrinol. *24*, 223–225.

Hall, T. R., Chadwick, A. (1984): Effects of synthetic mammalian TRH, somatostatin and dopamine on the secretion of prolactin and growth hormone from amphibian and reptilian pituitary glands incubated *in vitro*. J. Endocrinol. *102*, 175–180.

Hall, T. R., Harvey, S., Chadwick, A. (1986a): Control of prolactin secretion in birds: a review. Gen. Comp. Endocrinol. *62*, 171–184.

Hall, T. R., Harvey, S., Scanes, C. G. (1986b): Control of growth hormone secretion in the vertebrates: a comparative survey. Comp. Biochem. Physiol. *84A*, 231–253.

Horrobin, D. F. (1977): In: Prolactin, Vol. 5. (D. F. Horrobin, ed.) Churchill Livingstone, Scotland.

Jackson, I. M. D., Reichlin, S. (1974): Thyrotropin-releasing hormone (TRH): Distribution in hypothalamic and extrahypothalamic brain tissues of mammalian and submammalian chordates. Endocrinology *95*, 854–862.

Jackson, I. M. D., Reichlin, S. (1977): Thyrotropin-releasing hormone: abundance in the skin of the frog *Rana pipiens*. Science *198*, 414–415.

Jackson, I. M. D., Reichlin, S. (1979): Thyrotropin-releasing hormone (TRH) in the blood of the frog, *Rana pipiens*: Its nature and possible derivation from regional locations in the skin. Endocrinology *104*, 1814–1821.

Kühn, E. R., Engelen, H. (1976): Seasonal variation in prolactin and TSH releasing activity in the hypothalamus of *Rana temporaria*. Gen. Comp. Endocrinol. *28*, 277–282.

Kühn, E. R., Kikuyama, S., Yamamoto, K., Darras, V. M. (1985): *In vivo* release of prolactin in *Rana ridibunda* following an intravenous injection of thyrotropin-releasing hormone. Gen. Comp. Endocrinol. *60*, 86–89.

Labella, F. S., Vivian, S. R. (1971): Effect of synthetic TRF on hormone release from bovine anterior pituitary *in vitro*. Endocrinology *88*, 787–789.

Malagón, M. M., García-Navarro, S., García-Herdugo, G., Gracia-Navarro, F. (1988a): Immunocytochemical and morphometrical study of thyrotropic cells of *Rana ridibunda*. Histochemistry *89*, 461–466.

Malagón, M. M., García-Navarro, S., Ruiz-Navarro, A., Garcia-Navarro, F. (1988b): Light and electron microscopic immunoidentification of prolactin-producing cells in the pituitary gland of *Rana ridibunda*. Z. mikrosk.-anat. Forsch. *102*, 935–944.

Malagón, M. M., García-Navarro, S., Ruiz-Navarro, A., Gracia-Navarro, F. (1988c): Morphometric evaluation of subcellular changes induced by *in vivo* TRH treatment in the pituitary gland of *Rana perezi*: effects on prolactin and thyrotropic cells. Cell Tissue Res. *256*, 391–398.

Mimnagh, K. M., Bolaffi, J. L., Montgomery, N. M., Kaltenbach, J. C. (1987): Thyrotropin-releasing hormone (TRH): Immunohistochemical distribution in tadpole and frog brain. Gen. Comp. Endocrinol. *66*, 394–404.

Norris, D. O. (1980): Vertebrate Endocrinology. Lea & Febiger, Philadelphia.

Porter, D., Licht, P. (1985): Pituitary responsiveness to superfused GnRH in two species of ranid frogs. Gen. Comp. Endocrinol. *59*, 308–315.

Rosenkilde, P. (1979): The thyroid hormones in Amphibia. In: Hormones and Evolution, Vol. 1 (E. J. W. Barrington, ed.), pp. 437–491. Acad. Press, New York.

Roth, J. (1983): The colloidal gold marker system for light and electron microscopic cytochemistry. In: Techniques in immunocytochemistry, vol. 2, (G. R. Bullock, P. Petrusz, eds.), p. 127, Acad. Press, London.

Sawin, C. T., Bolaffi, J. L., Callard, I. P., Bacharach, P., Jackson, I. M. D. (1978): Induced metamorphosis in *Ambystoma mexicanum*: Lack of effects of triiodothyronine on tissue or blood level of thyrotropin-releasing hormone (TRH). Gen. Comp. Endocrinol. *37*, 427–432.

Seki, T., Kikuyama, S. (1982): *In vitro* studies on the regulation of prolactin secretion in the bullfrog pituitary gland. Gen. Comp. Endocrinol. *46*, 473–479.

Seki, T., Kikuyama, S. (1984): *In vitro* stimulation of bullfrog prolactin release by hypothalamic extract. Zool. Sci. *1*, 969.

Seki, T., Kikuyama, S. (1986): Effect of thyrotropin-releasing hormone and dopamine on the *in vitro* secretion of prolactin by the bullfrog pituitary gland. Gen. Comp. Endocrinol. *61(2)*, 197–202.

Seki, T., Nakai, Y., Shioda, S., Mitsuma, T., Kikuyama, S. (1983): Distribution of immunoreactive thyrotropin-releasing hormone in the forebrain and hypophysis of the bullfrog, *Rana catesbeiana*. Cell Tissue Res. *233*, 507–516.

Taurog, A., Oliver, C., Eskay, R. L., Porter, J. C., McKenzie, J. M. (1974): The role of TRH in the neoteny of the Mexican axolotl (*Ambystoma mexicanum*). Gen. Comp. Endocrinol. *24*, 267–279.

Vale, W., Rivier, C., Brown, M. (1977): Regulatory peptides of the hypothalamus. Ann. Rev. Physiol. *39*, 473–527.

Vandesande, F., Aspeslagh, M. R. (1974): Failure of thyrotropin-releasing hormone to increase ^{125}I uptake by the thyroid in *Rana temporaria*. Gen. Comp. Endocrinol. *23*, 355–356.

Weibel, E. R. (1979): Stereological methods, Vol. 1: Practical methods for biological morphometry. Acad. Press, London.

Fortschritte der Zoologie, Band/Vol. 38 · Hanke, W. (Hrsg.), Biology and Physiology of Amphibians
Gustav Fischer Verlag · Stuttgart · New York · 1990

Melanotrope cell function in the neuroendocrine regulation of dermal melanophores

Bruce G. Jenks and Ingrid D. van Zoest

Dept. Animal Physiology, University of Nijmegen, Toernooiveld, 6525 ED Nijmegen, The Netherlands

1. Introduction

The melanotrope cells of the amphibian pars intermedia constitute a key link in the neuroendocrine system regulating pigment dispersion in dermal melanophores. The regulation of secretion of α-melanophore stimulating hormone (α-MSH) from these cells appears to be very intricate, involving multiple factors of hypothalamic origin. Moreover, the secretory signal of the melanotroph cells is very complex, involving release of not only α-MSH but also other peptides derived from the precursor protein proopiomelanocortin. This survey considers the implications of these complexities for the physiological functioning of the melanotrope cells. In addition, evidence is presented for the involvement of a β-adrenergic receptor mechanism, functioning at the level of dermal melanophores, in the regulation of pigment dispersion during the process of background adaptation.

2. Melanotrope cell function

2.1. The classic view

Most amphibians have the ability to regulate the degree of pigment dispersion in their dermal melanophores and thus alter the coloration of their skin. The best example of this phenomena can be seen during the process of background adaptation in which amphibians regulate pigment dispersion according to the color of their background. This topic has been widely reviewed (Waring, 1963; Bagnara and Hadley, 1973) and is often cited as an example of a neuroendocrine reflex. Placing an animal on a black background leads to release of the peptide α-melanophore stimulating hormone (α-MSH) from the pars intermedia of the pituitary gland. This hormone induces a rapid dispersion of pigment containing organelles, the melanosomes, within the melanophores. These organelles contain the black pigment melanin and, as a consequence of their dispersion, there is a darkening of the skin. In animals placed on a white background release of α-MSH is terminated and consequently the melanosomes aggregate to a perinuclear position within the melanophore thus leading to blanching of the skin. As stated above, the neuroendocrine regulation of pigment dispersion seems to be a simple process which would involve a stimulation of α-MSH release from the pars intermedia of animals on black background and an inhibition of hormone release in animals on white background. Etkin (1962) established that the hypothalamus exerts primarily an inhibitory influence on the pars intermedia. Many early studies concerned the possible involvement of aminergic fibers innervating the pars intermedia of amphibians (Enemar and Falk, 1965; Iturriza, 1966;

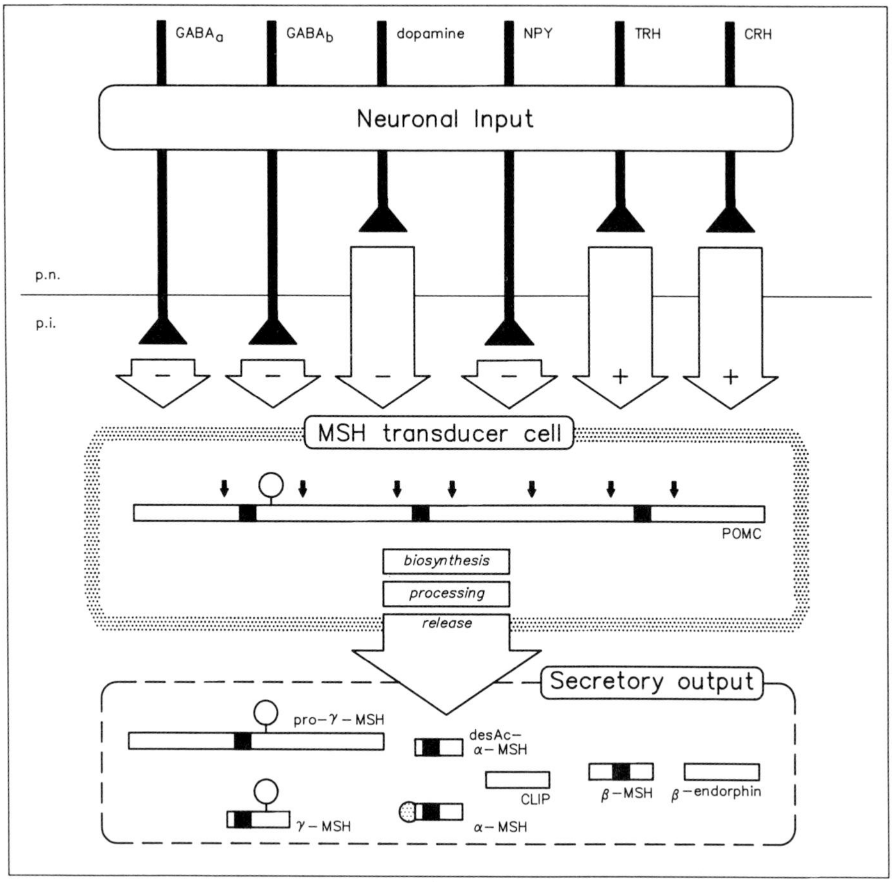

Fig. 1: Schematic representation of the MSH cell of *Xenopus laevis* giving an overview of the hypothalamic neuronal systems involved in the regulation of the secretory process of this cell and indicating the diversity in the peptide content of its secretory signal. The horizontal line indicates the boarder between the pars nervosa (pn) and pars intermedia (pi) and the bold vertical lines represent nerve fibers: the neurotransmitter gamma-aminobutyric acid (GABA) inhibits secretion through $GABA_a$ and $GABA_b$ receptors; dopamine inhibits through dopamine d_2 receptors; neuropeptide Y (NPY) inhibits secretion and the peptides thyrotropin releasing hormone (TRH) and corticotropin releasing hormone (CRH) stimulates secretion. The MSH cell generates its secretory signal from the multifunctional precursor protein proopiomelanocortin (POMC); small arrows indicate the location of proteolytic cleavage sites within the precursor protein and the circle gives the location of the single glycosylation site within the precursor. Among the peptides identified in the secretory signal are: the N-terminal fragment of POMC (pro-γ-MSH), γ-MSH, both the non-acetylated and acetylated form of α-MSH (desacetyl-α-MSH and α-MSH respectively), corticotropin-like intermediate lobe peptide (CLIP), β-MSH and β-endorphin. The filled region within various peptides indicates the location of a tetrapeptide sequence common to these peptides.

Jørgensen and Larson, 1967; Terlou and Ploemacher, 1973). Indeed, catecholamines including adrenalin and dopamine were found to be potent inhibitors of α-MSH secretion (Iturriza, 1966, 1969; Goos, 1969; Bower et al. 1974). From these studies evolved the classical view of regulation of the intermediate lobe melanotrope cells, with central integration of neuronal input from the eyes leading to an activation (white background) or inactivation (black background) of an inhibitory catecholaminergic system innervating the pars intermedia.

2.2. The current view

It was already appreciated in the early 1970's that regulation of secretion from the melanotrope cell was probably very complex, and involvement of a number of regulatory neurotransmitters was indicated (Hadley et al. 1975 a, b; Hadley and Bagnara, 1975). At present, the most complete picture of melanotrope cell regulation has been established for the species *Rana ridibunda* and *Xenopus laevis* (for reviews see Tonon et al. 1988; Jenks et al. 1988). Models for this regulation have been constructed on the basis of immunocytochemical studies, which were used to establish the morphological basis of hypothalamic regulation, and *in vitro* superfusion experiments with intermediate lobe tissue, where the effect of potential secretagogues on the release of α-MSH could be determined. These studies reveal that the pars intermedia of amphibians is regulated by multiple factors, both classical neurotransmitters and neuropeptides. These factors reach the pars intermedia either through direct innervation of the gland, or, in some cases, through diffusion from nerves terminating in the pars nervosa. While some species differences have been found in both the nature of the innervation of the neurointermediate lobes and in the effects of secretagogues on α-MSH release, it can be said that both *Rana* and *Xenopus* have developed similar strategies in the regulation of α-MSH release. This regulation has both inhibitory and stimulatory components. The current model for regulation of α-MSH secretion from the melanotrope cell of *Xenopus laevis* is given in Fig. 1.

An additional complexity in considering the functioning of melanotrope cells of amphibians was the discovery that MSH is produced from the multifunctional precursor protein proopiomelanocortin (POMC). This precursor was first characterized in mammals (reviews: Eipper and Mains, 1980; Herbert, 1981), and subsequently shown to be synthesized by melanotrope cells of amphibians (Loh and Gainer, 1977; Loh, 1979; Martens et al. 1982; Martens, 1986; Vaudry et al. 1986). The full structure of an amphibian POMC has been revealed by the application of recombinant DNA techniques (Martens, 1986). Pulse-chase analysis of biosynthetic events in intermediate lobes of amphibians have shown that processing of POMC to form secretory peptides occurs in a pattern very similar to that established for the mammalian pars intermedia (review: Jenks et al. 1988). This same analysis shows that there is a concomitant release of the POMC-derived peptides from melanotroph cells of amphibians. Therefore, the secretory signal of these cells is very complex, consisting of a mixture of acetylated and nonacetylated α-MSH, β-MSH, pro-γ-MSH, γ-MSH, CLIP and β-endorphin related peptides (see Fig. 1).

3. Physiological implications of the complex regulation of melanotrope cells

In the classic view of melanotrope cell function this endocrine cell is primarily under inhibitory control. This view is supported by the observation that α-MSH is spontaneously released if the pars intermedia is isolated from hypothalamic influence, either through severing connections of this tissue with the hypothalamus (*in vivo* lesion experiments or ectopic transplant experiments) or removing the tissue and incubating it *in vitro* (review: Hadley and Bagnara, 1975; Tonon et al. 1988). One may therefore question the physiological significance of secretagogues which stimulate α-MSH secretion. It can only be assumed that, in the intact hypothalamo-hypophyseal system, endocrine output from melanotrope cells must be regulated through a careful balance of stimulatory and inhibitory influences. There are morphological indications that melanotrope cells of black adapted animals, which are often considered to display maximal biosynthetic and secretory activity, infact undergo a further activation when brought to the *in vitro* situation (Hopkins, 1970). This suggests that in the living animal these cells must function under somewhat constrained conditions in which stimulatory factors may be required to override tonic inhibitory influences.

As mentioned earlier, regulation of melanotrope cell function during the process of background adaptation would appear to be a simple problem: stimulation of hormone secretion in animals on black background and inhibition of secretion in animals on white background. With this in mind the question arise, are all the neuronal systems and their associated secretagogues indeed utilized for regulation of melanotrope cells during background adaptations? While it is too early to give a definitive answer, there is some evidence to suggest that this may not be the case. It has been shown that injection of white adapted *Xenopus* with sulpiride, a dopamine D_2-receptor antagonist, has almost no effect on pigment dispersion in dermal melanophores (Verburg et al. 1986b). If dopamine played a major role in the inhibition of MSH secretion in such animals then one would have expected pigment dispersion with such treatment. That sulpiride itself is an appropriate receptor antagonist for such experiments has been demonstrated both *in vitro* (sulpiride blocks the inhibitory effect of dopamine and all other catecholamines on the release of MSH) and *in vivo* (sulpiride blocks the blanching effect of dopamine injected into black adapted animals). Thus, the possibility must be entertained that in the species *Xenopus laevis* the neurotransmitter dopamine may not be involved in the inhibition of MSH secretion in animals on white background. This is a surprising finding in that dopamine is considered to be the most important MSH release inhibiting factor in the classic view of melanotrope cell regulation.

In considering the complex nature of the system that has evolved for the regulation of the melanotrope cells, it is conceivable that parameters other than the color of background could also be involved in regulating α-MSH release. In this view, the complex nature of hypothalamic regulation would reflect the diverse nature of environmental and other inputs to the pars intermedia, with each of the inputs utilizing a different element of the neuronal networks converging on the pars intermedia. The melanotrope cell itself would function to integrate these diverse inputs to determine endocrine output. Concerning the nature of such inputs to the pars intermedia, one can only speculate. It is known that pigment dispersion in dermal melanophores displays an endogenous day-night rhythm (see Waring, 1963). It remains to be determined if this phenomenon reflects a rhythmic mode of secretory activity in the pars intermedia. Other potential sources of input to the pars intermedia could be criteria concerning temperature, season, and aspects of stress. This latter possibility is of interest in that it has been suggested for both fish (Malo-Michele, 1980; Balm et al. 1987; Wendelaar Bonga and Balm, 1988) and mammals (Berkenbosch et al. 1984) that the pars intermedia may be involved in the endocrine responses to stress.

4. Physiological implications of the complex secretory signal of the melanotrope cells

In view of the potential of POMC-producing cells to deliver a wide range of bioactive peptides, a relevant question concerning melanotroph cells is whether the qualitative nature of the secretory signal can be regulated (i.e. regulation of which peptides are infact synthesized and released). We have indeed found evidence that the amphibian melanotroph cells are capable of altering their secretory signal. This evidence comes from the study of the acetylation process in which desacetyl-α-MSH is converted to α-MSH. In two species of amphibians, *Rana ridibunda* (Vaudry et al. 1983; Jenks et al. 1985) and *Xenopus laevis* (Martens et al. 1981; Verburg et al., 1987), it has been shown that the acetylation process is associated with the release process. For the latter species it has also been demonstrated that, for black adapted animals, the major secretory form of the peptide is α-MSH; transferring animals to white background leads to a rapid inhibition of the acetylation process (Verburg et al., 1987). This physiologically induced modulation in the composition of the secretory signal correlates well with the function of the cells in that the acetylated form of MSH is reported to have up to 46 times the melanotropic potency of the nonacetylated peptide (Guttmann and Boissonnas, 1961; Rudman et al. 1983). It has also been demonstrated *in vitro* that dopamine and GABA inhibit not only the secretion of MSH but also the acetylation process (Jenks et al. 1985; Verburg et al. 1987). This indicates that factors that regulate the rate of secretion from melanotroph cells can also affect the peptide profile of the secretory signal.

In considering the complex secretory signal of the melanotroph cells, one question that immediately rises is the possibility of coordinate action of these peptides at the level of the target tissue. For example, for the secretory products of the POMC-producing corticotroph cells of the pars distalis it has been suggested that γ-MSH could function in mammals as a potentiating factor for ACTH (Pedersen and Brownie, 1980) or as trophic factor for the adrenal cell growth (Lowry et al., 1984). Concerning the amphibian melanophore, the suggestion has been made that the C-terminal tetrapeptide of β-endorphin could function as a MSH-potentiating factor (Carter et al. 1979), although others have been unable to confirm this activity (Eberle, 1988). While γ-MSH itself has proven to be a weak melanotropin (Ling et al. 1979), to our knowledge no studies have been conducted to test possible potentiating activity of this peptide at the level of the melanophore.

Another aspect for future consideration is the possibility that tissues other than dermal melanophores of the skin could be target tissues for the complex secretory signal of melanotroph cells. In this regard it is worth noting that α-MSH has been shown to possess weak corticotropic activity when tested on amphibian adrenal tissue (Delarue et al. 1988). Given the potential of melanotrope cells to modulate the qualitative nature of their secretory signal, this cell may well be capable of producing a potent corticotropic signal.

5. Dermal melanophore function: The possible significance of β-adrenergic receptors

Besides receptors for MSH, the dermal melanophores of amphibians also possess β-adrenergic receptors, activation of which causes pigment dispersion (Lerner et al. 1954; Graham, 1961; Hadley and Goldman, 1970). It would seem that during periods of acute stress (e.g. handling) these receptors are sensitive to circulating catecholamines in that many amphibians, including *Xenopus*, undergo a slight and transitory darkening, termed «excitement darkening» (Burgers, 1953). We have recently found evidence that the β-adrenergic receptor may have a physiological function during the early stages of black background adaptation in the species *Xenopus* (van Zoest, manuscript in preparation). Among the evidence was the observation that white adapted animals treated with the β-adrenergic receptor antagonist propranolol showed retarded expansion of pigment in dermal melanophores when placed on black background (Fig. 2). Previous *in vitro* studies demonstrate that β-adrenergic receptor agonists and antagonists have no direct effect on MSH secretion from neurointermediate lobes (Verburg et al. 1986a), suggesting that the above action of propranolol could be at the level of the dermal melanophores.

There are several potential sources of catecholamines for physiological regulation of melanophores. Involvement of circulating catecholamines from the adrenal gland would seem unlikely in that there is only a very slight pigment expansion in dermal melanophores during acute stress, a period when circulating catecholamines would be expected to be elevated. While there is no evidence for direct autonomic innervation of melanophores in *Xenopus*, the skin is reported to be rich in catecholamines (Brouwer and van de Veerdonk, 1969), probably located in skin glands whose secretion is under autonomic control. It is conceivable that catecholamines in such secretions or from nerve terminals in the vicinity of the melanophores could generate a local catecholamine concentration of sufficient magnitude to have a physiological function during background adaptation. To investigate this we have recently conducted *in vivo* experiments whereby skin was excised from the webs, thus severing any autonomic nerve fibers, and transplanted to the back of the animal. Vascularization of the autotransplant was re-established within a few days,

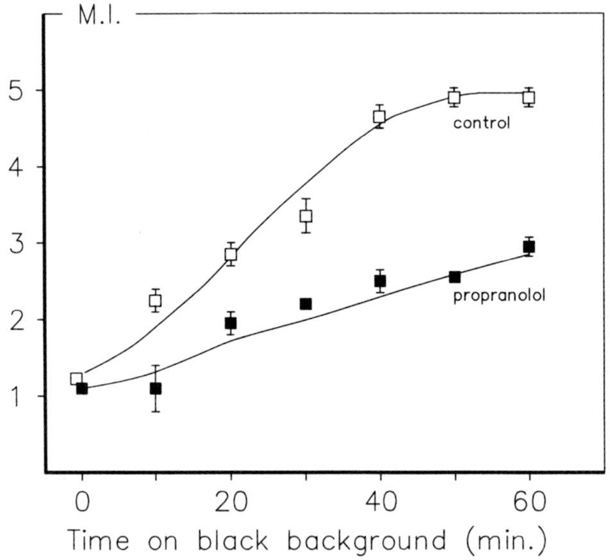

Fig. 2: The effect of the β-adrenergic receptor antagonist propranolol on the dispersion of pigment in dermal melanophores of *Xenopus laevis* during adaptation to black background. White background adapted animals were injected i.p. with saline (control) or propranolol solution (5×10^{-9}mol./g body weight) and then placed on black background. The degree of dispersion of pigment in web melanophores was recorded following this transfer (M.I. is melanophore index: M.I. = 1 represents fully accumulated pigment, M.I. = 5 represents fully dispersed pigment). Bars represent S.E.M., n = 5.

demonstrated by the fact that the melanophores of the transplant were fully responsive to injections of α-MSH. In contrast, these melanophores showed retarded pigment expansion when the animal was placed on black background (Fig. 3), an observation which lends support to the concept that the action of nerve terminals could be an important element in inducing pigment expansion during physiological adaptations.

In considering the possible physiological significance of the involvement of a β-adrenergic receptor mechanism for the stimulation of pigment expansion in *Xenopus laevis*, it is important to realize that the capacity of melanotrope cells to synthesize MSH is acquired only very slowly during adaptation to black background. Following transfer to black background, it takes a number of days for the melanotrope cells to acquire the high biosynthetic capacity which they exhibit in long-term black adapted animals (Loh and Gainer, 1977; Jenks et al. 1977). There is evidence that the hormone stores possessed by animals on white background are quickly depleted during the adaptive process (Verburg et al. 1987) and yet, despite this depletion, the animals are capable of rapid and sustained pigment dispersion. For the species *Xenopus* at least, regulation of dermal melanophores may be viewed as a cooperative effort, with a β-adrenergic mechanism playing an important role in short-term events during which time the melanotrope cells of the neuroendocrine system acquire the biosynthetic capacity to maintain pigment dispersion.

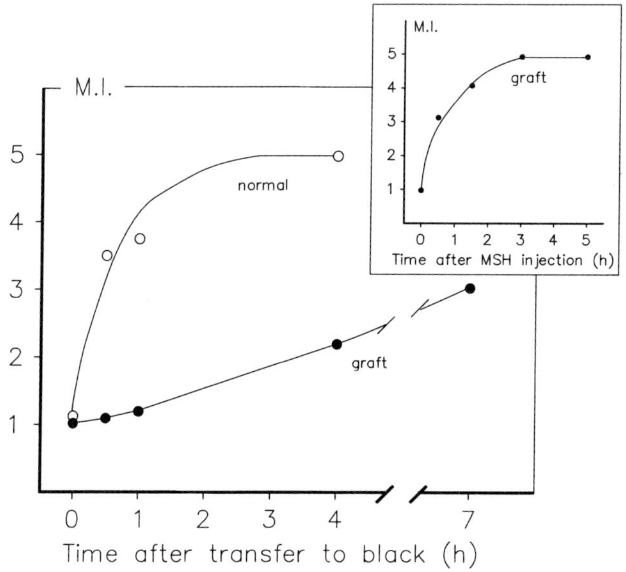

Fig. 3: Pigment dispersion in melanophores of intact web and excised web segment grafted to a dorsal site of *Xenopus laevis*. The animal used was fully adapted to white background and transferred to black background 3 days after the graft was implanted. Melanophores of web were found to be fully responsive to injection of α-MSH (insert), indicating that vascular connections had been made within the 3 days. Data shown is from a single experiment; this experiment has been repeated once with essentially the same results.

Concluding remarks

The melanotrope cells of amphibians are neuroendocrine transducer cells which are the focal point for a number of regulatory neuronal systems of hypothalamic origin. Therefore, these cells can be considered a major center of neuroendocrine integration which, through the secretion of the peptide α-MSH, play a major role in physiological background adaptations. In view of the complexity of these cells, from the standpoint of the complex nature of their hypothalamic regulation and their potential to generate diverse biological signals, it seems unlikely that their function would be limited to their role in background adaptations. Indeed, our understanding of these cells at a cellular and biochemical level seems to have surpassed our appreciation of their physiological significance.

Acknowledgments

We gratefully acknowledge support from Netherlands Organization for Advancement of Scientific Research (NWO) (grants 426.263 & 426.901P) and the European Economic Community (contract ST2J-0468-C).

References

Bagnara, J. T., Hadley, M. E. (1973): Chromatophores and Color Change: The Comparative Physiology of Animal Pigmentation. Prentice Hall, Englewood Cliff, New Jersey.

Balm, P. H. H., Lamers, A., Jenks, B. G., Wendelaar Bonga, S. E. (1987): The role of α-MSH in the regulation of Tilapia interrenal function. Gen. Comp. Endocrinology 66, 12.

Berkenbosch, F., Vermes, I., Tilders, F. J. H. (1984): The β-adrenoreceptor-blocking drug propranolol prevents secretion of immunoreactive β-endorphin and α-melanocyte-stimulating hormone in response to certain stress stimuli. Endocrinology *115*, 1051–1059.

Bower, A., Hadley, M. E., Hruby, V. J. (1974): Biogenic amines and control of melanophore stimulating hormone release. Science *184*, 70–72.

Brouwer, E., van der Veerdonk, F. C. G. (1969): Identification of a catecholamine in the skin of the toad, *Xenopus laevis*, and the relation to the physiological melanophore reaction. Experientia *25*, 391–392.

Burgers, A. C. J., Boschman, Th. A. C., van de Kamer, J. C. (1953): Excitement darkening and the effect of adrenalin on the melanophores of *Xenopus laevis*. Acta Endocrinology 14, 72–82.

Carter, R. J., Schuster, S., Morley, J. S. (1979): Melanotropic potentiating factor is the C-terminal tetrapeptide of human lipotropin. Nature *279*, 74–75.

Delarue, C., Leboulenger, F., Netchitaïlo, P., Lihrman, I., Feuilloley, M., Idres, S., Morra, M., Larcher, A., Lefebvre, H., Vaudry, H. (1988): Neuroendocrine regulation of adrenalcortical cells in amphibians. Abstract in the proceedings of the symposium Biology and Physiology of Amphibians, Karlsruhe, Aug. 31–Sept. 3, 1988.

Eberle, A. N. (1988): The Melanotropins: Chemistry, Physiology and Mechanisms of Action. Karger, Basel.

Eipper, B. A., Mains, R. E. (1980): Structure and biosynthesis of pro-adrenocorticotropin/endorphin and related peptides. Endocrine Rev. *1*, 1–27.

Enemar, A., Falk, B. (1965): On the presence of adrenergic nerves in the pars intermedia of the frog, *Rana temporaria*, Gen. Comp. Endocrinology *5*, 577–583.

Etkin, W. (1962): Hypothalamic inhibition of pars intermedia activity in the frog. Gen. Comp. Endocrinol. *1*, 148–159.

Goos, H. J. Th. (1969): Hypothalamic control of the pars intermedia in *Xenopus laevis* tadpoles, Z. Zellforsch. *97*, 118–124.

Graham, J. D. P. (1961): The response to catecholamines of the melanophores of *Xenopus laevis*. J. Physiol. (London) *8*, 5–6.

Guttmann, S. T., Boissonnas, B. A. (1961): Influence of the N-terminal extremity of α-MSH on the melanophore stimulating activity of this hormone, Experientia *17*, 265–267.

Hadley, M. E., Bagnara, J. T. (1975): Regulation of release and mechanism of action of MSH. In: Trends in Comparative Endocrinology, Amer. Zoologist Suppl. (E. J. W. Barington ed., pp. 81–104, Griffiths, New York (1975).

Hadley, M. E., Goldman, J. M. (1970): Adrenergic receptors and geographic variation in *Rana pipiens* chromatophore responses. Am. J. Physiol. *219*, 72–77 (1970).

Hadley, M. E., Bower, A., Hruby, V. J. (1975 a): Regulation of melanophore-stimulating hormone (MSH) release. Yale J. Biol. Med. *46*, 602–616.

Hadley, M. E., Hruby, V. J., Bower, A. (175 b): Cellular mechanisms controlling melanophore stimulating hormone release. Gen. Comp. Endocrinol. *26*, 24–35.

Herbert, E. (1981): Discovery of pro-opiomelanocortin: a cellular polyprotein. Trends in Biochem. Sci. *6*, 184–188.

Hopkins, C. R. (1970): Studies on secretory activity in the pars intermedia of *Xenopus laevis*. III. The synthesis and release of melanocyte stimulating hormone (MSH) *in vitro*. Tissue and Cell *2*, 83–98.

Iturriza, F. C. (1966): Monoamines and control of the pars intermedia of the toad pituitary, Gen. Comp. Endocrinology *6*, 19–25.

Iturriza, F. C. (1969): Further evidence for the blocking effect of catecholamines on the secretion of melanocyte-stimulating hormone in toads. Gen. Comp. Endocrinol. *12*, 417–426.

Jenks, B. G., van Overbeeke, A. P., McStay, B. F. (1977): Synthesis, storage and release of MSH in the pars intermedia of the pituitary gland of *Xenopus laevis* during background adaptation. Can. J. Zool. *55*, 922–927.

Jenks, B. G., Verburg-van Kemenade, B. M. L., Tonon, M. C., Vaudry, H. (1985): Regulation of biosynthesis and release of pars intermedia peptides in *Rana ridibunda*: dopamine affects both acetylation and release of α-MSH. Peptides *6*, 913–921.

Jenks, B. G., Verburg-van Kemenade, B. M. L., Martens, G. J. M. (1988): Proopiomelanocortin in the amphibian pars intermedia: a neuroendocrine model system. In: The Melanotropic Peptides. Volume 1: Source, synthesis, Chemistry, Circulation and Metabolism. M. E. Hadley, ed. pp. 103–126, CRC Press, Boca Raton, Florida U.S.A.

Jørgensen, C. B., Larsen, O. J. (1967): Neuroendocrine mechanisms in lower vertebrates. In: Neuroendocrinology Vol. II (L. Martini, W. F. Ganong, eds.) pp. 485–528. Academic Press, N. Y.

Lerner, A. B., Shizume, K., Buding, I. (1954): The mechanism of endocrine control of melanin pigmentation. J. Clin. Endocrinol. Metab. *14*, 1463–1490.

Loh, Y. P. (1979): Immunological evidence for two common precursors to corticotropins, endorphins, and melanotropin in the neurointermediate lobe of the toad. Proc. Natn. Acad. Sci. U.S.A. *76*, 796–800.

Loh, Y. P., Gainer, H. (1977): Biosynthesis, processing, and control of release of melanotropic peptides in the neurointermediate lobe of Xenopus laevis. J. Gen. Physiol. *70*, 37–58.

Lowry, P. J., Estivariz, F. E., Silas, L., Linton, E. A., McLean, C., Crombe, K. (1984): The case for pro-γ-MSH as the adrenal growth factor. Endocrine Research *10*, 243–258.

Ling, N., Ying, S., Minick, S., Guillemin, R. (1979): Synthesis and biological activity of four γ-melanotropin peptides derived from the cryptic region of the adrenocorticotropin*.165-lipotropin precursor. Life Sci. *25*, 1773–1780.

Malo-Michele, M. (1980): Stimulation des cellules cortico-melanotropes de la pars intermedia de l'hypophyse de la saupe, *Boops salpa* (téleostéen marin) soumise à un stress neurogène sonore. Gen. Comp. Endocrinol. *42*, 101–104.

Martens, G. J. M. (1986): Expression of two proopiomelanocortin genes in the pituitary gland of *Xenopus laevis*: complete structures of the two preprohormones. Nucleic Acids Res. *14*, 3791–3798.

Martens, G. J. M., Biermans, P. P. J., Jenks, B. G., van Overbeeke, A. P. (1982): Biosynthesis of two structurally different pro-opiomelanocortins in the pars intermedia of the amphibian pituitary gland, Eur. J. Biochem. *126*, 23–28.

Martens, G. J. M., Jenks, B. G., van Overbeeke, A. P. (1981): Nα-acetylation is linked to α-MSH release from pars intermedia of the amphibian pituitary gland. Nature *294*, 558–560.

Pedersen, R. C., Brownie, A. C. (1980): Adrenalcortical response to corticotropin is potentiated by part of the amino-terminal region of pro-corticotropin/endorphin. Proc. Natl. Acad. Sci. (U. S. A.) *77*, 2239–2243.

Rudman, D., Hollins, B. M., Kutner, M. H., Moffitt, S. D. (1983): Three types of α-melanocyte-stimulating hormone: bioactivities and half-lives, Am. J. Physiol. *245 E*, 47–54.

Terlou, M., Ploemacher, R. E. (1973): The distribution of monoamines in the tel-, di-, and mesencephalon of *Xenopus laevis* tadpoles, with special reference to the hypothalamo-hypophysial system, Z. Zellforsch. Mikrosk. Anat. *137*, 521–540.

Tonon, M. C., Danger, J. M., Lamacz, M., Leroux, P., Adjeroud, S., Anderson, A., Verburg-van Kemenade, B. M. L., Jenks, B. G., Pelletier, G., Stoekel, L., Burlet, A., Kupryszewski, G., Vaudry, H. (1988): Multihormonal control of melanotropin secretion in cold-blooded vertebrates. In: The Melanotropic Peptides. Volume 1: Source, synthesis, Chemistry, Circulation and Metabolism. M. E. Hadley, ed.), pp. 127–170 CRC Press, Boca Raton, Florida U. S. A.

Vaudry, H., Jenks, B. G., van Overbeeke, A. P. (1983): The frog pars intermedia contains only the non-acetylated form of α-MSH: acetylation to generate α-MSH occurs during the release process. Life Sciences *33*, 97–100.

Vaudry, H., Jenks, B. G., Verburg-van Kemenade, B. M. L., Tonon, M. C. (1986): Effects of tunicamycin on biosynthesis, processing and release of proopiomelanocortin-derived peptides in the intermediate lobe of the frog *Rana ridibunda*, Peptides 7, 163–169.

Verburg-van Kemenade, B. M. L., Jenks, B. G., van Overbeeke, A. P. (1986 a): Regulation of melanotropin release from the pars intermedia of the amphibian *Xenopus laevis*: evaluation of the involvement of serotonergic, cholinergic, or adrenergic receptor mechanisms. Gen. Comp. Endocrinol. *63*, 471–481.

Verburg-van Kemenade, B. M. L., Jenks, B. G., Smits, R. J. M. (1987): N-terminal acetylation of MSH in the pars intermedia of *Xenopus laevis* is a physiologically regulated process. Neuroendocrinology. *46*, 289–296.

Verburg-van Kemenade, B. M. L., Tonon, M. C., Jenks, B. G., Vaudry, H. (1986 b): Characteristics of receptors for dopamine in the pars intermedia of the amphibian *Xenopus laevis*. Neuroendocrinology *44*, 446–456.

Waring, H. (1963): Color Change Mechanisms of Cold-Blooded Vertebrates, Academic Press, New York.

Wendelaar Bonga, S. E., Balm, P. H. H. (1988): Endocrine responses to acid stress in fish. In: Acid Toxicity and Aquatic Animals. (R. Morris, E. W. Taylor, A. Brown, eds.) Cambridge University Press, London and New York.

Fortschritte der Zoologie, Band/Vol. 38 · Hanke, W. (Hrsg.), Biology and Physiology of Amphibians
Gustav Fischer Verlag · Stuttgart · New York · 1990

Binding sites of atrial natriuretic peptide and [Val^{-5}]-Angiotensin II in the kidney of *Xenopus laevis*. Localization and quantification by *in vitro* autoradiography*

Werner Kloas[1], Eberhard Fuchs[2] and Wilfried Hanke[1]

[1] Department of Zoology, Kaiserstr. 12, D-7500 Karlsruhe, FRG;
[2] German Primate Center, Kellnerweg 4, D-3400 Göttingen, FRG

1. Introduction

De Bold et al. (1981) demonstrated that administration of rat atrial homogenates causes a massive and rapid diuresis and natriuresis in recipient rats. This observation led to the discovery and characterization of the atrial natriuretic peptides (ANPs) which is a generic name given to a family of peptides isolated from cardiocytes of mammalian atria. These peptides are derived from a common precursor which undergoes proteolytic cleavage to generate the circulating form of ANP (99–126), which has diuretic and natriuretic effects in mammals. Main target organs in mammals are the kidneys, where ANP causes diuresis and natriuresis, and the adrenals, where ANP inhibits aldosterone synthesis (Genest and Cantin, 1988). In these organs ANP acts as a «physiological antagonist» to angiotensin II (A II).

In lower vertebrates such as fish and amphibians an ANP-like peptide which is immunologically and biochemically related to mammalian ANP is produced in the cardiocytes of atria and ventricles (Reinecke et al., 1985, 1987; Netchitaïlo et al., 1986, 1988). Furthermore, extracts from the frog heart have been shown to induce natriuresis in the rat (De Bold and Salerno, 1983) and Sakata et al. (1988) were able to sequence the ANP of the bull frog (*Rana catesbeiana*). 24- and 21-amino acid peptides were found to elicit diuretic-natriuretic and vasorelaxant activity in rats, and were named «frog ANP-24» and «frog ANP-21», respectively. Frog ANP-21 is a form related to frog ANP-24 by deletion of the three N-terminal amino acids. A remarkable homology between frog ANP and mammalian ANP exists, thus supporting the hypothesis that ANP is a conservative hormone.

Recently, some studies dealing with the effects and binding sites of ANP in lower vertebrates investigated a possible role of this peptide in osmomineral regulation. In bony fish, ANP binding sites are localized in gill and interrenal tissue, but not in the kidney itself (Kloas et al., 1987); acclimation to saltwater induces changes of immunoreactive ANP content in serum (Kloas et al., in prep.). On the contrary, the cyclostome *Myxine glutinosa* has ANP binding sites in the glomeruli (Kloas et al., 1988), but there are no binding sites for A II (unpublished observation). These findings led to the question whether an antagonism of ANP and A II exists in amphibians as it does in mammals.

* This work was supported by DFG grant Ha 78/36–1.

Lihrmann et al. (1988) have studied the effects of synthetic ANP (101–126) on the interrenal of *Rana ridibunda* measuring corticosterone and aldosterone secretion of perifused interrenal slices to investigate a possible role of ANP in the control of corticosteroid biosynthesis in amphibians. No direct effect of synthetic ANP (101–126) on corticosteroid production could be observed. Only ACTH- or A II-stimulated corticosteroid release was inhibited by synthetic ANP (101–126). The immunocytochemical localization of ANP fibers among interrenal cells led to the suggestion that ANP may take part in the regulation of corticosteroidogenesis.

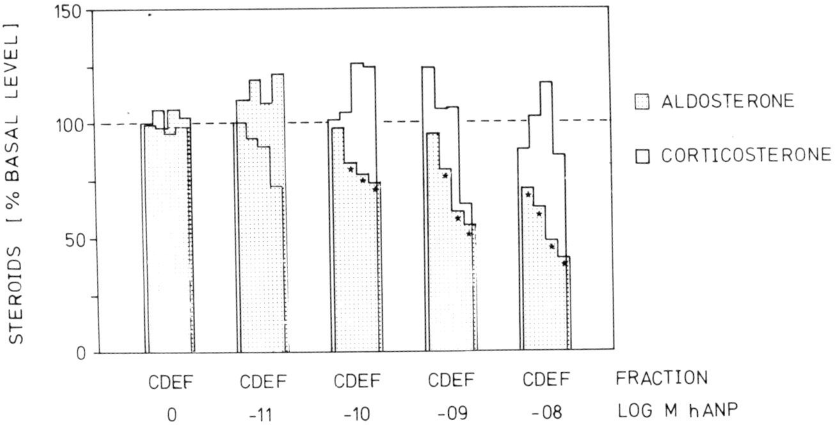

Fig. 1: Steroid secretion–response to human ANP (99–126): Changes of steroid secretions in % basal level by addition of human ANP (99–126) in varying concentrations to the medium with fraction C. Every fraction represents a time period of 15 min. Statistical significances are calculated with Wilcoxon-test for paired values and marked with * ($p < 0.05$).

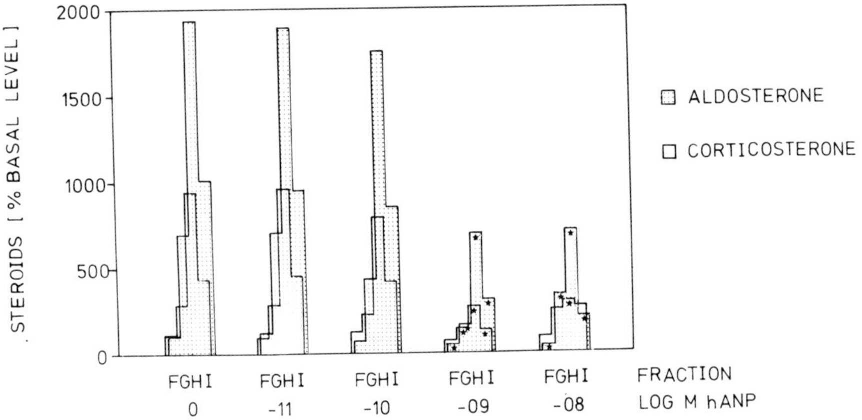

Fig. 2: Steroid scretion–response to ACTID (ACTH 1–28) simultaneous with human ANP (99–126): Changes of steroid secretions in % basal level after addition of $3*10^{-9}$M ACTID for 5 min. to fraction G under varying concentrations of human ANP (99–126). Every fraction represents a time period of 15 min. Statistical calculation is done with t-test comparing the same fractions to the control-fractions and significances are marked with * ($p < 0.05$).

On the contrary, our group found a direct effect of human ANP (99–126) on the interrenal of *Xenopus laevis* using a perifusion technique (Thurmond et al., 1986) to measure corticosterone and aldosterone release (Kloas et al., 1989). We observed a clear inhibition of aldosterone biosynthesis (with 10^{-10}M human ANP (99–126)) in a dose-dependent manner, whereas corticosterone release is hardly influenced by application of human ANP (99–126). Higher doses of ANP (10^{-9} and 10^{-8}M) inhibit the ACTH-stimulated secretion of both steroids (Fig. 1, 2).

Another species-specific difference between interrenals of *Rana spec.* and *Xenopus laevis* exists in their distinct reactivity to A II. It is well established that the interrenals of *Rana temporaria* have an increased corticosteroid biosynthesis following applications of A II (Hanke, 1984; Hanke et al., 1989). However, the interrenal of *Xenopus laevis* only responds to pharmacological doses of A II with a slight increase of corticosteroid secretion (Kloas et al., 1989).

To get a better insight into the mechanisms of actions on the cellular level and to study the question if in amphibian kidney a similar «physiological antagonism» exists between ANP and A II comparable to that in mammals, we investigated the distributions and properties of the binding sites for both peptides in the kidney of *Xenopus laevis* by quantitative *in vitro* autoradiography. In comparison to the mammalian kidney, the amphibian kidney has the advantage of unifying two types of tissues: The renal and, on the ventromedian side, the interrenal tissue which is homologous to the adrenal cortex in higher vertebrates; therefore it is possible to study both organs simultaneously.

2. Experimental procedure for the investigation of binding sites by quantitative *in vitro* autoradiography (QAR)

In our study we investigated renal tissue from nine clawed toad (*Xenopus laevis*) kidneys. The animals were about one year old, weighing around 20 g and were kept under constant environmental conditions. After sacrificing, the kidneys were removed, covered with embedding medium (Tissue Tek) immediately frozen in liquid nitrogen, and stored until use at −80 °C. Frozen 16 μm sections were cut at −19 °C on a cryostat, thaw-mounted onto gelatine coated slides, and placed under vacuum over night.

Schematically the procedure is depicted in Fig. 3; the general principles of the method for QAR were recently described by Boast et al. (1987).

2.1. Saturation experiments

To determine total binding, consecutive sections were incubated at room temperature in a buffer with increasing concentrations of ^{125}I-rat ANP (99–126) or ^{125}I-[Val^5]-A II. The incubation for ^{125}I-rat ANP was done according to Quirion et al. (1984); the details for the ^{125}I-A II incubation were described by Israel et al. (1985). Nonspecific binding was determined on alternate sections in the presence of a 1000-fold excess of unlabeled rat ANP (99–126) or [Val^5]-A II, respectively. After incubation, the slides were gently washed in ice-cold buffer and dried under cold air. The slides were exposed together with ^{125}I-standards to ^{3}H-Ultrofilm (LKB, Munich) and developed after one to four days. Tissue structures which bind the labeled ligand are visualized as grey areas on the film. The amount of bound ligand can be quantified by computerized microdensitometry (ASBA, Leitz, Köln, FRG) in comparison to ^{125}I-standards (Davenport and Hall, 1988). The specific binding was calculated as the difference of total and nonspecific binding and resulted in a saturation curve.

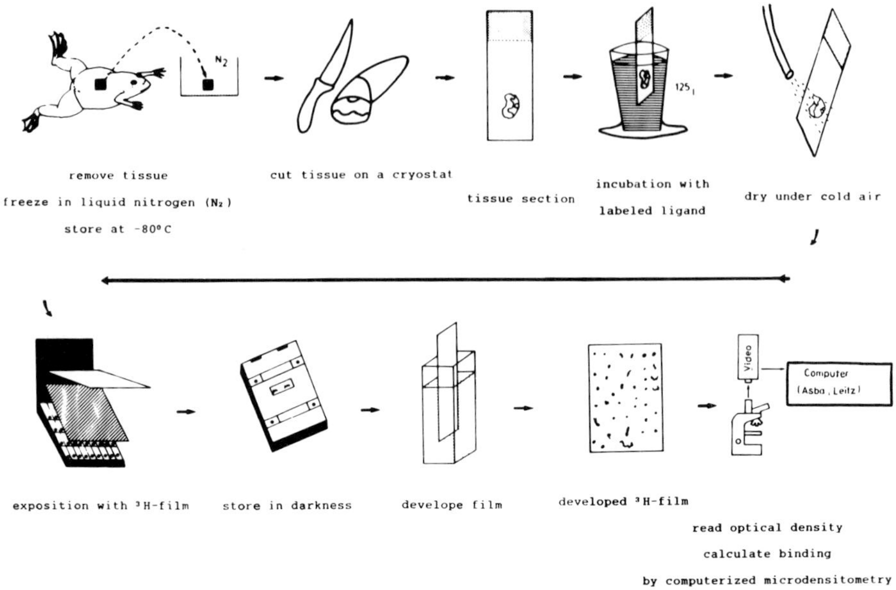

Fig. 3: Method – quantitative in vitro autoradiography.

Following incubation, the tissue sections can be stained. Upon comparison with the corresponding autoradiograph, the binding sites could be associated with definite structures. Thus, QAR is a technique to localize and quantify binding sites in tissue sections concommitant with nearly intact histology of the tissue investigated.

2.2. Displacement experiments

Displacement experiments are performed to test the specificity of the binding sites. Consecutive sections were incubated with a half-saturation concentration of labeled peptide in the presence of increasing amounts (10^{-12} to 10^{-6}M) of unlabeled peptides which are related or unrelated to the labeled ligand.

3. Characterization of the binding sites studied by quantitative *in vitro* autoradiography (QAR)

The results of the experiments in which we studied the distribution as well as properties of the binding sites for ANP and A II in the kidney of *Xenopus laevis* by QAR are summarized in the following section.

3.1. Localization

The histology of a transverse section of a clawed toad kidney stained with Azan showing tubuli, glomeruli and interrenal tissue is represented in Fig. 4.1. Comparison with the corresponding autoradiography for total binding of ^{125}I-rat ANP (99–126) (Fig. 4.2) indicates that ANP binding sites exist in glomeruli and interrenal tissue of *Xenopus laevis*.

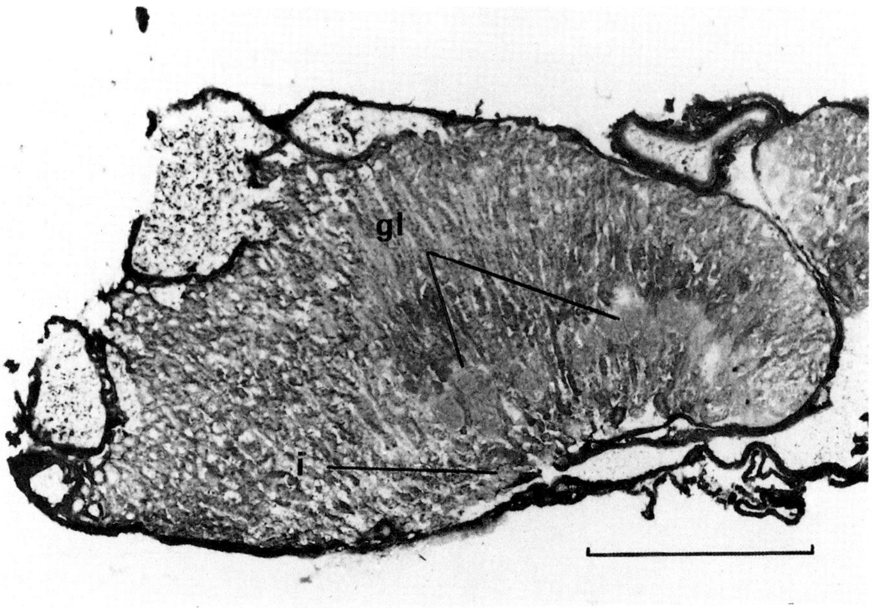

Fig. 4.1: Photomicrograph of a transverse 16 μm section of a *Xenopus laevis* kidney. The section was incubated with 150 pM ^{125}I-rat ANP (99–126) and stained afterwards with Azan. Bar represents 1 mm. gl – glomeruli; i – interrenal tissue.

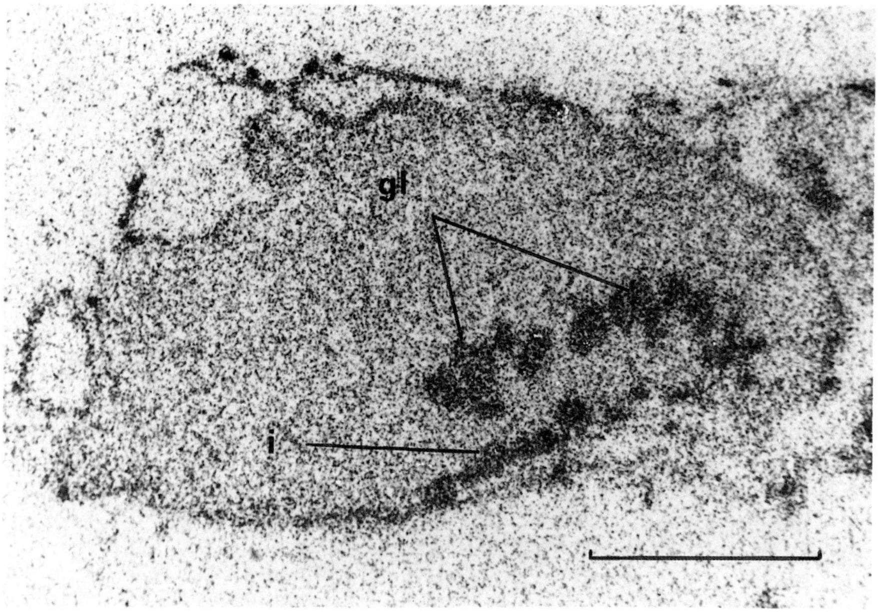

Fig. 4.2: Corresponding autoradiograph for total ^{125}I-rat ANP (99–126) binding with the distribution of binding sites which are localized in glomeruli (gl) and interrenal tissue (i).

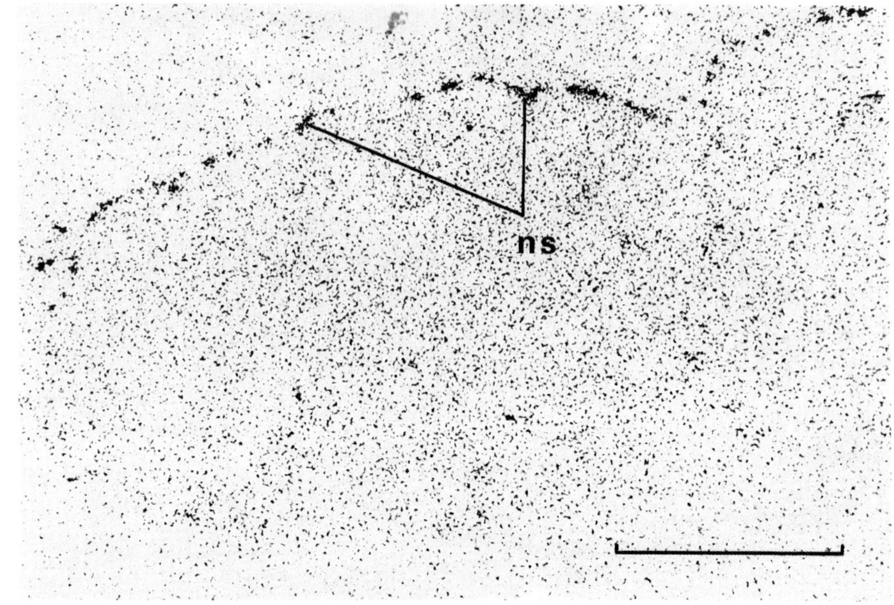

Fig. 4.3: Autoradiograph for nonspecific binding which was determined on the adjacent section of Fig. 4.1. Incubation was carried out with 150 pM ^{125}I-rat ANP (99–126) in the presence of a 1000-fold excess of unlabeled rat ANP (99–126). Only small areas of nonspecific binding can be detected in the surrounding connective tissue (marked with lines: ns – nonspecific binding).

Nonspecific binding was determined on the adjacent section with the same concentration of ^{125}I-rat ANP (99–126) and 1000-fold excess of unlabeled rat ANP (99–126). The autoradiograph for nonspecific binding (Fig. 4.3) demonstrates that nonspecific binding is located only in small areas of the surrounding connective tissue.

The distribution of the ^{125}I-[Val^5]-A II binding sites shows a different pattern. Comparison of the histology (Fig. 5.1) with the corresponding autoradiograph for total binding (Fig. 5.2) indicates that binding sites are only localized in the glomeruli, but not in the interrenal tissue. Small areas of nonspecific binding exist only in the surrounding connective tissue (see Fig. 5.3).

3.2. Quantification

3.2.1. Saturation curves

The quantification of specific binding sites after incubation with increasing amounts of ^{125}I-rat ANP (99–126) (Fig. 6) shows that the binding is saturable in the glomeruli and in the interrenal tissue, the latter providing a higher binding capacity for ANP. The curve form for both tissues is comparable and provides evidence for a positive cooperation of binding sites. This question is subject of ongoing investigations.

The specific binding sites for ^{125}[Val^5]-A II in the glomeruli are saturable (Fig. 7) and have a similar binding capacity but a lower affinity than ^{125}I-rat ANP (99–126). The curve form seems to demonstrate a positive cooperation of binding sites comparable to our results for ANP.

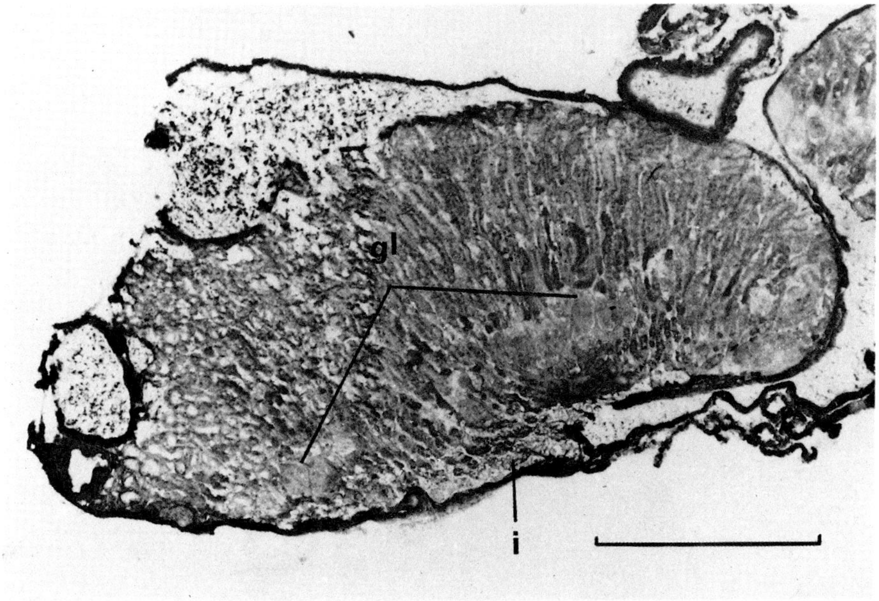

Fig. 5.1: Histology of a transverse 16 μm section of a *Xenopus laevis* kidney stained with Azan after incubation with 2 nM ^{125}[Val^5]-A II. Glomeruli (gl) and interrenal tissue (i) are marked. Bar represents 1 mm.

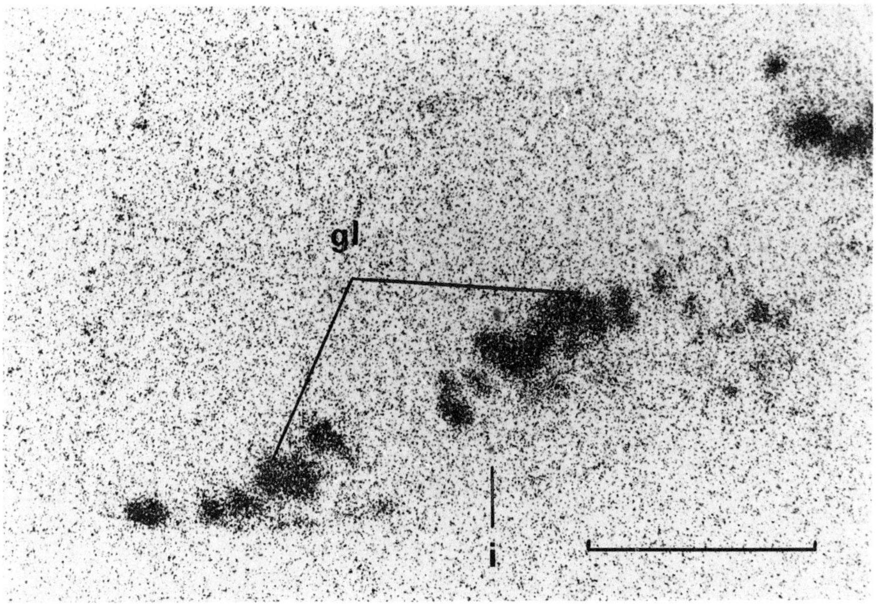

Fig. 5.2: Corresponding autoradiograph for total binding to Fig. 5.1. Binding sites for ^{125}I-[Val^5]-A II are only localized in the glomeruli (gl).

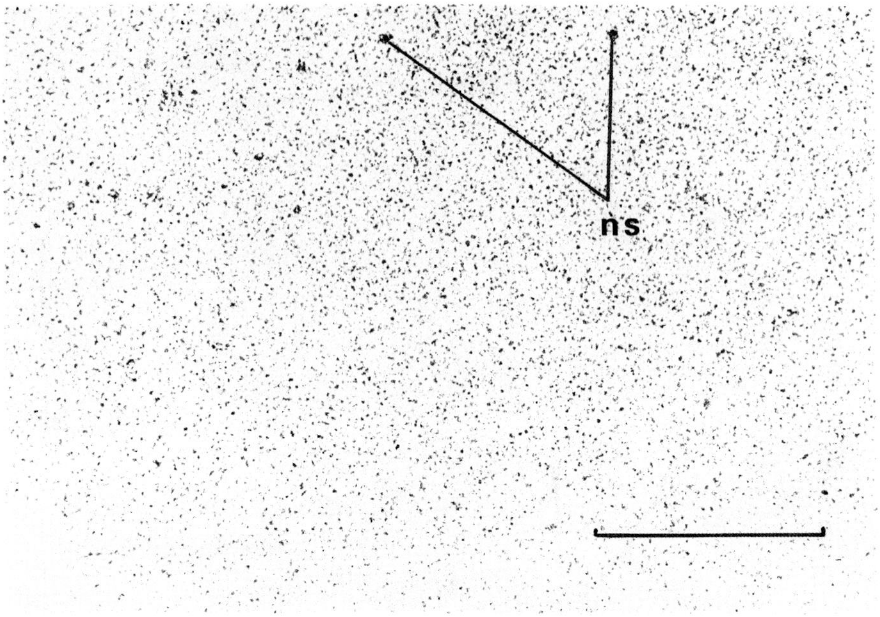

Fig. 5.3: Autoradiograph for nonspecific binding of the following section to Fig. 5.1. which was incubated with 2 nM ^{125}I-[Val^5]-A II in the presence of a 1000-fold excess of unlabeled [Val^5]-A II. As for ANP, nonspecific binding (ns) only exists in small areas of kidneys surrounding connective tissue.

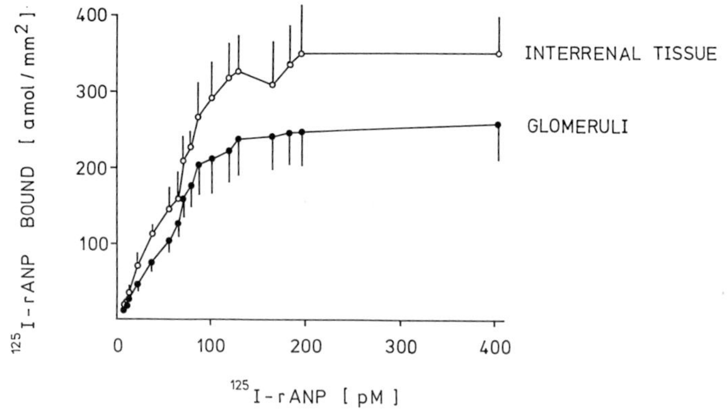

Fig. 6; Saturation curves of specific ^{125}I-rat ANP (99–126) binding in glomeruli and interrenal tissue of *Xenopus laevis*. X-axis shows the concentration of labeled ligand and y-axis represents the amount of bound labeled peptide in amol/mm^2 according to Davenport and Hall (1988). Points are mean values with standard deviation of 9 animals.

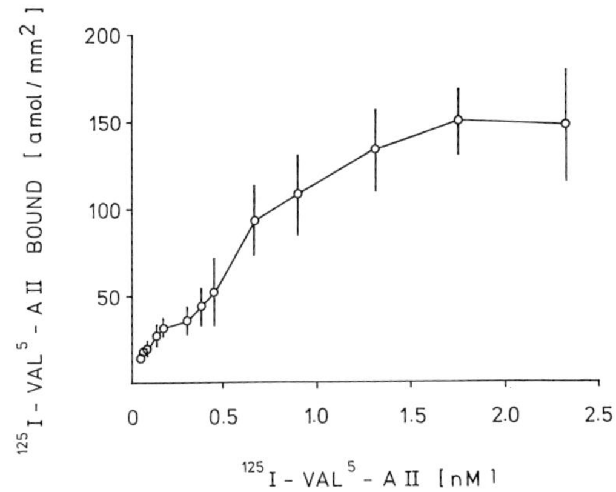

Fig. 7: Saturation curve of specific ^{125}I-[Val^5]-A II in glomeruli of *Xenopus laevis*. Points represent the mean values with the standard deviation of the same 9 animals of Fig. 6.

3.2.2. Displacement experiments

To study the specifity of ^{125}I-rat ANP (99–126) binding sites, we incubated consecutive sections with 55 pM ^{125}I-rat ANP (99–126) in the presence of increasing amounts of unlabeled peptides. Fig. 8 clearly indicates that only biologically active ANP with an intact disulfide bridge can displace the labeled ligand from the binding sites. No differences in the affinities of the biologically active ANPs (rat ANP(99–126), human ANP and atriopeptin II(103–125) could be observed. The N-terminal ANP-fragment(99–109) and the C-terminal ANP-fragment(116–126), which both lack biological activity in mammals, only show small displacing effects in high concentrations. Unrelated peptides such as A II, arginine vasotocin (AVT), adrenocorticotropic hormone (ACTH) or substance P are not

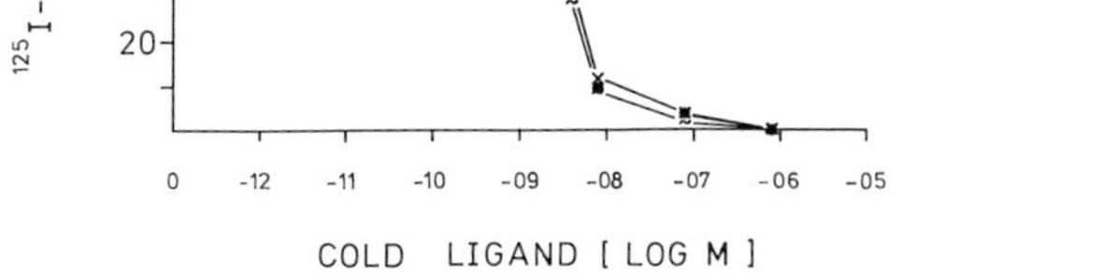

Fig. 8: Displacement curves of specific ^{125}I-rat ANP (99–126) binding on glomeruli of *Xenopus laevis* kidney. Incubations were carried out with 55 pM labeled ANP in the presence of different concentrations (ranging from 10^{-12} to 10^{-6}M) of various unlabeled peptides. X-axis shows the concentration of the unlabeled ligands and y-axis represents the specific ^{125}I-rat ANP (99–126) binding in percent of binding without competing ligand. Points are mean values of 6 animals.

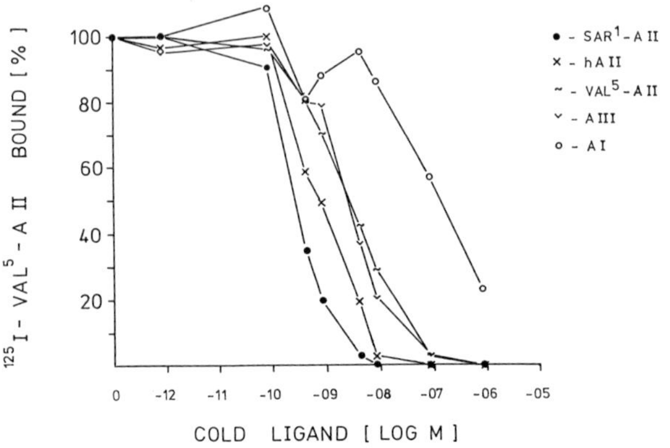

Fig. 9: Displacement curves of specific ^{125}I-[Val^5]-A II binding in glomeruli of *Xenopus laevis* kidney. Incubations were performed with 475 pM ^{125}I-[Val^5]-A II and different concentrations of unlabeled ligands. Scales are due to Fig. 8 and points are the mean values of the same 6 animals as used for the ANP displacement experiments.

effective (results not shown). No significant difference exists between binding sites in glomeruli and in interrenal tissue.

To test the specificity of A II binding sites, consecutive sections were incubated with 475 pM ^{125}I-[Val^5]-A II in the presence of increasing amounts of unlabeled peptides. Here, we found differences in the affinities of angiotensin analogs (Fig. 9) to the binding sites. Sar^1-A II, which is known to be an angiotensin inhibitor in mammals, has the highest affinity, followed by human A II and with a lower affinity by [Val^5]-A II. No significant difference in the affinities could be observed between [Val^5]-A II and human A III. The decapeptide A I has only displaceable effects in high concentrations, this may possibly be due to a partial degradation of A I to A II. Unrelated peptides such as ANP, AVT, ACTH and bradykinin did not cause any displacement (results not shown).

4. Discussion

This study demonstrates for the first time the localization and characterization of binding sites for ANP and A II in an amphibian kidney (*Xenopus laevis*).

Specific ANP binding sites are located in the glomeruli and interrenal tissue of the clawed toad. These binding sites are saturable and highly specific for biologically active ANP. A II binding sites are only present in the glomeruli, but not in the interrenal tissue. They are also saturable and specific, but various angiotensin analogs have different affinities. One important finding is that there are two independent populations of binding sites for ANP and angiotensin, since no crossreaction between the two ligands could be observed in the displacement experiments.

Our results in the kidney of *Xenopus laevis* indicate that in the glomeruli a «physiological antagonism» of ANP and A II may exist solely in the glomeruli, a situation similar to that in mammals.

The findings that the interrenal tissue of the clawed toad has binding sites for ANP, but not for A II, confirm our studies with the perifusion system in measuring corticosterone and aldosterone release during ANP or A II treatment (Kloas et al., 1989). Therefore, we conclude that the corticosteroidogenesis in the interrenal of *Xenopus laevis* is directly controlled by ANP, but not by A II. Nevertheless, there may exist an indirect influence of A II on renal haemodynamic effects. In *Xenopus laevis* the effect of ANP on the interrenal tissue is similar to the action of the peptide on the adrenal gland in mammals. Several groups have reported a decrease in aldosterone biosynthesis in rat or bovine zona glomerulosa cells after ANP treatment (Campbell et al., 1985; Goodfriend et al., 1984).

In the interrenals of *Rana ridibunda* Lihrmann et al. (1988) were not able to find a direct physiological effect of synthetic ANP (101–126). This contrast to our results can be explained as a species-specific difference in receptor properties between *Xenopus laevis* and *Rana ridibunda.* This hypothesis is supported by preliminary results from QAR studies on ANP binding sites in the kidney of *Rana temporaria.* Here, ANP binding is localized mainly in the glomeruli. There is, however, faint binding in the interrenals. The localization of these ANP binding sites resembles the areas where, recently, immunocytochemical localization of ANP fibers in *Rana ridibunda* were detected by Lihrmann et al. (1988). It is obviously not possible to generalize the results of ANP effects for the whole amphibian group.

ANP and A II may both play an important role in the osmomineral regulation in *Xenopus laevis* by influencing the glomerular filtration rate similar to its action in mammals. However, ANP seems to be more important, as it acts directly on the interrenal tissue by decreasing aldosterone release and through inhibition of ACTH-reactivity.

References

Boast, C. A., Snowhill, E. W., Altar, C. A. (eds.) (1987): Quantitative receptor autoradiography. Neurology and Neurobiology, Vol. *19*. Academic Press.

Campbell, W. B., Currie, M. G., Needleman, P. (1985): Inhibition of aldosterone biosynthesis by atriopeptins in rat adrenal cells. Circ. Res. *57*, 113–118.

De Bold, A. J., Salerno, T. A. (1983): Natriuretic activity of extracts obtained from hearts of different species and from various rat tissues. Canad. E. Physiol. Pharmacol. *61*, 127–130.

De Bold, A. J., Borenstein, H. B., Veress, A. T., Sonnenberg, H. (1981): A rapid and potent natriuretic response to intravenous injection of atria myocardial extract in rats. Life Sci. *28*, 89–94.

Davenport, A. P., Hall, M. D. (1988): Comparison between brain paste and polymer [^{125}I]-standards for quantitative receptor autoradiography. J. Neurosci. Meth. *25*, 75–82.

Genest, J., Cantin, M. (1988): The atrial natriuretic factor: Its physiology and biochemistry. Rev. Physiol. Biochem. Pharmacol. *110*.

Goodfriend, T. L., Elliott, M. E., Atlas, S. A. (1984): Actions of synthetic atrial natriuretic factor on bovine adrenal glomerulosa. Life Sci. *35*, 1675–1682.

Hanke, W. (1984): Changes of the biology of the adrenal cortex in the vertebrate evolution. Nova Acta Leopoldina 56, *255*, 363–378.

Hanke, W., Kaltenhäuser, U., Maser-Gluth, C., Pathak, V. (1989, in press).: Regulation of interrenal activity by electrolytes and peptide hormones. Fortschritte der Zoologie, vol.

Israel, A., Niwa, M., Plunkett, L. M., Saavedra, J. M. (1985): High affinity angiotensin receptors in rat adrenal medulla. Peptides *11*, 236–243.

Kloas, W., Hanke, W., Fuchs, E. (1987): Binding sites of the atrial natriuretic peptide (ANP) in the excretion organs of *Cyprinus carpio, Sarotherodon mossambicus, Xenopus laevis*, and *Rana temporaria*. Verh. Dtsch. Zool. Ges. *80*, 170–171.

Kloas, W., Flügge, G., Fuchs, E., Stolte, H. (1988): Binding sites for atrial natriuretic peptide in the kidney and aorta of the hagfish (*Myxine glutinosa*). Comp. Biochem. Physiol. *91 A*, 4, 685–688.

Kloas, W., Fuchs, E., Hanke, W. (1989, in press): Comparison of binding sites and effects of atrial natriuretic peptide (ANP) and Val^5-angiotensin II (A II) in fish and *Amphibia*. Proceedings of the 14th conference of european comparative endocrinologists 1988. Gen. Comp. Endocrinol.

Lihrmann, I., Netchitaïlo, P., Feuilloley, M., Cantin, M., Delarue, C., Leboulenger, F., De Lean, A., Vaudry, H. (1988): Effect of atrial natriuretic factor on corticosteroid production by perifused frog interrenal slices. Gen. Comp. Endocrinol. *71*, 55–62.

Netchitaïlo, P., Feuilloley, M., Pelletier, G., Cantin, M., De Lean, A., Leboulenger, F., Vaudry, H. (1986): Localization and characterization of atrial natriuretic factor (ANF)-like peptide in the frog atrium. Peptides *7*, 573–579.

Netchitaïlo, P., Feuilloley, L. M., Pelletier, G., De Lean, A., Ong, H., Cantin, M., Gutkowska, J., Leboulenger, F., Vaudry, H. (1988): Localization and characterization of atrial natriuretic factor (ANF) in the frog ventricle. Peptides *9*, 1–6.

Quirion, R., Dalpe, A., De Lean, A., Gutkowska, J., Cantin, M., Genest, J. (1984): Atrial natriuretic factor (ANF) binding sites in brain and related structures. Peptides *5*, 1167–1172.

Reinecke, M., Nehls, M., Forssmann, W. G. (1985): Phylogenetic aspects of cardiac hormones as revealed by immunocytochemistry, electron-microscopy, and bioassay. Peptides *6*, 321–331.

Reinecke, M., Betzler, D., Forssmann, W. G. (1987): Immunocytochemistry of cardiac polypeptide hormones (cardiodilatin / atrial natriuretic polypeptide) in brain and hearts of *Myxine glutinosa (Cyclostomata)*. Histochemistry *86*, 233–239.

Sakata, J., Kangawa, K., Matsuo, H. (1988): Identification of new atrial natriuretic peptides in frog heart. Biochem. Biophys. Res. Com. *155,3*, 1338–1345.

Thurmond, W., Kloas, W., Hanke, W. (1986): Daily rhythm of interrenal activity in *Xenopus laevis*. Gen. Comp. Endocrinol. *61*, 260–271.

Fortschritte der Zoologie, Band/Vol. 38 · Hanke, W. (Hrsg.), Biology and Physiology of Amphibians
Gustav Fischer Verlag · Stuttgart · New York · 1990

Regulation of interrenal activity by electrolytes and peptide hormones

WILFRIED HANKE, URSULA KALTENHÄUSER, CHRISTIANE MASER-GLUTH, VISHNU PATHAK

Department of Zoology, University, D 7500 Karlsruhe, FRG

Direct effects on interrenal secretion can be studied by using an *in vitro* perifusion system. The interrenals taken from the organisms produce and secrete corticosteroids for several hours if they are superfused by an adequate medium. Such superfusion systems have been introduced for mammalian adrenal cortex by several authors (e.g. Tait et al., 1970, 1980a, 1980b, Tait and Tait, 1979) for amphibian tissue (Delarue et al., 1979; 1980, 1981a, 1981b, 1984; Maser et al., 1982; Hanke and Maser-Gluth, 1985; Hanke and Yousri, 1988; Thurmond et al., 1986a, 1986b) and for teleost interrenals (Rance and Baker, 1981; Vetter and Hanke, 1985; Hanke et al., 1986). In all cases, the *in vitro* systems were used to test the influence of ACTH, electrolyte concentrations, inhibitors of steroid biosynthesis, other peptide hormones etc. on the secretion rate. The interpretation of the cytological events is difficult in so far, as the secretion rate does not allow to distinguish between release of stored material or production of steroids and release. Furthermore, it is difficult to decide whether the released products are secreted in the same manner as *in vivo*. The superfusion system may not contain the same quality of mediators for the secretion of steroids as the fluid *in vivo*.

The amphibian interrenal tissue secretes the two main steroids, corticosterone and aldosterone. The titres of these corticosteroids in the peripheral blood are about 5 ng/ml corticosterone and 0.5 ng/ml aldosterone. The titres depend on the secretion rate and the rate of removal of the corticosteroids from the peripheral blood. Since the ratio of the concentrations C/A is about 10 in the blood it has been found that the interrenals of the common frog secrete more aldosterone than corticosterone, concentration ratio about 0.6. It is doubtful whether the difference between blood titre and *in vitro* secretion is due to an easier secretion of the aldosterone than the corticosterone molecule under in vitro condition or to a faster metabolization rate of aldosterone than corticosterone *in vivo*.

This clearly demonstrates that the two facts cannot be explained by the *in vitro* technique as it stands. It is an open question which amount the tissue just releases and which is produced. The problem exists if the secretion rate of both steroids is similar *in vitro* as *in vivo*. This does not touch the fact that shifts of the C/A release ratio from control to experimentally influenced conditions elucidate probably cytological mechanisms (Kloas and Hanke, 1986).

This paper deals with the comparison of three different interrenal systems, that of the common frog, *Rana temporaria*, the clawed toad, *Xenopus laevis*, and the axolotl, *Ambys-*

toma mexicanum. Three problems should be reviewed or elucidated under the light of new results:

1. Are the characteristics of the secretion rate and the response to ACTH similar in these tissues?

2. What is known about the influence of the 4 important cations, Na^+, K^+, Ca^{++}, Mg^{++} and different osmolality on the secretion rate?

3. What is the influence of two peptides discussed as stimulators on interrenal secretion: angiotensin II (ANG) and the hypophysial nonapeptide, arginine vasotocin (AVT).

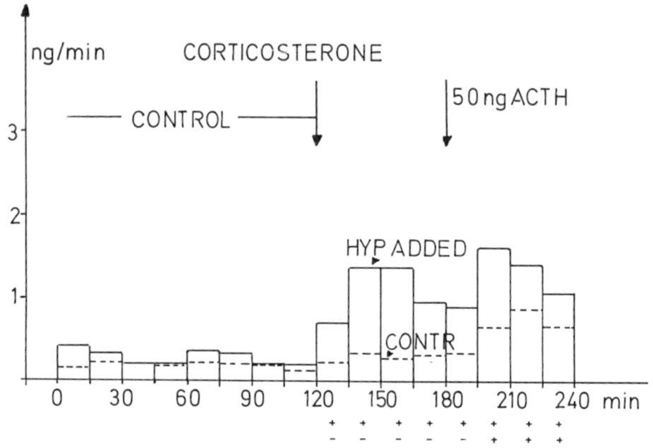

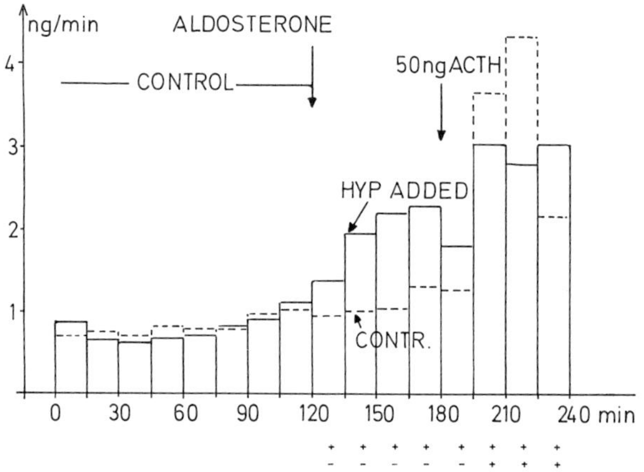

Fig. 1: The amounts of corticosterone (above) and aldosterone (below) released from interrenals of *Rana temporaria.* A control period of 120 min is followed by addition of a pituitary (HYP) to half of the runs. After 60 min (time 180) 50 ng of mammalian ACTH is added. The plus or minus beneath the columns indicate whether the value is statistically significant different from the control period (the upper line for the group with pituitaries, the lower line without these). For both steroids, the release increases statistically significant after addition of one pituitary or 50 ng ACTH ($p < 0.05$ Wilcoxon test for paired values, $n = 12$).

1. The response of the interrenal preparation of different species to ACTH

The response of the interrenals of *Rana temporaria* to mammalian ACTH is similar to the response on the own pituitary. It has been shown that the secretion of corticosterone and aldosterone is constant for 180 min. The level in one experiment was about 0.3 ng/min corticosterone and 0.8 ng/min aldosterone. When 50 ng mammalian ACTH (1–28) was given, an increase of the release of both corticosteroids was seen after 15 min. This time lack suggests that the increase is due to a stimulation of production. The same happens after addition of a pituitary (Fig. 1, Hanke and Yousri, 1988). The result is in accordance to that found by Delarue et al. (1979) and Leboulenger et al. (1978) for *R. ridibunda.*

A similar experiment was done with interrenals of *Xenopus laevis* showing the same results after addition of ACTH or pituitary. The ratio for C/A was 2.5 during the control period. A clear increase of the secretion rate was seen after addition of ACTH (Fig. 2) or pituitary (Thurmond et al., 1986b).

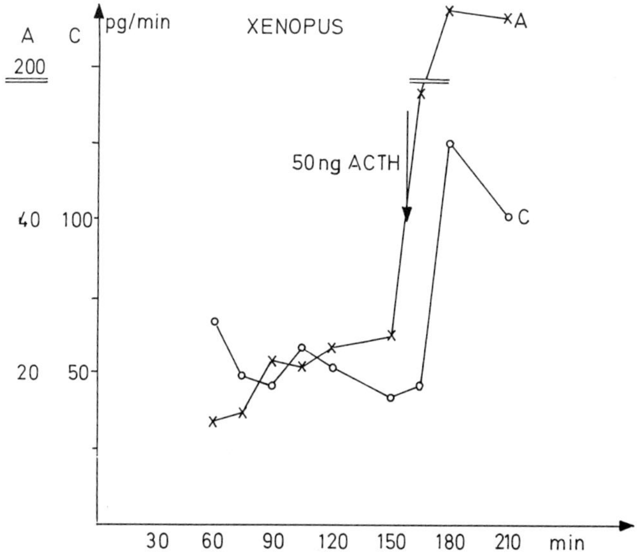

Fig. 2: The amounts of corticosterone (C) and aldosterone (A) released from interrenals of *Xenopus laevis*. A control period of 150 min is followed by addition of 50 ng of mammalian ACTH. The changes after ACTH are certainly statistically significant ($p < 0.05$ Wilcoxon test for paired values, $n = 12$).

The situation found for interrenals of axolotl is confusing. In a first set of experiments, it was found that the response to ACTH could not clearly be established. A more careful recent analysis shows two characteristics of the interrenal response to ACTH (mammalian ACTH was used). Firstly, the stimulation of corticosterone release was clearly seen while the increase of aldosterone was moderate or absent. Secondly, the augmentation of corticosterone release was biphasic. A small response was seen immediately after addition of ACTH while a sharp increase followed 2 hrs after addition. The background of this delay is not clear. The best explanation for it is that the gland is quite inactive under normal conditions. Therefore, a longer time is necessary to build up the apparatus for the production of steroids (Fig. 3).

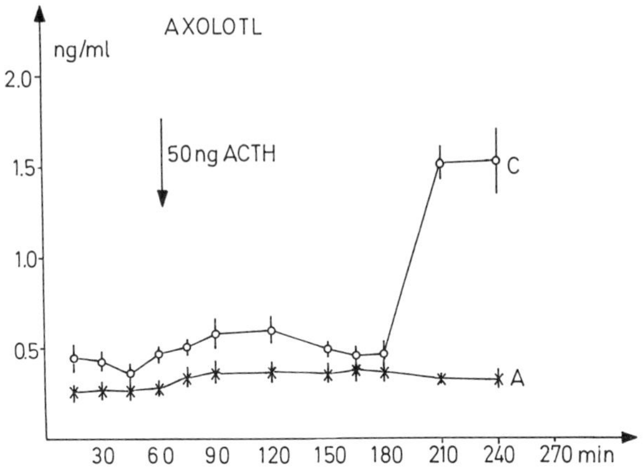

Fig. 3: The amounts of corticosterone (C) and aldosterone (A) released from interrenals of axolotl. A control period of 60 min is followed by addition of 50 ng of mammalian ACTH. The changes after ACTH are biphasic. A small peak follows 30 to 60 min after addition, but the main response is seen 150 min after addition. Only the response of corticosterone is statistically significant ($p < 0.05$ Wilcoxon test for paired values, $n = 12$).

Compared to the results obtained with the tissue of *Rana temporaria* or *Xenopus laevis*, the effect of stimulation by ACTH seems to be different in axolotl. Generally, the biosynthesis of steroids runs roughly described from cholesterol via pregnenolone to corticosterone and then to aldosterone. Both corticosteroids, corticosterone and aldosterone, are released from the tissue. The ratio of the released amounts depends on the medium, especially on the protein content of it. The protein can be regarded as carrier for non polar substances. In *Rana* preparations, corticosterone (C) release is less than that of aldosterone (A), the ratio of C/A is between 1 and 0.3. In axolotl as in *Xenopus*, this ratio can be larger than 1, which means that more corticosterone is released than aldosterone. Stimulatory influences can affect the steps before corticosterone leading to a higher release of it if the steps between C and A are rate limiting. They can also affect the steps between C and A preferentially. Then, the release of aldosterone can be enhanced.

The differences between frog and axolotl interrenal tissue might be suggested as follows. The stimulation of biosynthesis in axolotl interrenal tissue mostly needs a setup of the whole organization which results in a longer delay and a pronounced release of the first product of synthesis. The stimulation of interrenal biosynthesis in frog tissue (*Rana spec.* and equally in *Xenopus laevis*) meets a working cellular apparatus and, therefore, the steps between C and A are more pronounced affected. Of course, it could be that the interrenals of axolotls are also found already in a higher stage of activity. In this case, the response is similar as in frogs (Fig. 4).

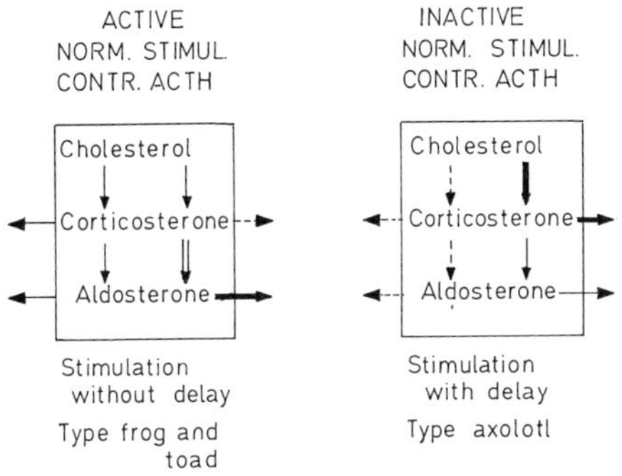

Fig. 4: Cellular events in both extremes of interrenal cells of Amphibia. Comparison of the response of active and inactive cells, explaining the results obtained in frog or axolotl preparations.

2. The response of the interrenal preparation to changes of electrolyte concentrations

The results obtained in the experiments done with the interrenal preparation of *Rana* tissue are mainly described in two former papers (Maser et al., 1982; Hanke and Maser-Gluth, 1985). In summarizing the results, it can be pointed out that an increase of the Na^+ concentration of the perifusion medium gradually decreased the release of corticosterone and aldosterone. The influences were investigated for Na^+ concentrations of 85-104-132-146-170-182 mM. The response was clearly seen 60 or 90 min after the variation of the medium (Maser et al., 1982).

An increase of the K^+ concentration of the medium (steps from 2.8-9.2-13.6-18.8-23.9-27.3 mM) resulted in a pronounced augmentation of corticosterone and aldosterone release. In both cases, inhibition by higher Na^+ concentrations or stimulation by higher K^+ concentrations, the release of aldosterone responds apparently more sensitive than the secretion of corticosterone (Fig. 5).

It was also found in these experiments that changes of the osmolality also affected the secretion rate. The clearest effects were obtained when mannitol was used as a non penetrating osmolyte in the external medium. A stimulation of the release was found at 227 m osm, while a clear inhibition occured at 375 m osm for the release of aldosterone. Again, stimulation and inhibition were more pronounced in the case of aldosterone release (Fig. 6). It must be pointed out that the response on variations of Na^+ or K^+ concentrations is not congruent with the changes following altered external osmolality and cannot be explained by those changes (Hanke and Maser-Gluth, 1985).

Axolotl tissue also reacts on changes of the electrolyte concentrations of the perifusion medium. In a set of experiments, the basal secretion rate was determined after a prerun of 30 min. The basal secretion is calculated as the mean of a 60 min period. The changes in relation to this basal secretion rate are demonstrated in Figs. 7–10. The relative changes are indicated for 5 periods of 30 min each (D–H). The last two periods are under the influence of ACTH. This was given for 5 min (50 ng) at the beginning of period G. The results demonstrate on the one hand the influence of the altered electrolyte concentration on the secretion rate (D, E, F), on the other hand the influence on the response following addition of ACTH is analyzed. A comparison of the absolute values is not possible because

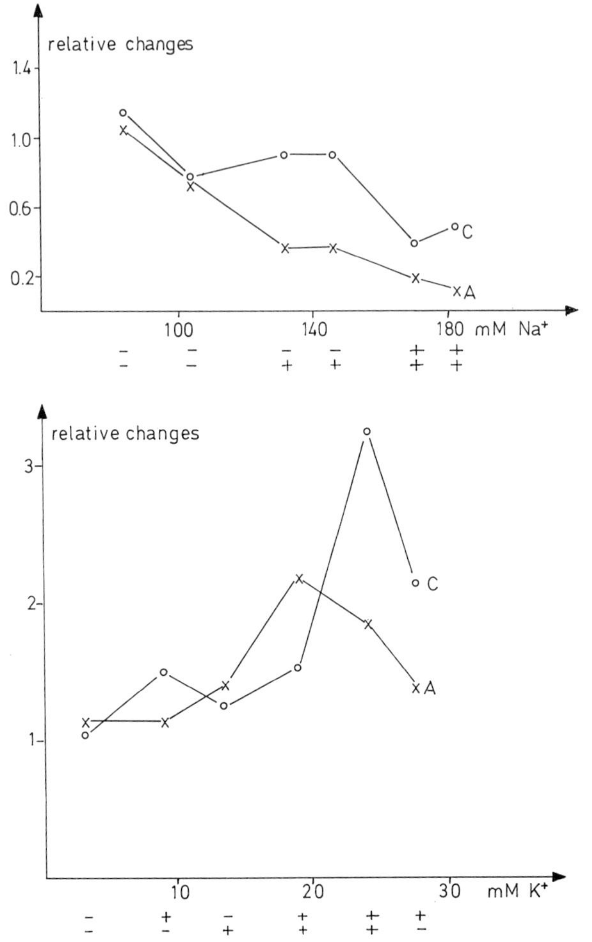

Fig. 5: Relative changes of the corticosterone (C) or aldosterone (A) secretion from *Rana* interrenals 39–90 min (2 periods of 30 min) after variation of the Na^+ (above) or K^+ (below) concentration of the medium. Means of the relative changes of the whole period are indicated. Plus or minus indicate statistical significance ($p < 0.05$) calculated by use of Wilcoxon test for paired values, upper row for C, lower row for A.

the basal secretion rate varies with the age, weight of the animal, size of the interrenals and other parameters.

The secretion rate of corticosterone increased when the Na^+ concentration was little elevated and the response on ACTH was relatively high (Na^+ 80–100 mM). The secretion rate of aldosterone did not change. A higher concentration of Na^+ (155 mM) clearly reduced the secretion rate and the effect of ACTH (Fig. 7).

Increasing concentrations of K^+ from 4 to 10 till 33 mM stimulated gradually the secretion rate of both corticosteroids depending on the dose. The ACTH response was also larger when higher K^+ concentrations were adjusted. It was clearly demonstrated that the corticosterone release is more significantly stimulated than the release of aldosterone. It is

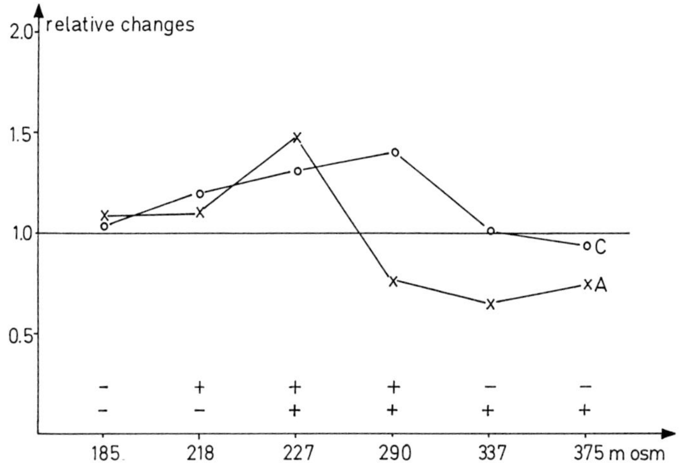

Fig. 6: Relative changes of the corticosterone (C) or aldosterone (A) secretion from *Rana* interrenals 0−90 min (3 periods of 30 min) after variation of the osmolality of the medium. Means of the relative changes of the whole period are indicated. Plus or minus indicate statistical significance ($p < 0.05$) calculated by use of Wilcoxon test for paired values, upper row for C, lower row for A.

typically for axolotl that the stimulation or inhibition of corticosterone release is more sensitive and clearer worked out than the change of aldosterone release (Fig. 8).

Reduction of Ca^{++} or Mg^{++} concentrations of the perifusion medium did not strongly change the secretion rate of the axolotl interrenals (Figs. 9, 10). This is in contrast to observations made with *Rana* tissue where a strong inhibition was found, when Ca^{++} or Mg^{++} was reduced (Hanke and Maser-Gluth, 1985; Hanke et al., 1986). In axolotl tissue, the lack of effect might be due to the fact that the removal of Ca^{++} from the external medium could not avoid the release of Ca^{++} from the mitochondria within the cell. An increase of the Ca^{++} concentration led to a pronounced stimulation of the corticosterone release. The response of aldosterone was moderate. The corticosterone effect did not depend on the concentration. Elevation to 3.88 mM had a similar effect as elevation to 6.61 mM. An increase of Mg^{++} to 6.62 mM caused a moderate stimulation of the corticosteroid release but the effect was not clear enough to be statistically significant in each case. Further increase to 13.33 mM did not show any results.

The response of teleost interrenals on cation changes is vague. There is evidence that a response on Na^{++} or K^{++} ion concentrations depends on the osmotic adaptation, steno- or euryhalinity. The stenohaline fresh water fishes respond to electrolyte changes while euryhaline fishes are not as sensitive. This has been investigated by comparing the stenohaline carp with the euryhaline tilapia. This result suggests that the effect of Na^{++} or K^{++} ion variations cannot be explained only by an influence on the membrane potential which alters the mechanism of hormone secretion. It might be that the influence of Ca^{++} and/or Mg^{++} is different. These ions could affect the steroid production and release via second messenger mechanisms.

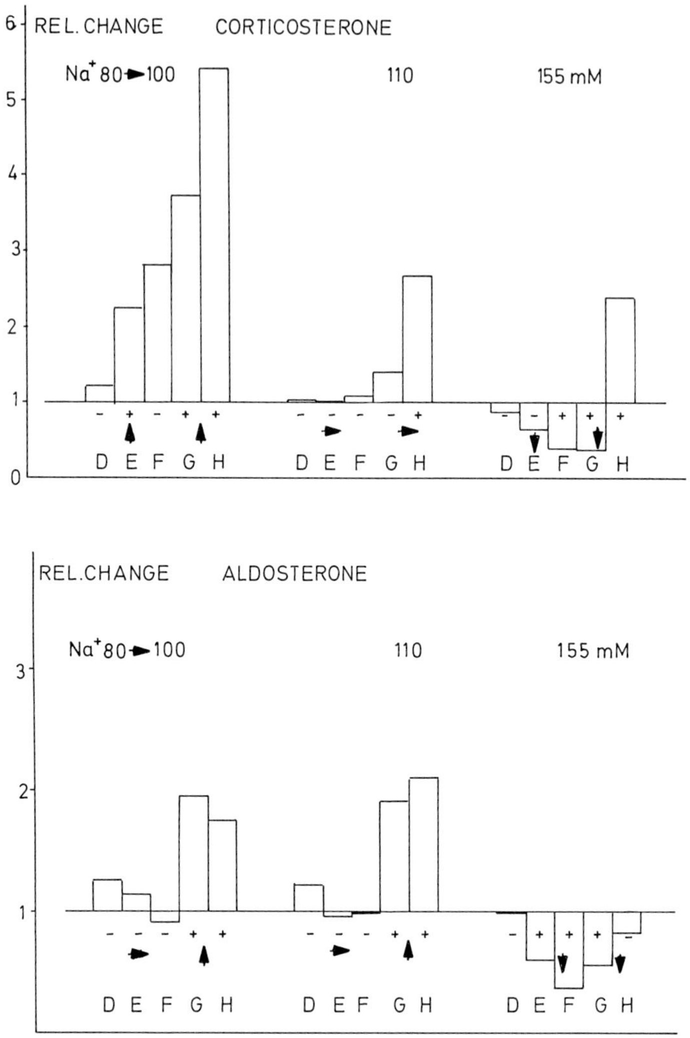

Fig. 7: Relative changes of the corticosterone (above) or aldosterone (below) secretion from axolotl interrenals in 5 periods of 30 min each after variation of the Na^+ concentration as indicated. Period D, E, F are under normal perifusion, G, H with addition of ACTH. Plus or minus indicate the significance ($p < 0.05$) of the changes compared with the basal secretion rate calculated by use of Wilcoxon test for paired values.

3. The response of the interrenal preparation to angiotensin II and arginine-vasotocin

It was demonstrated in former experiments with *Rana* interrenals that two well known hormonal peptides, angiotensin II (ANG) and arginine-vasotocin (AVT) stimulate the release of corticosterone and aldosterone (Hanke, 1984; Hanke and Maser, 1985).

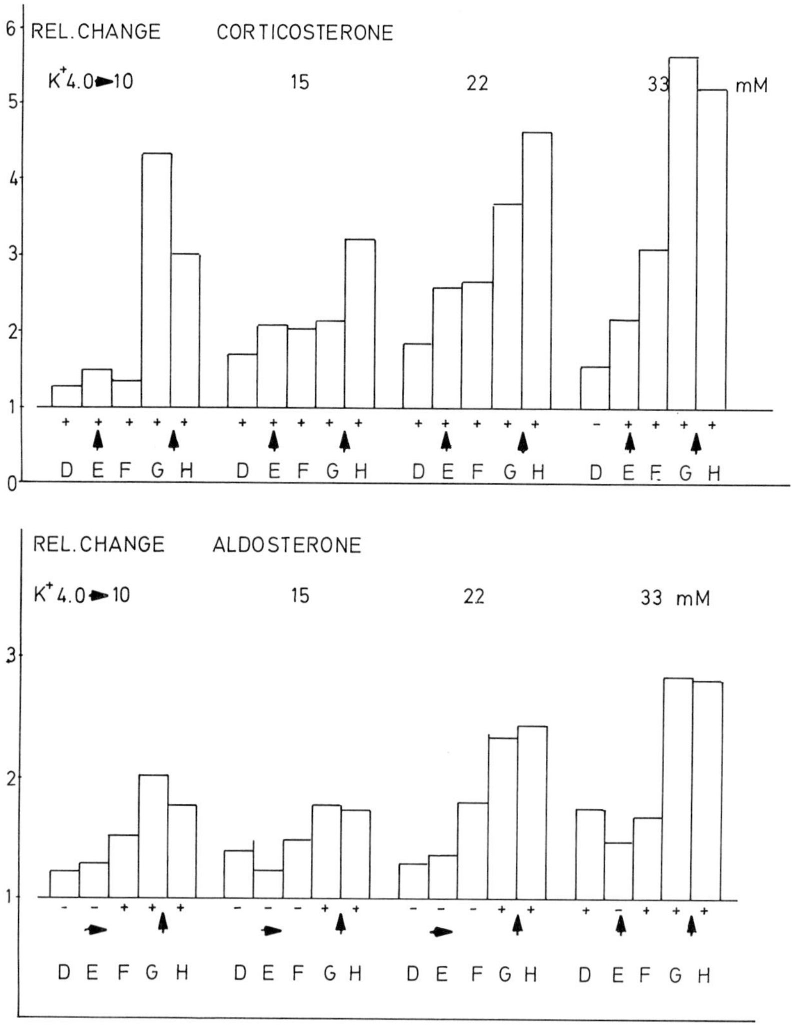

Fig. 8: Relative changes of the corticosterone (above) or aldosterone (below) secretion from axolotl interrenals in 5 periods of 30 min each after variation of the K^+ concentration as indicated. Period D, E, F are under normal perifusion, G, H with addition of ACTH. Plus and minus indicate the significance ($p < 0.05$) of the changes compared with the basal secretion rate calculated by use of Wilcoxon test for paired values.

10–100 ng of each of the two compounds were effective, when given in 5 min. The response lasted for about 60–90 min. Fig. 11 gives the relative changes of aldosterone and corticosterone release for three 30 min periods subsequent to the addition of 10 ng ANG or AVT. Two angiotensins with different amino acid sequence were used in this case: 1-Asp-5-Ile-ANG and 1-Sar-5-Val-ANG. The latter is known to be bound potently at the receptors for vascular regulations and is used as antagonist in therapy. In comparison, AVT seems to be more effective than each of the both angiotensins.

Since it was known that angiotensin and AVT do not have clear effects on cortisol secretion in fish (Vetter and Hanke, 1985; Hanke et al., 1986), it was especially interesting to study the effect of these both substances on axolotl interrenals. In this case, 1-Asp-5-Val-ANG and 1-Asn-5-Val-ANG were used, because it is well established that a 5-Val-ANG is the original compound in teleost fish (Nishimura, 1980; Sakakibara et al., 1985). The 1-Asp analogue is present in eel and bullfrog while the 1-Asn compound might be the active form in salmon and goosefish.

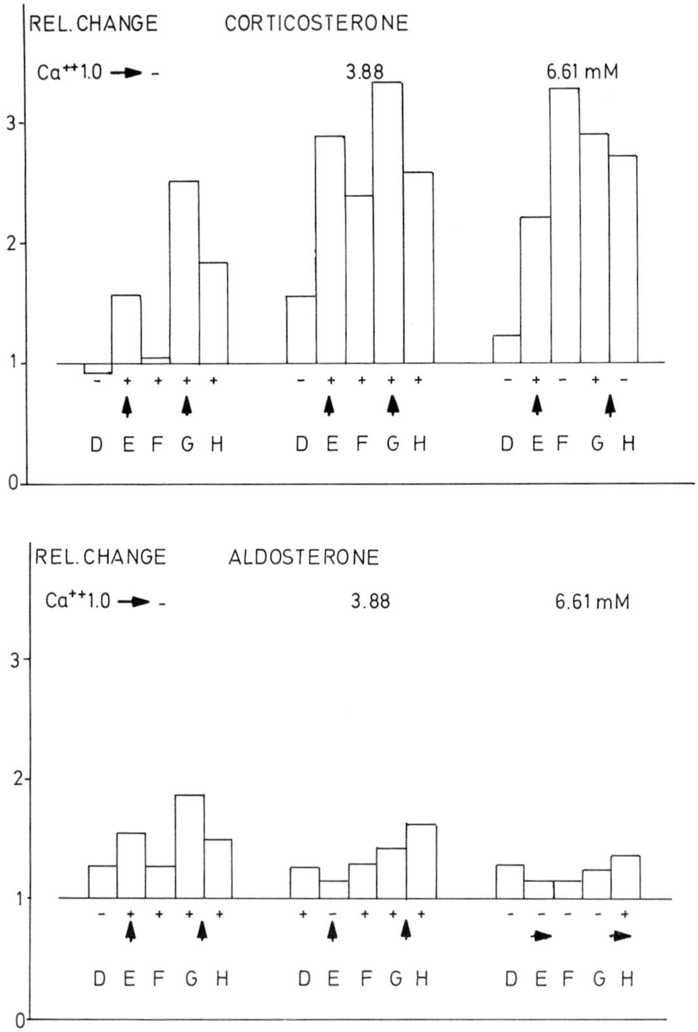

Fig. 9: Relative changes of the corticosterone (above) or aldosterone (below) secretion from axolotl interrenals in 5 periods of 30 min each after variation of the Ca^{++} concentration as indicated. Period D, E, F are under normal perifusion, G, H with addition of ACTH. Plus or minus indicate the significance ($p < 0.05$) of the changes compared with the basal secretion rate calculated by use of Wilcoxon test for paired values.

The relative changes during 90 min after the addition of 1-Asp-5-Val-ANG in different doses are shown in Fig. 12. The compound is not effective in a dose of 10 or 50 ng as in frog interrenals, but it stimulates at higher doses of 100 ng. It is also evident that 50 ng increases more pronounced the aldosterone release as expected from the studies with frog preparation. Similar results are found after different doses of 1-Asn-5-Val-ANG.

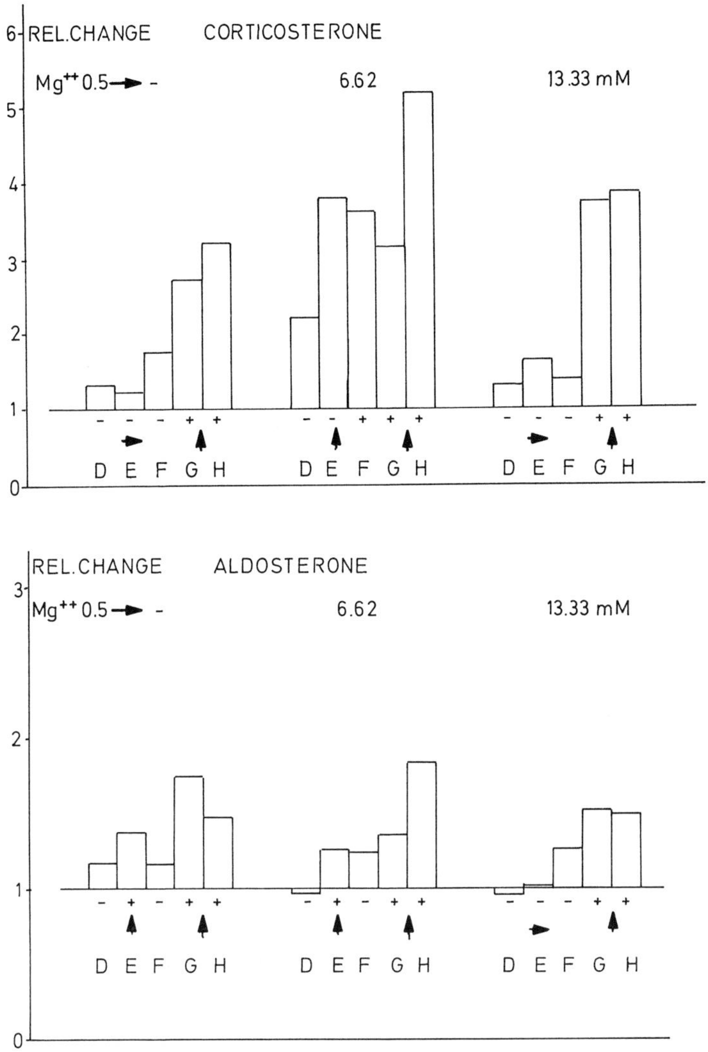

Fig. 10: Relative changes of the corticosterone (above) or aldosterone (below) secretion from axolotl interrenals in 5 periods of 30 min each after variation of the Mg^{++} concentration as indicated. Period D, E, F are under normal perifusion, G, H with addition of ACTH. Plus or minus indicate the significance ($p < 0.05$) of the changes compared with the basal secretion rate calculated by use of Wilcoxon test for paired values.

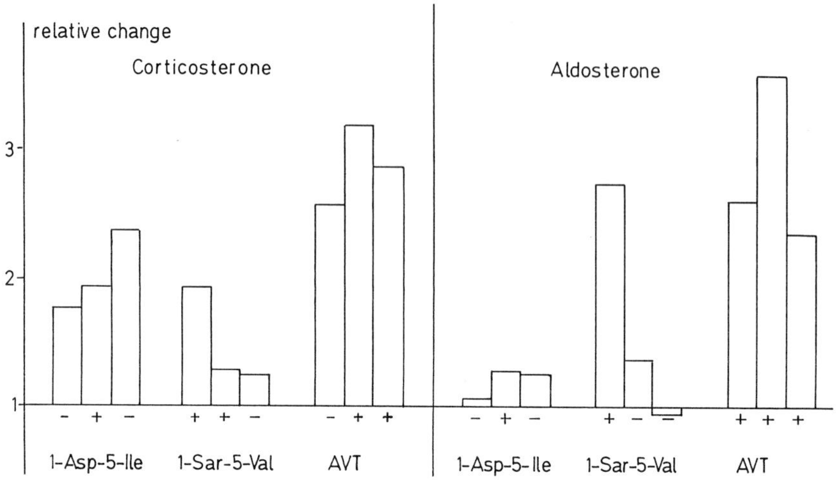

Fig. 11: Relative changes of the corticosterone (left) or aldosterone (right) secretion from *Rana* interrenals in 3 periods of 30 min each after addition of 2 different angiotensins or AVT. Plus and minus indicate the significance ($p < 0.05$) of the changes compared with the basal secretion rate calculated by use of Wilcoxon test for paired values.

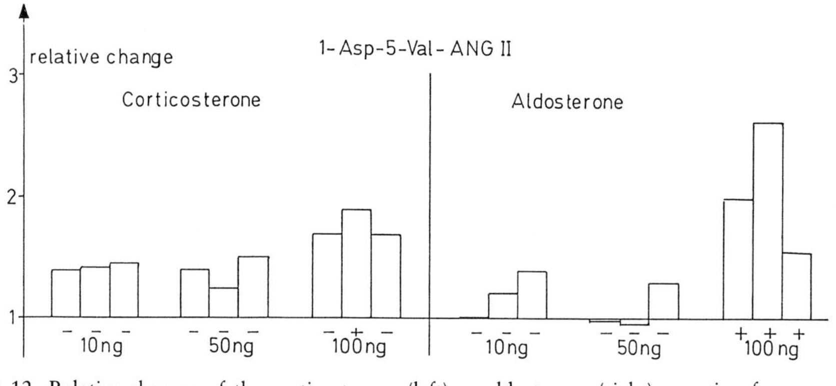

Fig. 12: Relative changes of the corticosterone (left) or aldosterone (right) secretion from axolotl interrenals in 3 periods of 30 min each after addition of 3 doses of 1-Asp-5-Val-ANG II. Plus and minus indicate the significance ($p < 0.05$) of the changes compared with the basal secretion rate calculated by use of Wilcoxon test for paired values.

The relative changes found after different doses of AVT in axolotl interrenals are shown in Fig. 13. The increase after 10 or 50 ng AVT is difficult to work out on a statistical basis because of the variability of the changes. It looks as if the response of corticosterone is more pronounced than that of aldosterone.

It is interesting to speculate about these effects of angiotensin II and AVT. The first compound is well known to stimulate the release of aldosterone in mammals. The cortisol secretion is not as pronounced affected in mammals. AVT is not known to charge directly

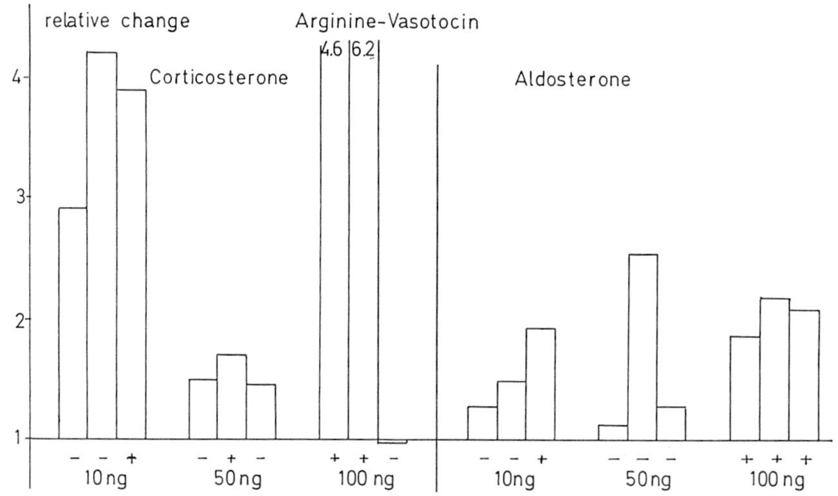

Fig. 13: Relative changes of the corticosterone (left) or aldosterone (right) secretion from axolotl interrenals in 3 periods of 30 min each after addition of 3 doses of AVT. Plus and minus indicate the significance ($p < 0.05$) of the changes compared with the basal secretion rate calculated by use of Wilcoxon test for paired values.

with the interrenal secretion in mammals. The effect of ANG on interrenal secretion can be seen from the phylogenetic step of Amphibia to mammals. It is found as well in frogs as in axolotls. In axolotls as in *Xenopus* (Kloas et al., 1990), relatively high doses are necessary to find the angiotensin effect. Taken in mind that no effects are found in teleost fish (except some preliminary results found by Kniehl, personal communication), it can be postulated that both the receptors for angiotensin at the interrenal cells and parallelly, the response of the interrenals on angiotensin start at the phylogenetic level of tetrapode evolution. It could be demonstrated by *in vitro*-receptor-autoradiography that binding sites for angiotensin existed at the interrenal cells of *Rana*. But, surprisingly, these are not found at the interrenals of *Xenopus* (Kloas et al., 1990).

The effect of AVT on amphibian interrenals which has no parallel to teleosts or other vertebrate groups, as far as it is known, can only be explained by an effect on Ca^{++} uptake. Such an effect of nonapeptides is found in some other tissues, smooth muscle systems, liver glycogenolysis in rats and possibly in Amphibia, too. Receptors for AVT at amphibian interrenal cells must be postulated which might induce the shift of Ca^{++} ions into the cell. The dependency of the AVT response on Ca^{++} is not studied, till now.

Conclusions

There are several influences which directly affect the corticosteroid release from amphibian interrenal tissue. The effect of changes in cation concentrations (Na^{+}, K^{+}, Ca^{++}, Mg^{++}) and osmolality are reported. The stimulatory or inhibitory influence of these changes seems to be especially pronounced in Amphibia, which might be due to the fact that these animals are very much dependent on osmoregulation because of the start of adaptation to living on land.

The effects of angiotensin, its stimulation of corticosteroid release, have also evolved in the group of the earliest land-living tetrapods. This hormone may have cardiovascular effects in teleosts but reaches its adrenocortical influence at the level of Amphibia. The effect of AVT is extraordinary and linked with a low specialized receptor system of this hormone.

An important complex is touched by the elaboration of secretory differences between both steroids after stimulation. It is not sure whether the differences between axolotl and frog or clawed toad interrenals are fundamental. Stimulation of axolotl tissue needs a longer delay till it responds in higher steroid release. The secretion of corticosterone is preferred. On the contrary, frog tissue acts in about 10 min and the stimulation of aldosterone is more sensitive. The easiest explanation for this difference is to suggest that the axolotl interrenals are in a less sensitive phase and need time for the organization of the apparatus for biosynthesis compared to frog interrenals (Fig. 4).

There seem to exist some quite clear effects between the regulation of teleost fish and Amphibia (Fig. 14). In euryhaline fresh water fish like tilapia (T) only ACTH has been found to stimulate the secretion of corticosteroids. The concentration of Na^+ or K^+ is only effective on the interrenals of the stenohaline carp (C). On the other hand the interrenal tissue of Amphibia has evolved to respond on several different influences. It cannot be decided if the other type of corticosteroid molecules produced in fish compared with Amphibia is important for the change of regulatory influences.

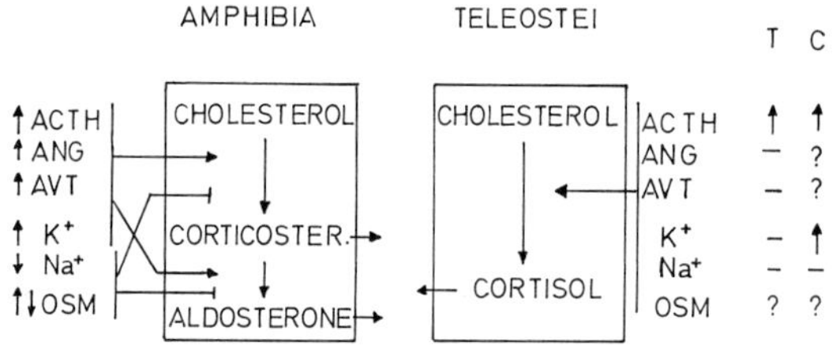

Fig. 14: Cellular events in interrenal cells of Amphibia or teleost fish (C carp, T tilapia). The stimulatory influences are indicated by ↑, the inhibitory influences by ↓.

References

Delarue, C., Tonon, M. C., Leboulenger, F., Jegou, S., Leroux, P., Vaudry, H. (1979): *In vitro* study of frog (*Rana ridibunda*, Pallas) interrenal function by use of a simplified perifusion system. II. Influence of adrenocorticotropin upon aldosteron production. Gen. Comp. Endocrinol. *38*, 399–409.

Delarue, C., Tonon, M. C., Jegou, S., Leroux, P., Netchitaïlo, P., Vaudry, H. (1980): *In vitro* study of frog (*Rana ridibunda*, Pallas) interrenal function by use of a simplified perifusion system. IV. Influence of metyrapone and aminoglutethimide upon aldosterone production. Gen. Comp. Endocrinol. *42*, 516–525.

Delarue, C., Netchitaïlo, P., Leboulenger, F., Perroteau, I., Roullet, M., Kusmierek, M. C., Capron, M. H., Vaudry, H. (1981 a): *In vitro* study of frog (*Rana ridibunda*, Pallas) interrenal function by use of a simplified perifusion system. VI. Inhibition of aldosterone biosynthesis by SC 14266. Journ. Steroid Biochem. *15*, 343–348.

Delarue, C., Perroteau, I., Leboulenger, F., Netchitaïlo, P., Leroux, P., Jegou, S., Belanger, A., Tonon, M. C., Vaudry, H. (1981 b): *In vitro* effect of prostaglandins on corticosterone and aldosterone production by frog interrenal gland. Biochem. Biophys. Research Communications *100*, 769–777.

Delarue, C., Netchitaïlo, P., Leboulenger, F., Perroteau, I., Escher, E., Vaudry, H. (1984): *In vitro* study of frog (*Rana ridibunda*, Pallas) interrenal function by use of a simplified perifusion system. VII. Lack of effect of somatostatin on angiotensin-induced corticosteroid production. Gen. Comp. Endocrinol. *54*, 333–348.

Hanke, W. (1984): Changes of the biology of the adrenal cortex in the vertebrate evolution. Nova acta Leopoldina NF 56, Nr. *255*, 363–378.

Hanke, W., Maser, C. (1985): Regulation of interrenal tissue in *Amphibia.* In: Current trends in comparative endocrinology (B. Lofts, W. N. Holmes, eds.) vol. 1, pp. 447–449.

Hanke, W., Maser-Gluth, C. (1985): The influence of osmolality and ions on the interrenal secretion in *Amphibia.* Zool. Jb. Physiol. *89*, 453–467.

Hanke, W., Yousri, R. (1988): Regulation of the pituitary-interrenal axis of *Rana temporaria.* Zool. Jb. Physiol. *92*, 429–445.

Hanke, W., Kloas, W., Gluth, C., Vetter, S., Kniehl, K., Thurmond, W., Pathak, V. (1986): The significance of the interrenal gland of poikilothermic vertebrates during the process of acclimation. Zool. Beitr. N. F. *30*, 279–296.

Kloas, W., Hanke, W. (1986): The influence of metopirone on the secretion of corticosteroids by the amphibian interrenal gland. Acta endocrinologica *111*, suppl. 274, 62–63.

Kloas, W., Fuchs, E., Hanke, W. (1990): Binding sites of atrial natriuretic peptide and (Val^5)-angiotensin II in the kidney of *Xenopus laevis* – localization and quantification by *in vitro* autoradiography. Progress in Zoology, vol. *38*, Stuttgart, Fischer, 229–240.

Leboulenger, F., Delarue, C., Tonon, M. C., Jegou, S., Vaudry, H. (1978): *In vitro* study of frog (*Rana ridibunda*, Pallas) interrenal function by use of a simplified perifusion system. I. Influence of adrenocorticotropin upon corticosterone release. Gen. Comp. Endocrinol. *36*, 327–338.

Nishimura, H. (1980): Evolution of the renin-angiotensin system. In: Evolution of vertebrate endocrine system (P. K. T. Pang and A. Epple, eds.) pp. 373–404. Texas Tech Press.

Maser, C., Janssens, P. A., Hanke, W. (1982): Stimulation of interrenal secretion in Amphibia. I. Direct effects of electrolyte concentration on steroid release. Gen. Comp. Endocrinol. *47*, 458–466.

Rance, T. A., Baker, B. I. (1981): The *in vitro* response of the trout interrenal to various fragments of ACTH. Gen. Comp. Endocrinol. *45*, 497–503.

Sakakibara, S., Sokabe, H., Nakajima, T., Koshla, M. C., Kumagaye, S., Watanabe, T. X. (1985): Evolution of angiotensins and some problems in their synthetic preparations. In: Current trends in comparative endocrinology (B. Lofts, W. N. Holmes, eds.) vol. 2, pp. 1157–1159.

Tait, J. F., Tait, S. A. S. (1979): Recent perspectives on the history of the adrenal cortex. J. Endocrinol. *83*, 3P–24P.

Tait, S. A. S., Schulster, D., Okamoto, M., Flood, C., Tait, J. F. (1970): Production of steroids by *in vitro* superfusion of endocrine tissue. II. Steroid output from bisected whole, capsular and decapsulated adrenals of normal intact, hypophysectomized and hypophysectomized-nephrectomized rats as a function of tissue on superfusion. Endocrinology *86*, 360–382.

Tait, J. F., Tait, S. A. S., Bell, J. B. G., Hyatt, P. J., Williams, B. C. (1980 a): Further studies on the stimulation of rat adrenal capsular cells: four types of response. J. Endocrinol. *87*, 11–27.

Tait, J. F., Tait, S. A. S., Bell, J. B. G. (1980 b): Steroid hormone production by mammalian adrenocortical dispersed cells. Essay in Biochemistry *16*, 99–174.

Thurmond, W., Kloas, W., Hanke, W. (1986 a): Circadian rhythm of interrenal activity in *Xenopus laevis.* Gen. Comp. Endocrinol. *61*, 260–271.

Thurmond, W., Kloas, W., Hanke, W. (1986 b): The distribution of interrenal stimulating activity in the brain of *Xenopus laevis.* Gen. Comp. Endocrinol. *63*, 117–124.

Vetter, S., Hanke, W. (1985): A study comparing *in vitro* adrenal cortex response of fish and Amphibia. Acta endocrinologica *108*, suppl. 267, 157.

Fortschritte der Zoologie, Band/Vol. 38 · Hanke, W. (Hrsg.), Biology and Physiology of Amphibians
Gustav Fischer Verlag · Stuttgart · New York · 1990

Evolution and development of the adrenal gland in amphibians

F. Accordi, E. Grassi Milano

Dipartimento di Biologia Animale e dell' Uomo, Università «La Sapienza», Viale dell' Università 32, 00185 Roma, Italy

1. Introduction

The structure of the adrenal gland of amphibians represents an important step in the evolution of this organ. Throughout the evolutionary history of Vertebrates, the adrenal gland, like and more than other endocrine glands, has undergone conspicuous morphological changes (Bellamy, 1971). It shows a strong evolutionary trend towards a concentrated arrangement, starting from conditions of great dispersion. The adrenal gland is composed of two types of tissue of separate origins, the interrenal and the chromaffin tissue. The former type, derived from intermediate mesoderm, secretes steroids hormones which affect the regulation of water and saline balance and glucidic and lipidic metabolism (Hanke, 1978). The chromaffin tissue, which is derived from the neural crest, produces catecholamines (adrenalin and noradrenalin) which enable the organism, by various mechanisms, to overcome difficult environmental conditions (Coupland, 1965). The gland is therefore involved in the regulation of autoecological and synecological relationships of the animal, in correlation with nervous and vascular systems. Other important connections are those between the single steroidogenic or chromaffin cells and between the two tissues. These connections are developed mainly in higher vertebrates, whereas different degrees of dispersion can be observed in lower vertebrates.

In amphibians the gland is always placed on the ventral surface of the kidney, to compose small glandular bodies or islets, never immersed in the renal tissue; chromaffin and steroidogenic cells are juxtaposed and arranged in cords. This pattern can be defined as «amphibian type». Within this type of organization, we observed in different species of anurans and urodeles some morphological and histological variations, which may be correlated to the amphibian phylogenesis.

We will refer about the variation in the adrenal structure observed at gross anatomical, histological and ultrastructural levels, in adults and during development, in various amphibian species belonging to families of different phyletic positions.

2. Gross anatomy

The adrenal gland of adult amphibians always lies on the ventral surface of the kidney. It is composed of small bodies or islets, of varying concentrations among the different species. No sexual differences are observed in any character studied. The adrenal gland is always in contact with the caval vein or efferent renal veins.

The differences observed in the structural pattern of the adrenal gland in the three amphibian orders relate mainly to the position of the gland on the ventral face of the kidney, its relationship with the renal vessels and the degree of dispersion of the islets. There are also minor differences in histological and cytological characteristics.

Available reports about the adrenal gland of gymnophionans are scarcer than those regarding anurans and urodeles. From the researches of Dittus (1935), Gabe (1971), Bhatta (pers. comm.) it appears that the adrenal gland is composed of small islets more or less aggregated and aligned along the medial margin of the kidney in close proximity to the caval vein (Fig. 1). The islets are composed of steroidogenic cells, among which are scattered groups of adrenalin- and noradrenalin-cells. According to Gabe (1971), this pattern is similar to that of urodeles' adrenals.

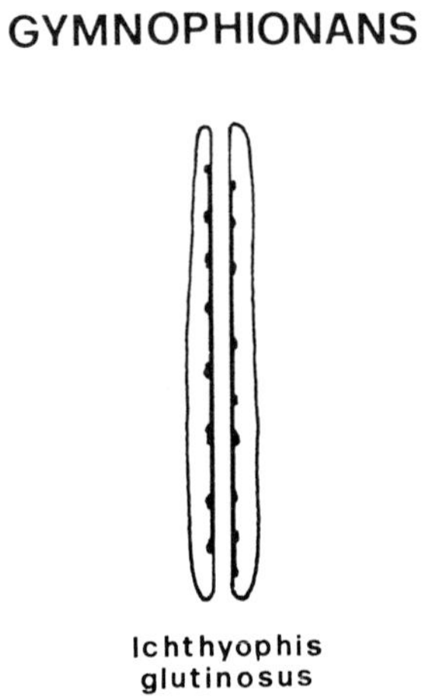

Fig. 1: Schematic drawing of the distribution of the adrenal gland of *Ichthyophis glutinosus*.

An examination of the topography of the adrenal gland in the numerous species of urodeles studied by us and by other authors (Certain, 1961; Mastrolia et al., 1976; Berchtold, 1972; Accordi et al., 1984; Setoguti et al., 1985; Grassi Milano and Accordi, 1986) reveals substantial variation which includes intrageneric variation. In most species the islets are small, close to the medial margin of the ventral face of the kidney, but the number, size and dispersion differ throughout the species, as shown in Fig. 2. The adrenal gland is always in contact with the efferent renal veins, at variable distance from the caval vein.

The adrenal gland of anurans (Grassi Milano and Accordi, 1983, 1986) is composed of islets, more closely grouped than in gymnophionans and urodeles, which form a yellow streak on the ventral renal surface. The position of the gland varies with respect to the median sagittal axis of the kidney. It is medial to this axis in archaeobatrachians, except in *Pelobates cultripes* where it is nearly coincident with it. In neobatrachians the gland is always lateral to this axis. The position, the length of the gland and the closeness of the islets are shown in Fig. 3. In gymnophionans, in urodeles and in archaeobatrachians, the islets are more dispersed than in neobatrachians, in which the texture of the gland is more compact. The glandular islets are in contact with wider efferent renal veins in the species in

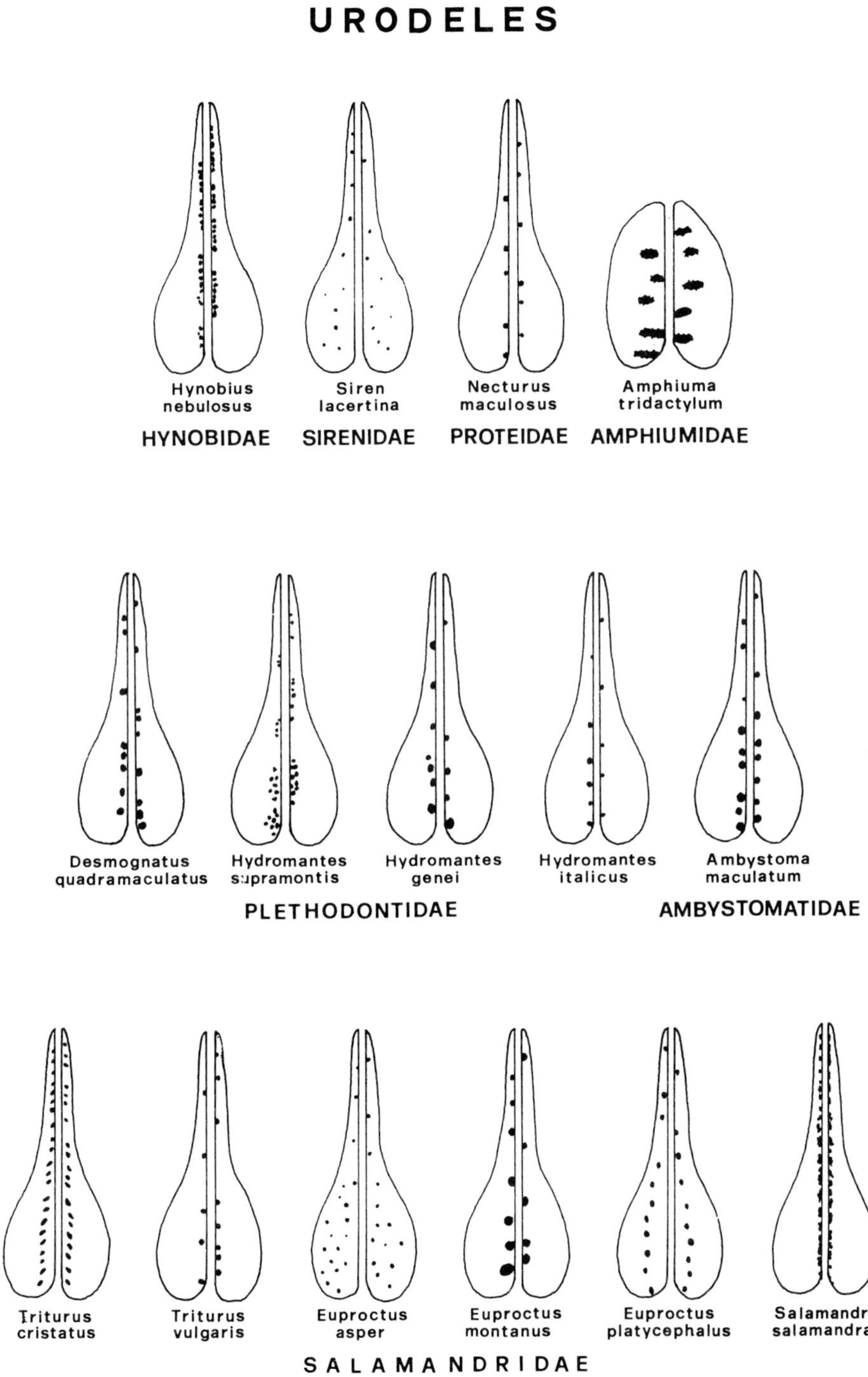

Fig. 2: Schematic drawing of the distribution of the adrenal gland of urodeles.

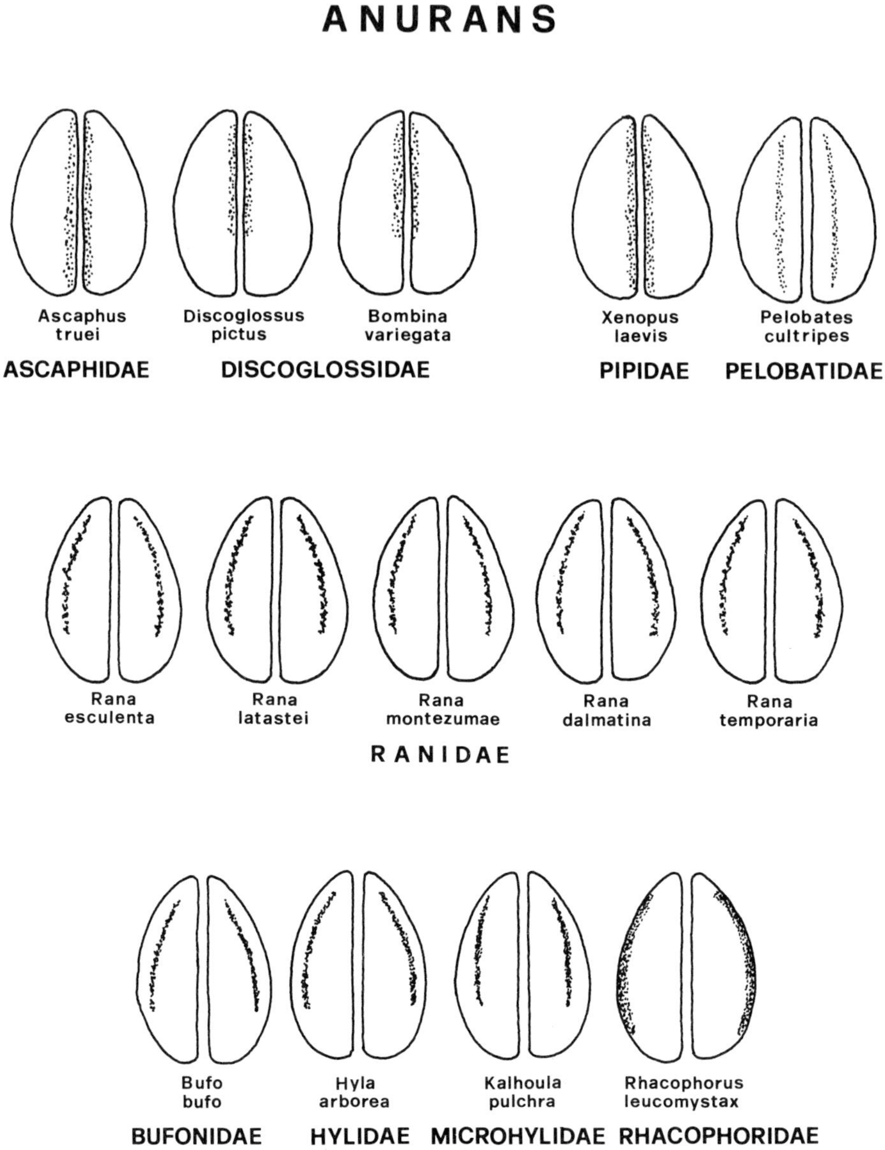

Fig. 3: Schematic drawing of the distribution of the adrenal gland of anurans: archaeobatrachians are grouped in the upper row, neobatrachians in the two lower rows.

which they are medial, and with narrower veins in the species in which they are lateral (Fig. 4). In archaeobatrachians the gland is frequently as long as the kidney, whereas in neobatrachians it is shorter than the kidney.

In frogs the adrenal morphology is steadier than in urodeles, since it does not vary within the genus and not even within different families.

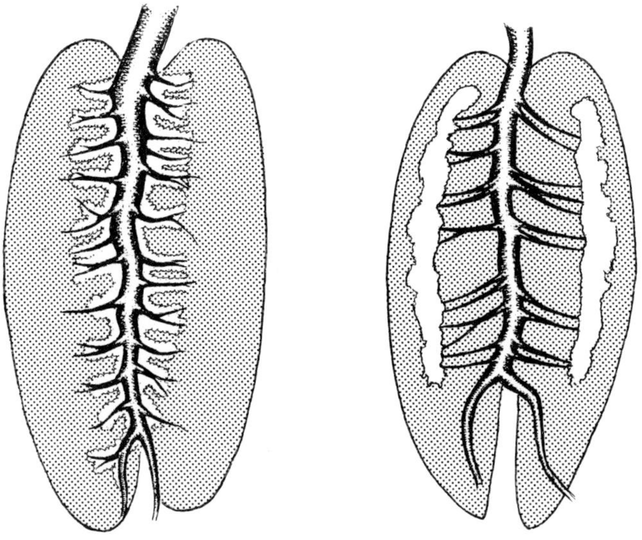

Fig. 4: In the archaeobatrachian *Xenopus laevis* the adrenal islets are in medial position, in contact with wider efferent renal veins. In the neobatrachian *Rana esculenta* the islets, located in lateral position, are in contact with narrower veins.

3. Histology

The amphibian adrenal gland is made up of cords surrounded by connective tissues, that separate them from one another and from the surrounding organs. The cords may be small, composed of a few cells arranged in a single layer or in small groups, as observed in gymnophionans (Gabe, 1971) in archaeobatrachian anurans and in most urodeles. In these cases the cords consist mainly of steroidogenic cells, whereas the chromaffin cells may be assembled in small groups on the periphery of the steroidogenic cords, or completely isolated from them (Fig. 5). In neobatrachians and in some neurodeles (*Triturus, Salamandra, Euproctus*) the cords are large and multilayered, composed of mingled chromaffin and steroidogenic cells forming large groups (Fig. 6) (Accordi et al., 1984; Grassi Milano and Accordi 1983, 1986).

4. Ultrastructure

At ultrastructural level, the steroidogenic cells show the typical cytological characteristics: rounded or polygonal shape, lobed nucleus with large chromatin masses, many rounded lipid droplets, mitochondria with tubular cristae, lysosomes, glycogen granules and well developed smooth endoplasmic reticulum. Some differences related to the seasonal activity can be observed in the number, size and content of lipid droplets, as well as in the arrangement of mitochondrial cristae and of endoplasmic reticulum.

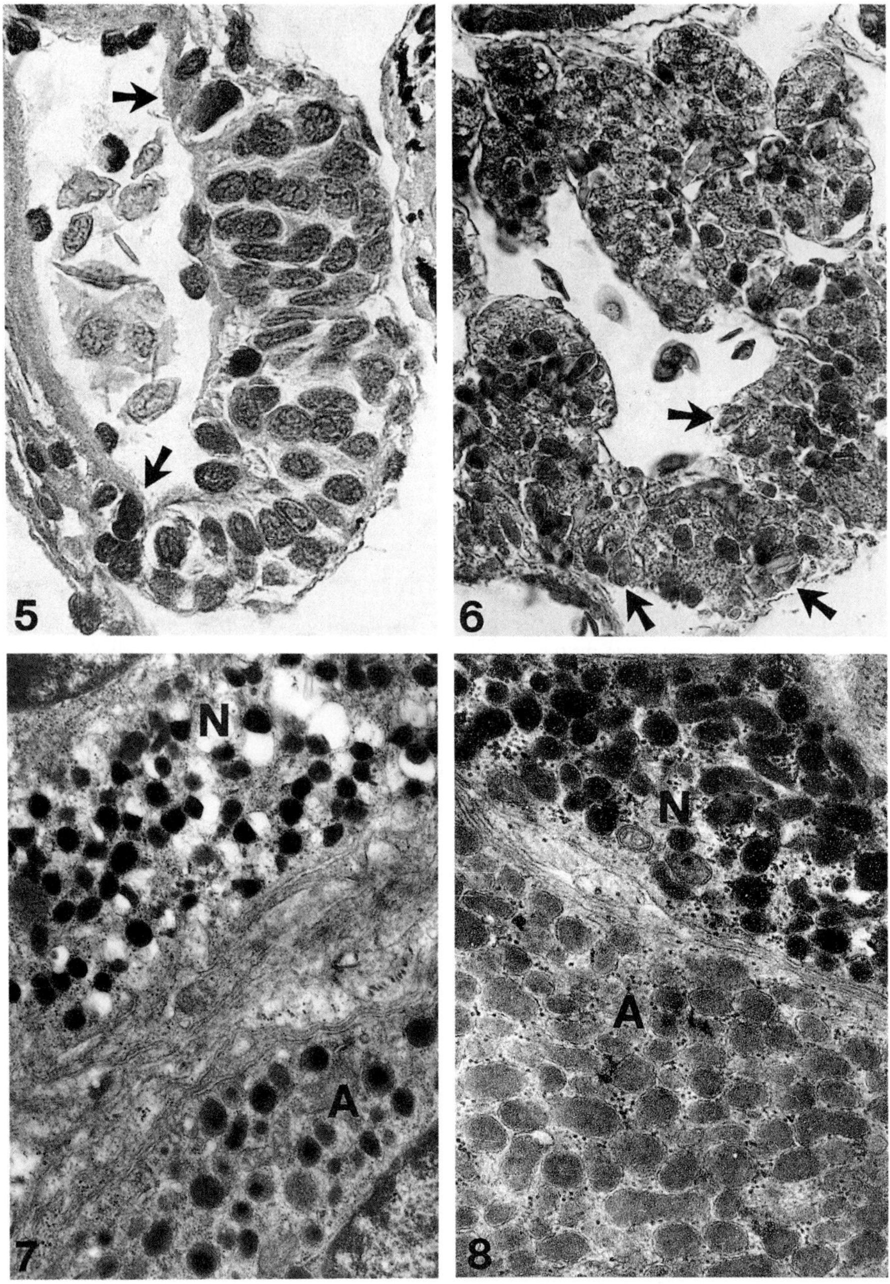
5
6
N
A
7
N
A
8

In the adrenals of some anurans (*Rana esculenta*, *Rana montezumae*, *Rhacophorus leucomystax*) we found the acidophilic Stilling's cells (Grassi Milano et al., 1979; Accordi and Cianfoni, 1981; Grassi Milano and Accordi, 1983), a particular cell type probably related to steroidogenesis. Their cytoplasm is filled with spherical, strongly electron-dense granules whose diameter varies between 0,4 and 0,8 μm. A few small sized mitochondria with lamellar cristae as well as small amounts of RER and SER also occur in the cytoplasm.

The chromaffin cells of anurans and urodeles can be distinguished into adrenalin-cells (A), containing weakly electron-dense, rounded granules and noradrenalin-cells (N), with strongly electron-dense granules of varied form. The difference between the two types of cells is slight in most urodeles (Fig. 7, 8).

The diameter of the chromaffin granules varies between 100 and 200 nm in urodeles and between 150 and 250 nm in anurans. In urodeles the size difference between A- and N-granules is lower than in anurans.

In many anurans (Accordi and Gallo, 1982) and, among the urodeles, in *Siren lacertina* (Accordi, 1987) and *Amphiuma tridactylum* (Accordi, 1988), a third chromaffin cell type was observed, i.e. the Small Granulated Chromaffin-cells (SGC-cells). These differ from A- and N-cells by containing small granules and by showing peculiar cytological characteristics such as a high nucleo/plasmatic ratio, a large amount of rough endoplasmic reticulum and many free ribosomes.

The chromaffin cells at the beginning of metamorphosis contain granules smaller than those in the adult and generally not distinguishable as A- and N-type on the basis of their electrondensity. The differentiation of granules into two types, the increase of their diameters and the segregation in different cells are completed during development.

5. Development

In anurans and urodeles the adrenal blastema is composed of cells of different embryonic origin i.e., presumptive steroidogenic cells derived from the mesoderm and chromaffin cells derived from neural crest. The embryonic mesodermic cells of the interrenal primordium migrate from their site of origin towards the ventral wall of the aorta where they form a median peduncle. Early chromaffin cells migrated from the neural crest invade interrenal primordium.

At the beginning of metamorphosis (early premetamorphosis) the glandular blastema is situated between the dorsal aorta, the caval vein and the dorsal renal surfaces. During

---

Fig. 5: In the urodele *Hydromantes italicus* the steroidogenic cells are grouped in small cords, the chromaffin cells are few and located at the periphery of the cords (arrows). 410 ×.

Fig. 6: In the neoobatrachian *Rana esculenta* the cords are large and multilayered, composed of mingled chromaffin (arrows), steroidogenic and Stilling cells. 410 ×.

Fig. 7: Adrenalin- (A) and noradrenalin-cell (N) in the adrenal gland of the urodele *Euproctus asper*. The difference between the two types of chromaffin granules is slight. 20.600 ×.

Fig. 8: Adrenalin- (A) and noradrenalin-cell (N) in the neobatrachian *Rana esculenta*. The two types of granules are well distinguishable. 24.700 ×.

metamorphosis the gland rotates and shifts ventrally and laterally (Fig. 9), at the same time organizing itself in cords. In most urodeles and in archaeobatrachian anurans the rotation stops at the end of metamorphosis (Accordi and Corbellini, 1987; Grassi Milano et al., 1985, 1986). In consequence, in juveniles as well as in adults the definitive position of the gland on the ventral renal face is medial. In neobatrachian anurans the gland continues its shift in the postmetamorphic period and then reaches its definitive lateral position (Fig. 9).

At the beginning of metamorphosis the chromaffin cells of *Rana esculenta* and *Bufo bufo* contain granules smaller than those of the adults and not distinguishable in A- and N-type on the basis of their electron-density. The differentiation of granules into two types, their increase in size and the segregation in different cells are gradually attained during metamorphosis (Accordi et al., 1975; Accordi and Grassi Milano, 1977). In *Discoglossus*

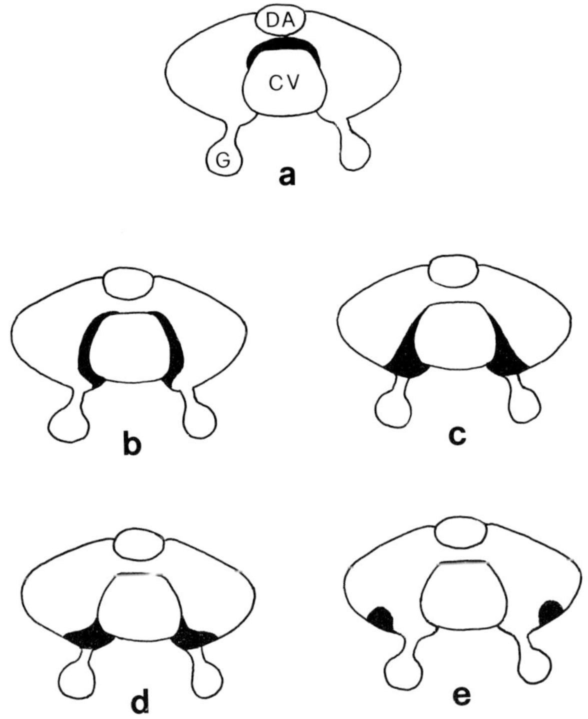

Fig. 9: The adrenal gland shifts during development:
a) In early metamorphosis it is dorsally located between dorsal aorta (DA) and caval vein (CV). G: gonads.
b) During the middle metamorphic period the gland shifts ventrally and laterally, along the walls of the caval vein, attaining the ventral renal surface.
c) During metamorphic climax the main part of the gland attains the renal surface, leaving the dorsal position.
d) At the end of metamorphosis, in adult urodeles and archaeobatrachians, the gland is located medially on the renal surface near the caval vein.
e) In neobatrachians the gland continues its shift in the postmetamorphic period and reaches a definitive lateral position.

pictus the differentiation and segregation of chromaffin granules seems to occur earlier than in the other species (Grassi Milano et al., 1988). The metamorphic adrenal shift occurs mainly by means of active cellular movements, indicated by the positive AChE reaction in the steroidogenic cells (Grassi Milano et al., 1985).

6. Discussion

The analysis of the structural variation of the adrenal gland in vertebrates indicates that a diffuse gland, dispersed inside the kidney and with little or no contact between the chromaffin and the steroidogenic tissues, constitutes a primitive trait. A comparison of the structural organization of the adrenal tissue throughout the fishes (Balment et al., 1980) indicates that, in all the species studied, the chromaffin and the steroidogenic cells are mostly separated and frequently dispersed inside the head kidney, surrounding veins. This leads one to infer that the condition of the adrenal tissue in all fishes is plesiomorphic to that found in amphibians. In Dipnoi, whose adrenal tissue has been considered as very similar to that of urodeles (Janssens et al., 1965; Chester Jones and Mosley, 1980; Balment et al., 1980), the steroidogenic cells are not on the renal surface because they are covered by perirenal tissue. Furthermore, the position of the chromaffin cells, as reported by Nilsson (1984) seems to make mingling of the two tissues impossible.

In the course of evolution, chromaffin and steroidogenic tissues emerge on the kidney surface, associate themselves to form a gland whose pattern can be generally defined as «amphibian type». This type of gland presents a more advanced evolutionary state compared to that of fish, because it is always on the renal surface, never immersed in the renal tissue, and because the chromaffin and steroidogenic tissues which compose the gland are juxtaposed. Within this type of organization we can recognize different evolutionary steps, a primitive one in which islets are small, scattered and composed of little groups of chromaffin and steroidogenic cells scarcely intermingled. The islets are generally disposed close to the medial margin of the kidney. This type of gland is present in gymnophionans, in many urodeles and in archaeobatrachians. A more advanced adrenal gland is composed of larger, numerous islets, in which conspicuous and multilayered cords of steroidogenic and chromaffin cells are intermixed. This type of gland can be observed in some neurodeles and in neobatrachians. In these latter the gland is located laterally to the median sagittal axis of the kidney, but in *Pelobates cultripes*, where the gland is nearly coincident with this axis. According to Duellman (1975), this anuran species is an archaeobatrachian. However, Lynch (1973) considers this species phylogenetically intermediate between archaeobatrachians and neobatrachians. More recent classifications (Laurent, 1979; Dubois, 1983) put Pelobatidae and Pipidae in intermediate suborders between archaic and advanced frogs.

The adrenals of urodeles are very variable, particularly in the degree of dispersion, the localization of the islets and in the extent of minglig between the chromaffin and the steroidogenic cells. There is also some intrageneric variation. There is no clear taxonomic pattern to this variation. In fact, in the representatives of the more advanced urodeles families i. e. Salamandridae and Plethodontidae, various evolutionary steps in the adrenal arrangement are observed, evidenced by the structural differences present in the three species of *Euproctus*, in the three italian species of *Hydromanthes* and in two species of *Triturus*. Furthermore, species distant from each other, e. g. *Euproctus asper* and *Siren lacertina* exhibit similar primitive organizational patterns (Fig. 2).

The higher variation in the adrenal arrangement in urodeles with respect to that of anurans could be attributed to their higher specifical isolation; many of them are perennibranchiate, other caverniculous, other have restricted geographic distribution. Few natural hibrids are found in urodeles with respect to anurans.

In anurans the variation of the adrenal gland generally agrees with the phyletic relationships of the frog families. The glandular structure is very similar among advanced anurans and intrageneric differences, common among urodeles, are not observed.

In neobatrachians the lateral position of the gland is attained by means of the protraction of morphogenesis during postmetaphorphosis. The evolutionary differences related to the position of the gland are then settled mainly by a change in the chronology of the development, that is, by means of a heterochronic process. Heterochrony can be defined as the process of morphological evolution due to alteration of timing and rates of development (Alberch, 1980; Atchley, 1987). The postmetamorphic shift brings the adrenal gland of advanced frogs in lateral position by a lenghtening of the period of cellular movement, important in the settling of evolutionary differences (Grassi Milano et al., 1985, 1986; Manelli et al., 1987).

The lateral position of the gland observed in neobatrachians may be more advantageous because the gland, being in contact with thin vessels, is more compact than that of archaeobatrachians which is divided in blocks by the wider vessels of the medial edge of the kidney (see Fig. 4 and Accordi et al., 1981). The compact structure of the gland, that is the close anatomical contact between the two cell types promotes their integration and allows a better functional control (Delarue et al., 1988 and this volume).

One can surmise that the anuran-urodele divergence occurred from an ancestral group which already possessed the «amphibian type» adrenal, i.e. placed on the kidney surface, rather than immersed in the renal tissue but still in a primitive diffuse condition. In gymnophionans (Gabe, 1971) the adrenal gland is like that of urodeles, and hence it is probable that the divergence of this order took place when the evolution of the gland in the ancestral stock was still at a primitive stage. According to this hypothesis, the high degree of mingling between chromaffin and steroidogenic cells, observed in a few urodeles, i.e. *Salamandra salamandra* (Berchtold, 1972) and *Triturus cristatus* was reached independently of the advanced anurans.

According to Balment et al. (1980) the evolution of the adrenal gland of vertebrates reflects the evolution of the mesonephric blastema, but in some cases this point of view cannot explain all observations. In fact, in both fishes and amphibians, the definitive kidney is the opisthonephros, but the relationships between the gland and the kidney vary in the different classes. On the other hand, the adrenal gland of chelonians, whose definitive kidney is a metanephros, is organized as in anurans. It seems therefore that the structure of the adrenal gland is regulated by some other factors besides the evolution of the kidney.

As regards hormonal production, aldosterone is generally present in amphibians. This hormone is infrequently identified in fishes, whereas is generally found in tetrapods (Balment et al., 1980; Hanke, 1984). Hence, the passage to a terrestrial life may be marked by integrated physiological and morphological modifications of the adrenal gland.

With evolutionary progress, the concentration of the organ increases and the two components assume a close and well-defined relationship. The gland continues its evolution, reducing the contact with the kidney. This type of adrenal gland, that is, the encapsulated gland of Amniotes, may be considered apomorphic or derived. In this way, the functional correlation between the catecholamines and the steroids (Delarue et al.1988) and hence the control of the metabolic activity of the organism can be reinforced. This control is also improved by more precise nervous control, as indicated by a higher percentage of innervated chromaffin cells in some neobatrachians as compared with archeobatrachians (Grassi Milano and Accordi, 1983). It is possible that the functional improvement, derived from the more complex organization of the anurans' glands, with respect to those of urodeles, may explain the wider geographical distribution of the former. Anurans have colonized the southern hemisphere and tropical regions besides the northern hemisphere, whereas urodeles, to whom has been attributed the inability to compete with tropical anurans (Darlington, 1957), are distributed almost exclusively in the northern hemisphere.

Acknowledgements

We wish to thank Prof. H. Manelli for his encouragement, Dr. N. Falchi and Mr F. Ventola for their skilful technical assistance.

References

Accordi, F. (1987): The chromaffin cells of *Siren lacertina* (Amphibia Urodela): cytological characteristics and evidence of exocytosis. J. Anat. *156*, 169–176.

Accordi, F. (1988): The adrenal gland of *Amphiuma tridactylum* (Amphibia, Urodela). Life Sci. Adv. (in press).

Accordi, F., Cianfoni, P. (1981): Histology and ultrastructure of the adrenal gland of *Rhacophorus leucomystax* (Amphibia, Anura). Boll. Zool. *48*, 277–284.

Accordi, F., Corbellini, F. (1987): Morphogenesis of the adrenal gland of *Triturus cristatus carnifex* during larval development and metamorphosis. Arch. Anat. Micr. Morph. Exp. 75(4), 241–251.

Accordi, F., Gallo, V. P. (1982): Adrenaline-, Noradrenaline-, and Small Granule Containing-Cells in the adrenal gland of *Discoglossus pictus* (Amphibia, Anura). J. Anat. 135, *1*, 5–12.

Accordi, F., Gallo, V. P., Grassi Milano, E. (1981): The adrenal gland of *Xenopus laevis* D. Some histological and ultrastructural observations. Monitore Zool. Ital. (NS) 15, 163–174.

Accordi, F., Grassi Milano, E. (1977): Catecholamine-secreting cells in the adrenal gland of *Bufo bufo* during metamorphosis and in the adult. Gen. Comp. Endocrinol. 33, 2, 187–195.

Accordi, F., Grassi Milano, E., Gallo, V. P. (1984): Adrenal gland of *Euproctus* (Urodela, Salamandridae): comparison among three species and phylogenetic inferences. J. Anat. 139, 2, 209–214.

Accordi, F., Mastrolia, L., Grassi Milano, E., Manelli, H. (1975): Electron microscopic observations of adrenal chromaffin cells in the frog *Rana esculenta* during embryonal development and metamorphosis. Riv. Biol., 68, 3, 35–163.

Alberch, P. (1980): Ontogenesis and morphological diversification. Amer. Zool., 20, 653–667.

Atchley, W. R. (1987): Developmental quantitative genetics and the evolution of ontogenesis. Evolution 41 (2), 316–330.

Balment, R. J., Henderson, I. W., Chester Jones, I. (1980): Adrenal cortex and its homologue in vertebrates: evolutionary considerations. In: General, Comparative, and Clinical Endocrinology of the Adrenal Cortex. (I. Chester Jones, I. W. Henderson, eds) Vol. III, pp. 525–562. Academic Press, London.

Bellamy, D. (1971): The evolution of Vertebrate endocrine system. In: Hormones in Development (M. Hamburg & E. J. W. Barrington, eds) pp. 821–839. Appleton Century Crofts, New York.

Berchtold, J. P. (1972): Le tissue interrenal (corticosurrenalien) des Amphibiens Urodeles: ultrastructure, aspects cytochimiques. These de Doctorat, Universite' Luis Pasteur, Strasbourg, Section Sciences.

Certain, Ph. (1961): Organogenese des formations interrenales chez le batracien Urodele *Pleurodeles waltlii* Michah. Bull. Biol. France Belgique 95, 134–149.

Chester Jones, I., Mosley, W. (1980): The interrenal gland in Pisces. Part I. Structure. In: General, Comparative, and Clinical Endocrinology of the Adrenal Cortex (I. Chester Jones and I. W. Henderson, eds) Vol. III, pp. 395–472. Academic Press, London.

Coupland, R. E. (1965): The natural history of the chromaffin cells. Longmans, London.
Darlington, P. J. jr. (1957): Zoogeography: the geographical distribution of animals. J. Wiley, New York.
Delarue, C., Leboulenger, F., Nechtitaïlo, P., Lihrmann, I., Feuilloley, M., Idres, S., Larcher, A., Morra, M., Vaudry, H. (1988): Neuroendocrine regulation of adrenocortical cells in Amphibians. Karlsruher Beitr. z. Zoophysiol. 14, 97–102.
Dittus, P. (1935): Interrenalsystem und Chromaffinzellen im Lebenslauf von *Ichthyophis glutinosus*. Z. Wiss. Zool. 147, 459–512.
Dubois, A. (1983): Classification et nomenclature supragenerique des Amphibiens Anoures. Bull. men. Soc. Linneenne Lyon, 52, 270–276.
Duellman, W. E. (1975): On the classification of frogs. Occasional Papers, Mus. Nat. History, University of Kansas, 42, 1–14.
Gabe, M. (1971): Donnees histologiques sur la glande surrenale d'*Ichthyophis glutinosus*. Arch. Biol. 82, 1–23.
Grassi Milano, E., Accordi, F. (1983): Comparative morphology of the adrenal gland of Anuran Amphibia. J. Anat. 136, 1, 165–174.
Grassi Milano, E., Accordi, F. (1986): Evolutionary trends in the adrenal gland of anurans and urodeles. J. Morph. 189, 249–259.
Grassi Milano, E., Accordi, F., Antuzzi, D., Rapisarda, R. (1979): Morphologic observations on the interrenal, Stilling and intermediary cells in the adrenal gland of *Rana esculenta* complex. Riv. Biol., 72, 1/2, 46–69.
Grassi Milano, E., Accordi, F., Arizzi, M., De Mattheis, L. (1988): Organogenesis of the adrenal gland of *Discoglossus pictus*. Acta Embr. Morph., Exp. (in press).
Grassi Milano, E., Arizzi, M., Bracci, M. A., Manelli, H. (1985): Active cell movements and embryonic cholinesterase in the postmetamorphic completion of the adrenal morphogenesis in frogs. Exp. Cell. Biol., 53, 328–334.
Grassi Milano, E., Bracci, M. A., Manelli, H. (1986): Morphogenesis and evolution of the adrenal gland in Anurans. Boll. Zool. 53 (suppl.), 41.
Hanke, W. (1978): The adrenal cortex of Amphibia. In: General, Comparative and Clinical Endocrinology of the Adrenal Cortex (I. Chester Jones and I. W. Henderson, eds): Vol. II, pp. 419–495. Academic Press, London.
Hanke, W. (1984): Changes of the biology of the adrenal cortex in the Vertebrate evolution. Nova Acta Leopoldina N. F., 56, 363–378.
Janssens, P. A., Vinson, G. P., Chester Jones, I., Mosley, W. (1965): Amphibian characteristics of the adrenal cortex of the african lungfish (*Protopterus* sp.). J. Endocrinol., 32, 373–382.
Laurent, R. F. (1979): Esquisse d'une phylogenese des Anoures. Bull. Soc. Zool. France, 104, 397–422.
Lynch, J. D. (1973): The transition from archaic to advanced frogs. In: J. L. Vial (ed), Evolutionary Biology of the Anurans. Contemporary Researches on Major Problems, pp. 133–182. University of Missouri Press, Columbia.
Manelli, H., Grassi Milano, E., Bracci, M. A. (1987): Comparative morphogenesis of the adrenal gland in Archaeobatrachia and Neobatrachia. Acta Embr. Morph. Exper. *8*, 411–418.
Mastrolia, L., Gallo, V., Manelli, H. (1976): Cytological and histochemical observations on chromaffin cells of the suprarenal gland of *Triturus cristatus* (Urodele Amphibian). Boll. Zool. 43, 27–36.
Nilsson, S. (1984): Adrenergic control systems in Fish. Marine Biology Letters 5, 127–146.
Setoguti, T., Shin, M., Inoue, Y., Matsumura, H., Chen, H. (1985): Ultrastructural changes in development and aging of the interrenal cell of the Salamander, *Hynobius nebulosus*. Arch. Histol. Japon. 48, 2, 199–211.

IV. Osmoregulation and Adaption

Fortschritte der Zoologie, Band/Vol. 38 · Hanke, W. (Hrsg.), Biology and Physiology of Amphibians
Gustav Fischer Verlag · Stuttgart · New York · 1990

Crowding in toads, are crowded toads stressed or not?

LIS OLESEN LARSEN, METTE BOHN CHRISTIANSEN, TERKEL DUE, SØREN HASTRUP, CHRISTIAN KAPEL, MARTIN SCIUTO, and ANNE METTE WULFF

Zoophysiological Laboratory A, August Krogh Institute, University of Copenhagen, DK 2100 Copenhagen, Denmark

1. Introduction

Stress responses can be quantified in various ways. In vertebrate physiological tradition various parameters related to activation of the sympathetic nervous system have been investigated: 1. Circulating catecholamines from nerve endings or from the adrenal medulla and their effects on e.g. blood glucose, blood lactate; 2. circulating opiates, corticotropin, corticosteroids or other hormones; their effects have normally not been used as parameters of stress, since they are not well known or easy to quantify. These parameters belong to a tradition focusing on a quantitative analysis of well defined parameters, which are expected to reflect the degree of stress precisely, and they necessitate blood sampling. Another, and much older tradition, is to watch the animals, register their food intake (appetite), their growth rate, their fertility, their appearance (epidermis, fur, feathers, scales), and their behaviour. These parameters are essential for animal production and are certainly affected by the hormonal, metabolic, and behavioural changes related to increased activity of the sympathetic nervous system. But there is rarely a clear cause-effect-relationship between the levels of one hormone or of one metabolite and these parameters.

In the present experiment we combined an investigation of two parameters, which are supposed to reflect increased sympathetic activity and increased corticotropin – corticosteroid secretion, with some easily measured parameters with complex regulatory mechanisms involved, like food intake, digestion, and growth.

The purpose of the experiment (performed as a student project) was to see whether forced crowding of toads would cause stress responses. Furthermore, aggressive behaviour and competitive feeding were expected, when the crowded toads were fed for only one hour each day, with amounts of mealworms supposed not to create long term satiety (Larsen, 1984).

It was decided to follow two easily observed functions of the skin: Stress causes the melanophore index in a toad kept on a black background to decrease from 5 towards 1 which causes the toad to become paler (Parker, 1948; Bagnara and Hadley, 1973), probably because of increased sympathetic activity. As another indicator of stress, moulting on the skin was chosen; in *Bufo bufo* moulting depends strictly on corticosteroids (Larsen, 1976), and corticosteroids in too low or at constant, high levels cause skin abnormalities (Larsen, 1976; Jørgensen, 1988). In stressed *Rana pipiens* corticosterone levels doubled (Laub et al., 1975). To get an idea of the general health of the toads, and to see if any feeding hierarchy developed, food intake and growth were measured, and behaviour was observed during the daily feeding periods.

2. Methods used to determine stress response in toads

Animals. Twenty small adult male *Bufo bufo*, with dark brown finger cornifications, were captured in Northern Jutland, Denmark, during late September or early October, and stored in a refrigerator at 2–3 °C until Oct. 20. On that date they were marked individually by toe clipping and placed in black boxes (17 × 22 × 6 cm) with transparent lids, tilted so that 60 ml of water covered about one fourth of the bottom (Fig. 1). The box also contained a tray for mealworms. The room had constant dim light (c. 100 lux) and constant temperature (23 °C).

Experimental plan. On Oct. 27 and 30 the toads were offered 10 mealworms each, and the 15 toads which ate most were selected for the experiment. On Oct. 30, 10 toads were placed under crowded conditions: 5 toads in each of two boxes (groups I and II), and 5 toads were kept singly (group III). For the next 4 weeks (except Sundays) groups I and II each day received 50 mealworms, and the toads in group III 10 mealworms each. Before the mealworms were offered, water was removed from the boxes in order to prevent drowning of mealworms when wet toads jumped into the mealworm tray. After one hour the remaining mealworms were removed and counted. During the feeding period the toads were observed by two persons, and the behaviour described, especially with regard to eating behaviour and social interactions. The individual toads were recognized by individual patterns of lipstick markings. In a few cases toads snapped at the mealworms in vain or got two worms in one snap. Skin moulting was registered daily (except on Sundays) by marking the skin of the neck with lipstick (Bendsen, 1956). When the lipstick disappears, a moult has occurred since last inspection. Once a week (5 times) the toads

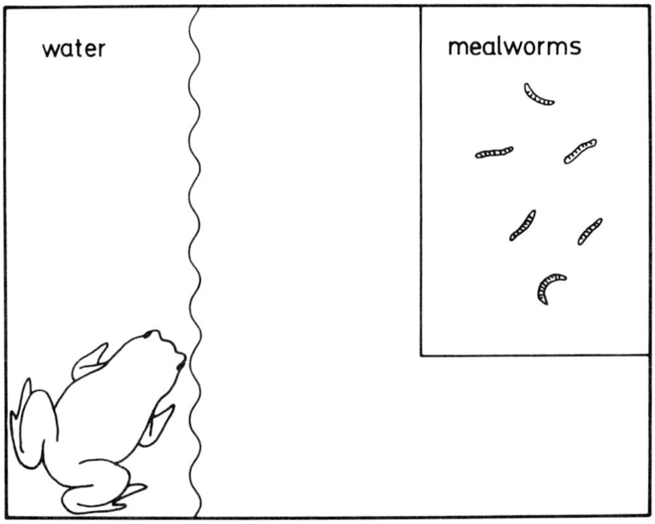

Fig. 1: The boxes used, with the correct proportional dimensions (see Methods).

were weighed after emptying the bladder for urine and their length recorded by placing them firmly on their backs along a scale in mm. Melanophore index according to Hogben and Slome (1931) was recorded by the same person on Nov. 13, 21, and 28. Since *Bufo bufo* has no hind-web, the melanophore index was read on the eyelid (method developed by Lis Olesen Larsen; involves pressing the eyeball gently so that the eyelid is raised without the eyeball being retracted).

Calculations. Condition index, reflecting nutritional condition = weight in g/length^3 × 1000 (g/cm^3 × 1000). Food conversion = g weight increase/g consumed food × 100%. Consumed food: Number of mealworms eaten × average weight: 200 mealworms were weighed; the average weight of one worm was 73.5 mg.

3. The influence of crowding on physiological and behavioural parameters

Table 1 summarizes the physiological parameters measured.

Melanophore index. Groups I and II had significantly lower indices than group III and thus showed paling in spite of a black background.

Moulting. There was no difference between the moulting intervals in the 3 groups. However, group I showed significantly more and group II a tendency to more variation than group III. Very regular moulting (range of intervals x – x+1 days) was only seen in 2 toads, from group III. Very irregular moulting (range x – x+5–7 days) was only seen in 2 toads from group I and 2 toads from group II. The large variation in group I is especially conspicuous, since this group showed little variation in growth and food intake when compared with groups II and III.

Growth. In all toads there was growth in length, and these was no significant difference between the groups. In all groups the small toads grew most. The time course of the length increase differed among individuals; some continued growth throughout the experiment, whereas others stopped growing in the latter part of the experiment. In this respect there seemed to be a difference between groups I and II, whereas group III resembled group I. The average weight increased in all groups, but 2 toads showed loss of weight or no increase.

Condition index. This measure of body proportions showed no difference between the groups and no consequent change with time.

Food intake. Group III showed a tendency (insignificant) to higher food intake than groups I and II. In no case, group I or II had eaten all the mealworms offered. The maximum number eaten by one toad was 19. In group III the individual toads varied much with respect to pattern of eating; one ate all mealworms on 20 out of 25 days, another toad never ate all mealworms. The time course of food intake was similar to the time course in growth in length: A majority of the toads showed a decrease in the latter part of the experiment, although no toad stopped feeding.

Food conversion. The average food conversion did not differ significantly between the groups, but variation was extreme in group II and very low in group I.

Behaviour. The behaviour observations were analyzed for signs of dominance/subordination in the feeding situation in groups I and II. From this analysis (Fig. 2) 3 toads (no. 1, 2, and 5) could be characterized as dominating and 4 toads (no. 7, 8, 9, and 10) as dominated toads, but this pattern of behaviour was not reflected in the physiological parameters. Toad no. 10 was twice observed to actively hinder the access of number 8 to the food tray. The only other sign of dominance or aggression was one toad which snapped at a toe of another toad (no. 2 at no. 4). In three toads no interaction with other toads was observed.

Table 1: Physiological parameters in toads kept under crowded conditions or singly for 4 weeks

Toad group		Growth increse in length, mm	Growth increse in weight, g	Condition index ($g/cm^3 \times 1000$) Oct. 30	Condition index ($g/cm^3 \times 1000$) Nov. 27	Food intake (number of mealworms)	Food conversion (weight increase/food intake × 100%)	Melanophore index (Nov. 13,21,28)	Moulting intervals (days)
I	mean ± S.D.	5.4 ± 3.8	5.3 ± 1.6	93	94	111 ± 22	64 ± 12	1.9 ± 1.5	5.1 ± 2.0
	range	3–11	3–7	69–103	84–103	74–129	52–84	1–5	2–11
(5 per box)	change with time	late stop in 4				decrease in 4		constant (3) or decrease (2)	no consistent
II	mean ± S.D.	5.6 ± 4.0	4.8 ± 6.1	97	91	116 ± 80	32 ± 69	2.1 ± 1.3	4.8 ± 1.6
	range	2–10	−3–13	88–105	82–98	41–233	−86–75	1–5	1–9
(5 per box)	change with time	late stop in 1				decrease in 4		constant (2) or varying (3)	no consistent
III	mean ± S.D.	5.8 ± 4.0	5.8 ± 6.0	98	86	147 ± 67	44 ± 34	4.0 ± 1.4	5.2 ± 1.1
	range	2–11	0–14	85–106	78–100	95–243	0–80	2–5	3–8
(5 singly)	change with time	late stop in 5				decrease in 4		constant (3) or increase (2)	no consistent
				Statistics					
	size at start of experiment	I 52–64 II 57–63 III 56–63	17–27 17–26 18–27	no significant difference between groups				Students's t-test: I v. III P < 1‰ II v. III P < 1‰	Variance ratio: I v. III P 1–5‰ II v. III P 5–10%
	size at end of experiment	I 61–68 II 60–69 III 64–68	22–30 21–30 23–31						

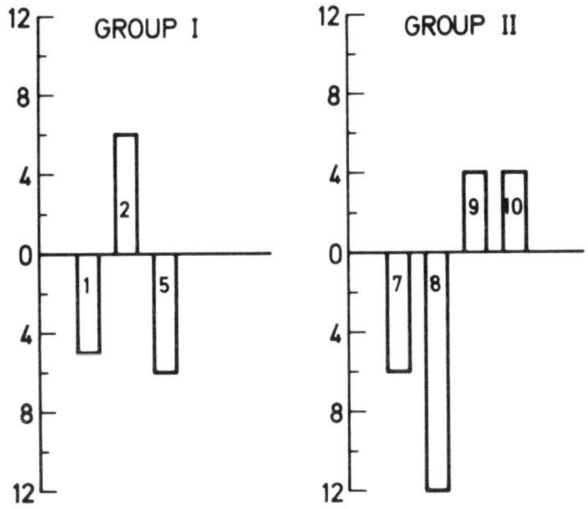

Fig. 2: The numbers on the y-axis above 0 indicate number of observations of toads which came first to the mealworm tray and stayed there for the whole hour; this was considered a sign of dominant behaviour. The numbers below 0 indicate the number of observations of toads which showed no interest in the food and exhibited dominated behaviour (retiring into a corner, digging with hindlegs, easily disturbed by moving objects or by sounds). Each column represents one toad.

General well-being. No toad seemed to be in bad health, which normally shows itself as lack of food intake or vomiting of ingested food, lack of growth, partial moulting leading to piling up of unshed cornified epithelium, and faeces with bad smell, not delivered in faecal sacs (general experience from our laboratory).

4. Discussion

Under the present conditions of crowding the toads were in good health, and no feeding hierarchy developed. The fact that the small toads grew most supports the idea that the few negative social interactions had no harmful effects on growth or other signs of health. The only results, which may be interpreted as signs of stress, were the low melanophore index on a black background, and the very irregular moulting intervals. If only these parameters, supposed to reflect increased sympathetic activity, had been measured, the conclusion would have been: The crowded toads are stressed. However, when all measured parameters are considered, the effects of crowding on melanophore index and moulting intervals may rather be interpreted as an excitement reaction, causing no harm to the toads.

There were very few observations of aggressive behaviour, and the snapping towards another toad's toe is probably a consequence of the toe movement, described by Radcliffe et al. (1986). Previous work on other toad species has also only revealed moderate aggressive behaviour and competitive feeding (Alexander, 1964; Tracy, 1973). The consequences for food intake and growth have not been investigated before.

Although crowding in this experiment did not influence the toads in a negative way, it may be important for the function of amphibia whether they are kept singly or together, as discussed by Gatten and Hill (1984). It must also be stressed that the water and the box have to be kept clean. Furthermore the toads should perhaps be followed for more than four weeks. However, the changes with time in the various parameters revealed no clear signs of adaptation or aggravation, indicating a stable situation.

In nature, toads often crowd during hibernation and during mating. At their feeding season, they often hide singly, each in one hiding place, e. g. in small holes between roots of big trees or in small holes in windfalls, but they may also hide two or more together (Poulsen and Pedersen, unpublished observations). This is in apparent contrast to the situation in our laboratory: When there are several big hiding places (plastic pots), we often see many toads in one pot and the rest of the pots empty. The essential thing for the toads may be to have the body surrounded by some material, preferably a «wall»; other toads may then substitute for that when the hiding place is too large. So optimal hiding places for toads should probably be of the size of the toad body. In this way the inflation of the lungs when they are grasped also makes sense: It makes it difficult for a mammal (or human being) to pull the toad out of its hiding place.

A few general comments on the physiological parameters seem warranted.

It has been suggested that the decrease in food intake (long term satiety) seen after some weeks of ample feeding is causally related to extremely large fat bodies, as reflected in a condition index well above 100 (Guha et al. 1980, Larsen, 1984). However, this cannot be the explanation in the present experiment, where the condition index remained constant; in this case the endogenous element of the normal growth cycle probably is at play (Jørgensen, 1986). The reason that the toads did not become fat may be that the food was offered only for one hour at a time; in previous experiments food was always offered for 24 hours at least. During a 24-h-period the toads often have several «meals» (Larsen, 1984).

Moulting frequency is differing between toads, but is normally rather regular in the same toad (Scharrer, 1958). Irregular moults have been observed after moving toads from one room to another, and sometimes the moult is skipped, and two cell layers are shed at the next moult (Jørgensen and Larsen, 1961). The very short moulting intervals (down to one day) observed here have not been seen before in *Bufo bufo*, and the mechanism involved is unknown.

The present study underlines the importance of measuring as many parameters as practically possible, both with relation to physiology and behaviour, before making conclusions with regard to effects of crowding or other types of stress factors; and the parameters used here may provide a more valid and easily obtained measure of stress than measurement of stress hormones in blood. Furthermore it is suggested that a slight activation of the sympathetic nervous system is not harmful.

Acknowledgement

The senior author expresses her gratitude towards Dr. Alan Pickering for helpful suggestions that led to clarification of thought.

References

Alexander, T. R. (1964): Observations on the feeding behavior of *Bufo marinus* (LINNE). Herpetology *20*, 255–259.

Bagnara, J. T., Hadley, M. E. (1973): Chromatophores and Color change, the Comparative Physiology of Animal Pigmentation. Prentice Hall, Inc., New Jersey. 202 pp.

Bendsen, J. (1956): Shedding of the skin in the common toad, *Bufo bufo*. Vidsk. Meddr. dansk naturh. Foren. *118*, 211–225.

Gatten, R. E., Hill, C. J. (1984): Social influence of thermal selection by *Hyla crucifer*. J. Herpetol. *18*, 87–88.

Hogben, L., Slome, D. (1931): The pigmentary effector system. IV. The dual character of endocrine co-ordination in amphibian colour change. Proc. Roy. Soc. B. *108*, 10–53.

Guha, K., Jørgensen, C. B., Larsen, L. O. (1980): Relationship between nutritional state and testes function, together with observations on patterns of feeding, in the toad, *Bufo bufo bufo*. J. Zool. Lond. *192*, 147–155.

Jørgensen, C. B. (1986): External and internal control patterns of feeding, growth and gonadal function in a temperate zone anuran, the toad *Bufo bufo*. J. Zool. Lond. (A) *210*, 211–241.

Jørgensen, C. B. (1988): Nature of moulting control in amphibians: Effects of cortisol implants in toads *Bufo bufo*. Gen. Comp. Endocrinol. *71*, 29–35.

Jørgensen, C. B., Larsen, L. O. (1961): Molting and its hormonal control in toads. Gen. Comp. Endocrinol. *1*, 145–153.

Larsen, L. O. (1976): Physiology of molting, In: Physiology of Amphibia *3* (B. Lofts, ed.), pp. 53–100. Academic Press, New York.

Larsen, L. O. (1984): Feeding in adult toads: Physiology, behaviour, ecology. Vidsk. Meddr. dansk naturh. Foren. *145*, 97–116.

Laub, J. M., Callard, G. V., Callard, I. P. (1975): The role of adrenal steroids in the negative feedback control of the amphibian adrenal gland. Gen. Comp. Endocrinol. *25*, 425–431.

Parker, G. H. (1948): Animal Colour Changes and their Neurohumours. The University Press, Cambridge. 337 pp.

Radcliffe, C. W., Chiszar, D., Estep, K., Murphy, J. B., Smith, H. M. (1986): Observations on pedal luring and pedal movements in leptodactylid frogs. J. Herpetol. *20*, 300–306.

Scharrer, E. (1958): Molting cycles in the toad, *Bufo marinus*. Anat. Record. *130*, 369 (abstract).

Tracy, C. R. (1973): Observations on social behavior in immature California toads (*Bufo boreas*) during feeding. Copeia *1973*, 342–345.

Fortschritte der Zoologie, Band/Vol. 38 · Hanke, W. (Hrsg.), Biology and Physiology of Amphibians
Gustav Fischer Verlag · Stuttgart · New York · 1990

Xenopus laevis South African clawed toad – A potential indicator for radioactive contamination in ecological systems?

MANUELA GIANNETTI, ANNEKE TRUX, BRUNO GIANNETTI, ZDZISLAW ZUBRZYCKI

Institut für Angewandte Zoologie der Universität Bonn; An der Immenburg 1; D-5300 Bonn 1, FRG

1. Introduction

Since the nuclear reactor catastrophy at Tschernobyl in 1986 there is an increasing interest in potential biological indicators for radioactive contamination in ecological systems. The aim of our study was to investigate, whether vertebrates could be used as indicators in aquatic systems and if the system «vertebrate» could provide a subsytem, whose parameters indicate radioactive contamination.

Xenopus laevis was chosen for two reasons: first because of the greater radiosensitivity of amphibians compared to fishes and second for the easy laboratory mantainance.

We investigated the reaction of several plasma parameters to the injection of 45-Ca. A further question was the survival rate of the offsprings from contaminated parents. 45-Ca was selected, because its physiological behaviour in the organism is comparable to that of 90-Strontium, one of the most important radioisotopes from reactor and nuclear weapon fallouts.

2. Material and methods

2μ CI 45-Ca in sterile physiological sodium-chloride were injected subcutaneously into the dorsal lymphsack of 9 males and 10 females of *Xenopus laevis*. The average body weight was 35 g (sd 10 g).

As the last step in the development of the oocytes should be under radioactive influence, the animals were stimulated to breed by hormonal treatment (human choriongonadotropin) prior to the injection of the isotope.

Thus it was ensured, that radiation exposure coincided with the development of the most oocystes up to stage VI.

Animals were examined on day 7, 10, 15, 19 and 55 after application of 45-Ca.

On day 55 three males and three females were treated again with choriongonadotropin to induce breeding. At mid-gastrula stage 200 viable eggs of each spawn were separated and grown up in non-contaminated water. Another spawn from untreated parents was used as a control-group. Survival rates of F_1 generation were followed up from the mid-gastrula stage to metamorphosis. All animals were kept under equal conditions (water quality, temperature, population density and food).

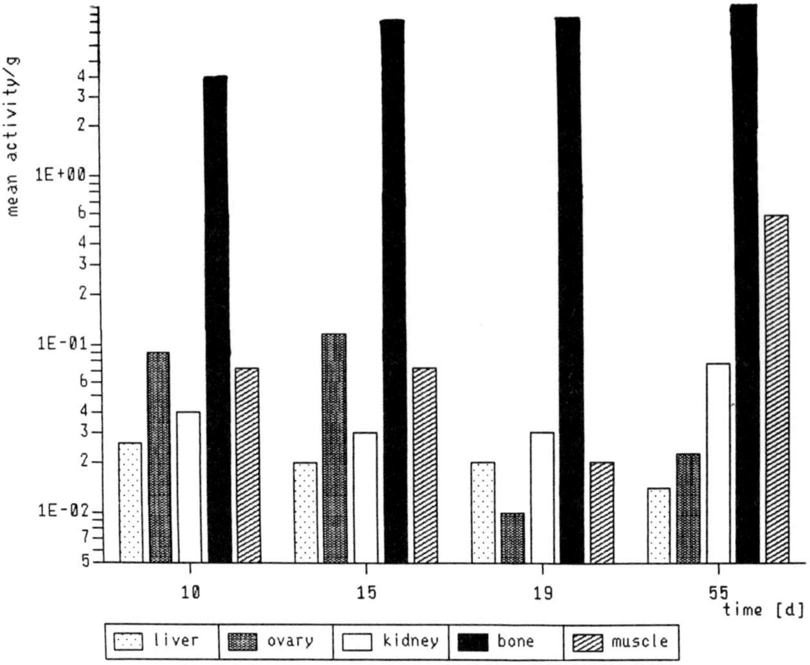

Fig. 1: 45-Ca uptake of several organs.

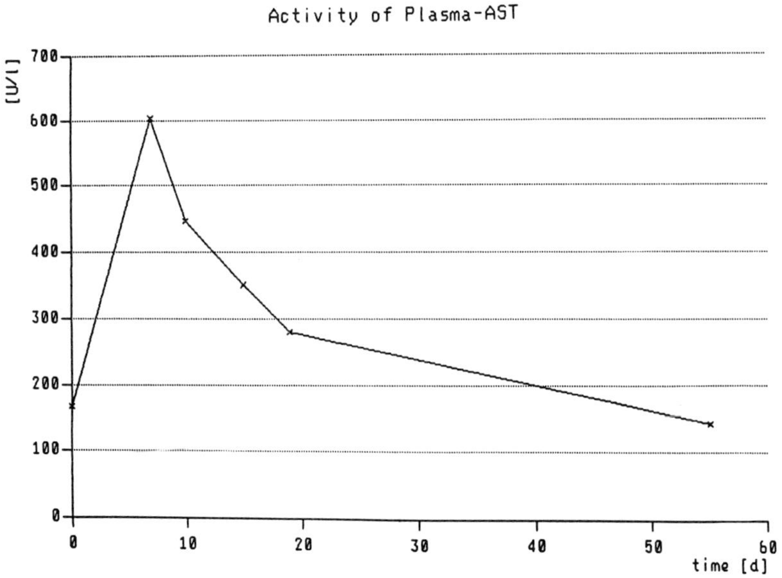

Fig. 2: Activity of Plasma-AST after application of 2 μCi45-Ca/g bodyweight.

3. Ca-distribution in the clawed toad and effects of 45-Ca

Fig. 1 shows the time-course of the specific activity of several organs during the experiment.

Liquid scintillation measurements of the specific organ activities showed an increasing accumulation of the isotope in muscles and bones, here up to 450 percent, whereas the uptake of 45-Ca in liver, ovary and kidney was below 5 percent with a tendency to decrease.

Data about LD 50 does concerning incorporated β-emitters are hardly available, but further investigations with higher applied activities, revealed the activities used in this experiment as markedly sublethal.

The liver is looked upon as a relative radiosensitive organ and it has the advantage, that its functional alterations can be checked by standardized laboratory methods usable also for amphibians.

As indicators for liver function we chose AST (Aspartat-Amino-Transferase), ALT (Alanin-Amino-Transferase), the membrane-bound γ-GT (γ-Glutamyl-Transferase) and urea.

According to Bacq and Alexander (1961) enzyme-release due to the breaking of bonds which hold the molecules in situ is an important mechanism by which small and medium doses of irradiation can produce their biological effects.

Fig. 2 shows the time-course of plasma-AST.

Between day 7 and day 15 after 45-Ca application plasma AST level rose significantly with a maximum of the 3,6 fold normal level on day seven. The same tendency was revealed by plasma-ALT levels (Fig. 3).

There is a significant increase of the plasma values between day 7 and 10 with a maximumo of 250% of the control value at day 10.

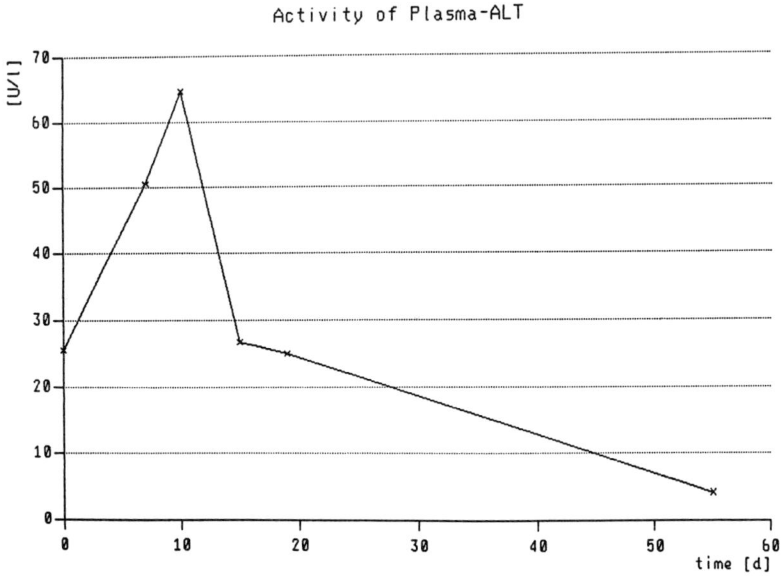

Fig. 3: Activity of Plasma-ALT after application of 2 μCi-45-Ca/g bodyweight.

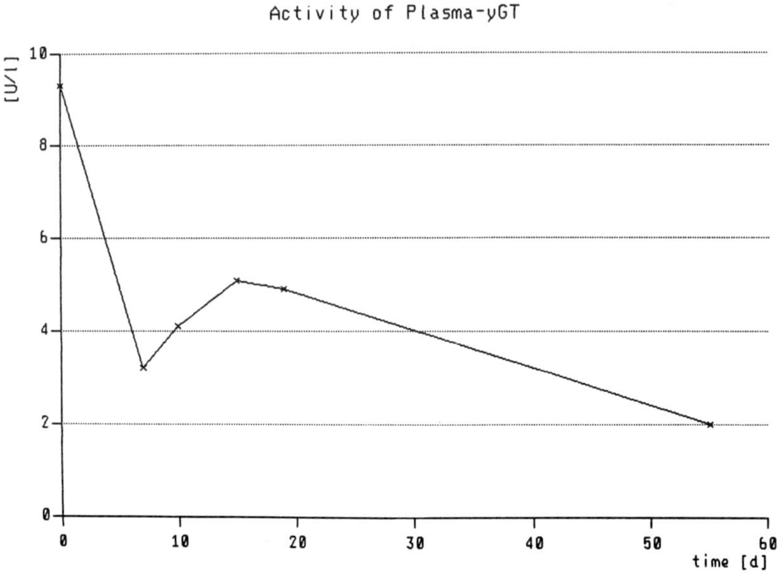

Fig. 4: Activity of Plasma γ-GT after application of 2 μCi 45-Ca/g bodyweight.

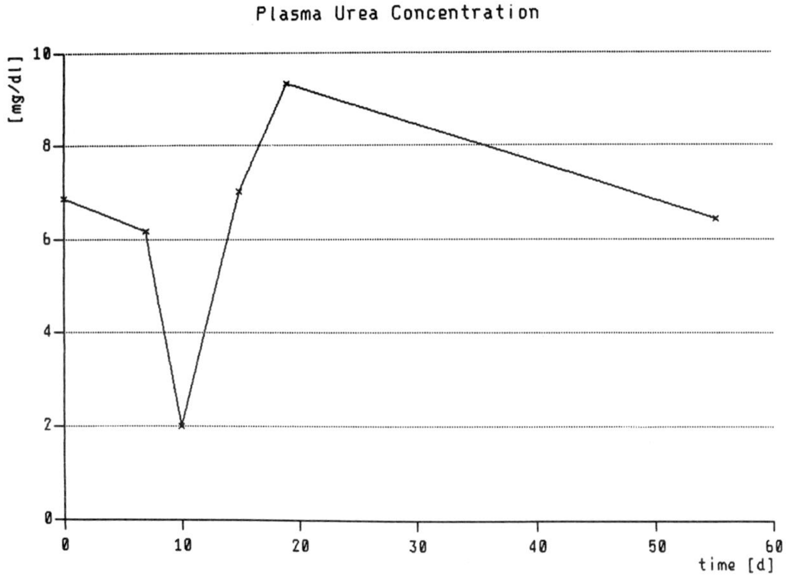

Fig. 5: Plasma Urea Concentration after application of 2 μCi 45-Ca/g bodyweight

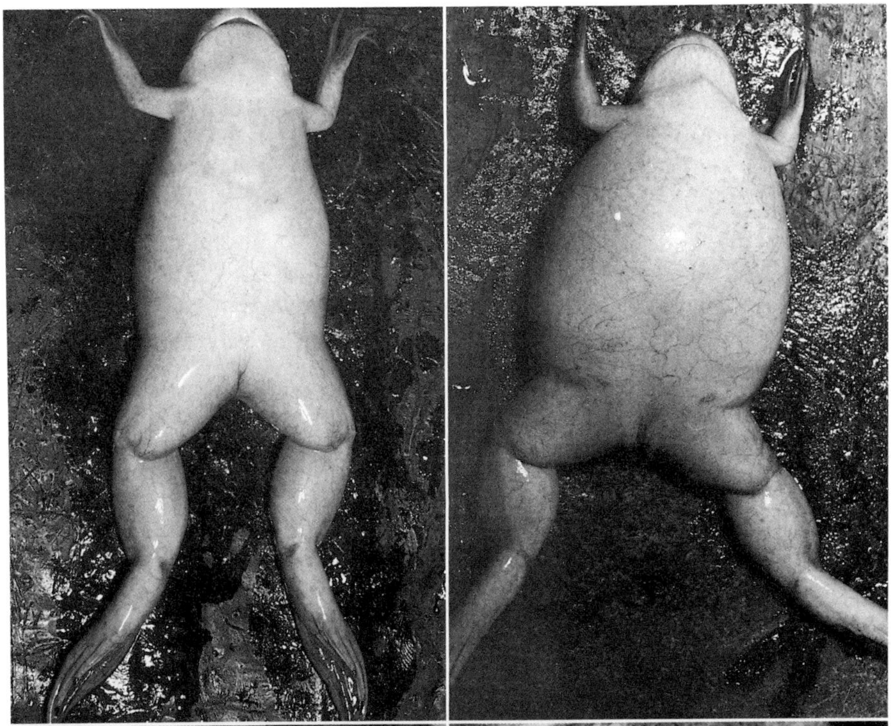

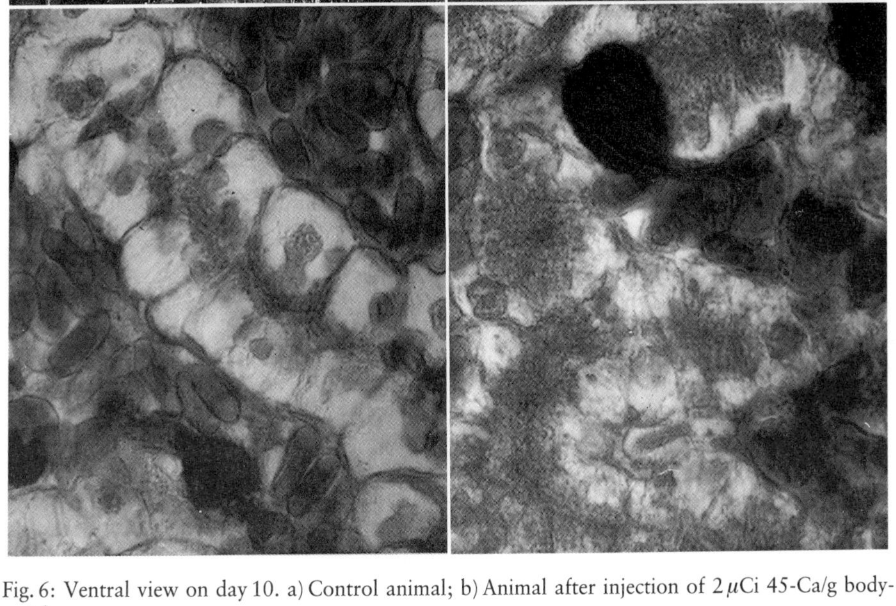

Fig. 6: Ventral view on day 10. a) Control animal; b) Animal after injection of 2 μCi 45-Ca/g bodyweight

Fig. 7: a) Control, liver, Azan 400 ×; b) day 7, liver, Azan 400 ×.

γ-GT (Fig. 4) showed a marked depression of activity on day 7 when compared with controls. This suppression of enzyme activity remained constant all over the observation period. Considering the reference range for serum enzymes, the γ-GT values are critical though not clearly pathological.

No change was observed in creatinine concentrations over the study period, while plasma urea (Fig. 5) was markedly decreased on day 10 after the application of 45-Ca and normalized at the end of the observation period. Decreased plasma urea levels can be a hint for acute liver dysfunction.

This speculation was supported by histological investigations of the liver (Fig. 6).

Normal hepatocytes show only narrow cytoplasmatic boarders. The remaining cell body is unstained due to the accumulation of glycogen granula which are resolved during preparation (Fig. 6a).

In contrast, the H. E. or Azan staining of hepatocytes from irradiated animals on day 7 suggests a lack of glycogen content. As we can see here cytoplasmatic boarders are twice as broad as in controls (Fig. 6b).

The alterations of plasma parameters between day 7 and 10 coincided with a severe ascites in 50% of the contaminated animals.

Fig. 7 shows a control animal and an animal 7 days after injection of 2μ Ci 45-Ca/g bodyweight.

The abdomina were enlarged and autopsy showed ovarian dropsy.

Considering the short latency period this diagnosis is surprising, because ascites after irradiation is looked upon as a chronic alteration resulting from portal hypertension. Another reason for ascites could be a decrease of the colloid-osmotic pressure as a consequence of hypalbuminemia.

Indeed we found the synthesis of albumin decreased. Normally the physiological quotient between serum albumin and globulines has a value of about 1,26; irradiated animals

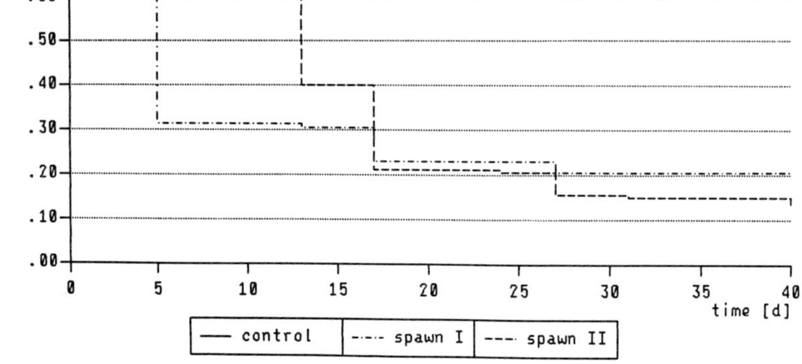

Fig. 8: Survival rate of the F_1-generation from contaminated parents

had a markedly decreased ratio of albumine to globulines of 0,47.

Examination of the F_1 generation showed a drastically reduced viability of spawns from contaminated parents (Fig. 8).

Mortality of controls up to the age of 40 days, respectivly st. 57/58 (Nieuwkoop-Faber) was 32%, whereas offsprings from irradiated parents had a mortality of 80–85%. Irrespectively of these results increased malformation or retardation in development, as it is known after early embryonic x-irradiation, could not be ascertained.

4. Discussion

We found highly significant alterations in plasma parameters as an acute reaction of liver function to sublethal radioactive contamination in amphibians. Increased levels of plasma transaminases as an acute reaction to external x-irradiation in the range of LD/50 up to lethal doses are known from rats. Therapeutic application of fractionated high liver doses between 3500 and 5900 rad cause an increase of plasma ALT and AST within the first two months after irradiation. The observed ascites probably developed as a result of the reduction in albumin syntheses and/or obliterative vascular inflammation, that is known as an early stage of the Budd-Chiari-syndrome after irradiation.

Liver function of *Xenopus* is highly sensitive to radioactive contamination, even with isotopes like 45-Ca, without a liver-specific accumulatin.

The effects presented here are acute and still reversible. The search of parameters as indicators long-term is our aim for further studies.

References

Bacq, Z.M., Alexander, P. (1961): Fundamentals of Radiology. Pergamon Press, London.

Nieuwkoop, P.D., Faber, J. (1967): Normal table of *Xenopus laevis* (Daudin). North Holland, Amsterdam.

Fortschritte der Zoologie, Band/Vol. 38 · Hanke, W. (Hrsg.), Biology and Physiology of Amphibians
Gustav Fischer Verlag · Stuttgart · New York · 1990

Influence of surface water acidification on amphibians*

JÜRGEN BÖHMER and HINRICH RAHMANN

Institute of Zoology, University of Stuttgart-Hohenheim, D-7000 Stuttgart 70, FRG

Abstract

Atmospheric pollution leads to increasing acidity in sensitive waters. Acidic water harms amphibians; especially the reproductive phase is effected: fertilization is inhibited, embryonic and larval mortality increases, deformities and abnormalities in development occur. Acid sensitivity varies with species but intraspecific differences also have been observed. This reflects genetical differences as well as different chemical properties of the water. The influence of acidity on mortality has been studied extensively but only very little is known about sublethal effects, like changes in gill morphology or aluminium accumulation in the gills, and their consequences. Larval mortality at low pH is mainly caused by disturbances of ion regulation. H^+ leads to changes of membranes and tight junctions of the epithelia causing increased ion efflux, decreased ion influx and subsequent death. Decreased reproductive success naturally affects distribution and abundance of amphibians. However acid induced changes in the whole ecosystem might be as important as the failure in recruitment, especially at sublethal pH values.

1. Introduction

During the last decades acidification of aquatic ecosystems has become one of the major environmental problems facing Europe and North America, where many poorly buffered waters have been seriously acidified. Acid rain is considered as the main cause by most of the authors (e.g. Battarbee and Charles, 1986; Davis and Stokes, 1986; Lehnhart and Steinberg, 1984). Pure unpolluted rain has a pH of 5.6 due to CO_2 in the atmosphere. But naturally occurring concentrations of contaminants like SO_2 and NO_x cause a further drop in the pH. Therefore the natural pH of rain water before industrialization probably was about 5.0 in general (Likens, 1976). Today, resulting from anthropogenous emissions, the average pH of precipitation is below 4.7 in large parts of Europe and North America (Schnoor et al., 1986; Kallend et al., 1983 in Lehnhart and Steinberg, 1984; Psenner, 1984; Likens and Bormann, 1974).

Acid producing processes in the vegetation and the soil of the catchment areas also contribute to the acidification of waters. The plants take up cations in exchange for H^+. During the decomposition of organic material in the upper layers of the soil humic acids

* Supported by the Umweltministerium Baden-Württemberg.

are formed. But what portion of the acidity of waters is due to natural processes and what is due to acid rain and has come with industrialization therefore?

Measurements of pH of soils and waters indicate that the pH is decreasing rapidly. However, former data are scarce and not easily comparable because the pH was determined colorimetrically whereas today the pH is measured electrochemically (Falkengreen-Grerup, 1987; Haines, 1981 and 1982; Howells, 1982). Therefore attempts have been made to reconstruct the pH-history of lakes using the remains of diatoms, cladocerans and other taxa in the sediments. In many lakes a decrease of species variety and an increase in number and abundance of acidophilic species of these taxa was observed in the upper layers of the sediment indicating a rapid decline of pH in the last two centuries, especially in the last decades (Battarbee and Charles, 1986; Davis and Stokes, 1986; Dixit et al., 1988; Henrikson et al., 1982). For the Huzenbachersee in the Black Forest/West Germany e.g. a slow decrease of pH was determined from about 6.5 at the end of the ice ages down to about 5.6 two hundred years ago, followed by a rapid decrease to about 4.5 in the last two centuries (Steinberg et al., 1986).

Low pH naturally effects the organisms of the aquatic habitats. Amphibians are especially vulnerable because they often breed in small or temporary ponds which are highly susceptible to acidification. These aquatic habitats are mainly supplied by acidic rain and even more acidic melt water, and there is only little contact with the soil buffering systems. In addition many Amphibians are spring breeders, i.e. that embryos and larvae develop at a time when water acidity is on its peak, because all the acidity accumulated in winter as frozen precipitation is quickly released at spring thaw. Effects of acid water on amphibians are not pH effects alone. Elevated concentrations of H^+-ions mobilize the highly toxic aluminium and heavy metals from the sediments and watershed soils.

Amphibians are important factors in many aquatic ecosystems. They may regulate types and quantities of algae in ponds and play a significant role in transferring energy and nutrients out of the aquatic into the terrestrial habitat (Seale, 1980; Dickmann, 1986; Wassersug, 1975).

This paper gives an overview on the effects of surface water acidification on amphibians. First pH-effects on newt populations are considered. In order to explain those effects it is necessary to look at the different phases in the life cycles of amphibians: adults, fertilization and development of eggs, embryonic and larval mortality and growth and development of larvae. In search of the causes of mortality in acid waters the possible mechanisms are discussed.

2. Effects of acidity on amphibian populations

Only very few studies have been carried out concerning amphibian populations in acidic waters. A field survey in the Netherlands revealed that the occurrence of amphibians was pH-dependant. The number of species as well as the percentage of waters which harbour a certain amphibian species is diminished in the extremely acid pH class (pH < 4.0; Leuven et al. 1987). A reduction in the number of amphibian species in acidic environments also was reported by Freda and Dunson (1985a, b), Strijbosch (1979), Saber and Dunson (1978) and Gosner and Black (1957). In the Black Forest/West Germany we found that *Bufo bufo* populations were absent in ponds with an average pH below 4.5, and *Triturus helveticus*, *Triturus alpestris*, *Rana temporaria* and *Rana dalmatina* were absent below pH 4.2, whereas these species were common in less acidic ponds (Tab. 1). *Triturus vulgaris* was absent in acidic ponds though eggs exposed in a pond at pH 5.6 developed normally (see later chapter for critical pH of this species). *Triturus vulgaris* was only found at metal

Table 1: Amphibian populations of 18 differently acidic ponds in the district of Freudenstadt in the northern Black Forest/West Germany in 1987 and 1988. (Rt = *Rana temporaria*, Th = *Triturus helveticus*, Ta = *Triturus alpestris*, Tv = *Triturus vulgaris*, Bb = *Bufo bufo*, Bc = *Bufo calamita*, * = reproduction but embryonic mortality > 15%, () = only few individuals encountered and no reproduction, n.p. = not present)

pond (area)	mean pH	hardness meq/l	species occurrence					
Sumpf 1 (0.5 m²)	3.7	0.04	n.p.	n.p.	n.p.	n.p.	n.p.	n.p.
Waldmulde (1.5 m²)	3.9	0.04	n.p.	n.p.	n.p.	n.p.	n.p.	n.p.
Baum (1.5 m²)	4.1	0.08	n.p.	n.p.	n.p.	n.p.	n.p.	n.p.
Sumpf 2 (0.5 m²)	4.1	0.20	(Rt)	n.p.	n.p.	n.p.	n.p.	n.p.
Herrenwiesersee (1.1 ha)	4.2	0.08	Rt*	Th*	Ta*	n.p.	n.p.	n.p.
Grasloch (2 m²)	4.2	0.16	Rt*	Th*	Ta*	n.p.	n.p.	n.p.
Schurmsee (1.4 m²)	4.3	0.08	Rt*	Th*	Ta*	n.p.	(Bb)	n.p.
Huzenbachersee (2.1 ha)	4.5	0.10	Rt*	Th*	Ta*	n.p.	Bb*	n.p.
Kaltenbachsee (0.4 ha)	4.7	0.15	Rt*	Th*	Ta*	n.p.	(Bb)	n.p.
Erdkrötenloch (1.5 m²)	4.7	–	Rt	Th	Ta	n.p.	Bb*	n.p.
Poppelsee (0.5 ha)	5.5	0.18	Rt	Th	Ta	n.p.	Bb	n.p.
Ellbachsee (0.4 ha)	5.6	0.18	Rt	Th	Ta	n.p.	Bb	n.p.
Sankenbachsee (2.4 ha)	5.6	0.15	Rt	Th	Ta	n.p.	Bb	n.p.
Kaltenbachteiche (0.1 ha)	5.9	0.31	Rt	Th	Ta	n.p.	n.p.	n.p.
Kuhbrunnen (200 m²)	6.2	0.43	Rt	Th	Ta	n.p.	Bb	n.p.
Dammerswiese (500 m²)	6.5	0.36	Rt	Th	Ta	n.p.	Bb	n.p.
Eisweiher (400 m²)	6.3–7.2	1.2	Rt	Th	Ta	Tv	Bb	n.p.
Buchholder (300 m²)	7.5	8.2	Rt	n.p.	Ta	Tv	Bb	Bc
Birre (0.1 ha)	8.1	3.6	Rt	n.p.	Ta	Tv	Bb	Bc

rich sites (hardness ≥ 1.2 meq/l) whereas *Triturus helveticus* was only found in very soft water (≤ 1.2 meq/l). Therefore we think that these two species of newts compete against each other in their habitat. *Triturus helveticus* is dominant in very soft water and *Triturus vulgaris* is dominant in harder waters which are protected against acidification.

The data of Strijbosch (1979) and Clark (1986) indicate that population densities of anurans are smaller in acidic ponds even though pH-levels were not low enough to cause acute toxicity to eggs or larvae. The population densities of newts in six similar ponds in the Black Forest, measured as trapping success in weir baskets, declined with decreasing mean pH of a pond (Fig. 1). In circumneutral and moderately acidic ponds the alpine newt *Triturus alpestris* was the dominant newt species whereas the palmate newt *Triturus helveticus* became increasingly dominant with decreasing pH (also Fig. 1).

3. Effects of acidity on subadults and adults

Acidity might act onto different stages of the complex life cycle of amphibians. Courtship, spawning, fertilization and development of embryos and larvae mainly occur in aquatic habitats whereas the adults and foreaging subadults use these habitats to a strongly varying degree depending on species or even strain.

Postmetamorphic amphibians seem to react similarly to acidity as fish (McDonald, 1983). Acid water causes a loss of ions, mainly sodium, potassium and chloride, through

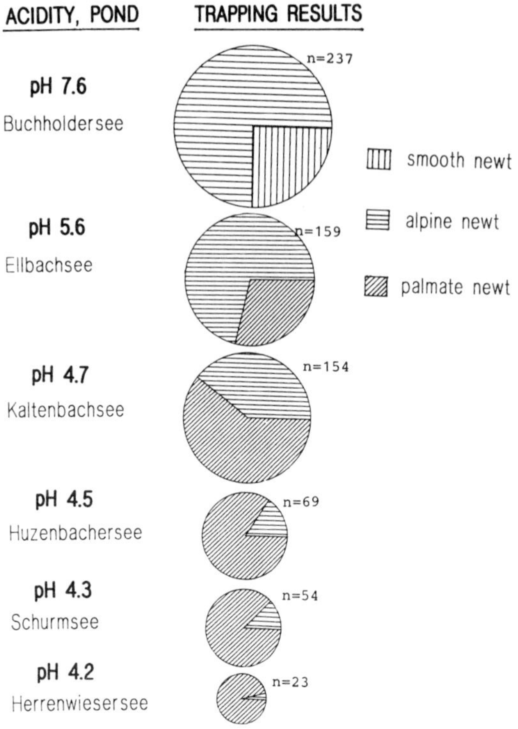

Fig. 1: Newt populations of six ponds in the northern Black Forest/West Germany in dependance of pH in 1987 and 1988 (n = number of trapped newts per trap and spawning season)

the skin. This effect is well established in isolated frog skin (van Driessche and Zeiske 1985) but there is no evidence that postmetamorphic amphibians are killed in acid water under natural conditions. They are still encountered in extremely acid waters (Clausnitzer, 1979; Leuven et al., 1987; Strijbosch, 1979) at pH-values at which premetamorphic stages of amphibians are harmed (see below). Adults and subadults seem to be less acid sensitive. Early and late stages of *Triturus alpestris* larvae were killed within a few hours at pH 3.7 whereas subadults two days after metamorphosis survived the five days of exposure in the same water without any visible harm (Tab. 2). The reason might be the resorption of the

Table 2: Times until the end of reactions (movements after touching) and survival times of two stages of larvae and subadults of the alpine newt *Triturus alpestris* in natural pond water of pH 3.7. (mean ± sd; n = 6)

	freshly hatched larvae	larvae at begin of metamorphosis	subadults two days after metamorphosis
time until end of reactions	298 ± 27 min	326 ± 26 min	> 5 days
time until death	395 ± 68 min	611 ± 123 min	> 5 days

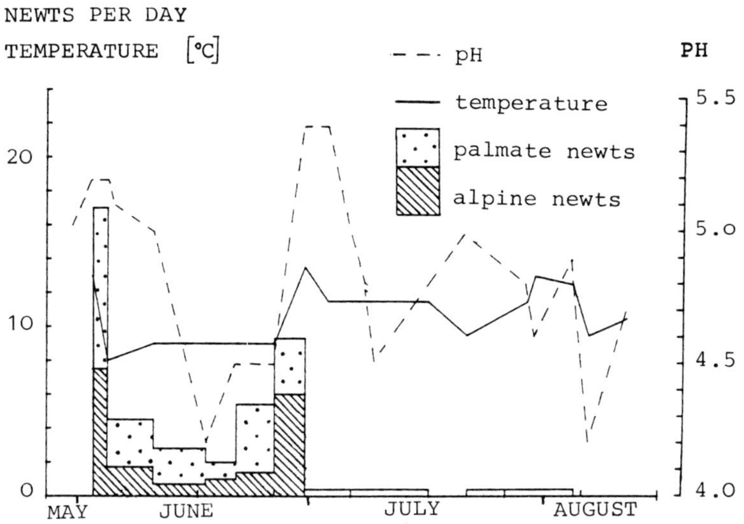

Fig. 2: Time course of trapping success in weir baskets, pH and temperature in the pond «Kaltenbachsee» in the northern Black Forest in 1987

gills and the changes in skin which occur during metamorphosis. In addition postmetamorphic amphibians may escape the harms of acid exposure by frequently leaving the water. Trapping results in the Black Forest/West Germany give evidence that less newts were in the water during a pH-depression (Fig. 2).

Obviously the occurrence of amphibians in acidic ponds is not limited by the acid resistance of the postmetamorphic stages. However, given other waters in the vicinity some amphibian species might avoid acidity by means of habitat selection (Strijbosch, 1979).

4. pH-effects on fertilization and development of eggs

The eggs of anurans are mostly fertilized externally in the water of the spawning habitat. Eggs and sperm are exposed to environmental conditions before and during gamete fusion. Sperm motility of *Rana pipiens* decreases with decreasing pH below 6.5–5.5 and stops below pH 4.5 (Schlichter, 1981). The sperm of Rana temporaria is even more acid sensitive. There was no motility below pH 6.0–6.3 (Gellhorn, 1927). Decreased sperm motility naturally leads to a smaller fertilization rate but the buffering capacity of jelly of the egg masses might lead to a higher pH in the egg clumps allowing fertilization despite a low pH in the water. The sperm of salamanders and newts is probably less affected since the spermatophore is exposed to ambient pH during pairing for a short time only and fertilization occurs internally.

Activation and cleavage of *Rana pipiens* eggs were less susceptible to low pH than fertilization (Schlichter, 1981). This is remarkable since most investigators have used fertilized eggs for acid toxicity tests and therefore probably underestimated the impact of acidity on amphibian reproduction.

Acid shock experiments revealed that exposure to low pH during any part of development of *Ambystoma jeffersonianum*, *Ambystoma maculatum* and *Xenopus laevis* caused increased mortality and an increased rate of abnormalities of hatchlings. Late developmental stages were slightly more susceptible to acid exposure than early stages (Tome and Pough, 1982). The authors therefore suggested that the lethal effects of acid media were concentrated on the superficial tissues. Amphibian embryos transferred to water of low pH were killed by two distinct processes: At extremely low pH levels embryos stopped developing soon after exposure to the test solutions whereas at more moderate but still lethal ph levels embryos became curled within the perivitelline membrane and failed to hatch. This has been called the curling defect (Freda and Dunson, 1985a; Pierce, 1987 and others, Fig. 3).

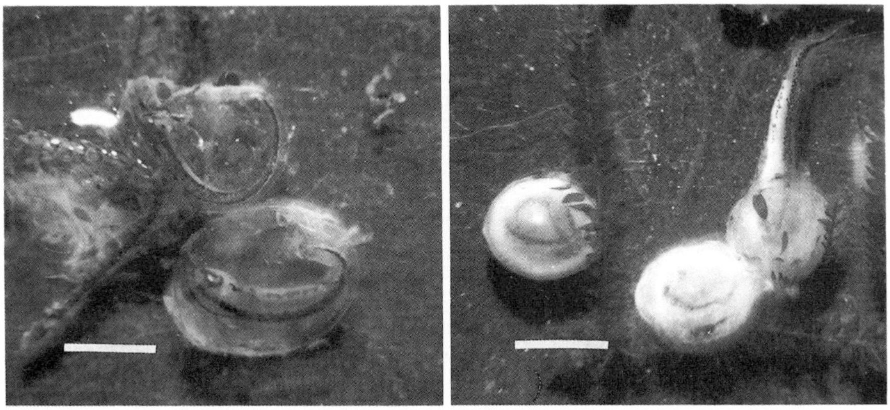

Fig. 3: Eggs of *Triturus vularis* at the beginning of hatching in pond water of pH 7 (a) and 4.4 (b). In strongly acidic water the developing embryos become curled within shrunken and opaque egg membranes (curling defect) and are often unable to hatch. (Bar = 0.25 cm)

Amphibian eggs are surrounded by the perivitelline membrane which consists of mostly protein and several jelly layers. Shortly after deposition of the egg the perivitelline membrane fits tightly around the ovum. As the embryo develops the perivitelline chamber increases keeping pace with the increasing length of the embryo. This process is thought to be caused by osmotic uptake of water through the perivitelline membrane. In later stages of development the outer jelly layers are ruptured by osmotic pressure in concert with a weakening of the membranes by a hatching enzyme which then further weakens the structure of the remaining membranes until they are ruptured by the movements of the embryo. Subsequent hatching occurs (Salthe, 1965; Carroll and Hedrick, 1974; Katagiri, 1963, 1972).

Acidity can interfere with these processes in several ways:

The jelly layers of the eggs become opaque at pH-values below 5 (Pierce, 1987, Fig. 3) indicating changes in physical and chemical properties.

The failure of the perivitelline chamber to expand during development (Freda and Dunson, 1985a; Dunson and Connell, 1982; Pough, 1976; Tome and Pough, 1982, Fig. 4) might be due to changes in membrane permeability or an increased resistance of the jelly layers against expansion.

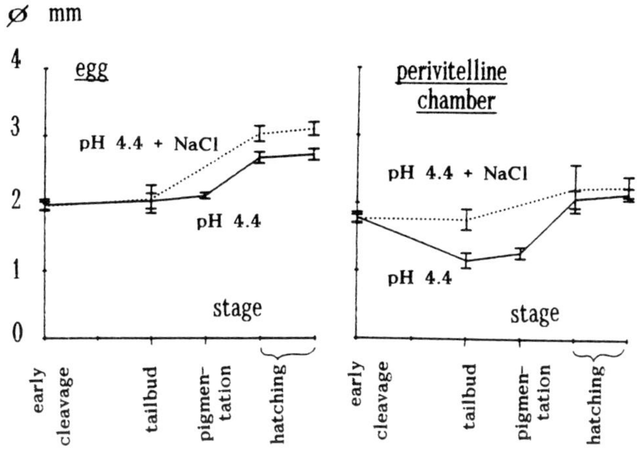

Fig. 4: Diameter of eggs and perivitelline chamber of *Triturus vulgaris* in pond water of pH 7 and 4.4 in dependance of development (mean ± sd, n = 5, natural pond water in aquariums at 20 °C

In vitro the hatching enzyme of *Xenopus laevis* is blocked at a pH near 4.0 (Urch and Hedrick, 1981 in Leuven et al., 1987).

For fish it has been shown that the lower activity levels of the embryos at low pH may also result in a failure to rupture the outer capsule membrane (Peterson et al., 1980 in Leuven et al., 1987). Anesthetization of *Xenopus laevis* embryos inhibited hatching (Carroll and Hedrick, 1974).

For all these reasons hatching of *Xenopus laevis* was blocked at pH 4.0. After artificial removal of the egg membranes, however, the larvae continued development (Dunson and Connell, 1982).

5. Effects of acidity on mortality of eggs

One important factor for the maintenance of a population is the reproductive success. Therefore many attempts have been made to assess the effects of acidity by investigating the pH dependance of embryonic mortality in the laboratory. Fewer experiments were carried out under field conditions. The pH sensitivity varies among the amphibian species but in general the critical pH for embryonic development is between 4 and 5 (Tab. 3).

Critical and lethal pH-values within a species often vary in different experiments indicating differences in intraspecific acid sensitivity or in experimental conditions. Therefore we investigated the embryonic pH-resistance of three newt species (*Triturus alpestris*, *T. helveticus*, *T. vulgaris*) undeer different experimental conditions: a) in water permeable boxes in the ponds (active monitoring), b) in aquariums filled with natural pond water and c) in aquarium filled with artificial soft water without aluminium or humic substances. In all cases embryonic mortality was low in neutral and moderately acid water but was rising sharply below a certain pH (Fig. 5 for *Triturus alpestris*, data for other species not shown). The lethal pH was 4.1 in natural water in field and laboratory whereas it was between 3.7 and 3.9 in artificial soft water. These results indicate that the chemical composition of the

Table 3: Critical pH (50% mortality) and lethal pH for development of amphibian embryos (data from field or laboratory studies)

species	critical pH	lethal pH	source
Acris gryllus	4.2–4.6	4.0–4.1	Gosner and Black, 1957
Ambystoma jeffersonianum	4.0–5.0	4.0–4.6	Gosner and Black, 1957 Cook, 1978 in Leuven et al., 1987
Ambystoma laterale		4.2	Karns, 1983 in Freda, 1986
Ambystoma maculatum	5.0–7.0	4.0–5.0	Cook, 1978 in Leuven et al., 1987 Freda and Dunson, 1985a, b Gosner and Black, 1957 Pough, 1976
Ambystoma texanum	5.0		Punzo, 1983 in Freda, 1986
Bufo americanus	4.1–4.2	4.0 3.8–4.2	Clark and Lazerte, 1985, Freda and Dunson, 1985a, b Freda, 1986
Bufo bufo	4.0–4.5	3.5–4.0	Leuven et al., 1987, Strijbosch, 1979,
Bufo boreas	4.0		Porter and Hakanson, 1976 in Freda, 1986
Bufo calamita		< 3.8	Strijbosch, 1979
Bufo woodhousei	4.2	4.0	Freda, 1986
Hyla andersoni	3.6–3.8	3.4–3.7	Gosner and Black, 1957; Freda, 1986
Hyla crucifer	4.0–4.2	3.8	Gosner and Black, 1957
Hyla versicolor	3.9–4.3	3.8	Gosner and Black, 1957
Rana arvalis	4.0–4.5	3.5–4.3	Leuven et al., 1987; Strijbosch, 1979
Rana catesbeiana	4.1–4.3	3.9	Gosner and Black, 1957; Saber and Dunson, 1978
Rana clamitans	3.8–4.3	3.7–3.8	Gosner and Black, 1957; Saber and Dunson, 1978
Rana dalmatina	3.1–>4.0	3.0–>4.0	Andrén et al., 1988, Gebhardt et al., 1987
Rana 'esculenta'	4.0–4.5	3.5–4.0	Leuven et al., 1987; Strijbosch, 1979
Rana palustris	4.2–4.4	3.9–4.0	Gosner and Black, 1957; Freda, 1986
Rana pipiens	<4.5–6.0	<4.5–5.8	Schlichter, 1981; Freda and Dunson, 1985a; Freda, 1986
Rana sylvatica	3.5–4.0	3.5–4.0	Gosner and Black, 1957; Freda and Dunson, 1985a; Tome and Pough, 1982
Rana sphenocephala	4.1		Pierce, 1987
Rana temporaria	4.0–4.5	3.5–4.0	Gebhardt et al., 1987; Leuven et al., 1987; Strijbosch, 1979
Rana utricularia	3.9–4.1	3.7	Gosner and Black, 1957
Rana virgatiopes	3.6–3.8	3.4	Gosner and Black, 1957
Triturus alpestris	4.0–4.3	3.7–4.1	Böhmer, 1988; Böhmer et al., 1988
Triturus helveticus	4.0–4.3	3.7–4.1	Böhmer, 1988
Triturus vulgaris	4.3–4.6	4.0–4.4	Böhmer, 1988
Pelobates fuscus		4.5	Strijbosch, 1979
Pseudacris nigrita	3.9–4.1	3.8	Gosner and Black, 1957
Pseudacris triseriata		4.2	Karns, 1983 in Freda, 1986
Xenopus laevis	3.5–4.7	3.0–4.3	Dunson and Connell, 1982; Saber and Dunson, 1978; Tome and Pough, 1982

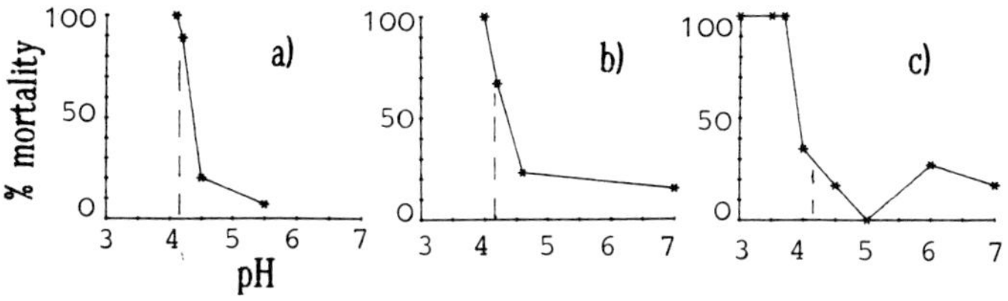

Fig. 5: Mortality of embryonic alpine newts in dependance of pH, a) exposure to natural pond water, b) to aquariums filled with water from ponds and c) to aquariums filled with artificial soft water. (N ≥ 2, n = 15)

water is more important for the pH-resistance than the temperature or other factors (field: 12–17 °C, pH varying around mean; aquarium: 21–22 °C, constant pH).

The reduced hatching success in natural water could be due to its aluminium content which was about 1 mgAl/l at pH 4.0. Aluminium accumulation in eggs of *Rana temporaria* was observed in acidic water. The aluminium concentration was 70–150 μg/g dry weight in one day old egg clumps at pH-values between 4.5 and 5.0 in the field (LFU 1988). For fish it was shown that aluminium toxicity varied with pH and the inorganic and organic complexes that it forms (Baker and Schofield, 1980; McCahon and Pascoe, 1989). Clark and Lazerte (1985) found that the addition of as little as 10 μg inorganic monomeric aluminium (IMAl)/l at pH ≤ 4.34 further reduced hatching success of *Bufo americanus*. Hatching success of *Rana sylvatica* was reduced by the addition of 20 μg IMAl/l at pH 4.14. Increasing aluminium concentrations at pH 4.14 seemed to have no further effect except at the highest level used (200 μg/l). IMAl that was toxic at pH ≤ 4.34 had no effect at pH ≥ 4.75. Aluminium toxicity did not depend on aluminium specification. Similar levels of $Al(OH)_x$, Al^{3+} and $Al(F)_x$ had the same effect. A significant rise in embryonic mortality of *Rana temporaria* at 92.5 and 185 μg IMAl/l compared with aluminium free treatments was reported by Leuven et al. (1987).

Hatching success at low pH also might be influenced by the ionic composition of the water. Freda and Dunson (1985 a) reported that the early mortality of embryos in acidic test solutions was reduced by increased concentrations of Ca, Mg and to a lesser extend Na. However, low pH and high concentrations of cations acted synergistically to reduce the volume of the perivitelline membrane leading to an increased curling defect. Since *Ambystoma maculatum* and *A. jeffersonianum* were generally able to hatch even though they became curled whereas *Rana sylvatica* remained trapped and died, hatching success at low pH was increased for the two *Ambystoma* species with higher cation concentrations and reduced for *Rana sylvatica*. Freda and Dunson (1985 a) tested 1, 10, 20, 40 and 80 mg of each cation/l. But cation levels in acidic waters are generally very low (< 2 mg/l). The addition of Na (6 mg/l) to natural pond water (< 0.5 mg/l of Na, K, Ca and Mg respectively) raised the hatching success of *Triturus vulgaris* by reducing the mortality of embryos and decreasing the portion of fully developed embryos remaining trapped in the eggs (Table 4). Sodium addition also caused an expansion of the perivitelline chamber during embryonic development (Fig. 6). However the differences between the Na-rich and Na-poor treatments vanished towards hatching. This might be due to an inhibitory effect of cations on the hatching enzyme at low pH as suggested by Freda and Dunson (1985 a) and Urch and Hedrick (1981).

These findings indicate that much caution is necessary in comparing the results of acid toxicity tests conducted in media of different composition.

Table 4: Mortality and percentage of fully developed embryos of *Triturus vulgaris* unable to hatch in aquariums with water from the pond «Schurmsee»/Black Forest with and without the addition of 6 mg Na/l as NaCl. (20 °C, constant pH, N = number of treatments, n = number of eggs)

	% mortality	% unable to hatch (concerning fully developed embryos)
pH 4.4	95 (N = 3, n = 52)	40
pH 4.4 + Na	53 (N = 2, n = 30)	30

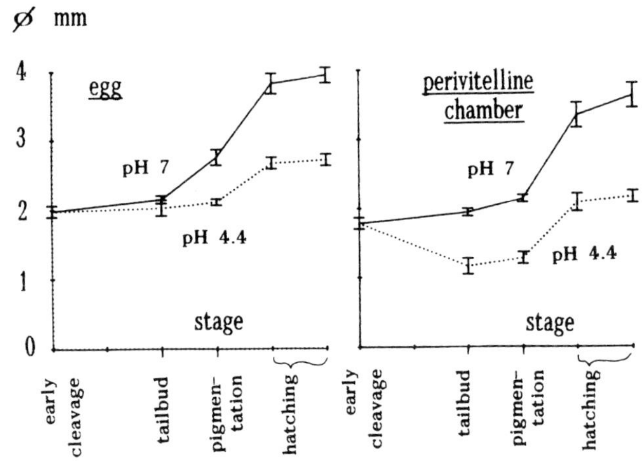

Fig. 6: Diameter of eggs and perivitelline chamber of Triturus vulgaris in pond water of pH 4.4 with 0.6 mg Na/l and 6.6 mg Na/l (addition of NaCl) in dependance of development (mean ± sd, n = 5, 20 °C).

6. Effects of acidity on mortality of larvae

Amphibian larvae tend to be less sensitive towards acidity than embryos (Gebhardt et al., 1987; Clark and Hall, 1985; Clark and Lazerte, 1985; Freda and Dunson, 1987b). Cummins (1986) raised *Rana temporaria* tadpoles from hatching until metamorphosis at pH 3.6 without losses whereas the critical pH for the embryos is about 4.5 (see Tab. 3). However those tadpoles had to be adapted over several days to increasingly acid conditions. But in nature sudden pH-drops occur, especially after heavy rainstorms. In another study *Rana temporaria* tadpoles suffered about 45% mortality within 72 hours after sudden exposure to pH 3.6 (Gebhardt et al., 1987). We observed high mortality of *Rana temporaria* tadpoles (estimated 30%) in a small pond after a short time pH-drop from pH 4.5 to 3.6. Mortality of newt larvae beeing raised in plastic screen cages in ponds also seemed to be more a result of sudden pH-drops rather than by the lowest occurring pH-value (Fig. 7). Obviously amphibian larvae can adapt to more acidity if the decline in pH is slow or in steps. This is also indicated by acid shock experiments: *Triturus helveticus* larvae acclimated to pH 4.4 survived longer in pH 3.6 water than larvae from neutral water (Table 5).

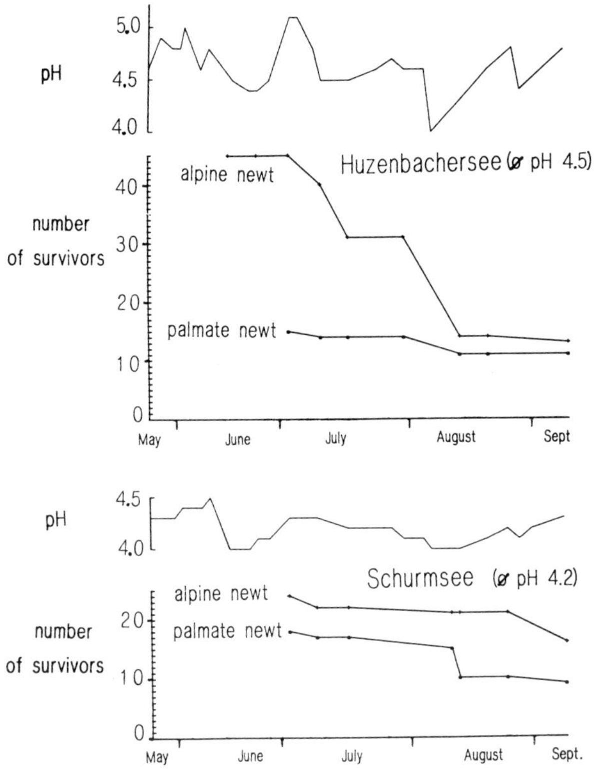

Fig. 7: PH and number of surviving newt larvae in exposure experiments in two acidic ponds in the Black Forest during 1987. In the Huzenbachersee most of the alpine newt larvae were killed during the two main pH-drops whereas in the Schurmsee with an always lower pH but without sudden pH-drops only few larvae died.

Table 5: Differences in survival time in pH 3.6 pond water between palmate newt larvae which had developed in neutral and pH 4.4 water. (Larvae 5 days after hatching, 20 °C, mean ± sd, n = 17)

larvae from	survival time (hours)
neutral water	6 ± 2
pH 4.4 water	19 ± 2

Mortality of different species of amphibian larvae at low pH has been reported by many studies but only very little is known about the portion of larvae reaching metamorphosis under chronic acid stress. We raised the larvae of three newt species in artificial soft water at different pH-values. More than 60% of the successfully hatched larvae metamorphized between pH 7 and 4.5 but the percentage dropped rapidly with decreasing pH and was zero at pH 3.75 (Fig. 8). However acid induced mortality might be compensated or enhanced under natural conditions in the field, e.g. due to different predator prey relationships. This has not been investigated yet.

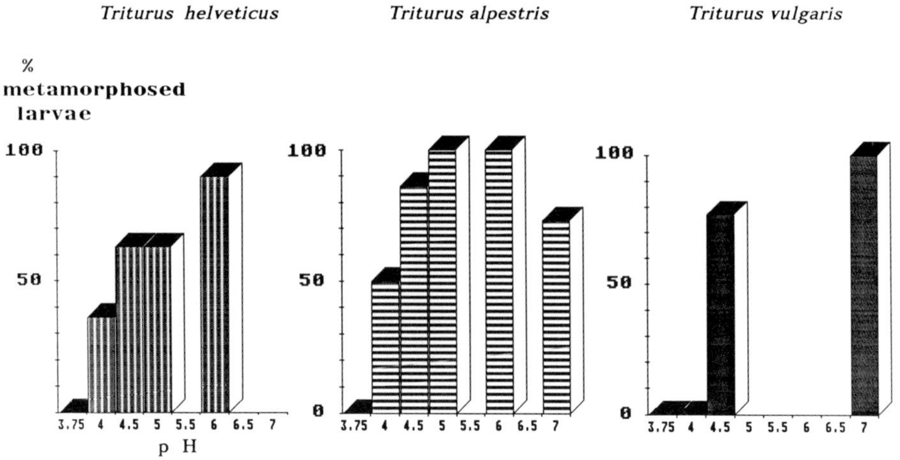

Fig. 8: Percentage of newt larvae reaching metamorphosis in dependance of pH in aquariums filled with artificial soft water. (21 °C, 12 h photoperiod)

Survival times of amphibian larvae under lethal acid stress are correlated with pH (e.g. Freda and Dunson, 1984) but ontogenetic changes in sensitivity may occur (Freda and Dunson, 1985b; Pierce et al., 1984, Tab. 2).

Survival also depends on cation concentration. Pilot experiments revealed that survival times of newt larvae in natural pond water of pH 3.6 are doubled after the addition of 6 mg Na/l (Tab. 6).

Table 6: Survival times of palmate newt larvae in pond water of pH 3.7 with 0.7 mg Na/l and 6.7 mg Na/l (addition of NaCl, larvae 5 days after hatching, 20 °C, mean ± sd, n = 5).

water	survival time
pH 3.7	223 ± 55 min
pH 3.7 + NaCl	423 ± 109 min

Calcium reduced larval mortality of *Rana sylvatica* at pH 4.5 and 7.4 μM total dissolved aluminium/l (Gascon et al., 1987).

Aluminium has been shown to increase larval mortality of several amphibian species at concentrations as frequently found in acidic waters (Andrén et al., 1988; Cummins, 1986; Leuven et al., 1987; Huckabee et al., 1975 in Andrén et al., 1988).

7. Differences in acid tolerance within species

Embryos coming from different acidic ponds varied in acid tolerance but hatching success was not dependant on the pH of the ponds whereas tadpoles from acidic ponds survived better in acidic solutions than tadpoles from neutral ponds (Pierce and Harvey,

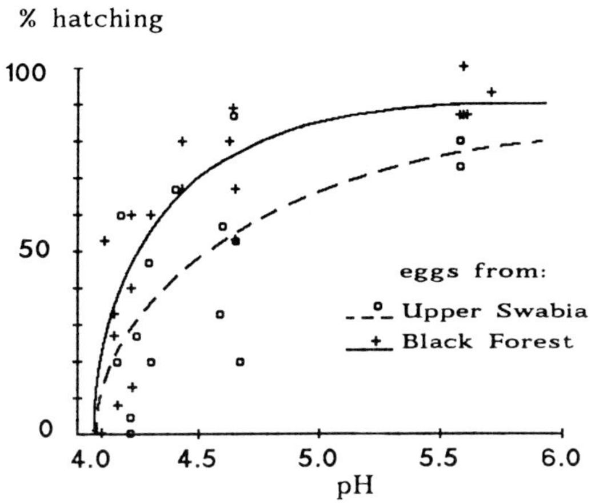

Fig. 9: Differences in hatching success of alpine newt larvae from differently acidic regions in southern Germany exposed in acidic ponds of the Black Forest (n = 15 eggs per assay)

1987). In another study salamander embryos from different acidic ponds did not differ in acid sensitivity whereas the offspring of different pairs of *Xenopus laevis* did (Tome and Pough, 1982). Controlled crosses among frogs indicated that individual differences in acid tolerance were genetically based (Pierce and Sikand, 1983).

In acidic ponds the hatching success of alpine newt embryos whose parents came from a region of West Germany with hard and neutral waters was lower than that of alpine newt embryos whose parents came from the Black Forest, a soft water region with many naturally acidic and also acidified ponds (Fig. 9).

These findings indicate that there is a genetical variation of acid tolerance within species but genetical adaptation did not appear as rapidly as many waters were acidified. But there might have evolved genetical adaptations to low ionic levels in soft water regions like a more efficient sodium uptake which increases tolerance of acid stress since acid sensitivity is dependant on osmoregulatory capabilities (see chapter 8).

8. Sublethal harms and physiological responses of amphibian embryos and larvae to acid stress

Acidity causes abnormalities in amphibian development. Eggs from ponds with pHs of 4.5 to 5.0 failed to retract yolk plugs whereas those from pH 5.5 developed normally through gastrulation but subsequently developed swellings on the chest and stunted gills (Tome and Pough, 1982). In chapter 4, we already described that amphibian embryos became curled in a shrunken perivitelline chamber (curling defect). If the embryos don't fail to hatch this can lead to delay in hatching (Andrén et al., 1988; Gascon et al., 1987) which could have consequences for the competitive ability and could also increase the risk of *Saprolegnia* infection (Leuven et al., 1987). The curling defect might also contribute to the significant increase in deformities of hatchlings (e.g. crooked vertebrate columns) at low pH which can reach 100% near the lethal pH (Andrén et al., 1988; Pierce et al., 1984; Gosner and Black, 1957). Acid stress on tadpoles can also lead to deformities of metamorphized tadpoles. Cummins (1986) reported the occurrence of acid-induced limb deformities. Based on his experiments he suggested that these deformities represented an extreme manifestation of a physiological disturbance.

Amphibian larvae exhibited abnormal behaviour under acid and aluminium stress like reeling uncoordinated swimming, diminished flight reactions, laying motionless on the ground (sometimes upside down) and not feeding (Gebhardt et al., 1987; Andrén et al., 1988; own observations). Therefore it is not surprising that growth rates and maximum body size were reduced and metamorphosis was delayed with decreasing pH for *Rana*

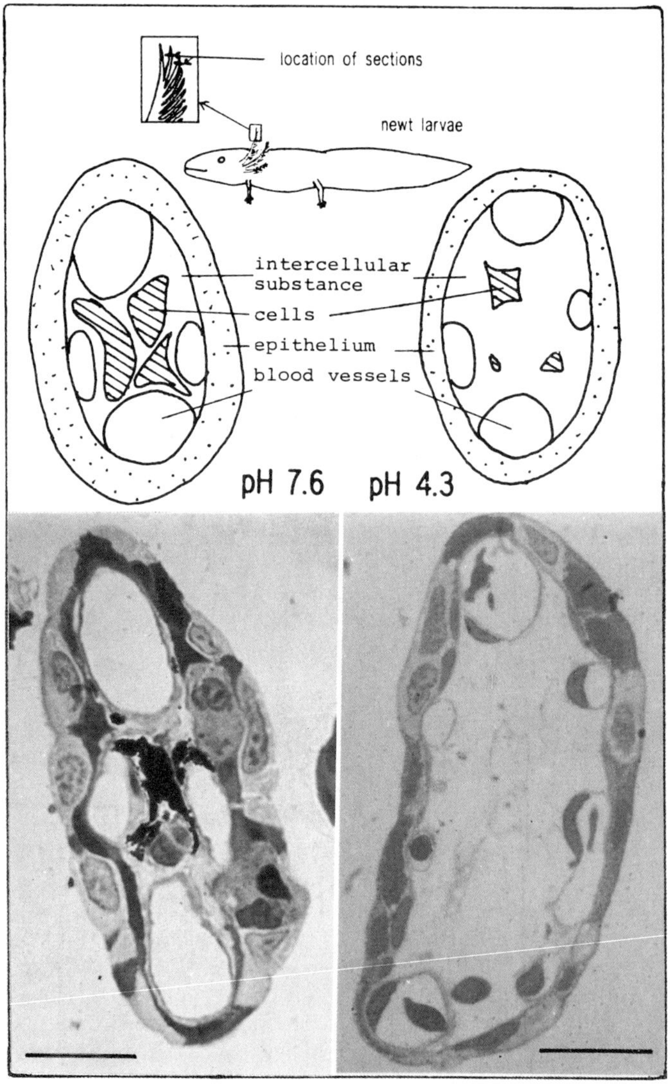

Fig. 10: Schematic drawings and photomicrographs of cross sections through the gills of alpine newt larvae from differently acidic ponds. (Bar = 50μm)

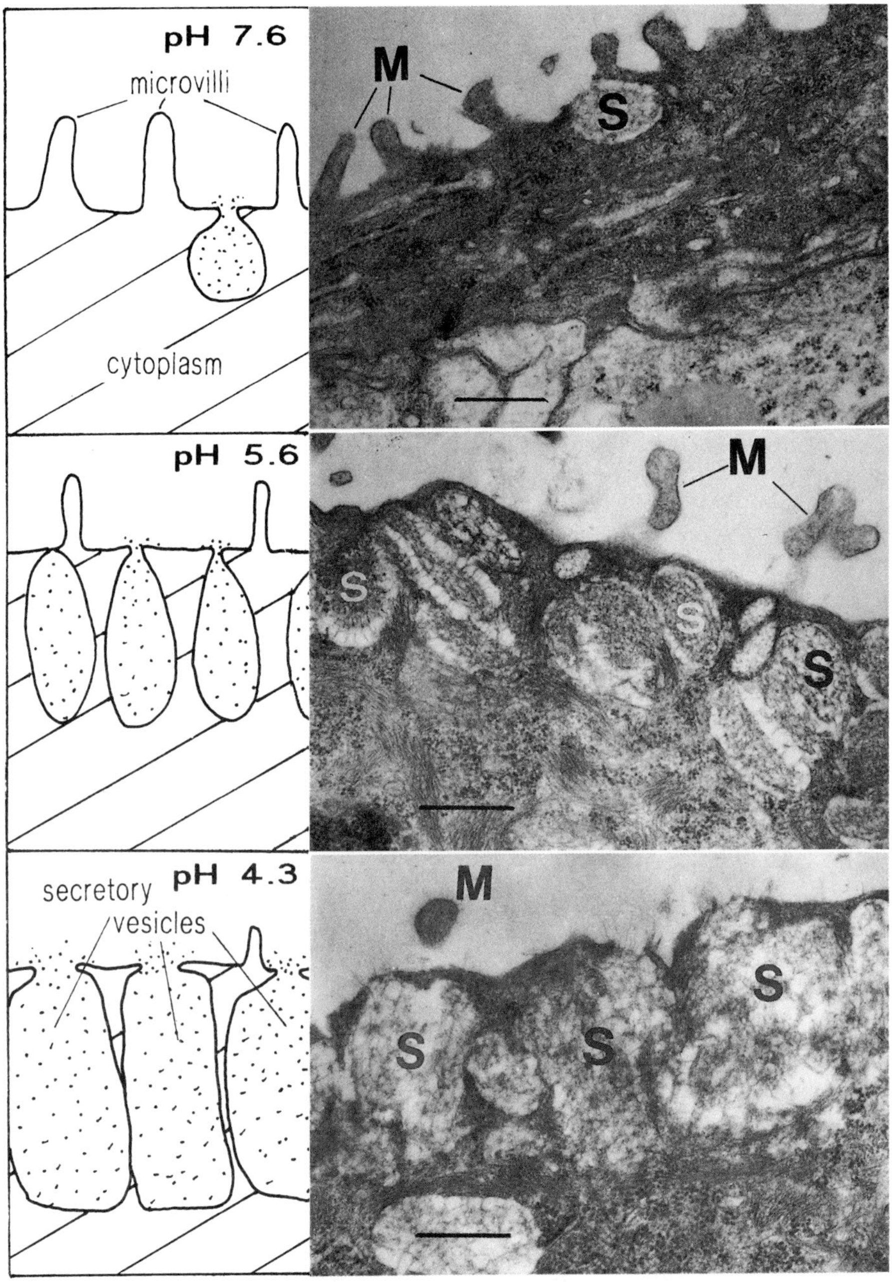

Fig. 11: Schematic drawings and photomicrographs of the surface of the gill epithelium of alpine newt larvae from differently acidic ponds. (Transmission electron microscope, bar = 0.5 μm)

temporaria tadpoles. Growth was depressed and metamorphosis delayed by 800 μg Al/l, too. At 1600 μg Al/l small tadpoles suffered arrested growth and development and eventually died while larger tadpoles metamorphosed without delay (Cummins, 1986). Gascon et al. (1987) showed that *Rana sylvatica* tadpoles in acid water with aluminium needed less time to reach metamorphosis but duration of metamorphosis was much longer than for tadpoles in neutral water.

How does acidity act onto amphibian larvae? One of the organs most likely to be directly affected by acidic water are the gills. The gill is important for oxygen uptake and osmoregulation. By means of light and electron microscopy we observed that gills from newt larvae from acid ponds had relatively much more intercellular substance in the connective tissue, smaller blood vessels and thinner epithelia than the gills from newt larvae from neutral water (Fig. 10). On the surface of the epithelia of the acid-affected gills much more and larger secretory vesicles were found and the number of microvilli became less with decreasing pH (Fig. 11). An increased mucous secretion also occurred on the skin of *Rana temporaria* tadpoles from acid water (Linnenbach et al., 1987). Aluminium is toxic for amphibian larvae (see chapter 6). By means of ESI (electron spectroscopic imaging) aluminium can be found in the gills of *Triturus* larvae from a pond with an average

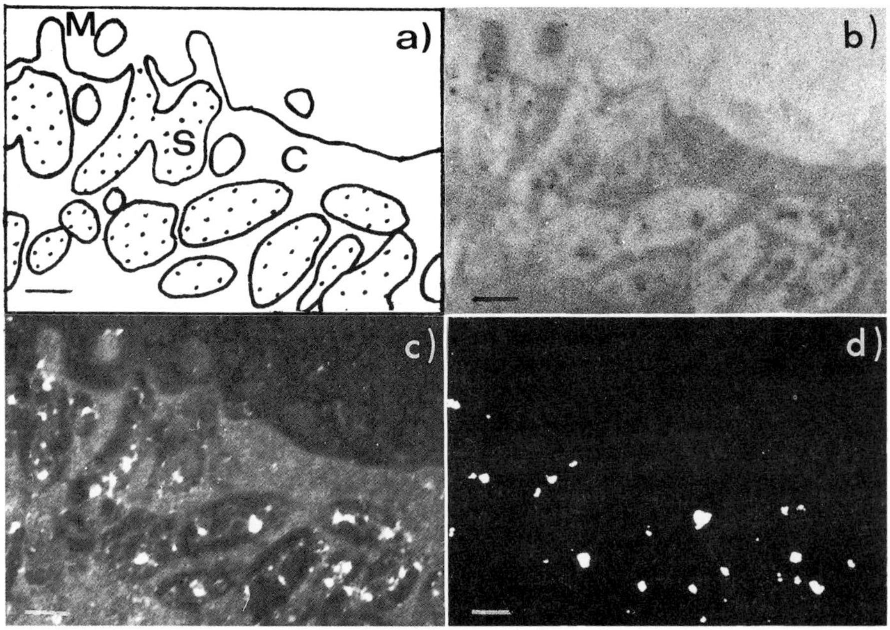

Fig. 12: Evidence of aluminium in the gill epithelium of *Triturum helveticus* larvae from the pond «Huzenbachersee» with an average pH of 4.6:

a) drawing of a part of an epithelial cell, b) regular transmission electron microscopic image of unstained ultrathin section (30 nm), c) ESI (electron spectroscopic imaging with the Zeiss CEM 902) created darkfield image of the same section as in b) produced by inelastcally scattered electrons of the energy loss of 250 eV and d) aluminium distribution image of the same section as b) and c). This image was obtained by computer assisted processing of ESI images above (1580 eV) and below (1540 eV) the aluminium specific energy loss. (Bar = 0,25 μm, S = secretory vesicle, M = microvilli, C = cytoplasm) pH of 4.6 and about 0.5 mg Al/l (Fig. 12). First and preliminary results indicate that the aluminium is located in the secretory vesicles of the epithelial cells, other vesicles in all cell types and in the intercellular substance.

The observed histological changes of skin and gills might interfere with respiratory function and osmoregulation. Disturbances of the osmoregulation, mainly losses of sodium and chloride are thought to be the main cause of death in acid water for amphibian larvae as well as for fish (Freda and Dunson, 1984; McDonald, 1983; McDonald et al., 1984). Alpine newt larvae under lethal acid stress (ph 3.6) lost 72% of their whole body sodium and 36% of their whole body potassium prior to death (Tab. 7).

Table 7: Relative whole body sodium and potassium content of alpine newt larvae prior to death after exposure to natural water of pH 3.6 (larvae were killed for analysis when blood circulation began to callpse; n = 3, mean ± sd)

	Na/dry weight (μg/mg)	K/dry weight (μg/mg)
control	19.4 ± 0.4	28.6 ± 1.4
pH 3.6	5.5 ± 0.4	21.1 ± 0.3
difference	13.9 (= 72% of control)	7.5 (= 36% of control)

Reduction of body sodium at death for three *Rana* species killed by acute acid exposure at pH 3.0 was about 50%. Chronic exposure to acid solutions resulted in a 21–62% reduction. Potassium contents did not change. These net ion losses were caused by a decrease in Na-influx and an increase in Na-efflux with decreasing pH. Elevated calcium concentrations (from 0.025 to 5 mM) reduced Na-efflux of *Rana pipiens* tadpoles during acute acid exposure significantly and increased the survival time fourfold (Freda and Dunson, 1984). McDonald et al. (1984) showed that net losses of Na, K, CL and Ca were mainly due to stimulation of efflux. Inhibition of Na-uptake also contributed to the net Na-loss while Cl-influx was not significantly reduced. Net ion losses largely disappeared within several hours of acid exposure. Acclimation to pH 5.0 for 12 days did not reduce net ion losses at pH 4.0 though ion efflux was slightly smaller. The reason was a more pronounced inhibition of the Na-uptake of the pH 5 acclimated tadpoles which could not be restored in neutral water. In contrast pH 7 acclimated animals showed an almost twofold increase in Na-uptake after the return from pH 4.0 to neutral water. Therefore the authors suggested that dormant ion carrier transport sites might have been activated by salt depletion. These dormant ion transporting sites might have been lost by low pH acclimated animals possibly as a result of some low level damage to the external epithelium.

Interspecific differences in acid tolerance seem to be correlated with differences in disturbance of ion regulation. In fish increasing sensitivity to exposure to low pH was characterized by shorter survival times and greater losses of whole-body ions. Na-efflux was the most important factor in determining survival (Freda and McDonald, 1988).

9. Possible mechanisms of disturbance of osmoregulation in acid water

Ion movements in tight epithelia (= epithelia with tight junctions and therefore low diffusion permeability of the apical cell junctions) have been mainly studied in isolated frog skin (reviewed by van Driessche and Zeiske, 1985). Active Na- and K-transport is limited to the basolateral membrane. Na-pumps accumulate Na in the intercellular spaces in exchange for potassium leading to a high potassium and low sodium concentration in the cells. Passive diffusion of potassium back into the intercellular space generates a negative potential inside the cells which together with the very low sodium concentration in the epithelial cells leads to a diffusion of sodium from the water into the cells. Sodium diffusion occurs through Na-specific channels in the apical membrane (Fig. 13). This step seems to be rate limiting for transepithelial Na-uptake.

The apical Na-channels are chemically gated (in contrast to the voltage dependent Na-channels of excitable membranes). Their most important properties are: sodium self inhibition, stimulation of the Na-current by low concentrations of metal cations (even heavy metals) and H^+ between pH 5 and 7 (probably by releasing the channels from Na self inhibition), inhibition of Na-influx at pH < 5 (by protonation of important functional groups and competitive inhibition) and an intracellular regulation of Na-transport by Ca and hormones.

At low pH the diffusional permeability of the tight junctions increases causing a loss of ions from the intercellular space through this so-called «paracellular pathway» (Ferreira and Hill 1982, Fig. 13). Presumably the protones displace Ca from negatively charged glycoproteines which seal the tight junctions.

Besides the direct effects of the protones on the properties of the ionic channels and the paracellular pathway indirect influences have to be considered. Bolis et al. (1984) reported about changes in fatty acid and phospholipid composition in the gills of trout after 48 hours at low pH. This might also effect membrane properties in respect of transepithelial ion movements.

The properties and reactions of tight epithelia reported in this chapter might explain a variety of reactions of acid stressed amphibians and fish which have been described in literature:

1. transepithelial net losses of sodium and other ions (McDonald, 1983; McDonald et al., 1984; Freda and Dunson, 1984; Freda and McDonald, 1988; several papers in Witters and Vanderborght, 1987) as a result of increased diffusional permeability of the tight junctions and a decreased permeability of the apical membrane (→ less influx, Fig. 13).
2. Elevated Ca concentrations decrease sodium losses, prolong survival times and decrease embryonic and larval mortality (e.g. Freda and Dunson, 1984 and 1985;

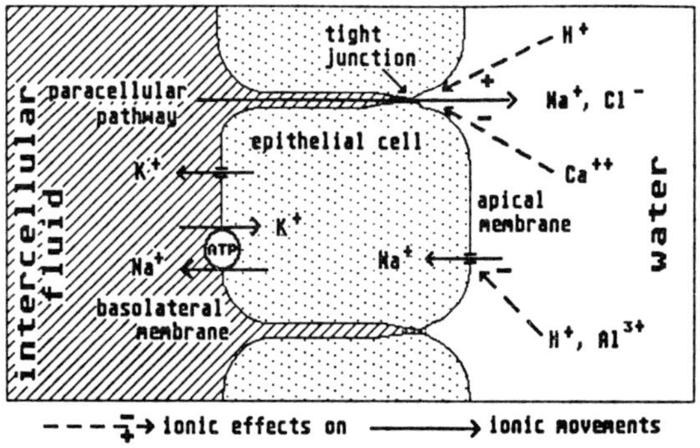

Fig. 13: Model of the ionic movements and the ionic effects influencing the sodium budget of amphibian epithelia.

Gascon et al., 1987 for amphibians; Brown, 1983; Sadler and Lynam, 1986; Wood and McDonald, 1987 and others for fish) by replacing displaced Ca in the tight junctions (Fig. 13).

3. Elevated external Na concentrations increase the diffusional gradient between epithelial cell and external medium thus thriving more sodium into the cell. Increasing Na concentration was shown to stimulate Na-uptake in fish (Bornancin et al. 1987) and to reduce amphibian embryonic mortality (Freda and Dunson, 1985a).
4. Salmonid larvae were killed in water of extremely low ionic strength within two weeks at pH 6.0. Mortality was low after slightly rising Na, Al or H^+ (pH > 4.5) concentrations (Hutchinson et al., 1987). The reason could be a diffusional loss of Ca from the tight junctions causing Na-losses and subsequent death. Na-losses after removal of external Ca were reported by Cuthbert and Maetz (1972) and Eddy (1975), both cited in McDonald (1983).

   Elevated but still low levels of H^+, Al, Na and other metal cations increase Na-channel permeability and subsequent Na-uptake. Higher Al-levels however decrease Na-uptake (Wood and McDonald, 1987).
5. *Rana clamitans* tadpoles were able to compensate sublethal ion losses at sublethal pH by enhancing Na-influx (hormonal regulation?) and diminishing Na-efflux. Chronically acid stressed larvae could less increase Na-influx (McDonald et al., 1984). We suggest that this might be an effect of the reduced surface area of the epithelial cells due to a loss of microvilli (Fig. 11). A smaller surface area could mean less Na-channels which limit maximum Na-uptake.

10. Relations between the different effects of acidity

Tab. 8 summarizes the autecological effects of acidity on amphibians. Aluminium and H^+ directly cause a variety of abnormalities like decreased fertilization, changes in egg membranes, disturbance of osmoregulation and epithelial structure. Consequently secondary and tertiary phenomena are likely to occur. Amphibian larvae are harmed in their anatomy (deformities), physiology (e.g. respiration and excretion through the epithelium)

Table 8: Autecological effects of acidity, especially H^+ and aluminium, on amphibians

acidic water directly or indirectly induces

- inhibition of fertilization
- alteration of egg membranes
- deformities of embryos, larvae and adults
- alterations in structure and ultrastructure of gills and other organs
- disturbances of osmoregulation, respiration, excretion and other physiological functions

resulting consequences are

- increased energy requirement to maintain metabolism and body functions
- deformities of adults
- disturbances of behaviour (e.g. flight from predators, feeding)
- reduction in growth
- decrease in reproductive success
- decrease in survival
- reduction in population size

and behaviour. More energy might be required to maintain normal body functions, growth is reduced and the competitive abilities of the animals are decreased. Subsequently less larvae survive until metamorphosis. Those which do metamorphize might have irreversible harms like deformities (Cummins, 1987) or other abnormalities which diminish the success in survival, competition and finally reproduction. As a consequence the population becomes smaller or even vanishes.

However, synecological aspects have to be considered, too. Acidity also effects other organisms of an ecosystem. Subsequently changes of the predator prey-relationships in the complex food web take place which are difficult to predict (Fig. 14). As an example amphibian population size might increase with decreasing pH when the fish fauna is extinguished as observed in the Swedish lake Tranevatten (Hagström, 1977 and 1980 in Leuven et al., 1987). Due to less fish carnivorous invertebrates might become more numerous. This, however, might decrease amphibian reproductive success again.

In conclusion amphibians are harmed in acidic waters. At sublethal pH synecological effects of acidity might be more important. With continuing acidification, however, embryonic and larval development finally fails leading to the extinction of amphibian populations in very acid sensitive waters.

Amphibians exhibit specific responses to acidity as discribed in this paper. Even the ultrastructure of cells reflects environmental conditions (Storch, 1987 and Fig. 11). Therefore amphibians could be useful tools for indicating water acidity. Mortality rates, abnormalities and morphological changes can be quantified and could indicate even short episodical events otherwise could be only assessed by continuous monitoring of water chemistry. However, more research is necessary to clearly distinguish between the effects of acidity and other possible factors.

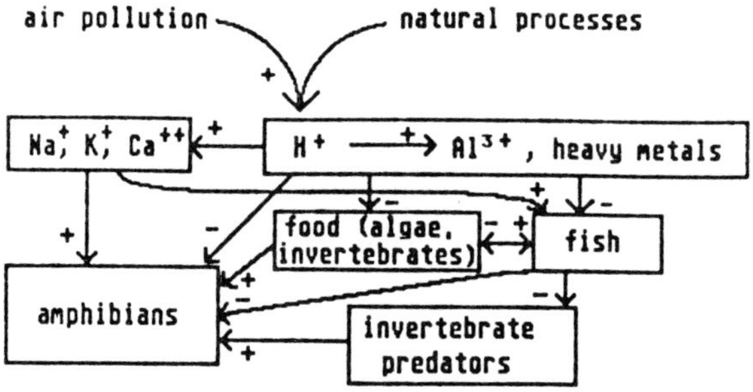

Fig. 14: Simplified model of synecological effects of acidification on amphibians

References

Andrén, C., Henrikson, L, Olsson, M., Nilson, G. (1988): Effects of pH and aluminium on embryonic and early larval stages of Swedish brown frogs *Rana arvalis*, *R. temporaria* and *R. dalmatina*. Holarctic Ecology, *11*, 127–135.

Baker, J. P. and Schofield, C. L. (1980): Aluminium toxicity of fish in acidic waters. Water Air and Soil Pollution *18*, 289–309.

Battarbee, R. W., Charles, D. F. (1986): Diatom-based pH reconstruction studies of acidic lakes in europe and north america: a synthesis. Water, Air and Soil Pollution *39*, 347–354.

Böhmer, J. (1988): Labor- und Feldstudien zum Einfluß niedriger pH-Werte auf die frühe Entwicklung von Molchen im Schwarzwald. Diploma thesis, University of Hohenheim, FRG, 91 pp.

Böhmer, J., Bauser-Eckstein, A., Rahmann, H. (1988): Labor- und Feldstudien zum Einfluß niedriger pH-Werte auf Molche. Abstract. In: Gefährdung und Schutz von Gewässern (Kohler, A. und Rahmann, H., eds.), pp. 225–228, Hohenheimer Arbeiten, Ulmer Verlag.

Bolis, C. L., Cambria, A., Fama, M. (1984): Effects of acid stress on fish gills. In: Toxins, Drugs and Pollutants in Marine Animals (Bolis et al., eds.), pp. 122–129, Springer-Verlag Berlin Heidelberg.

Bornancin, M. A., Gardaire, E., Nance, J.-M., Isaia, J., Masoni, A., Mayer-Gostan, N. (1987): Sodium and potassium influx in freshwater trout: the influence of acclimation to various freshwater environments on gill structure and sodium branchial uptake. In: Ecophysiology of acid stress in aquatic organisms (H. Witters, O. Vanderborght, eds.). Annls. Soc. r. Belg. 117.

Brown, D. J. A. (1983): Effect of calcium and aluminium concentrationon the survival of brown trout (*Salmo trutta*) at low pH. Bull. Environ. Contam. Toxicol. *30*, 582–587.

Carroll, E. J. Jr., Hedrick, J. L. (1974): Hatching in the toad *Xenopus laevis*: morphological events and evidence for a hatching enzyme. Develop. Biol. *38*, 1–13.

Clark, K. (1986): Distribution of anuran populations in central Ontario relative to habitat acidity. Water, Air and Soil Pollution *30*, 727–734.

Clark, K. L., Hall, R. J. (1985): Effects of elevated hydrogen ion and aluminium concentrations on amphibian embryos and larvae. Can. J. Zool. *63*, 116–123.

Clark, K. L., LaZerte, B. D. (1985): A laboratory study of the effects of aluminium and pH on amphibian eggs and tadpoles. Can. J. Fish. Aquat. Sci. *42*, 1544–1551.

Clausnitzer, H.-J. (1979): Durch Umwelteinflüsse gestörte Entwicklung beim Laich des Moorfrosches (*Rana arvalis* L.). Beitr. Naturk. Niedersachsens *32*, 68–78.

Cook, R. P. (1978): Effects of acid precipitation on embryonic mortality of spotted salamanders (*Ambystoma maculatum*) and Jefferson salamander (*A. jeffersonianum*) in the connecticut valley of Massachusetts. Thesis, University of Massachusetts, Amherst.

Cummins, C. P. (1986): Effects of aluminium and low pH on growth and development of *Rana temporaria* tadpoles. Oecologia *69*, 248–252.

Cuthbert, A. W., Maetz, J. (1972): The effects of calcium and magnesium on sodium fluxes through the gills of *Carassius auratus*. J. Physiol. (London) *221*, 633–643.

Davis, R. B., Stokes, P. M. (1986): Overview of historical and palaeoecological studies of acidic air pollution and its effects. Water Air and Soil Pollution *30*, 311–318.

Dickmann, M. (1968): The effect of grazing by tadpoles on the structure of a periphyton community. Ecology *49*, 1188–1190.

Dixit, S. S., Dixit, A. S., Evans, R. D. (1988): Chrysophyte scales in lake sediments provide evidence of recent acidification in two Quebec (Canada) lakes. Water, Air and Soil Pollution *38*, 97–104.

Dunson, W. A., Connell, J. (1982): Specific inhibition of hatching in amphibian embryos by low pH. Journal of herpetology *16*, 314–316.

Eddy, F. B. (1975): The effect of calcium on gill potentials and on sodium and chloride fluxes in the goldfish *Carassius auratus*. J. Comp. Phys. *96*, 131–142.

Falkengren-Grerup, U. (1987): Long-term changes in pH of forest soils in southern Sweden. Environmental Pollution *43*, 79–90.

Ferreira, K. T. G., Hill, B. S. (1982): The effect of low external pH on properties of the paracellular pathway and junctional structure in isolated frog skin. J. Physiol. *332*, 59–67.

Freda, J. (1986): The influence of acidic pond water on amphibians: a review Water, Air and Soil Pollution *30*, 439–450.

Freda, J., Dunson, W. A. (1984): Sodium balance of amphibian larvae exposed to low environmental pH. Physiol. Zool. *57*, 435–443.

Freda, J., Dunson, W. A. (1985 a): The influence of external cation concentration on the hatching of amphibian embryos in water of low pH. Can. J. Zool. *63*, 2649–2656.

Freda, J., Dunson, W. A. (1985 b): Field and laboratory studies of ion balance and growth rates of ranid tadpoles chronically exposed to low pH. Copeia 2, 415–423.

Freda, J., McDonald, D. G. (1988): Physiological correlates of interspecific variation in acid tolerance in fish. J. exp. Biol. *136*, 243–258.

Gascon, C., Planas, D., Moreau, G. (1987): The interaction of pH, calcium and aluminium concentrations on the survival and development of wood frog (*Rana sylvatica*) eggs and tadpoles. In:

Witters, H. and Vanderborght, O. (eds.): Ecophysiology of acid stress in aquatic organisms. Annls. Soc. r. Belg. *117*, 189–199.
Gebhardt,·, Kreimes, K., Linnenbach, M. (1987): Untersuchungen zur Beeinträchtigung der Ei- und Larvalstadien von Amphibien in sauren Gewässern. Natur und Landschaft 62, 20–23.
Gellhorn, E. (1927): Studien zru Tonenphysiologie an den Spermatozoen und Eiern von *Strongylocentrotus lividus*. Pflügers Arch. ges. Physiol. *216*, 198–219.
Gosner, K. L., Black, I. H. (1957): The effects of acidity on the development and hatching of New Jersey frogs. Ecology *38*, 256–262.
Hagström, T. (1977): The extinction of frogs in a lake acidified by atmospheric pollution. Sver. Nat. *11*, 367–369 (in Swedish).
Hagström, T. (1980): Reproductive strategy and success of amphibians in waters acidified by atmospheric pollution. Proc. Eur. Herp. Symp. C. W. L. P. Oxford, 55–57.
Haines, T. A. (1981): Acidic precipitation and its consequences for aquatic ecosystems: a review. Trans. Amer. Fisher. Soc. *110*, 669–707.
Haines, T. A. (1982): Interpretation of aquatic pH trends. Trans. Amer. Fisher. Soc. *111*, 779–786.
Henrikson, L., Olofsson, H. G., Oscarson, H. G. (1982): The impact of acidification on chironomidae (Diptera) as indicated by subfossil stratification. Hydrobiologica *86*, 223–229.
Howells, G. (1982): Interpretation of aquatic pH trends. Trans. Amer. Fish. Soc. *111*, 779–786.
Huckabee, J. W., Goodyear, C. P., Jones, R. D. (1975): Acid rocks in the great smokies: Unanticipated impact on aquatic biota of road constructions in regions of sulfide mineralization. Trans. Am. Fish. Soc. *104*, 677–684.
Hutchinson, N., Holtze, K., Munro, J., Pawson, T. (1987): Lethal responses of salmonid early life stages to H^+ and Al in dilute waters. In: Witters, H. and Vanderborght, O. (eds.): Ecophysiology of acid stress in aquatic organisms. Annls. Soc. r. Belg. 117.
Kallend, A. S., Marsh, A. R. W., Pickles, J. H., Proctor, M. V. (1983): Acidity of rain in Europe. Atmospheric Environment *17*, 127–137.
Karns, D. R. (1983): Toxic bog water in northern Minnesota peatlands: Ecological and evolutionary consequences for breeding amphibians. Ph. D. Thesis, University of Minnesota, Minneapolis, MN
Katagiri, C. (1963): On the fertilizability of the frog egg. III. Removal of egg envelopes from unfertilized egg. J. Fac. Sci. Hokkaido Univ. Ser. VI Zool. *15*, 202–211.
Katagiri, C. (1972): A method for assaying the jelly digesting activity of the hatching enzyme from frog embryos. J. Fac. Sci. Hokkaido Univ. Ser. VI Zool. *18*, 461–468.
Lehnhart, B., Steinberg, C. (1984): Limnochemische und limnobiologische Auswirkungen der Versauerung von kalkarmen Oberflächengewässern. Informationsberichte Bayer. Landesamt f. Wasserwirtschaft *4/84*, 210 pp.
Leuven, R. S. E. W., den Hartog, C., Chritiaans, M. M. C., Heijligers, W. H. C. (1987): Effects of water acidification on the distribution pattern and the reproductive success of amphibians. Experientia *42*, 495–503.
LFU (Landesanstalt für Umweltschutz, ed., 1988): Immissionsökologisches Wirkungskataster Baden-Württemberg. Jahresbericht der Landesanstalt für Umweltschutz (Institut für Ökologie und Naturschutz), Karlsruhe FRG, 240 pp.
Likens, G. E. (1976): Acid precipitation. Chemical and engineering news *54*, 29–44.
Likens, G. E., Bormann, F. H. (1974): Acid rain: a serious environmental problem. Science *184*, 1176–1179.
Linnenbach, M., Marthaler, R., Gebhardt, H. (1987): Effects of acid water on gills and epidermis in brown trout (*Salmo trutta*) and in tadpoles of the common frog (*Rana temporaria*). In: Witters, H., Vanderborght, O. (eds.): Ecophysiology of acid stress in aquatic organisms. Annals. Soc. r. Zool. Belg. *117*, 365–374.
McCahon, C. P., Pascoe, D. (1989): Short-term experimental acidification of a welsh stream: Toxicity of different forms of aluminium at low pH to fish and invertebrates. Arch. Environ. Contam. Toxicol. *18*, 233–242.
McDonald, D. G. (1983): The effects of H^+ upon the gills of freshwater fish. Can. J. Zool. *61*, 691–703.
McDonald, D. G., Ozog, J. L., Simons, B. P. (1984): The influence of low pH environments on ion regulation in the larval stages of the anuran amphibian, *Rana clamitans*. Can. J. Zool. *62*, 2171–2177.

Peterson, R. H., Daye, P. G., Metcalfe, J. L. (1980): The effects of low pH on hatching of atlantic salmon eggs. In: Ecological Impact of Acid Precipitation (D. Drablos, A. Tollan, eds.) Proc. Int. Conf. Ecol. Impact Acid.

Pierce, B. A. (1987): The effect of acid rain on amphibians. The American Biology Teacher *49*, 342–247.

Pierce, B. A., Harvey, J. M. (1987): Geographic variation in acid tolerance of Connecticut wood frogs. Copeia *1*, 94–103.

Pierce, B. A., Sikand, N. (1985): Variation in acid tolerance of Connecticut wood frogs: genetic and maternal effects. Can. J. Zool. *63*, 1647–1651.

Pierce, B. A., Hoskins, J. B., Epstein, E. (1984): Acid tolerance in Connecticut wood frogs (*Rana sylvatica*). Journal of Herpetology *18*, 159–167.

Porter, K. R., Hakanson, D. E. (1976): Toxicity of mine drainage to embryonic toads (Bufonidae *Bufo boreas*). Copeia *2*, 327–331.

Pough, F. H. (1976): Acid precipitation and embryonic mortality of spotted salamanders *Ambystoma maculatum*. Science *192*, 68–72.

Psenner, R. (1984): Saurer Regen – eine Gefahr für unsere Gewässer? Österreichs Fischerei *37*, 184–194.

Punzo, F. (1983): Effects of environmental pH and temperature on embryonic survival capacity and metabolic rates in the smallmouth salamander, *Ambystoma texanum*. Bulletin of Environmental Contamination and Toxicology *31*, 467–473.

Saber, P. A., Dunson, W. A. (1978): Toxicity of bog water to embryonic and larval anuran amphibians. J. Exp. Zool. *204*, 33–42.

Sadler, K., Lynam, S. (1986): Some effects of low pH and calcium on the growth and tissue mineral content of yearling brown trout, *Salmo trutta*. J. Fish Biol. *29*, 313–324.

Salthe, S. N. (1965): Increase in volume of the perivitelline chamber during development of *Rana pipiens* Schreber. Physiol. Zool. *38*, 80–98.

Schlichter, L. C. (1981): Low pH affects the fertilization and development of *Rana pipiens* eggs. Can. J. Zool. *59*, 1693–1699.

Schnoor, J. L., Nikolaidis, N. P., Glass, G. E. (1986): Lake resources at risk to acidic deposition in the upper midwest. Journal Water pollution Control *58*, 139–148.

Seale, D. B. (1980): Influence of amphibian larvae on primary production, nutrient flux and competition. Ecology *61*, 1531–1550.

Steinberg, C., Arzet, K., Krause-Dellin, D., Sanides, S., Frenzel, B. (in press): Lonig core study on natural and anthropogenic acidification of Huzenbachersee, Black Forest, Federal Republic of Germany. Global Biogeochemical Cycles.

Storch, V.: Zelle und Umwelt (1987): eine Verbindung von Morphologie und Ökologie. Ruperto Carola *77*, 31–41.

Strijbosch, H. (1979): Habitat selection of amphibians during their aquatic phase. Oikos *33*, 363–372.

Tome, M. A., Pough, E. H. (1982): Responses of amphibians to acid precipitation. In: Johnson, R. E. (ed.): Acid Rain and Fisheries. American Fisheries Society, Bethesda, Md., 245–254.

Urch, U. A., Hedrick, J. L. (1981): Isolation and characterization of the hatching enzyme from the amphibian *Xenopus laevis*. Biophys. *206*, 424–431.

Van Driessche, W., Zeiske, W. (1985): Ionic channels in epithelial cell membranes. Physiol. Rev. *65*, 833–903.

Wassersug, R. J. (1975): The adaptive significance of the tadpole stage with comments on the maintenance of complex life cycles in anurans. American Zoologist *15*, 405–417.

Witters, H., Vanderborght, O. (eds., 1987): Ecophysiology of acid stress in aquatic organisms. Annals. Soc. r. Zool. Belg. *117*.

Wood, C. M., McDonald, D. (1987): The physiology of acid/aluminium and toxic effects on atlantic salmon. In: Witters, H., Vanderborght, O. (eds.): Ecophysiology of acid stress in aquatic organisms. Annals. Soc. r. Zool. Belg. *117*.

Fortschritte der Zoologie, Band/Vol. 38 · Hanke, W. (Hrsg.), Biology and Physiology of Amphibians
Gustav Fischer Verlag · Stuttgart · New York · 1990

Effects of starvation in Xenopus

Siegbert Merkle

Department of Zoology, University of Karlsruhe, Karlsruhe, FRG

1. Introduction

In climates with cold winters or prolonged and severe dry seasons, amphibians generally are subjected to long periods of starvation. Representatives of the northern, temperate or subarctic regions either do not feed at all, or only to a negligible extent during winter and the following spawning season (Itämies and Koskela, 1970). Also for anurans living in arid or semiarid regions, food is unavailable during droughts when most animals escape the very demanding dry season conditions by burrowing in the ground. This is also true for the South African clawed toad, *Xenopus laevis*, which in part inhabits temporary pools drying up as a result of evaporation. In this case the animals are forced to aestivate in the mud at the bottom, waiting for the seasonal rains when the ponds fill up again with water, plant and animal life. As a consequence of these environmental conditions, the ability to tolerate long periods of total food deprivation has to be expected for amphibians. Indeed, *Rana esculenta* is known to withstand fasting for more than 18 months under laboratory conditions (Grably and Piery, 1981 a and 1981 b). Several considerations indicate that at least some individuals of a population of *Scaphiopus couchii* can survive two or more years without food (Seymour, 1973).

A great deal of work on starvation has been done in fishes and mammals. In amphibians, generally, the results are rather scarce. Some clues to the adaptations of the metabolism of starving amphibians may doubtless be obtained from the numerous and detailed studies concerning seasonal changes of physiological parameters (ref. see Nagano et al., 1975); however, superimposition of other environmental factors than feeding conditions complicates the interpretation. Recently, some studies have been published dealing with starvation in *Xenopus* under controlled, artificial conditions (Woof and Janssens, 1978; Merkle and Hanke, 1988 a, b). Despite this only small number of investigations, among amphibians *Xenopus* seems to be one of the best studied species under controlled conditions and therefore has increased our knowledge about adaptations occurring in starving amphibians.

2. General metabolism during starvation

During starvation *Xenopus*, as other animals, fulfill their energy demand by depleting tissues and stored reserve substances. The resulting loss of body weight after 12 months of starvation at 20 °C is approximately 35% and 45% of the initial body weight in males and females, respectively (Merkle and Hanke, 1988 a), and thus is comparable with weight losses observed in starving fish. The higher weight loss in females compared to males is consistent with higher nitrogen-excretion rates of this sex during starvation (Fig. 2) and seems at least in part to be due to sex-related differences in motor activity and energy metabolism both of fed and starved adult animals. The differences in motor activity are assumed to be again an outcome of distinct food requirements of sexes: adult females evidently need more food for gametogenesis and body growth than males and consequently have to be the more active predators (Merkle, 1989 a). The response to starvation in *Xenopus* thus depends not only on the age or weight of the animals (Woof and Janssens, 1978), but also is markedly influenced by the sex. The following statements are essentially concerned to adult, female animals with a body weight of 30–80 g.

The analysis of oxygen consumption measured in fed and starving frogs (Fig. 1) points to two important findings. First, *Xenopus* exhibits a pronounced diurnal oxygen-consumption cycle with values about 2.5 fold higher during the night than during the day. As many other amphibians, it seems to be a nocturnal animal. In the laboratory, undisturbed frogs usually remain fairly motionless at the bottom of their basins, only occasionally swimming to surface to gulp air. During darkness they actively swim around the basin. As a consequence, an estimation of spontaneous motor activity during the night is possible which uses the difference between the oxygen consumption during the night and day. Moreover, the time course of mean oxygen consumption indicates a division in the period of long-term starvation into two distinct phases. Merkle and Hanke (1988 a) designated the phase lasting from the beginning of fasting until the fourth to sixth month of starvation as ‹starvation period I›, and the subsequent as ‹starvation period II›. Period I is characterized by a 30% reduced mean oxygen consumption compared to the fed state. The reduction occurs within 2 weeks after the cessation of feeding and is maintained throughout period I. Comparable short-term fasting effects have been observed in other anurans (Warren, 1940; Stangenberg, 1955). It is clear that the reduced demand in part comprises oxygen required for digestion of food. However, the concommitantly decreased difference

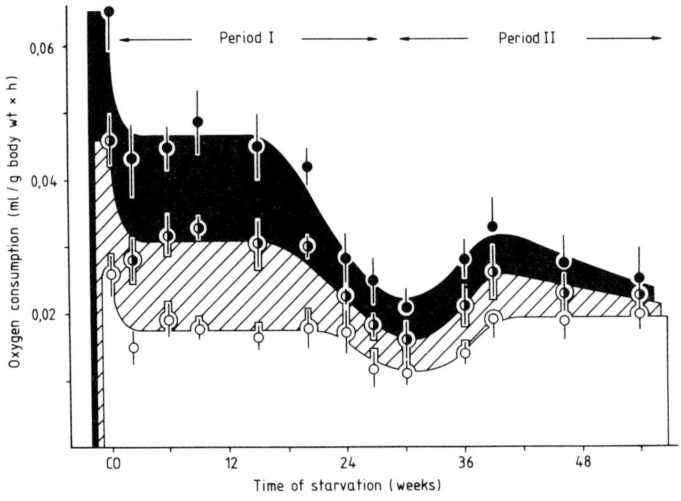

Fig. 1: Oxygen consumption of female *X. laevis* during starvation. Data of scotophase, photophase and the whole day are given in closed, open and half-closed symbols, respectively. From Merkle and Hanke (1988 a).

of oxygen consumption between the scoto- and photophases (Merkle and Hanke, 1988 a) during this period suggests that this reduction is mainly a result of a decreased motor activity. In this context it is interesting that in a variety of fishes a similar general metabolic decline due to a reduced motor activity is regarded as the major adaptive strategy in response to starvation (Love, 1980). The question may arise whether this reduction of motor activity is a general difference between poikilothermic and homoiothermic animals subjected to starvation. The latter respond to food deprivation with an increase in locomotory activity which is commonly described as «food seeking» (Wald and Jackson, 1944). However, such a generalized comparison between lower and higher vertebrates is tenuous and maybe premature due to the limited data base and the great diversity among lower vertebrates themselves. Nevertheless, for cold blooded animals with comparably low metabolic rates, high proportions of active to resting metabolism and marked seasonal variations in food availability, the use of mechanisms which reduce motor activity but maintain the capability to metabolize food when it becomes available would allow the animal to adjust its energy metabolism efficiently. Such a strategy would, therefore, increase the ability to survive severe environmental conditions.

During prolonged starvation in *Xenopus* this first adaptation of oxygen consumption to starving conditions is followed by a further decline in this parameter. The animals seem to pass through an energy crisis. Again mainly the restriction of activity seems to result in a decline of respiratory rate. Also since at precisely this point in time, the fat body is nearly totally depleted and the total gonadal weight has decreased markedly and glycogen stores have been largely consumed (Fig. 4, 5, 6) the exhaustion of carbohydrate and lipid stores are probably responsible for this crisis. During the following starvation period II, a new but only slight increase of oxygen consumption indicates the use of a different source of energy. A similar rise in oxygen consumption is reported in *Protopterus aethiopicus* fasted for five months (Smith, 1930) and regarded as an increase in protein catabolism. In starving mammals such an increase has long been suggested to be a terminal feature, marking the end of lipid and carbohydrate reserves. Indeed, in *Xenopus* during starvation

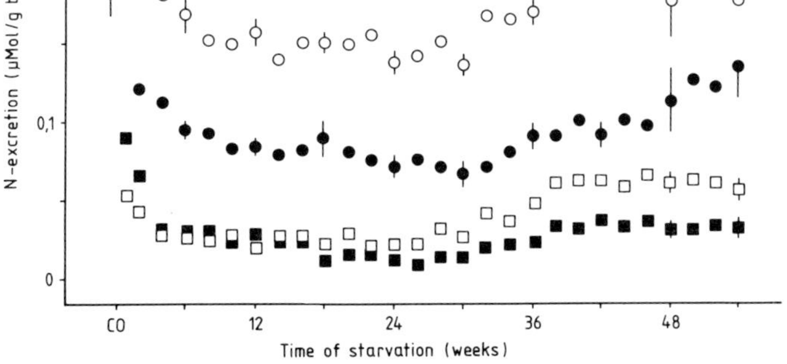

Fig. 2: Nitrogen excretion of *X. laevis* during starvation. From Merkle and Hanke (1988 a).

period II increasing nitrogen-excretion rates and decreasing concentrations of muscle proteins (Merkle and Hanke, 1988 b) are indications of a forced mobilisation of proteins, especially from muscle. However, the observed increase in the mean rate of oxygen consumption is directly followed by an continuous reduction of this parameter. In frogs starved for 12 months, the calculated motor activity is reduced to less than 20% of normal activity (Merkle and Hanke, 1988 a) a finding which is consistent with the lethargic behaviour of these animals.

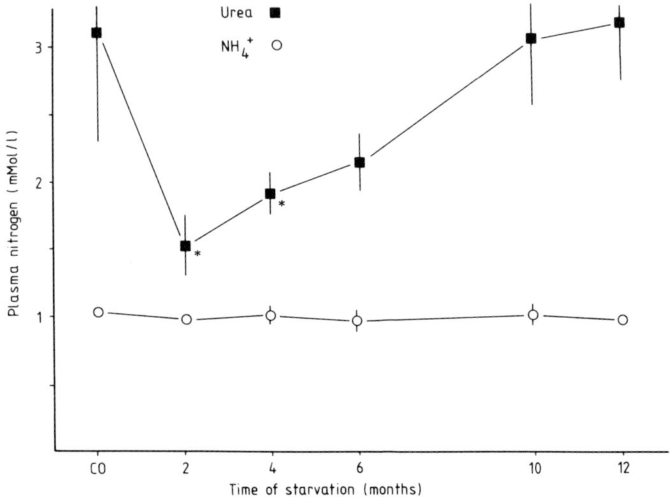

Fig. 3: Concentrations of ammonia and urea in the plasma of female *X. laevis* during starvation. From Merkle and Hanke (1988 a).

3. Source of metabolized substrates during starvation

It is well known that the predominant nitrogenous end-products of protein breakdown in *Xenopus* are ammonia and urea. The excretion rate of these compounds may, therefore, be used as a quantitative measure of protein catabolism. Fig. 2 shows that the excretion of both ammonia and urea declines sharply during the first few days after cessation of feeding when the stomach empties. The decline continues slowly to a constant level which is maintained throughout the next seven to eight months of starvation in females. Consequently, the protein dependent metabolism during this phase decreases to 40–50% in comparison to about 100% in fed animals (Merkle and Hanke, 1988 a). Subsequently, this basal level of protein catabolism is followed by a new rise of nitrogen excretion rates, but without reaching values found under conditions of normal feeding. However, the protein dependent metabolism is again 100%; that is, the combustion of proteins accounts for all of the oxygen consumption during this late phase of starvation. It is interesting that the observed alterations of urea and ammonia excretion correlate with alterations of urea but not with those of ammonia in plasma (Fig. 3). The different behaviour in these compounds may be explained by their main sites of formation in the organism. Urea is mainly produced by the liver whereas ammonia may be formed essentially by the kidney for purpose of cation conservation and regulation of acid-base balance. The reduction of protein catabolism described during long-term starvation is in agreement with earlier investigations of Balinsky and Baldwin (1961) and Unsworth (1965) in short-term fasted *Xenopus*. Contradictory findings of Woof and Janssens (1978), which indicated no difference in nitrogen excretion between fed adult male and those fasted for four months, are difficult to interprete since no clear indications of feeding conditions shortly prior to the start of the experiment are given and the «fed» animals might have been already in a short-term fasted state. The observation of feeding is important since our observations indicate that recently handled or disturbed male animals do not feed.

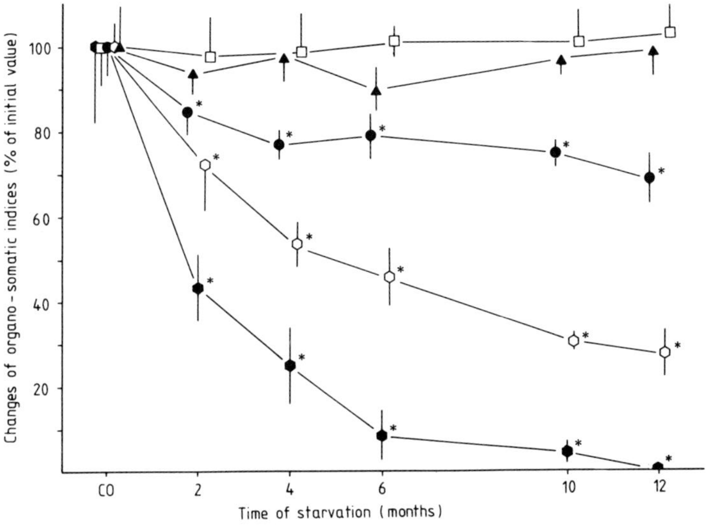

Fig. 4: Changes of organo-somatic indices of the heart (□), kidney (▲), liver (●), ovaries (○) and fat body (⬢) in female *X. laevis* during starvation. From Merkle and Hanke (1988b).

A further question concerns the sources of utilized proteins and of other substrates metabolized during the phase of reduced protein dependent metabolism. Decreasing somatic indices of ovaries and fat body during starvation period I (Fig. 4) suggest that a further early response to starvation is the mobilisation of lipids stored in the ovaries and the fat body. The latter source has long been recognized as an energy depot in frogs and toads. Apart from proteins and lipids, carbohydrates are depleted during the early starvation period. Glycogen in liver, ovaries, and muscle but not in kidney declines steadily during the first months of starvation (Fig. 5 and 6). Observations in *Xenopus* males reveal decreases of glycogen concentration in liver and muscle after a four month fast which, however, are not statistically significant (Woof and Janssens, 1978). Regarding the weight losses of tissues, the reduction of glycogen during starvation period I in females accounts for 80–90% of the initial carbohydrate. The consistent release of glucose ensures to maintain glucose homeostasis in plasma at least during «short» periods of starvation (Woof and Janssens, 1978; Merkle and Hanke, 1988 a).

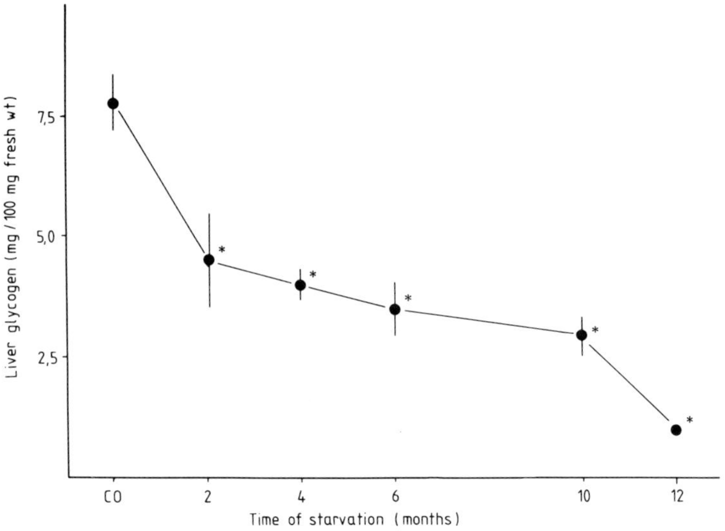

Fig. 5: The glycogen concentration of the liver of female X. *laevis* during starvation. From Merkle and Hanke (1988 a).

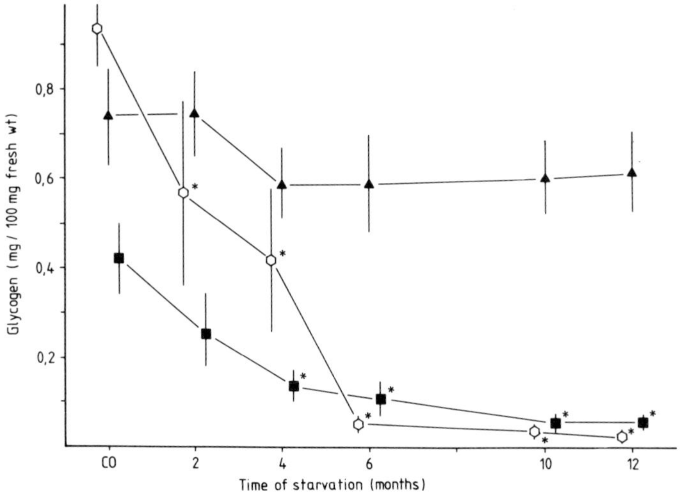

Fig. 6: The glycogen concentration of the kidney (▲), muscle (■) and ovaries (○) of female X. *laevis* during starvation. From Merkle and Hanke (1988 b).

The time course of alterations of somatic indices furthermore demonstrates that beside the overall reduction of organ weights mainly the depletion of ovarial proteins must be the principal source of proteins utilized during starvation period I. In contrast during period II the observed increase of water content and concommitantly decrease of protein concentration in muscle (Merkle and Hanke, 1988b) suggests a depletion of muscle proteins. This inverse dynamic relationship between the two main constituents of muscle is known as the «protein-water line» in starving fish (Love, 1980). It is of interest whether this increase of tissue water results from increases of intracellular or extracellular water spaces. Changes in these spaces may be indirectly estimated by changes of muscle sodium, a largely extracellular ion, and corresponding changes of potassium which is intracellular. However, since the concentration of these ions decreases in starving *Xenopus* (Merkle and Hanke, 1988a) such data are ambiguous. Nevertheless, the increase of the Na^+/K^+ ratio which accompanies the initial increase of muscle water indicates an increase of the extracellular space during early starvation period II, which comparably occurs in long-term starved carp (Gas, 1972). Decreases in plasma protein concentrations during this phase (Merkle and Hanke, 1988a) are consistent with oedema due to a reduced colloid osmotic pressure of plasma. However, the increase of extracellular water is insufficient on its own to account for all of the increased water content, especially during the late phase of this period. The constant or slowly decreasing Na^+/K^+ ratio combined with the steadily increasing water content of muscle lead to the conclusion that, in addition, intracellular water is elevated. This may be a consequence of depletion of single protein filaments as observed in starving carp (Gas, 1972) which may occur beneath the utilization of enzymatic material. The latter is indicated by a generalized reduction in muscle enzyme activity during the late starvation phase II (Fig. 7).

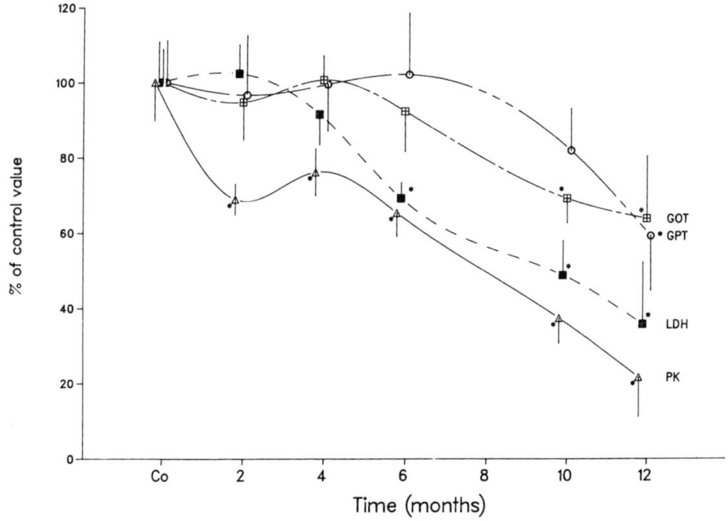

Fig. 7: Time course of enzymatic activity of pyruvate kinase (PK), glutamate-pyruvate transaminase (GPT), glutamate-oxaloacetate transaminase (GOT), and lactate dehydrogenase (LDH) in muscle of female *X. laevis* during starvation. From Merkle (1989b).

4. Enzyme activities during starvation

Changes in the nutritional state of an organism affect metabolic pathways and therefore may be reflected in altered enzyme activities. Woof and Janssens (1978) investigated some hepatic enzymes involved in carbohydrate and protein metabolism in adult male *Xenopus* fasted for 60 and 130 days. Fasting in this anuran species results in a decrease of the activity of glutamate-pyruvate transaminase (GPT) after 60 and 130 days of starvation. Fructose-1,6-diphosphatase (FPDase), glucose-6-phosphatase and carbamylphosphate synthetase are reduced only after 130 days of fasting. In contrast, phosphoenolpyruvate carboxykinase and glutamate dehydrogenase activities remain unchanged. The authors concluded from these results that some decline of activity in the pathways leading to glucose and urea formation occurs after the onset of starvation. Some of these results and the conclusion drawn are essentially in agreement with those obtained in starving female *Xenopus*. As seen in Fig. 8, GPT and oxaloacetate transaminase (GOT) in liver decrease after the cessation of feeding. In the case of GPT, the activity increases again during prolonged starvation whereas GOT remains at the reduced level. A similar response of GPT can be observed in kidney (Merkle, 1989b) but not in muscle (Fig. 7). Thus, the alterations in transaminase activities at least in part appear to reflect the changes of protein utilization and possibly of gluconeogenesis in liver and kidney. Following the data of nitrogen-excretion, carbohydrate utilization and metabolic activity, the latter pathway is assumed to decline during the early starvation phase in *Xenopus* and to increase again throughout the later phase. During prolonged starvation when carbohydrate stores are exhausted, gluconeogenesis is probably the sole source of glucose for tissues in which metabolism mainly depends on this metabolite. This expectation is not consistent with the further reduced values of the gluconeogenic enzyme FDPase during this phase (Fig. 8) which, however, is less likely to be a regulation point in gluconeogenesis of *Xenopus* (Woof and Janssens, 1978).

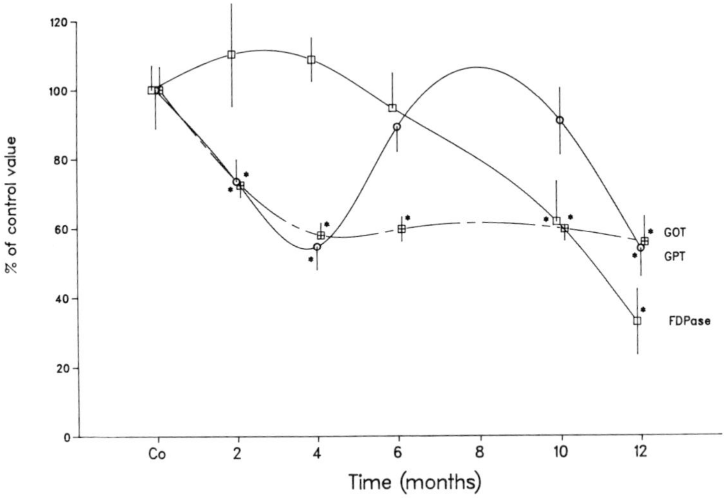

Fig. 8: Time course of enzymatic activity of glutamate-pyruvate transaminase (GPT), glutamate-oxaloacetate transaminase (GOT) and fructose-1,6-diphosphatase (FDPase) in liver of female *X. laevis* during starvation. From Merkle (1989b).

Another characteristic effect during starvation is the steady decline in activity of glucose-6-phosphate dehydrogenase both in liver (Fig. 9) and in kidney (Merkle, 1989b). The reduction of this enzyme seems to be a general feature of starving vertebrates and is thought to be related to reduced or absent lipogenesis during starvation. The behaviour of pyruvate kinase in muscle should also be mentioned (Fig. 7). The time course of activity of this enzyme essentially follows the time course of oxygen consumption and motor activity during starvation, possibly indicating a role of this enzyme in the regulation of the glycolytic pathway which supplies the most energy for activity. It should be pointed out that a relationship between the decline of major glycolytic enzyme activities in both muscle types and the general metabolic decline was already suggested in starving fish (Moon and Johnston, 1979).

Finally, changes of activity of enzymes during starvation may be divided into two categories; i.e., those changes which appear to be true adaptations of the organism to the altered nutritional state occurring during early and middle periods of starvation, and those which are probably a result of the overall protein depletion in the tissues predominantly occurring during the latter starvation phases.

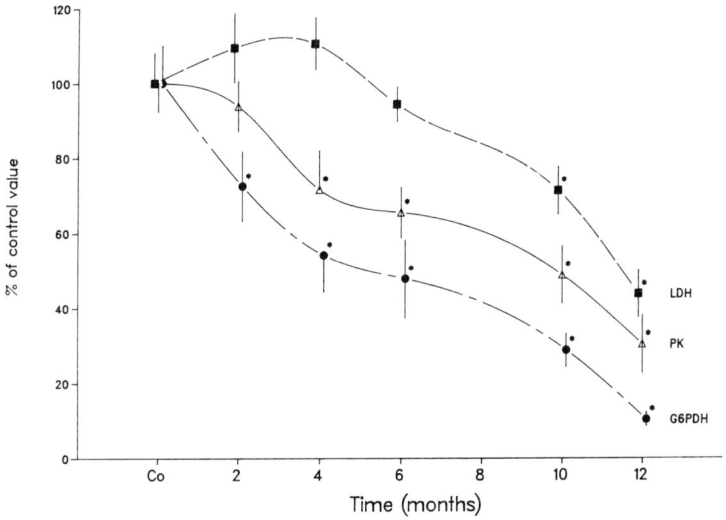

Fig. 9: Time course of enzymatic activity of glucose-6-phosphate dehydrogenase (G6PDH), pyruvate kinase (PK) and lactate dehydrogenase (LDH) in liver of female *X. laevis* during starvation. From Merkle (1989b).

References

Balinsky, J. B., Baldwin, E. (1961): The mode of excretion of ammonia and urea in *Xenopus laevis*. J. Exp. Biol. *38*, 695–705.

Gas, N. (1972): Structural alterations in the white muscle of carp (*Cyprinus carpio* L.) during prolonged starvation. C. r. hebd. Seanc. Acad. Sci. Paris, Ser. D. 275, 1403–1406.

Grably, S., Piery, Y. (1981a): Weight and tissue changes in long term starved frogs *Rana esculenta*. Comp. Biochem. Physiol. 69A, 683–688.

Grably, S., Piery, Y. (1981 b): Glycogen phosphorylase and hexokinase in skeletal and heart muscles of *Rana esculenta* submitted to imposed long-term starvation. Comp. Biochem. Physiol. 70 B, 587–594.
Itämies, J., Koskela, P. (1970): On the diet of the common frog (*Rana temporaria* L.). Aquilo, Ser. Zool. *10*, 53–60.
Love, R. M. (1980): *The Chemical Biology of Fishes*, Academic Press, London.
Merkle, S. (1989 a): Sexual differences as adaptation to the different gender roles in the frog *Xenopus laevis* Daudin. J. Comp. Physiol. B *159*, 473–480.
Merkle, S. (1989 b): Long-term starvation in *Xenopus laevis* Daudin – III. Effects on enzymes in several tissues. Comp. Biochem. Physiol. *94 b*, 783–788.
Merkle, S., Hanke, W. (1988 a): Long-term starvation in *Xenopus laevis* Daudin – I. Effects on general metabolism. Comp. Biochem. Physiol. 89 B, 719–730.
Merkle, S., Hanke, W. (1988 b): Long-term starvation in *Xenopus laevis* Daudin – II. Effects on several organs. Comp. Biochem. Physiol. 90 A, 491–495.
Moon, T. W., Johnston, I. A. (1979): Starvation and enzyme activities in the skeletal muscles and liver of a teleost fish (*Pleuronectes platessa*). Biochem. Soc. Trans. Cambr. 7, 1045–1046.
Nagano, H., Itoh, H., Shukuya, R. (1975): Seasonal variation in hepatic PEPCK activity of bullfrog, *Rana catesbeiana*. Comp. Biochem. Physiol. 51 B, 255–256.
Seymour, R. S. (1973): Energy metabolism of dormant spadefoot toads (*Scaphiopus*). Copeia *3*, 435–445.
Smith, H. L. W. (1930): Metabolism of the lungfish *Protopterus aethiopicus*. J. Biol. Chem. *88*, 97–130.
Stangenberg, G. (1955): Der Temperatureinfluß auf Lebensprozesse und den Cytochrom c-Gehalt beim Wasserfrosch. Pflüg. Arch. ges. Physiol. *260*, 320–332.
Unsworth, B. R. (1965): The metabolism of amino nitrogen in *Xenopus laevis* with special reference to the excretory products. Ph. D. Thesis, London University.
Wald, G., Jackson, B. (1944): Activity and nutritional deprivation. Physiology 30, 255–263.
Warren, M. K. (1940): Studies on the effect of experimental hyperthyroidism on the adult frog *Rana pipiens*, Schreber. J. Exp. Zool. 83, 127–159.
Woof, C., Janssens, P. A. (1978): Effects of fasting and cortisol administration on carbohydrate metabolism in *Xenopus laevis* Daudin. Gen. Comp. Endocr. 36, 346–359.

Fortschritte der Zoologie, Band/Vol. 38 · Hanke, W. (Hrsg.), Biology and Physiology of Amphibians
Gustav Fischer Verlag · Stuttgart · New York · 1990

Magnetic field effects in larvae of Xenopus laevis

Thomas Leucht

Zoologisches Institut II der Universität Würzburg, FRG

1. Introduction

It is now well established that a variety of animals is able to use the Earth's magnetic field (EMF) as a physical source of information. Potentially, the EMF provides a set of different parameters that may be used by the animal. The vector product of constant, terrestrial parameters – the horizontal and vertical components – is defined by the intensity and inclination of the magnetic field lines (Intensity: ca. 45 000 nT, inclination: ca. 65° in central Europe). Both, intensity and inclination, vary considerably with latitude, thus providing information about the geographical location. Superimposed on these steady components are small magnetic variations in the order of less than 100 nT that are mostly due to solar activity and position. Apart from singular events like magnetic storms these variations are of periodical nature with diurnal, lunar and annual cycles. Intensity as well as the time course of the fluctuations can be perceived by animals and used for orientation in space and in time (Keeton et al., 1974; Martin et al., 1983).

Since the pioneering work of Fromme (1961) on birds and of Lindauer and Martin (1968) on honeybees the influence of magnetic stimuli on orientational behaviour has been described in a great number of animals thus showing the wide abundance of magnetic field detection and associated behavioural patterns (For review see: Adey, 1981; Lindauer and Martin, 1985). In amphibians, experimental evidence for the capability to orient with respect to magnetic fields (MF) is restricted to only a few species. In urodeles the first demonstration of MF-related orientation has been shown in the cave salamander, *Eurycea lucifuga* (Plethodontidae) living in the twilight and aphotic regions of limestone caves (Phillips, 1977). More detailed information on the mechanisms guiding magnetic orientation has been derived from laboratory experiments with the migratory eastern red-spotted newt, *Notophthalmus viridescens* (Phillips, 1986a). Artificial rotation of the horizontal alignment of the ambient MF resulted in consistent orientational responses to the MF. Depending on the behavioural context the newts display a simple compass orientation by referring to the inclination of the MF (axial sensitivity) or, in the case of homing, to the horizontal polarity (polar sensitivity) (Phillips, 1986b). In anurans Sinsch (1987) has shown that the initial homing orientation of *Bufo bufo* is subject to magnetic influences. Attachment of small bar magnets to the head of the animals, thus disturbing the EMF, causes an increased dispersion, i.e. no specific homing direction could be observed. In addition, MF effects have been observed in two other toad species, *B. spinulosus* and *B. calamita* (Sinsch, 1988a, b).

The question where the magnetic stimulus is detected and how it is transduced is not yet understood. One reason for the weak information on magnetic stimulus transduction is that behavioural studies have the disadvantage that the processes involved in magnetoreception are difficult to follow in the big black box of an intact animal. A way to overcome the problem is to use a reaction where the steps from the input of a magnetic stimulus to the output can be discretely defined. A second possibility is to study single organs, tissues or other components of the organism that may be involved in the processing of magnetic information. Experimental strategies like this have provided results that indicate – though controversial – that the sensory structures involved in optical and gravitational information processing may also detect magnetic stimuli (Leucht, 1984; Olcese et al., 1985; Semm et al., 1984; Semm and Demaine, 1986; Korall and Martin, 1987; Sinsch, 1988 a). On the physiological level there is now substantial evidence that the mechanisms regulating calcium permeability of membranes are affected by MF (Ossenkopp and Kavaliers, 1988). The importance of calcium ions in the transduction of endocrinological and neuronal information is well known. Yet, the biophysical and biochemical basis of MF-induced changes in calcium conductance has not been evaluated.

Using ethological and endocrinological techniques it was tried to analyze simple patterns of anuran behaviour sensitive to influences of weak MF and to find out more about the topology and physiology of MF-effects by isolating single parts of the chain leading from the sensory input to the behavioural response.

2. Magnetic field effects on gravity-oriented behaviour

The tadpoles of *X. laevis* exhibit a typical head-down body axis orientation comprising an angle of 50–60° with respect to the horizontal. Using this behaviour as a test paradigm, the possible interactions of magnetic and gravitational stimuli were considered. To this end, groups of 15 tadpoles of stage 51–53 (Nieuwkoop and Faber, 1967) were placed in a narrow glass cuvette (height: 20 cm; width: 20 cm; depth: 1 cm) that was adjusted in N-S direction. In order to exclude directional light information the cuvette was covered with white cardboard on top, bottom and side walls. The container with the animals was centered between two pairs of Helmholtz-coils that were used to manipulate the EMF by selectively generating horizontal and vertical MF components according to the required stimulus conditions. The larvae were observed with a video-camera and the angle of body axis orientation was measured by single-frame analysis using a protractor mounted on the screen of video-monitor. Only those tadpoles were used for analysis whose body axis was parallel or antiparallel to the N-S direction.

The results obtained show that the angular inclination of the larvae predominantly refers to the perception of the direction of gravity. However, the animals can also use the MF as a source of directional information. An artificial change of the magnetic inclination is accompanied by a corresponding change of body axis orientation. When the inclination of the MF is increased from 65° to 90° by compensating the horizontal component of the EMF and simultaneously amplifying the vertical component, the animals respond with a steeper angle of body axis orientation when compared with controls (+3.12°; $P < 0.05$). Switching the inclination down to 0° the angle of body axis of the larvae decreases by −2.66° ($P < 0.001$). Similar, but more pronounced responses are observed, when the magnetic inclination is reduced from 65° to 35° resulting in a decrease of the angle of orientation by − 3.84° when compared with controls (Fig. 1 a). A comparison of animals heading north and south revealed that tadpoles heading in northern direction consistently hold a steeper angle of body axis orientation when compared with larvae oriented 180° opposite.

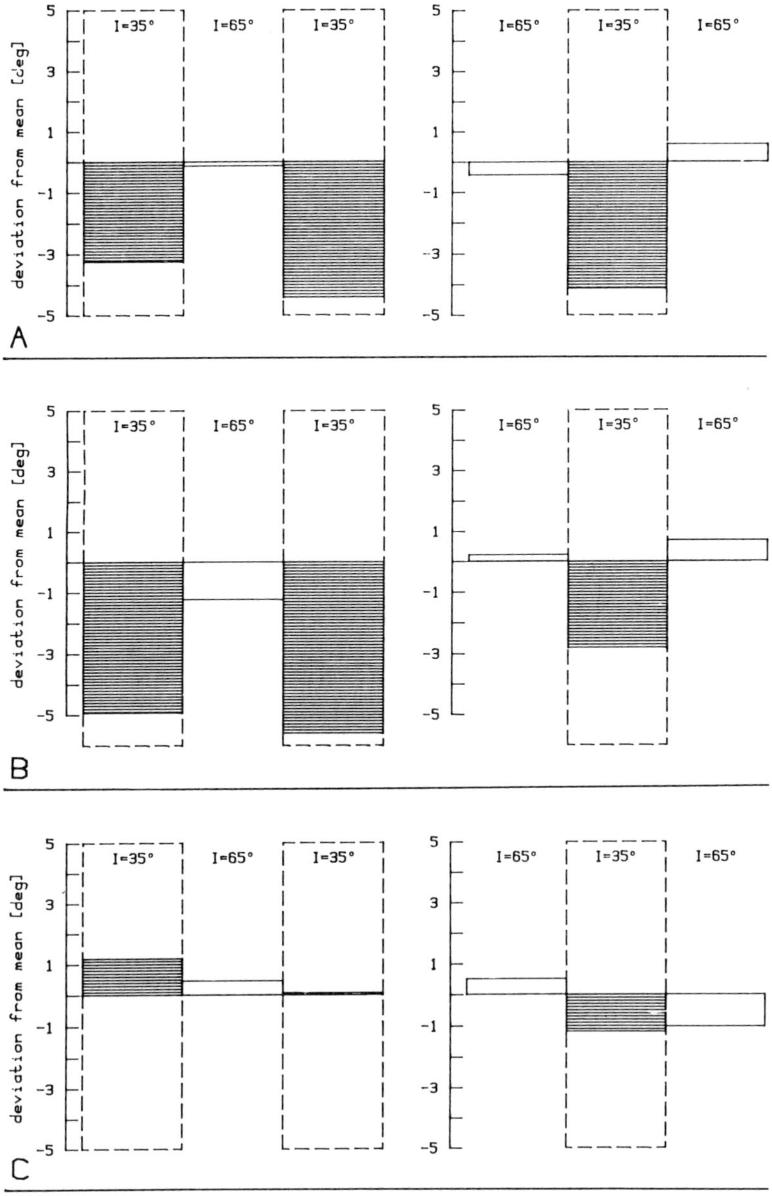

Fig. 1: Angle of body axis orientation with respect to the horizontal in the natural EMF (inclination: 65°; intensity: 42000 nT) and in an artificial MF (inclination: 35°; intensity: 76000 nT). Ordinate: Angular deviation of body axis orientation from the mean of controls. White columns: Results in the natural EMF. hatched columns in stippled rectangles: Results in the artificial MF. Each bar represents the mean of measurements of an observation-period of 45 min. Fig. 1a: Intact animals. Fig. 1b: sham-operated animals. Fig. 1c: Animals with the N. opticus cut. From Leucht (1989).

In an attempt to localize the pathways of information processing that are controlling the described MF-influenced behaviour, tests were repeated with animals whom the optic nerve had been cut, thus interrupting the functional connection between the eyes and the CNS. A control group has been sham-operated. As mentioned above, previous experimental work as well as theoretical considerations (Leask, 1977; Schulten and Windemuth, 1986) have given evidence that the eyes might be structures involved in the detection of MF. Comparison of the responses of intact and operated larvae revealed that the observations concerning MF-induced modulations of body posture do not hold for blinded tadpoles. Changing the inclination of the MF from 65° to 35° the animals did not respond to the magnetic stimulus (Fig. 1 c). Thus it may be inferred that the optical system is involved in the reception and/or processing of environmental MF-information.

Under the described conditions of stimulus application – a rapid switch of MF-inclination accompanied by an amplification from 42 μT to 76 μT within less than 1 ms – intact animals show no sign of behavioural delay, i.e. they respond immediately to the altered magnetic situation. What happens if these alterations are slowly in time and small in amplitude? An answer is given by long term observations of the body axis orientation of *X. laevis* larvae, indicating that the influence of MF may not merely be restricted to artificially induced artifacts. In Fig. 2 a, c the results of measurements over periods of 48 hrs are shown and compared with the variations of the intensity of the horizontal component of the EMF. Fig. 2 a gives an example of a recording period with pronounced variations and shows that there is a correlation between these fluctuations and the course of deviation from the mean of body axis orientation with respect to gravity. Furthermore,

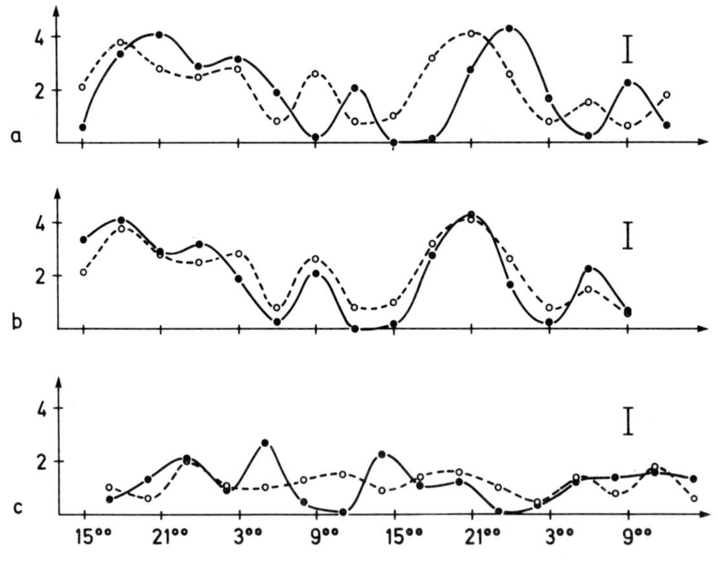

Fig. 2: Long term observations of body axis orientation during 6/25-6/27/88 (Fig. 2 a and 2 b) and 10/30-11/1/87 (Fig. 2 c). Abscissa: Solid lines and closed symbols: deviation of body axis orientation from mean in degrees. Broken lines and open symbols: difference between maximum and minimum intensity of the horizontal component of the EMF during the preceding 3 hrs. Vertical bar: 13.5 nT. In Fig. 2 b the curve for body axis orientation has been shifted 3 hrs backwards to show correlation between the dynamics of MF variation and changes of body posture.

the slope of both curves demonstrates a delay in the behavioural response to the changing intensity of variation. This observation closely resembles hysteresis-effects like those being observed in the honeybee (Martin and Lindauer, 1977). Fig. 2c illustrates the results of measurements during a magnetically quiet period. Under these conditions, the time-slope of MF-variation and body orientation shows no apparent coherence. Comparison of results under magnetically quiet and noisy conditions allows for an estimation of threshold values of magnetic intensity under natural conditions. From Fig. 2a, b it can be seen that magnetic variations of more than 50 nT are followed by a significant reaction of the tadpoles. Thus, it can be concluded that the larvae can respond to intensity variations around 0.1% of the total intensity of the EMF.

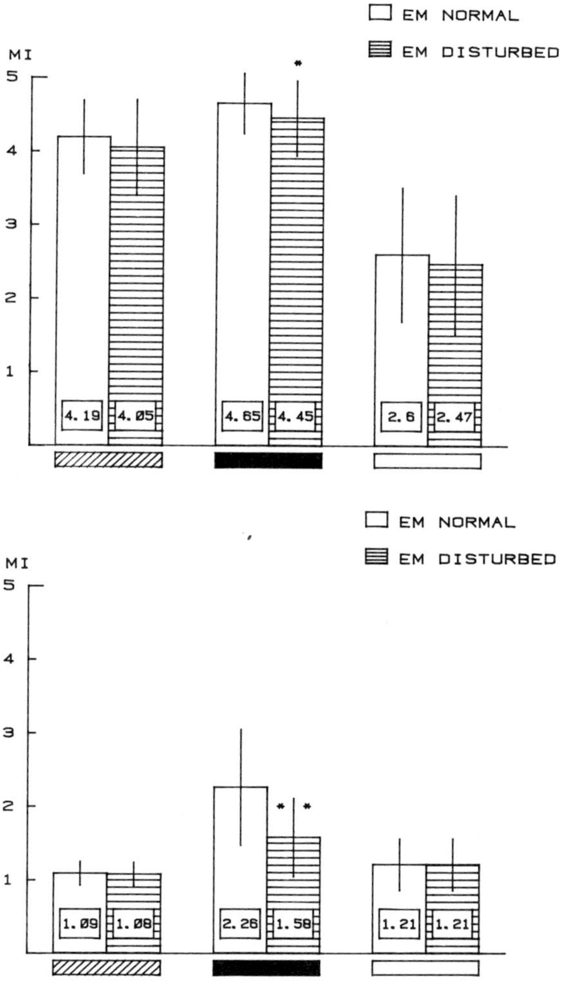

Fig. 3: Effects of a disturbed MF on pigment migration in X. laevis in the head region (Fig. 3a, above) and in the tail-fin region (Fig. 3b, below). Abscissa: Melanophore-Index (MI; according to Hogben and Slome, 1931). Bars indicate S.D..

Level of significance: **: $P < 0.0001$, *: $P < 0.002$. Background of container: medium: ▨; black: ■; white: □. White columns: MF normal; hatched columns: MF disturbed. From Leucht (1987a).

3. Modulation of background adaptation by MF in vivo

The ability of background adaptation in tadpoles of *X. laevis* is exclusively triggered by optical inputs. The effector system, pigment containing melanophores in the dermis of the animals, are thought to be controlled by α-Melanophore Stimulating Hormone (MSH) mediating pigment dispersion and by melatonin that causes aggregation of melanin granules inside the melanophores. The secretion of both hormones is regulated by optical stimuli. Apart from this «secondary response» of pigment cells (Weber, 1983) there exists a «primary response», in which the cell directly responds to incident light, i.e. the melanin granules inside the cells aggregate upon illumination. This is the case for the melanophores of the ventral tail-fin of *X. laevis* (Lek, 1967).

To test the possible influence of MF on background adaptation groups of 10 animals were placed in transparent containers with medium, black and white coloured bottom. The animals were allowed to adapt to the different brightness of the background for 1 hr and subsequently the dispersion of melanophores was assessed using the melanophore index of Hogben and Slome (1931). Two different areas of pigment cells were observed: one in the headregion of the larvae and another one in the ventral tail-fin. The artificial magnetic stimuli used in these experiments were a distortion of the EMF by simultaneously changing the N-S axis, decreasing the degree of inclination and amplifying the field to nearly twice the value of the EMF. A second magnetic test parameter was the compensation of the EMF down to less than 4% of total intensity.

The experimental results obtained under these test conditions clearly show that background adaptation is affected by disturbing the ambient MF. The adaptation to a black background is significantly decreased. The effect is most pronounced in melanophores of the tail-fin region, where a reduction of pigment-dispersion by 30.09% due to the artificial MF is observed, when compared with controls (Fig. 3). In the pigment cell population of the head region a weaker, although significant response is measured. These MF induced modulations are restricted to adaptational responses on a black background.

No effects are obtained, when the EMF is compensated to less than 4% of total intensity. There is a slight increase in melanin dispersion, when the animals are standing over a black background but the effect is not significant.

4. MF effects on melanophores *in vitro*

The significant difference concerning the inhibition of pigment migration in the head- and ventral tail fin region due to altered MF conditions led me to consider whether the MF directly affects the responsiveness of melanophores to hormonal stimulation. Experiments were performed with isolated pieces (1.5* 1.5 mm) of melanophore tissue from the ventral tail fin of tadpoles. The pigment cells were incubated in Ringer's solution containing MSH and the reaction, i.e. the pigment dispersion of a population of approximately 50 cells was observed by measuring the intensity of a light beam passing the probe. The increasing light absorption due to the spreading of pigment inside the cells was monitored radiometrically over a period of 30 min and recorded with a pen-writer or, using A/D conversion, with a computer.

A comparison of results obtained in the natural EMF and in an amplified MF (intensity: 84000 nT; inclination and direction of the field unchanged) shows that melanophores respond to varying MF in vitro (Leucht, 1987 b). Stimulation with different concentrations of MSH (1.25; 1.67; and 2.00 ng/ml) show a dose dependent effect in the natural EMF. Fig. 4 a gives an example. The application of the artificial MF is followed by a decrease of

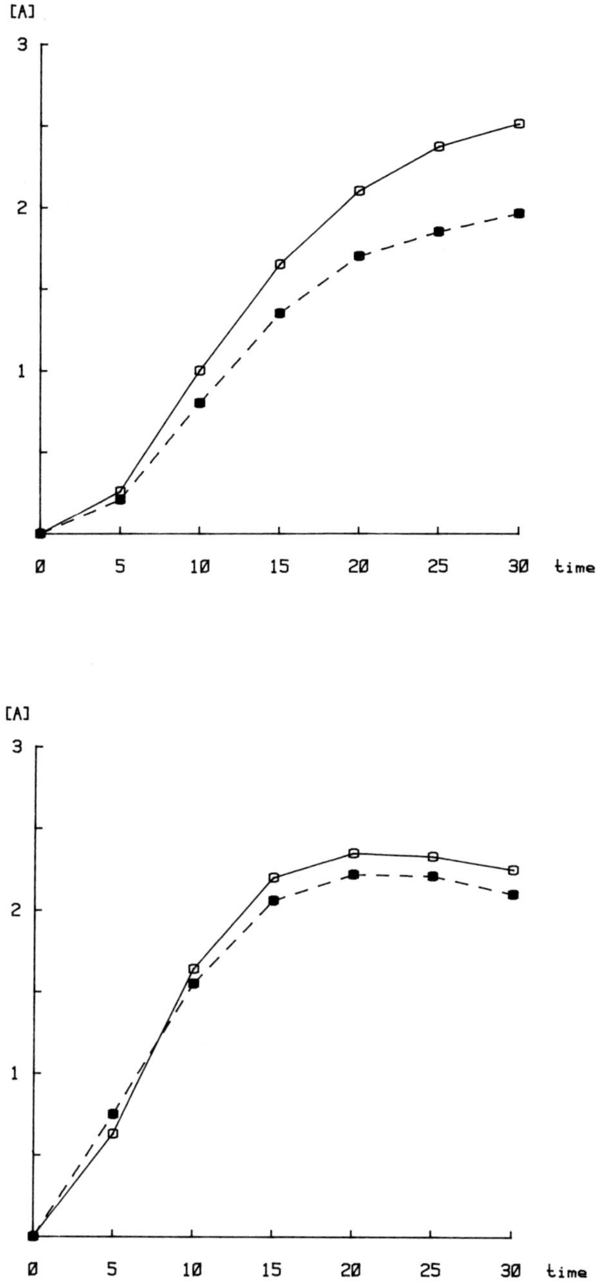

Fig. 4: Effect of MF on pigment migration in excised melanophore tissue of ventral tail fin. Fig. 4a (above): Stimulation with 1.67 ng/ml a-MSH. From Leucht (1987b). Fig. 4b (below): Stimulation with $1*10^{-6}$ M forskolin. Abscissa: Absorption due to pigment migration (arbitrary units). Ordinate: Time in minutes. Solid lines and open symbols: Natural EMF; broken lines and closed symbols: MF amplified.

pigment dispersion of 22–24% at all three concentrations tested. – If the pigment migration is measured after 30 min of incubation (1 ng/ml MSH) in darkness, similar results are obtained, i.e. amplification of the MF yields a reduction of pigment dispersion by 23% when compared with controls in the natural MF. The dynamics of subsequent pigment aggregation due to illumination is not affected by different MF conditions. Thus it can be concluded that the observed MF effect results in a modification of the «secondary response» mechanism alone.

Hormonal signal transduction in *Xenopus* melanophores is thought to be mediated by a second messenger mechanism via the hormone receptor, a G-protein, and adenylate cyclase that catalyzes formation of cAMP (White et al., 1987). In order to further localize the site of MF action in *Xenopus* melanophores and to find out more about the possible role of calcium in the MF-induced changes of pigment migration, the effect of stimulation with the diterpene forskolin was studied. The ability of forskolin to stimulate adenylate cyclase directly has been shown in the rat (Seamon et al., 1981) and in *Xenopus* (deGraan et al., 1984). Incubation of ventral melanophore tissue with forskolin at a concentration of $1*10^{-6}$ M is followed by a marked dispersion of melanin granules comparable to the effect obtained with 1.67 ng/ml MSH. Maximum response shows up after 20 min of incubation followed by a slight decrease of pigment dispersion. If the ambient MF is artificially amplified to 84000 nT no effect can be observed when compared with the natural EMF. In a second series of experiments, using a concentration of forskolin of $5*10^{-7}$ M, again no difference between data collected in the ambient EMF and the amplified MF was observed. Comparison with the results obtained with MSH under identical MF conditions indicates that the MF induced modulation of pigment migration is due to a membrane bound step in signal transduction.

5. Discussion

From the experimental results described above it may be inferred that larvae of *X. laevis* are subject to influences of MF on the behavioural and on the physiological level as well.

The observations concerning the interaction of gravity and MF stimuli show the modulatory influence of electromagnetic fields on orientational behaviour related to gravity. Apart from the described effects due to artificial changes of magnetic inclination this becomes especially apparent in long time observations that show responses to very weak fluctuations of the EMF. The ability to detect minute MF intensities in the nT-range also has been demonstrated in invertebrates, e.g. in the honeybee (Martin and Lindauer, 1977; Korall et al., 1988) and in vertebrates (Wiltschko et al., 1986, Kowalski et al., 1988). A behavioural parallel with respect to the influence of MF on body posture is given in the honeybee, where the direction indication of the dancing bee, i.e. the angular orientation with respect to gravity, exhibits periodical mistakes that are correlated with the daily variation of the EMF intensity. Here again effects of hysteresis show up, pointing to summative computing of single events over time.

On the background of relatively small quantitative effects on the observed behaviour it has to be asked for the biological significance of MF perception. Apart from the influence on spatial orientation in this context it may be referred to the function of MF as exogeneous «Zeitgeber». As Martin et al. (1983) demonstrated in the honeybee, variation of the EMF substantially influences the orientation of the animals in time. In vertebrates the pineal gland seems to be the most important organ to communicate rhythmic changes of the physical environment, i.e. the photoperiod (for review see Collin et al., 1988). This can either be achieved by direct photodetection or via information coming from the peripheral eyes. In both, eyes as well as pineal, melatonin is synthesized at a rate dependent on photocycle. In Xenopus, Besharse and Iuvone (1983) could show that the activity of N-Acetyltransferase (NAT), an enzyme catalyzing the production of melatonin, is subject to rhythmic changes correlated to the dark-light cycle of the environment. Yet, the activity of NAT as well as of Hydroxyindole-O-Methyltransferase, another enzyme catalyzing melatonin synthesis, is also due to changes of the MF. This has been demonstrated in the retina and pineal gland of chicken (Cremer-Bartels et al., 1984), and in the pineal of pigeons (Reuss and Semm, 1987) and of the rat (Reuss and Olcese, 1986). Besides the influence of MF on retinal hormone synthesis, effects on neuronal activity coming from the retina have been demonstrated by Olcese et al. (1985) and Semm et al. (1984). The extinction of MF induced effects on gravity related orientation described here by cutting the N. opticus gives additional evidence that the eyes might be involved in the detection of MF. The MF effects shown in background adaptation in vivo, a behaviour exclusively triggered by optical inputs, may point in the same direction.

First steps to elucidate the action of MF on the cellular level have been done in the experiments with isolated tail-fin tissue of *X. laevis*. The marked influence of MF during stimulation of melanophores with MSH and the lack of a response when stimulating with forskolin indicates that membrane-bound events are involved. DeGraan et al. (1984) showed in melanophores of *X. laevis* that the binding of MSH to its receptor and the pathway transducing the hormonal signal to adenylate cyclase require calcium. In contrast, the activity of adenylate cyclase does not depend on calcium. The fact that the transport of calcium can be affected by varying MF has been shown in experiments with the terrestrial snail, *Cepaea nemoralis* (Kavaliers and Ossenkopp, 1988) concerning opioid receptors and in vertebrates on the behavioural and physiological level (Blackman et al., 1985; Kavaliers and Ossenkopp, 1986). The two rather distinct locations – eyes and melanophores – which are involved in the perception of MF both require calcium for light signal processing and also for the transfer of the hormonal stimulus, respectively (de Graan et al., 1984; Stieve, 1988).

It may be speculated that cells equipped with these mechanisms of signal transduction generally are sensitive to MF, i.e. that MF reception does not depend on specialized sensory structures but is a basic property of the living cell. Results of experiments on the development of *X. laevis* under different MF conditions support this interpretation (Imgrund et al., 1989), showing that the velocity of growth and differentiation is influenced by MF before the development of sensory organs and neural structures is finished. Thus, whether the effects of MF are expressed on the behavioural level of the animal may not be primarily a question of the reception of MF but of appropriate neuronal wiring.

References

Adey, W. R. (1981): Tissue Interactions With Non-Ionizing Radiation. Physiol. Rev. *61*, 435–514.

Besharse, J. C., Iuvone, P. M. (1983): Circadian clock in Xenopus eye controlling retinal serotonin N-acetyltransferase. Nature *305*, 133–135.

Blackman, C. F., Benane, S. G., Rabinowotz, J. R., House, D. E., Joines, W. T. (1985): A Role for the Magnetic Field in the Radiation-Induced Efflux of Calcium Ions From Brain Tissue *In Vitro*. Bioelectromagnetics *6*, 327–337.

Collin, J.-P., Arendt, J., Gern, W. A. (1988): Le «troisieme oeil». La Recherche *19*, 1154–1156.

Cremer-Bartels, G., Krause, K., Mitoskas, G., Brodersen, D. (1984): Magnetic Field of the Earth as Additional Zeitgeber for Endogeneous Rhythms? Naturwissenschaften *71*, 567–574.

Fromme, H. G. (1961): Untersuchungen über das Orientierungsvermögen nächtlich ziehender Kleinvögel (*Erithacus rubecula, Sylvia communis*). Z. Tierpsych. *18*, 205–220.
deGraan, P. N. E., van de Kamp, A. J., Hup, D. R. W., Gispen, W. H., van de Veerdonk, F. C. G. (1984): Calcium Requirement for a-MSH Action on Melanophores: Studies with Forskolin. J. Rec. Res. *4*, 521–536.
Hogben, L. T., Slome, D. (1931): The pigmentary effector system VI. The dual character of the endocrine co-ordination in Amphibian colour change. Proc. R. Soc. London *B. 108*, 10–53.
Imgrund, U., Leucht, T., Martin, H. (1989): Der Einfluß unterschiedlicher Magnetfeldbedingungen auf die larvale Entwicklung von *Xenopus laevis*. Zool. Jahrb. Physiol. *93*, 397–405.
Kavaliers, M., Ossenkopp, K. P. (1986): Magnetic Field Inhibition of Morphine-Induced Analgesia and Behavioural Activity in Mice: Evidence for Involvement of Calcium Ions. Brain Res. *379*, 30–38.
– (1988): Magnetic fields inhibit opioid-mediated «analgesic» behaviours of the terrestrial snail, *Cepaea nemoralis*. J. Comp. Physiol. A *162*, 551–558.
Keeton, W. T., Larkin, T. S., Windsor, D. M. (1974): Normal Fluctuations in the Earth's Magnetic Field Influence Pigeon Orientation. J. Comp. Physiol. *95*, 95–103.
Korall, H., Martin, H. (1987): Responses of bristle field sensilla in *Apis mellifica* to geomagnetic and astrophysical fields. J. Comp. Physiol. A *161*, 1–22.
Korall, H., Leucht, T., Martin, H. (1988): Bursts of magnetic fields induce jumps of misdirection in bees by a mechanism of magnetic resonance. J. Comp. Physiol. A *162*, 279–284.
Kowalski, U., Wiltschko, R., Füller, E. (1988): Normal fluctuations of the geomagnetic field may affect initial orientation in pigeons. J. Comp. Physiol. A *163*, 593–600.
Leask, M. J. M. (1977): A physicochemical mechanism for magnetic field detection by migratory birds and homing pigeons. Nature *267*, 144–145.
Lek, B. v. D. (1967): Photosensitive Melanophores. Bronder-Offset, Rotterdam.
Leucht, T. (1984): Responses to light under varying magnetic conditions in the honeybee, *Apis mellifica*. J. Comp. Physiol. A. *154*, 865–870.
– (1987a): Effects of Weak Magnetic Fields on Background Adaptation in *Xenopus laevis*. Naturwissenschaften *74*, 192–193.
– (1987b): Magnetic Effects on Tail-Fin Melanophores of *Xenopus laevis* Tadpoles *in vitro*. Naturwissenschaften *74*, 441–443.
– (1989): Interactions of light and gravity reception with weak magnetic fields in *Xenopus laevis*. J. exp. Biology, in press.
Lindauer, M., Martin, H. (1968): Die Schwereorientierung der Bienen unter dem Einfluß des Erdmagnetfeldes. Z. vergl. Physiol. *60*, 219–243.
– (1985): The Biological Significance of the Earths Magnetic Field. In: Progress in Sensory Physiology, Vol. 5 (D. Ottoson, ed.), pp. 119–145. Springer, Berlin, Heidelberg, New York.
Martin, H., Lindauer, M. (1977): Der Einfluß des Erdmagnetfeldes auf die Schwereorientierung der Honigbiene (*Apis mellifica*). J. Comp. Physiol. *122*, 145–187.
Martin, H., Lindauer, M., Martin, U. (1983): «Zeitsinn» und Aktivitätsrhythmus der Honigbiene – endogen oder exogen gesteuert? In: Bayerische Akademie der Wissenschaften, Mathematisch-Naturwissenschaftliche Klasse. Sitzungsberichte, 1982. München.
Nieuwkoop, P. D., Faber, J. (1967): Normal Table of *Xenopus laevis* (Daudin). North-Holland, Amsterdam.
Olcese, J., Reuss, S., Vollrath, L. (1985): Evidence for the involvement of the visual system in mediating magnetic field effects on pineal melatonin synthesis in the rat. Brain Res. *333*, 382–384.
Phillips, J. B. (1977): Use of the Earth's Magnetic Field by Orienting Cave Salamanders (*Eurycea lucifuga*) J. Comp. Physiol. *121*, 273–288.
– (1986a): Magnetic compass orientation in the Eastern red-spotted newt (*Notophthalmus viridescens]. J. Comp. Physiol. A 158*, 103–109.
– (1986b): Two Magnetoreception Pathways in a Migratory Salamander. Science *233*, 765–767.
Reuss, S., Olcese, J. (1986): Magnetic Field Effects On the Rat Pineal Gland: Role Of Retinal Activation By Light. Neurosc. Lett. *64*, 97–101.
Reuss, S., Semm, P. (1987): Effects of Earth-strength Magnetic Field on Pineal Melatonin Synthesis in Pigeons. Naturwissenschaften *74*, 38–39.

Schulten, K., Windemuth, A. (1986): Model for a Physiological Magnetic Compass. In: Biophysical Effects of Steady Magnetic Fields (G. Maret, N. Boccara, J. Kiepenheuer, eds.), pp. 99–106, Springer Proceedings in Physics, Vol. 11. Springer, Berlin, Heidelberg, New York.
Seamon, K. B., Padgett, W., Daly, J. W. (1981): Forskolin: Unique diterpene activator of adenylate cyclase in membranes and in intact cells. Proc. Natl. Acad. Sci. USA *78*, 3363–3367.
Semm, P., Demaine, C. (1986): Neurophysiological properties of magnetic cells in the pigeon's visual system. J. Comp. Physiol. A *159*, 619–625.
Semm, P., Nohr, D., Demaine, C., Wiltschko, W. (1984): Neural basis of the magnetic compass: interactions of visual, magnetic and vestibular inputs in the pigeon's brain. J. Comp. Physiol. A *155*, 283–288.
Sinsch, U. (1987): Orientation behaviour of toads (*Bufo bufo*) displaced from the breeding site. J. Comp. Physiol. A *161*, 175–727.
Sinsch, U. (1988 a): El sapo andino *Bufo spinulosus*: anáeisis preliminar de sa orientación hacia sus lugares de reproducción. Boletin de Lima *57*, 83–91.
– (1988 b): The initial orientation of three toad species (Bufo) displaced from the breeding site. In: Symposium Biology and Physiology of Amphibians. (W. Hanke, ed), pp. 86–87, Karlsruher Beiträge zur Zoophysiologie, Vol. 14.
Stieve, H. (1988): Was wissen wir über den molekularen Mechanismus der Erregung von Lichtsinneszellen? Naturwissenschaften *75*, 288–296.
Weber, W. (1983): Photosensitivity of Chromatophores. Amer. Zool. *23*, 495–506.
White, B. H., Sekura, R. D., Rollag, M. D. (1987): Pertussis toxin blocks melatonin-induced pigment aggregation in Xenopus dermal melanophores. J. Comp. Physiol. B *157*, 153–159.
Wiltschko, W., Nohr, D., Füller, E., Wiltschko, R. (1986): Pigeon Homing: The Use of Magnetic Information in Position Finding. In: Biophysical Effects of Steady Magnetic Fields (G. Maret, N. Boccara, J. Kiepenheuer, eds.), pp. 154–162, Springer Proceedings in Physics, Vol. 11. Springer, Berlin, Heidelberg, New York.

Fortschritte der Zoologie, Band/Vol. 38 · Hanke, W. (Hrsg.), Biology and Physiology of Amphibians
Gustav Fischer Verlag · Stuttgart · New York · 1990

Salt and water balance during hibernation in anurans

K. Hvidtfeldt Nielsen and C. Barker Jørgensen

Zoophysiological Laboratory A. August Krogh Institute, 13 Universitetsparken, DK-2100 Copenhagen Ø, DK

1. Introduction

During hibernation, frogs and toads accumulate sodium chloride and water, and they emerge from hibernation with distended cutaneous lymph sacs (Barthélémy, 1926; de Haan, 1927). The state is usually referred to as oedematous, and it has been suggested to result from deficient osmotic regulation at low temperature (Jørgensen, 1950a; Zamachowski, 1966; Gordon, 1982). This suggestion seemed supported by the finding that frogs, *Rana esculenta*, at low temperature efficiently eliminated a water load, but not a salt load. When frogs were injected with hypertonic solutions of sodium chloride, they retained the salt and established a positive water balance until normal osmotic pressure of the body fluids was reestablished. This response to hypertonic salt solutions was observed even in frogs that had already substantially expanded their extracellular fluid volume by cutaneous uptake of salt and water, salt loads thus aggrevating the oedematous state. Upon retransfer to room temperature the excess of salt and water was rapidly eliminated (Jørgensen, 1950a). The expansion of the extracellular fluid volume in anurans at low temperature has even been compared to the oedematous state that may develop in patients suffering, e.g. from congestive heart failure (Gayton, 1978). However, several circumstances suggest that the accumulation of salt and water in hibernating anurans should be interpreted in adaptational rather than in pathological terms. Thus, the ‹oedematous› state seems related to breeding. Only after the end of the breeding period following hibernation does osmotic regulation return to the pattern typical of the non-hibernating state. Moreover, the retention of salt and water at low temperature is only observed in healthy animals in a good nutritional condition, and not in emaciated animals (Jørgensen et al., 1978). To further elucidate the nature of the anuran hibernation oedema, the temporal changes in water and salt balance were analysed in detail in toads exposed to simulated hibernation for a period of about 5 months.

2. Methodical design to elucidate anuran hibernation oedema

Experiments were carried out on adult female toads collected in Vendsyssel, Denmark, in the beginning of September and kept in plastic trays with tapwater in a refrigerator at 2 °C in order to keep the toads in a good nutritional condition until the start of the experiment. On October 25 the toads were transferred to room temperature for acclimation during three days. During this period they eliminated the salt and water they had accumulated in the refrigerator. Finally, they were transferred to a thermostatted room at 4 °C and kept in frog's Ringer diluted 1:25 as a substitute for freshwater. The medium was changed as required so that the concentration of NaCl never dropped below 2 mmol l^{-1}.

Experiments were made on two groups of 10 toads each kept in plastic trays with 1 l medium, as well as on four single toads kept in plastic boxes with 25 ml medium. Handling, including emptying of the bladder by catheterization and other types of ‹stress›, causes salt loss and may affect the cutaneous ion uptake (Jørgensen et al., 1978). The one group of 10 toads, of mean body mass 51 ± 7.7 (S.D.) g (Group K) therefore served as controls that were only handled at the start of the experiment, when all animals were weighed after catheterization of the bladder and samples of lymph were taken. In this experiment only net changes in the ionic balance of the 10 toads were determined by analysis of the medium for content of Na^+, Cl^- and K^+. The other group of 10 toads, of mean body mass 48 ± 7.0 g (Group A) as well as the four single toads (Group B) were sampled repeatedly. Changes in body mass were determined by weighing after catheterization of the bladder. If obtained in sufficient quantities the urine was analysed for concentrations of Na^+, Cl^- and K^+.

Moreover, the concentration of these ions was followed in lymph drawn by suction from the dorsal lymph sac through a heparinized hypodermic needle attatched to 4 mm plastic tubing. Mostly, 50 or 100μl samples could be recovered. The four single toads were treated similarly. They served to elucidate individual variability in the response to handling.

Urinary losses of Na^+, Cl^- and K^+ were estimated from the concentration of the ions multiplied by the rate of urine flow, which at steady state equals the rate of cutaneous water uptake, or 0.048 ml cm^{-2} at 4 °C (Jørgensen, unpublished). From the measured net changes in contents of Na^+ and Cl^- in the bodies and calculated urinary losses the cutaneous influxes could be estimated.

The stay at 4 °C lasted to mid March, when the toads were retransferred to room temperature and placed individually in 25 ml of distilled water. The water was changed repeatedly in connection with weighing of the toads and sampling of urine and lymph, in order to follow the reestablishment of the high temperature water and salt balance in the toads, and to measure the amounts of water and sodium chloride accumulated during the stay at low temperature. All toads were healthy at the end of the experiment.

Na^+ and K^+ determinations were made by means of an Eppendorf emission flame photometer and Cl^- by means of a chloride titrator (CMT, Radiometer).

3. Response of toads under simulated hibernation

3.1. Accumulation phase at 4 °C

The immediate response of the toads to transfer from about 20 to 4 °C was an increase in body mass, amounting in Group A to 6.0 ± 1.0% after 3 days (Fig. 1). This increase in body water was reflected in declining ion concentrations in the lymph, *i.e.*, the blood plasma. The concentration of Na^+ dropped from 119 to 110 mM, or about 7% and Cl^- from 105 to 101 mM, or about 4% (Fig. 4). The changes in total body Na^+ and Cl^- were small (Fig. 2). During the following week body mass increased further to reach a level about 10% above the initial mass. The rate of accumulation of Na^+ and Cl^- peaked during this week, but accumulation continued at a declining rate throughout the stay at 4 °C, both in the group of handled and in the undisturbed toads (Fig. 2). In fact, the handled toads exhibited a larger and more steady increase in the body pools of Na^+ and

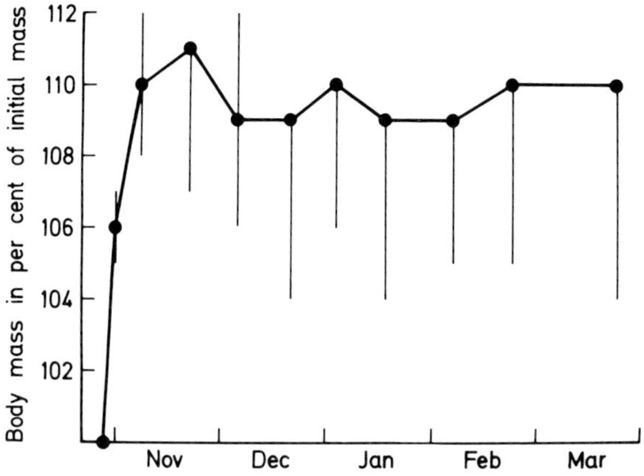

Fig. 1: Temporal changes in body mass of a group of 10 female toads, kept in 1/25 frog Ringer, upon transfer from 20 °C to 4 °C. Vertical bars indicate standard deviations of the means.

Cl^-. Both groups eventually accumulated more Cl^- than Na^+. K^+ was lost in both groups, the loss being greater in the handled than in the control toads (Fig. 2).

This pattern in mean temporal changes in water and salt balance was repeated in the single toads. At the transfer from 20 to 4 °C the body mass increased by 7.8 ± 1.3% and Na^+ and Cl^- decreased by 7 and 5%, respectively. All four toads showed the sigmoid pattern of salt accumulation, but the variation was great, both in the temporal changes in body mass and salt accumulation. Fig. 3 A and B show two examples, in one of which the accumulation was temporarily strongly reduced or negative. This period was terminated by a moult. The same relationship between moulting and a preceding period of declining

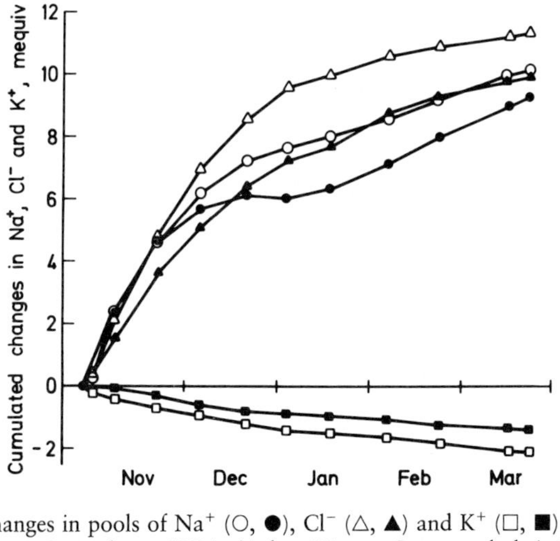

Fig. 2: Cumulated changes in pools of Na^+ (○, ●), Cl^- (△, ▲) and K^+ (□, ■) in two groups of 10 female toads kept about 5 months at 4 °C in 1/25 frog Ringer. Open symbols indicate handled toads, filled symbols control toads.

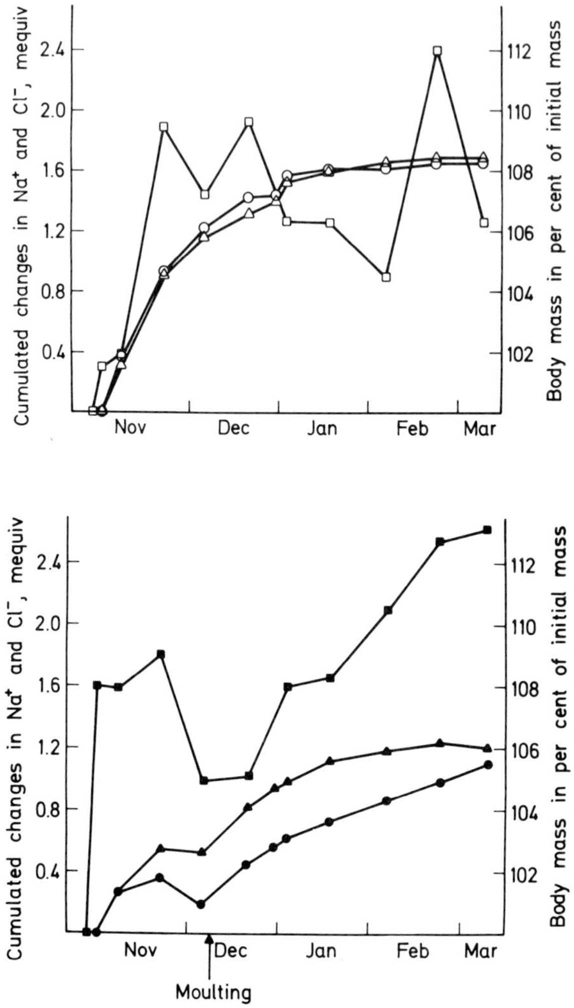

Fig. 3 A, B: Cumulated changes in pools of Na^+ (○) and Cl^- (△), as well as changes in body mass (□), in two toads kept at 4 °C in 1/25 frog Ringer. Open symbols: toads without moult; closed symbols: toads with interruption by a moult.

uptake and eventually loss of salt was also observed in two other toads, whereas such irregular uptake was absent in the fourth toad that did not moult during the period of accumulation (Fig. 3 A).

Concurrently with the accumulation of Na^+ and Cl^-, the concentration of the ions in the lymph increased to reach levels that exceeded the initial. The increase in Cl^- was particularly pronounced. In Group A the concentration rose from 79 to about 100 mM (Fig. 4).

Potassium in the lymph behaved differently from Na^+ and Cl^-. At transition from room temperature to 4 °C, the K^+ concentration in Group A declined within 3 days from 3.0 ± 0.25 mM to 1.9 ± 0.31 mM, or 37%. The concentration remained at this level throughout

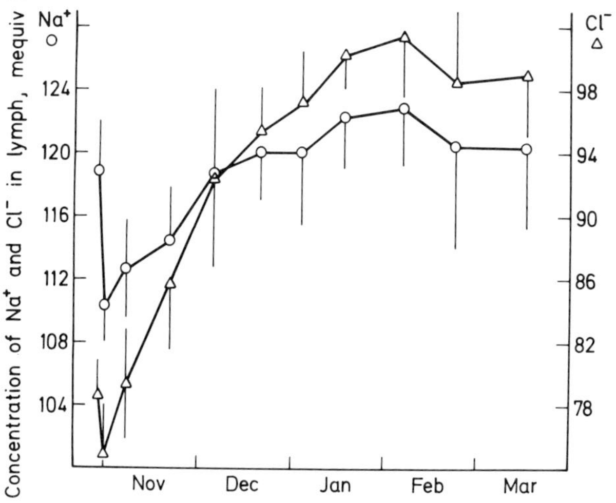

Fig. 4: Concentration of Na^+ (○) and Cl^- (△) in the lymph of a group of 10 female toads kept about 5 months at 4 °C in 1/25 frog Ringer. Vertical bars indicate standard deviations of the means.

the stay at the hibernation temperature, the mean concentration being 1.85 mM (range 1.7 ± 0.28 to 2.0 ± 0.41) (Fig. 5). In group B the decline was from 3.6 ± 1.1 to 1.7 ± 0.48, or 52%. The concentration of K^+ thus declined much more than corresponding to the increased hydration of the body.

The temporal pattern in ion balances during the phase of accumulation was analysed in more detail by following the net changes in accumulation and urinary losses. The sum of these constitutes a minimum figure for the cutaneous influx of the ion. The net uptake rates are fairly accurately determined, whereas the urinary losses can only be roughly

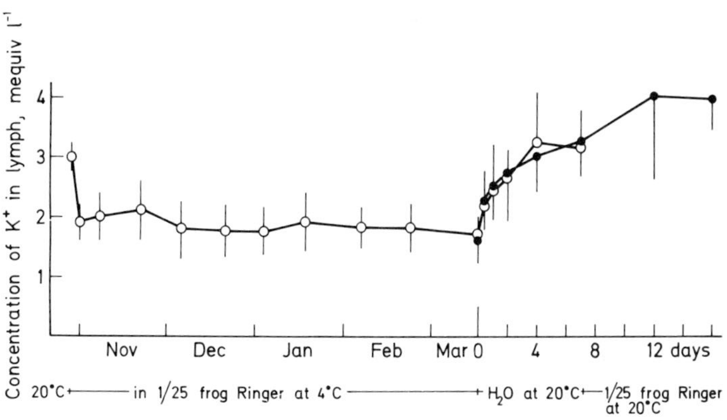

Fig. 5: Concentration of K^+ in lymph of a group of 10 female toads (○) before, during and after exposure to 4 °C for about 5 months. Five of the toads (●) were followed for 16 days after retransfer to 20 °C. Vertical bars indicate standard deviations of the means.

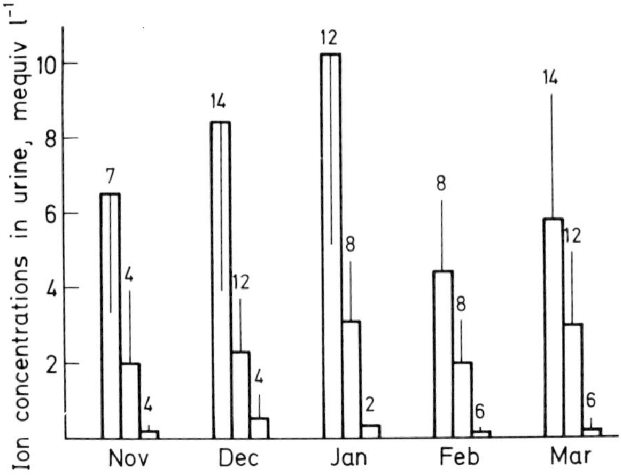

Fig. 6: Concentrations of Na^+, Cl^- and K^+ in the urine of female toads kept about 5 months at 4 °C in 1/25 frog Ringer. Columns to the left are Na^+ and to the right K^+. Figures above columns indicate numbers of determinations. Vertical bars indicate standard deviations of the means.

estimated, mainly because of the large fluctuations in the concentrations of the ions, particularly Na^+. The monthly means ± SD of all measured ionic concentrations are shown in Fig. 6. The concentration of Na^+ was consistently higher than that of Cl^-, typically 2–3 times higher. The concentrations of both ions tended to increase during the period of accumulation to reach maximum values in January, when also the concentrations in the lymph reached their highest values (Fig. 4).

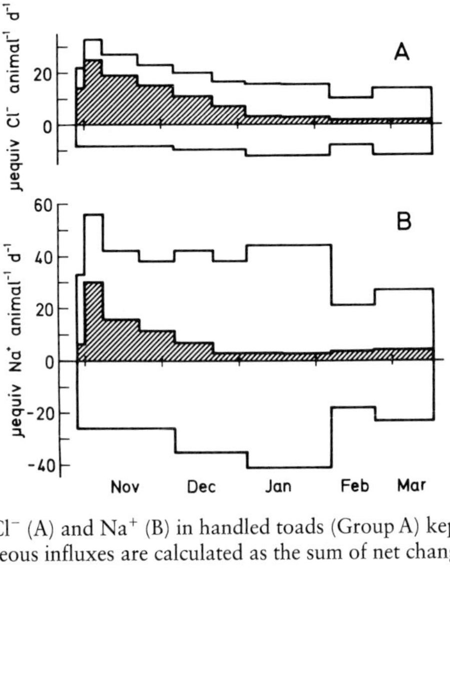

Fig. 7 A, B: Balances of Cl^- (A) and Na^+ (B) in handled toads (Group A) kept about 5 months at 4 °C in 1/25 frog Ringer. Cutaneous influxes are calculated as the sum of net changes (hatched) and urinary losses.

Measured net uptake rates, estimated urinary losses and calculated influx rates are shown in Fig. 7 for the group of handled toads (A) and in Fig. 8 for the undisturbed controls (K). The estimates of Na^+ and Cl^- excreted with the urine are based on all measurements available. Fig. 7 indicates that the delay of some days before the net uptake rates reach their maximum values is correlated with a gradual increase in influx of both ions rather than a decrease in urinary losses. The decreasing net uptake is correlated both with rising urinary losses and declining influxes. Because of the relatively high concentrations in the urine, net uptake rates of Na^+ were lower than the simultaneous loss in the urine, except during the peak uptake rates of days 4 to 11 after transfer to hibernation conditions, whereas the net uptake rates of Cl^- exceeded or equalled the urinary losses for more than a month.

This general picture of the temporal patterns in net uptake, urinary losses and influx was further corroborated by the observations on the single toads. In these, sufficient numbers of samples of urine were obtained from two toads to allow estimates to be made of individual urinary losses.

Both toads showed a clear delay before peak net uptake rates of Na^+ and Cl^- (Figs. 9 and 10). In the toad that did not moult during simulated hibernation (it had moulted just before the transfer to the cold room, the further development in ion balance closely corresponded to the general pattern (Fig. 9). The toad, shown in Fig. 3 B, that did moult is particularly instructive in indicating that the approaching moult affected the cutaneous transport properties several weeks in advance of the actual moult (Fig. 10). The net uptake rate dropped to low levels after one week of high uptake rate. In the period from late November to early December the net uptake of Cl^- was close to zero whereas Na^+ was actually lost from the body. The toad moulted within the last 3 days of the period. If influxes were calculated from measured net changes and urinary losses the result suggested drastic declines throughout the period of 4 weeks. However, moulting is known to be preceded by a high cutaneous permeability to ions, which are lost by cutaneous diffusion (Jørgensen, 1949). Such losses are not included in the calculated influxes which therefore

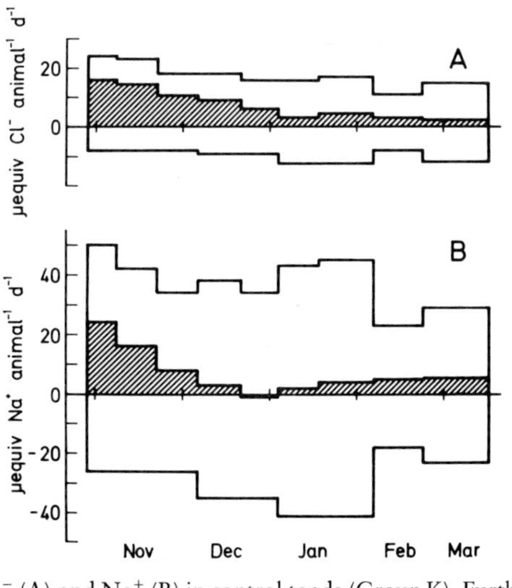

Fig. 8 A, B: Balances of Cl^- (A) and Na^+ (B) in control toads (Group K). Further explanation in legend to Fig. 7 A, B.

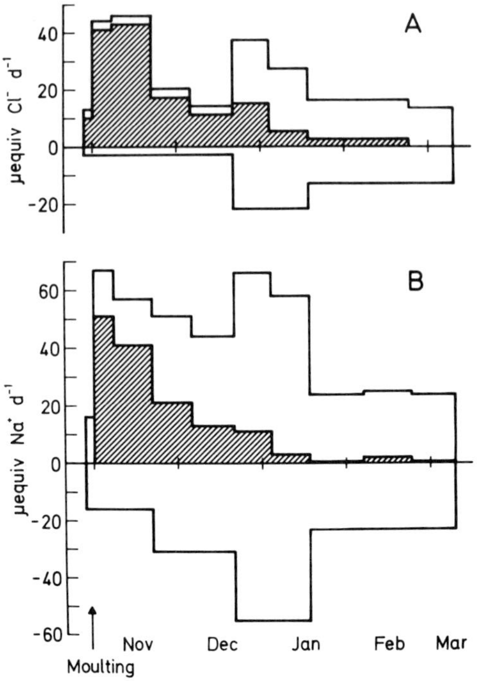

Fig. 9: Balances of Cl^- (A) and Na^+ (B) in a toad that did not moult during the stay at 4 °C. Further explanation in legend to Fig. 7 A, B.

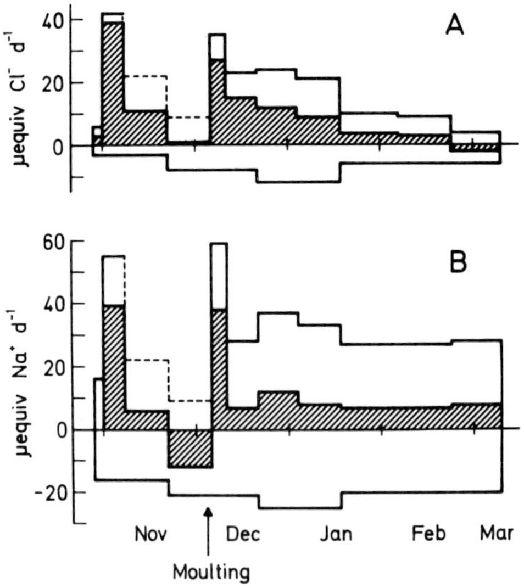

Fig. 10: Balances of Cl^- (A) and Na^+ (B) in a toad that moulted during the stay at 4 °C, indicated by the arrow. Further explanation in legend to Fig. 7 A, B.

underestimate the true influxes, as indicated by the use of hatched lines in Fig. 10. Actually influxes are doubled or more during moulting (Jørgensen, 1949).

In the period of 5 days following the moult, the rates of net uptake approached the early peak values, subsequently to decline to more moderate levels. For Na^+ this level was maintained until the end of the period of observation, whereas net uptakes of Cl^- continued to decline to become negative during the last 2 weeks, presumably because of a declining influx.

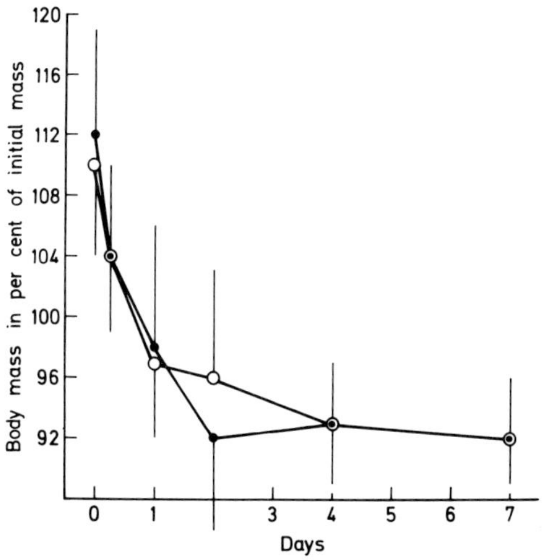

Fig. 11: Changes in body mass in group of handled (○) and control (●) toads upon retransfer to 20 °C.

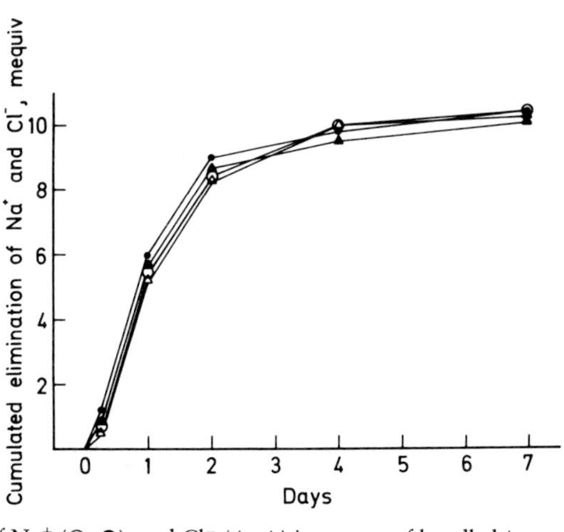

Fig. 12: Elimination of Na^+ (○, ●), and Cl^- (△, ▲) in groups of handled (open symbols) and control (closed symbols) toads upon retransfer to 20 °C.

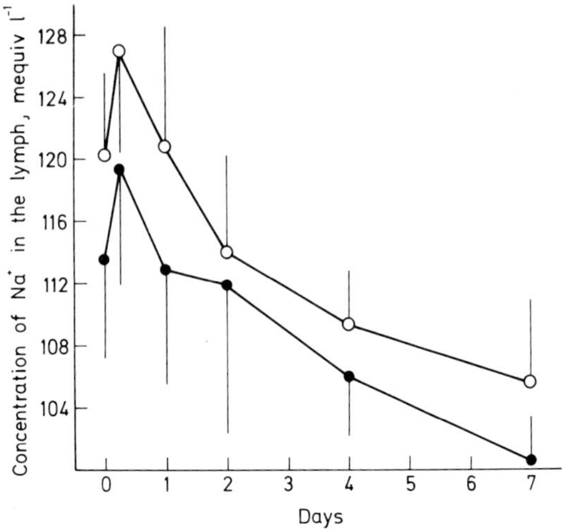

Fig. 13: Temporal changes in concentration of Na^+ in the lymph of groups of handled (○) and control (●) toads upon retransfer to 20 °C. Vertical bars indicate standard deviations of the means.

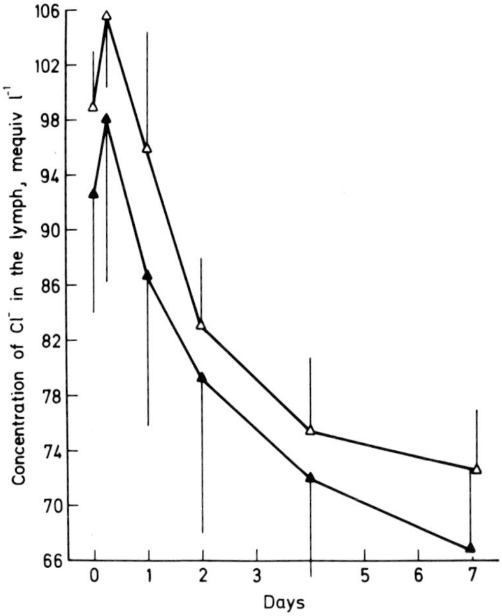

Fig. 14: Temporal changes in concentration of Cl^- in the lymph of groups of handled (△) and control (▲) toads upon retransfer to 20 °C. Vertical bars indicate standard deviations of the means.

3.2. Elimination phase at 20 °C

When the toads returned to room temperature they immediately began to eliminate salt and water. The elimination of water, measured as loss in body mass, abated within 2–4 days (Fig. 11), whereas Na^+ and Cl^- continued to be eliminated at a low rate at each change of the distilled water (Fig. 12). Fig. 12 also shows that elimination of salt was relatively slow during the first period of 6 hours, in contrast to the elimination of water, which peaked in the same period. This difference in pattern of elimination of salt and water is reflected in the changes observed in the concentrations of Na^+ and Cl^- in the lymph during the elimination phase (Figs. 13 and 14). Both ions increased in concentration during the first 6 hours before they began to decline. The decline in lymph concentrations continued throughout the period of observation of 7 days.

In order to assess how closely the toads at the end of the 7 days period had approached equilibration with freshwater at 20 °C, 5 toads from Group K were placed in 1/25 Ringer, and the water and salt balance was followed for 9 days. There was a slight further mean loss of Na^+ and a small gain in Cl^-. More importantly, elimination of water was resumed, resulting in an actual increase in lymph concentrations of as well Na^+ as Cl^- (Figs. 15 and 16).

With the return to the high temperature the K^+ concentration in the lymph rose again. The pattern in the increase in Groups A and K is shown in Fig. 5. In Group B, the concentration rose from 1.5 ± 0.34 mM to 2.6 ± 0.96 mM on day 7. Three mM thus seems to represent the level of K^+ in the blood plasma at 20 °C, against 2 mM or less at 4 °C.

3.3. Relation between Na^+ and Cl^-

During the period of ion accumulation in the cold the concentration of Cl^- in the lymph increased faster than did that of Na^+ (Fig. 4) and *vice versa* during the subsequent elimina-

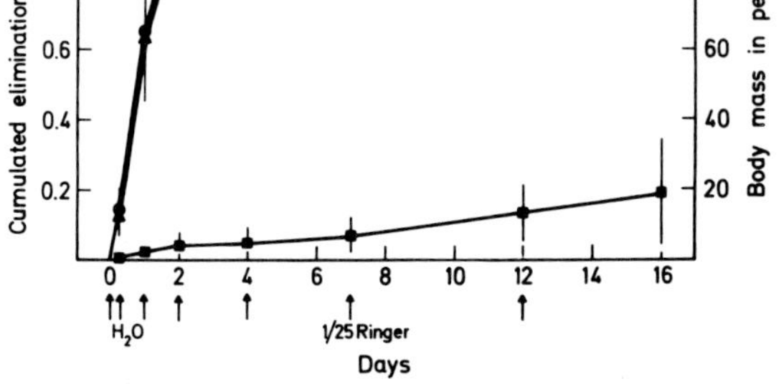

Fig. 15: Cumulated elimination of Na^+ (●), Cl^- (▲) and K^+ (■), as well as changes in body mass (+), in five control toads upon retransfer to 20 °C. Arrows indicate change of medium, initially distilled water, later 1/25 frog Ringer. Vertical bars indicate standard deviations of the means. Most standard deviations for Cl^- are omitted for the sake of clarity, they are similar to those for Na^+.

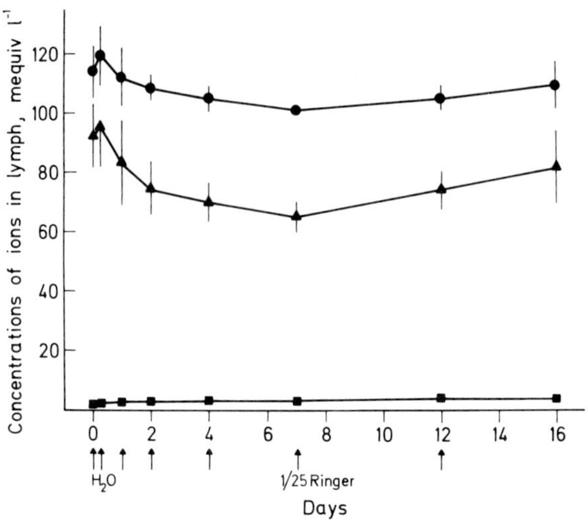

Fig. 16: Temporal changes in the concentrations of Na^+ (●), Cl^- (▲) and K^+ (■) in the lymph of five control toads upon retransfer to 20 °C. Arrows indicate change of medium, initially distilled water, later 1/25 frog Ringer. Vertical bars indicate standard deviations of the means.

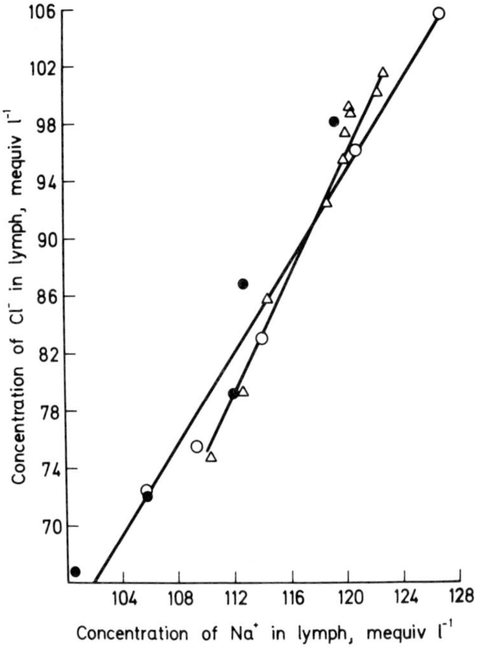

Fig. 17: Relation between concentration of Na^+ and Cl^- in the lymph of handled toads during 5 months of salt accumulation at 4 °C (△) and in handled (○) and control (●) toads during 7 days of elimination after retransfer to 20 °C.

tion of ions upon return to room temperature (Fig. 16). It was therefore of interest to determine the relationship between the concentrations of the two ions. Fig. 17 shows that the relationship differed during the two periods. Both relations could be described by linear regression equations, but with different slopes. The plot of Cl^- concentration on Na^+ concentration during the period of accumulation could be described by the equation $[Cl^-] = -164 + 2.17\,[Na^+]$ ($r = 0.99$), when the concentrations are expressed as mequiv l^{-1}. The same relation during the elimination phase could be described by the equation $[Cl^-] = -95 + 1.58\,[Na^+]$ ($r = 0.98$). The difference between the two slopes was statistically significant ($P < 0.01$).

4. Discussion of the observations

4.1. Temporal pattern in osmoregulatory adjustments at low temperature

When toads, in contact with water, are transferred from high to low temperatures they retain water, thus reducing the osmotic pressure of the body fluids. This response may be general in amphibians, both anurans and urodeles (Jørgensen, 1950a; Schmidt-Nielsen and Forster, 1954; Miller et al., 1968; Brown et al., 1984).

The positive water balance established in warm acclimated anurans exposed to low temperature results from reduced or discontinued urine production (Schmidt-Nielsen and Forster, 1954) as well as from a relatively high cutaneous water uptake (Hevesy et al., 1935; Jørgensen et al., 1978). Lowering of the body temperature in the toad thus initiates processes that result in antidiuresis and increased rates of water uptake. The full renal and cutaneous effects are only reached several hours after the temperature of the toad has reached that of the environment. The antidiuresis and increased rates of water uptake can be prevented by prior injection of water in amounts corresponding to that retained in response to the change in temperature (Jørgensen, unpublished).

When exposed to hibernation temperatures toads thus react as if they are dehydrated, or hypertonic, by reducing urine production and increasing the cutaneous water permeability until a new equilibrium for osmoregulation has become established at a lower set point, as has been suggested previously for frogs (Jørgensen, 1950a; Miller et al., 1968).

After a few days at the low temperature the osmoregulatory pattern again changed, as revealed by an increasing rate of net uptake of Na^+ and Cl^-. The rates culminated after about 10 days and remained high for some weeks before they declined to low levels. Presumably, the high rates of uptake resulted from high influxes of the ions. Even though these influxes were not precisely determined, because of only inaccurately determined urinary losses, the trends were clear. The influxes remained high after the decline in net uptake rates, correlated with increasing urinary losses.

The estimated influxes of Na^+ in the toads exposed to 4 °C may be compared with influxes measured in toads acclimated to room temperature, as determined by means of ^{24}Na (Jørgensen, 1950b). At 20 °C the influx in a 50 g toad amounted to about 40 μequiv Na^+ per 24 hours or substantially less than the peak values estimated early during the period spent at 4 °C. After the initial osmoregulatory response to a low temperature the toads thus reacted as if they were salt depleted by increasing the influx of Na^+ and Cl^- (Jørgensen, 1950b).

The high influx of Na^+ (and Cl^-) after 1–2 weeks stay at 4 °C is consistent with the finding of Lagerspetz and Skytta (1979) that Na^+ fluxes, as estimated from the short circuit currents of the isolated ventral skin of frogs, *Rana temporaria*, acclimated to 6 °C for 2–4 weeks, were the same as those in frogs acclimated for similar periods of time at 12 and 23 °C.

Within some months at the hibernation temperature a new steady state developed in water and salt balance, concurrently with the reestablishment of high concentrations of Na^+ and Cl^- in the extracellular fluid. As the steady state was approached influxes of Na^+ decreased to values about half those measured in toads acclimated to room temperature.

The character of a well regulated sequence of events was strikingly demonstrated in the osmoregulatory responses correlated with a moult. As mentioned, moulting is preceded by a salt loss due to a high cutaneous permeability to Na^+ and Cl^- (Jørgensen, 1949). Immediately after the actual moult these losses were compensated for by increased influxes of Na^+ and Cl^-, to restore the osmoregulatory status prevailing before moulting affected the salt and water balance.

4.2. Pool sizes

In order to estimate the relative increases in body water and salt accumulated during the simulated hibernation we should know the contents of water as well as sodium and chloride ions in the bodies prior to exposure to the hibernation conditions. The water content of the lean body mass, *i.e.*, body mass corrected for fat depots and, in females, vitellogenic ovaries, was 81.3 ± 1.0% in toads acclimated to room temperature (20 °C). The water content was independent of sex and season (based on data from Wind-Larsen & Jørgensen, 1987). This value agrees with the about 80% body water found by Zamachowski (1977) in *Bufo bufo*. At this initial water content, the weight loss upon retransfer to room temperature corresponded to a 25% increase in body water during the stay at 4 °C.

The initial size of the pool of sodium ions is not known, but if we assume that the sodium space approximates the inulin space of 30% of the body mass (Jørgensen et al., 1978), pool sizes can be estimated from the concentrations of Na^+ in the lymph. Such estimates were made separately for the three experimental groups of toads. Table 1 shows that the mean pool sizes in the groups varied from 3.4 to 3.6 mmol Na^+ per 100 g body mass.

At the end of simulated hibernation the pool sizes had increased to 4.7–5.1 mmol/100 g, or by about 40–45%. From the concentration of Na^+ in the lymph, spaces of about 42–44% could be calculated. After the toads returned to room temperature most of the accumulated sodium was again excreted. At the low concentrations of Na^+ in the lymph, the Na^+ space remained relatively high, about 35–37% (Table 1).

The chloride pool in toads, *Bufo bufo*, acclimated to room temperature is 36.4 ± 3.7 μmol per g body mass (Jørgensen, unpublished). From the concentrations of Cl^- in the lymph, spaces were calculated to correspond to 46–50% of the body mass (Table 1). At acclimation at 4 °C the pools had increased to 51–54 μmol/g, or up to 50%, and spaces to 55% of the body mass. Seven days after return to room temperature significant amounts of accumulated Cl^- still remained in the bodies, and because of the low Cl^- concentrations in the lymph, the Cl^- spaces had increased even further, to 57–59% (Table 1).

The changes in lymph concentrations and in pool and space sizes were similar in all three groups of experimental animals, so there were no obvious effects on water and salt balance at low temperature of the handling of the toads or of keeping the animals separate or in groups.

Potassium was lost slowly during the stay at 4 °C. If we assume a K^+ space corresponding to the intracellular volume, amounting to 80–30 = 50% of the body water, the losses at the end of the stay amounted to 5.6 μmol per liter of intracellular water in Group K,

Table 1: Pools and spaces of sodium and chloride ions in toads, *Bufo bufo*, acclimated to low salinities (1/25 frog Ringer) at 20 °C and at 4 °C for five months (simulated hibernation)

Period	Group	Na^+ Conc. in lymph mM	Na^+ Pool mmol/100 g	Na^+ Space % b.m.	Cl^- Conc. in lymph mM	Cl^- Pool mmol/100 g	Cl^- Space % b.m.
Prior to exposure to 4 °C	K	114 ± 4.9	3.4	30	74 ± 12.4	3.6	49.5
	A	118 ± 3.3	3.6	30	79 ± 2.2	3.6	46.3
	B	116 ± 3.2	3.5	30	79 ± 1.7	3.6	45.5
At end of exposure to 4 °C	K	113 ± 6.6	4.7	41.9	93 ± 9.2	5.1	54.8
	A	120 ± 5.1	5.1	42.7	99 ± 4.0	5.4	54.7
	B	115 ± 3.8	5.1	43.8	97 ± 1.2	5.4	55.3
After return to 20 °C	K	101 ± 3.1	3.5	34.7	67 ± 6.3	3.9	59.0
	A	106 ± 5.2	3.8	36.2	73 ± 4.4	4.2	57.8
	B	105 ± 4.8	3.9	36.7	72 ± 10.0	4.1	57.1

8.9 μmol per liter of in Group A and 9.8 μM in Group B. It is noteworthy that the rate of K^+ elimination increased greatly on return to room temperature. During 7 days at 20 °C the loss of K^+ amounted to about half the total loss during the almost 5 months stay at 4 °C.

Intracellular (muscular) concentrations of K^+ in anurans are comparable to extracellular concentrations of Na^+ (Shaw and Simon, 1955; Miller et al., 1968). A loss of about 6 μmol K^+ per litre of intracellular fluid during hibernation would therefore constitute a decline in concentration of 6% or less.

4.3. Restoration of high temperature water and salt balance

At retransfer to room temperature in mid March, elimination of the water and salt that was accumulated during the about 5 months of simulated hibernation began immediately. It is thus indicated that the physiological conditions of the breeding phase, characterized by maintenance of the expanded extracellular fluid, had not (yet?) been established.

The pattern of elimination was basically the reverse of that prevailing at the transfer to the low temperature. Initially, excretion of water dominated, resulting in a passing increase in the already high extracellular concentrations of Na^+ and Cl^-. The toads thus reacted as if they were hypotonic and/or hypervolumic. After some hours the excretion of salt predominated over that of water and during some days the concentrations of Na^+ and Cl^- had fallen to low values. During this period the organism reacted as if it was hyperosmotic. During the second week normal concentrations were restored due to resumed elimination of water. The period of elimination of excess extracellular fluid is thus characterized by a highly dynamic state of changing ‹set points› for extracellular volume and osmotic pressure before steady state conditions are reestablished.

5. Summary and conclusions

In order to elucidate the nature of the anuran hibernation oedema, the temporal changes in water and salt balance were analysed in toads exposed to simulated hibernation for a period of about 5 months, starting at the end of October. The toads were kept in frog's Ringer diluted 1:25 as a substitute for freshwater. The immediate response to transfer from room temperature (20 °C) to 4 °C was an increase in body water, resulting both from a reduced diuresis and a relatively high cutaneous uptake of water. When exposed to a hibernation temperature warm adapted toads thus reacted as if they were dehydrated (hypertonic). After a few days at the low temperature Na^+ and Cl^- influxes increased strongly, resulting in high net uptake rates of salt. The rates reached a maximum after about 10 days and remained high for some weeks. During this period the toads thus reacted as if they were salt depleted. Within some months in simulated hibernation a new steady state developed in water and salt balance, concurrently with declining influxes and re-establishment of high concentrations of Na^+ and Cl^- in the extracellular fluid. At this steady state body Na^+ had increased by 40–45%, Cl^- by about 50% and water about 25%.

At return to room temperature, in mid March, elimination of accumulated water and salt began immediately. The pattern of elimination was basically the reverse of that prevailing at the transfer to the low temperature. The periods of acclimation to hibernation conditions and returns to summer conditions are thus characterised by highly dynamic states of changing ‹set points› for extracellular volume and osmotic pressure (ion concentrations), the time constants in the osmoregulatory cybernetics scaling from minutes to months.

When toads, acclimated to freshwater (dilute salt solution) at room temperature, are exposed to a low temperature (simulated hibernation) a sequence of osmoregulatory processes is initiated that eventually establish the greatly expanded volume of extracellular fluid, including distended lymphsacs, that are characteristic of posthibernating anurans during the breeding season. These oedema thus do not reflect deficient osmoregulation in hibernating anurans, an interpretation that is supported by the finding of normal regulatory function of the cardiovascular system in frogs, *Rana catesbeiana*, at low temperature (Weathers, 1975; Lillo, 1980).

References

Barthélémy, H. (1926): Recherches biometriques et expérimentales sur l'hibernation, la maturation et la surmaturation de la Grenouille rousse (*Rana fusca*). C.R. Acad. Sci. *182*, 1653–1654.

Brown, P.S., Brown, S.C., Specker, J.L. (1984): Osmoregulatory changes during the aquatic-to-terrestrial transition in the rough-skinned newt, *Taricha granulosa*: the roles of temperature and ACTH. Gen. Comp. Endocrinol. *56*, 130–139.

Gayton, A.C. (1978): Discussion. In *Osmotic and Volume Regulation* (C.B. Jørgensen, E. Skadhauge eds.), pp. 78–79. Copenhagen: Munksgaard.

Gordon, M.S. (1982): Water and solute metabolism. In: *Animal Physiology: Principles and Adaptations* (M.S. Gordon ed.) 4. ed., pp. 272–332. MacMillan, New York.

de Haan, J. (1927): Schwankungen in Blut und Gewebeflüssigkeit bei Sommer- und Winterfröschen. Biol. gen. *3*, 1–14.

Hevesy, G.v., Hofer, E., Krogh, A. (1935): The permeability of the skin of frogs to water as determined by D_2O and H_2O. Skand. Arch. Physiol. 72, 199–214.

Jørgensen, C.B. (1949): Permeability of the amphibian skin. II. Effects of moulting of the skin of anurans on the permeability to water and electrolytes. Acta. Physiol. Scand. *18*, 171–180.

Jørgensen, C. B. (1950a): Osmotic regulation in the frog, *Rana esculenta* (L.), at low temperatures. Acta Physiol. Scand. *20*, 46–55.

– (1950b): The influence of salt loss on the osmotic regulation in anurans. Acta Physiol. Scand. *20*, 56–61.

Jørgensen, C. B., Brems, K., Geckler, P. (1978): Volume and osmotic regulation in the toad *Bufo bufo* (L.) at low temperature, with special reference to amphibian hibernation. In: *Osmotic and Volume Regulation* (C. B. Jørgensen, E. Skadhauge, eds.) pp. 62–79. Copenhagen: Munksgaard.

Lagerspetz, K. Y. H., Skyttä, M. (1979): Temperature compensation of sodium transport and ATPase activity in frog skin. Acta Physiol. Scand. *106*, 151–158.

Lillo, R. S. (1980): Heart rate and blood pressure in bullfrogs during prolonged maintenance at low temperature. Comp. Biochem. Physiol. *65 A*, 251–253.

Miller, D. A., Standish, M. L., Thurman, Jr., A. E. (1968): Effects of temperature on water and electrolyte balance in the frog. Physiol. Zool. *41*, 500–506.

Schmidt-Nielsen, B., Forster, R. P. (1954): The effect of dehydration and low temperature on renal function in the bullfrog. J. Cell. Comp. Physiol. *44*, 233–246.

Weathers, W. W. (1975): Circulatory responses of *Rana catesbeiana* to temperature, season and previous thermal history. Comp. Biochem. Physiol. *51 A*, 43–52.

Wind-Larsen, H., Jørgensen, C. B. (1987): Hormonal control of seasonal growth in a temperate zone toad *Bufo bufo*. Acta Zoologica (Stockh.) *68*, 39–56.

Zamachowski, W. (1966): Changes in the weight of the body of the common frog (*Rana temporaria* L.) during the period of hibernation. Acta Biologica Cracoviensia. Ser. Zool. *9*, 199–206.

Zamachowski, W. (1977): The water economy in some European species of anuran amphibians during the annual cycle. I. Water content of the organism. Acta Biologica Cracoviensia. Ser. Zool. 20, 181–189.

Fortschritte der Zoologie, Band/Vol. 38 · Hanke, W. (Hrsg.), Biology and Physiology of Amphibians
Gustav Fischer Verlag · Stuttgart · New York · 1990

Changing plasma osmolality – a strategy of adaptation of anuran amphibia to water scarcity under burrowing conditions

URI KATZ and JOY HOFFMAN

Dept. of Biology, Technion, Israel Institute of Technology, Haifa, Israel

1. Introduction

Anuran Amphibia depend to a large extent on water proximity. Only a small number have been reported from arid regions or brackish water and none in sea water (Bentley, 1971). A few can, however, endure long periods of time without free water under certain conditions. Two principal strategies can be distinguished amongst these species: I. those which are exposed to the environmental challenge without special protection, such as *Scaphiopus ssp.*, *Xenopus laevis*, and *Bufo viridis*, but are able to tolerate large variations in the osmolality of their body fluids (Bentley, 1971; Balinsky, 1981). II. those, such as *Chiromantis ssp.* and *Phyllomedusa ssp.*, which can become protected from the hostile environment by spreading wax over their integument, thus diminishing the water evaporation through their skin; they become also uricotelic for the elimination of the nitrogenous waste (Shoemaker and Nagy, 1977). *Rana cancrivora* (Gordon et al., 1961), *Bufo viridis* (Schoffeniels and Tercafs, 1965; Gordon, 1962; Katz, 1973) and *Xenopus laevis* (McBean and Goldstein, 1970; Schlisio et al., 1973) employ the former strategy; they may be considered truly euryhaline and can be adapted to high salinities. These and other anurans which belong to this group have to cope with conditions of water restriction. Burrowing behaviour is quite common among the Amphibia, particularly *Bufonidae*; it seems however to fulfil various functions such as defence against predators, aestivation and a means for water economy. In this paper, we discuss the mechanisms which underly the ability of *Bufo viridis* to endure long periods of time without access to free water, under burrowing conditions and compare it to *Scaphiopus couchi*. The significance of this particular strategy lies in that it provides larger flexibility under environment stressful conditions, despite the limited osmoregulatory capacity which is common to Amphibia in general (Table 1).

2. Adaptation of *Bufo viridis* for conditions of dehydration

Bufo viridis distributes through a large variety of geographical and environmental conditions (Gislen & Kauri, 1959). It is found in Scandinavia in the North and distributes in the South, to North Africa and the Arabian peninsula. It does not seem to possess any special protective mechanism against water loss, and when devoid of free water, it will dehydrate and die like other Amphibians. The species, which is the common toad in Israel,

Table 1: Plasma osmolality and urea concentration in anuran Amphibia under salt and burrowing conditions. (S – is 400 mmol/l NaCl in the first group – I, and 115–150 mmol/l in II. B – indicates water restriction under borrowing conditions for 2–3 months). Mean ± SE.

Species	Control Conditions Osmolality (mOsm)	Control Conditions Urea (mmol/l)	Salt or Burrowing Conditions Osmolality (mOsm)	Salt or Burrowing Conditions Urea (mmol/l)	Reference
I.					
Rana cancrivora (S)	290	40	830	350	Gordon et al. (1961)
Xenopus laevis (S)	230	10	545	155	Schlisio et al. (1973)
Bufo viridis (S)	270	22	810	310	Katz (1973)
(B)		–	1000	500	Hoffman et al. (1988)
Bufo woodhousei (Dry)	–	13	–	120	Jones (1982)
Scaphiopus couchi (B)	305	40	720	200	McClanahan (1967)
	274 ± 19	25 ± 7	781 ± 83	272 ± 64	
II.					
Bufo bufo (S)	213	12	380	10	Schoffeniels & Tercafs (1965)
Rana pipiens (S)	260	12	294	20	Jungreis (1971)
Rana temporaria (S)	218	3	262	13	Ackrill et al. (1969)
Rana esculenta (S)	239	1.5	388	22	Garcia-Romeu et al. (1981)
	232 ± 12	7.1 ± 3.3	331 ± 30	16 ± 3	

distributes both in the mesic an the semi arid zones of the country (Katz et al., 1984). It shows high tolerance to extreme environmental conditions, which is related to its ability to elevate the blood osmolality to very high values under osmotically stressful conditions. Urea is the principal contributing osmolyte under such conditions. *Scaphiopus couchi*, which was studied quite extensively by McClanahan and others (McClanahan, 1967, 1972), seems to share common features with *Bufo viridis*, although they differ markedly in their life history and specific responses to the external conditions. Unfortunately, the knowledge on other burrowing species is rather limited, based on behavioural observations and the natural history.

Bufo viridis will burrow when put on soil under laboratory conditions. It loses some water (weight) in the first few days, but keeps its weight constant thereafter for extended periods of time (Hoffman et al., 1988). This should resemble its natural behaviour, since burrowing toads were found in the midst of the summer in places where no free water was available. The toads maintain normal hydration despite the absence of free water, as evidenced by the water content of the various tissues which remains nearly constant throughout (Katz and Gabbay, 1986). The most dramatic changes are seen, however, in the osmolality and composition of the plasma and body fluids (Degani et al., 1984). Plasma osmolality of over 1000 mOsm was found in toads which were burrowed for over 7 weeks (Fig. 1), depending on the water content of the soil. *Scaphiopus couchi* on the other hand, may burrow for the greater part of the year (McClanahan, 1972) and its plasma osmolality will increase likewise up to 650 mOsm (Table 2). The principal and

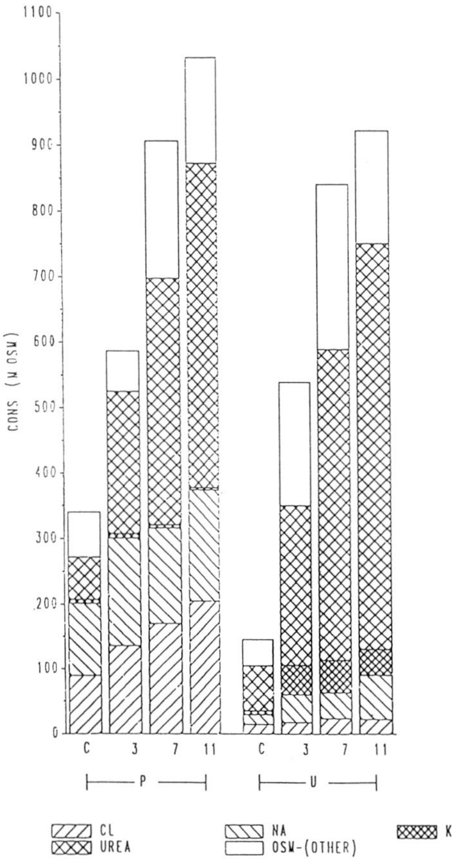

Fig. 1: Mean values of osmolality and compositions of plasma (P) and urine (U) of toads (*Bufo viridis*), burrowed for 3, 7 and 11 weeks in soil with 11.5% water content (C – control values). The blank spaces represent undetermined osmolyte(s).

nearly exclusive changing osmolyte unter these conditions in both species, is urea. This is a common feature to all the adaptable species (Balinsky, 1981), which belong to this category (see above). Urea retention and accumulation should therefore be of prime importance, under conditions of osmotic stress (Balinsky, 1981; Katz et al., 1984).

The toads become in fact a closed system under the burrowing conditions: urine voidance ceases, thus minimizing water and urea loss which recycle from the urinary bladder to the body fluids, while kidney function is maintained. The increase in the plasma osmolality facilitates retention of body water, against the soil water potential, while cellular osmotic stress is circumvented, since urea which is a highly permeant molecule, equilibrates with the cell interior. However, the retention of urea does not suffice to account for the increase in the urea concentration in the body fluids and urea synthesis should be greatly accelerated. This is achieved in part, through increase in the activity of the urea cycle enzymes (Balinsky, 1981). We have recorded also a great increase in the liver weight, following two weeks under burrowing conditions. There is indication also, that muscle

Table 2: A Comparison of Plasma and Urine Composition of *Bufo viridis* and *Scaphiopus couchi** in the Laboratory under Simulated Burrowing Conditions

	Plasma					Urine				
	Osm	Urea	Na^+	K^+	Cl^-	Osm	Urea	Na^+	K^+	Cl^-
	mOsm	mmol/l				mOsm	mmol/l			
1) Start of Experiments										
B. viridis	340	64	112	6	89	145	69	14	6	15
B. couchi	300	33	148	5	104	164	43	6	2	12
2) 2–3 month High water content soil**										
B. viridis	636	149	189	5	195	600	266	44	25	17
S. couchi	340	112	163	7	162	127	90	4	7	3
3) 2–3 month Low water content soil***										
B. viridis	1034	495	169	4	205	922	621	67	40	23
S. couchi	453	126	162	7	137	261	125	14	40	17

* Source: McClanahan (1972). *S. couchi* suffered from 30% mortality under both low and high water content soil conditions.

	B. viridis	*S. couchi*
	Water potential (atmospheres)	
** High water contained soil	2	< 1
*** Low water contained soil	5	10

proteins are broken down, which can thus contribute to the urea synthesis. Rather important metabolic changes therefore take place under the water restricted burrowing conditions. It facilitates the accumulation of large ammounts of urea in the body fluids, aiding greatly the increase in the plasma osmolality. The changes are differential and selective: the electrolytes (sodium and chloride) are efficiently conserved, and almost absent from the urine (nearly completely reabsorbed by the kidneys).

The regulatory basis for these changes is completely obscure. One could imagine that changes in blood osmolality or a particular constituent i.e. sodium, would stimulate release of certain hormone(s) which will initiate the reactions leading to the increased urea concentration in the body fluids. Short- and long-term regulations must be involved and should await a detailed study.

The Elasmobranchii is the only other class employing similar strategy, namely using a non-ionic osmolyte to compensate for the increase in the plasma osmolality (Smith, 1936). Since urea is the common molecule used for this purpose, it is evidently not toxic to the organism. Yancey et al. (1982), have suggested that a specific proportion of such osmolytes (urea and TMAO for example) stabilizes the structure of proteins under extreme conditions. The counter osmolyte has not been identified however, yet, in the Amphibia. Moreover, there is another important difference between the two groups: in the adaptable Amphibia, urea and plasma osmolality change widely depending on the environmental conditions (Balinsky, 1981), while in the Elasmobranchii it is maintained continually high.

Behaviouraly speaking, *Bufo viridis* which does not have spades, is not specifically adapted for burrowing. *Pelobates syriacus* on the other hand, which does possess them, exemplifies a similar, alas, apparently a lesser ability than *B. viridis*, for increasing plasma osmolality and urea concentration (Degani et al., 1986). It seems therefore that burrowing is a rather opportunistic response and any generalization will be premature at the moment, requiring more species in various habitats to be studied. *Scaphiopus sp.*, which burrows for long periods of time continually, becomes dormant (McClanahan et al., 1972), while *B. viridis* seems to be a periodic and rather active burrower. Burrowing, as has been mentioned above, may serve various purposes. It is rather disappointing then, that our knowledge on its distribution amongst species, as well as its possible ecological implications are so limited. A report on experimental burrowing of *Bufo marinus* (Boutilier et al., 1979) indicates regulatory response to disturbances in the acid-base status, but did not address the problem of plasma osmolality.

A comparison of the plasma osmolality and composition in several species, both euryhaline and burrowing (Table 1), shows that all the adaptable species have the capacity for a large increase in the plasma urea concentration under the osmotic stressful conditions. The plasma osmolality of the other species change only a little and the concentration of urea does not increase more than 40 mmol/l. Lower concentrations are not considered therefore in this context (Schmid, 1968). Amphibia is the only class of vertebrates, where large changes in the osmolality and composition of body fluids occur in response to environmental challenge. This is an intriguing strategy, particularly in species which maintain their activity such as *Bufo viridis*, rather than becoming dormant and deserves a thorough study of the underlying mechanisms. Only a survey of more species on a larger scale, will show how generally this hypothesis may hold.

3. Conclusions and summary

Bufo viridis, Scaphiopus couchi and a few other anuran Amphibia can live without free water under burrowing conditions for extended periods of time. The underlying principle common to these and the salt adaptable euryhaline species, is their ability to accumulate large quantities of urea in their body fluids. The physiological and biochemical mechanisms involved are therefore directed towards urea accumulation. Urea, a non-ionic and highly permeable solute, contributes to the increase in the plasma osmolality, thus facilitating water retention against the external high water potential conditions. Osmotic stress on the cells is avoided since urea equilibrates with the cell interior. The burrowing behaviour is discussed in the light of its adaptational significance for water economy and a distinction is made between the adaptable and non-adaptable species on the basis of their ability for increasing the plasma urea concentration.

References

Ackrill, P., Hornby, R., Thomas, S. (1969): Responses of *Rana temporaria* and *Rana esculenta* to prolonged exposure to a saline environment. Comp. Biochem. Physiol. *38*, 1317–1329.

Balinsky, J. B. (1981): Adaptation of nitrogen metabolism to hypertonic environment in Amphibia. J. Exp. Zool. *215*, 335–350.

Bentley, P. J. (1971): Endocrines and osmoregulation. Springer, Berlin, Heidelberg, N. Y.

Boutilier, R. G., Randall, D. J., Shelton, G., Toews, D. P. (1979): Acid-base relationships in the blood of the toad, *Bufo marinus*. III. The effect of burrowing. J. exp. Biol. *82*, 357–365.

Degani, G., Goldenberg, S., Warburg, M. R. (1986): Changes in ion, urea concentrations and blood plasma osmolarity of *Pelobates syriacus* juveniles under varying conditions. Comp. Biochem. Physiol. *75A*, 619–623.

Degani, G., Silanikove, N., Shkolnik, A. (1984): Adaptation of green toad (*Bufo viridis*) to terrestrial life by urea accumulation. Comp. Biochem. Physiol. *77A*, 585–587.

Garcia-Romeu, F., Masoni, A., Isaia, J. (1981): Active urea transport through isolated skins of frog and toad. Am. J. Physiol. *241*, R114–R123.

Gislen, T., Kauri, H. (1959): Zoogeography of the Swedish Amphibians and reptiles. Acta vertebratica *1*, 191–397.

Gordon, M. S. (1962): Osmotic regulation in the green toad (*Bufo viridis*) J. exp. Biol. *39*, 261–270.

Gordon, M. S., Schmidt-Nielsen, K., Kelly, H. M. (1961): Osmotic regulation in the crab-eating frog *Rana cancrivora*. J. exp. Biol. *38*, 659–678.

Hoffman, J., Eilat, U., Katz, U. (1988): *Bufo viridis*: physiological responses to osmotic stress (burrowing and salt acclimation). Israel J. Zool. *35*, 103–104.

Jones, R. M. (1982): Urea synthesis and osmotic stress in the terrestrial anurans *Bufo woodhousei* and *Hyla cadaverina*. Comp. Biochem. Physiol. *71A*, 293–297.

Jungreis, A. M. (1971): Seasonal effects of hyper-osmotic sodium chloride on urea production in the frog, *Rana pipiens*. J. exp. Zool. *178*, 403–414.

Katz, U. (1973): Studies on the adaptation of the euryhaline toad *Bufo viridis* to high salinities: oxygen consumption, plasma concentration and water content of the tissues. J. exp. Biol. *58*, 785–796.

Katz, U., Gabbay, S. (1986): Water retention and plasma and urine composition in toads (*Bufo viridis* L.) under burrowing conditions. J. Comp. Physiol. *B156*, 735–740.

Katz, U., Degani, G., Gabbay, S. (1984): Acclimation of the euryhaline toad *Bufo viridis* to hyperosmotic solution (NaCl, urea and mannitol). J. exp. Biol. *108*, 403–409.

McBean, R. L., Goldstein, L. (1970): Renal function during osmotic stress in the aquatic toad *Xenopus laevis*. Am. J. Physiol. *219*, 1115–1123.

McClanahan, L. L. (1967): Adaptations of the spadefoot toad *Scaphiopus couchi*, to desert conditions. Comp. Biochem. Physiol. *20*, 73–99.

McClanahan, L. L. (1972): Changes in body fluids of burrowed spadefoot toads as a function of water potential. Copeia *1972*, 209–216.

Schlisio, W., Jurss, K., Spannhof, L. (1973): Osmotic and ionic regulation in *Xenopus laevis* Daud. during adaptation to different osmotic environment. I. Tolerance and water economy. Zool. Jb. Physiol. 77, 275–290.

Schmid, W. D. (1968): Natural variations in nitrogen excretion in Amphibians from different habitats Ecology *49*, 180–185.

Schoffeniels, E., Tercafs, R. R. (1965): L'osmoregulation chez les Batraciens. Ann. Soc. Roy. Zool. Belg. 96, 23–39.

Shoemaker, V. H., Nagy, K. A. (1977): Osmoregulation in Amphibians and reptiles. Ann. Rev. Physiol. 39, 449–471.

Smith, H. (1936): The retention and physiological role of urea in the Elasmobranchii. Biol. Revs. 11, 49–82.

Yancey, P. H., Clark, M. E., Hand, S. C., Bowlus, D. R., Somero, G. N. (1982): Living with water stress: evolution of osmolyte systems. Science 217, 1214–1222.

Fortschritte der Zoologie, Band/Vol. 38 · Hanke, W. (Hrsg.), Biology and Physiology of Amphibians
Gustav Fischer Verlag · Stuttgart · New York · 1990

Hormonal regulation of Ca^{++}-uptake and distribution in Xenopus laevis

ULRIKE STENGEL, WILFRIED HANKE

Department of Zoology, University, D 7500 Karlsruhe, FRG

1. Introduction

The regulation of Ca^{++} uptake and distribution in Amphibia depends on the stage and the life situation. During the aquatic life of larvae, the Ca^{++} exchange system is an «open» system (Dacke, 1979) in which a more or less continuous uptake by the skin is possible provided the Ca^{++} content of the environment is not too low. On the contrary, the adult land-living stages resemble a «closed» system in which stores of Ca^{++} within the body exchange Ca^{++} to keep the Ca^{++} level of the blood constant. A constant Ca^{++} level of the blood is important for several physiological events, e.g. muscle contraction, cell metabolism and for the regulation of several physiological processes.

An intensive study of the hormonal regulation of the Ca^{++} homeostasis of *Rana pipiens* and *R. catesbeiana* has been reported by Robertson (1968, 1969a, 1969b, 1970, 1971a, 1971b, 1971c, 1972a, 1972b, 1974, 1975a, 1977). It has been shown that the Ca^{++} homeostasis is influenced and sustained by the secreted hormones of the ultimobranchial body and the parathyroid gland. Additionally, the vitamin D complex plays an essential role. Adult frogs depend mainly on Ca^{++} uptake by food. Furthermore, they mobilize Ca^{++} under Ca^{++} deficiency from stores, e.g. the paravertebral lime sacs or the bones. On the contrary Ca^{++} is shifted into the stores when hypercalcemia exists. It is not clear whether other hormonal systems apart from those mentioned play any role in the regulation of Ca^{++} levels in these frogs.

Xenopus laevis is peculiar in several respects. The toads still live in water after metamorphosis and might therefore keep the characteristics of an «open» system for their whole life. The target systems for the regulation of Ca^{++} homeostasis are the uptake mechanisms by the skin and the distribution into stores, like muscle, skin and bones. In our observations, we could not identify paravertebral lime sacs and therefore we concluded that they do not exist. It can be expected that the clawed toads have a very effective Ca^{++} uptake system in the skin.

The effects of hormones or vitamin D and its metabolites on Ca^{++} regulation in *Xenopus* have not been investigated extensively. Vitamin D or the active metabolite $1{,}25(OH)_2-D_3$ (calcitriol) control the Ca^{++}-resorption by the intestine in terrestrial Anura. Excessive doses of vitamin D_3 induce hypercalcemia (Schlumberger and Burk, 1953). It is doubtful whether *Xenopus* has developed ultimobranchial bodies after metamorphosis (Sterba, 1950; Saxén and Toivonen, 1955; Sehe, 1960). Despite of a good vascularized parathyroid gland in clawed toads, injection of parathyroid hormone (PTH) did not change the concentration of Ca^{++} in the plasma. Pang and Yee (1980) stated that PTH will cause hypercalcemia only in terrestrial Amphibia.

It would be of interest to study the regulation of Ca^{++} uptake and distribution in the aquatic *Xenopus* in order to compare another model of Ca^{++} regulation in Amphibia with the well defined system of terrestrial Ranidae.

This paper will focus on several problems. First, normal and hypophysectomized clawed toads recieved Ca^{++} injections and were influenced by hypo- or hypercalcitonicity of the environment. The Ca^{++} distribution in both types of toads were analyzed in order to study the regulation of Ca^{++} distribution by the pituitary. Second, the effects of hypophysectomy and 1,25 $(OH)_2$-vitamin D_3 (calcitriol) on Ca^{++} permeability of the skin are measured using Ussing chambers to study the regulation of Ca^{++} uptake. Third, receptors for calcitriol and concentrations of 25(OH)-vitamin D_3 (calcidiol) and calcitriol are determined in order to study the significance of these hormones with another approach.

2. Ca^{++} distribution in the juvenile clawed toad under Ca^{++} deficiency and Ca^{++} load

In *Xenopus*, different main compartments exist among which Ca^{++} is distributed. These are the plasma, the muscles, the bone, and to a minor extent the skin. Paravertebral lime sacs were not recognized. Normally, these are parts of the endolymphatic system and are located parallel to the vertebrae column. Clawed toads represent an open system in which Ca^{++} is taken up by the skin (and intestine) and shifted from the plasma to the muscle and bone. The main Ca^{++} pool is the bone which takes up and releases the Ca^{++} ions quite easily.

The concentration of Ca^{++} in the plasma is 2.05 mM (mean of our experiments). This is in fresh water (environmental Calcium: 2.87 mM) and varies only slightly (SEM 0.08).

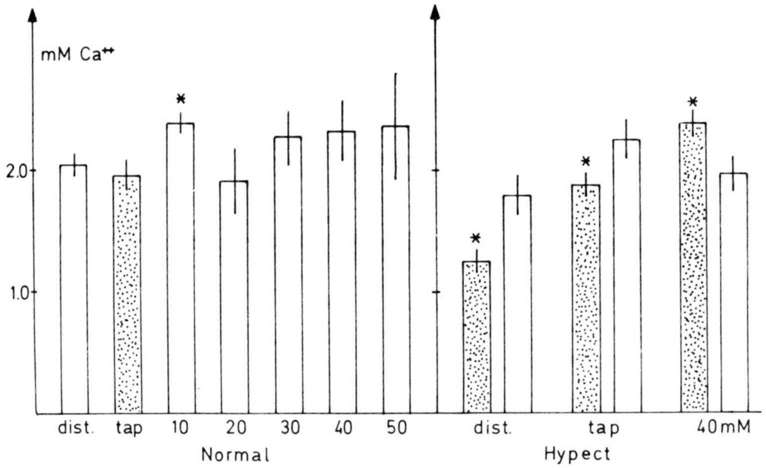

Fig. 1: Left: Variations of the plasma Ca^{++} concentration in distilled water or in 10–50 mM external Ca^{++} compared to those in tap water (dotted column, external Ca^{++}: 2.87 mM) after 3 days of acclimation. Right: Comparison between normal and hypophysectomized toads (dotted columns); n = 5, asterisk $p < 0.05$).

The muscles of our clawed toads contain 11.52 m mol/kg dry weight. The mean Ca^{++} concentration of the femur was 1969.23 m mol/kg dry weight. This last value is relatively low which might be due to the fact that juvenile toads were used in these experiments.

2.1. Ca^{++} distribution at acclimation to different external Ca^{++} concentrations

Low external Ca^{++} concentration as found in distilled water does not change the plasma Ca^{++} concentration when the animals are acclimated for 3 days. Hypertonicity of Ca^{++} increases the plasma concentration, but the effects are variable and therefore often not significant after acclimation for 3 days (Fig. 1). Hypophysectomy significantly lowers the Ca^{++} concentration of the plasma in toads acclimated for 3 days to normal Ca^{++} levels or to distilled water. Acclimation to higher Ca^{++} significantly increases the plasma Ca^{++} concentration in hpyophysectomized animals. These results demonstrate that the pituitary is important for the regulation of Ca^{++} homeostasis in clawed toads.

The Ca^{++} content of muscles significantly increased after treatment with 20 mM excess of Ca^{++}. The bone decreased the Ca^{++} content after acclimation to distilled water. In this case the effect in the muscle was found after 3 days, in the bone after 15 days of acclimation (Fig. 2). No evidence was found for an effect of hypophysectomy on the Ca^{++} content after the acclimation period.

It is reasonable to assume that the adjustment of the Ca^{++} levels in the plasma, muscle and bone is time dependent. This can be better demonstrated if the uptake of $^{45}Ca^{++}$ is measured dependent on time of acclimation to 40 mM Ca^{++}. There is a rapid increase in the plasma for 90 min followed by a slower increase for 24 hrs and a reduction after that time. The same characteristicss are found for muscle tissue at a much lower level. In the femur as an example for bone, a continuous incorporation of $^{45}Ca^{++}$ is seen for 48 hrs which increases to very high levels (Fig. 3). Hypophysectomy clearly lowers the amount of $^{45}Ca^{++}$ present on the first day in all three tissues. Plasma and muscles have higher $^{45}Ca^{++}$ levels after 48 hrs while the bone remains at lower incorporation after 48 hrs (Figs. 4, 5, 6).

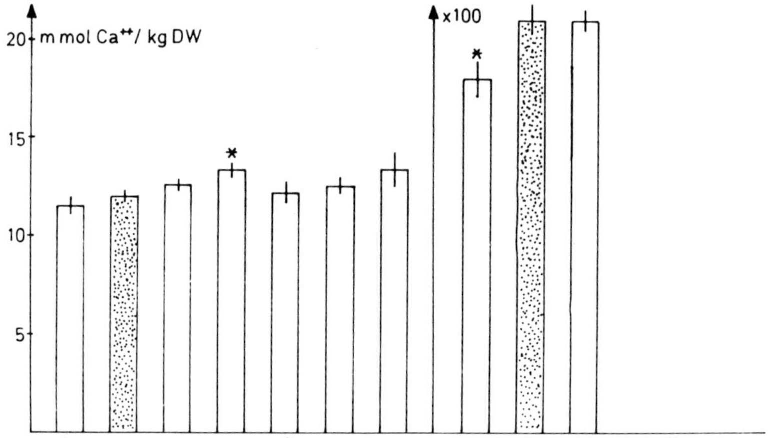

Fig. 2: Variation of the Ca^{++} concentration in m mol/kg dry weight (DW) of the muscle (left) and bone (right) compared to tap water (dotted columns); n = 5, asterisk $p < 0.05$.

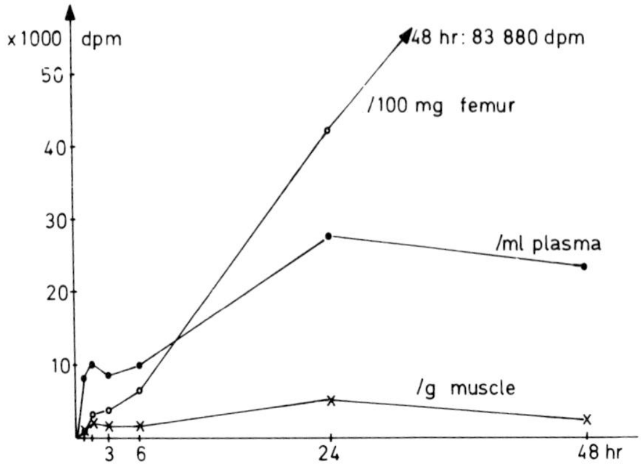

Fig. 3: Time course of distribution of $^{45}Ca^{++}$ in the plasma (per ml), muscle (per g) or femur (per 100 mg) during acclimation to 40 mM Ca^{++}, n = 3.

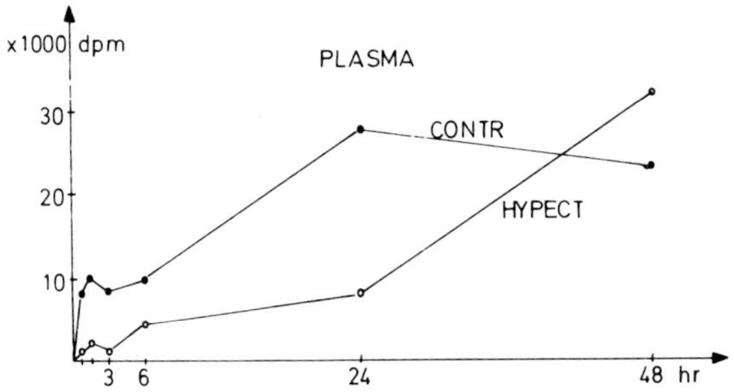

Fig. 4: Time course of distribution of $^{45}Ca^{++}$ in the plasma (per ml) of normal control or hypophysectomized toads during acclimation to 40 mM Ca^{++}, n = 3.

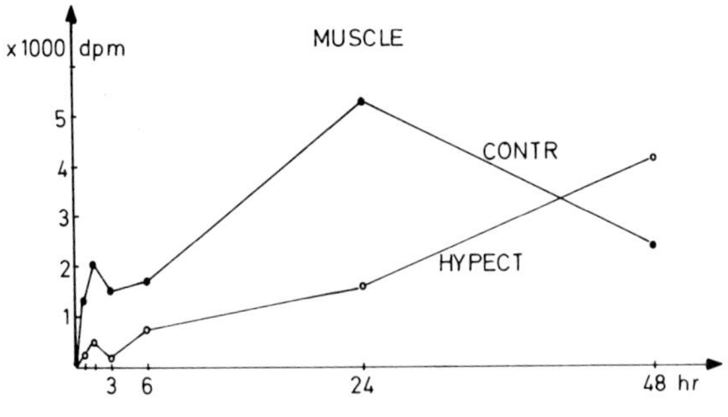

Fig. 5: Time course of distribution of $^{45}Ca^{++}$ in the muscle (per g) of normal control or hypophysectomized toads during acclimation to 40 mM Ca^{++}, n = 3.

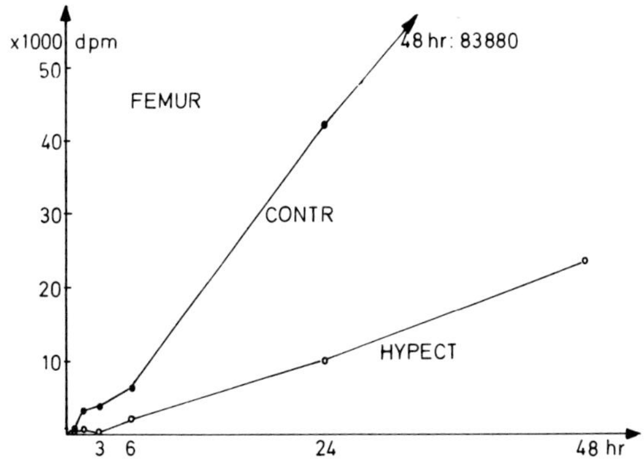

Fig. 6: Time course of distribution of $^{45}Ca^{++}$ in the femur (per 100 mg) of normal control or hypophysectomized toads during acclimation to 40 mM Ca^{++}, n = 3.

The experiments describing the Ca^{++} content of plasma, muscle or bone after 3 or 15 days of acclimation demonstrate the equilibrium at that time. The experiments showing the distribution of $^{45}Ca^{++}$ reflect the rate of uptake by the skin and by the muscle or bone. Both types of experiments are necessary to demonstrate the significance of the pituitary.

A comparison of these results with those found in other Amphibia shows the peculiarities of the clawed toad. The homeostasis of the Ca^{++} concentration found in juvenile *Xenopus* is in agreement with that found for tadpoles of *R. catesbeiana* (Uchiyama and Pang, 1981; Robertson, 1971 c). The premetamorphic animals display normal Ca^{++} values when acclimated to hypercalcemic media. The same was found by Sasayama et al. (1983) for *R. catesbeiana* and *R. nigromaculata* tadpoles. The plasma Mg^{++} level may not be as strongly controlled.

The tadpoles drink water and the Ca^{++} is mainly taken up by the intestine. It is not surprising that tadpoles of *Rana* species maintain a good homeostasis because they can shift excess Ca^{++} easily to the paravertebral lime sacs (Schlumberger and Burk, 1953; Pilkington and Simkiss, 1966; Robertson 1971 a). Calcitonin is suggested to be responsible for this transport of Ca^{++} into the stores (Sasayama and Oguro, 1982). Robertson (1971 b) found with histological methods that the ultimobranchial follicles of tadpoles of *R. catesbeiana* were very active during hypercalcemic acclimation. Removal of the ultimobranchial bodies resulted in further uptake of Ca^{++} from the hypercalcemic environment but in less storage of Ca^{++} in the endolymphatic system.

In adult frogs, which do not drink as much water, the food must be considered as the main source for Ca^{++}. The ultimobranchial gland is also involved in the Ca^{++} regulation along with other glands. The Ca^{++} regulation resembles a «closed» system.

Xenopus is regarded as the only anuran which reduces the ultimobranchial gland after metamorphosis. Calcitonin injection does not result in an uptake of Ca^{++} in paravertebral lime sacs (McWhinnie and Scopelliti, 1978). The results of our experiments demonstrated that the bone acts as a store for Ca^{++}. An effect of calcitonin injection was not seen. The muscle does not appear to be strongly involved in the regulation processes.

Hormones of the pituitary must lower the rate of uptake, but must also regulate the homeostatis in the Ca^{++} distribution system, which is called an «open» system.

It is well known that the pituitary influences the Ca^{++} homeostasis in teleost fish (Pang 1973, 1981; Wendelaar Bonga and Greven, 1978). Injection of high doses of prolactin can prevent the reduction of the plasma Ca^{++} level in hypophysectomized fresh water fish (Pang et al., 1970; Bern et al., 1981). It has been suggested that because of similarities of the life style the hypophysis is also necessary for the regulation of the Ca^{++} level in larval anurans and urodeles. In adults, parathyroid hormone then regulates the Ca^{++} homeostasis in connection with calcitonin and calcitriol.

One week after hypophysectomy, the Ca^{++} level in the plasma of tadpoles of *Rana catesbeiana* is significantly lowered (Ushiyama and Pang, 1981, 1982; Sasayama and Oguro, 1982). Prolactin or pituitary extract prevents this decrease. Injection of parathyroid hormone does not cause any significant effect in *Xenopus laevis*. The same seems to be true for tadpoles of *Rana catesbeiana* even though there is a functioning parathyroid in these tadpoles (Sasayama and Oguro, 1975; 1981).

Another influence on the Ca^{++} level may be the effect of estrogens. Since the ovary of reproductively active females contains high amounts of Ca^{++}, this must be considered as another possible compartment. This is the reason that in the experiments mentioned above juvenile toads were investigated.

2.2. Ca^{++} distribution after injection of Ca^{++} ions

An injection of high doses of Ca^{++} ions estimated to increase the plasma Ca^{++} concentration 5-fold (example: juveniles of 6 g weight receive an injection of 25 μM Ca^{++}) is tolerated. The Ca^{++} concentration clearly increases after such an injection. It needs 18–24 hrs to return to the normal level (Fig. 7). The muscle immediately takes up some of the excess amount of Ca^{++} and releases it again following the same timing as its disappearance from the plasma (Fig. 8).

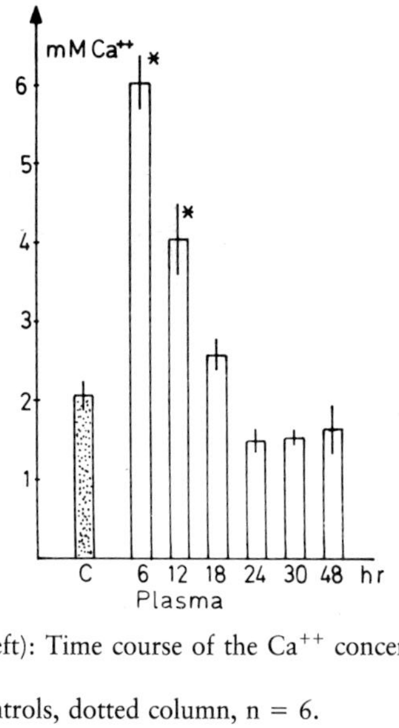

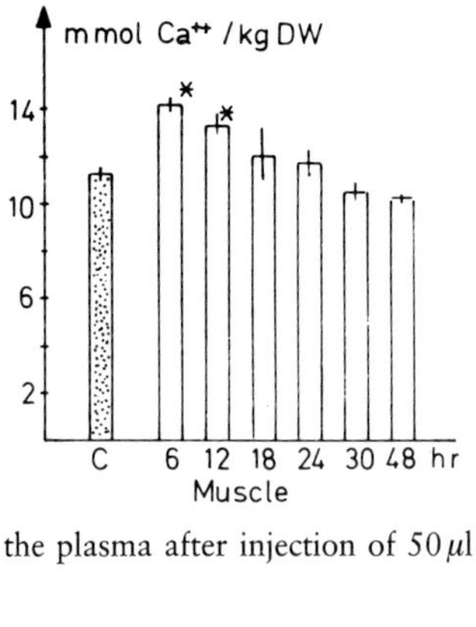

Fig. 7 (left): Time course of the Ca^{++} concentration in the plasma after injection of 50 μl of 0.5 M $CaCl_2$.
C = controls, dotted column, n = 6.

Fig. 8 (right): Time course of the Ca^{++} concentration in the muscle after injection of 50 μl of 0.5 M $CaCl_2$.
C = controls, dotted column, n = 6.

To check the distribution between plasma, muscle and bone more carefully, 0.2 Ci $^{45}Ca^{++}$ in 50 l of 0.5 M $CaCl_2$ (25 μM Ca^{++}) were injected in 6 g animals. The results clearly demonstrate that the radioactivity is quickly reduced in the plasma, is also decreased after a short increase in the muscle, and increases continuously in the bone (Fig. 9). The radioactivity reveals the distribution of Ca^{++} after a Ca^{++} load to maintain homeostasis.

Hypophysectomy influences the distribution of injected Ca^{++} as expected (Figs. 10, 11, 12). The drop of Ca^{++} in the plasma is not changed very much. It slopes a little more slowly, but it is difficult to demonstrate this convincingly. The uptake of radioactivity in the muscle is much slower and the release is not as fast in hypophysectomized clawed toads as in controls. In the same way, the uptake of radioactivity by the bone is significantly less than in controls.

3. Ca^{++} penetration through the skin of the juvenile clawed toad

The influx of $^{45}Ca^{++}$ through the skin can be measured in vitro using special types of Ussing chambers. The efflux of $^{45}Ca^{++}$ is relatively low and can be neglected. The uptake of $^{45}Ca^{++}$ or the non radioactive isotop can be assumed to be equal and so the total influx from a 1 mM Ca^{++} containing Ringer solution can be calculated.

3.1. Influence of hypophysectomy

The influx of $^{45}Ca^{++}$ *in vitro* is much lower through the skin of hypophysectomized toads compared to normal toads. In these experiments, the hypophysectomy was generally performed a fortnight before the skin was investigated. The reduction is true only for Ca^{++} influx. A comparison to changes for inulin uptake shows that it is not a reduction due to general structural changes (Fig. 13).

3.2. Influence of calcitriol injections

Juvenile toads received 3 equal injections of calcitriol (RO 21-5535, Hoffmann-La Roche) 48, 24 and 12 hrs before investigation of the skin. The whole dose given with these 3 injections was 0.1 or 1.0 g calcitriol.

It is demonstrated that both doses clearly enhance the uptake of Ca^{++} by the skin. In both cases the permeability for inulin was not changed significantly despite a slight increase in the uptake rate in one of the experiments. A dose-effect relationship was not suggested from these two experiments (Figs. 14, 15).

4. Ca^{++} regulation by calcidiol and calcitriol

The significance of calcidiol and calcitriol was studied by determination of their receptors in the intestine and skin. Furthermore, the level of calcitriol was determined in dependency on the environment. The experiments did not reveal clear differences in the calcitriol levels, it was only found that the level was much higher in fed compared to starved clawed toads. All the experiments described in this section were done in collaboration with other laboratories (Merke et al., 1989).

The cytosol of the mucosa of the intestine was homogenized in a buffer solution and then 1,25 ^3H-$(OH)_2D_3$ (tritiated calcitriol) was added. The receptor binding was analyzed

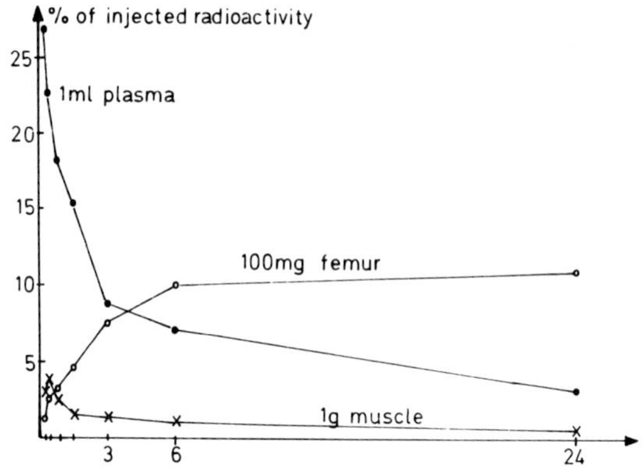

Fig. 9: Time course of the changes of the percentage of radioactivity after injection of 0.2 μCi $^{45}Ca^{++}$ in 50 μl of 0.5 M $CaCl_2$. n = 3.

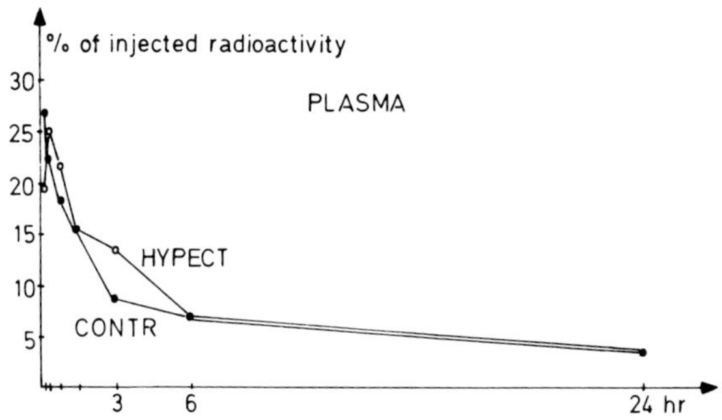

Fig. 10: Time course of the changes of the percentage of radioactivity in the plasma of control or hypophysectomized clawed toads. Injection as in Fig. 9. n = 3.

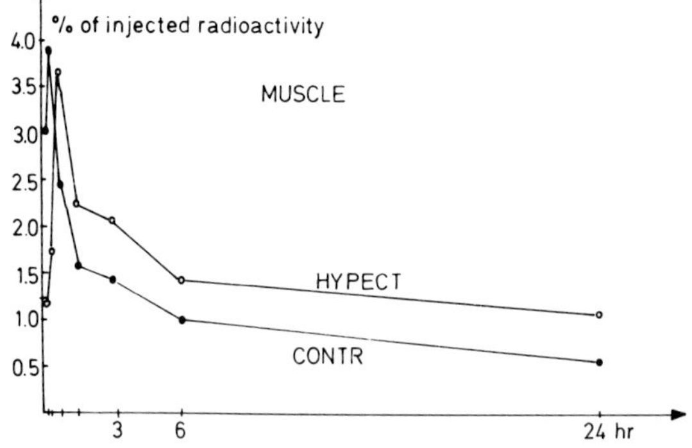

Fig. 11: Time course of the changes of the percentage of radioactivity in the muscle of control or hypophysectomized clawed toads. Injection as in Fig. 9. n = 3.

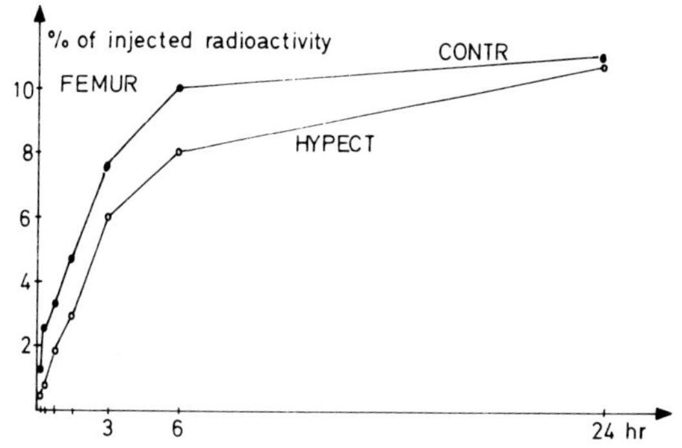

Fig. 12: Time course of the changes of the percentage of radioactivity in the femur of control or hypophysectomized clawed toads. Injection as in Fig. 9. n = 3.

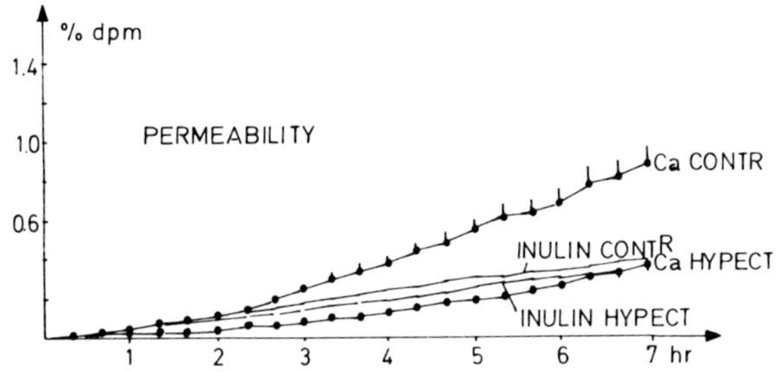

Fig. 13: Permeability and uptake of $^{45}Ca^{++}$ or ^{3}H-inulin by the skin of control or hypophysectomized clawed toads. n = 10. Ringer-solution on both sides of the skin, $^{45}Ca^{++}$ was added at the epidermal chamber. n = 10.

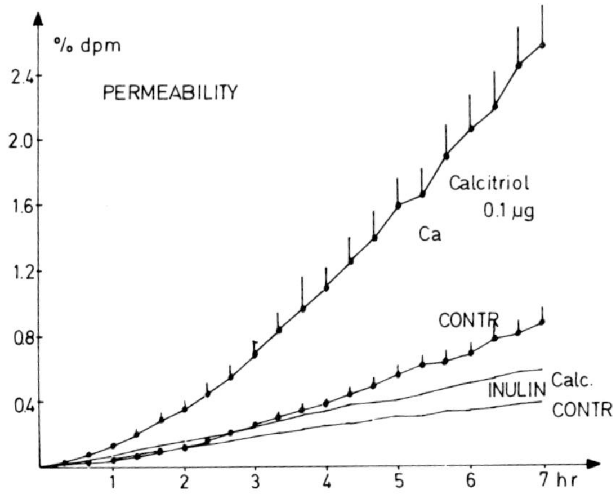

Fig. 14: Permeability and uptake of Ca^{++} or inulin by the skin of control or calcitriol treated (3 injections with total 0.1 μg). Experimental procedure like that in Fig. 13. n = 10.

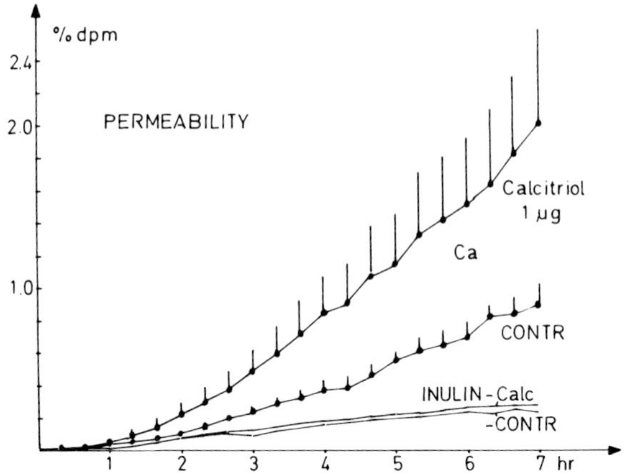

Fig. 15: Permeability and uptake of Ca^{++} or inulin by the skin of control or calcitriol treated (3 injections with total 1.0 µg). Experimental procedure like that in Fig. 13. n = 10.

by a sucrose density gradient centrifugation (Merke et al., 1983). A peak of the radioactivity was found at 3.2 S. Addition of excess (100 fold) tritiated 25 $(OH)D_3$ (calcidiol), did not suppress the binding of calcitriol which demonstrates the specificity of this receptor. On the other hand, excess of labeled calcitriol reduced the binding capacity (Fig. 16). No binding was found in a preparation of the serosa. Calcidiol was bound at a receptor, the Svedberg constant of which was 4.8. But, this binding was not due to a specific receptor because excess of calcidiol did not reduce the bound radioactivity.

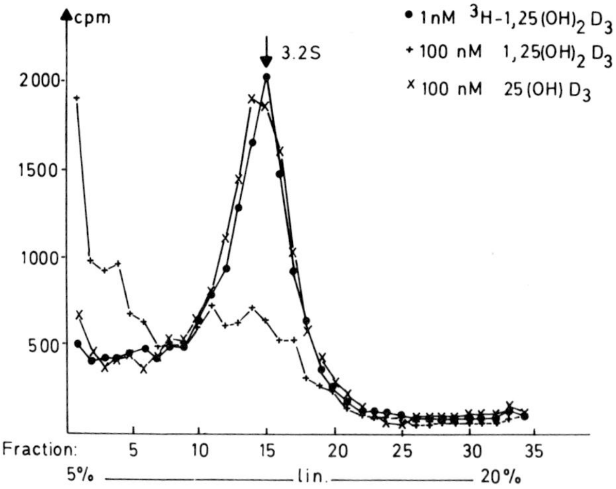

Fig. 16: Analysis of the receptors for 1,25 $(OH)_2$-D_3 in the mucosal cytosol by sucrose density gradient analysis. The labeled compound and additionally excess of the unlabeled substance or 25 (OH)-D_3.

The same situation was found in a preparation of epidermal cytosol, where a specific receptor binds labeled calcitriol (at 3.2 S, Fig. 17), while calcidiol is only bound unspecifically at 4.8 S.

The preparation of mucosal and epidermal cytosol is not an easy procedure. Nevertheless, the results demonstrate quite clearly that receptors for calcitriol exist in the tissue responsible for the uptake of Ca^{++}. A good hypothesis which must be evaluated would be that pituitary hormones regulate these receptors and thus indirectly influence the Ca^{++} uptake.

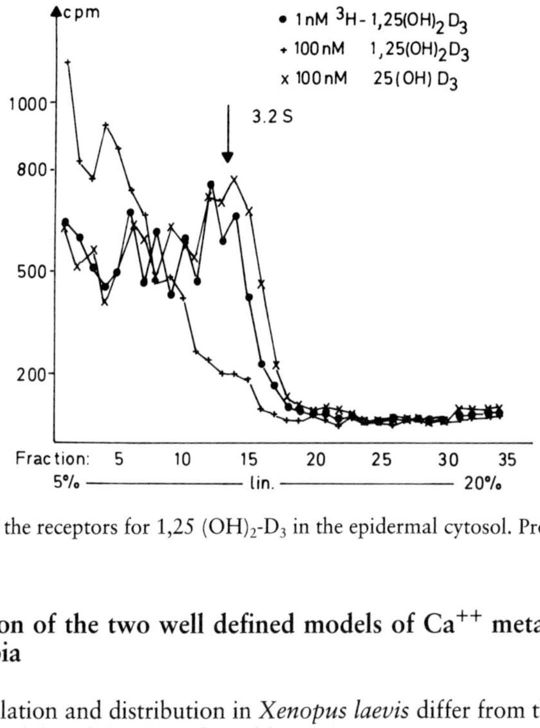

Fig. 17: Analysis of the receptors for 1,25 $(OH)_2$-D_3 in the epidermal cytosol. Procedure like Fig. 16.

5. Comparison of the two well defined models of Ca^{++} metabolism in amphibia

The Ca^{++} regulation and distribution in *Xenopus laevis* differ from the system in *Rana spec.* Larvae and adults of the clawed toad have no apparent paravertebral lime sacs for Ca^{++} storage. Primitive amphibians like the labyrinthodonts were well ossified. The modern urodeles and anurans, compared with these ancient members, show evidence of skeletal degeneracy. Ca^{++} is therefore not stored in bones of most recent Amphibia. It is accumulated in modified structures of the *ductus endolymphaticus* termed paravertebral lime sacs. These structures are located between the vertrebrae and build enlarged multifollicular systems. Ca^{++} is accumulated in these lime sacs during the larval phase and later used for the ossification of the bones.

Lime sacs have not been described for urodeles and *Xenopus laevis* which therefore differ from the system of Ca^{++} regulation, and distribution described for frogs. Removal of ultimobranchial glands results in hypercalcemia in frogs, larvae or adults. On the contrary, calcitonin stimulates the uptake of Ca^{++} by the lime sacs and induces hypocalcemia. In *Xenopus laevis*, calcitonin has no clear effects, which might be explained by the absence of lime sacs. Calcitriol has strong effects on Ca^{++} uptake by the skin and intestine of the clawed toad. This type of stimulation was only found in frogs after removal of the ultimobranchial gland.

The added table 1 summarizes the differences of the Ca^{++} regulation between *Xenopus* and *Rana.*

Table 1: Differences of the Ca^{++} regulation between *Xenopus* and *Rana*

Main pool	*Rana spec.*	*Xenopus laevis*
Main pool of Ca^{++}	paravertebral lime sacs	bone
system	more or less "closed"	"open"
stimulation of Ca^{++} uptake	calcitriol in ultimo-branchialectomized animals	strongly by calcitriol
source of Ca^{++}	food, uptake by the intestine	uptake mechanisms in skin and intestine
effects of calcitonin	hypocalcemia	no clear effects
effects of parathyroid hormone	pronounced hyper-calcemia	slight hypercalcemia
effects of pituitary hormones	not clear	regulation of Ca^{++} homeostasis

Acknowledgement

This work was done in several laboratories besides that of the authors. Prof. V. Volf, IGF, Kernforschungszentrum Karlsruhe, provided the possibility to work with radioactive Ca^{++}, Dr. E. Merke, Prof. E. Ritz and D. Schwittay, University of Heidelberg, made possible to analyse the vitamin D receptors and Prof. Schmidt-Gayk, University of Heidelberg measured the titres of calcidiol and calcitriol. All these supports are gratefully acknowledged.

References

Bern, H.A., Bisbee, C.A., Collie, N.L., Foskett, J.K., Hughes, B., Loretz, C.A., Marshall, W.S. (1981): Failure of ovine prolactin to elicit rapid responses by osmoregulatory surfaces. Gen. Comp. Endocr. *44*, 128–130.

Dacke, C.G. (1979): Calcium regulation in sub-mammalian vertebrates. Academic Press, London, New York, San Francisco.

McWhinnie, D.J., Scopelliti, T.G. (1978): A comparative study of the influence of calcitonin on plasma mineral and volume dynamics in the amphibians *Rana pipiens* and *Xenopus laevis*, and the rat. Comp. Biochem. Physiol. *61* A, 487–495.

Merke, J., Kreusser, W., Bier, B., Ritz, E. (1983): Demonstration of a testicular receptor for 1,25-dihydroxycholecalciferol in the rat. Eur. J. Biochem. *130*, 303–308.
Merke, J., Gabel, S., Stengel, U., Hanke, W., Ritz, E. (1989): Receptors for and action of 1,25-dihydroxyvitamin D_3 in submammalian vertebrates. Acta Endocrinologica, vol. 120, Suppl. *1*, 92–93.
Pang, P.K.T. (1973): Endocrine control of calcium metabolism in teleosts. Am. Zool. *23*, 719–727.
Pang, P.K.T. (1981): Hypercalcemic effects of ovine prolactin on the intact killifish *Fundulus heteroclitus*, subjected to different environmental calcium chalenges. Gen. Comp. Endocr. *43*, 252–255.
Pang, P.K.T., Yee, J.A. (1980): Evolution of the endocrine control of vertebrate hypercalcemic regulation. In: Hormones, Adaptation and Evolution. S. Ishii, T. Hirano and M. Wada (Hrsg.), Japan Sci. Soc. Press, Tokyo and Springer Verlag, Berlin, 103–111.
Pang, P.K.T., Griffith, R., Pickford, G.E. (1970): Hypocalcemia and tetanic seizures in hypophysectomized killifish, *Fundulus heteroclitus*. Proc. Soc. Exp. Biol. Med. *136*, 85–87.
Pilkington, J.B., Simkiss, K. (1966): The mobilization of the calcium carbonate deposits in the endolymphatic sacs of metamorphosing frogs. J. exp. Biol. *45*, 329–341.
Robertson, D.R. (1968): The ultimobranchial body in *Rana pipiens* Zeitschr. f. Zellforsch. *85*, 453–465.
Robertson, D.R. (1969a): The ultimobranchial body of *Rana pipiens*. VIII. Effects of extirpation upon calcium distribution and bone cell types. Gen. Comp. Endocr. *12*, 479–490.
Robertson, D.R. (1969b): The ultimobranchial body of *Rana pipiens*. X. Effect of glandular extirpation on fracture healing. J. exp. Zool. *172*, 425–442.
Robertson, D.R. (1970): The ultimobranchial body of *Rana pipiens*. XI. Response to dietary calcium – evidence of possible physiological function. Endocrinology *87*, 1041–1050.
Robertson, D.R. (1971a): Endocrinology of amphibian ultimobranchial glands. J. exp. Zool. *178*, 101–114.
Robertson, D.R. (1971b): Calcitonin in amphibians and the relationship of the paravertebral lime sacs with carbonic anhydrase. In: Intern. Congress Series. Excerpta Medica, Amsterdam *243*, 15–19.
Robertson, D.R. (1971c): Cytological and physiological activity of the ultimobranchial glands in the premetamorphotic anuran *Rana catesbeiana*. Gen. Comp. Endocr. *16*, 329–341.
Robertson, D.R. (1972a): Calcitonin in amphibians and the relationship of the paravertebral lime sacs with carbonic anhydrase. In: Calcium, Parathyroid Hormone and the Calcitonins. R.V. Talmage and P.L. Munson (eds.), Excerpta Medica Amsterdam, 21–28.
Robertson, D.R. (1972b): Influence of the parathyroids and ultimobranchial glands in the frog (*Rana pipiens*) during respiratory acidosis. Gen. Comp. Endocr. *3*, Suppl., 421–429.
Robertson, D.R. (1974): Effects of ultimobranchial and parathyroid glands on sodium and water excretion in the frog. Endocrinology *94*, 940–946.
Robertson, D.R. (1975a): Effects of the ultimobranchial and parathyroid glands and vitamins D_2, D_3 and dihydrotachysterol$_2$ on blood calcium and intestina calcium transport in the frog (*R. pipiens*). Endocrinology *96*(4), 934–940.
Robertson, D.R. (1975b): The *in vitro* transport of calcium by the frog intestine and the effect of vitamin D_3. Comp. Biochem. Physiol. *51* A, 705–710.
Robertson, D.R. (1977): The annual pattern of plasma-calcium in the frog and the seasonal effect of ultimobranchialectomy and parathyroidectomy. Gen. Comp. Endocr. *33*, 336–343.
Sasayama, Y., Oguro, C. (1975): Effects of parathyroidectomy on calcium and sodium concentrations of serum and coelomic fluid in the bullfrog tadpoles. J. exp. Zool. *192*, 293–298.
Sasayama, Y., Oguro, C. (1981): Effects of hypophysectomy and replacement therapy with pituitary homogenates or ovine prolactin on serum calcium, sodium and magnesium concentrations in bullfrog tadpoles. Gen. Comp. Endocr. *46*, 75–80.
Sasayama, Y., Oguro, C. (1982): The role of ultimobranchial glands on calcium balance in bullfrog tadpoles. Proc. IX Int. Symp. Comp. Endocr., University Press, Hong Kong.
Sasayama, Y., Nakayama, T., Maki, Y., Demoto, M., Oguro, C. (1983): Effects of environmental Mg- and Ca-levels on the serum Mg- and Ca-concentrations in tadpoles and frogs. Comp. Biochem. Physiol. *74* A, 577–578.
Saxen, L., Toivonen, S. (1955): The development of the ultimobranchialbody in *Xenopus laevis* Daudin and its relation to the thyroid gland and epithelial bodies. J. Embryol. Exp. Morph. *3*, 376–384.

Schlumberger, H. B., Burk, D. H. (1953): Comparative study of the reaction to injury: II. Hypervitaminosis D in the frog with special reference to the lime sacs. Archives of Pathology *56* (2), 103–125.

Sehe, L. (1960): Radioautographic studies on the ultimobranchial body and thyroid gland in vertebrates: Fishes and amphibians. Endocrinology *67*, 674–684.

Sterba, G. (1950): Über die morphologischen und histogenetischen Thymusprobleme bei *Xenopus laevis* Daudin nebst einigen Bemerkungen über die Morphologie der Kaulquappen. Akad. Verlag, Berlin, 1–54.

Ushiyama, M., Pang, P. K. T. (1981): Endocrine influence on hypercalcemic regulation in bullfrog tadpoles. Gen. Comp. Endocr. *44*, 428–435.

Ushiyama, M., Pang, P. K. T. (1982): Replacement therapy and plasma calcium concentrations in hypophysectomized bullfrog tadpoles, *Rana catesbeiana*. Gen. Comp. Endocr. *47*, 351–356.

Wendelaar Bonga, S. E., Greven, J. A. (1978): The relationship between prolactin cell activity, environmental calcium and plasma calcium in the teleost *Gasterosteus aculeatus*. Observations on stanniectomized fish. Gen. Comp. Endocr. *36*, 90–102.

Fortschritte der Zoologie, Band/Vol. 38 · Hanke, W. (Hrsg.), Biology and Physiology of Amphibians
Gustav Fischer Verlag · Stuttgart · New York · 1990

Hypothalamo-hypophysial axis in osmoregulation

M. Olivereau[1], J. M. Olivereau[2], S. Kikuyama[3] and K. Yamamoto[3]

[1] Laboratoire de Physiologie, Institut Océanographique, 195, rue Saint-Jacques, F-75005 Paris, France
[2] Laboratoire de Psychobiologie Environnementale, Université René Descartes, 106, quai de Clichy, F-92110, Clichy, France
[3] Waseda University, Department of Biology, School of Education, Nishi-Waseda 1-6-1, Tokyo 160, Japan

1. General influences of hormones on osmoregulation

Amphibians can be found in various environments throughout the world, and show a varying capacity for osmotic regulation. Some species can be adapted to deionized water (DW), such as *Ambystoma tigrinum* (Wittouck, 1973); others can tolerate a moderate salinity, for example an external medium isosmotic to plasma (*Pleurodeles waltlii*, Olivereau et al., 1977). Some euryhaline species live in variable salinities as reported in the early experimental studies in *Rana cancrivora* (Gordon et al., 1961) and *Bufo viridis* (Stoicovici and Pora, 1951; Gordon, 1962).

Several physico-chemical mechanisms participate in the adaptation to natural and artificial environmental conditions. Many experiments were performed on sodium and water transport through the skin and the urinary bladder, changes in permeability to sodium and urea, and responses of the short-circuit current through these epithelia as well as on the function of the kidney during adaptation to various external conditions. In short, acclimation of euryhaline amphibians to hyperosmotic saline solutions results in an increase in plasma osmolarity, sodium, chloride and urea concentrations (e.g. Gordon et al., 1961; Gordon, 1962; Dicker and Elliott, 1973; Jürss and Schlisio, 1975; Balinsky, 1981; Degani et al., 1984; Katz et al., 1984; Liggins and Grigg, 1985). However, these increases may be more or less marked and no urea retention occurs in some species such as *Rana temporaria* (Bolton and Henderson, 1987). Water permeability of the skin is variably affected, and sodium permeability reduced. Adaptation to high salinities also induces an increase in osmolarity, sodium and urea concentration in urine, a greatly reduced urine excretion and an increase in urea permeability of the urinary bladder, a retention of urea in the tissues and an increase in urea cycle enzymes (Dicker and Elliott, 1973; Giunta et al., 1973; Jürss and Schlisio, 1975; Lee et al., 1982).

Adaptation of *Ambystoma* to DW induces a loss of sodium and chloride and an increase in plasma urea (Wittouck, 1973) although somewhat divergent results are also reported (Kerstetter and Kirschner, 1971).

Several hormones appear to be involved in these physiological responses. Most studies deal with the effect of arginine vasotocin and occasionally with that of mesotocin (Bentley, 1980; Sawyer, 1987) and prolactin (Brown and Brown, 1987; Hirano et al., 1987) during adaptation to hypo- or hyperosmotic environments. Transfer of *Rana esculenta* from hypo- to isotonic medium or the reverse greatly affects the osmolarity and sodium content of the urine whereas urine flow and glomerular filtration are only slightly altered. These responses are probably controlled by neurohypophysial and adrenocortical hormones (Mayer, 1969).

Dessication by air of different anuran species results in an increase of urea concentration, osmolality and hematocrit. Dehydration by external salinity causes an increase of sodium and urea concentration and osmolality but a decrease of hematocrit. However, frogs and toads show opposite responses of the diffusional permeability of the skin, and the mechanisms involved in these responses are somewhat modulated by the ecological situation of each species (Mack and Hanke, 1977a). In the same species, vasopressin and oxytocin have similar effects on hematocrit, osmolality, sodium, ammonia and urea concentration in the blood, but diffusional permeabilities through the skin show opposite responses to vasotocin (Mack and Hanke, 1977b).

Other hormones also modulate the permeability of the skin, urinary bladder and the functioning of the kidney, such as the corticotropic hormone (ACTH) acting by the production of corticosteroids (Garland and Henderson, 1975; Yorio and Bentley, 1978), aldosterone and the renin-angiotensin system (Bolton and Henderson, 1987) and catecholamines (Bastide et al., 1967; Yokota and Hillman, 1984). A possible mediation of the oesophagus and gut in osmoregulation, such as that described in teleost fish, is not apparent in amphibians. They do not respond to angiotensin II by drinking while most of the tetrapods respond to angiotensin II (Kobayashi et al., 1979).

Few studies deal with the changes occurring in the brain (neuropeptides and neurohypophysial hormones) and the pituitary (adeno- and neurohypophysial hormones and nerve terminals containing neuropeptides, neurotransmitters and catecholamines) of amphibians adapted to hypo- or hyperosmotic milieux. This review will further focus on cytological and immunocytochemical data reported in the hypothalamo-hypophysial axis of amphibians in relation to osmoregulatory processes.

2. The influence of the atrial natriuretic peptide (ANP)

The ANP identified in mammals is affected by dehydration (Samson, 1985) and inhibits vasopressin secretion (Samson, 1985; Samson et al., 1987). Receptors of ANP present in kidney glomeruli, the glomerular zone of the adrenals, and the choroid plexus respond to changes in the fluid balance (Lynch et al., 1986). A similar neuropeptide is identified in the ventricle, atrium and central nervous system of *Rana ridibunda* (Netchitaïlo et al., 1986, 1987, 1988). Binding sites for ^{125}I-ANP are demonstrated in the interrenal tissue and renal glomeruli of *Xenopus*, suggesting that ANP could affect the glomerular function and homeostatic regulation (Kloas et al., 1989). ANP also binds in the brain and pituitary of the frog, mainly in the neurohypophysis (NH) (Netchitaïlo et al., 1989), but not in the intermediate lobe (IL). The injection of rat ANP has no apparent effect on renal fractional excretion of sodium in *Rana esculenta* tested in winter and in summer (Frick and Toygar, 1988).

In a perifusion system of interrenal slices of *Rana*, synthetic ANP does not affect the spontaneous secretion of corticosterone and aldosterone. ANP inhibits the ACTH- and angiotensin II-stimulated corticosteroid production. ANP released by the heart may act as a hormone, and that contained in splanchnic nerve fibers as a neurohormone to regulate corticosteroid secretion (Lihrmann et al., 1988). Similarly, perifusion of *Xenopus* interrenal with ANP decreases the aldosterone release but does not influence that of corticosterone (Kloas et al., 1989).

The role of ANP present in the central nervous system, the median eminence and the posterior lobe of the hypophysis remains to be elucidated, and a putative action on ACTH secretion has not yet been investigated. *In vitro* perifusion of the frog neurointermediate lobe with ANP increases α-MSH release (Lamarcz et al., 1987).

Studies are needed to explore the putative actions of ANP in other species kept under different external conditions, and the possible changes of the concentrations of ANP in the tissues and plasma must be investigated by using radioimmunoassays and immunocytochemical techniques.

3. The influence of arginine vasotocin (AVT)

AVT promotes water retention in amphibian species kept in an hyperosmotic milieu by acting on sodium fluxes, skin and bladder permeability to water and water excretion by the kidney (e.g. Alvarado and Johnson, 1966, Sawyer, 1987). AVT promotes water reabsorption by the bladder, decreases the glomerular filtration rate (Brown and Brown, 1980) and increases urea permeability of the bladder (Dicker and Elliott, 1973) in *Taricha* and *Triturus* respectively. During dehydration in *Rana ridibunda*, the plasma level of AVT increases whereas that of mesotocin is not significantly affected (Nouwen and Kühn, 1983).

Dehydration of *Rana temporaria* for 10 days induces a gradual increase in the mean nuclear diameter of the magnocellular perikarya of the praeoptic nucleus (PON). These are divided into three areas (ventral 1 and 2, and dorsal). Karyometric studies strongly suggest that the whole nucleus is involved in the mechanism of osmoregulation, but some differences are detected in the type of reaction of the three areas examined (Dierickx et al., 1964). In the same species, dehydration for 7 days induces a decrease of the aldehyde-fuchsin (AF) material in the PON, median eminence (ME) and NH. Incorporation of ^{3}H-cystine, difficult to evaluate accurately in the PON, increases in the NH although AF material decreases. The AF material as well as the labeling are often concentrated around portal blood vessels indicating an enhanced release after dehydration. However, the ventral border of the outer zone of the ME does not show any appreciable amount of radioactive labeling in dehydrated and control animals. These data suggest that synthesis of AF material is enhanced in the PON and that its transport is accelerated towards the NH where it is released (Vullings and Diederen, 1986).

In *Xenopus*, after a progressive and long-term adaptation (a few weeks and up to 6 months) to a saline environment (NaCl 1.25 g/l), the amount of AF neurosecretory material (including AVT, mesotocin and their respective neurophysins) increases in enlarged perikarya of the PON (Spannhof and Jönsson, 1969). However, fluorescence microscopical studies in *Xenopus* tadpoles gradually adapted to 0.75% NaCl for a few days (maximum 14 days) reveal that the loss of neurosecretory material stained by the pseudoisocyanin is restricted to the cells of the caudo-dorsal region of the PON. These cells seem to be involved in the synthesis of the neurohypophysial hormones (Notenboom, 1972). These two results suggest that neurohypophysial hormones are initially released by the PON perikarya, but this depletion is no more apparent in long-term adapted *Xenopus* because of an increased synthesis. In addition, the local response of the PON in *Xenopus* tadpoles dehydrated by saline immersion compared to the global reaction of the praeoptic nucleus after dehydration of *Rana* spec. in a continually aerated room suggests that the hypothalamic system is more stimulated in the second experimental condition.

Pleurodeles waltlii (larval stage 53 in the table of Gallien and Durocher) can be adapted to a saline solution (NaCl 9 g/l) for 15 days (20 °C, photoperiod 12L:12D). Immunocytochemical studies were performed in our laboratory using an antiserum against vasotocin (given by Dr. B. I. Baker, University of Bath) at a 1/1000 dilution to see whether environmental salinity affects the AVT system. In control *Pleurodeles* kept in fresh water under similar laboratory conditions, these techniques demonstrate abundant and well labeled perikarya in the PON and numerous immunoreactive fibers reaching the ME and ending in the NH. In saline-adapted *Pleurodeles*, the labeling is reduced in most perikarya of the PON, in the ME and NH. The amount of neurosecretory AF material is lower than in controls. These data suggest that AVT storage in perikarya is reduced and axonal transport is increased, as well as the release by neurohypophysial nerve endings, at least after a 15-day acclimation. It would be interesting to follow these changes at different stages during the adaptation to obtain more information on the kinetics of the response of AVT, an increased synthesis probably occuring at the beginning of the experiment as suggested by the results reported in other species.

Axolotls (*Ambystoma tigrinum*) can live in DW for 25 days at least. Their hypothalamo-hypophysial system was compared to that of controls kept in fresh water. Longitudinal sections corresponding to different levels of the PON and ME were immunostained. No clear difference is observed in immunoreactive AVT in the brain and NH between the two groups of animals.

If AVT is involved in acclimation to saline environments and dehydration, it does not seem to play a major role in adaptation to a hyposmotic milieu. As no evident changes are detected in *Ambystoma* after 25 days in DW, and knowing the rapid response of AVT, it is possible that AVT is released initially and that its synthesis is increased subsequently. However, this hypothesis is not supported by the findings of Kerstetter and Kirschner (1971), showing that NH is not necessary for the regulation of sodium fluxes in larval *Ambystoma*. Removal of the pituitary gland and destruction of the PON has little or no effect on active transport in animals adapted to pond water or after salt depletion. However, an increase in the plasma level of neurohypophysial hormones is detected in *Bufo chilensis* kept for 15 days in DW (Rojas et al., 1987).

4. The influence of prolactin (PRL)

Prolactin shows a wide spectrum of actions in *Amphibia*, either related to growth processes or to osmoregulation. Their involvement in osmoregulation was recently reviewed (Brown and Brown, 1987; Hirano et al., 1987). The main action of PRL is to promote sodium retention by decreasing the water turnover and urinary Na^+ loss (Robinson and Ewig, 1983) and increasing active Na^+ transport through the skin (*Rana* spec., Takada, 1986) and bladder (*Bufo marinus*, Snart and Dalton, 1973). Ovine PRL decreases urea excretion in tadpoles of *Rana catesbeiana* and *R. grylio* (Medda and Frieden, 1972). PRL binding sites are present in the brain, kidney, bladder, epidermis, liver and testes (White, 1981; Lüthy et al., 1985; D'Istria et al., 1987, Guardabassi et al., 1987, Tarpey and Nicoll, 1978) of different species. PRL binding on kidney and skin membranes is reduced in dehydrated *Xenopus* (Guardabassi et al., 1987) and PRL receptors disappear in hypophysectomized frogs (D'Istria et al., 1987).

PRLs used in these experiments are of mammalian origin and known to be slightly contaminated by vasopressin. Amphibian PRLs have been isolated from *Rana catesbeiana* (Yamamoto and Kikuyama, 1981), *Bufo japonicus* (Yamamoto et al., 1986) and *Cynops pyrrhogaster* (Matsuda et al., 1988). If these PRLs are available in sufficient amounts, it will be important to compare their biological effects on water and electrolyte metabolism with those shown by mammalian PRL. According to the results of the experiment in which bovine and bullfrog PRL were tested for transepithelial potential-reducing activity in *Notophtalmus viridescens* efts, both PRL showed an equipotent activity (Brown et al., unpublished).

In *Pleurodeles*, PRL cells are identified by using an antiserum against ovine PRL (Olivereau et al., 1976) and mainly localized in the antero-ventral area of the pars distalis. They correspond to the large orangeophilic cells of the cephalic part of the distal lobe. This location is now confirmed by the use of an anti-bullfrog PRL at a 1/1000 dilution, a rostro-ventral location similar to that described in other species of anurans and urodeles (Doerr-Schott, 1976). In control *Pleurodeles* kept in fresh water, the large PRL cells are intensely labeled. In saline-adapted *Pleurodeles*, PRL cells appear smaller in size and show darkly stained nuclei with a significant decrease of their cross-sectional area (Olivereau et al., 1977). The immunostaining is reduced or more heterogeneous in some larger cells, and granules are sometimes concentrated around the nucleus. A few small cells remain intensely labeled. These data suggest that PRL cell activity, mainly PRL synthesis, is reduced after a 15-day saline acclimation. The reduction in nuclear size suggests that PRL secretion is also lower.

Rana cancrivora can live in 50% and 75% sea water. In these milieus plasma osmolarity increases, largely due to an increase of plasma urea concentration. Decrease in plasma PRL levels in the frogs kept in saline for 48 hrs suggests that PRL is involved in the osmoregulation of this species (Kikuyama et al., 1987) (table 1).

Table 1: Effect of sea water adaptation on plasma PRL of *Rana cancrivora*

	Fresh water	50% sea water	75% sea water
Osmolality in mOsm/kg	339 ± 10	556 ± 2	735 ± 8
PRL concentration in ng/ml	158 ± 39	56 ± 10	29 ± 8

In *Ambystoma* kept in fresh water, immunoreactive PRL cells are elongated, with a small amount of cytoplasm at both extremities of a long and thin nucleus. Their columnar shape, their size, as well as the intensity of their immunostaining are not clearly affected in animals kept in DW for 25 days. These negative results seem to agree with the findings of Kerstetter and Kirschner (1971) showing that pituitary, and then endogenous PRL, is not absolutely necessary for a correct osmoregulation and sodium transport in DW-adapted axolotls. Indices of an increase in PRL synthesis and/or release are not apparent although ovine PRL appears able to compensate at least partially for the plasma Na^+ decrease of *Ambystoma* either hypophysectomized or kept in DW (Wittouck, 1973).

The role of PRL in maintaining plasma sodium levels after hypophysectomy or in an hyposmotic environment is not always evident. Ovine PRL may increase plasma sodium in some cases, or decrease it or else show no effect. Brown and Brown (1987) emphasize that in amphibians, plasma sodium alone does not adequately reflect changes in the sodium balance. Moreover, the sodium retaining effect of mammalian PRLs in aquatic amphibians may be secondary to their role in fluid volume control. A lack of consistency in responses to a PRL treatment is often observed in experiments on *Ambystoma*. The response of the

PRL cells to a deionized milieu must be investigated in other species sensitive to PRL administration.

The skin is a target organ for PRL (Brown and Brown, 1987) which affects the transepithelial potential (Brown et al., 1986) and the production of mucus in some species. Dehydration in *Xenopus* reduces the glycoprotein content of the skin mucous cells (Campantico et al., 1978). In the newts, *Cynops pyrrhogaster*, pile-up of skin gland secretion is often observed at the openings of the duct of the glands under a scanning electron microscope. Hypophysectomy decreases secretory activity but PRL treatment restores the activity (Kikuyama et al. 1975).

5. The influence of thyrotropic hormone (TSH)

TSH cells are easily identified by immunocytochemistry with an antiserum against human beta TSH (Niaddk, Bethesda) at a 1/1000 dilution. TSH cells are mainly located among PRL cells in the cephalic lobe of the pars distalis. They are larger, more intensely immunostained and appeared more active in saline-adapted *Pleurodeles* than in those kept in fresh water. Indices of thyroid stimulation are also reported in saline-adapted *Pleurodeles* (Olivereau et al., 1977) and *Xenopus* raised in a 12.5 g NaCl solution (Spannhof and Spittler, 1974).

Similar results are obtained on *Cynops pyrrhogaster* kept for 15 days in 0.11 M NaCl or 0,22 M mannitol in February. These treatments increase the molting frequency and epithelial cell height in thyroid follicles (table 2). Indirect evidence of an increased thyroid activity in *Cynops* kept in 0.11 M NaCl is given in table 3. Animals were studied for 30 days (February–March) after thyroidectomy or hypophysectomy or sham-operation. No molting is observed in freshwater or NaCl-adapted animals during the last 25 days after thyroidectomy or hypophysectomy, but molting can be induced in these animals, by intraperitoneal injections of 0.2 μg of thyroxine for 4 successive days, starting 31 days after the operation. In sham-operated *Cynops*, molting frequency increases in a saline solution and can be considered as an indirect but reliable indication of thyroid activity.

In *Ambystoma* kept in DW, only 50% of the animals possess some enlarged TSH cells. In the other animals TSH cells remain similar in size and immunostaining to those of freshwater controls.

Dehydration seems to reduce the size of type I basophiles of *Xenopus*, but has no clear effect on the cytological aspect of the thyroid gland. The return to fresh water does not seem to affect the pituitary-thyroid axis (Guardabassi et al., 1978).

Attempts have been made to interprete the thyroid hormone-PRL antagonism in amphibian metamorphosis (Etkin and Gona, 1967) from the point of view that these two

Table 2: Effect of environmental osmolality on molting and thyroid gland of *Cynops pyrrhogaster*.

Environmental water	mOsm/kg	Number of animals	Number of molting/10 days	Thyroid follicular cell height (µm)
Tap water	3	13 ♂	0.67 ± 0.15	13.9 ± 0.5
NaCl	208	13 ♂	1.79 ± 0.16	20.0 ± 1.4
Mannitol	206	13 ♂	2.25 ± 0.14	18.8 ± 0.7

Table 3: Effect of thyroidectomy and hypophysectomy on molting in newts, *Cynops pyrrhogaster* during salt water adaptation

Operation	Number	Environmental water	NNumber of molting/ 10 days
Thyroidectomy	7 ♀	Tap water	0.29 ± 0.09
	7 ♀	NaCl	0.19 ± 0.07
Sham-Thyroidectomy	7 ♀	Tap water	0.95 ± 0.13
	7 ♀	NaCl	2.05 ± 0.15
Hypophysectomy	7 ♀	Tap water	0.24 ± 0.06
	7 ♀	NaCl	0.19 ± 0.07
Sham-Hypophysectomy	7 ♀	Tap water	0.81 ± 0.14
	7 ♀	NaCl	1.90 ± 0.14

hormones act oppositely in terms of osmoregulation (Platt et al., 1978; White and Nicoll, 1981). Thyroid hormone causes a loss of water and sodium from the larval tissues whereas PRL promotes water and sodium retention (Platt and Christopher, 1977; Eddy, 1979). There is an evidence that fluid loss from larval tissue may facilitate metamorphic changes (Platt and LiCause, 1980).

Enzymes involved in the urea metabolism increase in saline-adapted amphibians (see introduction). These enzymes appear earlier in metamorphosing tadpoles treated with thyroxine (Cohen, 1970). These data are in accordance with the increased thyroid hormone secretion in saline-adapted amphibians.

6. The influence of growth hormone (GH)

In mammals as well as in fishes, GH cells are stained with orange G whereas PRL cells appear erythrosinophilic. An inverse situation occurs in amphibians, creating some misinterpretations of these two cell types until immunocytochemical techniques became available. Despite species specificity of adenohypophysial hormones in submammalian species, immunostaining of GH cells is possible with anti-human GH (Olivereau et al., 1976), at least in some species. GH cells are often smaller than PRL cells and mainly located in the dorso-caudal part of the distal lobe and close to the intermediate lobe. They are mixed with some PRL cells in the central area of the adenohypophysis. Cytological studies show that GH cells possess enlarged nuclei and are often more granulated in saline-adapted *Pleurodeles* than in freshwater controls (Olivereau et al., 1977). Immunocytochemical techniques (anti-human GH, NIADDK, used at a 1/1000 dilution), confirm that GH cells are larger and oftend contain more immunoreactive granules in the NaCl-adapted group than in the control one.

In *Xenopus* kept in dry conditions for 7 days, these cells formerly called type II acidophils appear larger and heavily granulated, suggesting an increased synthesis. This aspect is still evident after the animals have been returned to tap water for one day, but after 7 days, GH cells are smaller, faintly granulated and similar to those of *Xenopus* kept in tap water (Guardabassi et al., 1978).

The role of GH in saline adaptation was first suspected in the trout (Smith, 1956) and recent evidence summarized by Brown and Brown (1987). In bullfrog tadpoles, GH decreases plasma Na^+ (Brown et al., 1986). Cytological data reported in *Pleurodeles* suggest that GH synthesis is increased in enlarged cells and probably released during saline adaptation. In *Ambystoma* kept in DW GH cells do not seem to be affected.

7. The influence of the corticotropin-releasing factor (CRF) and corticotropin (ACTH)

A CRF system is described in various amphibian species (Olivereau et al., 1984, 1987). In *Pleurodeles* and *Ambystoma*, immunoreactive perikary are located mainly in the praeoptic nucleus and the interpeduncular nucleus. Fibers running into the tuberal area end in the median eminence and occasionally in the neural lobe (antiCRF given by Dr Vandesande, Leuven, and used at a 1/1000 or 1/2000 dilution). ACTH cells are labeled with antisera against $^{1-24}$ACTH, $^{17-39}$ACTH (Olivereau et al., 1976) and $^{1-39}$ACTH (Immunonuclear) at a 1/500 dilution. ACTH cells are located in the rostral area, close to the ME containing CRF-like fibers. Cells of the IL are also labeled with anti-ACTH sera. In saline-adapted *Pleurodeles*, changes are not apparent in the immunoreactivity of the CRF system. The size and immunostaining of ACTH cells is quite similar to that noted in freshwater controls. The coexistence of CRF and AVT is not demonstrated in preoptic perikarya of amphibia. Saline adaptation induces a depletion of AVT without clear changes in CRF-like material, substantiating the hypothesis of their separate location in brain perikarya and their independent release. However, these studies were performed after a 15-day adaptation. The CRF-ACTH axis generally responds rapidly to various stimuli, and changes in immunoreactive CRF and/or ACTH may occur soon after the transfer to the saline milieu. The release of AVT detected after 15 days has no apparent effect on ACTH cells, although AVT is known to stimulate ACTH release.

Gradual dehydration for 7 days does not affect the cytological aspect of type III basophils (ACTH cells) of *Xenopus* (Guardabassi et al., 1978). However, it induces a loss of sudanophilic material in the interrenal cells, a decrease in the glycogen content of kidney tubules (Campantico et al., 1978), and an increase in Na^+-K^+-ATPase activity in the kidney whereas this enzyme decreases in the skin and muscle (Giunta et al., 1978). Dehydration, as well as an increase in external salinity, causes a short-term rise of corticosteroid levels, more evident with higher salinities (Hanke, 1989). Angiotensin II stimulates the release of hormones from the interrenal tissue (Lihrmann et al., 1988; Hanke et al., 1986) but receptors for angiotensin II are not detected in the interrenal tissue of *Xenopus* (Kloas et al., 1989).

In *Ambystoma* adapted to DW, 50% of the animals show a reduced amount of immunoreactive CRF in the ME. No clear changes are detected though in the CRF-like material of the PON and interpeduncular nucleus. ACTH cells do not react significantly. Plasma aldosterone and corticosterone increase in *Ambystoma* kept in DW (Heney and Stiffler, 1983; Stiffler et al., 1986) and plasma Na^+ decreases. This effect on Na^+ is mostly compensated by aldosterone and corticosterone (Heney and Stiffler, 1983), but not by ACTH (De Ruyter and Stiffler, 1986).

An ACTH-like activity is present in the brain of amphibians, probably due to α-MSH (Thurmond et al., 1987). Its participation in osmoregulation has not yet been investigated.

8. The influence of the intermediate lobe and the melanotropin (MSH)

In saline-adapted *Pleurodeles*, MSH cells appear darkly stained and the nuclear cross-sectional area is significantly reduced compared to freshwater controls, but no changes are detected in the pigmentation (Olivereau et al., 1977). A similar hypoactivity is noted in *Xenopus* kept in hyperosmotic milieu (Ireland and Simons, 1976). It is known that α-MSH, β-MSH and β-LPH can stimulate aldosterone secretion even in hypophysectomized rats (Brown and Brown, 1987). Very few data are available for amphibians. In *Bufo arenarum*, administration of α-MSH increases heart Na^+ uptake (Iturriza et al., 1973), an effect which could partly explain the reduced activity of MSH cells in two species kept in a saline environment.

In *Ambystoma* kept in DW changes are not apparent in the IL. This lobe contains no PAS+ cells similar to those present in teleost IL, which react strongly to DW at least in the eel and the goldfish.

9. Conclusions

Several organs are involved in osmoregulation: skin, urinary bladder, kidney, but their relative importance varies in different species, according to their developmental stage and their aquatic or terrestrial life. The permeability to water and electrolytes of these tissues is modulated by different hormones. During adaptation to a saline environment, the release of AVT is evident and its effects are well documented. Decreased synthesis and release of PRL are also apparent in saline-adapted amphibians. These results are in accordance with the effects reported after treatment with PRL, although a possible contamination with AVT may alter the validity of some data. A study of the biological effects of amphibian PRLs is certainly needed.

The ANP does not influence the kidney function of the frog. Its effects must be investigated in other species kept under different experimental conditions. The TSH-thyroid axis seems to be stimulated in several amphibian species kept in NaCl solutions. More studies are necessary before we can speculate on the role of thyroid hormones in osmoregulation. The stimulation of GH cells is evident in saline-adapted *Pleurodeles* and in dehydrated *Xenopus*. Effects of mammalian GH were mainly investigated in relation to growth and results were more or less affected by a simultaneous water retention (Brown and Brown, 1987). A highly purified amphibian GH has been obtained (Kobayashi et al., 1989). The study of its action on osmoregulatory processes will be most interesting as well as its determination in biological fluids during osmotic adjustments. More investigations are also needed to clarify the role of the CRF-ACTH system in saline adaptation, mainly in short-term experiments in eury- and stenohaline species. The same observation also applies to the MSH cell response and the study of possible effects of MSH on water and electrolyte regulation.

If saline adaptation induces several changes in the hypothalamo-hypophysial system of the few species studied so far, the maintenance of *Ambystoma* in DW does not clearly affect the amount of AVT. As *Ambystoma* can live in DW, even after hypophysectomy (Kerstetter and Kirschner, 1971), it seems that endogeneous adenohypophysial hormones do not play a major role in the osmoregulation of this species. Experiments on other species, after metamorphosis, may reveal pituitaries more responsive to this artificial milieu. Owing to their large capacity to adapt to different environmental conditions, amphibian species represent interesting models for a comparative study on osmoregulatory processes.

Acknowledgements

The excellent assistance of Jacqueline Olivereau from the Centre National de la Recherche Scientifique is gratefully acknowledged, as well as the gift of antisera against vasotocin (Dr. B. I. Baker, University of Bath, England), human beta TSH and human GH (NIADDK, Bethesda, USA) and CRF (F. Vandesande, Leuven University, Belgium).

References

Alvarado, R. H., Johnson, S. R. (1966): The effects of neurohypophysial hormones on water and sodium balance in larval and adult bullfrogs (*Rana catesbeiana*). Comp. Biochem. Physiol. *18*, 549–561.

Balinsky, J. B. (1981): Adaptation of nitrogen metabolism to hyperosmotic environment in Amphibia. J. Exp. Zool. *215*, 335–350.

Bastide, F., Jard, S., Morel, F. (1967): Action de la noradrénaline sur le flux net de sodium et la perméabilité à l'eau de la peau de grenouille. J. Physiol. *59*, 340.

Bentley, P. J. (1980): Hormones and transepithelial ion transport in non-mammalian vertebrates. In Epithelial Transport in the lower Vertebrates B. Lahlou Ed. Cambridge Univ. Press 319–329.

Bolton, J. P., Henderson, I. W. (1987): Water uptake by *Rana temporaria*: effects of diuretics, and the renin-angiotensin system, and nephrectomy. Gen. Comp. Endocr. *67*, 155–162.

Brown, S. C. (1988): Electrophysiology of newt skin: effects of prolactin. Gen. Comp. Endocr. *72*, 161–167.

Brown, S. C., Brown, P. S. (1980): Water balance in the california newt *Taricha torosa*. Am. J. Physiol. *238*, R113–R118.

Brown, P. S., Brown, S. C. (1987): Osmoregulatory actions of prolactin and other adenohypophysial hormones. Vertebrate Endocrinology: Fundamentals and Biomedical Implications. P. K. T. Pang and M. P. Schreibman Eds Academic Press, New York 2, 45–84.

Brown, S. C., Morgan, E. A., Savage, L. M., Brown, P. S. (1986): Changes in body water and plasma constituents during bullfrog development. J. Exp. Zool. *237*, 25–33.

Campantico, E., Guardabassi, A., Torassa, R. (1978): Histological changes in *Xenopus laevis* Daudin specimens kept under dry conditions, then moved back to their natural aquatic environment. II Skin, kidney and interrenal. Arch. Sci. Biol. *62*, 63–76.

Cohen, P. P. (1970): Biochemical differentiation during amphibian metamorphosis. Science *168*, 533–543.

Degani, G., Silanikova, N., Shkolnik, A. (1984): Adaptation of green toad (*Bufo viridis*) to terrestrial life by urea accumulation. Comp. Biochem. Physiol. *77A*, 585–587.

De Ruyter, M. L., Stiffler, D. F. (1986): Interrenal function in larval *Ambystoma tigrinum*. II Control of aldosterone secretion and electrolyte balance by ACTH. Gen. Comp. Endocr. *62*, 298–305.

Dicker, S. E., Elliott, A. B. (1973): Neurohypophysial hormones and homeostasis in the crab-eating frog, *Rana cancrivora*. Horm. Res. 4, 224–260.

Dierickx, K., Vandesande, F., Roggen, D. (1964): The reaction of different areas of the magnocellular preoptic nucleus of *Rana temporaria* upon progressive dehydration. Z. Zellforsch. *62*, 98–101.

D'Istria, M., Fasano, S., Delrio, G. (1987): Prolactin receptors in the male *Rana esculenta*. Gen. Comp. Endocr. *68*, 6–11.

Doerr-Schott, J. (1976): Immunohistochemical detection by light and electron microscopy of pituitary hormones in cold-blooded vertebrates. I. Fish and amphibians. Gen. Comp. Endocr. *28*, 487–512.

Eddy, L. J. (1979): Prolactin action on extracellular fluid volume in tails of stage XII bullfrog tadpoles. Gen. Comp. Endocr. *37*, 369–373.

Etkin, W., Gona, A. G. (1967): Antagonism between prolactin and thyroid hormone in amphibian development. J. Exp. Zool. *165*, 249–258.

Frick, A., Toygar, A. (1988): Lack of effect of rat atrial natriuretic factor (rANF) on the renal function in frogs. Comp. Biochem. Physiol. *90A*, 465–469.

Garland, H. O., Henderson, I. W. (1975): Influence of environmental salinity on renal and adrenocortical function in the toad, *Bufo marinus*. Gen. Comp. Endocr. *27*, 136–143.
Giunta, C., Campantico, E., Bianchero, F., Perone, A. C., Vietti, M. (1973): Biochemical data on some organs from normal or prolactin-treated *Xenopus laevis* adults reared in fresh and in salt water. Gen. Comp. Endocr. *20*, 183–189.
Giunta, C., Gaudino, G., Guardabassi, A., Piovano, P. (1978): Na^+/K^+-dependent adenosine triphosphatase activity in the skin, kidney and muscle in *Xenopus laevis* adult specimens under different experimental conditions. Arch. Sci. Biol. *62*, 21–30.
Gordon, M. S. (1962): Osmotic regulation in the green toad (*Bufo viridis*). J. Exp. Biol. *39*, 261–270.
Gordon, M. S., Schmidt-Nielsen, K., Kelly, H. M. (1961): Osmotic regulation in the crab-eating frog (*Rana cancrivora*). J. Exp. Biol. *38*, 659–678.
Guardabassi, A., Campantico, E., Panebianco, I. (1978): Histological changes in *Xenopus laevis* specimens kept under dry conditions, then moved back to their natural aquatic environment. I. Pituitary, thyroid and testis. Arch. Sci. Biol. *62*, 51–61.
Guardabassi, A., Muccioli, G., Pattono, P., Belussi, G. (1987): Prolactin binding site in *Xenopus laevis* tissues: comparison between normal and dehydrated animals. Gen. Comp. Endocr. *65*, 40–47.
Hanke, W. (1989): Regulation of interrenal activity by electrolytes and peptide hormones. Fortsch. Zool. in press.
Hanke, W., Kloas, W., Gluth, C., Vetter, S., Kniehl, K., Thurmond, W., Pathak, V. (1986): The significance of the interrenal gland of poikilothermic vertebrates during the process of acclimation. Zool. Beitr. N.F. 30, 279–296.
Heney, H. W., Stiffler, D. F. (1983): The effects of aldosterone on sodium and potassium metabolism in larval *Ambystoma tigrinum*. Gen. Comp. Endocr. *49*, 122–127.
Hirano, T., Ogasawara, T., Bolton, J. P., Collie, N. L., Hasegawa, s., Iwata, M. (1987): Osmoregulatory role of prolactin in lower vertebrates. Comparative Physiology of Environmental Adaptation (R. Kirsch and B. Lahlou, eds.), Karger Basel, 112–124.
Ireland, M. P., Simons, I. M. (1976): Adaptation of the neotenous urodele axolotl (*Ambystoma mexicanum*) to a hyperosmotic medium. Gen. Comp. Endocr. *29*, 284.
Iturriza, F. C., Levitin, H., Estivariz, F. (1973): A new extrapigmentary effect of α-MSH. Promotion of sodium uptake in the heart of toads and rats. Horm. Metab. Res. *5*, 143–144.
Jürss, K., Schlisio, W. (1975): Osmo- und Ionenregulation von *Xenopus laevis* Daud. nach Adaptation in verschiedenen osmotisch wirksamen Lösungen. IV. Veränderungen des Stickstoffexkretion, Harnstoff- und Glykogenkonzentration der Leber sowie des Blutzuckers. Zool. Jb. Physiol. *79*, 1–8.
Katz, U., Degani, G., Gabbay, S. (1984): Acclimation of the euryhaline toad *Bufo viridis* to hyperosmotic solutions (NaCl, urea and mannitol). J. Exp. Biol. *108*, 403–410.
Kerstetter, T. H., Kirschner, L. B. (1971): The role of the hypothalamo-neurohypophysial system in maintaining hydromineral balance in larval salamanders. Comp. Biochem. Physiol. *40A*, 373–384.
Kikuyama, S., Hashimoto, K., Hataba, Y. (1975): Effect of prolactin on integument of the newt. Zool. Mag. *84*, 464.
Kikuyama, S., Yamamoto, K., Matsuda, K., Ogasawara, T., Hasegawa, S., Hirano, T. (1987): Plasma prolactin and osmolality in crab-eating frogs. Zool. Sci. *4*, 1086.
Kobayashi, H., Uemura, H., Wada, M., Takei, Y. (1979): Ecological adaptation of angiotensin-induced thirst mechanism in tetrapods. Gen. Comp. Endocr. *38*, 93–104.
Kobayashi, T., Kikuyama, S., Yasuda, A., Kawauchi, K., Yamaguchi, K., Yokoo, Y. (1989): Purification and characterization of bullfrog growth hormone. Gen. Comp. Endocr. *73*, in press.
Kloas, W., Fuchs, E., Hanke, W. (1989): Binding sites for atrial natriuretic peptide. Fortschr. Zool. in press.
Lamacz, M., Netchitaïlo, P., Tonon, M. C., Feuilloley, M., Ling, N., Pelletier, G., Vaudry, H. (1987): Atrial natriuretic factor (ANF) stimulates the release of α-MSH from frog neurointermediate lobe in vitro. Interaction with dopamine, GABA and neuropeptide Y. Life Sci. *40*, 1853–1858.
Lee, A. R., Silove, M., Katz, U., Balinsky, J. B. (1982): Urea cycle enzymes and glutamate dehydrogenase in *Xenopus laevis* and *Bufo viridis* adapted to high salinity. J. Exp. Zool. *221*, 169–172.
Liggins, G. W., Grigg, G. C. (1985): Osmoregulation of the cane toad, *Bufo marinus*, in salt water. Comp. Biochem. Physiol. *82A*, 613–619.

Lihrmann, I., Netchitaïlo, P., Feuilloley, M., Cantin, M., Delarue, C., Leboulenger, F., de Léan, A., Vaudry, H. (1988): Effect of atrial natriuretic factor on corticosteroid production by perifused frog interrenal slices. Gen. Comp. Endocr. *71*, 55–62.

Lüthy, I. A., Segura, E. T., Lüthy, V. I., Charreau, E. H., Calandra, R. S. (1985): Prolactin binding sites in the brain and kidneys of the toad, *Bufo arenarum* Hensel. J. Comp. Physiol. *155 B*, 611–614.

Lynch, D. R., Braas, K. M., Snyder, S. H. (1986): Atrial natriuretic factor receptors in rat kidney, adrenal gland, and brain: autoradiographic localization and fluid balance dependent changes. Proc. Nat. Acad. Sci. USA *83*, 3557–3561.

Mack, G., Hanke, W. (1977 a): Studies on anuran osmomineral regulation. I. Comparison of the reaction on dessication in different anuran species. Zool. Jb. Physiol. *81*, 112–129.

Mack, G., Hanke, W. (1977 b): Studies on anuran osmomineral regulation II. Comparison of the effects of octopeptides in different anuran species. Zool. Jb. Physiol. *81*, 177–190.

Matsuda, K., Yamamoto, K., Kikuyama, S. (1988): Purification and properties of newt prolactin and development of radioimmunoassay. Zool. Sci. *5* (in press).

Mayer, N. (1969): Adaptation de *Rana esculenta* à des milieux variés. Etude spéciale de l'excrétion rénale de l'eau et des électrolytes au cours des changements de milieux. Comp. Biochem. Physiol. *29*, 27–50.

Medda, A. K., Frieden, E. (1972): Effect of prolactin and growth hormone on the ammonia excretion of bullfrog tadpoles during normal and induced metamorphosis. Gen. Comp. Endocr. *19*, 212–217.

Netchitaïlo, P., Feuilloley, M., Pelletier, G., Cantin, M., De Lean, A., Leboulenger, F., Vaudry, H. (1986): Localization and characterization of atrial natriuretic factor (ANF)-like peptide in the frog atrium. Peptides *7*, 573–579.

Netchitaïlo, P., Leboulenger, F., Cantin, M., Gutkowska, J., Vaudry, H. (1987): Atrial natriuretic factor-like immunoreactivity in the central nervous system of the frog. Neurosci. *22*, 341–360.

Netchitaïlo, P., De Léan, A., Ong, H., Cantin, M., Gutkowska, J., Leboulenger, F., Vaudry, H. (1988): Localization and identification of immunoreactive atrial natriuretic factor (ANF) in the frog ventricle. Peptides *9*, 1–6.

Netchitaïlo, P., Yiai, T., Feuilloley, M., Leboulenger, F., Andersen, A., Pelletier, G., Cantin, M., Vaudry, H. (1989): Distribution of atrial natriuretic factor (ANF)-like immunoreactivity and ANF binding sites in the brain and pituitary of amphibians. Gen. Comp. Endocr. *74*, 290.

Notenboom, C. D. (1972): The reaction of the preoptic nucleus of *Xenopus laevis* tadpoles to osmotic stimulation. A fluorescence microscopical investigation. Z. Zellforsch. 134, 383–402.

Nouwen, E. J., Kühn, E. R. (1983): Radioimmunoassay of arginine vasotocin and mesotocin in serum of the frog, *Rana ridibunda*. Gen. Comp. Endocr. *50*, 242–251.

Olivereau, M., Bugnon, C., Fellmann, D., Olivereau, J. M., Aimar, C. (1976): Etude cytoimmunologique de l'hypophyse du Pleurodèle. C. R. Soc. Biol. *170*, 1147–1151.

Olivereau, M., Olivereau, J. M., Aimar, C. (1977): Modifications hypophysaires et thyroïdiennes chez le Pleurodèle en milieu salin. Gen. Comp. Endocr. *32*, 195–204.

Olivereau, M., Vandesande, F., Boucique, E., Ollevier, F., Olivereau, J. M. (1984): Mise en évidence immunocytochimique d'un système peptidergique de type CRF dans le cerveau des Amphibiens. C. R. Acad. Sci. *299, III*, 871–876.

Olivereau, M., Vandesande, F., Boucique, E., Ollevier, F., Olivereau, J. M. (1987): Immunocytochemical localization and spatial relation to the adenohypophysis of a somatostatin-like and a corticotropin-releasing factor-like peptide in the brain of four amphibian species. Cell Tissue Res., *247*, 317–324.

Platt, J. E., Christopher, M. A. (1977): Effects of prolactin on the water and sodium content of larval tissues from neotenic and metamorphosing *Ambystoma tigrinum*. Gen. Comp. Endocr. *31*, 243–248.

Platt, J. E., Christopher, M. A., Sullivan, C. A. (1978): The role of prolactin in blocking thyroxine-induced differentiation of tail tissue in larval and neotenic *Ambystoma tigrinum*. Gen. Comp. Endocr. *35*, 402–408.

Platt, J. E., LiCause, M. J. (1980): Effects of oxytocin in larval *Ambystoma tigrinum*: acceleration of induced metamorphosis and inhibition of the antimetamorphic action of prolactin. Gen. Comp. Endocr. *41*, 84–91.

Robinson, G. D., Ewig, J. E. (1983): Water fluxes in red efts, prolactin-injected efts and newts (*Notophthalmus viridescens*) exposed to freshwater. Comp. Biochem. Physiol. *74A*, 927–931.

Rojas, M., Gonzales, T., Preller, A. (1987): Effect of salt depletion on sodium concentration in serum and urine of *Bufo chilensis*. Evidence for increased levels of neurohypophysial principles in their plasma. Comp. Biochem. Physiol. *86A*, 225–228.

Samson, W. K. (1985): Dehydration-induced alterations in rat brain vasopressin and atrial natriuretic factor immunoreactivity. Endocrinology *117*, 1279–1281.

Samson, W. K., Aguila, M. C., Martinovic, J., Antunes-Rodrigues, J., Norris, M. (1987): Hypothalamic action of natriuretic factor to inhibit vasopressin secretion. Peptides *8*, 449–454.

Sawyer, W. H. (1987): Neurohypophysial hormones and osmoregulatory adaptations. Comparative Physiology of Environmental Adaptations. R. Kirsch and B. Lahlou, eds. pp. 76–82, Karger, Basel.

Smith, D. C. W. (1956): The role of the endocrine organs in the salinity tolerance of trout. Mem. Soc. Endocrinol. *5*, 83–101.

Snart, R. S., Dalton, T. (1973): Response of toad bladder to prolactin. Comp. Biochem. Physiol. *45A*, 307–311.

Spannhof, L., Jönsson, N. (1969): Beziehungen zwischen ventrikulärer Neurosekretion und Osmoregulation beim Krallenfrosch (*Xenopus laevis*). Zirkumventrikuläre Organe und Liquor, V. G. Fischer Verlag, G. Sterba Ed. Iena, 261–264.

Spannhof, L., Spittler, P. (1974): Osmo- und Ionenregulation von *Xenopus laevis* Daud. nach Adaptation in verschiedenen osmotisch wirksamen Lösungen. III. Änderungen des Schilddrüsenaktivität. Zool. Jb. Physiol. *78*, 242–254.

Stiffler, D. F., De Ruyter, M. L., Hanson, P. B., Marshall, M. (1986): Interrenal function in larval *Ambystoma tigrinum*. Responses to alterations in external electrolyte concentrations. Gen. Comp. Endocr. 62, 290–297.

Stoicovici, F., Pora, E. A. (1951): Comportarea la variatiuni de salinitate. Nota XXX. Stud. Cercet. Stiint., Acad. Rep. Pop. Romane, Fil. Cluj 2, 159–219.

Takada, M. (1986): The short-term effect of prolactin on the active Na transport system of the tadpole skin during metamorphosis. Comp. Biochem. Physiol. *85A*, 755–760.

Tarpey, J. F., Nicoll, C. S. (1987): Characterization of renal prolactin-binding sites of two amphibians (*Ambystoma tigrinum* and *Rana catesbeiana*) and a reptile (*Pseudemys scripta elegans*). J. Exp. Zool. *241*, 317–325.

Thurmond, W., Kloas, W., Hanke, W. (1986): The distribution of interrenal stimulating activity in the brain of *Xenopus laevis*. Gen. Comp. Endocrinol. *63*, 117–124.

Vullings, H. G. B., Diederen, J. H. B. (1986): The hypothalamo-hypophyseal system of *Rana temporaria* under osmotic stimulation with special reference to the hypothalamo-median eminence-distal lobe axis. Comp. Biochem. Physiol. *84A*, 665–667.

White, B. A. (1981): Occurrence and binding affinity of prolactin receptors in amphibian tissues. Gen. Comp. Endocr. *45*, 153–161.

White, B. A., Nicoll, C. S. (1981): Hormonal control of amphibian metamorphosis. Metamorphosis. I. L. Gilbert and E. Frieden Eds, Plenum Press, New York 366–396.

Wittouck, P. (1973): Recherches concernant l'influence de la prolactine sur la régulation ionique chez l'axolotl. Doct. Sci. Nat. Leuven.

Yamamoto, K., Kikuyama, S. (1981): Purification and properties of bullfrog prolactin. Endocr. Jap. *28*, 59–64.

Yamamoto, K., Kobayashi, T., Kikuyama, S. (1986): Purification and characterization of toad prolactin. Gen. Comp. Endocr. *63*, 104–109.

Yokota, S. D., Hillman, S. S. (1984): Adrenergic control of the anuran cutaneous hydroosmotic response. Gen. Comp. Endocr. *53*, 309–314.

Yorio, T., Bentley, P. J. (1978): Stimulation of the short-circuit current (sodium transport) across the skin of the frog by corticosteroids: structure-activity relationships. J. Endocr. *78*, 283–290.

Fortschritte der Zoologie, Band/Vol. 38 · Hanke, W. (Hrsg.), Biology and Physiology of Amphibians
Gustav Fischer Verlag · Stuttgart · New York · 1990

Ion and water balance and their endocrine control in the aquatic amphibians

M. R. Warburg and M. Rosenberg

Department of Biology, Technion Haifa 32000, Israel

1. Introduction

The amphibians are an extremely diverse group inhabiting both aquatic and terrestrial environments. Many species appear to be far more terrestrial than aquatic, spending a very short period in water during their lifetime. Several species inhabit xeric environments, even deserts, some of their special adaptations have been discussed recently (Warburg, 1988).

Early amphibians possibly inhabited swampy freshwater habitats during the Devon era (Johnson, 1980). The first amphibians were dependent on permanent water and presumably possessed moist skin (Thomson, 1980). Ammonia was excreted through the gills as in fishes, and urea was synthesized and stored as in ancient gnathostomes. The low plasma osmolality enabled their survival in freshwater (Thomson, 1971), and the high osmolality due to urea accumulation later facilitated emergence on land (Balinsky, 1970). Although, amphibians were the first vertebrate group on land (Bogart, 1981), they are still «handicapped» in many ways, especially in their reproductive modes (Goin, 1960) as most species must inhabit an aquatic environment during at least one stage of their life.

Amphibians, inhabiting the aquatic environment, belong to 4 different categories. Firstly, the anuran tadpoles or the urodele larvae which grow, differentiate and metamorphose. They spend a limited time in water, generally a few to several weeks.

The second group are the larvae (largely urodeles) that fail to metamorphose in time. These are the neotenous amphibians. Some of them become sexually mature, although they still retain larval traits. These are the paedomorphic amphibians. Both neotenous and paedomorphic Amphibia are aquatic.

The phenomena of neoteny and paedogenesis in amphibians are only known from urodeles. Anuran tadpoles may sometimes grow into gigantic dimensions (*Pelobates*, Boschwitz, 1957), but are not neotenous and eventually metamorphose. Some of them are incapable of responding to thyroid hormones (*Necturus*, *Siren*, *Proteus*) although in some cases triiodothyronine (T_3) and thyroxine (T_4) are produced by their own thyroid glands (*Proteus*). Others are capable of responding, and their thyroxine may induce the completion of metamorphosis (*Eurycea*, Kezer, 1952; *Ambystoma*, Prahlad and de Lanney, 1965). Other urodeles permanently retain their larval form and become paedogenic (*Ambystoma*, Patterson, 1978). There does not seem to be any cytological defect in their pituitary. These phenomena may be caused by both environmental or internal factors (Snyder, 1956; Dent, 1968; Wasserburg, 1975; Semlitsch, 1987). Sprules (1974) suggested that under harsh conditions of temperature fluctuations and low humidity, perhaps urodeles better survived when permanently staying in water and thus became neotenous and eventually paedomorphic.

Thirdly, there are those amphibians who as adults remain in water even after metamorphosis. These are both anurans (*Rana*, *Pipa*, *Discoglossus*, *Xenopus*) and urodeles (*Cryptobranchus*, *Amphiuma*).

Finally, there are many amphibian species where the adults return to water in order to breed. The breeding period can be short or extends for several weeks. However, in most amphibian species their aquatic phase is not of long duration. Thus, in some salamanders (*Salamandra*) it may last not more than 2% of its entire life span including the 2–3 months long larval period. In others newts (*Triturus*), pelobatids, bufonids and the aquatic phase may last up to 5% of their life.

After a period of a few to several days largely depending on temperature conditions the embryo hatches and the tadpole or larva starts its life as an independent individual in the aquatic environment.

Etkin (1963) recognized 3 major phases during the metamorphic cycle of anurans. Premetamorphosis: a period during which most growth takes place with some differentiation, ending with the emergence of the hindlimbs. This is followed by prometamorphosis, a period of intense differentiation and growth of the hindlimbs, ending with the emergence of the forelimbs. Finally, the metamorphic climax is reached with the resorption of gills and tail and the emergence on land.

The return to water of a fully grown amphibian may be an annual event during the breeding season or sometimes less frequent. The event was largely studied in the newt, *Notophthalmus viridescens*, returning to breed in water after 2–3 years on land (Dent, 1968). This so called «water drive» is found in other amphibians as well although not studied as much.

Apparently, the main stimulus for the «water drive» in *Notophthalmus viridescens* is induced by prolactin (PRL) causing a preference for an aquatic habitat. This is brought about by an increased serum osmolality resulting in water uptake (Moriya and Dent, 1986), which causes the animal to «sink» to the bottom of the pond once it reached it, due

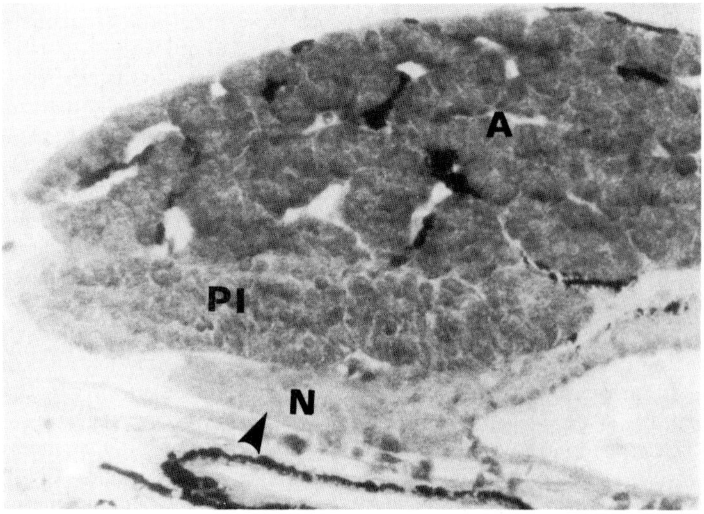

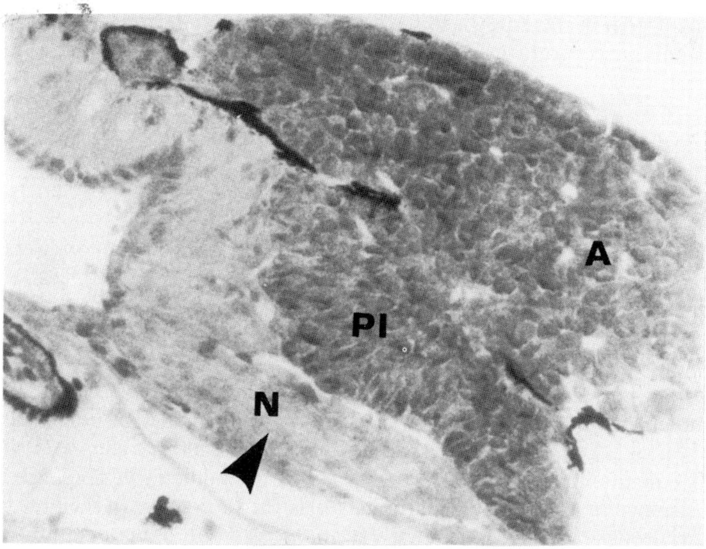

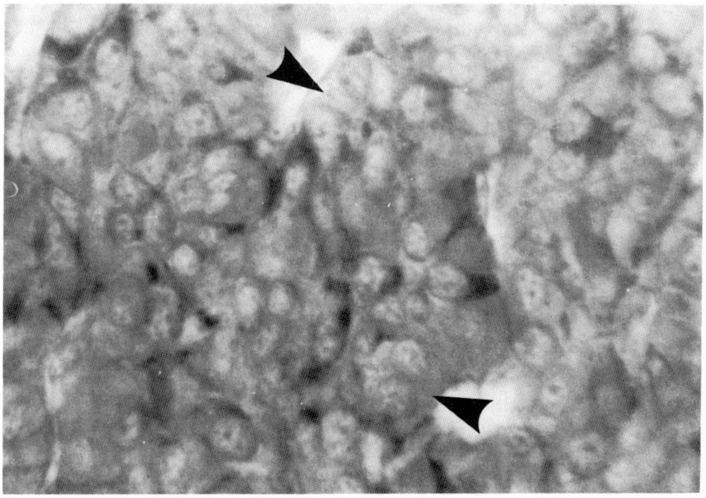

Figs. 1–3: Hypophysis of *Pelobates syriacus* tadpoles. Fig. 1 (p. 386) – Two-limbs (× 125). Fig. 2 (above) – Four-limbs (× 125, note the well developed neurohypophysis – arrow). Fig. 3 (below) – adenohypophysis of a two-limbed tadpole (× 625), note the putative PRL cells – arrows). A – Adenohypophysis – PI – Pars Intermedia – N – Neurohypophysis.

to its increased specific gravity. T_4 lowered both the osmolality and the specific gravity perhaps by lowering PRL levels, and the newt could float and eventually returns to land. AVT was found to be a stimulator for sexual behaviour (Zoeller and Moore, 1988). So far, we lack more quantitative physiological information about the response of sexually mature adult amphibians towards their breeding ponds.

The main purpose of this study is to find out to what extent the ionic and water balance, and their endocrine control vary among these different categories of aquatic amphibians.

2. Hormones and their effects on ion and water balance

2.1. Thyroid hormones

The circulating levels of thyroid hormones change during metamorphosis in *Rana pipiens*. Thus, between stages IX and XV the T_4-level is low (0.002 g/l – 0.02 g/l) increasing to 0.2 g/l at stage XIX and reaching a peak of 0.6 g/l at stage XXI (Kollros, 1961). Apparently, after metamorphic climax the level of hormone drops. T_3 follows the same pattern as T_4 with a time lag (Mondou and Kaltenbach, 1979). In *Rana catesbeiana* T_3 can be the more important hormone for metamorphosis (Miyauchi et al., 1977).

In *Hynobius nigrescens* larvae, T_4, reached its peak at metamorphic climax with 1.96 ng/ml (Suzuki, 1987). T_3 was detectable only at metamorphic climax. T_4 levels were much higher in the aquatic-prespawning phase of the adult newt compared with the aquatic-postspawning phase. Thus thyroxine levels vary according to the breeding conditions in the urodele. In another newt, *Hynobius retardatus*, temperature affects the metamorphic rate. Thyroxine administration could accelerate metamorphosis at low (10 °C) temperatures (Moriya, 1983 a). It should be of interest to study thyroxine levels in neotenous urodeles and compare them with normal larval ones.

In winter *Notophthalmus viridescens* specimen, T_4-treatment increased water permeability of the skin (Brown and Brown, 1973). It also increased Na^+-K^+-ATPase levels in the epidermis (Kawada et al., 1972). However, T_4 is not considered as an important hormone for hydromineral regulation (Grau, 1987).

2.2. The hypophyseal hormones

The hypophysis contains six different cell types based on their tinctorial affinities and EM granular structure. One of them is located in the pars intermedia and the rest in the pars distalis (Doerr-Schott, 1974; van Oordt, 1974). Some cells only appear in the larvae, others appear after metamorphosis (Holmes and Ball, 1974). The pars intermedia cells release MSH (Hanke, 1976). Whereas the adenohypophysial cells produce and release different hormones, among them: PRL, ACTH, STH, TSH (Figs. 1–3).

MSH is released at the very early stage of tail-bud promotion (Etkin, 1941), whereas TSH, ACTH and STH start at prometamorphosis (stages 46–48). Thus, at premetamorphosis very low levels of TSH and thyroid hormones are present as well as high amounts of PRL. The levels of the former hormones increase at prometamorphosis whereas PRL level decreases. Finally, at metamorphic climax TRH, TSH and T_4 levels are reduced (Hanke, 1976). The pars distalis volume increases during development and decreases towards metamorphic climax (Garcia-Navarro et al., 1988).

Hansen and Hansen (1981) found 2 different cell types in the pars distalis: STH and PRL cells (in *Lepidosiren paradoxa*, *Rana temporaria* and *Ambystoma mexicanum*).

In *Rana catesbeiana*, pituitary PRL levels were found to rise slowly from the emergence of the forelimbs through stage XXIII and to increase markedly at stage XXIV. Circulating plasma levels were similar to pituitary PRL release (Clemons and Nicoll, 1977). In *Pelobates cultripes* and *Rana perezi*, PRL appears to be synthetised and stored during pre- and prometamorphosis and released at metamorphic climax (Garcia-Navarro et al., 1988). In neotenic *Ambystoma tigrinum*, PRL levels are significantly higher than in larvae or post-metamorphic salamanders (Norris et al., 1973). Furthermore, evidence in fish indicates that changes in daylength could modify patterns of PRL release (Sage and de Vlaming, 1975).

2.2.1. *The neurohypophysial hormones and their effects*

The subject has been reviewed by Sawyer and Pang (1979, 1987) and Goldenberg and Warburg (1983).

Arginine vasotocin (AVT) was located in the neurohypophysis of *Rana catesbeiana* (Bentley, 1969). The amounts found in the tadpoles are ¼ of those found in the adults (Bentley and Greenwald, 1970). Mild dehydration of adult *Rana catesbeiana* caused an increase in AVT level in serum (Nouwen and Kühn, 1983). Dehydration affects the level of AVT in the ventral preoptic area of the newt *Taricha granulosa*, whereas in other brain areas it remained unchanged (Zoeller and Moore, 1986). In the male newt, AVT levels were low in summer, fall and winter and high during the breeding season in spring. Nothing is known about AVT circulating levels in neotenous urodeles. Are they similar to the larval levels? Even more significantly does the AVT level drop in the aquatic phase of the newt after reaching high levels in the terrestrial newts?

In the tadpoles of *Rana catesbeiana*, AVT caused a water uptake which increased towards metamorphosis (Bentley and Greenwald, 1970). This response started at the 2-limb stage in *Rana ridibunda* (Goldenberg and Warburg, 1977b) (see Fig. 4). In *Rana catesbeiana* it reached its peak after metamorphosis (Alvarado and Johnson, 1966). The weight gain appears to be a result of antidiuresis in the larvae of *Ambystoma tigrinum*, due to reduced GFR (Alvarado and Johnson, 1965). AVT caused sodium accumulation in larval *Ambystoma* (Alvarado and Kirschner, 1963), and caused sodium uptake in *Rana catesbeiana* tadpoles (Alvarado and Johnson, 1965). However, Bentley and Baldwin (1980) did not find that AVT affected sodium influx whereas it caused increased permeability of the skin in *Ambystoma tigrinum* larvae.

In the adult amphibians, AVT caused reduced GFR resulting in reduced water excretion (Sawyer, 1972; Sawyer and Pang, 1979). In the larval salamander, *Ambystoma tigrinum*, it caused antidiuresis due to reduced GFR, whereas in the adult it stimulated Na^+ uptake (Alvarado and Johnson, 1965). However, in the more aquatic species, *Necturus*, it did not

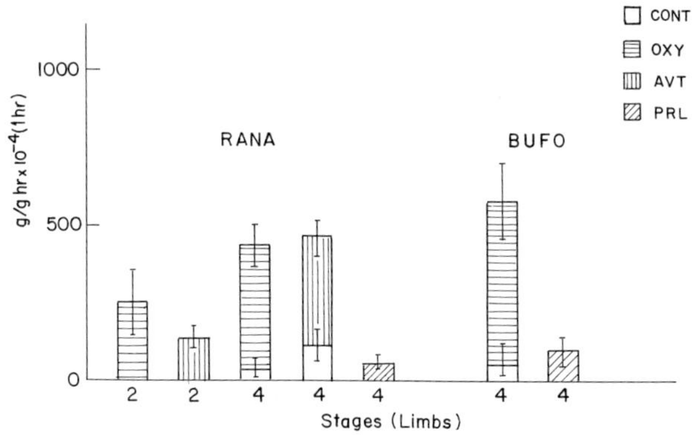

Fig. 4: Water retention response in *Rana ridibunda* and *Bufo viridis* tadpoles following injections of oxytocin (OXY), arginine vasotocin (AVT) or prolactin (PRL). Further discussions see Goldenberg and Warburg (1983). 2 – Two limbs stage – 4 – Four limbs stage.

cause any changes in Na^+ balance (Heller and Bentley, 1965). It caused some sodium transport in *Xenopus* (Bentley, 1966), but no water uptake. Nor did it affect water uptake in other amphibians like *Siren*, *Amphiuma* or *Discoglossus* (Heller and Bentley, 1965), or newts (*Notophthalmus viridescens*) in their aquatic phase (Brown et al., 1983). There appears to be some water retention in *Siren* and *Amphiuma* (Bentley, 1973), but only a third of that found in *Rana catesbeiana*. This is a result of the antidiuretic effect of AVT as found in *Necturus maculosus* (Garland et al., 1975), and not an effect on the bladder (Bentley, 1971). AVT also caused dermal gland secretion in *Xenopus* (Ireland, 1973). The subject has been reviewed by Sawyer & Pang (1979, 1987).

Although mesotocin (MT) rather than oxytocin (OXY) is naturally occuring in amphibians (in serum of *Rana ridibunda* adult frogs, Nouwen and Kühn, 1983), most studies were conducted on oxytocin. Mesotocin caused diuresis in *Rana catesbeiana* adults (Sawyer and Pang, 1979) as a result of increased GFR. It was found that *Rana ridibunda*, from 2-limb tadpoles onwards, responded to oxytocin by weight increase, whereas *Bufo viridis* only responded after metamorphic climax (Goldenberg and Warburg, 1976 and Fig. 4). *Rana catesbeiana* tadpoles responded to oxytocin from stage XXII onwards (Alvarado and Johnson, 1966).

In the urodele *Salamandra salamandra* young premetamorphic larvae responded to OXY by water uptake (Warburg and Goldenberg, 1978 a and Fig. 5). Likewise, the aquatic phase of the newt, *Triturus vittatus* (Warburg and Goldenberg, 1978 a), and *Notophthalmus viridescens*, responded to oxytocin by only half of their response to vasopressin (AVP, Brown and Brown, 1977). AVP does not naturally occur in amphibian hypophysis (Jørgensen and Larsen, 1967).

There appears to be a seasonal difference in the response to oxytocin of *Rana ridibunda* tadpoles. During summer it was much higher as compared to their response in winter (Goldenberg and Warburg, 1976 and Fig. 6). This could perhaps be related to a recent study by Nouwen (1984) that AVT (and MT) show a cyclic presence in the serum of adult *Rana ridibunda*.

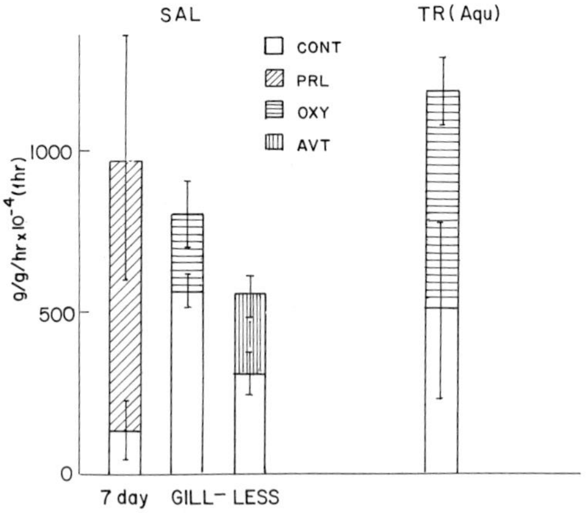

Fig. 5: Water retention responses in *Salamandra salamandra* larvae and the aquatic phase of *Triturus vittatus* following injections of oxytocin (OXY), arginine vasotocin (AVT) or prolactin (PRL). Further discussions see Warburg and Goldenberg (1978 a, b).

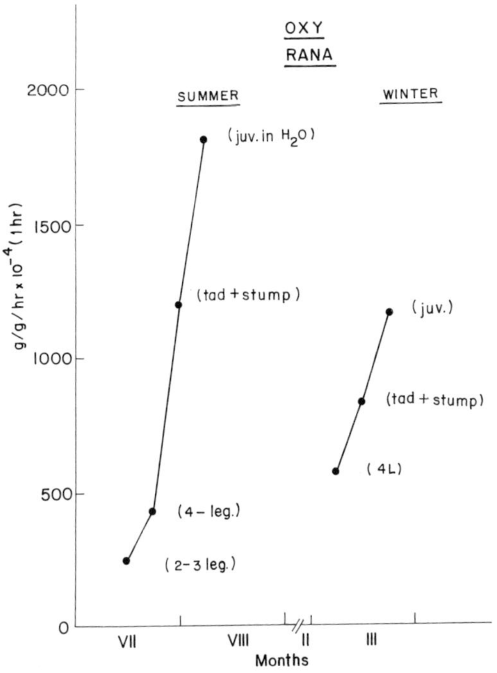

Fig. 6: Water retention response following injection of oxytocin (OXY) in *Rana ridibunda* tadpoles and juveniles during summer and winter. Note the higher response during summer (Further discussion in Goldenberg and Warburg, 1976).

Notophthalmus viridescens responded to AVP by increased water uptake, decreased urinary loss due to decreased GFR and increased bladder reabsorption (Brown and Brown, 1977). The isolated bladder showed an increase in water permeability as a response to AVP.

2.2.2. *The adenohypophysial hormones and their effects*

Prolactin's role in osmoregulation was reviewed by Bern (1975), Goldenberg and Warburg (1983) and Brown and Brown (1987). Apparently the neotenic *Ambystoma tigrinum* contained more PRL than either the larva or the adult (Norris et al., 1973). Prolactin release was high in winter breeding newts (*Triturus cristatus*, Lodi et al., 1978). There seems to be a rhythmic PRL release entrained by the daily photoperiod (Meier, 1975), and the response of frogs varied markedly during the day. When *Xenopus* was kept outside the water prolactin, although snythetized, was not released (Guardabassi et al., 1978).

Prolactin increased the ion absorbing ability of salamander (*Ambystoma*) gills (Wittouck, 1972). It caused water uptake in *Rana ridibunda* tadpoles towards climax and in *Bufo viridis* tadpoles in the 4-limb stage (Goldenberg and Warburg, 1977a and Fig. 4). It affected water movement in *Xenopus* tadpoles as well (Schultheiss et al., 1972). PRL caused an increase in body water and sodium in *Ambystoma tigrinum* larvae (Platt and Christopher, 1977). It also caused an increase in sodium and water content of the tail tissue in *Rana catesbeiana* stage XII tadpoles (Eddy, 1979). This might have been caused by the effect on the hydrophylic nature of the mucopolysaccharide layer in the skin (in the salamander *Hynobius*, Moriya, 1982). PRL also prevented the weight loss experienced by tadpoles of *Rana catesbeiana* when transferred from cold (5 °C) to warm (18 °C) temperature (Brown et al., 1986).

In hypophysectomized *Necturus maculosus* sodium was lost but could be restored by treatment with PRL (Pang and Sawyer, 1974). In the aquatic forms, adult *Xenopus* were not affected by PRL when in water, but only when outside on moss (Giunta et al., 1974–75). PRL is known in newts to induce the «water drive» phenomenon. Thus in *Triturus cristatus* it induced the return to water when the newts were 4–5 years old (Reinke and Chadwick, 1940). Gonads or the thyroid had no effect on this response. PRL caused water drive in 50% of the red efts (*Notophthalmus viridescens*, Meier et al., 1971), and in the salamander *Hynobius retardatus* (Moriya, 1982). PRL lowered the levels of circulating T_4 in *Notophthalmus* (Anderson and Dent, 1982).

PRL apparently affected the integument by causing a drop in water uptake through the integument in the aquatic phase of the newt *Notophthalmus viridescens* (Brown et al., 1983). It also depressed sodium transport through isolated skin in *Triturus cristatus* (Lodi and Biciotti, 1975/76; Lodi et al., 1982). PRL initiated change from granular to smooth skin in *Taricha torosa* (Grant and Grant, 1958; Harlow, 1977), and caused thick mucus formation (Brown and Brown, 1973). However, both aquatic and terrestrial skins responded in the same way to sodium and water movements in response to PRL (Harlow, 1977). For a detailed discussion see Brown & Brown (1987).

2.2.3. *Corticosteroids, the interrenal hormones*

Interrenal hormones or corticosteroids regulate water balance (and metabolism of carbohydrates), and are dependent upon the ACTH (Adrenocorticotropic hormone) producing cells (basophils type 3) in the pars distalis of the pituitary (van Kemenade, 1974).

Corticosterone concentration in *Rana catesbeiana* tadpoles was low prior to metamorphic climax (stage XX). At later stages XXI–XXIV corticosteroid levels in the plasma were elevated (Jaffe, 1981).

In *Xenopus*, Leist (1970) noted a decrease in the secreting activity of the interrenals towards the beginning of metamorphic climax. On the other hand, Jolivet-Jaudet and Leloup-Hatey (1984) found that both corticosterone and aldosterone levels reached a peak at the beginning of metamorphic climax (in *Xenopus*). They found maximal levels of hormones in plasma at this stage.

In *Rana pipiens*, the concentration of corticosterone was higher in summer (Jørgensen et al., 1967), and dehydration caused a decline in this concentration. On the other hand in *Rana esculenta* the peak of concentration of corticosterone coincides with the spawning season in late spring (Leboulenger et al., 1979). Apparently, blood sugar levels are highest during the peak breeding season in spring and in fall in *Rana temporaria* (Hanke et al., 1969).

Changes in both osmolality and sodium or potassium ion concentration affected the internal secretion in *Rana temporaria* (Hanke and Maser-Gluth, 1985).

Corticosterone was found to cause a decline in sodium efflux in *Ambystoma tigrinum* (Brown et al., 1986). It caused a decrease in water content of *Xenopus* tadpoles (Leist, 1970). An increased water uptake followed ACTH treatment of the aquatic phase of the newt (*Notophthalmus viridescens*) as well as increased transepithelial potential (TEP) (Brown et al., 1983). Apparently, the daily variations in the water drive caused by PRL are synchronized by the circadian rhythm of the interrenal hormonal secretion (Meier et al., 1971).

Aldosterone was found to stimulate reabsorption of sodium and the secretion of K^+ (Stiffler et al., 1986) in *Ambystoma tigrinum*. The short circuit current (SCC) through the isolated bladder in *Necturus* was affected by aldosterone (Bentley, 1971). Aldosterone was found to stimulate sodium influx in larvae of *Ambystoma tigrinum* (Alvarado and Kirschner, 1963). ACTH affected this response as well (de Ruyter and Stiffler, 1986). Leist (1970) found aldosterone to be ineffective on water balance or nitrogen metabolism in *Xenopus* tadpoles.

Finally, corticosterone stimulated storage of glucose in the liver (Hanke, 1974; Leist, 1970) and with aldosterone regulated moulting (Jørgensen and Larsen, 1967).

To conclude, ACTH and corticosteroides as well as thyroid hormones are responsible for protein synthesis, cornification of the skin and reduction of H_2O content.

3. Ion transport and water permeability

In the anuran tadpole, the development of the sodium pump is coincident with the development of the tadpole and metamorphosis (Robinson and Mills, 1987). Major changes take place in the epidermis of the tadpoles starting with a 2–3 layered epithelium with 2–3 cell types, and ending with a 4–5 layered epithelium with well defined strata (Fahrmann 1971 a, b; Warburg and Lewinson, 1977; Rosenberg and Warburg, 1978; Lewinson et al., 1983). Some cells are typically larval (Leydig cells in urodele larvae, Rosenberg et al., 1982), whereas others are typical of the adult epidermis (flask cells, Lewinson et al., 1982 and Fig. 7). During prometamorphosis the stratification of the epidermis becomes more advanced and towards the metamorphic climax the stratum corneum is well formed.

The ion transport phenomena are related to these structural changes of the epidermis. Furthermore, during moulting the transport of ions and water permeability change markedly (Larsen, 1976). The subject has been recently reviewed by Katz (1986). During the early stages of the metamorphic cycle there is only a passive Na^+ pathway (in *Rana catesbeiana* tadpoles). Active sodium transport through the integument first appeared at

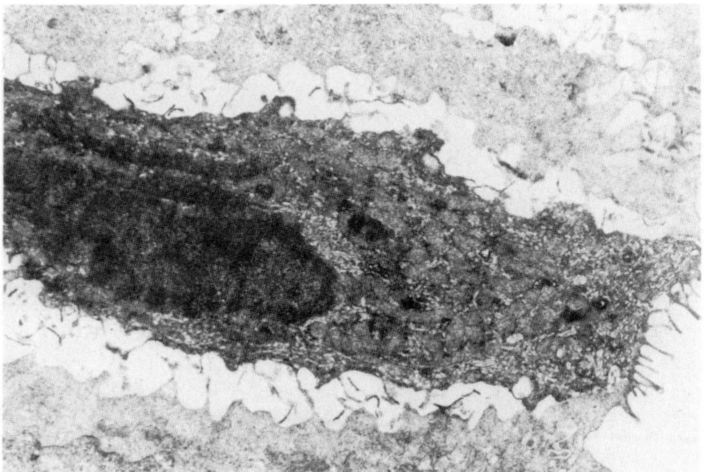

Fig. 7: Epidermal mitochondria – rich cell in a 2 week old *Salamandra salamandra* larva (× 4000).

stage XXI when potential difference and short circuit current were measurable (Takada, 1985). Thus, no transepithelial potential was observed until several days after emergence of forelimbs (stage XXI), increasing thereafter towards metamorphic crisis (Taylor and Barker, 1965). This was also noticed by Alvarado and Moody (1970) and Cox and Alvarado (1979) who measured active Na^+ and Cl^--ion movement into the body fluids from stage XXII onwards.

ATPase levels were low in *Rana catesbeiana* tadpoles (Kawada et al., 1969), but increased before there was any noticeable potential difference across the skin (Casada and Nichols, 1986), although they remained ¼ to ⅓ of the levels found in adult frogs (Kawada et al., 1969). The low level of Na^+-K^+-ATPase explains the low rate of transcutaneous Na^+ transport (Kawada et al., 1969). The current through Na^+ channels did not increase significantly during late metamorphosis (Hyllyard et al., 1982). ATPase activity increased greatly between stages 30–44 in *Calyptocephalella* tadpoles (Greenwald, 1972). We have observed cytochemical indication of ATPase activity in the epidermal cells of *Pelobates syriacus* tadpoles until metamorphic climax during the onset of tail resorption (Fig. 8). Apparently the outer layer of the epidermis is the main site of the sodium pump (Robinson and Mills, 1987). In the gills, ATPase activity was high in *Rana catesbeiana* tadpoles (Boonkoom and Alvarado, 1971) and in *Calyptocephalella caudiverbera* tadpoles (Gonzales et al., 1979). Gills are the major site of ammonia excretion in aquatic amphibian larvae (Maetz, 1972).

In the urodele larvae (studies are based largely on *Ambystoma tigrinum*) there seem to be fewer Na^+ channels than in the adults (Bentley and Baldwin, 1980). However, Na^+ and Cl^--concentrations were higher in the larvae (Alvarado and Kirschner, 1963). They are capable of transporting both Na^+ and Cl^- inward and the transepithelial potential (TEP) is generated by this active sodium transport (Dietz et al., 1967). Uptake of Cl^- is independent and a non-electrogenic mechanism. In the neotenous axolotl (*Ambystoma mexicanum*), SCC and TEP were very low, increasing after metamorphosis (Takada and Hara, 1988).

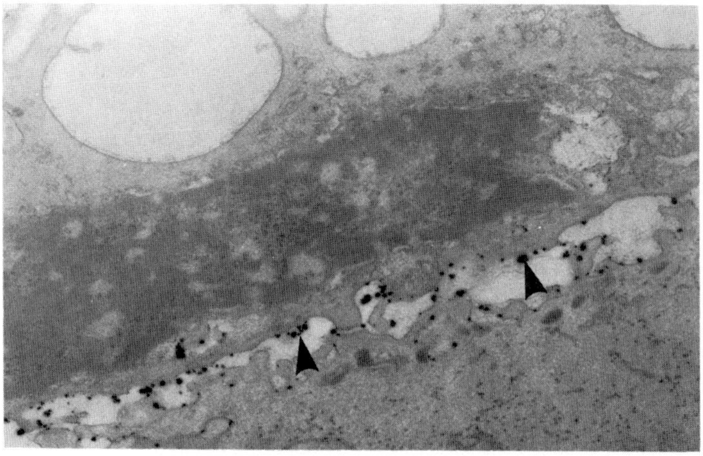

Fig. 8: Epidermal surface cells in *Pelobates syriacus* tadpole at metamorphic stage (× 15 000), showing cytochemical reaction for ATPase (arrows).

The urodele larvae take up water at a rate of 26% of their body weight per day (adults 32%) (Alvarado and Kirschner, 1963). However, in the more terrestrial forms of amphibians the decreased water permeability of the skin coincides with the degree of terrestrialism (Warburg, 1972, 1988).

The larva apparently has a lower skin permeability than the adult (in *Ambystoma tigrinum*, Bentley and Baldwin, 1980). A similar phenomenon is also seen in anurans where skin of the aquatic frog, *Rana septentrionalis*, is less (by 50%) permeable to water than the terrestrial *Bufo hemiophrys* (Schmid and Barden, 1965). On the other hand, the epidermis of the aquatic phase of the newt, (*Triturus vittatus*), responded much less than the terrestrial one to treatment with oxytocin (Warburg, 1971 and Fig. 9). The bladder seems to be the main target organ for OXY in the aquatic phase. This animal largely responded to AVT as well (Warburg, 1971; Fig. 9).

Adult species from aquatic habitats endure hydration for longer periods than the terrestrial ones (Schmid, 1965). In frogs that overwinter in water under the ice, the water content of the tadpole (of *Rana muscosa*) during their first month in water increased by 5.7% whereas the extracellular osmolality declined by 13.6% (Bradford, 1984). The tadpoles were more hydrated than the adults overwintering under the same conditions.

The osmolality of blood in aquatic species was lower (180–200 mM/l in *Rana catesbeiana* tadpoles (Just et al., 1977) than in terrestrial ones. In the salt water tadpoles of *Rana cancrivora*, salt is excreted actively through the gills (Gordon and Tucker, 1965).

In other aquatic species the adults show a low efflux of Na^+ and Cl^- (*Xenopus*, Yorio and Bentley, 1978; reviewed in Gordon, 1964). There is also a low Na^+ uptake (Greenwald, 1972). The water permeability of *Xenopus* changed during metamorphosis dropping towards metamorphic climax (Schultheiss et al., 1972).

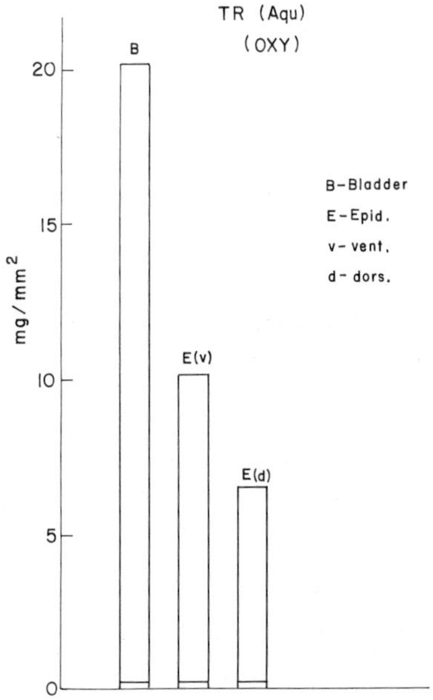

Fig. 9: Response (in vitro) of urinary bladder and epidermis of the aquatic phase of the newt *Triturus vittatus* to oxytocin. Further discussion in Warburg (1971).

Low levels of Na^+ transport and osmotic permeability were also found in the aquatic (winter) phase of the newt *Triturus cristatus* (Lodi et al., 1982). Apparently the aquatic phase of the newt has a lower SCC than the terrestrial phase (Mazzi, 1970). Similarly, TEP is lower in the aquatic (breeding phase) of *Notophthalmus viridescens* (Brown et al., 1983), as well as in plasma sodium (Brown and Brown, 1973). The structural changes that take place in the epidermis of amphibians (*Bufo*, *Rana*, *Triturus*) in their aquatic phase have been studied recently (Greven, 1987), and previously by us (Warburg and Lewinson, 1977; Rosenberg and Warburg, 1978).

In the aquatic urodeles net trans-cutaneous sodium flux was zero in *Necturus* (Bentley and Yorio, 1977), whereas in *Amphiuma* it was 0.09. In the neotenous axolotl (*Ambystoma tigrinum*) larvae it was 0.13 (Bentley and Baldwin, 1980). The three aquatic urodeles *Amphiuma*, *Necturus* and *Siren* have low levels of sodium uptake and loss (Greenwald, 1972). Their isolated skin has lower osmotic permeability (Bentley, 1966).

Both *Necturus* and the axolotl are known to absorb water (and Na^+) across their integuments (Bentley, 1973; Baldwin and Bentley, 1982). However, the exchange of ions across the skin is much lower (in *Amphiuma* and *Siren*) than that of the frogs (Bentley, 1975).

There appears to be some seasonal variations in transport phenomena. Thus in *Necturus*, SCC is higher in spring than in winter (Bentley, 1971). *Cynops pyrrhogaster* migrating from water to land in autumn have higher TEP than the «spring» newts (Takada and Komozaki, 1988).

4. Hormonal effects on transport phenomena

T_4 and PRL accelerated the appearance of the transepithelial potential (TEP) in *Rana catesbeiana* tadpoles (Taylor and Barker, 1965). Levels of K^+-pNPPase increased 3-fold in thyroxine-treated tadpoles of *Rana perezi* (stage 39) and peaked before metamorphotic climax (Burón and Navas, 1988). Prolactin was shown to cause increased Na^+ transport SCC across the skin in *Rana catesbeiana* tadpoles (Takada, 1986). This reaction increased towards metamorphic climax (stage XXII–XXV). Apparently prolactin affected the electromotive force of the active Na^+ current and the resistence to the current.

In *Salamandra* larvae prolactin already affected water uptake in the young larva (Warburg and Goldenberg, 1978 b). No response was noticeable in *Pelobates syriacus* tadpoles injected with OXY (Warburg, 1972). The aquatic phase of the newt (*Triturus vittatus*) responded much less to OXY than to AVT. Some response was noticeable in *Salamandra* larvae towards metamorphic climax (Warburg and Goldenberg, 1978 a and Fig. 5).

Apparently the frog tadpoles (stages X–XXV) were less sensitive to ADH than the adults (Cox and Alvarado, 1979). They were also less sensitive to ouabain or ameloride.

The effect of AVT on *Ambystoma tigrinum* larvae has shown that Na^+ influx (and water permeability) remained unchanged (Bentley and Baldwin, 1980; Baldwin and Bentley, 1982). The same was true of other aquatic amphibians (*Amphiuma*, *Necturus*, *Siren*, Bentley 1975; Bentley and Yorio, 1977). Thus no effect could be observed on isolated skins of *Notophthalmus* (Brown and Brown, 1977). However, in *Necturus* sodium transport was affected by AVT (Baldwin and Bentley, 1982), and water uptake by the bladder was affected in *Trituras vittatus* (aquatic phase) (see Warburg 1971).

In the adult newt (*Triturus cristatus*) PRL caused a reduction of Na^+ transport through the integument (Lodi and Biciotti, 1975–76), and affected SCC as well (Lodi et al., 1978). In the aquatic (breeding) phase of *Notophthalmus viridescens*, PRL caused a decreased TEP in the skin during winter (Brown et al., 1983). The same phenomenon was observed in *Cynops pyrrhogaster* when PRL blocked the sodium channels (Takada and Komazaki, 1988). Perhaps this is related to the fact that PRL caused increased mucous secretion of the dermal glands in Amphibia (Dent, 1975).

ACTH caused an increased water uptake through the integument of the aquatic phase of *Notophthalmus* (Brown et al., 1983).

Table 1: Hypophysial hormones present in the animal and the hormones affecting water and ion balance in aquatic amphibians

The Aquatic Amphibians	Hormones Present	Hormones Affecting Water Retention	Hormones Affecting Ion Transport
Premetamorphic tadpole or larvae	PRL	AVT OXY PRL	None
Tadpoles or larvae at metamorphic climax	MT AVT (25% of adults) PRL	AVT OXY PRL (–) MT	AVT, PRL (–) *Ambystoma* Aldosterone
Neotonous urodeles	PRL AVT (?)	PRL (–) MT	(–) AVT
Adult aquatic anurans	AVT MT PRL (high)	(–) OXY (–) MT	(–) AVT
Aquatic phase of adult newts	?	OXY PRL	?

(–) No effect

5. Conclusions

Amphibians vary in the length of time they spend in water during their lifetime. Not taking into account the terrestrial breeders, some species spend as little as 2% of their life in water, including their larval period (*Salamandra*). Most other amphibians spend about 5–10% of their life in water (bufonids, pelobatids). Still other species are completely aquatic (*Pipa*, *Discoglossus*, *Xenopus*, *Necturus*, *Amphiuma*, *Siren*). In some species there are larvae who fail to metamorphose. These neotenous species (*Ambystoma*) sometimes turn out to become paedogenic and reproduce as they are sexually mature in spite of their other larval traits.

During metamorphosis, endocrine glands develop gradually until their maturation at metamorphic climax. At the same time circulating hormonal levels increase. This is true for thyroid turnover. Only little is known about hypophysial hormone levels during pre- and prometamorphosis. Presumably, some of the hypophysial hormones are secreted only after the emergence on land (AVT), whereas other are secreted before (PRL, MT).

There is also a need for information about the difference in circulating levels of some hormones (PRL, AVT, MT) in aquatic versus terrestrial phases of the newts. Does the aquatic environment change the normal (terrestrial) pattern of hormonal balance in the newts?

The ionic and water balance of metamorphosing Amphibia develops gradually. Thus ion transport is detectable only upon metamorphosis. Apparently most aquatic urodeles (neotenous) show very little evidence of transport. A similar situation is found in the aquatic phase of the newts. It is likely that other areas of ion transport are functional (gills, kidney, gut?).

References

Alvarado, R. H., Johnson, S. R. (1965): The effects of arginine vasotocin and oxytocin on sodium and water balance in *Ambystoma*. Comp. Biochem. Physiol. *16*, 531–546.

Alvarado, R. H., Johnson, S. R. (1966): The effects of neurohypophysial hormones on water and sodium balance in larval and adult bullfrogs (*Rana catesbeiana*). Comp. Biochem. Physiol. *18*, 549–561.

Alvarado, R. H., Kirschner, L. R. (1963): Osmotic and ionic regulation in *Ambystoma tigrinum*. Comp. Biochem. Physiol. *10*, 55–67.

Alvarado, R. H., Moody, A. (1970): Sodium and chloride transport in tadpoles of the bullfrog *Rana catesbeiana*. Am. J. Physiol. *218*, 1510–1516.

Anderson, S. L., Dent, J. N. (1982): Increased loss of thyroxine from the blood streams of newts after injection with ovine prolactin. Gen. Comp. Endocrinol. *47*, 276–279.

Baldwin, G. F., Bentley, P. J. (1982): Roles of the skin and gills in sodium and water exchanges in neotenic urodele amphibians. Am. J. Physiol. *242*, R94–R96.

Balinsky, J. B. (1970): Nitrogen metabolism in amphibians. In: Comparative Biochemistry of Nitrogen Metabolism, vol. 2, The Vertebrates (J. W. Campbell, ed.), pp. 519–637 Acad Press.

Bentley, P. J. (1966): The physiology of the urinary bladder of Amphibia. Biol. Rev. *41*, 275–316.

Bentley, P. J. (1969): Neurohypophyseal hormones in Amphibia: A comparison of their actions and storage. Gen. Comp. Endocrinol. *13*, 39–44.

Bentley, P. J. (1971): Sodium and water movement across the urinary bladder of a urodele amphibian (the mudpuppy *Necturus maculosus*): Studies with vasotocin and aldosterone. Gen. Comp. Endocrinol. *16*, 356–362.

Bentley, J. J. (1973): Osmoregulation in the aquatic urodeles *Amphiuma means* (the Congo eel) and *Siren lacertina* (the mud eel). Effects of vasotocin. Gen. Comp. Endocrinol. *20*, 386–391.

Bentley, P. J. (1975): The electrical P.D. across the integument of some neotenous urodele amphibians. Comp. Biochem. Physiol. *50a*, 639–643.

Bentley, P. J. (1977): Endocrines and Osmoregulation. 300 pp. Springer.

Bentley, P. J., Baldwin, G. F. (1980): Comparison of transcutaneous permeability in skins of larval and adult salamanders (*Ambystoma tigrinum]. Am. J. Physiol. 239*, R505–R508.

Bentley, P. J., Greenwald, L. (1970): Neurohypophysial function in bullfrog (*Rana catesbeiana*) tadpoles. Gen. Comp. Endocrinol. *14*, 412–415.

Bentley, P. J., Yorio, T. (1977): The permeability of the skin of a neotenous urodele amphibian, the mudpuppy *Necturus maculosus*. J. Physiol. *265*, 537–547.

Bern, H. A. (1975): Prolactin and Osmoregulation. Amer. Zool. *15*, 937–948.

Bogart, J. P. (1981): How many times has terrestrial breeding evolved in anuran amphibians? Monit. Zool. Ital. N. S. Suppl. XV *3*, 29–40.

Boonkoom, V., Alvarado, R. H. (1971): Adenosinetriphosphatase activity in gills of larval *Rana catesbeiana*. Am. J. Physiol. *220*, 1820–1824.

Boschwitz, D. (1957): Thyroidless tadpoles of *Pelobates syriacus*. Copeia *1957*, 310–311.

Bradford, D. F. (1984): Water and osmotic balance in overwintering tadpoles and frogs, *Rana muscosa*. Physiol. Zool. *57*, 474–480.

Brown, P. S., Brown, S. C. (1973): Prolactin and thyroid hormone interactions in salt and water balance in the newt Notophthalmus viridescens. Gen. Comp. Endocrinol. *20*, 456–466.

Brown, P. S., Brown, S. C. (1977): Water balance responses to dehydration and neurohypophysial peptides in the salamander, *Notophthalmus viridescens.* Gen. Comp. Endocrinol. *31*, 189–201.

Brown, P. S., Brown, S. C. (1987): Osmoregulatory actions of prolactin and other adenohypophysial hormones, In: Vertebrate Endocrinology: Fundametals and Biomedical Implications Vol. 2 Regulation of Water and Electrolytes (P. K. T. Pang, M. P. Schreibman, eds.) pp. 45–84, Acad Press.

Brown, P. S., Brown, S. C., Bisceglio, I. T., Lemke, S. M. (1983): Breeding condition, temperature, and the regulation of salt and water by pituitary hormones in the red-spotted newt, *Notophthalmus viridescens.* Gen. Comp. Endocrinol. *51*, 292–302.

Brown, S. C., Horgan, E. A., Savage, L. M., Brown, P. S. (1986): Changes in body water and plasma constituents during bullfrog development: Effects of temperature and hormones. J. Exp. Zool. *237*, 25–33.

Burón, M. I., Navas, P. (1988): Thyroxin specifically stimulates anuran larvae epidermal sodium pump during metamorphosis. Comp. Biochem. Physiol. *91 A*, 693–695.

Campantico, E., Olivero, M., Guardabassi, A., Rinaudo, M. T., Giunta, C., Bruno, R. (1971): Effects of prolactin on arginase activity in the liver of *Bufo bufo* larvae under different experimental conditions. Gen. Comp. Endocrinol. *17*, 287–292.

Casada, J. H., Nichols, J. R. (1986): Interrelationships among epidermal Na-K ATPase, developmental stage and length of *Rana catesbeiana* tadpoles. Comp. Biochem. Physiol. *85 A*, 429–433.

Clemons, G. K., Nicoll, C. S. (1977): Development and preliminary application of a homologous radioimmunoassay for bullfrog prolactin. Gen. Comp. Endocrinol. *32*, 531–535.

Cox, T. C., Alvarado, R. H. (1979): Electrical and transport characteristics of skin of larval *Rana catesbeiana.* Am. J. Physiol. *237*, R74–R79.

Dent, J. N. (1968): Survey of amphibian metamorphosis, 271–311 In Metamorphosis (W. Etkin, L. I. Gilbert eds.) 459 pp. Appleton.

Dent, J. N. (1975): Integumentary effects of prolactin in the lower vertebrates. Amer. Zool. *15*, 923–935.

Dietz, T. H., Kirschner, L. B., Porter, D. (1967): The roles of sodium transport and anion permeability in generating transepithelial potential differences in larval salamanders. J. Exp. Biol. *46*, 85–96.

Doerr-Schott, J. (1974): Cyto-immunochemical study of the hypophysial cells of amphibians by light- and electron-microscopy. Fortschr. der Zool. *22*, 245–267.

Eddy, L. J. (1979): Prolactin action on extracellular fluid volume in tails of stage XII bullfrog tadpoles. Gen. Comp. Endocrinol. *37*, 369–373.

Etkin, W. (1941): The first appearance of functional activity in the pars intermedia in the frog, *Xenopus.* Proc. Soc. Exp. Biol. Med. *47*, 425–428.

Etkin, W. (1963): Metamorphosis-activating system of the frog. Science *139*, 810–814.

Fährmann, W. (1971 a): Die Morphodynamik der Epiderims des Axolots (*Siredon mexicanum* Shaw) unter dem Einfluß von exogen appliziertem Thyroxin. I. Die Epidermis des neotenen Axolotls, Z. Mikr. Anat. Forsch. *83*, 472–506.

Fährmann, W. (1971 b): Die Morphodynamik der Epidermis des Axolotls (*Siredon mexicanum* Shaw) unter dem Einfluß von exogen appliziertem Thyroxin. II. Die Epidermis während der Metamorphose. Z. mikr. anat. Forsch. *83*, 535–568.

Fox, H. (1981): Cytological and morphological changes during amphibian metamorphosis, In: Metamorphosis (L. I. Gilbert, E. Frieden eds.) pp. 327–362 Plenum.

Garcia-Navarro, S., Malagon, M. M., Garcia-Herdugo, G., Gracia-Navarro, F. (1988): Immunocytochemical and morphometric study of prolactin cells during amphibian morphogenesis. Gen. Comp. Endocrinol. *69*, 188–196.

Garland, H. O., Henderson, I. W., Brown, J. A. (1975): Micropuncture study of the renal responses of the urodele amphibian *Necturus maculosus* to injections of arginine vasotocin and an anti-aldosterone compound. J. Exp. Biol. *63*, 249–264.

Giunta, C., Campantico, E., Gay, V., Dore, B. (1974–1975): Further biochemical data concerning normal and prolactin-treated *Xenopus laevis* (Daudin) adults reared in water or moist moss. Atti. del. Accad. dell. Sci. di Torino. *109*, 311–326.

Goin, C. J. (1960): Amphibians, pioneers of terrestrial breeding habits. Smithsonian Rep. *1959*, 427–445.

Goldenberg, S., Warburg, M. R. (1976): Changes in the response to oxytocin followed throughout ontogenesis in two anuran species. Comp. Biochem. Physiol. *53c*, 105–113.
Goldenberg, S., Warburg, M. R. (1977a): Osmoregulatory effect of prolactin during ontogenesis in two anurans. Comp. Biochem. Physiol. *56a*, 137–143.
Goldenberg, S., Warburg, M. R. (1977b): Changes in the effect of vasotocin on water balance of *Rana ridibunda* during ontogenesis. Comp. Biochem. Physiol. *57A*, 451–455.
Goldenberg, S., Warburg, M. R. (1983): Water balance of five amphibian species at different stages and phases as affected by hypophysial hormones. Comp. Biochem. Physiol. *75A*, 447–455.
Gonzales, M., Morales, M., Zambrano, F. (1979): Sulfatide content and (Na^++K^+)-ATPase activity of skin and gill during larval development of the Chilean frog, *Calyptocephalella caudiverbera*. J. Membrane Biol. *51*, 347–359.
Gordon, M. S. (1964): Animals in aquatic environments: fishes and amphibians. pp. 697–713. Handbook of Physiology – Environment.
Gordon, M. S., Tucker, V. A. (1965): Osmotic regulation in the tadpoles of the crab-eating frog (*Rana cancrivora*). J. Exp. Biol. *42*, 437–445.
Grant, W. C. (1961): Special aspects of the metamorphic process: second metamorphosis. Amer. Zool. *1*, 163–171.
Grant, W. C., Grant, J. A. (1958): Water drive studies on hypophysectomized efts of *Diemictylus viridescens* Part I. The role of the lactogenic hormone. Biol. Bull. *114*, 1–9.
Grau, E. G. (1987): Thyroid hormones, In: Vertebrate Endocrinology: Fundamentals and Biomedical Implications vol. 2. Regulation of water and Electrolytes. (P. K. T. Pang, M. P. Schreibman, eds.) pp. 85–102. Acad. Press.
Greenwald, L. (1972): Sodium balance in amphibians from different habitats. Physiol. Zool. *45*, 229–237.
Greven, H. (1987): Skin texture and specific gravity of three amphibian species during their aquatic and terrestrial phase. 155–158 In Proc. 4th Ord. Gen. Meet. Soc. Europ. Herpetol. Nijmegen.
Guardabassi, A., Campantico, E., Panebianco, I. (1978): Histological changes in *Xenopus laevis* Daudin specimens kept under dry conditions, then moved back to their natural aquatic environment. I. Pituitary, thyroid and testis. Arch. Sci. Biol. *62*, 51–61.
Hanke, W. (1976): Neuroendocrinology, In Frog Neurobiology (R. Llinas, W. Precht, eds.) pp. 975–1020, Springer Verlag.
Hanke, W., Maser-Gluth, C. (1985): The influence of osmolality and ions on the interrenal secretion in Amphibia. Zool. Jb. Physiol. *89*, 453–467.
Hanke, W., Bergerhoff, K., Neumann, U. (1969): Die Wirkung des Interrenalorgans auf den Kohlenhydratstoffwechsel bei Amphibien. Z. Vergl. Physiol. *65*, 351–367.
Hansen, G. N., Hansen, B. L. (1981): Comparative immunocytochemical localization of prolactin and somatotropin in the pituitaries of *Lepidosiren paradoxa*, *Rana temporaria* and *Ambystoma mexicanum*. Cell Tiss. Res. *217*, 127–141.
Harlow, H. J. (1977): Effects of prolactin on cutaneous water and sodium transport in newts. Copeia *1977*, 745–746.
Heller, H., Bentley, P. J. (1965): Phylogenetic distribution of the effects of neurohypophysial hormones on water and sodium metabolism. Gen. Comp. Endocrinol. *5*, 96–108.
Hillyard, S. D., Zeiske, W., van Driessche, W. (1982): A fluctuation analysis study of the development of amiloride-sensitive Na^+ transport in the skin of larval bullfrogs (*Rana catesbeiana*). Biochem. Biphys. Acta *692*, 455–461.
Holmes, R. L., Ball, J. N. (1974): The pituitary gland in amphibians, In: The Pituitary Gland. A Comparative Account. (R. L. Holmes, J. N. Ball eds.) pp. 235–287 Cambridge University Press.
Ireland, M. P. (1973): Effects of arginine vasotocin on sodium and potassium metabolism in *Xenopus laevis* after skin gland stimulation and symphatetic blockade. Comp. Biochem. Physiol. *44A*, 487–493.
Jaffe, R. C. (1981): Plasma concentration of corticosterone during *Rana catesbeiana* tadpole metamorphosis. Gen. Comp. Endocrinol. *44*, 314–318.
Johnson, G. A. L. (1980): Carboniferous geography and terrestrial migration routes, In: The Terrestrial Environment and the Origin of Land Vertebrates (A. L. Panchen, ed.) pp. 41–54 Acad. Press.
Jolivet-Jaudet, G., Leloup Hatey, J. (1984): Variations in aldosterone and corticosterone plasma levels during metamorphosis in *Xenopus laevis* tadpoles. Gen. Comp. Endocrinol. *56*, 59–65.

Jorgensen, C. B., Larsen, L. O. (1967): Neuroendocrine mechanisms in lower vertebrates. In Neuroendocrinology (L. Martini, W. F. Ganong, eds.) pp. 485–528, Acad Press.

Jungreiss, A. M., Huibregtse, W. H., Ungar, F. (1970): Corticosteroid identification and corticosterone concentration in serum of *Rana pipiens* during dehydration in winter and summer. Comp. Biochem. Physiol. *34*, 683–689.

Just, J. J., Sperka, R., Strange, S. (1977): A quantitative analysis of plasma osmotic pressure during metamorphosis of the bullfrog, *Rana catesbeiana*. Experientia *33*, 1503–1505.

Katz, U. (1986): The Role of amphibian epidermis in osmoregulation and its adaptive response to changing environment. In: Biology of the Integument, vol. 2: Vertebrates. (J. Bereiter-Hahn, A. G. Matoltsy, K. S. Richards, eds. pp. 472–498, Springer.

Kawada, J., Taylor, R. E., Barker, S. B. (1969): Measurement of Na-K ATPase in the separated epidermis of *Rana catesbeiana* frogs and tadpoles. Comp. Biochem. Physiol. *30*, 965–975.

Kemenade, J. A. M. van (1974): Regulation of the interrenal gland and demonstration of cell types in the pars distalis of Amphibia. Fortschr. der Zool. *22*, 228–244.

Kerstetter, T. H., Kirschner, L. B. (1971): The role of the hypothalamo-neurohypophysial system in maintaining hydromineral balance in larval salamanders (*Ambystoma tigrinum*). Comp. Biochem. Physiol. *40A*, 373–384.

Kezer, J. (1952): Thyroxin-induced metamorphosis of the neotenic salamanders *Eurycea tynerensis* and *Eurycea neotenes*. Copeia *1952*, 234–237.

Kollros, J. J. (1961): Mechanisms of amphibian metamorphosis: Hormones. Am. Zool. *1*, 107–114.

Larsen, L. (1976): Physiology of molting. In: Physiology of the Amphibia vol. III (B. Lofts, ed.) pp. 53–100, Acad. Press.

Leboulenger, F., Delarue, C., Tonon, M. C., Jegou, S., Leroux, P., Vaudry, H. (1979): Seasonal study of the interrenal function of the European green frog, in vivo and in vitro. Gen. Comp. Endocrinol. *39*, 388–396.

Leist, K. H. (1970): Die Bedeutung des Adenohypophysen-Interrenal-Systems für den Osmomineral-Haushalt des Krallenfrosches (*Xenopus laevis* Daudin) im Verlauf der Metamorphose. Zool. Jb. Physiol. *75*, 375–401.

Lewinson, D., Rosenberg, M., Warburg, M. R. (1982): Mitochondria-rich cells in salamander larva epidermis; Ultrastructural description and carbonic anhydrase activity. Biol. of the Cell *46*, 75–84.

Lewinson, D., Rosenberg, M., Warburg, M. R. (1983): Developmental changes in the epidermal surface cells of salamander larva. Acta Zool. *64*, 191–197.

Lodi, G., Biciotti, M. (1975–1976): Ricerche preliminari sul transporto attivo del sodio nel tegumegnto del Tritone crestato in condizioni sperimentali diverse. Atti dell. Accad. Dell. Sci. di Torino. *110*, 141–146.

Lodi, G., Biciotti, M., Sacerdote, M. (1978): Osmoregulatory activity of prolactin in the skin of the crested newt. Gen. Comp. Endocrinol. *36*, 7–15.

Lodi, G., Biciotti, M., Viotto, B. (1982): Cutaneous osmoregulation in *Triturus cristatus carnifex* (Laur.) (Urodela). Gen. Comp. Endocrinol. *46*, 452–457.

Maetz, J. (1972): Interaction of salt and ammonia transport in aquatic organisms, In: Nitrogen Metabolism and the Environment (J. W. Campbell, L. Goldstein, eds.) pp. 105–154. Acad. Press.

Mazzi, V. (1970): The hypothalamus as a thermodependent neuroendocrine center in urodeles, In: The Hypothalamus (L. Martini, M. Motta, F. Fraschini, eds.) pp. 663–676. Acad. Press.

Meier, A. H., Garcia, L. E., Joseph, M. M. (1971): Corticosterone phases a circadian water-drive response to prolactin in the spotted newt, *Notophthalmus viridescens*. Biol. Bull. *141*, 331–336.

Meier, A. H. (1975): Chronophysiology of prolactin in the lower vertebrates. Amer. Zool. *15*, 905–916.

Miyauchi, H., LaRochelle, F. T., Suzuki, M., Freeman, M., Frieden, E. (1977): Studies on thyroid hormones and their binding in bullfrog tadpole plasma during metamorphosis. Gen. Comp. Endocrinol. *33*, 254–266.

Mondou, P. M., Kaltenbach, J. C. (1979): Thyroxine concentrations in blood serum and pericardial fluid of metamorphosing tadpoles and of adult frogs. Gen. Comp. Endocrinol. *39*, 343–349.

Moriya, T. (1982): Prolactin induces increase in the specific gravity of salamander, *Hynobius retardatus*, that raises adaptability to water. J. Exp. Zool. *223*, 83–88.

Moriya, T. (1983): The effect of temperature on the action of thyroid hormone and prolactin in larvae of the salamander *Hynobius retardatus*. Gen. Comp. Endocrinol. *49*, 1–7.

Moriya, T., Dent, J.N. (1986): Hormonal interaction in the mechanism of migratory movement in the newt, *Notophthalmus viridescens*. Zool. Sci. *3*, 669–676.

Norris, D.O., Jones, R.E., Criley, B.B. (1973): Pituitary prolactin levels in larval, neotenic and metamorphosed salamanders (*Ambystoma tigrinum*). Gen. Comp. Endocrinol. *20*, 437–442.

Nouwen, E.J. (1984): Aspects of the neurohypophysial secretion in adult anurans. A radioimmunological study. Med. Kon. Acad. Weten. Lett. Schone Kunst. Belgie *46*, 73–93.

Nouwen, E.J., Kühn, E.R. (1983): Radioimmunoassay of arginine vasotocin and mesotocin in serum of the frog *Rana ridibunda*. Gen. Comp. Endocrinol. *50*, 242–251.

Oordt, P.G.W.J. van (1974): Cytology of the adenohypophysis. In: Physiology of the Amphibia, vol. II. (B. Lofts, ed.) pp. 53–106. Acad. Press.

Pang, P.K.T. (1977): Osmoregulatory functions of neurohypophysial hormones in fishes and amphibians. Amer. Zool. *17*, 739–749.

Pang, P.K.T., Sawyer, W.H. (1974): Effects of prolactin on hypophysectiomized mud puppies *Necturus maculosus*. Amer. J. Physiol. *226*, 458–462.

Patterson, K.K. (1978): Life history aspects of paedogenic populations of the mole salamander, *Ambystoma talpoideum*. Copeia *1978*, 649–655.

Platt, J.E., Christopher, M.A. (1977): Effects of prolactin on the water and sodium content of larval tissues from neotenic and metamorphosing *Ambystoma tigrinum*. Gen. Comp. Endocrinol. *31*, 243–248.

Prahlad, K.V., DeLanney, L.E. (1965): A study of induced metamorphosis in the axolotl. J. Exp. Zool. *160*, 137–146.

Reinke, E.E., Chadwick, C.S. (1940): The origin of the water drive in *Triturus viridescens*. J. Exp. Zool. *83*, 223–233.

Robinson, D.H., Mills, J.W. (1987): Ouabain binding in tadpole ventral skin. II. Localization of Na pump sites. Am. J. Physiol. *253*, R410–R417.

Rosenberg, M., Warburg, M.R. (1978): Changes in structure of ventral epidermis of *Rana ridibunda* during metamorphosis. Cell Tiss. Res. *195*, 111–112.

Rosenberg, M., Lewinson, D., Warburg, M.R. (1982): Ultrastructural studies of the epidermal Leydig cell in larvae of *Salamandra salamandra* (Caudata, Salamandrida). J. Morphol. *174*, 275–281.

Ruyter, M.L. de, Stiffler, D.F. (1986): Interrenal function in larval *Ambystoma tigrinum*. II Control of aldosterone secretion and electrolyte balance by ACTH. Gen. Comp. Endocrinol. 62, 298–305.

Sage, M., de Vlaming, V.L. (1975): Seasonal changes in prolactin physiology. Amer. Zool. *15*, 917–922.

Sawyer, W.H. (1972): Lungfishes and amphibians: endocrine adaptation and the transition from aquatic to terrestrial life. Fed. Proc. *31*, 1609–1614.

Sawyer, W.H., Pang, P.K.T. (1979): Responses of vertebrates to neurohypophysial principles, In: Hormones and Evolution, vol. 2 (E.J.W. Barrington, ed.) pp. 493–523 Acad. Press.

Sawyer, W.H., Pang, P.K.T. (1987): Endocrine osmoregulation and vertebrate evolution. In: Vertebrate Endocrinology: Fundamentals and Biomedical Implications, vol. 2. Regulation of Water and Electrolytes. (P.K.T. Pang, M.P. Schreibman, eds.) pp. 293–305 Acad. Press.

Schmid, W.D. (1965): Some aspects of the water economies of nine species of amphibians. Ecology *46*, 261–269.

Schmid, W.D., Barden, R.E. (1965): Water permeability and lipid content of amphibian skin. Comp. Biochem. Physiol. *15*, 423–427.

Schultheiss, H. (1973): Der Einfluß von ACTH und Corticosteroiden auf den Stickstoff-Stoffwechsel während der Metamorphose des Mexikanischen Axolotl (*Ambystoma mexicanum* Cope) Zool. Jb. Physiol. *77*, 199–227.

Schultheiss, H., Hanke, W., Maetz, J. (1972): Hormonal regulation of the skin diffusional permeability to water during development and metamorphosis of *Xenopus laevis* Daudin. Gen. Comp. Endocrinol. *18*, 400–404.

Semlitsch, R.D. (1987): Paedomorphosis in *Ambystoma talpoideum*: effects of density, food and pond drying. Ecology *68*, 994–1002.

Snyder, R.C. (1956): Comparative features of the life histories of *Ambystoma gracile* (Baird) from populations at low and high altitudes. Copeia *1956*, 40–50.

Sprules, W. G. (1974): The adaptive significance of paedogenesis in North American species of *Ambystoma* (Amphibia; Caudata): an hypothesis. Can. J. Zool. *52*, 393–400.

Stiffler, D. F., deRuyter, M. L., Hanson, P. B., Marshall, M. (1986): Interrenal function in larval *Ambystoma tigrinum*. I. Responses to alterations in external electrolyte concentrations. Gen. Comp. Endocrinol. *62*, 290–297.

Suzuki, S. (1987): Plasma thyroid hormone levels in metamorphosing larvae and adults of a salamander, *Hynobius nigrescens*. Zool. Sci. *4*, 849–854.

Takada, M. (1985): Differentiation of the active sodium transport system during metamorphosis in *Rana catesbeiana* skin in relation to cadmium – and amiloride – induced responses. Jap. J. Physiol. *35*, 525–534.

Takada, M. (1986): The short-term effect of prolactin on the active Na transport system of the tadpoles skin during metamorphosis. Comp. Biochem. Physiol. *85 A*, 755–759.

Takada, M., Hara, K. (1988): T_3-induced differentiation of the electromotive force related to active Na transport across the skin of the neotenous urodele, *Ambystoma mexicanum*. Comp. Biochem. Physiol. *89 A*, 157–161.

Takada, M., Komazaki, S. (1988): Effect of prolactin on transcutaneous Na transport in the Japanese newt, *Cynops pyrrhogaster*. Gen. Comp. Endocrinol. *69*, 141–145.

Taylor, A. C., Kollros, J. J. (1946): Stages in the normal development of *Rana pipiens* larvae. Anat. Rec. *94*, 7–23.

Taylor, R. E., Barker, S. B. (1965): Transepidermal potential difference: Development in anuran larvae. Science *148*, 1612–1613.

Thomson, K. S. (1971): The adaptation and evolution of early fishes. Quart. Rev. Biol. *46*, 139–166.

Thomson, K. S. (1980): The ecology of Devonian lobe-finned fishes. In: The Terrestrial Environment and the Origin of Land Vertebrates. (A. L. Panchen, ed.) pp. 187–222, Acad. Press.

Warburg, M. R. (1971): The water economy of Israel amphibians: The urodeles *Triturus vittatus* (Jenyns) and *Salamandra salamandra* (L.) Comp. Biochem. Physiol. *40 A*, 1055–1063.

Warburg, M. R. (1972): Water economy and thermal balance of Israeli and Australian Amphibia from xeric habitats. Symp. Zool Soc. Lond. *31*, 79–111.

Warburg, M. R. (1988): Adaptation of amphibians to life in xeric habitats, In: Ecophysiology of Desert Vertebrates (P. K. Ghosh, I. Prakash, eds.) pp. 59–98, Scientific Publ. Jodhpur, India.

Warburg, M. R., Goldenberg, S. (1978 a): Effect of oxytocin and vasotocin on water balance in two urodeles followed throughout their life cycle. Comp. Biochem. Physiol. *60 A*, 113–116.

Warburg, M. R., Goldenberg, S. (1978 b): The changes in osmoregulatory effects of prolactin during the life cycle of two urodeles. Comp. Biochem. Physiol. *61 A*, 321–324.

Warburg, M. R., Lewinson, D. (1977): Ultrastructure of epidermis of *Salamandra salamandra* followed throughout ontogenesis. Cell Tiss. Res. *181*, 369–393.

Wasserburg, R. J. (1975): The adaptive significance of the tadpole stage with comments on the maintenance of complex life cycles in anurans. Amer. Zool. *15*, 405–417.

Wittouck, P. J. (1972): Intensification par la prolactine de l'absorption d'ion sodium ou niveau des branchies isolées de larves d'*Ambystoma mexicanum*. Arch. Int. Physiol. Biochim. *80*, 825–827.

Yorio, T., Bentley, P. J. (1978): The permeability of the skin of the aquatic anuran *Xenopus laevis* (Pipidae). J. Exp. Biol. *72*, 285–289.

Zoeller, R. T., Moore, F. L. (1986): Correlation between immuoreactive vasotocin in optic tectum and seasonal changes in reproductive behaviors of male rough-skinned newts. Hormones and Behavior *20*, 148–154.

Zoeller, R. T., Moore, F. L. (1988): Brain arginine vasotocin concentrations related to sexual behaviors and hydromineral balance in an amphibian. Hormones and Behavior 22, 66–75.

Species index

Subject index